ArtScroll Halachah Series®

Rabbi Nosson Scherman / Rabbi Meir Zlotowitz
General Editors

THE LAWS

Published by

Mesorah Publications, ltd

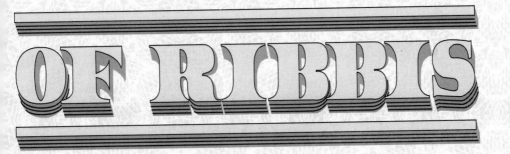

THE LAWS OF INTEREST
AND THEIR APPLICATION
TO EVERYDAY LIFE
AND BUSINESS

BY RABBI YISROEL REISMAN
FOREWORD BY RABBI AVROHOM PAM

FIRST EDITION
First Impression . . . May 1995

Published and Distributed by
MESORAH PUBLICATIONS, Ltd.
4401 Second Avenue
Brooklyn, New York 11232

Distributed in Europe by
J. LEHMANN HEBREW BOOKSELLERS
20 Cambridge Terrace
Gateshead, Tyne and Wear
England NE8 1RP

Distributed in Israel by
SIFRIATI / A. GITLER—BOOKS
4 Bilu Street
P.O.B. 14075
Tel Aviv 61140

Distributed in Australia & New Zealand by
GOLDS BOOK & GIFT CO.
36 William Street
Balaclava 3183, Vic., Australia

Distributed in South Africa by
KOLLEL BOOKSHOP
22 Muller Street
Yeoville 2198, Johannesburg, South Africa

ARTSCROLL HALACHAH SERIES ®
THE LAWS OF RIBBIS

Typography by Compuscribe at ArtScroll Studios, Ltd.

Printed in the United States of America by Noble Book Press
Bound by Sefercraft, Quality Bookbinders, Ltd. Brooklyn, N.Y.

THE LAWS OF RIBBIS

עולם

Dedicated to the memory of

My grandparents

ר׳ ישראל ב״ר בנימין ע״ה

כ׳ ניסן תש״ב

מרת חנה בת ר׳ יוסף דוב הי״ד

י״ג סיון תש״ד

ר׳ נתן ב״ר צבי אלימלך ע״ה

ה׳ כסלו תשכ״ז

מרת מלכה מירל בת ר׳ אריה לייביש ע״ה

י״ד טבת תשמ״ב

My brother

משה פתחיה ע״ה

כ״ט סיון תשמ״ו

לזכר

And my uncles, aunts and cousins
who perished during the Holocaust

דודי: בנימין ב״ר ישראל ע״ה

— ה׳ תמוז תש״ח

אשתו: שרה חנה בת ר׳ אליהו ע״ה
ובניהם: אליהו, יוסף דוב, יצחק אייזיק, פנחס, ושמואל הי״ד

— י״ג סיון תש״ד

דודי: משה יעקב ב״ר ישראל הי״ד
אשתו: גאלדא בת ר׳ שמחה הי״ד
וילדיהם: עזריאל צבי, ושאשע הי״ד

— י״ג סיון תש״ד

דודתי: רייזל בת ר׳ ישראל הי״ד
ובעלה: עוזר
וילדיהם: בנימין, יוסף דוב, וחיה, הי״ד

— י״ג סיון תש״ד

דודתי: אסתר מלכה בת ר׳ ישראל הי״ד

— י״ג סיון תש״ד

דודי: אהרון צבי ב״ר ישראל הי״ד

— י״ג סיון תש״ד

דודתי: שפרינצא בת ר׳ ישראל ע״ה

— ל׳ טבת תרצ״ט

דודי: אלימלך מרדכי ב״ר ישראל הי״ד

— ח׳ שבט תש״ה

תהא נשמתם צרורה בצרור החיים

הסכמת מורי ורבי
מרן הגאון ראש ישיבת תורה ודעת שליט"א

אברהם פאם
RABBI ABRAHAM PAM
582 EAST SEVENTH STREET
BROOKLYN, NEW YORK, N. Y.
11218

בס"ד יום עש"ק לס' לאמ"ש תשמ"ה

הנה ראיתי קצת קונ[ט]רסים מהחבור היקר על הלכות בית
שתתני יובו תחירי, מצו[תי] תהרי הכולו שלנו, הרב המומחה
בתורה והוראה, כא"א הרב ר' ישראל אברהם יצחק ... ...
... מעבר כי כל חולי לכאן, שאמתתא אליהם בלבטא.

ואמ[רו] שאמתי להבאתכי ל[צ]חק לעולם, ותתורה ... ...
... שלא, לדרך בין כבית לכליידם ופרטיהם ובקלוקיהם ...
... לאשה. וכבר ... כבר כתוב לכל ... ...
... במצורת ... ולתורה ... ... כ"ל ...
... מכח נתן ... טעם ובאת ... מקורות בהלכות,
... על ... ... כבר ... ...
... כש אנכי ... כל ... ...
... ... בכ"ג נ... כלבב. ... ...
... ...
... כנוגר בתנ... בנפש ... ...

מברכם יעקב הכהן כ/מ/ק

∾§ Table of Contents

Number(s) in parentheses indicate paragraph number(s)

(Ribbis Mukdemes / Ribbis Me'ucheres / haaramas Ribbis / Ribbis B'Shas *Perayon*) (27).

Introduction

(In the prophetic vision of Yechezkel,) four heavenly winds came forth
and opened the treasure room of the souls. Each spirit was returned to his
body of flesh and they all stood on their feet, except for one man. The
prophet asked, "Creator of the universe, what of this man?"
G-d responded, "He took Ribbis. . ."
(Pirkei DeR' Eliezer 33)

In Europe, a moneylender, who made his fortune by collecting Ribbis
payments from the poor people in town, passed away.
In vengeance, the Chevra Kadisha refused to bury him unless
an exorbitant amount of money was paid for the grave. The heirs
were incensed at the unjust treatment.
The matter was brought to the attention of R' Akiva Eiger. "How
appropriate," he responded. "The normal price of a grave assumes that the
purchaser will use it for a limited time, until *techiyas hameisim*, when the
dead will be brought back to life. But we are taught that people who
collect Ribbis will not be included in that resurrection. This man will
remain in the grave for eternity. Since he has far longer use of the grave,
it's certainly appropriate for him to pay more for this piece of land!"

Although this book is the product of my pen, it is the child of
Yeshivah Torah Vodaath, where it was conceived, nurtured and
finally saw the light of day. When the Kollel of our Yeshivah undertook
the study of the laws of Ribbis, we quickly realized that these laws are
not easily mastered. After much sweat and toil, we became acquainted
with the laws of Ribbis; later I had the privilege of reviewing Hilchos
Ribbis with Rabbi Avrohom Moshe Lewanoni, one of the extraordinary
talmidei chachamim of our Kollel, who has become an expert in this
field.

During the course of our study, we were disturbed to find that since
few people have the opportunity to study these laws in depth, there
is a great amount of confusion regarding their practical application.

Consequently, many people act in violation of the laws of Ribbis in their everyday personal and business affairs.

This book is meant to address these problems. Common situations are presented, the Ribbis issue is addressed, and solutions are offered for avoiding these problems. I look to break no new ground; I do not offer personal opinions or unique interpretations of the law. This is a collection of the laws of Ribbis as they apply to everyday life, culled from the poskim of the last four centuries, from the *Shulchan Aruch* to the poskim of present times. Each halachah is presented with a source; whenever I present my own thoughts, they appear in brackets. I have tried to present these halachos in a clear, comprehensible style, suitable for the layman, while providing insights and references for the scholar. I trust that both will find this work interesting and informative.

The laws of Ribbis are extensive; the reader may find himself overwhelmed by the size and extent of these laws. The first chapter of this work contains a list of everyday Ribbis situations that apply on a regular basis. I urge the reader to first limit himself to understanding the laws presented there; a further in-depth study can follow. Chapter 22, in particular, is important for anyone using a Heter Iska, since most poskim hold that a Heter Iska may only be used by individuals who understand its concept.

In deciding matters of dispute, I have generally followed the ruling of *Bris Yehudah*, a contemporary encyclopedic work on the laws of Ribbis, which has gained worldwide recognition as the definitive work on the laws of Ribbis. I have also leaned heavily on *Mishnas Ribbis*, an excellent work in which most contemporary issues are discussed clearly and concisely.

This book is graced by a foreword by my *Rebbe*, the Rosh Hayeshivah of Yeshivah Torah Vodaath, Harav Avrohom Pam. This essay does not deal with the laws of Ribbis per sé; it addresses the underlying problem of individuals who leave *halachah* behind when entering the business world. This attitude affects the observance of both the laws of Ribbis and the laws of *Choshen Mishpat*. The purpose of this book, and of the essay, is to make people more conscious of the importance of observing *halachah* in the marketplace.

It is my hope and prayer that this work will contribute to an increased awareness of the relevance of Hilchos Ribbis.

ACKNOWLEDGMENTS

I am indebted to my *Rebbe*, HARAV AVROHOM PAM שליט"א, who has encouraged me to publish this work. Harav Pam has lovingly given me of his precious time and broad wisdom, and has guided me in virtually every aspect of *Yahadus* that has crossed my path over the last seventeen years. May he continue to be a beacon of light and wisdom לאורך ימים ושנים.

I express appreciation to my long-time *chavrusa*, RABBI SCHACHNE WEINBERGER, with whom I studied these halachos, and to RABBI LABEL WULLIGER, our Rosh Kollel. RABBI AVROHOM MOSHE LEWANONI, the author of *Mishnas Ribbis*, was kind enough to review this manuscript, and to make corrections wherever they were necessary. RABBI MOSHE SILVERBERG, RABBI YITZCHOK ISBEE and RABBI CHAIM WILNER reviewed portions of this book; I thank them.

I am beholden to my wife, parents and in-laws, whose dedication, support and encouragement have made my studies possible; and to Yeshivah Torah Vodaath, where I have been fortunate to spend over two decades, כן ירבו, *bikoslei beis hamidrash*.

I am grateful to my *chaveirim* at Agudath Israel of Madison; and, in particular to those who attend my Sunday morning *Yoreh De'ah* shiur. Our study of the laws of Ribbis and the many questions and challenges put forth at the shiur, have contributed greatly to this volume.

This book has been improved by the expert editing of RABBI MOSHE GANS and RABBI AVROHOM BIDERMAN and by the meticulous work of the staff at ArtScroll/Mesorah.

The vision of RABBI NOSSON SCHERMAN and RABBI MEIR ZLOTOWITZ has brought forth a revolution in Jewish reading, making books on the broadest range of subjects available to the English-speaking public. I am grateful for my association with ArtScroll, and for the magnanimous manner in which they have dealt with me. No, Rabbi Zlotowitz, the privilege is *mine*.

I close with a deep sense of gratitude to the *Ribono Shel Olam*, Who has chosen the Jewish people from among the nations and given us His Torah,

Yisroel Reisman

Lag B'Omer 5755

Foreword

By Rabbi Avrohom Pam

נָשָׂאתָ וְנָתַתָּ בֶּאֱמוּנָה?
Did You Conduct Your Business Affairs With Faith?

◄§ The Questions

After a person has lived his years on earth, he must appear before the Beis Din Shel Maalah (Heavenly Tribunal) and answer, among other questions: "נָשָׂאתָ וְנָתַתָּ בֶּאֱמוּנָה" — *Did you conduct your business affairs with faith? (usually taken to mean 'with integrity'),* קָבַעְתָּ עִתִּים לַתּוֹרָה — *Did you establish set times for studying Torah?. . .* צָפִיתָ לִישׁוּעָה. — *Did you anticipate the redemption?" (Shabbos 31a). Interestingly, another source in the Talmud (Kiddushin 40b, Sanhedrin 7a) says that a person is first judged in regard to Torah which, as Tosafos points out, is an apparent contradiction. Tosafos then explains that while in judgment, business conduct takes precedence over Torah study. Retribution is in a different sequence: Punishment for neglecting Torah study comes first. The reason? The cause of a person's misconduct in business is a lack of proper knowledge of Torah and a lack of loyalty to its teachings. All else is built upon that foundation. . . . The questioning starts with a man's integrity in personal relationships with others but punishment begins at the source — laxity in Torah study.*

◄§ Why This Topic?

At first glance, a discussion of honesty and correct business practices may appear to be out of order, since such fundamental principles of Torah could well be taken for granted. It is interesting to note, how- ever, that the *Gemara* uses the term "בֶּאֱמוּנָה" — "Did you conduct your affairs with *emunah* — with faith?" — instead of "tzedek," "mishpat" or "din" — Were you *righteous,* or *just,* or *lawful,* in your business affairs? The reason might be because *emunah* has a two-fold meaning — integrity, and faith in God. Complete trust in God would prompt one to act even

---

This essay first appeared in Hebrew in the HaMesifta Journal, and in English in the Jewish Observer. Both were written by Rabbi Matis Blum, based on a speech delivered by Rav Pam to Torah Vodaath alumni.

לִפְנִים מִשּׁוּרַת הַדִּין, *beyond the letter of the law*, and imbue him with a higher sense of ethics; his faith dispels any apprehensions about loss of income resulting from ethical conduct.

The Chofetz Chaim declared that a God-fearing man entering the field of commerce is obliged to carefully study the second section of *Choshen Mishpat* (the section of the Codes dealing with monetary matters), especially those halachos dealing with cheating, and the possibility of an error in sale (227-238). Just as a *shochet* is obligated to learn the laws of ritual slaughter, and a *sofer* must be an expert in the field of Torah script, so too must a merchant be equally proficient in the halachos pertinent to his profession. It would be wonderful if just as ordination is granted to Rabbis to permit them to enter the rabbinate, so too would some form of *semichah* in הִלְכוֹת מֶקָח וּמִמְכָּר (*Laws of Commerce*) be instituted for people entering the business field.

> A shochet once told Reb Yisrael Salanter, "I'm giving up my position because I find the responsibility of slaughtering properly too much for my conscience to bear. If I make but one mistake, imagine how many people would be eating non-kosher meat because of me!"
>
> Asked Reb Yisrael: "What will you do for a living?"
>
> Replied the man, "I'll open up a small business.
>
> To which Reb Yisrael said: "Do you really think that that's preferable? As a shochet you have one responsibility — people should not transgress 'You shall not eat any meat improperly slaughtered' (Deuteronomy 14:21), and that makes you tremble. If you would be involved in business, do you know how many positive and negative commands you would be dealing with, how careful you would have to be not to violate any of them?"

❧ ❧ ❧

The Chofetz Chaim cites a few examples of halachos that are of extreme import to those engaged in business.

Some Common Examples

◄§ Defects in Sales

When selling an item, a person must be very careful that it does not have any flaw in it, or that it be lacking in any way. And should it be flawed, he must notify the would-be purchaser in advance, for if he does not, the sale may be invalid. If it is a defect that would cause a person to reconsider the purchase, not informing the purchaser would be deemed deception. This consideration applies whether the purchaser is a Jew or a Gentile, for one may not take their money under a false pretext — *gezel akum* is forbidden. (The Chofetz Chaim cites various sources; the *Rambam, Hilchos Geneivah* 7:8, among others.) Should a person have made this kind of invalid sale, he must return the money.

Similarly, a person is not permitted to cheat anybody — Jew and non-Jew alike — in any manner, in keeping with the passage: "Do not commit an injustice in measures, weights or volume" (*Leviticus* 19:36). You must make an exact accounting with the person who buys. "Committing such an injustice is an abomination before God" (*Deuteronomy* 25:16).

✍§ Defective Merchandise

The Chofetz Chaim also cites examples dealing with the purchaser: When a person who has discovered that an item he purchased has a defect, and uses it anyway, he may not bring it back for a refund, for use implies acceptance (*Choshen Mishpat* 232:3). Of course, if the defect is discovered after the item is used, it is a different matter, and a refund is in order. But the purchaser *must* be certain that he did not cause the flaw. (A person may feel that the shopkeeper will return the item to the manufacturer, and the manufacturer has thousands of such items; what difference does one more make? This type of rationalization is, of course, invalid and self-deceiving.)

Similarly, when examining an article one must be careful not to damage it in any way. When people purchase a *lulav,* and they examine it for defects, such as a split down the spine, they may well cause the split by examining it carelessly; and then say, "I don't want this one. Let me see another one, please." This is a common occurrence, and one should be exceptionally careful about it.

The Chofetz Chaim's son, Reb Leib, wrote that when the *Sefer Chofetz Chaim* was being printed, his father spent weeks on end in the printshop in Warsaw to make certain that there should be no error in the printing or the binding; he was truly frightened that perhaps someone would purchase a faulty copy which might constitute *gezel* (unintentionally defrauding the purchaser).

In 1906, when the Chofetz Chaim was publishing his Mishnah Berurah he asked Reb Leib, who had moved to Warsaw, to supervise the production of the sefer. Later, somebody purchased a set of Mishnah Berurah with one section printed incorrectly. The man sent a complaint to the Chofetz Chaim, who immediately wrote to his son, protesting: "What have you done to me, my son? All my days I was concerned that I be spared from even the remotest likeness of gezel. Never did I think I would be caught in outright gezel! And now, because of you, I fell into the trap of full-fledged gezel." He commanded his son to print a number of extra copies of this section without the inversion in it, for fear that others were similarly "defrauded," and he put a notice in the newspaper to the effect that: "Whoever purchased the Sefer Mishnah Berurah containing a misplaced section should please write me, and I'll send you a corrected section," which he did.

Reb Avrohom Horowitz zt"l, a true tzaddik, ran a bedding-supplies store in the East New York section of Brooklyn. When someone would ask, "Do you have a nice mattress?" he would say, "Nice? I don't know. Maybe others have better merchandise. I can only show you what I have."

Once he was in the back room of the store, and as his wife showed a particular mattress to a purchaser, he called out to her, "Did you show the customer the damage on that? Please show her."

He was always wary of defrauding the customer or misleading him in any way. (Offering a person advice that is to his disadvantage is a transgression of the Torah command: "Do not place a stumbling block before a blind person. . ." (Leviticus 19:14).

If someone asks a salesman for an item, specifying a desired color or fabric, and that particular item is not in stock, the salesman may not say, "They stopped making those. But I can show you something else that is much better," unless that is actually the case.

✑ Specifying Details of Agreement Beforehand

The Chofetz Chaim stresses (in Sefas Tamim, and also at the end of Ahavas Chessed, Section I) that when two people enter an agreement for some contracted work, it is extremely important that they both spell out precisely what each expects from the other in terms of work and payment. Frequently people say, "Start now. When the job's done, we'll get together." Then, upon completion of the job, disputes arise regarding payment, or how well the job was done; and when they part company, each one claims that he was short-changed by the other party . . . . Worse yet, some people prefer not to argue and let things go — but one party does not really forgive the other for the money withheld or overpaid, and thus ends up with possibilities of *gezel.*

Should such a dispute arise, the *Shulchan Aruch* rules that payment should be determined by the prevailing custom of the locality in regard to such work. If someone pays one cent less than required, then "the Torah considers this man dishonest, and guilty of withholding the wages of his worker."

However, it is usually difficult to ascertain the prevailing customs which govern a particular type of work. Therefore, it is best that the two parties spell out precisely what each expects from the other before entering into a contract.

The Deep-seated Attributes

◄§ Charity and Justice

In his introduction to *Ahavas Chessed*, the Chofetz Chaim comments on G-d's reference to Avraham Avinu: "I love him because he will command his children and his household after him, that they will keep the way of G-d, to do charity and justice" (*Genesis* 18:19). "Justice" refers to doing things correctly, in keeping with the law. "Charity" involves yielding to somebody else's needs beyond the requirements of the law. How are these two expressions to apply simultaneously?

The Chofetz Chaim explains that in dealing with somebody else, one must not say, "He won't mind if I pay him a little less for the item." Or when sending out an order, "He won't mind if I short-supply him slightly." With regard to fulfilling one's obligation to somebody else, the rule should be *mishpat*, justice — adhering to the letter of the law, no matter how insignificant the amount. On the other hand, in your expectations from others, the rule should be *tzedakah* — tend to be generous and waive your rights in minor matters. Thus, *tzedakah* and *mishpat* can both reside within the same person.

In the *Chut HaMeshulash*, the children of the *Kesav Sofer* (R' Shmuel Binyomin Schreiber zt"l) recorded how their father was so cautious in regard to other people's money he would not rely on seventy reasons for <u>heter</u> (permission) against one reason for <u>issur</u> (prohibition).

◌§ The Extra Measure of Caution

> In 1872, when Reb Yisroel Meir HaKohen was ready to
> print the sefer bearing the name by which he eventually
> became known, Chofetz Chaim, he traveled to various
> communities neighboring his own Radin for advance orders.
> Normally, people make some payment, but he refused to
> accept any money. When his son, Reb Leib, asked him why
> he had so refused, the Chofetz Chaim explained, "Perhaps
> some of these people will move, or even die, by the time the
> sefer is finished. How will I be able to trace their heirs, or
> find them if they are alive in other cities? It is better that I
> take orders without money." So his son asked, "Then tell
> me, why do you go to the trouble of getting orders altogether?
> Print the sefarim and then travel around and sell them." His
> father replied, "I have to borrow from others to finance this
> undertaking. What right do I have to ask others to lend me
> money on a risk, unless I have some idea of how many
> sefarim I am going to sell?"

When two people verbally enter a business agreement, without any
exchange of money or merchandise, either of the principals could change
his mind, but it is "contrary to the wishes of the Sages" (*Bava Metzia*
48a). There is a difference of opinion between two authorities, however,
whether or not this type of conduct renders a person מְחוּסָר אֱמוּנָה,
lacking in integrity, and halachic authorities decide according to the
more stringent view (Rav Yochanan). Thus, if two people enter into an
agreement — no money was taken, no contract was signed, no deposit
was made — and later one changes his mind, he is not acting according
to the strict requirements of halachah. The situation often arises when
someone selects merchandise but has no money, and says, "I'm going to
buy it," and the proprietor says, "Okay, it's yours. Come back tomorrow
with the money." He returns the next day and the item is gone; or *he* is
guilty of not returning the next day. Such practices are frowned upon by
our Sages. (Some authorities say that these restrictions do not apply when
the price of the item has changed — *Choshen Mishpat* end of Ch. 202,
but it is a minority view.) Integrity means being faithful to your word.
When a person fails to do this, he is not "conducting his affairs with
emunah."

✺§ Faithful in Thought

There is yet another, higher degree of *emunah*, of faithfulness in transactions: R' Safra fulfilled "speaking truth in his heart" (*Psalms* 15:2).

> *In addition to "not going back on his word," R' Safra never went back on his thoughts: A customer once entered R' Safra's store to make a purchase. He offered a price, but R' Safra was saying Kri'as Shema and did not answer. He raised the offer several times and R' Safra still did not comment. When R' Safra completed the Shema, he said, "I'll accept the first price." Said the man, "But I'm willing to pay the last." R' Safra replied, "Yes, but I was willing to accept the first. And since in my heart I said 'yes,' although I could not speak, I will not change my mind"* (She'iltos D'Rav Achai, Vayechi, 36). "Speaking honestly in one's heart" is an extremely high level of integrity.

The same *She'iltos* quotes a Midrash that comments on the passage: "My [i.e., G-d's] eyes are on the trusted, that they dwell together with Me" (*Psalms* 101:6). In this regard, the Midrash (on *Shmuel*) relates how the celebrated *Amora* Shmuel was named:

> *Shmuel's father had been a merchant. Rabbi Yehudah ben Beseira asked him to put aside a measure of silk for him, but he did not pay for it, nor give a deposit. A long period of time transpired, until Shmuel's father had occasion to bring it to Rabbi Yehudah. Rabbi Yehudah was surprised. "Why did you keep this merchandise for me?" he asked. "After all, we only exchanged words. I didn't pick up the silk, nor did I give you money." Answered the merchant, "An honorable man's word is as good as money." Reb Yehudah marveled at this man's concept of integrity, and he blessed him: "Because you trusted in me, may you be worthy of begetting a son like the prophet Shmuel, about whom the Scripture testifies, 'And all Israel from Dan to Beer Sheva knew that Shmuel was a trusted prophet of G-d' (Samuel I 3:20)." When his son was born, the merchant named him Shmuel.*

Perhaps that is what is meant by "dwelling within the boundaries of G-d." Being worthy of bringing Shmuel into the world is the equivalent of dwelling with G-d.

ᵉ✑ The Blessings of Trust

"A man of trust is many times blessed, but (one who is) anxious for wealth is never clean" (*Proverbs* 28:20). While the first part of the passage is an obvious truth, the second part is more subtle, referring to someone who is impatient for G-d's blessings, and wants to become rich immediately; he will never emerge clean from the stain of sin.

"The man of trust is many times blessed" refers to Moshe Rabbeinu. Indeed, every endeavor that he undertook, or for which he served as treasurer, was blessed. To demonstrate his trustworthiness, Moshe called together *Klal Yisrael* for an accounting when the building of the *Mishkan* (portable Sanctuary) was completed. This was surely unnecessary, for G-d Himself testified that "My servant Moshe is trusted throughout My house" (*Numbers* 12:7). The Midrash explains that Moshe did this to avoid the suspicion that he had become wealthy from handling the funds used for building the *Mishkan*.

It seems strange that someone trusted by G-d still was not satisfied until he had proved himself clean in the eyes of man. Yet, this is of extreme importance. The Talmud reports that the proceeds of the *shekalim* were stored in huge vats, and periodically an official would remove some of the coins to make purchases for the *Beis HaMikdash*. He was not permitted to wear a hemmed garment, shoes, or an amulet around his neck because it would offer an opportunity for him to smuggle out some coins for himself. Then, should he become poor, people would say: "Do you know why he became poor? He was punished because he stole from the treasury." And in case he becomes wealthy, people would say: "Do you know how he became rich? Because he stole from the treasury" (*Shekalim* 3:2). He must ascertain that his actions are beyond suspicion. In this regard it says: "And you shall be clean before G-d and Israel" (*Numbers* 32:22). Then, the *Mishnah* cites an additional passage: "And you should find favor and good understanding in the eyes of G-d and man" (*Proverbs* 3:4).

Tiferes Yisrael explains that both passages are needed. The first one ("And you shall be clean . . .") teaches us that we must avoid acting in a manner which could cause suspicion. But it is insufficient to clarify our actions after they are done. We must "find favor and good understanding" in everyone's eyes, so that people have no reason to question our actions before or after they occur. This is what we learn from the second verse.

✑§ A Twofold Obligation

The Chasam Sofer (R' Moshe Schreiber) writes (*Collected Responsa* 59):

> All my days I was in anguish over the passage: "And you shall be clean in the eyes of G-d and Israel." These two obligations are like two millstones weighing on my neck. It is possible to absolve oneself of the first — that is, to be clean in the eyes of G-d — much more easily than it is to satisfy people, for they imagine bizarre plots; and the punishment for failing to satisfy others is far more severe than for not satisfying G-d ח"ו. Indeed, the Gemara (end of Yoma) tells us that there is no atonement for Chillul Hashem — desecration of G-d's Name (which results from misrepresenting the high standards demanded by the Torah). Unfortunately, too often we hear people say: "Imagine that a Torah scholar such as he should be guilty of such-and-such!" even though it is pure speculation that leads them to judge him so. I often wonder whether any man has actually fulfilled this obligation to his fullest. Perhaps this is what King Solomon had in mind when he said: "There is no fully righteous man on earth who had done right and not sinned" — meaning that even though a man had done only good, it is impossible that he should not have "sinned" in somehow falling short of having his actions understood by others.

The Chasam Sofer adds that while the Tribes of Reuvain and Gad more than fulfilled their obligation of "And you shall be clean ..." by fighting on the front lines of *Bnei Yisrael* when they conquered Canaan, it is unlikely that they could completely clean themselves in the eyes of their brethren. It may well be for this reason that these tribes were later exiled before the remaining ten tribes were.

✑§ A Peaceful Hereafter

The Chofetz Chaim points out that when Yisro advised Moshe in regard to setting up a judiciary system, he concluded his words with: "If you follow this approach, then you will be able to withstand the pressures. All these people will return to their place *beshalom* — in peace" (*Exodus* 18:23). It is strange that Yisro spoke of the people returning "*in* peace," when this is a terminology usually reserved for the blessing for ultimate peace wished to a person who had died [as opposed to *leshalom*] (*Berachos* 64a). The Chofetz Chaim explains that when somebody is guilty of some type of cheating and dies without returning the money to its original owner, he has no rest in the World to Come until somehow the moneys are restored to the original owners or their heirs. Thus, Yisro assured Moshe that if he sets up a proper judiciary system, justice will prevail. Then when the people ultimately die, they will find eternal rest and not be troubled by unfulfilled financial obligations.

◄§ Pleasing to the Eye . . . Acceptable to the Heart

In spelling out the exact details of the construction of the *Mishkan*, G-d gave Moshe precise instructions in how to drape the material used in covering the Sanctuary (*Exodus* 26:13); to which Rashi comments: "The Torah here teaches us proper conduct — that a man should be concerned with the aesthetic."

A yeshivah student who has absorbed the light of Torah within himself radiates a special beauty of his own. It is this beauty that he should preserve with the utmost care. Even a small stain can mar it. Especially in our times, when people are so quick to find fault with the Torah and its students, *bnei yeshivah* must endeavor all the more to present the beauty of the Torah in all its aspects.

Thus it is insufficient to simply meet the requirements of *din* (Torah law), but one must strive for ever higher levels in faith, until one can respond positively to the query: "Did you conduct your business affairs with faith?" in all its possible implications ... *Were you among the faithful of the earth upon whom "the eyes of G-d gaze"?* Thus, the judgment of the rabbis, that a scholar with a stain on his garment is among those who "cause disenchantment with religion" (*Shabbos* 114a; *Rambam Dei'os* 5:9), certainly applies to misconduct in human relations and general unethical behavior.

Upon completion of the *Mishkan*, Moshe blessed the people (*Exodus* 39:43); according to *Rashi*, he said, "May it be the will of G-d that the *Shechinah* (Divine Presence) rest on all your activities," implying that the *Shechinah* not be limited to the Sanctuary but be found everywhere, in all their endeavors. This fulfills the command: "And you shall love G-d," which refers to being so exemplary in conduct that it inspires love and appreciation for G-d; people will say, "How graceful are the ways, how perfect are the acts of so-and-so who has studied Torah!" (*Yoma* 86a).

Fortunate is he who inspires others to the love of G-d and enhances Torah in their eyes.

Common Ribbis Problems

Introduction

The study of the laws of Ribbis must begin with the realization that these laws apply on a constant basis. While Ribbis problems are most common in business situations, there are many applications of the laws of Ribbis which apply to people when they are not in the business world. Some of these laws are presented in this chapter.

1. **When someone lends money to a friend,** they become borrower and lender. Their relationship is restricted by the laws of Ribbis, which prohibit the borrower from benefiting the lender. Still, their relationship does not have to change entirely. A favor which the borrower had often extended to the lender prior to the existence of the loan may be extended again afterwards.[1]

   Similarly, when the lender and borrower are close friends, even favors which had not previously been extended may be offered. This is permitted whenever it is clear that the favor would have been offered regardless of the loan.[2]

2. Although friends are generally permitted to benefit each other in this manner, this leniency does not apply to a favor or gift which is offered in public (this is called *befarhesya*). A borrower may not benefit his lender in a publicly noticeable manner, even if he had been doing him favors prior to the existence of the loan. For example, the borrower may not allow the lender to live in his home without charging him rent.[3] He may not offer the lender free use of his maid or worker, nor may he purchase an *aliyah* for him in the synagogue.

---

1. Y.D. 160:7. This applies both to benefits which involve a financial expense (such as inviting the lender for a meal) and to benefits with no expense (such as tutoring the lender) (*S.A. Harav* §11).

   Darkei Teshuvah 166:4, defining the Hebrew term which is used here ('*rogil*' ; this translates as 'often'), rules that this applies to favors which had been extended on more than two occasions before the loan was extended. *Pri Megadim* to O.C. 368:1 (in another context) defines this term in the same manner. Cf. *Shach* Y.D. 226:11.

2. *Shach* 166:1. This is permitted only when the borrower extends the favor as an expression of friendship. But if this is done in gratitude for the loan which was extended, it is prohibited even in the cases described here (*S.A. Harav* §11, *Bris Yehudah* 10:8).

3. Y.D. 160:7 and *Shach* 9, *Shach* 166:1. The borrower must charge a rental fee which is consistent with market prices [although he is permitted to charge a fee which is on the lower range of market rates] (*Mishnas Ribbis* 3:17; see also *Bris Yehudah* 10:n17).

3. When the friendship between the borrower and lender is so well known that it is obvious that the gifts are not being given because of the loan, many poskim hold that this is permitted even in a *befarhesya* situation.[4] One may rely on this opinion only when the borrower had extended the particular favor in a *befarhesya* manner, prior to the existence of the loan. For example, when the lender was living in the borrower's home before the loan was given, he may continue to live there after the loan.[5]

4. There is a second limitation on the relationship of friends when a loan passes between them. Ordinarily, a person is permitted to use his friend's utensil without receiving his expressed permission, as long as he is absolutely certain that his friend does not mind (as in the case of a person who frequently borrows the item).[6] However, once a loan has passed between them, the lender must avoid appearing as if he is making demands of the borrower because of the loan. He is therefore prohibited from using the borrower's property without requesting permission.[7]

In the Home

5. Borrowing household items: The prohibition of Ribbis is not limited to situations involving cash loans. Neighbors routinely

---

4. Shach 166:1 records a dispute regarding this. He cites an opinion quoted by *Rosh* who permits this, and the opinion of *Yam Shel Shlomo* who prohibits.

5. Yam Shel Shlomo (*Bava Kama* 9:9) concedes that this is permitted. This is also the ruling of S.A. Harav §11 and Bris Yehudah 10:7. Cf. *Chochmas Adam* 131:16 who rules leniently even if the borrower had not previously extended the favor, as long as they are extremely close friends. (See also Chapter 3, Note 2.)

6. Shach C.M. 358:1; see also *Aishel Avraham* (Butchech) to O.C. 14:1, s.v. *sham hagah*.

7. Y.D. 160:7. When the lender uses an item without permission, it may appear that he feels free to do so because of the loan which he had extended (*Shach* 11).

S.A. Harav §12 maintains that friends who are so close that they regularly use each other's utensils without permission may continue to do so even after a loan has passed between them. See also *Bris Yehudah* 10:n17 who cites a source for this in *Nimukei Yosef*.

[It seems difficult to interpret the *Shulchan Aruch* in a manner which supports this leniency. There is a basic Talmudic rule that *shoel shelo medaas ganav hu*, one who borrows without permission is a thief. Thus the prohibition which would apply to a lender can only be referring to situations where it is clear that permission would have been granted if it had been requested. It would appear that this leniency can be applied only where the friendship is publicly known, so that the appearance of Ribbis is avoided. This would mirror the *S.A. Harav's* leniency quoted above, Note 5.]

borrow household items (such as a cup of milk or a dozen eggs) from each other. The prohibition of Ribbis applies here as well. This means that the borrower may return only the amount which was actually borrowed. Anything added to the payment would constitute Ribbis.[8]

If someone borrowed a loaf of bread, he may repay his friend with a different loaf, even if the new loaf is slightly larger. This leniency applies only where the size difference is insignificant.[9] However, if he borrowed a number of items (such as six eggs), he may return only the same number which were borrowed.[10]

6. If the borrower is uncertain of the precise amount he borrowed, he may return an amount which is great enough to assure that the loan

---

8. *Bris Yehudah* 17:n6, based on Y.D. 160:17.

   Shulchan Aruch allows an exception for Talmudic scholars who are familiar with the laws of Ribbis and are certain that the added amount is intended as a gift and not as payment for the loan. Even these individuals may only add a small amount to the payment and only when foodstuffs were borrowed. As a matter of practical halachah, one should not rely on this exception (see *Bris Yehudah* 2:69 that this exception is limited to extraordinary scholars).

9. *Bris Yehudah* 17:n6.

10. *Mishnas Ribbis* 6:n5 points out that when a greater number of an item is returned, this difference is always considered to be a significant one. Still, *Mishnas Ribbis* quotes others who permit this when eggs are inexpensive, and the borrower and lender do not pay attention to the exact amount being borrowed and returned.

   If someone borrowed a dozen eggs and found that one of them had a blood spot which rendered it non-kosher, he would still be permitted to return a dozen eggs. Anytime a person buys a dozen eggs, there is a possibility that some of them have blood spots. The market value of the eggs which were borrowed took this into account. The eggs which are being returned have the identical value, since some of them might contain blood spots. (See *Mishnas Ribbis* ibid. who adds that according to the opinion of *Taz* 160:2 one is permitted to add a small amount to any payment. Although most poskim reject this ruling, it can be used here as a secondary reason to rule leniently.)

   If someone borrowed an item which is available in both regular and generic brands, he should return the same type of item which he borrowed. If, for example, he borrowed a generic brand of disposable diapers, he may not return a quality brand. If the difference in price between the items is minimal, to the degree that people do not generally care which item is used, he may return the better quality. Even in this case, the borrower should not deliberately return a better item if he is doing so in appreciation for the loan. (See *Mishnas Ribbis* ibid. who compares this to the ruling of *Minchas Yitzchak* 9:88, quoted below, Note 30. This means that when the borrower has a particular brand available to him, he is not obligated to shop around for the exact brand which he borrowed. In addition, the aforementioned ruling of the *Taz* can also be used here as a secondary basis for ruling leniently.)

is paid up. Although it is possible that he is actually returning more than he borrowed, this does not constitute Ribbis.[11]

7. When businessmen trade merchandise, its value is established by the prevailing market value. For example, a person borrows a hundred pounds of sugar when the prevailing cost is 35¢ per pound. A month later, when he returns the sugar, the cost has risen to 40¢ per pound. In this case, the borrower may not return the full hundred pounds, since he is returning something of greater value than what he borrowed.[12]

This limitation does not apply to neighbors or friends who borrow small amounts of merchandise from each other. For example, a neighbor who borrowed a five-pound bag of sugar may later return a five-pound bag of sugar, even if the price of sugar had gone up in the interval.[13]

8. An exception: Many neighbors are in the habit of borrowing from each other, without being careful to return everything they borrow. When neighbors have this type of relationship, none of the prohibitions of Ribbis apply. This is because there are no loans taking place. When these neighbors 'borrow' from each other, they are actually offering gifts. The prohibition of Ribbis therefore does not apply.[14]

---

11. The borrower is not obligated to do so. A basic Talmudic principle is that in cases of doubt, the burden of proof always rests with the person who is seeking payment (*hamotzi meichaveiro alav haraayah*). Still, the borrower satisfies a moral obligation when he makes an additional payment to insure that the loan is fully paid (*Bris Yehudah* 5:35).

It is preferable that the borrower stipulate that if he is overpaying, the extra money is an outright gift and is not given in gratitude of the loan (*Minchas Yitzchak* 9:88).

12. Y.D. 162:1. This is a general rule, which is discussed at greater length below, in Chapter 14. There are significant exceptions to this rule, as we will see there.

13. *Rema* 162:1. *Mishnah Berurah* (450:2) explains that this is permitted because prices tend to fluctuate by small amounts, and people generally do not take notice of this small difference (unlike businessmen, who do take notice of small price fluctuations). [*Mishnah Berurah* implies that even if there was a great fluctuation in the price, this would still be permitted. Since prices *generally* tend to fluctuate only slightly, people pay no attention to the market value of the items they borrow from each other (see *Divrei Sofrim* 162:19).]

14. If a neighbor were to voluntarily return an item, he may return more than he took. However, had the neighbor obligated himself to return what he borrowed (by pledging to do so when taking the item), he would not be permitted to return more than he actually received.

Borrowing Utensils

9. In the cases under discussion in the previous paragraphs, the borrower consumes the item which was borrowed. Payment is made when the borrower purchases another package of the same item and returns it to his neighbor. The prohibition on Ribbis applies in these cases.

Borrowing a tool or utensil (such as a hammer or a pot) is different; the borrower must return the very same tool to its owner. There is no prohibition of Ribbis in this case.[15]

10. Borrowing a Car: The Ribbis prohibitions also do not apply when someone borrows a vehicle such as a car or truck. This is also a tool which must be returned after it is used. Therefore, someone who borrows a car may fill the gas tank or do repairs to the car before returning it to its owner.[16]

Trading Meals

11. Individuals may not agree to trade meals, where one provides food one day while the other provides it the next day. The reason for this is that after the first person provides a meal, he is owed a meal in return. If this second meal were more elaborate than the first, it would constitute Ribbis. To avoid this problem, individuals should not make agreements to trade meals.

When there is no official agreement to trade meals, a person is permitted to offer a meal (even a more elaborate one) to a friend who

---

15. Y.D. 176:2. The owner of the tool is even permitted to charge for the use of his tool. This constitutes a rental payment rather than Ribbis.

This applies whenever the object which is borrowed loses value as it is used. Appliances, clothing, tools and mechanical instruments are examples of items whose value decreases as they are used. Items such as jewelry, precious stones and rare coins do not decrease in value when they are used. These items may be rented only under the conditions outlined in Chapter 11, Paragraph 4.

16. One could argue that the person who borrows a car is also borrowing the gas which is in the gas tank. and when he refills the tank, he is returning something which was consumed. As we have seen earlier, Ribbis prohibitions *do* apply when the item which is borrowed is consumed. Still, this is permitted because it is readily apparent to all that the extra amount is added in gratitude for use of the car, not for the gasoline (*Mishnas Ribbis* 6:n5; cf. *Chayei HaLevi* 2:53 who requires that the borrower state explicitly that the extra gas is in gratitude for use of the car. However, where the person lending the car does not require that the gas be returned, such as when it is lent for a short ride, he concedes that an explicit statement is not necessary; see also *Lehoros Nosson* 6:75).

had fed him. However, when inviting the friend, he may not use language which implies that he is repaying him for the first meal.[17]

When Shopping

12. A business may not set two prices for the same item, charging one price for items purchased with cash and a higher price for items purchased on credit. This is Ribbis, because the person paying the higher price is actually paying for credit.

A customer in this situation is permitted to make a cash purchase (at the lower price), but may not purchase on credit.[18]

Businesses are also prohibited from charging more for purchases which are made with a credit card. In this situation too, a customer may only make cash purchases (at the lower price).[19]

13. Sale prices: Many businesses limit their sale prices to cash purchases. In this case too, the credit customer is actually paying an additional fee for credit.[20] Therefore, he may purchase the item for cash only.

14. Prepayment: A buyer must pay a merchant after he receives the merchandise. When payment is made at a later time, the cost of the merchandise is considered a loan to the customer. The reverse is also true. If a merchant receives payment *before* the item is delivered, he is

---

17. *Rema* O.C. 170:13. If this meal were more elaborate than the first one, it might appear as Ribbis. This is not actually Ribbis, since the first meal was provided free, without any stipulation that it be repaid. Still, this is prohibited because it gives an appearance of Ribbis (*Mishnah Berurah* 170:31).

Some poskim permit an invitation to be phrased in the following manner: "Come eat with me. I'll eat with you some other time." This is understood to be a method of persuasion rather than an agreement to trade meals. In this case, the second meal may be more elaborate than the first one (*Rema*, ibid.). *Taz* (O.C. 170:7) disagrees and prohibits this. *Aruch HaShulchan* and *Bris Yehudah* 2:25 accept the ruling of *Rema* (*Mishnah Berurah* cites both opinions).

18. Y.D. 173:1, *Rema* 173:3. This is discussed in greater detail in Chapter 6, Paragraphs 5-14.

19. *Bris Yehudah* 22:n18. This is true even though the credit is extended by the credit card company, and not by the businessman who is selling the merchandise. Still, the businessman does not receive payment from the card company until later. In the interim, he is actually the one who is extending credit to the customer.

Businesses which incur expenses in the processing of credit card vouchers are permitted to pass along these expenses to their credit card customers. However, the charge may not exceed the actual cost to the business.

20. *Mishnas Ribbis* 7:3, based on the halachah outlined in the previous paragraph.

actually receiving a loan. He is prohibited from benefiting the customer in exchange for this loan.

This prohibition has two common applications:

a) A customer who orders merchandise for future delivery may wish to lock in today's price for that merchandise. This protects him from future price increases. Although a seller is normally permitted to guarantee a specific price for future delivery, he may not do so if a condition of the sale is that payment be made in advance. This is a Rabbinically prohibited form of Ribbis.[21]

---

21. Anytime money is advanced as part of a business transaction, the prohibitions which apply are only Rabbinic prohibitions (*Rema* 161:1).

Some exceptions to this prohibition:

• When the customer pays for an item which the seller does not have in his possession, the payment is considered an advance payment. However, if the seller has the merchandise in stock and ready for delivery at the time of payment, this is similar to a conventional sale, and the seller is permitted to guarantee the price of the item (*Y.D.* 175:4). This is true even if the customer does not receive legal title to the merchandise when he makes payment, and even though the merchant does not plan to deliver that same piece of merchandise which he has in stock (*Teshuvos R' Akiva Eiger* 1:52, *S.A. Harav* §34, *Chazon Ish* 76:1). Still, since the payment binds the seller to honor the sale agreement, this is considered a conventional payment for immediate purchase.

Additional details regarding this rule are found below, Chapter 8, Paragraphs 5-8.

• A price may be guaranteed, if the item being purchased has no set market value. Common examples of items with no set market value are precious stones, used cars and custom furniture. These items are appraised individually and their value can fluctuate greatly. Since these items have no clear market price, when a price is guaranteed this is not a clear benefit. This is therefore permitted. In this case, the seller is even permitted to offer a discounted price (*Rema* 173:7, *Chochmas Adam* 139:14, *Bris Yehudah* 23:3).

Additional details regarding this rule are found in Chapter 8, Paragraph 23.

• Prices may be guaranteed for merchandise which is readily available at a set market price. When this merchandise is sold, a seller is permitted to guarantee the market price, even if delivery will be made at a time when the price tends to be higher (*Y.D.* 175:1).

Additional details regarding this rule are found in Chapter 8, Paragraphs 10-12.

• If the money is advanced to the merchant and held by him, but he is not permitted to use the money until delivery is made, no loan has taken place. Therefore, if the merchant requests advance payment only because he wants to be sure that the customer will not default on payment, he may stipulate that the customer deposit funds in escrow, pending delivery. He would be permitted to offer the customer a financial incentive (such as guaranteeing his prices) for doing so.

• These prohibitions apply only where advance payment is *required*. When a customer is guaranteed a price, and he then makes advance payment on his own, this is permitted.

b) The seller is prohibited from offering benefits to those customers who agree to pay in advance. This means that a business may not set up a two-tier price system, offering a lower price to those who pay in advance.[22]

Trial Periods

15. Businesses sometimes allow a person to purchase an item and use it for a period of time. If the customer is not satisfied with the product, he can then return it for a refund. When this happens, the original sale is voided and the money is returned to the buyer.

This situation presents a Ribbis problem. The money which was originally given to the seller is in his possession on a contingency basis. If the customer decides to keep the product, the money would be used for payment. But if the sale is canceled, the money would be returned and it would turn out that this money was actually in the seller's possession on loan. In this case, the seller is considered to have borrowed the buyer's money, and is prohibited from benefiting the buyer in return. However, he *has* benefited the customer by allowing him to use his item for a period of time. This is considered Ribbis.

If the buyer returns the item after using it for a trial period, the businessman may not offer a full refund. He would be required to deduct a fair charge for the customer's use of the item.[23]

How to Avoid This Problem

16. The problem with permitting merchandise to be returned after a trial period is that the sale is invalidated retroactively, causing the original moneys to be considered a loan to the seller. This creates a borrower-lender situation and the Ribbis restrictions apply.

• According to *Igros Moshe* (2:63), whenever the seller is a corporation, these prohibitions do not apply (see Chapter 7, Paragraph 5). However, since this ruling is a matter of dispute it is preferable that a deal be designed to avoid this problem.

22. Y.D. 173:7. This type of Ribbis is also prohibited by Rabbinic law. Whenever Ribbis is part of a purchase agreement and not part of a conventional loan, it is not Biblically prohibited (*Rema* 161:1).

Many of the exceptions outlined in the previous note apply here as well. See Chapter 7, Paragraphs 3-18, for a full explanation.

23. *S.A. Harav* §55, *Minchas Elazar* 1:46, *Bris Yehudah* 28:4. If the *seller* has the option of voiding the sale by refunding the purchase price, these prohibitions also apply (Y.D. 174:1 in regard to real estate sales; *S.A. Harav* §54 and *Har Tzvi* 139 extend this to the sale of merchandise as well).

Most poskim hold that this entire problem is avoided if the original sale is completed in a manner which does not allow for it to be invalidated retroactively. Instead, the seller stipulates that if the customer is not satisfied with the product he will purchase it back from him. This language calls for a new sale rather than for return of the property. This allows the customer to return the product and recover his money, without a Ribbis problem.[24]

17. Another way to avoid this problem is to require the customer to retain the item for a specific number of days before he would be permitted to return it. The buyer now has irrevocable control of the item for a specified period of time. This makes it clear that the sale is a final one and that the property is his. Any subsequent transaction would then be a new sale.[25]

---

24. *Machneh Ephraim* §13, *Chavos Daas* 174:1, *Noda BeYehudah* 2:75, *Kreisi* 168:10 and 169:18, *Bris Yehudah* 28:8. Cf. *Har Tzvi* Y.D. 139. [Most of these poskim are discussing situations which involve the sale of real estate. The law is the same for the sale of merchandise.]

[*Chavos Daas* offers an alternative analysis. He explains that the problem with returning merchandise lies in the fact that when an item is returned, the sale is invalidated retroactively. Because of this, the original moneys, which were extended to the seller, are viewed as a loan. If the language which is used at the time of sale would not allow the sale to be voided retroactively, there would be no Ribbis problem.

Thus, *Chavos Daas* maintains that one may sell an item on the condition that the buyer retains the right to return the item. This is known as a *mechirah al minas lehachzir*, where a sale is considered final providing that the conditions of sale are met. According to this analysis, if a sale is made on the condition that the customer be permitted to return the item, the original sale is not invalidated when the property is later returned. (On the contrary, if the seller *does not* accept the property when it is returned, this would invalidate the sale, since the conditions of sale were not honored!)

Based on this, *Chavos Daas* rules that it would be sufficient for a business to use the following language: "The sale is made on the condition that the customer be permitted to return the merchandise within (a number) days for a full refund." The crucial point, according to *Chavos Daas*, is that the sale be made *conditional* to the right of the buyer to return the property.]

There are some poskim who disagree with this leniency (see *Bris Yehudah* 28:8). Although one may rely on the opinion of most poskim (who rule leniently), it is recommended that one also use the method of avoiding Ribbis which is outlined in the following paragraph.

25. *Sma* C.M. 207:11. Many poskim maintain that this condition alone would be sufficient to remove the Ribbis problems which are caused by an escape clause (*Bris Yehudah* 28:6 refers to this as a majority opinion). Still, since *Chavos Daas* 174:1 and S.A. *Harav* §54 reject this, it is preferable that this language be combined with the version of the escape clause outlined previously. The combined language should be acceptable according to all poskim.

To avoid a question of Ribbis, it is preferable that a business use both methods. A business should post the following:

Return Policy

If a customer is not satisfied with any product which is purchased here, the management will purchase it back from him, seven days after purchase.

18. Exchange Policy: Many businesses do not offer refunds, but allow customers to exchange damaged merchandise for another one of that same item. (This is common in the electronics and computer industries, as well as in the sale of eyeglasses.) This policy is permitted (see note below).[26]

Routine Transactions

19. Cashing a check: A person in need of cash may write a check and ask someone to cash it for him. However, he may not offer a discount to induce the person to cash the check (i.e., he may not sell a $100 check for $90). This is permitted only in certain circumstances (see note below).[27]

---

26. *Lehoros Nosson* 6:72 explains that when this happens, the original payment is considered a prepayment for the merchandise which is delivered at the later time (i.e., when the merchandise is exchanged). The question of Ribbis involves the possibility that the value of the item has gone up after the original payment, and that the consumer is therefore receiving a discount due to the fact that he offered the payment at an earlier time.

This is nevertheless permitted. As we have seen in Note 21, prepayments are permitted for items which are in the possession of the seller (*yesh lo*) at the time of payment; or even if they are not in his possession, this is permitted when the item is readily available in the marketplace at stable prices. This is almost always the case in regard to the consumer purchases discussed here.

27. *Bris Yehudah* 15:17 rules that this is permitted under the following conditions:

a) There are adequate funds in the account to cover the check. If there are no funds in the account, a person could not sell a check which is written on that account, even if he has overdraft privileges. In this case, the person is actually borrowing money and using the check as collateral. Since the bank owes him no money, he would not be selling a debt, but creating new debt.

b) The person who receives the check must accept a degree of risk, so that he would be liable in certain cases of loss. For example, if the check could not be cashed due to bank failure, the receiver would take the loss. [The receiver is not obligated to

20. Foreign Currency: All credit must be tied to the value of the local currency. Foreign currency is considered a commodity, and debt may not be tied to the value of a commodity.

For example, $100 worth of merchandise is purchased in the United States, on credit, at a time that this is worth $85 in Canadian currency. The buyer agrees to pay the supplier eighty-five Canadian dollars at a later date. However, thirty days later when the debt is paid, $100 in American currency is only worth $84 in Canadian currency. The customer may not pay the extra Canadian dollar, because this would mean that he is paying more than the $100 which he owes.[28]

---

accept liability if the check is not honored due to the lack of funds in the account (*Bris Yehudah*).]

c) The check is not postdated. If it is postdated, the check may not be sold at a discount, even if there are funds in the account.

Where all these conditions are present, *Bris Yehudah* rules that a person may offer to sell his own check, at a discount.

Mishnas Ribbis (13:n14) suggests that the ruling of *Bris Yehudah* applies only in Israel, and not in the United States. Under American law, an individual who passes a check is entitled to subsequently go to his bank and issue a stop payment order, which prevents the bank from honoring the check. Thus, the depositor retains legal rights to the money even after selling the check. Because of this, when a check is cashed, the bank's obligation is not truly sold to the buyer. This is not true in Israel (and in much of Europe), where it is a crime to stop a check without cause. There, bank laws require that cause be shown before a stop order can be issued. A more detailed analysis of American law appears below, as an Appendix to Chapter 12.

This is an issue related to the Biblical prohibition of Ribbis; therefore one must avoid this practice when a check is drawn on a U.S. bank.

Where a third party's check is offered for sale, many poskim hold that a discount may be offered, providing that the person who buys the check takes on the risk of the check being returned. If the check is returned, he would have to pursue the person who issued the check (and not the seller) for a refund. One may rely on these poskim in countries (such as Israel, England and France) where a depositor is not entitled to stop payment on his checks without cause. See Chapter 12, Paragraphs 26-28, where this is discussed in detail.

In the United States, where banking regulations permit a depositor to stop payment on his check, third-party checks should not be sold at discount (see Chapter 12, Paragraph 32). A Heter Iska may be used to permit this.

28. *Bris Yehudah* 22:n33. Debt is always established in the local currency. This customer therefore owes 100 American dollars, regardless of how the payment is made. At the time of payment, the seller should receive this amount and not more.

Bris Yehudah adds that if the customer had this foreign currency in his possession at the time that he received the merchandise, he could guarantee payment in that currency. (This is because of the exception of *yesh lo;* this concept is explained at length in Chapter 8, Paragraphs 5-8.)

We have the same rule when a person living in the United States borrows foreign currency. For example, he borrows eighty-five Canadian dollars at a time that it is worth $100 in American currency. If the Canadian currency decreases in value before the loan is repaid, the borrower would still owe $100, or the Canadian equivalent at the time that the loan was paid.[29]

"Keep the Change"

21. When paying a loan, the borrower does not always have the exact change with which to pay. He may wish to pay the loan with whatever bills or coins he has at hand, and allow the lender to keep the difference. This is prohibited except in cases where the amount of change is totally insignificant.[30]

22. When paying for a purchase: Reuven asks Shimon to purchase something on his behalf. Shimon buys the item, laying out his own money for the purchase. Later, when Shimon returns with the item, Reuven pays for it. In this case, it is common for Reuven to give Shimon a greater amount of money (sometimes rounding the bill upwards to an even amount) and tell him to keep the change.[31]

---

29. See *Minchas Yitzchak* 6:161 and *Bris Yehudah* 5:n35.

Igros Moshe Y.D. 3:37 rules that the dollar is considered a local currency in Israel, since businessmen (and even the government) commonly tie their agreements to the value of the dollar. Rabbi Y.S. Eliyashev Shlita (quoted in *Toras Ribbis* 19:8) concurs with this ruling. According to this view, loans could be tied to the dollar, even when they are extended in Israel. [Cf. *Bris Yehudah* 18:n15, who disputes this ruling.]

Toras Ribbis points out that these rulings were issued in the late 1970s when the Israeli economy suffered from hyperinflation. At that time, virtually all transactions were linked to the value of the dollar. Today, with inflation in check, Israelis deal in *shekalim*. Consequently, the dollar would no longer be viewed as currency.

R' Moshe Shternbuch Shlita (in *Kitzur Dinei Ribbis*) rules that when Israeli law prohibits the banks from trading dollars, this could not be considered a currency.

30. *Minchas Yitzchak* 9:88. *Minchas Yitzchak* rules that a slight overpayment is permitted in a case where neither the borrower nor lender would consider the amount significant, in that they would not search for that amount of money if they had dropped it on the floor.

31. Where the amount of change is insignificant, there is no problem (as in the previous note). The discussion here refers to situations where a meaningful sum of money is involved.

The laws outlined here also apply where Reuven sent Shimon to pick up an item that belongs to Reuven (e.g., clothing from the cleaners or a utensil from the repair shop). In this case too, if Shimon used his own money for payment, he may only be reimbursed for the actual cost.

If Shimon's intention was to purchase the item for Reuven, the item belongs to Reuven at the moment of purchase. Shimon's payment was actually a loan to Reuven. Reuven is therefore prohibited from benefiting Shimon. If Shimon had explicitly intended to acquire the item for himself, with the intention of selling it to Reuven at the time of delivery, no loan would have taken place. However, in general, we assume that Shimon's intention was to acquire the item for Reuven and to take possession for him.[32] Reuven is therefore prohibited from benefiting Shimon.[33]

---

32. C.M. 183:4 rules that when Reuven sends Shimon to purchase an item on his behalf, and Shimon uses his own money for the purchase, the item belongs to Reuven. If after purchasing the item, Shimon desires to keep it for himself, he would not be entitled to do so. See also *Machneh Ephraim Shiluchin* 18 and *Chazon Ish* to *Bava Kama* 21:11 who explain this ruling.

An application of this halachah appears in *Divrei Chaim* (C.M. 2:21). In the case presented there, someone was sent to purchase a lottery ticket. Before delivering the ticket, he discovered that it had won the lottery. The messenger decided to keep the ticket (and the prize) for himself. *Divrei Chaim* ruled that he may not do so, and that the ticket was the property of the sender from the moment it was purchased.

In our discussion of Ribbis, we have the same question: Who owns the item at the time of purchase?

If we were to assume that Shimon wants to become the legal owner of the item (and that he does not intend to acquire it for Reuven), when Shimon later delivers the item to Reuven he is actually selling it to him. Since no loan took place, there is no question of Ribbis and Reuven may pay any price for it.

However, since we assume that Shimon acquires the item as Reuven's agent and that the item belongs to Reuven from the moment of purchase, this means that when Shimon paid for the item, he was actually paying Reuven's bill. This is a loan, and Reuven is prohibited from benefiting Shimon.

33. There are two exceptions to this rule:

- Where Reuven is a relative who is accustomed to giving gifts to Shimon, Shimon may accept the additional money. This is based on *Shach* 160:4 who allows money to be added at the time of payment except where the added moneys appear to be Ribbis. In a case involving a close relative, it is obvious that the giver intends the additional money as a gift. (This is common in the case of parents who send their children on errands and allow them to keep the change.)

- Where Reuven explicitly states that Shimon may keep the change in recognition of the effort which he exerted in running the errand. In this case too, Shimon may keep the extra money.

[**Where the seller was a non-Jew:** It is not clear if this discussion would apply to cases where Shimon purchased the item from a non-Jewish merchant. This would depend on a complex halachic concept known as *shelucho shel baal hamamon*, which may require that when Shimon purchases an item for Reuven, Reuven must serve as an agent of the seller if he wishes to confer title to the Shimon. This would seem to exclude cases involving a non-Jewish seller, since a non-Jew does not confer legal agency (*shelichus*). A ruling on this issue is beyond the scope of this work (and this author).]

However, if Shimon purchased two pieces of the particular item, one for himself and one for Reuven, neither piece is designated for Reuven. It therefore cannot be said that Reuven has acquired the item. Rather, both pieces belong to Shimon until he actually delivers one to Reuven.[34] In this case, no loan took place and Reuven is not prohibited from benefiting Shimon.

"Fair" Ribbis Is also Ribbis

23. There is a common misconception that Ribbis is prohibited because it places an unfair burden on the borrower. This leads to a serious error in cases where Ribbis payments are considered fair, and are therefore paid.[35]

A common example involves a lender who has money in an interest-earning bank account. If he withdraws this money to lend it to a friend, he may not be reimbursed for the lost earnings.[36] The borrower may not

---

34. *Pischei Choshen Hil. Pikadon* 12:n63.

35. The Talmud alludes to this in B.M. 75b, "(Lenders who charge Ribbis) say that if the Torah had realized the profits involved, it would not have written (that Ribbis is prohibited)."

Taz 160:1 explains that this refers to people who justify charging Ribbis when the borrower is able to earn great profits by using the borrowed money. They rationalize that in such cases Ribbis payments are fair and justifiable. The Talmud speaks disparagingly of this attitude.

36. *Rashba* (Responsa 3:227) prohibits reimbursements and adds that if this were permitted, "all Ribbis would be permitted, because every loan causes a loss since (the lender) is unable to profit by other investments during the time (that the money is outstanding)."

Igros Moshe (Y.D. 3:93) applies this to our case. *Bris Yehudah* 3:n4 calls this a common problem, since "people don't realize" that this can be Ribbis Ketzutzah (Biblically prohibited Ribbis).

When one lends money, he fulfills a positive Biblical mitzvah. Since Jews are happy to forgo financial gain in the performance of mitzvos, a lender should view his lost interest as money well spent on an important mitzvah.

Igros Moshe (ibid.) rules that when the loan was offered to a poor person who is eligible to receive charity, the lost revenue may be considered a charitable donation which may be deducted from one's *maaser* (tithing) account. However, this applies only when the loan was a large one, which one is not technically obligated to offer, since the loss of interest is substantial. Where the lost interest is only a minimal sum, it is considered the cost of performing a mitzvah and not a contribution to charity.

It should be noted that in most cases a Heter Iska can be used to effectively permit reimbursement. The standard Heter Iska would be used. This appears below, in Chapter 23.

When a term deposit (such as a CD) is prematurely withdrawn, penalties are incurred. When this premature withdrawal was made solely for the purpose of lending the funds to another Jew, there is a question if the penalties may be passed on to the borrower. (The details of this are discussed in Chapter 4, Paragraph 9.)

reimburse the lender for this loss of profit, even if he fails to repay the loan on time.[37]

Similarly, a lawyer is often given funds which are to be placed in an interest-bearing escrow account. A Jewish lawyer may not be given permission to use these funds, if he is required to reimburse the lost interest which would have been earned in the account.[38]

Brokerage Accounts

24. When money is held in a brokerage account, and the funds are not actually being used to purchase stocks, interest is earned by the account. If the brokerage is owned by Jews, many poskim prohibit these interest payments.[39] However, if the brokerage is incorporated as a corporation, some poskim permit these payments.[40]

Buying Stocks on Margin

25. When purchasing stocks through a brokerage, a customer is usually given the option of buying on margin. When buying on margin, the customer actually advances cash for only a portion of the purchase price of the stocks. The remainder of the purchase cost is paid by the brokerage. Later, when the stock is sold, the brokerage takes back

---

37. *Rashba* in Responsa 3:227. *Beis Hillel* Y.D. 170 rules that reimbursement is permitted when a loan is not repaid on time. Still, most poskim follow the *Rashba* in prohibiting this (see *Beis Yitzchak* 2:1, *Imrei Yosher* 1:149, *Bris Yehudah* 2:15).

When failure to pay on time actually caused a loss; see Chapter 4, Paragraphs 6 and 7.

38. Additional details regarding escrow funds appear below, Chapter 13, Paragraphs 5 and 6.

39. *Vechai Achicha Imach* 8:94, *Mishnas Ribbis* 2:n10.

40. **Where a brokerage is owned by Jewish and non-Jewish partners:** The status of this type of company is a subject of dispute. Where a majority of the stocks in a particular company are owned by Jews, one should follow the stringent opinion and consider this a Jewish entity. However, where most are non-Jews, one may follow the lenient opinion, providing that the Jewish minority are not actually running the firm (R' Moshe Feinstein zt"l, quoted in *Mishnas Ribbis* 2:n7; See below, Chapter 5, Paragraph 26, for additional details regarding this dispute).

Igros Moshe Y.D. 2:63 maintains that corporations are permitted to pay interest for money which they borrow. This ruling appears to have an earlier source, in *Rivash* 305 and 308. This was also the opinion of *Maharshag* (in a letter published in the Noam Journal 5719:2; see also his Responsa Y.D. 3). This ruling is disputed by many contemporary poskim. Therefore, wherever possible, one should avoid this situation by using a Heter Iska.

its loan, plus an interest charge for the time that the stocks had been purchased. This interest payment constitutes Ribbis and is prohibited (when the brokerage is a Jewish company).[41]

---

41. *Vechai Achicha Imach* ibid., *Mishnas Ribbis* ibid. A Heter Iska may be used to permit this (*Vechai Achicha Imach* ibid.).

Where the brokerage is a corporation, this prohibition would still apply. Although *Igros Moshe* allows a corporation to pay Ribbis, he rules that Ribbis payments may not be made to corporations with Jewish owners.

Where funding is provided by outside financial institutions: The rules presented here assume that funding for stock purchases is provided by the brokerage itself. The same rules apply to cases where the brokerage borrows money from other institutions to fund these purchases. However, in cases where the brokerage arranges for outside (non-Jewish) institutions to lend money directly to customers who purchase on margin, these restrictions do not apply. [The stock may be used as collateral for this loan. However, the brokerage may act as guarantor for the loan only under the conditions outlined in Chapter 15.]

CHAPTER 2

The Different Categories of Ribbis

A. Biblically prohibited Ribbis (1-15)

- ☐ Ribbis Ketzutzah (1-2)
- ☐ The extent of the prohibition (3-5)
- ☐ Lending goods or services (6-9)
- ☐ Penalty clauses (10)
- ☐ Entering into agreements which call for Ribbis (11-12)
- ☐ Tzad echod beRibbis (13-14)
- ☐ Witnesses and lawyers to a Ribbis transaction (15)

B. Rabbinically prohibited Ribbis (16-24)

- ☐ Ribbis DeRabbanan (16-17)
- ☐ Ribbis bederech mekach u'memkar (18)
- ☐ Ribbis Mukdemes (19-21)
- ☐ Ribbis Me'ucheres (22-25)
- ☐ A Ribbis contract (26)

Introduction

Someone who lends money for Ribbis violates numerous Biblical prohibitions. *Rambam* (*Hil. Malveh* 4:2) lists six distinct prohibitions; *Ramban* (notes to *Sefer HaMitzvos, shoresh* 6) adds a seventh. These Biblical prohibitions apply only in specific cases and to specific benefits. The Rabbinic prohibition is broader, and applies to virtually all benefits which a borrower might extend to a lender. In this chapter, we will delineate the rules for determining whether a loan is Biblically or Rabbinically prohibited. This determination is important, because there are many differences between Biblically and Rabbinically prohibited Ribbis.[1]

---

1. There are numerous areas in halachah where a distinction is made between Biblical and Rabbinic Ribbis. They include the following;

    a) The Rabbinic prohibitions were not extended to charities. Funds which belong to charitable organizations or to orphans may be lent under conditions which call for Ribbis payments, provided that these payments are not Biblically prohibited (*Rema* 160:18). This rule (and its applications) is presented in Chapter 5, Paragraphs 13-16.

    b) Where a lender receives Ribbis in the form of a sefer or other mitzvah-related object, this is permitted, provided that the Ribbis is not a form which is Biblically prohibited (*Rema* 172:1). This rule (and its applications) is presented in Chapter 5, Paragraph 22. [According to most poskim, this does not apply to a mitzvah need of the borrower; see Chapter 5, Paragraph 21.]

    c) One who receives Biblically prohibited Ribbis may be compelled to return it. This does not apply to Rabbinically prohibited Ribbis (Y.D. 161:2).

    d) A lawyer is prohibited from preparing legal documents to facilitate a loan between Jews, if the loan agreement calls for Ribbis payments. Where only Rabbinically prohibited Ribbis is involved, this is permitted under specific circumstances. These circumstances are outlined below, Note 25.

    e) Certain leniencies are permitted only in cases of Rabbinically prohibited Ribbis. These include certain types of penalty clauses (see Chapter 9, Paragraph 7). Another example involves a customer who buys on credit. He may show his gratitude to the merchant by adding a small amount to the payment, provided that he does not explicitly state that this money is being added in appreciation of the credit which was extended (*Rema* 160:4, *Shach* 160:4 and 5). This rule is presented in Chapter 4, Paragraphs 22-23.

    f) A general Talmudic principle for cases involving doubt is that issues which involve Biblical law must be decided stringently, while issues which involve questions of Rabbinic law may be decided leniently. This is a recurring theme in the laws of Ribbis as well; where a ruling is a matter of doubt we rule stringently in cases involving Ribbis Ketzutzah, but we are lenient in cases involving Rabbinic Ribbis.

A unique aspect of the laws of Ribbis is that there are Biblical prohibitions on both the borrower and the lender. *Rambam* counts two Biblical prohibitions which apply to someone who borrows money for Ribbis. This sets the laws of Ribbis apart from virtually all finance-related prohibitions, where someone who is willing to sustain a loss may waive his financial rights. *Tur* (Y.D. 160) sees this as an indication of the severity of the prohibition of Ribbis.

Ribbis is often translated as interest. The term 'interest' is commonly used to refer to a per annum payment, usually for a specific percentage of the outstanding balance of a loan. It should be noted that this definition is not reflected in the Hebrew term Ribbis. *Any payment* which is made for a loan in excess of the amount borrowed constitutes Ribbis.

A. Biblically prohibited Ribbis

Ribbis Ketzutzah

1. Biblically prohibited Ribbis is called Ribbis Ketzutzah (lit., pre-arranged Ribbis). This is because the Torah prohibits Ribbis only when arrangements for the payments were made at the time that the loan was extended. In the case of a free loan, however, where the borrower delivers a gift to the lender at the time of payment, the only prohibition is by Rabbinic law, since there was no prearranged commitment to offer the gift.[2]

The Biblical prohibition applies regardless of when payment is actually made. Even if the agreement calls for Ribbis to be paid long after the loan was paid up, the prohibition applies.[3]

2. There are two other cases of Ribbis Ketzutzah:

The money was already in the borrower's possession. For example, he had been holding it for safekeeping. If the owner of the funds later

---

2. This is based on the verse, *Your moneys you shall not give him as neshech, and for interest you shall not give your foodstuffs* (Lev. 25:37).

The verse twice uses the phrase '*you shall not give.*' This indicates that the commitment to pay Ribbis already existed at the time that the loan was given. In the case of a free loan, when there is no agreement to pay Ribbis, the loan was not 'given' for interest. Therefore it is not Biblically prohibited (*Shach* 166:7, quoting *Magid Mishnah*).

3. *Bris Yehudah* 5:1. The crucial point in defining Ribbis Ketzutzah is that the agreement to pay already existed at the time of the loan. The timing of the payment itself does not determine if Ribbis is Biblically or Rabbinically prohibited.

agrees to allow the borrower to use the funds in exchange for payment, this is Ribbis Ketzutzah.[4]

An interest-free loan originated with a payment date. Later, the lender agreed to extend the term of the loan in exchange for interest payments. Since the commitment to pay Ribbis was made at the time that the extension was granted, it is considered Ribbis Ketzutzah.[5]

The Extent of the Prohibition

3. The prohibition applies no matter how much Ribbis is being charged. Even if the borrower pays interest at a rate which is tied to inflation or to the Consumer Price Index, this constitutes Ribbis Ketzutzah.[6]

---

4. R' Akiva Eiger to *Shach* 166:7, *Erech Shai* 177:7. In this case, the money became a loan at the time that permission was granted for its use. Since an agreement to pay Ribbis was established at that time, this constitutes Ribbis Ketzutzah.

If money was originally given as an investment, through the use of a Heter Iska, and after the termination of the Iska the money was lent to the receiver (for Ribbis), this too constitutes Ribbis Ketzutzah (*Erech Shai*).

5. This is actually a subject of dispute between *Rambam* and *Raavid* in *Hil. Malveh* 6:3. Both opinions are quoted in Y.D. 166:2. *Shach* and all subsequent poskim follow the stringent opinion of *Raavid*, quoted here.

Kreisi 166 and *Bris Yehudah* (3:6 and Note 14) limit this prohibition to cases where the extension was granted after the payment had already come due. Since the borrower was then obligated to return the borrowed funds, any payment for an extension is considered to be made at the time that a loan (i.e., the extension) was made. If (for example) the original loan called for payment to be made at the end of twelve months, and the twelve months had already passed when the extension was requested, a Ribbis agreement would then be considered Ribbis Ketzutzah. However, where payment was due at the end of twelve months, but after the first six months the borrower paid the lender to extend the due date, this is not Ribbis Ketzutzah. (This is based on *Meiri* to *Kiddushin* 6b.)

If a loan is payable on demand, any extension is considered as if it were made at the time that the loan was due. Even if provisions of the loan required the lender to give prior notice (for example, to give three months' notice that he was demanding payment) and no such notice was offered, payment for an extension is considered Ribbis Ketzutzah (*Teshuvos R' Akiva Eiger* 1:53).

6. *Chazon Ish* Y.D. 24:5, *Igros Moshe* Y.D. 2:114, *Minchas Yitzchak* 6:61. Ribbis is prohibited even if it represents compensation for lost value.

If the currency was devalued during the term of the loan, may the borrower compensate the lender for the loss in value?

This is a subject of dispute among the poskim, see C.M. 74:7. One should follow the stringent opinion and only the moneys borrowed should be repaid. For example, someone borrows ten *shekalim* in Israel at the time that they were worth $4. Later,

4. The prohibition applies regardless of how the interest payment is made. It makes no difference if it is a per annum payment or a one-time payment; if it is linked to the amount of outstanding balance or not; or if the payment is linked to the length of time that the loan is outstanding. Even when a loan is interest free for an initial period and interest payments are only required afterwards, the prohibition of Ribbis Ketzutzah applies.[7]

Even when an agreement does not mention interest payments, but it requires that the borrower give the lender a gift, this is Ribbis Ketzutzah.[8]

5. This prohibition applies regardless of whether the borrower is wealthy or not.[9] Even if the borrower is perfectly willing to pay the Ribbis, it is prohibited.[10]

---

they were devalued and the ten *shekalim* are worth only $3. At the time of payment the borrower should pay only ten *shekalim*, despite the fact that the *shekel* is now worth less (*Minchas Yitzchak* ibid., *Bris Yehudah* 5:n35). See also Chapter 8, Paragraph 27.

7. *Bris Yehudah* 3:1.

Ribbis Ketzutzah also applies in cases where the precise amount of Ribbis is not set at the time of the loan. For example, one has money which is earning interest in a bank and a borrower asks that the funds be loaned to him, with the pledge that he will replace the lost earnings at the same rate that the bank would have paid. Although no precise payment was set, this constitutes Ribbis Ketzutzah. *Bris Yehudah* 3:n4 bemoans the lack of awareness of this prohibition: "This is very common and people do not realize (that a Heter Iska is required)."

[We have already seen (in Chapter 1, Paragraph 23) that even though this payment is compensation for lost revenue, this does not affect its status as Ribbis Ketzutzah.]

8. *Pischei Teshuvah* 160:5, quoting *Teshuvah MeAhavah* 1:54-58, reports the following arrangement:

Reuven told Shimon, "I hereby give you $100 as an outright gift. However, this presentation is contingent on you giving me a gift of $120 in thirty days."

By stipulating that the funds which were given are gifts, Reuven hoped to avoid the prohibition on Ribbis. After a lengthy discussion, *Teshuvah MeAhavah* concludes that this is a form of Ribbis Ketzutzah, despite the fact that the principals never used the word "loan."

See Chapter 17, Paragraph 24, regarding a Charitable Remainder Trust, which is a financial arrangement similar to the arrangement described by *Teshuvah MeAhavah*.

9. *Rema* 160:1.

10. Even if the borrower waives his rights to protection from having to pay Ribbis, it is prohibited, "...for every case of Ribbis involves waiving (of the prohibition); but the Torah did not waive, and indeed prohibits, the waiving (of this prohibition). Therefore waiving one's rights does not help at all, even in regard to Rabbinically prohibited Ribbis" (*Tur* 160).

Lending Goods or Services

6. The prohibition of Ribbis Ketzutzah applies to the lending of goods as well. For example, one may not borrow ten bushels of apples and stipulate that he will return eleven bushels at a later time.[11]

7. This prohibition also applies to the bartering of services. For example, one may not paint a house and stipulate that the homeowner will repay him by painting a larger house at a later time. However, it is not clear if this is a Biblical form of Ribbis.[12]

8. Credit for purchases: Interest payments which are paid for credit on purchases are a Rabbinically prohibited form of Ribbis.[13] However, when a customer is late with payment and Ribbis is charged in return for an extension of credit time, this payment is Ribbis Ketzutzah.[14]

9. Cashing a check for less than its face value may also entail Ribbis Ketzutzah. The halachos which relate to this are presented at length below, Chapter 12, Paragraphs 26 - 31.

10. Penalty Clauses: These clauses require a borrower to make additional payments if the loan is not repaid on time. Most penalty clauses do involve Ribbis violations. This is discussed at length in Chapter 9. A distinction is drawn between two types of prohibited penalty clauses. When the clause calls for a one-time penalty, this is Rabbinically prohibited.[15] However, where the penalty requires the

---

11. *Bava Metzia* 60b: If the price of apples goes down, so that the fair market value of eleven bushels at the time of payment is equal to ten bushels at the time of the loan, the borrower may return eleven bushels because he is returning the same value that he received. If the fair market value does not fluctuate in this way, the extra payment is considered Ribbis Ketzutzah. (See Chapter 14, Paragraphs 15 and 16.)

12. Y.D. 176:7. See *Divrei Sofrim* (*Beur Halachah* at the end of 162) who discusses whether this is Biblically prohibited.

Chavos Daas (161: end of 1) points out that any Ribbis which is paid as a result of a sale or employment (rather than an outright loan) is only Rabbinically prohibited. (See also *Chavos Daas* 162:1.)

13. *Rema* 161:1. These are considered purchase payments rather than loan payments. The Biblical prohibition is limited to interest for loans.

Chavos Daas 161:1 applies this to credit for services as well.

14. *Chavos Daas* 166:4, *S.A. Harav* §4. When negotiating for an extension, the parties are establishing the debt. Subsequent payments are considered debt payments rather than purchase payments and the Ribbis prohibitions apply. When a Heter Iska is used, it is permitted.

15. Y.D. 167:14.

borrower to pay interest which increases based on the length of the
delay, it is Ribbis Ketzutzah.[16]

Entering Into Agreements Which Call for Ribbis

11. A lender may prefer to bluff his borrower by including a penalty
clause in the loan document. The lender, being an observant Jew,
has no intention of ever collecting this penalty. His intention is to
pressure the borrower (who may be unaware of this prohibition) to
repay the loan on time.

Many poskim rule that this is prohibited, because setting a Ribbis
obligation is itself a Biblical prohibition, even if it is never enforced.[17]

12. These prohibitions apply even when the borrower is using the
funds to realize a profit.[18] Even when the buyer purchases
merchandise on credit, for the purpose of selling it at a profit, the seller
is prohibited from sharing the profits with his creditor.[19]

---

16. Y.D. 167:16 and *Shach* 33.

17. This is based on the verse, *And you shall not place neshech on him* (*Ex.* 22:24). The
verse prohibits contracting for Ribbis, and does not mention the actual Ribbis payment.
This is understood to be a separate prohibition against the setting of Ribbis obligations.
Poskim dispute the extent of this prohibition. Some poskim maintain that this
prohibition is violated only if the Ribbis is ultimately paid (*Shaar Deah* 177:11 and
Avnei Nezer 144:1). According to this opinion, it would be permitted to sign a contract
which calls for Ribbis payments if this clause is never actually enforced.

Others disagree and maintain that stipulating Ribbis is a separate prohibition which
is violated even if the payment is never made (*Bach*, quoted by *Shaar Deah* 159:1 and
177:11, *Imrei Yosher* 1:149:3; this also appears to be the opinion of *Igros Moshe* Y.D.
2:65). According to this opinion, it would not be permitted to sign a contract which calls
for Ribbis payments, even if this clause is never actually enforced (*Maharsham* 4:138,
s.v. *u'ma she'shaal*). This opinion is presented here. Because the prohibition under
discussion is Biblical, one must follow the stringent opinion.

A second case: This type of situation can also occur in a reverse form. *Imrei Yosher*
(ibid.) deals with the case of a borrower who is unable to get a loan, except from a Jew
who demands Ribbis payments. He wishes to sign a contract obligating himself to pay
Ribbis, and plans to refuse to pay the Ribbis portion when it comes due. *Imrei Yosher*
forbids this for two reasons. First, the prohibition on paying Ribbis would be violated by
signing the commitment, even if Ribbis were never paid. Second, one may not commit
to an agreement unless he intends to comply with its terms. Agreeing to terms with the
intent of failing to fulfill them is a form of deceit which is tantamount to thievery.

To summarize: Neither borrower nor lender may make a commitment to pay Ribbis,
even if the payment is never made.

18. *Taz* 160:1.

19. Y.D. 177:1. In Chapter 22, we will see that cash or merchandise may be offered as an
investment rather than as a loan. When the deal is structured in this manner, profits (and
losses, if there are any) are shared between the parties.

Tzad Echod BeRibbis

13. The Biblical prohibition of Ribbis only applies to cases where the arrangements for Ribbis payments were made at the time that the loan was extended. If the original agreement was a conditional one, calling for Ribbis payments to be made only if certain conditions were met, this is called *tzad echod beRibbis*, an agreement which allows a possibility of Ribbis.[20] There is a dispute regarding the status of this type of agreement; some consider it to be Ribbis Ketzutzah, while others view it as Ribbis DeRabbanan.[21]

---

20. This is a concept which appears numerous times in the Talmud. To cite one example: The Talmud (*Megillah* 27b) discusses the case of a synagogue which had been sold. The purchase agreement included an escape clause, which allows the seller to reclaim the synagogue by returning the purchase price. If this escape clause is exercised, there would be a Ribbis problem. This is because it would then turn out that the buyer had extended funds to the seller for a period of time. This is a loan. In exchange, the buyer had use of the building for that period of time (until the clause was exercised) without paying rent. This is considered *tzad echod beRibbis* because the agreement results in Ribbis only if the escape clause is used. If the sellers do not reclaim the building, no loan will have taken place. This is prohibited; the only question is whether the prohibition is Biblical in nature.

[It should be noted that this is not limited to a situation which involves the sale of a synagogue. This halachah applies to the sale of any home (Y.D. 174:1; see Chapter 13, Paragraph 19).]

An exception: The concept of *tzad echod beRibbis* applies only to an agreement that allows the individuals who are involved to affect the outcome of their transaction. Sometimes, an agreement is completed, and market fluctuations will determine whether the agreement calls for Ribbis. *Tosafos* (B.M. 63a, s.v. *tzad echod*) explains that this is not considered a case of *tzad echod beRibbis*.

For example, someone borrows merchandise and pledges to return similar merchandise at a later time. If the value of the merchandise goes up in the interval, the payment would constitute Ribbis because it is worth more than the loan. This is known as *seah b'seah* and is prohibited. Is this a case of *tzad echod beRibbis*?

In this case, the original agreement may or may not cause a Ribbis payment. But this determination is not dependent on the people involved; instead, this depends solely on market fluctuations (i.e., whether the value of the merchandise goes up). This is not considered a case of *tzad echod beRibbis*. (Other applications of this rule include the cases outlined in Paragraphs 6 and 7, above.)

21. *Taz* 174:1 (based on the language of *Shulchan Aruch*) rules that this is Ribbis Ketzutzah.

Shach 172:29 disagrees and rules that this is only Ribbis DeRabbanan. See also *Shach* 174:1, who explains the language of *Shulchan Aruch* according to his own opinion.

14. In all the cases outlined here, there is no difference whether it is the lender who requested Ribbis or if the borrower offered to pay. In either case, the agreement is considered Ribbis Ketzutzah.[22]

Witnesses and Lawyers to a Ribbis Deal

15. The Biblical prohibition of Ribbis also applies to someone who acts as a witness to a transaction involving Ribbis Ketzutzah.[23] This also extends to those who prepare the documents necessary for this transaction.[24] It is therefore prohibited to act as a lawyer who prepares the documents for a transaction involving Ribbis.[25]

---

22. *Rema* 160:14. If the lender was prepared to offer the loan even if no Ribbis were paid, and he then accepts the borrower's offer to pay Ribbis, this would be a Rabbinic prohibition (*Mabit* 1:51, *Bris Yehudah* 3:n10).

23. Y.D. 160:1. Witnesses are in violation of the verse, *And you shall not place neshech on him* (*Ex.* 22:24). The verse prohibits contracting for Ribbis, and applies to anyone involved in establishing the Ribbis contract (*Bava Metzia* 75b).

Sometimes a lender is not willing to offer a loan if there are no witnesses. In this case, the witnesses are in violation of the additional Biblical prohibition of *Lifnei iver lo setain michshol* (lit., before a blind person do not place a stumbling block). This is a general prohibition on causing someone to violate any Biblical law. This applies when someone causes a violation of the laws of Ribbis as well (Y.D. 160:1).

If a loan would be extended even if no witnesses are found, the prohibition of *Lifnei iver* does not apply. [If other people are available to serve as witnesses, does the prohibition of *Lifnei iver* apply? See Chapter 15, Note 6, where this is discussed at length.]

24. *Shach* 160:1.

A difficulty: While it is clear that the one who prepares the documents for a Ribbis transaction is in violation of Biblical law ("all poskim agree to this "; *Shach*), it is not clear why this is so. The Ribbis prohibition also applies to loans which are extended on oral agreement, without any document. If so, why is the document related to the prohibition? See *Bris Yehudah* 1:n54 who deals with this question.

One might argue that this prohibition applies to the person preparing the document only where the loan would not have been extended otherwise. However, it is clear from *Tosafos* (to *Bava Metzia* 75b s.v. *areiv*) that the prohibition of *And you shall not place neshech on him* even applies to cases where the loan would have been extended even without documents..

25. See *Divrei Sofrim* 160: *Emek Davar* 31.

When a lawyer does not actually help prepare legal documents, may he be involved in facilitating a Ribbis transaction, or collecting Ribbis payments? Similarly, may a Jewish bookkeeper bill for Ribbis payments on behalf of his Jewish employer?

Where the payments involve Ribbis Ketzutzah, it is prohibited to facilitate a Ribbis transaction or to collect Ribbis payments, because of the Biblical prohibition of *Lifnei iver lo setain michshol*, which is a general prohibition on causing someone to violate *any*

B. Rabbinically prohibited Ribbis

16. We have seen that the Biblical prohibition on Ribbis applies only when there was a commitment to pay Ribbis at the time that the loan was given. By Rabbinic law, the borrower is prohibited from paying interest or offering a gift to the lender even if he had not previously committed himself to do so. These payments constitute Ribbis D'Rabbanan.[26]

Biblical law. This applies when someone causes a violation of the laws of Ribbis as well (Y.D. 160:1).

However, the Biblical prohibition of *Lifnei iver* applies only when a person is involved in a transgression which would not have happened without his involvement (see Chapter 15, Note 6, for an elaboration on this point). Therefore, in cases where the agreement would be completed or the Ribbis collected, without the assistance of the Jewish lawyer or employee (e.g., the employer himself would have pursued collection or he would have hired non-Jews to act as lawyers), there is no Biblical violation of *Lifnei iver.* However, there is another violation: the Rabbinic prohibition of *mesayeia ovrei aveirah,* aiding sinners. A person must therefore avoid these situations.

In cases where a lawyer or employee finds it difficult to avoid this situation (for example, if this would cause animosity between him and his employer), he may be involved in these Ribbis transactions. This is based on the ruling of *Meishiv Davar* 2:31 and *Maharsham* 2:93 who rules leniently in situations involving *mesayeia ovrei aveirah,* when a person is involved in arrangements for a transgression but not in the act of the transgression itself. Here too, the lawyer or employee could not actually sign the Ribbis agreement or take possession of the Ribbis payment, but he may make the arrangements for these to take place (see also *Binyan Zion* 1:15).

Where the payments involve Ribbis DeRabbanan, and the collection could be made by others, there are additional factors which would be grounds for leniency. *Pri Megadim* (O.C. 163:2, and cited by *Mishnah Berurah* 163:12) questions whether the prohibition of *mesayeia ovrei aveirah* applies to a person who aids another to transgress a Rabbinic law. This question is discussed by many poskim (see *Beis Yehudah* Y.D. 1:17 who rules leniently; see also *Tuv Tam Vodaas* 3:2:31, *Sdei Chemed* Vol. 2 and Vol. 6 and *Yechaveh Daas* 3:67). Additionally, when the borrower and lender are deliberately violating the law, many poskim hold that the prohibition of *mesayeia ovrei aveirah* does not apply (see *Shach* 151:6 and *Dagul MeiRivavah*). In these cases, therefore, one may act leniently.

Salesmen or brokers may not arrange business dealings which involve Ribbis payments (*Shach* ibid.).

26. Y.D. 160:4 and *Shach* 6. At the time that the loan is paid, the borrower is prohibited from adding to the payment in any way. This prohibition is more stringent than the general prohibition against benefiting the lender during the course of a loan, in two ways. First, this prohibition is violated even if the lender and borrower are friends and are accustomed to sending gifts to each other. In addition, this prohibition is violated even if the gift is a small one which might have been sent even if there was no loan (*S.A. Harav* §7).

17. During the entire period of the loan, the borrower may not give a gift to the lender, even if he does not mention the gift in connection with the loan.[27]

Ribbis Bederech Mekach U'memkar

18. Where a credit arrangement is part of a business deal, the prohibition of paying Ribbis is Rabbinic in nature. This is known as *Ribbis bederech mekach u'memkar*, Ribbis which is part of a business transaction and is one of the more lenient forms of Rabbinic Ribbis.[28] For this reason, there are various leniencies which are permitted in regard to purchase credit, which would not be permitted in cases involving loans.[29]

---

27. *Beis Yosef* 160, *Shach* 166:9, *Bris Yehudah* 5:n7.

If the borrower and lender are close friends, even favors which had not previously been extended may be offered. Such a favor is permitted only if it is clear that the favor would have been offered irrespective of the loan (*Shach* 166:1). See Chapter 1, Paragraphs 1-4, where this was discussed at length.

28. For example, businessmen who purchase merchandise from a wholesaler often do so on credit, agreeing to make payment at a later date. If a businessman were to arrange to pay interest for this credit period, this would be considered Ribbis DeRabbanan since the debt originated as credit for a purchase.

29. This is true of the many leniencies delineated in Chapters 6, 7, 8, 12 and 13.

For example, we will see that in many cases a seller is permitted to sell an item at a higher price when he is offering credit, provided that he does not state explicitly that the price was raised due to the credit terms. This is permitted even if the seller and buyer know full well that the price is tied to the credit arrangements. Still, this is permitted because it is not obvious to outsiders that the price is tied to the credit.

This leniency does not apply in other cases of Ribbis DeRabbanan. For example, when a loan passes between friends, the borrower may extend favors to the lender whenever it is clear that the favors would have been offered irrespective of the loan (as in Chapter 1, Paragraph 1). However, this is prohibited when the person knows that he is extending the favor in gratitude for the loan, even if it is not obvious to outsiders that the benefit is tied to the loan (*S.A. Harav* §11, *Bris Yehudah* 10:8).

Why does halachah treat *Ribbis bederech mekach u'memkar* more leniently than other Rabbinically prohibited forms of Ribbis?

R' Akiva Eiger (to *Bava Metzia* 64b s.v. *bemasnisan*) explains: "When it is in the manner of a purchase, Ribbis is not prohibited by Biblical law, since there was no loan. The Rabbis prohibited this, because the purchase was not completed immediately and the [outstanding] funds are similar to a loan. But this was prohibited only where it is obvious that something is being done because of the credit, but where it is not obvious, no [prohibition exists]. This is true even if a person knows in his mind that he is doing something because of the credit; still there is no prohibition since there was no loan. A prohibition exists only because this appears to be Ribbis, and therefore if no extra benefit is obvious, this is not prohibited. But regarding other types of Rabbinic Ribbis, for

Before the Loan Is Given

19. *Ribbis Mukdemes* (Preloan gifts): One may not send a gift to a potential lender with the hope that this will influence him favorably to offer a loan.[30]

If a gift is given on the expressed condition that a loan be offered, the gift is Ribbis Ketzutzah.[31]

20. The extent of this prohibition: Some poskim hold that the prohibition on *Ribbis Mukdemes* applies even if the gift is small and it might have been given even if there was no potential for a loan. As long as the sender's intent is to influence the recipient to offer a loan, it is prohibited.[32]

Others permit small gifts, even with the intent of influencing the lender, as long as no mention of the loan is made when giving the gift and it is not obvious that the sender has an ulterior motive (e.g., he is a friend who would send gifts irrespective of his need for a loan). One may rely on this opinion.[33]

21. One who receives a gift from a friend as part of a normal friendly relationship may subsequently lend him money.[34] Some poskim even permit the lender to state that the loan is in gratitude for a gift or favor.[35] However, if the gift is given with the clear intent of influencing

---

example when payments are not arranged at the time of the loan, where it is a Rabbinic decree that Ribbis not be paid here even where it is not obvious [to outsiders that the gift is being given as Ribbis], if a person knows in his mind that he is doing this because of the loan, this remains prohibited. This is because this prohibition is not due to an appearance of Ribbis. Rather, it is itself a prohibition to give Ribbis because of a loan." See also *Avnei Nezer* 175:7 who offers a similar explanation and provides numerous applications of this distinction between *Ribbis bederech mekach u'memkar* and other Ribbis DeRabbanan.

30. Y.D. 160:6.

31. R' Akiva Eiger to 160:6, *Chavos Daas* 160:3.

32. *Shach* 160:10, *Chochmas Adam* 131:89.

33. *Rema* 160:6, *Taz* 160:3, R' Akiva Eiger to *Shach* 160:10.
  S.A. Harav §7 rules that one should follow the *Shach's* opinion as a personal stringency (but may rule leniently for others). Since the prohibition under discussion is Rabbinic in nature, one may rely on the *Rema's* leniency. This is also the ruling of *Bris Yehudah* 5:6.

34. *Radvaz* (3:233) explains that since most loans are offered to friends because of a close personal relationship, small gifts are not considered Ribbis.

35. *Mishnas Ribbis* 3:n12, quoting contemporary poskim.

the lender to offer the loan, the lender may not subsequently extend a loan to the sender.[36]

Ribbis Me'ucheres: After the Loan Is Repaid

22. *Ribbis Me'ucheres* (Postpayment Ribbis): After the loan has been repaid, the borrower may not send a gift to the lender if he stipulates that it is in gratitude for the loan.[37]

23. When a short period of time has elapsed after the loan was repaid, the borrower is permitted to send gifts to the lender, provided that the gift is of minimal value (so that it is not obvious that the gift is related to the loan) and no mention of the loan is made.[38] According to most poskim, this is permitted even when the borrower actually intends the gift to be an expression of gratitude for the loan.[39]

24. When a longer period of time has passed after the loan was repaid, even a large gift may be sent to the lender, provided that no mention is made of the loan.[40]

25. Even after many years have passed, the borrower may not send a gift to the lender if he explicitly states that he is doing so in gratitude for the loan.[41]

---

36. *Bris Yehudah* 5:n9.

37. Y.D. 160:6.

38. *Rema* 160:6 and *Shach* 8.
    S.A. *Harav* §7 defines a minimal gift as something "many people routinely send to a friend." [*Shach* 160:9 implies that gifts are routine when their existence is not something that people would be moved to discuss publicly.]
Any gift which obviously would not have been given if no loan had been made is considered a large gift (*Shach* ibid.). Naturally, this varies from situation to situation.

39. *Shach* 160:10 and *Chochmas Adam* 131:8-9 prohibit any type of gift where the borrower intends it as gratitude for the loan. The authorities quoted above, Note 33 in regard to *Ribbis Mukdemes*, dispute this ruling as well, and the ruling of S.A. *Harav* (quoted there) applies here as well. One may therefore rely on the lenient opinion.

40. *Shach* 160:10. *Chochmas Adam* 131:8 defines a longer period of time as "many days." *Shevet HaLevi* (2:69) maintains that this varies, depending on the situation. For example, if the borrower and lender have had other [significant] business dealings immediately after the loan was repaid, they may even consider a few days as a long time after payment.

41. *Mishnas Ribbis* 3:8.

After a Ribbis Contract Is Signed

26. If a contract calling for Ribbis payments is written, it may not be honored. The lender is prohibited from keeping the contract in his possession, even if he wishes to use it for the purpose of collecting the principal. The contract must be destroyed.[42]

---

42. *Rema* 161:11. The reason for this is twofold. First, we are concerned that the contract will be used to collect Ribbis payments (*Rema*). In addition, there is a general prohibition on retaining documents which call for improper payments (*Taz* 161:9; see *Chochmas Adam* 133:5 who sees this as a second reason). [The Talmud (*Kesubos* 19a) quotes the verse, *Do not allow injustice to dwell in your tents* (Job 11:14), and applies the term "injustice" to contracts which could be used to improperly collect payment.]

This obligation is not limited to the lender himself; anyone who comes into contact with the contract is obligated to destroy it, to ensure that it is not used to collect Ribbis (*Rema*). However, if one is afraid that the lender will harm him if he destroys the contract, he is not obligated to do so (*Chochmas Adam* 133:5).

CHAPTER THREE

Benefits Which Are Prohibited

- Mitzvah-related gifts or services (*mishloach manos, pidyon haben,* teaching Torah, returning lost objects) (1-4)
- Charitable donations (5-6)
- Business transactions (7-9)
- Ribbis Devarim (10-13)
- Thanking the lender (14-18)
- Borrowing utensils (19)
- Trading loans (20-24)
- Tovas Hanaah (25-29)
- Using a Heter Iska (30-31)
- Restructuring debt (32-34)
- Discounting a debt (35)

Introduction

The prohibition on paying Ribbis is not limited to conventional interest payments. There is a common misconception that other types of favors or non-financial benefits are permitted. In this chapter, we will examine the other forms of benefit which are included in this prohibition. Later, in Chapter 4, we will examine the types of benefit which are permitted.

Mitzvah-related Gifts or Services

1. Someone who has taken a loan is prohibited from benefiting his lender even if he is performing a mitzvah when doing so. For example, the borrower may not send *mishloach manos* (Purim gifts) to the lender.[1] If the lender is a Kohen and the borrower has a firstborn son to redeem, he may not give the *pidyon haben* coins to the lender.[2] Similarly,

---

1. *Mishnas Ribbis* 3:n18, based on Y.D. 160:10. If the borrower had been accustomed to sending *mishloach manos* to the lender in previous years (before the loan), he may continue to do so afterwards as well (Y.D. 160:7).

2. *Rosh* (quoted by *Beis Yosef*, end of 160) rules that a Kohen who offers a loan, but requires that the borrower give him *terumah* in exchange for the loan, violates the prohibition of Ribbis Ketzutzah.

If the Kohen does not stipulate that these gifts be given, the Biblical prohibition is removed. Still, if the borrower voluntarily offers these gifts, this would constitute Ribbis DeRabbanan.

Ksav Sofer (Y.D. 146) rules that this applies to the coins of *pidyon haben* as well. A Kohen may not offer a loan and stipulate that the borrower use his services when performing the mitzvah of *pidyon haben*.

Ksav Sofer discusses the case of a Kohen who lent the coins which are used for *pidyon haben* to a father, for use in performing this mitzvah. The father did not have cash with which to pay for the coins, so the Kohen gave them to him on credit. However, the Kohen stipulated that the coins were being lent on the condition that he be the Kohen who receives this gift. *Ksav Sofer* rules that a *pidyon haben* which is performed under these circumstances is not valid and that it must be repeated (using another Kohen). (This ruling is based on the Talmudic principle of *mitzvah habaah b'aveirah*.)

It is not clear if *Ksav Sofer* would have required that the *pidyon haben* be repeated if the Kohen had made no such stipulation and the borrower had voluntarily chosen to use him for the *pidyon haben*.

It is common for the Kohen to sell the necessary coins for *pidyon haben*. One should be careful to pay for the coins before the *pidyon haben*, so that he will no longer owe the Kohen money at the time of the *pidyon*. [However, if arrangements had already been made to use this Kohen, the Kohen may subsequently lend these coins to the father.]

a loan may not be offered on the condition that the borrower will allow the lender to use his *lulav* to perform the mitzvah of *lulov* on *Succos*.[3]

2. Service benefits: The borrower is also prohibited from offering free services to the lender, even when these services are related to the performance of mitzvos. For example, the borrower may not tutor the lender (or his child) in the study of Torah unless he is paid for doing so.[4] If the borrower had been tutoring the lender without compensation, prior to the existence of the loan, he may continue doing so, even after the loan.[5]

3. The type of mitzvos in the cases mentioned above (*mishloach manos*, *pidyon haben* and teaching Torah) do not require that a specific

---

If the Kohen gave the coins to the father as a gift, these restrictions do not apply (*Ksav Sofer*).

When the Kohen is a close friend: There is a general rule that when it is clear that the borrower would have benefited the lender even if no loan had been given (for example, where they are relatives or close friends), he is permitted to benefit the lender (*Shach* 166:1). This does *not* apply to benefits that are publicly observed (*befarhesya*) (Y.D. 160:7 and *Shach* 166:1). Since the mitzvah of *pidyon haben* is usually performed publicly, it is therefore prohibited for the father of the baby to give the coins to a Kohen who extended him a loan even if they are relatives or close friends. But if the father pays the loan before the *pidyon haben*, this Kohen may be used.

In case of great need, for example, where the lender is a close relative who would be insulted if he were not honored to serve as the Kohen at the *pidyon haben*, a Rav should be consulted. [It would appear that in cases of great need, one may rely on the opinion of *Chochmas Adam* 131:16 who rules that a borrower may extend a favor to a lender, even when the favor is publicly observed, if they are such close friends that it is obvious that the favor would have been extended regardless of the loan.]

3. *Bris Yehudah*, *hashmatos* to 11:n49. [If the borrower often loans his *lulav* to others, and this is not a condition of the loan, the borrower may lend his *lulav* to the lender, provided that it is not done in a public way (*befarhesya*).]

4. Y.D. 160:10. Since a father is obligated to teach Torah to his son (or to hire a tutor to do so), the borrower is directly benefiting the lender by teaching the child (*Shach* 160:15). The father's obligation continues even after the child is bar mitzvah (*S.A. Harav* in *kuntres achron* to Hil. *Talmud Torah* 1:1; see also *Dibros Moshe Kiddushin* 50:7 who adds that the obligation to teach a son has no limit and that it applies to all facets of Torah study). The prohibition of tutoring the lender's child therefore continues past bar mitzvah as well.

[Although the Talmud (*Kiddushin* 30a) implies that a father is only obligated to teach his son the Written Torah (*Torah She'be'ksav*), numerous poskim explain that this obligation actually applies to other areas of study as well (see *Gra* Y.D. 245:7, *S.A. Harav* Hil. *Talmud Torah* 1:1, *Chazon Ish* Y.D. 152:1).]

5. Y.D. 160:10. This is permitted only if the favor is not intended as an expression of gratitude for the loan (*S.A. Harav* §11, *Bris Yehudah* 10:8).

Yad Dovid (quoted by *Darkei Teshuvah* 160:69) maintains that the borrower may

individual be involved in performing the mitzvah. There are other mitzvos, however, where a specific individual is required to perform the mitzvah. These mitzvos may be performed, even when they benefit the lender. For example, a borrower finds an object which was lost by the lender. Since the Torah obligates him to return it, he may do so.[6]

4. A person who finds a lost object is not always obligated to return it to the owner.[7] Still, even in these cases, Jews who are scrupulous in performing mitzvos will voluntarily return the lost object. In these cases, if the person who finds the object has borrowed money from its owner, it is questionable if he may return the object to him. However, it is clear that if the finder is someone who would always return a lost object in such a situation, he would also be permitted to return it here.[8]

Charitable Donations

5. The prohibitions of Ribbis apply even when the lender is a poor person who is eligible to receive charity. During the time that the loan is outstanding, the borrower may not offer a donation to the lender, unless he had already been accustomed to doing so before the loan was made.[9]

---

continue tutoring the lender (or his child), only in private. To do so publicly is prohibited because it creates an appearance of Ribbis (cf. *Bris Yehudah* 10:n13 who questions this ruling).

6. *Bris Yehudah* 10:n2 (s.v. *u'ale'inyan*) and 11:n40. See Note 17, below, for another example of this.

7. For example, when an object is lost in an area which is traveled mostly by people who would not usually return lost objects which they find. In this case, the person who lost the object certainly despaired of having it returned to him. Anytime that an owner despairs of having his object returned to him, the object becomes the property of whoever finds it.

8. The object may only be returned in a private manner. If it would be returned in a public manner (*befarhesya*), this would create an appearance of Ribbis (Y.D. 160:7).

9. *Shitah Mekubetzes* to *Kesuvos* 108a, *S.A. Harav* §14. *Bris Yehudah* 11:n50 discusses a case where the poor person does not have food to eat, and the borrower is the only person with the ability to help him. [In this case, it would seem that there is a simple option: The borrower may give the lender money as a partial payment of the loan. In this way, the poor person is provided for without his having received a donation from the borrower.]

Once the loan is paid and a short period of time has elapsed, the borrower may offer a routine donation to the lender. This is permitted only if no statement is made connecting the donation to the loan.

6. The borrower may not tell the lender that if he lends him money, the borrower will make a donation to charity. Even if the lender instructs the borrower to pay the entire principal to charity, he may not ask the borrower to pay more than the amount which was borrowed.[10]

Transactions Between Borrower and Lender

7. The borrower may not sell goods to the lender at a discount. He must charge the regular market price. Similarly, he may not perform services for him at a reduced fee.[11]

8. Similarly, the borrower may not purchase goods from the lender at more than the market price, nor may the borrower pay more than the usual fee for the lender's services.[12]

9. When a loan is requested, the lender may give merchandise to the borrower and instruct him to sell the merchandise and accept the income as a loan. However, since the lender is benefiting from the sale, the borrower must be compensated for his effort and expenses.[13]

Sometimes, the lender instructs the borrower to sell the merchandise in a town or market other than the one in which the borrower will be taking possession of the property, because the merchandise will have greater value there. Since the borrower takes responsibility for the merchandise in the place in which it is worth less, the borrower may only pay the lender

---

10. *Rema* 160:14, R' Akiva Eiger (to *Rema*). This prohibition applies to any lender who directs the borrower to make a contribution to charity.

A third party may be paid (or may direct that a payment be made to charity) to influence the lender to offer a loan (Y.D. 160:16).

11. *Shach* 160:37. If this were a condition of the loan, it would be Ribbis Ketzutzah (Biblically prohibited Ribbis). Even if it were not a condition of the loan, if this discount was offered in order to induce the lender to extend the date on which this is due, this would be Ribbis Ketzutzah (ibid.). Where the lender and borrower are friends, and the borrower had previously extended discounts to the lender, see Chapter 1 paragraphs 1-3.

12. *Shach* 173:6. If this were a condition of the loan, many poskim would consider it Ribbis Ketzutzah (Biblically prohibited Ribbis), and obligate the lender to return the extra payment to the borrower (ibid.).

13. *Mishnas Ribbis* 4:8, based on Y.D. 173:15. Most poskim rule that it is not necessary to pay full wages for the work and effort which the borrower expended to sell the merchandise, but that a token payment is sufficient. This is because the borrower expended this effort for his own benefit (i.e., to receive the cash which he then used as a loan). Although the lender also gained from the sale, he is not required to pay the full value of the effort. He is only required to offer a token payment [a one-dollar payment would suffice] (*Taz* 173:24, *Chavos Daas* 173:23, *S.A. Harav* §19, *Har Tzvi* Y.D. 130, *Bris Yehudah* 11:15; cf. *Shach* 173:30).

the value at the time and place he received it. Later, it is the borrower who causes the merchandise to increase in value when he transports it; therefore the lender is not entitled to this increase. If the additional amount is paid, this is Ribbis.[14]

Ribbis Devarim

10. The Rabbinic prohibition of Ribbis extends even to benefits which have no financial value. For example, if the borrower had not been accustomed to greeting the lender before the loan was given, he may not begin to do so afterwards. Even if he had greeted him previously,[15] he may not begin to greet him in a warmer or more elaborate manner.[16]

This is known as *Ribbis Devarim*, Ribbis involving words.

11. This prohibition applies when the borrower extends greetings. However, if the lender extends greetings, the borrower is permitted to return the greeting.[17]

---

14. Y.D. 173:15.

An option for the lender to receive the full value: The lender has the option of accepting responsibility for the merchandise, so that if it were to become damaged or devalued during transport to the second market he would absorb the loss. If he does this, the merchandise is still considered his while it is being transported. [Liability is considered an indication of ownership; this is a basic principle which applies in many areas of the laws of Ribbis. See, for example, Chapter 15, Paragraph 10 and Chapter 17, Paragraph 7.] In this case, when the item is sold, the entire revenue belongs to the lender. The borrower would then borrow this money and be required to return the same amount to the lender (Y.D., ibid.).

15. *Tosefta*, cited by *Gra* 160:14, implies that even if the borrower had greeted him just once before, this is sufficient to permit him to continue greeting the lender after the loan (*Divrei Sofrim* 160:61).

16. Y.D. 160:11. The Talmud (B.M. 75b) finds a source for this in the Biblical verse *Neshech kol davar* (lit., Ribbis of any sort). This verse can be translated homiletically, to mean 'Ribbis of any (spoken) word.' Despite this source, *Ribbis Devarim* is only prohibited by Rabbinic law. [This is certainly so in most cases, because a loan is not usually given on the condition that gratitude be expressed, and any Ribbis which is not a condition of the loan is not Ribbis Ketzutzah. Even in cases where the loan was given on the specific condition that the borrower befriend the lender, it would only be Ribbis DeRabbanan (*Ran* to *Kesubos* 46a. *Bris Yehudah* 11:n62 accepts this as the opinion of most poskim).]

This applies even to a simple "Good morning" greeting. If the borrower is a person who greets all of the people he meets, he may greet the lender as well (*Bris Yehudah* 10:22). If the borrower and lender later become friends, for reasons which have no connection to the loan (for example, they become relatives through marriage), *Bris Yehudah* suggests that they would be permitted to greet each other.

17. *Divrei Sofrim* 160:63, *Mishnas Ribbis* 4:n19. [This also fits well with the language of

12. The borrower may not praise, compliment or offer a blessing to the lender for extending the loan. This is also considered *Ribbis Devarim*. When the borrower approaches the lender to request an extension on the loan, he may not try to influence him with praise and compliments, in order to secure the extension. He must limit his words to expressions of personal request and a statement of his own need.[18]

13. The borrower may praise the lender to others, when not in the presence of the lender[19] [except where it is clear that his words will be repeated to the lender].

Other Forms of Ribbis Devarim

14. **Thanking the lender:** According to some poskim, the rule of *Ribbis Devarim* prohibits the borrower from thanking the lender for the loan. Many contemporary poskim disagree and rule that a simple thank-you is permitted.[20]

15. When someone borrows money to cover the cost of publishing a sefer, he may not show his appreciation by printing a note of thanks to the lender in the book.[21]

Shulchan Aruch, which explicitly limits the prohibition to *lehakdim lo shalom*, greeting (the lender) first with *shalom*.]

The Talmud (*Berachos* 6b) teaches that when one person is greeted by another, he is obligated to return the greeting. This is a mitzvah which can only be satisfied by responding to the lender. We have already seen (in Paragraph 3) that when a mitzvah requires a person to benefit the lender, this is permitted. This rule applies here as well. Responding to a greeting is therefore not only permitted, but is actually obligatory.

18. *S.A. Harav* §9.

19. *Bris Yehudah* 11:n63, based on *S.A. Harav* ibid.

20. *Beis Yosef* (160, s.v. *v'afelu*) seems to prohibit this. This is also the ruling of *Igros Moshe* Y.D. 1:80.

Others permit the borrower to say, "Thank you." R' Shlomo Zalman Auerbach zt"l (in *Minchas Shlomo* 27) maintains that the prohibition on *Ribbis Devarim* applies only when the borrower extends words of blessing to the lender and not when he says a simple thank-you. R' Y.S. Eliyashev Shlita is also quoted (in *Mishnas Ribbis* 4:n21) as permitting this. *Torah Temimah* (to Devarim 23:20) notes that it is the custom to thank the lender for the loan. He suggests that this is permitted because the thanks is offered for the physical exertion or inconvenience endured by the lender to facilitate the loan, and not for the loan itself.

To summarize: This question is a subject of dispute. Therefore, the borrower should state clearly that he is thanking the lender for exerting himself on his behalf. All would agree that this is permitted (*Mishnas Ribbis* ibid.).

21. *Erech Shai* 2:160, *Igros Moshe* Y.D. 1:80. *Igros Moshe* permits a limited form of recognition if it does not include an expression of thanks. He permits the citation to state

16. Common courtesies which people routinely extend to others may be extended to the lender as well.[22]

Although the borrower is permitted to extend these favors on his own, the lender may not request any favor from the borrower, even if it is a simple favor which involves no cost. For example, if the lender is awaiting the arrival of a guest, he may not ask the borrower to notify him when the guest arrives. This is prohibited even when it involves no exertion on the part of the borrower and even if the loan was not mentioned in connection to the request.[23]

17. Simple requests which are made in the course of conversation are permitted. For example, if the lender asks for the time, the borrower may respond.[24]

18. The prohibitions of *Ribbis Devarim* apply only while a loan is outstanding. Once a loan has been repaid, these prohibitions do not apply.[25]

---

that the loan was extended and the fact that Heaven will bless the lender for his deed. ("God's blessings are extended to Mr. _____ who performed a kind deed by lending funds for the publication of this volume.")

Cf. Rabbi Y.S. Eliyashev Shlita (quoted in *Mishnas Ribbis* 4:n21), who raises serious objections to this leniency. See also *Darkei Teshuvah* and *Tzitz Eliezer* 9:15.

22. *Bris Yehudah* 10:n22.

23. Y.D. 160:12 and *S.A. Harav* §10. When the lender requests a favor from the borrower it may appear that he feels entitled to make demands on account of the loan. The right to demand a favor is considered a form of *Ribbis Devarim* (*Taz* 160:5).

Darkei Teshuvah 160:80 maintains that this prohibition applies only where the request was phrased as a demand. If the lender makes the request in a soft, non-demanding manner, the borrower may comply since there is no impression that the request is based on his position as a lender. Some poskim question this leniency (see *Bris Yehudah* 11:n30; the language of *Shulchan Aruch* also does not appear to allow for the distinction made by *Darkei Teshuvah*).

24. *Beis David*, quoted by *Darkei Teshuvah* 160:80. This is permitted only if the borrower would have responded even if there had been no loan (ibid.). *Beis David* explains that, in the case cited in the previous paragraph, the borrower is prohibited from informing the lender that a guest had arrived, only because he had been told to go and notify the lender. If the lender had asked, in the course of conversation, whether a guest had arrived, it is permitted.

25. This is an exception to the regular rule of Ribbis. All other forms of Ribbis are prohibited even after the loan has been repaid, under the rules for *Ribbis Me'ucheres* (these rules have been outlined in the preceding chapter). *Ribbis Devarim* is a more lenient form of Ribbis because it does not involve financial benefits. Therefore, it is permitted after a loan is repaid. *Birkei Yosef* (160:11 and printed in the column of the popular edition of *Shulchan Aruch*) states, "After repayment, this is permitted, for it is

Borrowing Utensils

19. The lender may not borrow utensils which belong to the borrower unless he had been accustomed to doing so prior to the loan. Articles which are easily identified as belonging to the borrower (such as a company vehicle with markings identifying its owner)[26] may not be used by the lender, even if he had been accustomed to using them in the past.[27]

Trading Loans

20. A borrower may not offer compensation for a loan. Instead, the borrower might wish to offer the following deal, "If you lend me money today, I will obligate myself to lend you money when you request it at some future time."

This is known as *halveini v'elveh loch* ('lend me and I'll lend you'), and is a subject of disagreement among earlier poskim. Most poskim rule that this is prohibited as Ribbis.[28]

21. Free Loan Funds which require that its members lend money to the fund in order to be eligible for a loan at a future time may be violating the concept of *halveini v'elveh loch*; see Chapter 19, Paragraph 7.

22. When a loan was given without conditions and it was repaid, the lender may later request that his former borrower lend him money. This second loan may be extended, even if the new lender is doing so only because he had previously received a loan. However, it is preferable that no mention of the previous loan be made in connection with the new one.[29]

---

illogical to say that once a loan is offered, the borrower is prohibited from greeting (the lender) for the rest of his life!" (See also *Darkei Teshuvah* 160:87.)

26. *Shearim HaMitzuyanim BeHalachah* 65:3. Where the borrower is a corporation, see below, Chapter 5, Paragraph 27.

27. Y.D. 160:7.

28. *Rema* 160:9 quotes two opinions. *Levush* 160:10, *Gra* 160:16, *S.A. Harav* §6 and *Kitzur Shulchan Aruch* 65:7 all rule stringently. Where the second loan is for a longer period of time (or for a greater amount of money; *S.A. Harav*), all would agree that this is prohibited as Ribbis (*Rema* ibid.).

The prohibition of *halveini v'elveh loch* also applies when merchandise is loaned; see Chapter 14, Paragraph 3.

29. Although we are stringent in regard to trading loans (see previous note), this ruling holds true only where there is an issue of Ribbis in its basic form. Once a loan has been repaid, benefits which are extended to the lender fall under the more lenient category of *Ribbis Me'ucheres*. In this case, we may rely on the opinion which

23. Some poskim permit this even when the second loan is for a larger sum of money than the first (or when it is offered for a longer period of time). Others prohibit this.[30] One may rely on the lenient opinion, provided that he does not mention the first loan in connection with the new one.[31]

24. A tenant who was late making rental payments or an employer who was behind in paying his employers may subsequently make up for this delay by making subsequent payments ahead of schedule. However, he may not explicitly mention his previous late payments in connection with his early payments.[32]

Other No-Cost Benefits: Tovas Hanaah

25. If the lender has a business, he may not stipulate that the borrower patronize his business in exchange for the loan. This is known as *tovas hanaah*, and this is a real benefit, which may not be offered to the lender.[33] Similarly, the lender may not offer a loan on the condition that

---

permits the trading of loans (*S.A. Harav* §6, *Kitzur Shulchan Aruch* 65:7, *Ben Ish Chai* to *V'eschanan* 7).

On this basis, the second loan might be permitted even if the lender mentioned explicitly that this was being offered to reciprocate for the first loan. Still, when the parties avoid mention of the previous loan, the prohibition of *Ribbis Me'ucheres* does not apply at all. Although we may rely on the lenient opinion, since one would satisfy all opinions by not mentioning the previous loan at all, it is preferable that it not be mentioned (*S.A. Harav*).

30. *Bris Yehudah* 11:5 rules leniently, based on *Kuntres HaSma* and *Maharam Shick* (*Y.D.* 157). *S.A. Harav* §6 and *Kitzur Shulchan Aruch* 65:7 prohibit this whenever the second loan is intended as gratitude for the first loan.

31. In this case, we may rely on the leniency that *Ribbis Me'ucheres* is permitted when no mention of the previous loan is made; see above, Chapter 2, Paragraph 23.

32. *Mishnas Ribbis* 4:n13, based on the sources cited in Note 29.

33. *Y.D.* 160:23. *Taz* 160:22 disputes this ruling (see Note 40, below), but all other poskim accept it. (Even *Taz* disputes this only on an academic level. As a matter of practical halachah, he rules stringently.)

There is a Talmudic dispute regarding the value of *tovas hanaah*. One opinion maintains that *tovas hanaah eino mamon*, that there is no intrinsic financial value in patronizing a business. (See *Chidushei R' Meir Simchah* to *Kiddushin* 58b for insight into this opinion.) Others disagree and hold that there is a true value to *tovas hanaah*. The question of whether this constitutes Ribbis Ketzutzah depends on this dispute (*Rema* 160:23; *Gra* 160:55 cites *Choshen Mishpat* where *Rema* himself rules that *tovas hanaah eino mamon*).

This prohibition applies to patronizing both a business which sells merchandise (such as a grocery store) and a business which offers a service (such as a repair shop) (*Bris Yehudah* 11:24 and 25).

he be given a job, even if he will be paid a fair salary for his work. This is another example of *tovas hanaah*.[34]

Even if no such stipulation was made, most poskim prohibit a borrower from patronizing the lender's business, unless he had been doing so before the loan was requested.[35] This applies even where the borrower pays a fair price for the goods or services which he receives from the lender.

Once the loan has been repaid, the borrower may begin to patronize his lender's business, provided that he does not mention that he is doing so in connection with the loan.[36]

26. Similarly, the lender may not require the borrower to refer other customers to his business.[37]

27. The lender is also prohibited from requiring the borrower to patronize a business which belongs to someone else (for example, a friend or relative), even if he has no financial benefit from it. In this case, however, if no stipulation was made, the borrower may subsequently patronize that business.[38]

28. If the borrower patronized the lender's business: If the lender stipulated at the time of the loan that the borrower patronize his business, this benefit would be considered Ribbis Ketzutzah. As with all

---

34. *S.A. Harav* §14. Even if the loan was given without any stipulation, the borrower may not hire the lender unless he would have done so even if the loan had not been offered (ibid.).

35. *S.A. Harav* §14, *Shaar Deah* 160:9, *Darkei Teshuvah* 160:185. This appears to be the ruling of *Rema* 160:23, although it is not clear if *Rema* means to prohibit this *lehalachah* or only according to the opinion which holds that *tovas hanaah* has an intrinsic financial value.

Mishnah LaMelech (to *Hil. Malveh* 7:11) disagrees and holds that this is permitted. However, this opinion is a difficult one. [As *Shaar Deah* points out, "This is (no better than) extending a greeting, where it is prohibited for him to greet (the lender) if he had not been accustomed to do so, even if this is not a stipulation. . .certainly then, we should prohibit patronizing his business."]

36. *Yad Avraham* 160:6, *Mishnas Ribbis* 4:23.

37. *Igros Moshe* Y.D. 3, in notes to *Hil. Ribbis* 160:18, points out that there is a market value for the service of acting as a broker to attract customers. Requiring the borrower to perform this service therefore constitutes Ribbis Ketzutzah, even according to those who rule that *tovas hanaah eino mamon*.

38. *Bris Yehudah* 11:n52. A borrower is permitted to benefit the family of the lender, as explained in Chapter 4, Paragraph 29.

[The borrower may not tell the lender that he is now patronizing the business, as this would present a problem of *Ribbis Devarim*.]

cases involving Ribbis Ketzutzah, the lender is obligated to return the value of this benefit to the borrower. However, he is *not* obligated to return all profits earned from the borrower's purchases. Rather, it would be sufficient for him to repay the amount which would be due a broker who generates this amount of business.[39]

A Permitted Form Of Tovas Hanaah

29. If the lender receives collateral for his loan, he may stipulate that if the borrower later sells the collateral, he may only sell it to him. This is permitted even if they agreed that the money which was given as a loan would be used as payment. However, the purchase price must reflect the true value of the item or property which is being sold.[40]

---

39. *Maharsham* 4:95, *Bris Yehudah* 11:n46. *Maharsham* discusses the case of a teacher who lent someone money and stipulated that the borrower send his children to study under him. Later, after the children had already switched to his school, the parties realized that this agreement involved Ribbis. *Maharsham* suggests that the lender pay a 2% fee to the borrower as compensation for inducing him to send the children to study under him. (*Maharsham* permits this fee to be deducted from the tuition bill which is owed the teacher.)

The reason that it is only necessary to return the broker's fee (and not the entire profit) is because the Ribbis aspect of this transaction is only the *tovas hanaah* (not the profit). Only the Ribbis must be paid back to the borrower.

40. Y.D. 172:4.

Taz 160:22 maintains that this ruling, which permits a *tovas hanaah* benefit to be extended to a lender, contradicts the ruling in 160:23 (quoted in Paragraph 25 which prohibits this. Since the ruling quoted here has a clear source (*Bava Metzia* 65b), *tovas hanaah* should be permitted in all cases where a fair price is paid for the lender's services. According to *Taz*, there should be no prohibition on patronizing the lender's business. [When the lender is a Kohen, *Taz* concedes that the borrower would be prohibited from giving *terumah* or *pidyon haben* gifts to him, in exchange for the loan. Although Rishonim also refer to this arrangement as *tovas hanaah*, it is prohibited because the lender receives something free in exchange for his loan. This is different from other cases, where the lender provides goods or services in exchange for payment.]

All subsequent poskim reject the argument of *Taz*, and accept the ruling of *Shulchan Aruch*, which prohibits *tovas hanaah* in virtually every form. These poskim reconcile the contradiction presented by *Taz* in various ways.

Nekudos HaKesef and *Kreisi* explain that *tovas hanaah* may be extended to the lender only in the case here, where the lender is guaranteed the right to make a purchase. In this case, the *tovas hanaah* does not create a financial gain, since the lender pays a fair price for the property. *Tovas hanaah* is prohibited in other cases, where the lender receives customers for his business. There, he realizes a financial gain, since he would not have these profits if the customers had not patronized the business. This form of *tovas hanaah* is prohibited.

Poskim offer additional explanations of the laws of *tovas hanaah* (see *Nekudos*

Using a Heter Iska

30. We will see (in Chapter 22) that there are two basic Heter Iska forms. The more prevalent form is known as *palga milveh u'palga pikadon*. The details of this Heter Iska will be explained later, but it is important to understand that this contract works by creating a half-loan/half-investment arrangement between the parties. Although this type of Heter Iska allows the sharing of profits, it nevertheless leaves the participants with a borrower-lender relationship. Only those benefits which are explicitly mentioned in the Heter Iska are permitted. The prohibitions outlined in this chapter remain prohibited even when this Heter Iska is used.[41]

31. The second type of Heter Iska is known as *kulo pikadon*. When this is used, the transaction between the parties is purely an investment transaction. The relationship between the parties is purely a business relationship. In this case, other benefits may be passed between the parties since no loan has taken place.[42]

Restructuring Debt

32. At the time a loan is given, the lender has the right to schedule payment in any manner he chooses. However, once the loan has been given, his ability to restructure the payment schedule is limited, as follows.

The lender may find that he is in need of some of the funds which he has loaned out. He would ask the borrower to prepay a portion of the loan. In exchange, the lender would be willing to extend the due date for the remainder of the debt. Many poskim prohibit this as a form of Ribbis. According to this view, when the borrower agrees to prepayment, he is actually giving a gift to the lender for the purpose of extending the due date. Paying for an extension of credit violates the laws of Ribbis.[43]

HaKesef, Chavos Daas 160:17 and 169:34 and *Tiferes LeMoshe*). As a matter of halachah, all agreements involving *tovas hanaah* are prohibited, with the exception of the one case outlined here.

41. *S.A. Harav* §39, *Tuv Tam Vodaas* 3:35, *Maharsham* 4:95.

42. *Mishnas Ribbis* 4:n29. The advantages of using one Heter Iska form over the other will be discussed in Chapter 23, Paragraphs 9-11.

43. *Bris Yehudah* 11:n15, quoting earlier poskim; cf. *Shaar Deah* 173:5 who rules that this is permitted.

If the benefits of prepayment are equal to (or outweighed by) the delay in payment of the remaining debt, *Bris Yehudah* concedes that this is permitted. For example, if a

33. This applies only when the restructuring of the debt includes both a prepayment requirement *and* an extension. Any restructuring which requires prepayment but does not extend the terms of the remainder of the loan is permitted. Similarly, it is permitted to restructure a loan by allowing later payments and not requiring a prepayment.

In addition, it is permitted to restructure a loan if the original loan agreement gave the lender an option of demanding prepayment.

34. This also applies to debt which is created by business transactions.

When payment is owed for goods or services, most poskim prohibit a restructuring of payments in the same way that this is prohibited when debt was created by a loan.[44]

Discounting a Debt

35. A lender may forgive part of the debt, on the condition that the borrower prepays the remainder. For example, if Reuven owes Shimon $1000, payable in six months, Shimon may offer to forgive the debt, for an immediate payment of $900.[45]

$1,000 loan is due in six months, the payment may be rescheduled so that $500 is due at the end of four months (two months early), while the remaining $500 is due after eight months (two months late). Cf. *Kitzur Dinei Ribbis* 2:13.

44. *Mishnas Ribbis* 4:n15. The leniency of *Bris Yehudah* (explained in Note 43) applies here as well.

45. Y.D. 173:3, in a case involving merchandise which was sold on credit. Once the sale has been completed, the seller is permitted to offer a discount for immediate payment. However, if the purchaser has not yet acquired the merchandise, the seller is prohibited from offering two prices, one if the sale is made on credit and another (cheaper) price for a cash sale (*Rema* 173:3). The details of this ruling are outlined at length in Chapter 7.

CHAPTER FOUR

Permitted Forms of Benefit

A. Charging for expenses (1-10)

B. Payments which are offered by a third party (11-16)

C. Payments which are made to a third party (17-20)

D. Additional leniencies (21-33)

- ☐ Adding to a payment (22-23)

- ☐ After the loan is repaid (24)

- ☐ When the balance is unknown (25)

- ☐ Rental fees (26-27)

- ☐ Cosigner fees (28)

- ☐ Benefiting the lender's family (29)

- ☐ Conditions of payment (30)

- ☐ Common courtesies (31)

- ☐ Security deposits (32)

- ☐ Returning stolen goods (33)

Introduction

When asked to summarize the laws of Ribbis, most people would respond by saying that the Torah prohibits a lender from receiving any benefit in exchange for extending a loan. While this is true as a general rule, we nevertheless find circumstances where particular forms of benefit are permitted. In this chapter, we will examine these exceptions.

The leniencies outlined in this chapter have been culled from diverse sections of the laws of Ribbis. It is for this reason that the guidelines which pertain to each of the leniencies tends to vary greatly. However, it should be noted that in virtually all the cases where benefits are permitted, the borrower is prohibited from stating explicitly that the benefit is being offered in gratitude for the loan.

A. Charging for Expenses

1. When extending a loan, a lender may incur expenses. Any expense which is related to the loan (except those noted in Paragraphs 5 and 9) may be passed on to the borrower. This includes charges for legal help in the drawing of a contract or a lien, costs involved in the transfer of funds, bank charges for returned checks, the cost of billing for payment, and Beis Din or court fees if they are needed to force payment.[1]

This does *not* include expenses which would have been incurred even if the loan had not taken place.[2]

---

1. The prohibition on Ribbis applies only when the lender (or someone he designates) profits from the loan. When the lender is reimbursed costs which he incurs because of the loan, he does not have a net profit. This is therefore permitted. This holds true even when the money is spent to benefit the lender, such as for the cost of a lien (C.M. 39:17; see also *Bris Yehudah* 9:1-8 at length).

This is not meant to imply that the borrower is required to pay all these expenses, only that he is permitted to do so (see C.M. ibid.).

2. For example, we will see (Paragraph 9, below) that when a person withdraws a term deposit (such as a CD) prematurely for the purpose of offering a loan, and penalties are incurred, the penalties may sometimes be passed on to the borrower.

However, if someone made a premature withdrawal because he thought that he would need the money for his personal use, and it later turned out that he did not need the money, the penalty may not be passed on to someone who subsequently borrows this money (*Bris Yehudah* 9:n3).

2. The lender may *not* be reimbursed for the time and effort he expended to extend the loan.[3]

3. Delivery charges: Under normal conditions, the lender may not charge for delivering the loan. However, if the delivery required an unusually long or difficult trip, such that most people would charge for it, the lender may be paid for the delivery.[4]

4. When expense payments are reimbursed by the borrower, it should be expressly stated that these are reimbursements and not interest payments.[5] The bill should list a separate balance for the debt and a separate balance for expenses.[6]

5. Interest expenses: A Jew may borrow money from a non-Jewish source and pay interest for the loan. If these moneys are being borrowed so that they can be passed on to a second Jew as a loan, the interest expense may not be passed on to him. Only the individual who actually borrowed the funds may pay interest for them.

A common example involves an individual who borrows a friend's credit card. When he uses the card, a loan is extended to the owner of the card. He, in turn, is allowing these funds to be used by his friend. Interest charges which accrue to the card owner may not be paid by the person using the card. This person may not pay the interest even if he makes payment directly to the lending institution involved.[7]

---

3. If the lender took time off from work to arrange the loan, it is not clear if his lost wages may be reimbursed by the borrower (*Bris Yehudah* 9:n18). The borrower should therefore not offer such payments.

4. *Bris Yehudah* 9:n18.
[Delivery services charge for any delivery. The criterion here is whether people who are not in the delivery business would normally make this type of delivery as a favor.]

5. *Doveiv Meisharim* Responsa 10, *Mishnas Ribbis* 1:n9.

6. *Bris Yehudah* 9:n13.

7. Y.D. 168:17 (see also 160:14). When Reuven borrows money from a bank, he is obligated to pay interest. If Reuven then lends these funds to Shimon, a second loan has taken place. This loan is between two Jews and no Ribbis may be paid. If Shimon were to pay interest directly to the bank, he would be satisfying Reuven's obligation. This is actually a payment to Reuven and is considered Ribbis.

If the borrower is a poor person who is eligible to receive *tzedakah*, interest charges which the lender incurs are regarded as charitable contributions and may be deducted from one's *maaser* (tithe) account (*Igros Moshe* 3:93).

Additional rules relating to the loaning of credit cards are found in Chapter 17, Paragraphs 15 and 16.

When the Loan Is Not Paid on Time

6. A borrower is obligated to pay his loan on time.[8] However, if he fails to do so and this causes the lender to lose an opportunity to profit, the borrower is prohibited from reimbursing him for this loss of profit.[9]

The borrower may regret causing the loss and wish to reimburse the lender. Although he is prohibited from doing so at the time of payment, he would be permitted to send the lender a gift at a later time (this is known as *Ribbis Me'ucheres*). However, the gift must be one of minimal value,[10] so that it is not obvious that it is connected to the loan. Additionally, the borrower may not stipulate that the gift is being sent in connection with the loan.[11]

7. Any financial damage caused by the borrower's failure to pay on time (other than loss of profit) may be reimbursed.[12] If the lender was

---

8. C.M. 97:4 and 359:8. *Bach* (C.M. 38) rules that someone who delays payment beyond the stipulated time is considered a thief, since he prevented the lender from using his money to earn profits. Many poskim rule that the lender is obligated to sell his nonessential property, in order to repay the loan (*Nesivos HaMishpat* 86:2, *S.A. Harav Rules of Loans* §5). See also *Ahavas Chessed* 2:24 who expounds on the severity of this obligation.

9. *Rashba* in Responsa 3:227. *Beis Hillel* Y.D. 170 rules that payment is permitted. Still, most poskim follow the *Rashba* in prohibiting this (see *Beis Yitzchok* 2:1, *Imrei Yosher* 1:149, *Bris Yehudah* 2:15).

10. This refers to a gift which "many people routinely send to their friends" (*S.A. Harav* §7).

11. Y.D. 160:6 and *Shach* 8. Most poskim permit this even when the gift is being sent in gratitude for the loan, as long as it is not mentioned explicitly (*Rema* 160:6, *Taz* 160:3, R' Akiva Eiger to *Shach* 160:1, *Bris Yehudah* 5:60; cf. *Shach* 160:10 and *Chochmas Adam* 131:8-9 who prohibit this. Since this prohibition under discussion is Rabbinic in nature, one may rely on the *Rema's* leniency).

S.A. Harav §7 rules that one should follow the *Shach's* opinion as a personal stringency (but may rule leniently for others).

If a long period of time has elapsed since the loan was repaid, it is permitted to send a large gift, providing that the loan is not mentioned in connection with the gift (*Shach* 160:10). *Chochmas Adam* 131:8 defines a long period of time as "many days." It would appear that this depends on the relationship which exists between the borrower and lender. If they have other personal or business dealings, there would be no obvious connection between the gift and the loan after a brief period of time. However, if they had no other relationship other than this loan, the connection would remain obvious for a long time (see *Shevet HaLevi* 2:69 and *Toras Ribbis* 3:18).

Additional details regarding *Ribbis Me'ucheres* have been outlined in Chapter 2, Paragraphs 22-25.

12. *Bris Yehudah* 9:13, based on *Taz* 170:3. This is not meant to imply that the borrower is *obligated* to do so, only that he is permitted to reimburse the lender.

in need of funds and borrowed money from a bank, the interest costs which he incurred may not be reimbursed.[13]

Bank Costs

8. If the lender has money which is earning interest in the bank and he withdraws this money to lend it to a friend, he may not be reimbursed for the lost earnings.[14]

9. Penalties for premature withdrawals: Banks offer higher interest rates to depositors who are willing to commit their funds to deposit for a longer period of time. Funds which are placed in these term deposits (commonly called CDs) may not be withdrawn prematurely. When they are withdrawn early, the depositor is assessed a penalty.

If the depositor withdraws funds prematurely, solely because he wishes to lend this money, he would want the borrower to reimburse him for this penalty. Whether he may do so depends on the type of penalty which is incurred.

If the penalty involves a loss of part of the principal which was deposited, the borrower may reimburse the lender for the loss.[15]

Often, the penalty involves only a loss of interest which the account had earned. For example, the penalty might call for the interest rate to be reduced, resulting in a loss of revenue for the depositor. Another common form of penalty is the forfeiture of thirty days' interest.

In these cases, reimbursement of the penalty is permitted only if the depositor was already in legal possession of the interest revenue, which is now taken from him as a penalty. When the depositor does not yet have the right to withdraw the interest, these funds have technically not actually come into his possession. Since this interest is not yet his, the penalty is actually a loss of potential revenue, which may not be reimbursed.[16]

---

13. *Taz* 170:3.

14. *Rashba* (Responsa 3:227) prohibits reimbursements and adds that if this were permitted, "all Ribbis would be permitted, for every loan causes loss since (the lender) is unable to profit by other investments during the time (that the money is outstanding)."

Igros Moshe (Y.D. 3:93) applies this to the case mentioned here. *Bris Yehudah* 3:n4 calls this a common problem, where "people don't realize" that this can be Ribbis Ketzutzah (Biblically prohibited Ribbis). See Chapter 1, Paragraph 23 (with notes) for additional details.

15. *Mishnas Ribbis* 1:n9.

16. *Mishnas Ribbis* ibid. Some time deposits credit interest at maturity. (This is often done to defer tax payments on the interest revenue.) In these cases, the borrower would not be permitted to reimburse the lender, since the lender never received these moneys.

[When the interest had already been credited to the depositor's account and he has the

10. A Free Loan Fund may pass on its expenses to those who take loans from the fund. The limitations which apply to these funds and the manner in which they may charge for their loans are outlined in Chapter 19.

B. Payments Which Are Offered by a Third Party

11. The Torah prohibits Ribbis only when the borrower is paying the lender for the loan. A third person may offer to pay the lender for extending a loan, providing that he has not arranged for the borrower to reimburse him.[17] This is permitted even where a father pays a lender to offer a loan to his son.[18]

---

right to withdraw this money, these funds have already come into his legal possession. It would seem that penalties which involve forfeiture of these funds may be reimbursed. Cf. *Mishnas Ribbis* ibid., who expresses uncertainty in this case.]

R' J. David Bleich Shlita disputes this ruling and maintains that premature withdrawal penalties may never be passed on to the borrower. He likens this to a lender who sells an item of furniture which he owns in order to procure cash, which he then extends as a loan. If he sold the furniture at less than market value because of his desire to receive the cash, he may not pass on this loss to the borrower. In the same way, someone who makes a premature withdrawal is actually purchasing his debt from the bank, at a discount. The penalty is actually a discount on the price of purchasing the debt. Accordingly, this may not be passed on to the borrower.

[This explanation seems inconsistent with the language of the bank agreement, which refers to the transaction as a withdrawal rather than a sale; and to the charge as a penalty, rather than a discount.]

17. Y.D. 160:13.

[This leniency has an important practical application. A common problem involves individuals who have contracted to pay Ribbis, and later realize that this is prohibited. In this case, the borrower might approach his Rabbi, who would rule that he may not make the Ribbis payments. This leaves the borrower in the uncomfortable position of having to renege on his agreement with the lender. This problem is especially serious when the lender is a non-observant Jew who insists on receiving payment, and cannot understand why the borrower would refuse to follow through on his agreement. A Rabbi can resolve this problem by contacting a close friend or relative of the borrower and explaining the problem to him. The Rabbi would suggest that the friend be kind enough to pay the lender, so that the borrower would not have to make a Ribbis payment. Since he is a third party to the loan, he is permitted to do so. The Rabbi can also point out to the third party that the borrower would be permitted to reimburse him at a later date (although he is not obligated to do so, and he may not even pledge to do so). If the friend agrees and makes the Ribbis payment, the lender will have been satisfied (since he does not care who pays the interest) and no prohibition will have been violated by the payment. Later, the borrower may reimburse his friend for his expenditure.]

18. *Darkei Teshuvah* 160:93.

12. When a loan comes due, a third person is permitted to pay the lender to extend the due date, so that the borrower will not have to repay the loan until a later time.[19]

13. Most poskim rule that a borrower is permitted to set up this situation, by convincing a third person to pay the lender for the loan (or for extending its due date).[20]

Reimbursing the Third Party

14. A third party may offer his own moneys to a lender, as an inducement for him to offer a loan. However, the borrower may not pay the third party to do so,[21] nor may he pledge to reimburse him at a later time.[22] The borrower is even prohibited from paying the third party for the time and effort which he spent on the borrower's behalf.[23]

15. Once the deal is completed, with the lender having accepted payment from the third party and having extended the loan to the borrower, most poskim permit the borrower to reimburse the third party for his expense. This means that the money which was paid to the lender is now being reimbursed by the borrower. If this payment had taken place before the loan was extended, it would constitute Ribbis. However, because the loan was already made in a permissible manner, there is no restriction on reimbursement.[24]

Restrictions

16. A third party is permitted to pay the lender to extend a loan only under the following conditions:

□ The third party is only permitted to offer a fixed payment for the loan. He may not obligate himself to make regular interest

---

19. *Yad Avraham* 160:13.

20. This ruling is the subject of a dispute between two opinions recorded in *Shulchan Aruch* (Y.D. 160:13). We may rely on the lenient opinion (*Shach* 160:18, *Chochmas Adam* 132:1, *S.A. Harav* §60). According to both opinions, the borrower must be careful not to intimate to the third person that he will reimburse him for his expense.

21. Y.D. 160:13. This is prohibited even when the reimbursement is only for a portion of the third party's expenditure (*Taz* 7).

22. *Nimukei Yosef* (B.M. 69b), *Chochmas Adam* 132:1.

23. *Rema* 160:16, *Taz* 160:7, see also *Chavos Daas* 6.

24. *Darkei Moshe* 170:6, *Chavos Daas* 160:6, *Chochmas Adam* 132:1, *Avnei Nezer* 150.

payments which continue to accrue for the duration of the loan.[25]

☐ The borrower should not tell the lender that a third party has agreed to pay him to offer the loan (or to extend the date when payment is due).[26]

☐ The third person may not take the loan from the lender and deliver it to the borrower. This would create an appearance of Ribbis, since both the loan and the payment are being passed between the same people.[27]

☐ The lender may not demand that the borrower find a third party to make this payment.[28]

C. Payments Which Are Made to a Third Party

17. The Torah prohibits Ribbis only when the borrower is paying the lender for a loan. Someone who is seeking a loan is permitted to hire a third person to influence the lender to offer a loan. This is even permitted when the son of the lender is paid to influence his father to offer a loan (provided that the son is an adult who does not live with his father).[29]

---

25. *Taz* 160:6. When the third party obligates himself to pay interest until the loan is repaid, he has assumed an open-ended obligation. The third person is actually accepting responsibility for payment of the principal, since his debt grows as long as it is not repaid. Since he carries the financial burden of repaying the loan, he has the status of a borrower and is prohibited from paying Ribbis. When the obligation to pay interest lasts for a fixed period of time (for example, if the obligation runs only for a year or two) and then ends, regardless of whether the principal has been paid, the third party may make the interest payments (*Mishnas Ribbis*, based on *Chavos Daas* 160:11 and 170:7).

See Chapter 15, Note 45, for another application of this concept.

[If the third person has not *obligated himself* to pay Ribbis, he may make regular monthly payments to the lender for as long as he chooses. Only an obligation to make monthly payments gives someone the status of a borrower.]

26. *Y.D.* 160:13, *S.A. Harav* §60; Cf., *Chavos Daas* 160:6 and *Pischei Teshuvah* 9 who maintain that this is subject to a dispute among Rishonim, and that those who rule leniently in Note 20 above would rule leniently here as well.

27. *Darkei Moshe* 170:6, *Binas Adam* §4, *Yad Avraham* 160:13.

28. *Mishnas Ribbis* based on *Y.D.* 160:15.

29. *Y.D.* 160:16. This is permitted despite the fact that the father gains satisfaction from the fact that the son was hired and paid. This is not prohibited as *Ribbis Devarim*

18. A person may offer to arrange loans through outside lenders, for a fee. This is permitted even when the lender knows that the agent was paid to arrange the loan.[30]

Restrictions

19. A person may be hired to influence someone to extend a loan only under the following conditions:

☐ The third person may subsequently influence the lender only by friendly persuasion. Although a third party is permitted to pay a lender to offer a loan (in Paragraph 11 above), this does not apply here. When the third party has been paid by the borrower to arrange a loan, he is prohibited from paying the lender.[31]

☐ The third person may not take the loan from the lender and deliver it to the borrower. This would create an appearance of Ribbis, since both the loan and the payment are being passed between the same people.[32]

☐ The lender may be aware that this payment was made. However, he may not tell the borrower to make this payment in order to secure the loan. See Chapter 3, Paragraph 27.[33]

20. Donations to charity: An individual who is extending a loan may not require that the borrower offer a donation to charity in exchange for the loan.[34] However, Rabbinical prohibitions of Ribbis do

---

(Ribbis without financial gain), because the payment was not made directly to the lender. See also Paragraph 29, below.

This third-party payment may not be made to the spouse of the lender (R' Akiva Eiger to *Taz* 160:16).

30. *Bris Yehudah* 6:n17.

31. *Rema* 160:6. If this were permitted, people could easily circumvent the prohibition on paying Ribbis by routing their payments through a third party. Most poskim therefore prohibit these payments under any condition. Cf. *Chavos Daas* 160:7 who permits payment under specific conditions. *Bris Yehudah* 6:n20 points out that other poskim clearly disagree with this leniency.

32. *Mishnah LaMelech* (to *Hil. Malveh* 4:14, s.v. *v'da*); this is identical to the ruling of *Binas Adam* and *Yad Avraham* in the situation described in Paragraph 14, above.

33. *Bris Yehudah* 6:n17, based on *Chavos Yair* 190 and *Mishnah LaMelech* (ibid.). *Bris Yehudah* points out that this may constitute Ribbis Ketzutzah (Biblically prohibited Ribbis).

34. *Rema* 160:14.

Where the borrower is required to raise money (from others) in exchange for the loan, see *Minchas Yitzchak* 6:78 who permits this. (See also *Bris Yehudah* 6:n29.)

not apply where a charity's moneys are involved. Therefore, a charitable organization such as a yeshivah or synagogue may invest its funds in ways which would otherwise be prohibited by Rabbinic law.[35]

Additionally, someone who receives a free loan from a charity may subsequently choose to show his appreciation by making a donation to the charity. This is permitted even if the donation is clearly being offered in gratitude for the loan.[36]

D. Additional Leniencies

21. Merchandise may be used to repay a loan, provided that this is acceptable to the lender. Most merchandise has a market value which fluctuates, within a range, from store to store. When using merchandise to repay a loan, the borrower may calculate its value at the lowest price at which it is commonly available. This benefits the lender, since he receives the merchandise at the best available price.

This benefit may only be extended at the time that the loan is paid. A loan may not be offered with the stipulation that it be repaid in this manner.[37]

Adding to a Payment

22. A customer may not pay for the privilege of purchasing on credit. However, if a merchant does allow him to buy on credit, the

---

35. *Rema* 160:18. Although *Shach* 26 writes that to his knowledge this leniency is not actually practiced, most poskim follow the ruling of *Rema*. *Noda BeYehudah* (Y.D. 1:40) writes, "I have often done this (when) lending the money of orphans . . . ." This is also the ruling of *Bris Yehudah* 7:1. A practical application of this leniency is presented in Chapter 5, Paragraph 16.

36. *Bris Yehudah* 7:n45. This is not Ribbis Ketzutzah since it was not a condition of the loan. [If a donation is made to charity, it is preferable that it be made before the loan is granted or after it is repaid, since these are more lenient forms of Ribbis DeRabbanan (ibid.).]

Other laws which pertain to charity funds are discussed in the next chapter.

37. *Shaar Deah* 166:1 and 173:2, *Bris Yehudah* 12:4 and Note 11. It is prohibited to extend a loan on the condition that merchandise will be delivered at a discounted price. This is a discount for advance payment, which constitutes Rabbinically prohibited Ribbis. We will learn that there are circumstances where even this is permitted, most notably, where the borrower has the merchandise in his possession at the time of the loan. The details of these laws are discussed below in Chapter 7.

[A second leniency mentioned by *Shaar Deah* is the subject of considerable dispute. We have not entered into this discussion because it applies only to situations which are uncommon today.]

customer may show his gratitude to the merchant by adding a small amount to the payment. Still, he may not explicitly state that this money is being added because of the loan.[38]

23. Limitations on this leniency:

☐ Although one is permitted to add a small amount when paying for a purchase, he may do so only if the debt is being paid in its entirety. When only a portion of the payment is made and the remainder of the debt is outstanding, this is prohibited.[39]

☐ Even when the entire debt is being paid, many poskim hold that it is permitted to add to the payment only when the payment is made in the form of merchandise, and not when a cash payment is made.[40]

☐ A significant sum of money may never be added to a payment (even in the form of additional merchandise). This is the equivalent of an expressed statement of thanks for the loan, and is therefore prohibited.[41]

☐ Where credit was extended for a purchase and the customer did not make payment by the due date, the credit takes on the status of a loan. In this case, nothing may be added at the time of payment.[42]

---

38. *Rema* 160:4, *Shach* 160:4 and 5, *Chavos Daas* 163:6, *S.A. Harav* §8; this also appears to be the opinion of *Taz* 160:12. Even when this is permitted, only a small amount may be added to the payment.

The reason for this leniency is that the small addition appears to be a gift to the seller, rather than an interest payment. By Biblical law, the rules of Ribbis apply only to situations where money has actually passed from lender to borrower. When this happens, even a small gift may not be added at the time of payment. However, when the debt resulted from a purchase, a small addition is permitted. The reason for this is that when money is owed as a result of a purchase, even outright interest payments are only prohibited by Rabbinic law; see Chapter 6, Note 1 (*Taz* 160:12, *Chochmas Adam* 131:6, *Divrei Sofrim* 160:*Emek Davar* 57).

39. *Tzemach Tzedek* Y.D. 82.

40. R' Akiva Eiger and *Beis Meir* to *Rema* 160:4, *Chochmas Adam* 131:6. According to this opinion, one is permitted to add to a payment only where it is not easily noticeable that an addition was made. Since businessmen sometimes calculate merchandise at discount prices for certain customers, when someone offers additional merchandise it is not considered a noticeable addition. However, when a customer pays with cash, it is unusual to pay more than billed. This is therefore a noticeable addition and is prohibited. *Bris Yehudah* 5:9 rules that one may follow the lenient opinion of *Rema*.

41. *S.A. Harav* §8.

42. *Chochmas Adam* 131:6.

Ribbis Me'ucheres

24. After the loan has been paid up, even if only a short period of time has elapsed, the borrower is permitted to send a gift to the lender. The gift must be one of minimal value, so that it would not be obvious that the gift is being sent because of the loan. In addition, the borrower may not stipulate that the gift is being sent in connection with the loan.[43]

When the Debt Balance Is Unknown

25. It is important that both the borrower and lender keep accurate records of how much is owed. When records are not kept, there may be uncertainty regarding the balance which is owed. In this case, the borrower may pay the lender an amount of money which is great enough to assure that the loan is paid up.[44] Although it is possible that he is actually returning more than he borrowed, this is not considered Ribbis. Preferably, the borrower should stipulate that if he is over-paying, the extra moneys are an outright gift and are not intended as a Ribbis payment.[45]

Rental Fees

26. Rental fees are permitted. This applies both to rentals for real estate[46] and to rentals for utensils.[47]

---

43. *Rema* 160:6 and *Shach* 8. See above, Paragraph 6, Notes 10 and 11. See also Chapter 10, Paragraph 12.

44. The borrower is not obligated to do so. Although a basic Talmudic principle is that in cases of doubt the burden of proof always rests with the person seeking payment, the borrower nevertheless satisfies a moral obligation by making an additional payment to insure that the loan is fully paid (*Bris Yehudah* 5:35).

45. *Avnei Nezer* C.M. 26, *Minchas Yitzchak* 6:161 and 9:88.

   When paying a small loan, the borrower may sometimes find that he does not have correct change. Often, the borrower might choose to let the lender keep the change, rather than to be bothered with finding someone to change his money. *Minchas Yitzchak* rules that when the amount of overpayment is insignificant to both the borrower and lender, this is permitted (provided that the extra amount is not intended as a sign of gratitude for the loan). An amount of money is considered insignificant when neither of them would bother to search for this amount of money if they had dropped it. Still, *Minchas Yitzchak* recommends that they stipulate that the overpayment be given to charity, as a donation of the borrower.

46. It is common to offer discounts to people who prepay for a month's use of a *mikveh*. Although it is generally prohibited to offer discounts in exchange for advance payment, it is permitted in the case of a rental. Thus, a person may receive a discount when paying the monthly fee for a *mikveh* (*Mishnas Ribbis* 9:32).

47. Y.D. 176:2. This applies whenever the object which is borrowed loses value as it is

When someone lends an object to another person, the borrower is permitted to pay him for the loan, even if the object was loaned without a request for payment. Thus, one who borrows a car may pay for its use or offer a gift to its owner, as explained in Chapter 1, Paragraph 10.

27. A borrower may pay another person to provide collateral for his loan.[48]

Cosigner Fees

28. One who serves as guarantor for a loan may be paid for offering this service.[49]

Benefiting the Lender's Family

29. The borrower may give a gift (for example, a *bar mitzvah* or wedding gift) to the child of the lender, if the child is over 13 years of age (12 years for a girl).[50] However, the gift must be an item which the father would not normally purchase for the child.[51]

---

used. Appliances, clothing, tools and motorized or mechanical instruments are examples of items whose value decreases as they are used. Items such as jewelry, precious stones and rare coins do not decrease in value when they are used. These items may be rented only under the conditions outlined in Chapter 11, Paragraph 4.

A rental occurs when the borrower must return the same item to the owner. However, if he will not be returning the actual item to the owner, this is not a rental and this leniency does not apply.

48. *Avnei Nezer* Y.D. 200, *Bris Yehudah* 9:21. The money which is paid is actually a fee for use of the collateral. This is similar to a cosigner fee, which is permitted.

49. See Chapter 15, Paragraphs 14 and 15, where this is discussed in greater detail.

50. When a child is younger than this, anything he acquires is the legal property of his father (C.M. 270). A *bar mitzvah* gift must therefore be presented *after* the child's thirteenth birthday.

51. *Bris Yehudah* 11:n43. For another application of this ruling, see Chapter 3, Paragraph 27.

The borrower is prohibited from benefiting the lender; thus he may only give a gift when he is benefiting the lender's son, not the lender himself. If the gift is an item which the father would normally purchase (for example, a book needed for school), the lender is benefiting from the gift, in that he saves the money which he would otherwise have spent to buy the item. This is therefore prohibited.

This ruling is based on *Shulchan Aruch* Y.D. 160:10, which rules that the borrower is prohibited from tutoring the son of the lender in the study of Torah. *Beis Yosef* (quoted by *Shach* 160:15) explains that this is prohibited because a father is obligated to teach his son Torah or to hire a tutor to do so. When the borrower teaches Torah to the lender's son, he is benefiting the lender himself, in that he is satisfying the lender's own obligation. *Bris Yehudah* deduces from here that when there is no benefit to the lender himself, it is permitted to benefit the child.

While the lender is certainly happy that his son is receiving this gift, this is only

The gift should be a type of item which is used by the recipient individually, such as a book or toy. A gift which would benefit the entire family, such as an air conditioner or radio, should not be given because the lender himself will derive a direct benefit from it.

Conditions of Payment

30. The conditions of payment may be drawn to accommodate the lender. The lender may stipulate that the loan be repaid at a specific location, despite the fact that this will make the borrower exert himself for the lender's convenience. Similarly, he may direct that payments be made directly to a specific bank account.[52]

Common Courtesies

31. Courtesies which people routinely extend to others may be extended to the lender as well.[53] The borrower may therefore offer a tissue to the lender or change money for him.

Security Deposits

32. Many companies require security deposits before offering service. For example, many utility companies do not allow customers to open an account unless a security deposit is provided. Regulations often allow the companies to use these funds. Therefore, these companies are actually receiving a loan, in exchange for their service. This is permitted because it is clear that the company requires the security as a means of

---

Ribbis Devarim (Ribbis without financial gain to the lender), which is permitted when it is not extended directly to the lender. [A similar case was discussed in Paragraph 17 above.]

52. *Bris Yehudah* 11:15 and notes. Cf. *Toras Ribbis* 5:3 and *Mishnas Ribbis* 4:n10.

If the borrower must suffer a financial loss to fulfill this condition (for example, where travel to the required location involves an expense), *Bris Yehudah* is uncertain as to whether this stipulation is permitted.

53. *Bris Yehudah* 10:n22. However, the lender may not request a favor from the borrower, even if it is a common courtesy. This is prohibited even when it involves no exertion on the part of the borrower and even if the loan is not mentioned in connection with the request (see Chapter 3, Note 23).

The prohibition on benefiting the lender extends even to greeting him. This is known as *Ribbis Devarim* (see Chapter 3, Paragraph 10). *Bris Yehudah* explains that it is prohibited only where the borrower is a type of person who does not normally greet everyone. If the borrower is a person who greets everyone whom he meets, he may greet the lender as well.

securing payment for its services. This is obviously not intended as a loan and is therefore permitted.[54]

For the same reason, deposits which are given to a storeowner for soda bottles or shopping carts are not considered loans.[55]

Returning Stolen Goods

33. A thief is obligated to return the goods which he stole. If the stolen items were consumed, the thief must pay for them. The value of these goods is pegged at their market value at the time they were stolen. Thus, if the value of the goods were to go up in the interim after they were stolen, the thief is only obligated to pay what they were worth at the time of the robbery.

If the thief wishes to replace the stolen goods by purchasing new ones (even after the price had gone up), he would be permitted to do so.[56]

---

54. *Bris Yehudah*, *hashmatos* to 11:n54.

55. Ibid.

56. *Bris Yehudah* 16:n18.

Bris Yehudah adds that these rules also apply when someone damaged another person's property. In this case too, he is only obligated to pay for the value of the item at the time it was damaged. Still, if he wishes to replace the damaged item, he is permitted to do so, even if this involves a greater expenditure. (*Machneh Ephraim*, in *Dinei Nizkei Mamon* §1, rules that someone who damages another person's property is obligated to replace the damaged goods, whatever the cost. According to this opinion, there is an *obligation* to pay the full current price of the damaged item. *Bris Yehudah* maintains that most poskim reject this ruling and hold that someone who damages property is only obligated to repay the property according to its value at the time that it is damaged. Still, if someone chooses to replace the property, he is permitted to do so.)

CHAPTER FIVE

Who Is Exempt
From the Laws of Ribbis?

In this chapter, we will examine the laws of
Ribbis as they apply to loans involving:

**A. Non-Jews, converts to Judaism and non-observant
Jews** (1-10)

B. Charities (11-25)

C. Partnerships, corporations and banks (26-32)

D. Family members and minors (33-39)

E. Trustees (40-42)

A. Non-Jews

1. The Torah prohibits Ribbis only in loans which involve a Jewish borrower and lender. When a non-Jew is involved, none of these restrictions apply.[1] A Jew is therefore permitted to accept Ribbis from a non-Jewish borrower,[2] or to pay Ribbis to a non-Jewish lender.[3]

2. A non-Jew who lends money to a Jew may stipulate that the interest payments be made to another Jew. In this case, it is permitted for a Jew to make interest payments to another Jew because they do not have a lender-borrower relationship.[4]

3. A Jew may not act as an agent for a non-Jew, to lend the non-Jew's money for Ribbis. Although this involves no Biblical prohibition, the Rabbis prohibited it because it might appear that the Jew is lending his own money for interest (this is known as *maris ayin*).[5]

---

1. **The reason** for this is explained in a note which appears in *Shulchan Aruch* (to 159:1). "Jews are bound by a mutual agreement, set out in the Torah, to join in a fraternity whose members offer free loans to each other, without taking interest. Non-Jews, who never joined in this fraternity, as well as Jews who completely remove themselves from it (this refers to the case outlined in Paragraph 10) do not have the rights which belong to its members."

Thus a non-Jew lacks the privilege of being protected against Ribbis charges, but also has the benefit of being permitted to collect Ribbis.

2. Y.D. 159:1. *Rambam* (*Hil. Malveh* 5:1) cites the verse in *Deut.* 23:20 as the source for this. *Tur* 159 cites a different verse, in *Lev.* 25:36 (see *Taz* 159:1 and *Mishneh LaMelech* 5:1).

[It is interesting that the words '*la'nochri sashich*, to a gentile you may (lend for) Ribbis' (*Deut.* 23:21) is not cited as the source for permitting loans to non-Jews (see *Mishneh LaMelech*, ibid.). Rather, this is understood to represent an additional prohibition on collecting Ribbis from a Jew (this is inferred from this verse which states that one may lend money for Ribbis to a gentile, but not to a Jew) (B.M. 70b).]

3. *Rambam Hil. Malveh* 5:1. It is not clear why *Shulchan Aruch* does not record this halachah. *Gedulei Terumah* suggests that this law was so obvious and well known that *Shulchan Aruch* did not deem it necessary to record it (*Bris Yehudah* 30:n2).

Concerning interest payments which benefit a church, see *Minchas Yitzchak* 4:88.

4. Y.D. 168:4. *Avnei Nezer* 189 rules that if the non-Jew directs that both the principal and interest be paid to a Jew, this would be prohibited. *Bris Yehudah* 31:n2 disagrees, and rules that as long as the debt has not been transferred (by means of a *kinyan*) to the second Jew, the interest is being paid for a non-Jew's loan and is permitted, even if both principal and interest are actually paid to a Jew.

5. Y.D. 168:23. This is prohibited even if the borrower (and any others who are present when the loan is given) is told explicitly that the funds belong to a non-Jew (*Chochmas Adam* 137:33 and *S.A. Harav* §74; see also Chapter 17, Note 4).

There are exceptions to this prohibition. For example, when a professional money

4. A Jew who is seeking to borrow money from a non-Jew may hire another Jew to arrange the loan for him (even if Ribbis will be paid).[6]

5. One who is faced with the choice of lending money to a non-Jew or to a Jew should perform the mitzvah of lending money to a fellow Jew rather than make an interest-earning loan to a non-Jew.[7]

However, where the amount of earnings which would be lost is significant to the lender, he is not obligated to do so.[8]

6. A Jew is generally prohibited from accepting payment for business which is transacted on Shabbos (or Yom Tov). Still, interest which accrues on Shabbos (or Yom Tov) may be accepted (with one exception — see note).[9]

---

manager issues the loan, people understand that he is lending someone else's money, thus avoiding the issue of *maris ayin* (*Rema* 168:23, *Shach* 71). See Chapter 17, Paragraph 2, for other situations where this prohibition does not apply.

6. Y.D. 168:17. The prohibition of *maris ayin* does not apply when a Jew acts as an agent of the borrower (*Darkei Moshe* 168:22, *Bris Yehudah* 31:n14).

7. *Bava Metzia* 71a. In contemporary terms, this means that a person should be willing to withdraw a deposit from an interest-bearing account, to offer a free loan to a fellow Jew. [The borrower would be prohibited from reimbursing him for his lost earnings (see Chapter 1, Paragraph 23).]

If the lender has reason to fear that his loan will never be repaid, he is not required to offer the loan (*Chochmas Shlomo* to C.M. 97:1, *Ahavas Chessed* 1:1:8; see also *Ahavas Chessed* 2:8).

8. *Ahavas Chessed* 1:5:3, *Igros Moshe* Y.D. 3:93. If the borrower is a poor person who is eligible to receive charity, the lender may offer the loan and count the lost interest as a charitable contribution which may be deducted from his *maaser* (tithing) calculation (*Igros Moshe*, ibid.).

9. Shabbos earnings may not be accepted even when they are earned in a passive manner (such as the case of interest which accrues on Shabbos). Still, the method banks use for calculating interest serves to permit this, for the following reason.

The concept of *havlaah* permits a Jew to accept earnings which accrue during a period of time which spans both Shabbos and a weekday. For example, a Jewish landlord may collect rent for an apartment (despite the fact that this includes payment for Shabbos rental), because the rent is paid for an entire week or month at one time. Similarly, interest which is paid at the end of a period of time which includes both Shabbos and weekdays may be collected. In the case of a bank account which pays interest on a day of deposit to day of withdrawal basis, interest is computed for each day. Still, because banks compute interest based on the secular day which runs from midnight to midnight, there is no 'day' which consists totally of Shabbos. (Saturday runs past sunset, into a time which the Jewish calendar regards as Sunday.)

The concept of *havlaah* therefore applies, and interest earned on Saturday may be accepted.

However, when Yom Tov falls on Sunday, this leniency does not apply. Since the secular day Saturday is part Shabbos and part Yom Tov, interest credited for this day may

A Ger (Convert to Judaism)

6. Someone who converts to Judaism is considered a Jew in all regards; therefore the laws of Ribbis apply to him.[10] However, this applies only to Ribbis which is collected after the <u>Geirus (conversion)</u>; he may keep any interest which he may have collected from Jews prior to the time he converted.[11]

7. If Geirus occurred during the term of a loan: If a non-Jew lent money to a Jew (and terms of the loan called for interest payments) and he subsequently became a Ger, he may collect Ribbis only if, while he was still a non-Jew, the principal and interest were totaled in one written bill (or promissory note). In this case, the total is viewed as an established debt from that time and may be collected even after the lender converts to Judaism.[12]

For example, a $100 loan was issued for a year, calling for $1 per month in interest. A promissory note was written, stating that the borrower owes $112, payable at the end of the year. If the non-Jew were to become a Ger during the year, he may collect the entire $112 at the year's end.[13]

---

not be accepted. (When Yom Tov falls on Friday, there is an identical problem. In this case, Friday is part Yom Tov and part Shabbos.) Since the banks do not have arrangements which allow for interest to be refused, the Jew should take the money which is credited for this day and donate it anonymously to charity (*Igros Moshe* O.C. 4:59).

10. To become a Jew, a gentile must agree to observe all of the mitzvos, be circumcised (if he is a male) and then immerse in a *mikveh* under the guidance of an Orthodox Beis Din. He does not have the status of a Jew until all three steps have been taken. (Regarding his status in the interim, see *Binyan Tzion* 1:92 and *Avnei Nezer* 351:4.)

11. If he collected an interest payment for a twelve-month loan and subsequently became a Ger during the twelve-month period, he is not obligated to return the part of the payment which was made for the time after his conversion (*Bris Yehudah* 30:n18).

12. Y.D. 171:1, with *Taz* and *Shach*. This means that even interest which accrued during the time that he was already a Jew may be collected, since it had already been established as debt.

13. This is permitted only when the terms of the loan do not allow the borrower to make prepayment during the year. If he does have the option of prepaying, only the interest which accrued prior to the time of Geirus may be collected. (When there is a prepayment option, the interest cannot be viewed as existing debt, because the borrower has an option of avoiding it. This would appear to be identical to the case in *Rema* 168:20, regarding debt which a non-Jew sells to a Jew. See *Bris Yehudah* 30:n14 and 31:n21.)

No matter what the terms are, if the borrower is unable to make payment at the end of the year, no additional interest may be charged for the period that the loan remains outstanding.

However, if the bill (or promissory note) was first issued after the lender became a Ger, he may collect only the $100 principal.[14]

8. If a Jew lends money to a non-Jew, and the non-Jewish borrower then converts to Judaism, the lender may not collect interest which accrues after the Geirus.[15] However, interest which accrued before the Geirus must be paid. In this case, there is no difference if the bill (or promissory note) was written before or after the borrower had become a Ger.[16]

Non-observant Jews

9. The prohibition of paying Ribbis to a Jew applies even when the lender is not an observant Jew.[17]

10. The prohibition of collecting Ribbis from a Jew applies even when the borrower is not an observant Jew, except in the following situation: When the borrower was raised in an observant home but has

---

14. Y.D. ibid. This means that interest which accrued *prior* to his becoming a Ger may also not be collected. Some poskim say that Ribbis which accrues *after* he became a Ger is considered Ribbis Ketzutzah (*Bris Yehudah* 30:16; however, this is difficult to understand since the Biblical prohibition applies only when an agreement [or *ketzitzah*] calling for Ribbis had been made. In this case, there was no agreement to pay Ribbis to a Jew. See also *Avnei Nezer* 189).

15. Y.D. 171:1.
Shaar Deah (171:2) rules that the lender may demand that the loan be repaid immediately. Since he made the loan on the assumption that he would be paid interest, and he is no longer able to do so, he may retract his commitment. *Shaar Deah* explains that this is why we are not concerned that the Geirus is motivated by the Ger's desire to gain financial benefit by being relieved of the obligation to pay Ribbis after the Geirus. In fact, the Ger does not gain because upon becoming a Ger, he stands to lose the loan entirely. (See also *Bris Yehudah* 31:n21.)

16. Y.D. ibid. The reason we require the Ger to pay this interest is that if we would allow a situation where Geirus would absolve a Ger from debt, this may create the suspicion that the Geirus was motivated by economic benefit.
In this case, there is no difference if the charges had already been formally totaled and billed before the Geirus or not (*Taz* 2).
[This is in contrast to the previous paragraph (where the Ger was a lender), where the halachah was determined by the date on which the principal and interest were formally totaled in a bill or promissory note.]
See *Bris Yehudah* 30:7 regarding a situation where no bill or promissory note was written at all.

17. Y.D. 159:2. A non-observant Jew who collected Ribbis and later became observant must return the Ribbis to the borrower (*Darkei Teshuvah* 159:19). There is one exception to this. When the repentant Jew had made many loans involving Ribbis, he may not be obligated to return these funds; see Chapter 20, Paragraphs 15-18.

become so far removed from his people that he no longer considers himself part of the Jewish nation, Ribbis may be collected.[18]

Even in this situation, where Ribbis may be charged, it is preferable to avoid any halachic question by using a Heter Iska.[19]

B. Charities

11. The Biblical prohibition of Ribbis applies to both individuals and to charities who are involved in loans. Therefore, a charity may not lend its funds on the condition that the recipient make a donation to that charity[20] or to a different charity.[21]

Similarly, a synagogue or free loan fund may not require that membership dues be paid in order to secure a loan.[22]

12. An individual who is extending a loan may not require a borrower to make a donation to charity in exchange for the loan.[23]

---

18. Y.D. 159:2 permits charging interest to a non-observant Jew. *Shach* explains that this applies only to one who is completely removed from the Jewish people. Although such an individual has the status of a Jew in virtually all other areas of halachah, the laws of Ribbis differ. [This is based on a Biblical verse — see *Taz* 159:1 and 3.]

Maharshag Y.D. 5 and *Chazon Ish* O.C. 87:14 limit this to individuals who grew up in an observant home. This is based on *Rema* 159:3 and *S. A. Harav* §79.

If this loan is later inherited by an observant son, see *Darkei Teshuvah* 159:11.

19. Where it is necessary to offer a loan, and the borrower does not agree to use a Heter Iska, see *Rema* 159:2, *Pischei Teshuvah* 159:4, *Igros Moshe* Y.D. 3:39.

The mitzvah of offering free loans: Ahavas Chessed 1:3 rules that there is a mitzvah to offer free loans only to observant Jews. He defines an observant Jew as "anyone who subscribes to the thirteen basic principles of our faith."

20. Y.D. 160:18. See also *Minchas Yitzchak* 6:78 and *Bris Yehudah* 6:n29.

Igros Moshe C.M. 1:80 also rules that synagogues and charity funds are also prohibited from paying Ribbis for their loans. Today, virtually all such organizations are incorporated. As we shall see (in Paragraph 27), *Igros Moshe* himself rules that corporations are not prohibited from paying interest. We must therefore assume that the Responsa quoted here is referring to the rare case of a synagogue which is not incorporated.

21. The Biblical prohibition applies whenever the lender requires that a payment be made, even if it is made to others (Y.D. 160:14).

22. *Bris Yehudah* 7:n45, *Mishnas Ribbis* 2:14. Dues which are used solely to cover loan-related expenses may be charged (as with expenses involved in any loan — see Chapter 4, Paragraphs 1-10). These laws are discussed at greater length in Chapter 19.

23. *Rema* 160:14; cf. *Birkei Yosef*, end of 161, quoting *Radvaz*.

Where the borrower is required to raise money (from others) in exchange for the loan, see *Minchas Yitzchak* 6:78 who permits this. (See also *Bris Yehudah* 6:n29.)

A common problem: A *gabbai tzedakah* is collecting money for a charity. He meets a person who wishes to contribute but does not have the funds in hand. May the

13. A leniency: Rabbinical prohibitions of Ribbis do not apply to the funds of a charity. Therefore, a charitable organization such as a yeshivah or synagogue may invest its funds in ways which would otherwise be prohibited by Rabbinic law. See the guidelines for these investments in Paragraphs 15-18.[24]

Additionally, someone who receives a free loan from a charity may subsequently show his appreciation by making a donation to the charity. This is permitted even if the donation is clearly being offered in gratitude for the loan.[25]

14. Similarly, the estate of an orphan (who lost his father) may lend out its money in ways which are considered Ribbis DeRabbanan. This is true even if the orphan is over thirteen years of age, as long as

---

collector lend his own money to the donor so that he can make the contribution? This would seem to be prohibited, since the loan is extended on the condition that the money is donated to charity. *Bris Yehudah* 6:n29 rules that this is permitted if the donor desired to make the donation even before a loan was offered. Since the donation is not being made in gratitude for the loan, it is permitted.

24. *Rema* 160:18. Although *Shach* 26 writes that to his knowledge this leniency is not actually practiced, most poskim follow the ruling of *Rema. Noda BeYehudah* (Y.D. 1:40) writes, "I have often done this (when) lending the money of orphans . . . ." This is also the ruling of *Chasam Sofer* Y.D. 135 and *Bris Yehudah* 7:1.

25. *Bris Yehudah* 7:n45. This is not Ribbis Ketzutzah since it was not a condition of the loan. [If a donation is made to charity, it is preferable that it be made before the loan is granted or after it is repaid, since these are more lenient forms of Ribbis DeRabbanan (ibid.).]

A common question: If someone who is receiving a free loan from a charity pledges to make a donation at a later time, may he subsequently make that donation?

This depends on whether this is considered Ribbis Ketzutzah. *Machneh Ephraim* §18 quotes a dispute among Rishonim in the case of a borrower who is given a loan unconditionally, but upon receipt of the loan, the borrower states that he will give the lender a gift for his kindness. While all agree that this is prohibited (in cases which do not involve charity funds), there is a dispute as to whether this is considered Ribbis Ketzutzah. (See also *Bris Yehudah* 3:n11 and 12.) This situation presents a unique problem. In general, where a question of Biblical law is involved we follow the more stringent opinion, so as to avoid the possibility of violating a Biblical prohibition. On the one hand, this would mean that the borrower should refrain from making a donation to the charity, since this may be a form of Ribbis Ketzutzah. On the other hand, if this is actually Ribbis DeRabbanan, the obligation stands. Failure to pay would violate the separate Biblical injunction on failing to pay one's pledge to charity.

It would seem that the borrower would have to find a way out of this dilemma, perhaps by telling a friend of his problem and hoping that the friend would make the donation on his behalf.

he is not yet old enough to deal with his finances in the manner of an adult.[26]

This leniency applies even where the orphans were left a large sum of money.[27]

15. An application of this leniency: Normally, when funds are invested in a business, the investor may not be guaranteed that his principal will be returned to him. An investor must accept risk to be entitled to a share of profits. When he risks nothing (that is, he is guaranteed a return of his principal), this transaction is viewed as a loan, not an investment. In this case, any profits which he collects are prohibited as Ribbis DeRabbanan.

Since this is only a Rabbinic prohibition, charity funds may be invested in this manner. The businessman who uses this money may guarantee the principal and still share the profits with the charity.[28]

16. Another application: A loan agreement may not contain a penalty clause which penalizes the borrower if he does not pay on time. However, where the clause calls for a one-time penalty, this is only prohibited by Rabbinic law. Therefore, when charity funds are loaned, this type of penalty clause may be included.[29]

17. When entering into an agreement which calls for the payment of Rabbinically prohibited Ribbis, the contract should state specifically that the moneys which are given belong to charity (or to orphans).[30]

---

26. Y.D. 160:18. [This leniency does *not* apply to the possessions of someone who was captured at war. Even if his estate is put into trusteeship, the funds may not be loaned for Ribbis DeRabbanan (*Divrei Sofrim* 160:E.D. 324, quoting *Gedulei Terumah*).]

27. *Bris Yehudah* 7:n9. Orphans who have been adopted or who have a stepfather are still considered orphans as regards this halachah. This is because stepparents are not legally bound (by halachah) to provide support for their stepchildren (ibid.).

Regarding a situation where there are wealthy grandparents, see *Sdei Chemed* Vol. 1, page 339.

28. As in *Bava Metzia* 70a. This type of arrangement is known as *karov leschar verachok lehefsed* [lit., (an investment where) profit is likely, but loss is unlikely]. The reason that this is not considered Ribbis Ketzutzah is because the profit is not guaranteed.

29. *Pischei Teshuvah* 177:4 cites the opinion of Rabbi Eliyahu Mizrachi, who permitted penalty clauses which call for continuous payment (for each month, as long as the loan is not repaid). However, many poskim hold that this is a Biblical form of Ribbis. It should therefore not be included in the loan agreement, even when charity funds are involved.

30. This was the practice of *Noda BeYehudah* (see Note 24), cited in *Pischei Teshuvah* (160:20).

18. A charity may *not* make an investment where both the principal and profit are guaranteed, since this is a Biblically prohibited form of Ribbis.[31]

19. When an orphan reaches adulthood (i.e., he is over thirteen years old and sufficiently mature to manage his finances in the manner of an adult), he should terminate any business deal in which he is receiving Ribbis DeRabbanan because of this dispensation. In the case outlined above (Paragraph 15), where payments are made to orphans based on profits generated by their moneys, some poskim permit the orphans to continue collecting profits based on the original agreement.[32]

20. **A Charitable Trust:**[33] A charitable trust is an account which is set up by a person who wishes to leave money to charity. This trust can take one of many forms.

Revocable Trusts: When a revocable trust is set up, the donor retains control of its funds. This trust is not considered a charity, in regard to the laws of Ribbis. Similarly, if the trust allows the donor to use the money in any way he chooses, but stipulates that after his death, the money automatically reverts to the designated charity, the trust itself is not considered a charity. This trust may not offer loans involving Ribbis DeRabbanan, since its owner may still decide to use the money for his own personal purposes.[34]

Irrevocable Trusts: When a trust is set up so that the donor can no longer control the funds of the trust, this is seen as a charity. If the donor has no direct benefit from the interest earned by the trust, the trust would be permitted to offer loans involving Ribbis DeRabbanan.

For Mitzvah Purposes

21. **For the borrower's mitzvah:** Some poskim extend this leniency further. They discuss a situation where someone is unable to

---

31. This arrangement is a loan, not an investment and the profit is therefore Ribbis Ketzutzah.

32. *Mishneh LaMelech* to Hil. *Milveh* 4:14, *Bris Yehudah* 7:7. The moneys may certainly not be reinvested for an additional period even with the same person.

33. The status of charitable trusts (specifically, the *Charitable Remainder Annuity Trust, Unitrust,* and the *Charitable Lead Trust*) is discussed in greater length below, in Chapter 17, Paragraphs 24 and 25.

34. Where the account is set up so that the interest or profits which are generated go to the charity and may not be used by the individual, see *Divrei Sofrim* 160:116 at length.

    A *Charitable Remainder Annuity Trust* may not offer loans involving Ribbis (this is the type of trust described by *Divrei Sofrim*, in *Emek Davar* 160:344).

perform a mitzvah due to lack of funds. According to these poskim, if he is unable to secure a free loan, he may borrow money on terms which call for Ribbis DeRabbanan so that he would be able to perform the mitzvah. One should *not* rely on these poskim.[35]

22. For the lender's mitzvah: When offering a loan, a lender may not require the borrower to provide him with a sefer or other mitzvah-related object. This constitutes Ribbis Ketzutzah. However, in situations involving only Ribbis DeRabbanan, it is permitted for the lender to acquire a sefer or other mitzvah related object in exchange for the loan.[36]

Charity-Box Funds

23. Money which has been set aside for charity, but is still in the donor's possession, may be borrowed by the donor for personal use. It is not necessary to obtain the consent of the charity.[37]

24. There is a dispute regarding the status of moneys which were placed in a charity box (commonly called a *pushka*) which is in a person's home and has not yet been given to the charity.

Some view this as money which already belongs to charity. In their view, since the box belongs to the charity, anything placed in it becomes the property of the charity. According to this opinion, one may not

---

35. This dispute centers on a *Yerushalmi* quoted by *Magen Avraham* 242:2. Many interpret this to permit loans which are given to enable one to perform a mitzvah (*S.A. Harav* 242:9 and *kuntres achron* §5, *Pischei Teshuvah* Y.D. 160:2, *Chasam Sofer* Y.D. 135 s.v. *lehachlit*, *Teshuvah MeAhavah* 3:242). Others disagree with this interpretation and prohibit loans which involve *any* type of Ribbis (*Pri Megadim* and *Machtzis HaShekel* to *Magen Avraham* ibid.). *Mishnah Berurah* 242:4 follows this opinion, prohibiting Ribbis, unless a Heter Iska is used. [Cf. *Gra* 160:43.] See also *Tzitz Eliezer* 9:15 although his comparison to *Rema* 172:1 seems to be in error, since there Rema discusses a situation where the *lender* is able to perform a mitzvah because of the loan (see next paragraph).

36. *Rema* 172:1 in a case involving collateral which is used for a mitzvah. It would seem that this leniency applies as well to other forms of Ribbis DeRabbanan. [For example, in cases involving credit on purchases, where interest is only prohibited by Rabbinic law; or where the loan contains a penalty clause calling for the lender to receive a sefer if payment is not made by the due date.]

In situations where the lender is permitted to charge Ribbis, there is no prohibition on borrowing (*Shaar Deah* 160:22, based on *Taz* 159:2). This loan is therefore permitted.

In this case, since it is permissible for the lender to charge Ribbis, the borrower may take the loan. In the previous case, however, where the borrower is using the money for his mitzvah, the lender remains prohibited to charge Ribbis.

37. Y.D. 259:1. See also *Ahavas Chessed*, note to beginning of Chapter 18.

borrow money from a charity box without the consent of the charity to which it belongs.

Others disagree. They see this as private money which was set aside to be donated to charity. According to this view, these moneys have been pledged to charity, but do not yet belong to charity. They may therefore be borrowed by their owner for personal use.[38]

When someone relies on this lenient opinion and borrows money from a charity box, he may make an additional donation when repaying the loan. Since the money was always his, no loan has taken place, and there can be no Ribbis problem. Additionally, even if we were to consider this as charity money, since there was no prior commitment to make this donation, it is (at worst) only Rabbinically prohibited Ribbis, which charities may accept. Thus, even according to the opinion that these moneys belong to charity, this donation does not constitute Ribbis.[39]

25. When someone else (other than the donor) borrows money from a charity box,[40] it is preferable that he refrain from adding a donation at the time that he repays the loan.[41]

If the charity box was in the possession of the charity (for example, it was in a synagogue or school), and its money was borrowed, all would agree that an additional donation may be added when the loan is repaid.[42]

---

38. This is a dispute between *Mamar Mordechai* (Responsa 14) and *Avnei Nezer* (Y.D. 293). *Beis Yitzchok* O.C. 21 and *Maharsham* 4:107 and 147 also discuss this dispute. See *Tzedakah U'Mishpat* 8:n25 for a synopsis of their opinions.

As a matter of practical halachah, this issue can be avoided if the people who have charity boxes in their home make their donations with the explicit condition that the funds remain theirs, so that they could borrow these moneys. It would not be necessary to express (or even think of) this condition each time a donation is made. It is sufficient to state clearly that this is their regular practice and intent, so long as the person has not forgotten that he made this stipulation.

39. It should be noted that according to this opinion the moneys may only be borrowed with the express consent of the charity.

40. It goes without saying that one may not borrow these funds without permission from the owner of the *pushka*.

41. Because, according to the opinion that the moneys do not yet belong to charity, these are private funds, and the laws of Ribbis apply. [One might dispute this. Although the funds are still the property of the donor, they are designated for charity. The added moneys would therefore constitute a charitable donation which may be made, since Ribbis Ketzutzah is not involved. Still, since this is not clear, one should act stringently.]

42. In this case, all would agree that the funds belong to charity. Rabbinically prohibited Ribbis may therefore be accepted for the loan. Since this donation was not required as a condition of the loan, it is permitted.

C. Partnerships, Corporations and Banks

26. Partnerships which involve Jews and non-Jews: The halachic status of a company which has both Jewish and non-Jewish shareholders has been the subject of great dispute for over a century. Some view such companies as non-Jewish entities to which the Ribbis prohibition does not apply. Others disagree and maintain that a company which has any degree of Jewish ownership may not be party to transactions involving Ribbis.[43]

Where a majority of the stocks in a particular company are owned by Jews, one should follow the stringent opinion and consider this a Jewish entity. However, where most of the shareholders are non-Jews, one may follow the lenient opinion,[44] provided that the Jewish minority is not actually running the firm.[45]

---

43. This issue was first debated in the 19th century. At that time, R' Shlomo Ganzfried published his *Kitzur Shulchan Aruch*. In it (65:28 and in *Lechem HaPanim*, his notes to the *Kitzur*), he rules stringently, considering corporations with Jewish shareholders to be a Jewish entity. R' Yosef Shaul Nathanson disagreed and in a letter (subsequently published in his *Shoel U'Meishiv* 1:3:31) he asked R' Ganzfried to retract his opinion in subsequent editions of the *Kitzur*. R' Ganzfried did not do so. *Maharam Shick* (Y.D. 158) disagreed with R' Nathanson's reasoning but concurred with his ruling due to other considerations. *Maharshag* (Y.D. 3) and *Melamed Lehoil* (2:59), both disciples of *Maharam Shick*, discuss his ruling. Others who discuss this include *Maharsham* (1:20) and *Minchas Elazar* 2:22. For a synopsis of their views, see *Bris Yehudah* 30:n43.

It should be noted that this discussion applies to large companies which have Jewish and non-Jewish shareholders. The laws which apply to small businesses which are owned by Jewish and non-Jewish partners are discussed in Chapter 16.

44. *Shaarei Tzedek* (124), *Maharam Shick* (158) quoted by *Maharsham* (1:20; see also the index page, Note 31), Rabbi Yisroel Salanter, quoted in *Teshuvos Vehanhagos* 2:421. *Bris Yehudah* (ibid.) accepts this as the opinion of most poskim. Cf. *Minchas Yitzchak* 3:1 and 6:77. [Wherever possible, a Heter Iska should be used so as to satisfy all opinions.]

45. Although *Bris Yehudah* rules leniently even in this case, we have followed the opinion of R' Moshe Feinstein *zt"l*, quoted in *Mishnas Ribbis* 2:n7, who ruled that when a Jewish minority shareholder has a significant holding in the company, to the extent that his opinion carries weight in management decisions, the Ribbis prohibitions do apply. This is also the opinion of R' Yecheskeil Roth Shlita (also quoted in *Mishnas Ribbis*, ibid.). [See also R' Akiva Eiger to Y.D. 168:21, citing *Maharit* 1:116, who also connects the control of the business to its status in regard to the laws of Ribbis.]

[This does not apply to situations where Jewish employees who are at management level own some company shares. In this situation, these people make decisions as employees, not as owners; this does not affect the status of the company. Rather, the reference here is to situations where Jews make management decisions because of their extensive level of ownership.]

27. Today, all banks and most large companies are incorporated. This means that owners of these businesses have no personal liability to depositors, lenders or creditors. R' Moshe Feinstein *zt"l* ruled that these corporations may pay Ribbis for deposits, loans or credits which they receive, even if the corporation is totally owned by Jews. The reason for this is that a borrower is defined as someone who has personal responsibility to pay a loan. When a loan is guaranteed by a company's assets, but not by any individual, there is no Jewish borrower and Ribbis may be paid by the corporation.[46]

Others dispute this leniency and maintain that even corporations are prohibited from paying Ribbis.[47]

Although one may rely on the lenient ruling of R' Moshe Feinstein *zt"l*, it is preferable that a Heter Iska be used.[48]

---

46. *Igros Moshe* Y.D. 2:63 (see also *Tzafnas Paneach* in Responsa 184). This ruling appears to have an earlier source, in *Rivash* 305 and 308.

This was also the opinion of *Maharshag* (in a letter published in the Noam Journal 5719:2; see also his Responsa Y.D. 3). *Igros Moshe* permits corporations to pay Ribbis (for the reason explained above) but prohibits individuals from paying Ribbis to a Jewish corporation. (Since the borrower is an individual who does accept personal responsibility to pay the loan, the leniency outlined above does not apply.) See also R' Yosef Eliyahu Henkin in *Eidus LeYisrael* p. 129 and in his collected writings 2:50.

Lending money to the corporation, with the personal guarantee of the owners, is prohibited even according to *Igros Moshe*.

Non-recourse loans also involve no personal liability. Even if it is an individual taking a non-recourse loan, *Igros Moshe* would hold that the Ribbis prohibition does not apply.

Regarding incorporated charities, see Note 20.

47. *Har Tzvi* Y.D. 126, *Minchas Yitzchak* 1:3 and 4:16 and *Bris Yehudah* 7:n66 prohibit the taking of Ribbis even when no personal liability is involved. See also R' Shlomo Zalman Auerbach *zt"l* in *Minchas Shlomo* 28.

48. It should be pointed out that many of those who disagree with R' Feinstein *zt"l* nevertheless concede that Ribbis paid by a corporation does not constitute Ribbis Ketzutzah (*Minchas Yitzchok* 4:16 and 17, *Chelkas Yaakov* 3:190). Since this is an issue of Rabbinic law, one may certainly rely on the opinion of *Igros Moshe*.

Still, wherever possible, one should satisfy both opinions by using a Heter Iska. In fact, most banks which are owned by Jews do use a Heter Iska for all their transactions involving Jews. [These banks use a Heter Iska Klali; see Chapter 23 where this is explained.]

Free gifts to depositors: Even when a bank uses a Heter Iska, it is questionable if a Jewish bank is permitted to offer free gifts to depositors, if the gifts are delivered at the time the deposit is made. This is because a Heter Iska works only for payments which are made *after* the investment has had the opportunity to earn a profit (*Bris Yehudah* 38:n10, based on *Maharsham* 2: notes to index 216). [If the gift is chosen at the time of deposit, but it is not delivered until later, this would be permitted.]

28. Even those who permit a corporation to pay Ribbis for its loans would prohibit a corporation from collecting Ribbis from Jewish borrowers unless a Heter Iska is used.[49]

Partnerships Involving Jews

29. Borrowing for a Partnership: When two Jews take a joint loan from a bank, each actually borrows only half the money. However, because it is a joint loan, each is liable for the entire loan. Since each of them is also responsible for his friend's portion of the loan, each is serving as a guarantor for the other. We will see (in Chapter 15, Paragraph 16) that this arrangement is prohibited.

When a loan is issued to a business owned by two Jewish partners, some poskim hold that the same restriction applies. According to this opinion, each of the partners could not guarantee the entire loan. Others hold that where the loan will be repaid from business moneys, this is permitted.[50]

Partners in a business which is incorporated, where the individuals have no personal liability for the loan, may certainly rely on the lenient opinion.[51]

30. Bonds issued by companies with Jewish owners may not be purchased (except where the exceptions outlined in the previous paragraphs apply). The Israeli Government uses a Heter Iska Klali to permit purchase of its bonds.[52]

Israeli Government Loans: The Israeli government offers loans to new immigrants, at low-interest rates. One may not pay Ribbis to any

---

49. *Igros Moshe* Y.D. 2:63; see also Note 46.

50. See Chapter 16, Paragraphs 1 - 5, where this is discussed in greater detail. Where only one partner is actually involved in running the business, he would certainly be permitted to arrange this type of loan.

51. In this case, one may certainly rely on the lenient opinion of *Igros Moshe* quoted above.

52. According to the opinion of *Igros Moshe* (in Paragraph 27), this would be permitted even without use of a Heter Iska, since no individual accepts responsibility for these bonds (*Bris Yehudah* 7:n68). This is also the opinion of *Har Tzvi* Y.D. 126. Cf. *Bris Yehudah* (ibid.) who questions whether it is appropriate for a government to use a Heter Iska. A Heter Iska permits Ribbis because of the possibility that profits will be generated by the investment. Since the government is not involved in generating profits, a Heter Iska would seem to be inappropriate. He nevertheless concedes that one who wishes to rely on the lenient opinion mentioned above may do so.

Jewish institution, including the Israeli government. A Heter Iska should therefore be used.[53]

Brokerage Firms

31. Many prominent brokerage firms are owned by Jews. These firms may not invest their customer's money in a manner which would require a Jew to pay interest to the firms. For example, one may not purchase stocks on margin through these firms.[54]

32. Many brokerage firms pay interest on money which is held on account between transactions. Since these firms are incorporated, it would be permitted to collect this interest, based on the ruling of R' Moshe Feinstein zt"l (Paragraph 26, above).

D. Loans to Family Members and Minors

33. The prohibitions of Ribbis also apply to loans which are made to members of one's immediate family. This is prohibited even if the lender intends to return the Ribbis at a later time.[55]

34. Similarly, one may not pay Ribbis to family members or children (even small children)[56] even when the Ribbis is intended as a gift and is not truly being given for the loan.[57]

Minors

35. Financial deals involving a child are not valid unless the child is at least six years old and understands business affairs.[58] Any

---

53. *Vechai Achicha Imach* §101.

54. *Mishnas Ribbis* 2:10. This is prohibited even when the firm is a corporation. As noted above, *Igros Moshe* permits Ribbis to be paid *by* a corporation which borrows money, but prohibits Ribbis payments to be made *to* a corporation.

[In fact, many brokerages are owned by Jews and many of their customers are unaware of this prohibition.]

55. *Taz* 160:4. [Although *Taz* and *Nekudos HaKesef* question whether the *Shulchan Aruch* is referring to this case, they do not dispute the fact that this is prohibited.]

56. *Bris Yehudah* 2:n70.

57. Y.D. 160:8. Although this is not technically Ribbis, the Talmud (*Bava Metzia* 75a) prohibits this because this is an improper chinuch for children. They would see that collecting Ribbis is an easy way to make money, and might later look to collect Ribbis even for loans involving non-family members.

58. C.M. 235:1.

agreement involving a child younger than this is not binding. Therefore, if a child under this age lends money for Ribbis, the Ribbis which
he collects is not considered Ribbis Ketzutzah. He is therefore not
obligated to return this Ribbis.[59]

36. A child who is older than six years old and understands business
affairs may enter into a binding agreement. Ribbis which he
collects must be returned. However, if he has already spent the Ribbis
which he collected, he cannot be compelled to repay it even if he has
other funds.[60]

Later, when he grows up, some hold that he is obligated to return the
Ribbis (*latzeis yidei shamayim*), but all agree that he cannot be
compelled to do so.[61]

37. If the Ribbis which the minor received is still in his possession, it
should be taken from him and returned to the borrower.[62]

38. If a minor borrowed money and paid Ribbis, the lender (even if he
is an adult) cannot be compelled to return it.[63] However, he should
do so on his own (*latzeis yidei shamayim*).[64]

A Minor and a Heter Iska

39. Bris Yehudah rules that a minor may act as an investor in a Heter
Iska agreement, but questions whether a minor may accept funds
as the managing partner in an Iska partnership.[65]

---

59. *Mishneh LaMelech*, to *Hil. Milveh* 4:14, s.v. *v'nireh*. This is because Ribbis is Biblically prohibited only when it is part of an agreement which would otherwise be binding.
60. *Rashba*, quoted by *Mishneh LaMelech* (*Hil. Milveh* 4:14, s.v. *v'eicha*h), *Rivash*,
quoted by *Beis Yosef* 160 and *R' Akiva Eiger* 160:20.
61. *Bris Yehudah* 8:n61. The case discussed there involves an agent who was appointed
to manage the minor's affairs and collected Ribbis for him. This should also apply to a
situation where the minor collected Ribbis on his own. Cf. *Bris Yehudah* 3:11, who
presents a dispute regarding such a situation, including the opinion of some poskim who
consider this to be Ribbis Ketzutzah, which must be returned.
62. *Rashba*, quoted by *Mishneh LaMelech* (ibid.). This is the ruling of Y.D. 160:20, as
explained by R' Akiva Eiger; *Gra* 160:49 apparently understood the *Shulchan Aruch*
differently, but nevertheless quotes this opinion. R' Akiva Eiger also quotes a dissenting
opinion which holds that a minor can never be compelled to return Ribbis.
63. *Bris Yehudah* 3:12, because this is not considered Ribbis Ketzutzah. [This applies to
Ribbis paid by a child who is at least six years old and understands business affairs.
Payments made by a younger child are not legal transactions and must be returned.]
64. This is also true regarding Rabbinically prohibited Ribbis which was collected (see
Chapter 20, where the laws of returning Ribbis are outlined).
65. *Bris Yehudah* 35:20.
[This ruling is not clear. *Bris Yehudah* prohibits a minor from managing an Iska

E. Trustees

40. A trustee is someone who has control of another person's moneys under specific guidelines. Often, he is instructed to keep the money in specific accounts and he is not entitled to borrow the funds for personal use or investment.

If a trustee deviates from the agreement and borrows these funds to make an investment, he is liable for any lost money. If this investment earns a profit, he is not obligated to share the profits with the owner of the money.[66] Still, if he wishes, he is permitted to share the profits. This is not considered Ribbis since he was never authorized to borrow the money.[67]

41. A trustee is prohibited from lending a Jew's money to another Jew for Ribbis. This is also true when the trustee is non-Jewish and he is dealing with the funds of a Jew.[68]

---

partnership because the agreement into which a minor enters is not a binding one. Once the Iska agreement is not binding, the funds which the minor receives is considered a loan, and the 'profits' would actually be Ribbis. In fact, we have seen that a minor who is six years old and understands business affairs may enter into a binding agreement. We must therefore assume that *Bris Yehudah* is referring to the highly unlikely case of a minor who does not understand business affairs and is nevertheless receiving funds as the managing partner of an investment!]

66. Y.D. 177:19. If the trustee pledged to invest these moneys on the owner's behalf and failed to do so, he is also not obligated to reimburse the owner for lost income (*Shach* to C.M. 61:10 and 292:15, *Chasam Sofer* C.M. 48).

67. Y.D. 177:19 as explained by *Gra* 41 (that the trustee was not entitled to use the money; Cf. *Kehunas Olam* to 176, quoted in *Bris Yehudah* 2:n37, who disagrees). This is also the ruling of *Chasam Sofer* C.M. 48.

[This ruling appears to contradict *Beis Yosef* in Y.D. 176 (and *Shach* 176:1) who rules that someone who uses funds without authorization is prohibited from paying the owner of the money. This contradiction is noted by *Shaar Deah* 176:1. Various resolutions are offered; see *Mekor Mayim Chaim* 176:1, *Atzei Levonah* 176:1 and *Bris Yehudah* 29:n6.]

When the trustee is entitled to use the money interest free: See *Rema* (and *Darkei Moshe*) C.M. 292:7 and *Sma* 21, that when the trustee is entitled to borrow the money for his own investments he is also permitted to share his profits. *Bris Yehudah* 2:16 accepts this ruling, but cites *Nachal Yitzchak* 81:32:7 who disagrees with this interpretation of *Rema* and *Sema*.

68. *Bris Yehudah* 33:n10. The laws of Ribbis apply whenever a non-Jew manages the money of a Jew (Y.D. 168:21 and 24). This would not hold true if the non-Jew is liable for the money which was loaned (ibid.). However, when the courts appoint a trustee, neither the courts nor the trustee is liable if the borrower were to default on the loan. (By law, a trustee is liable only for "gross negligence or willful misconduct.") This is therefore considered the Jew's loan, and Ribbis may not be accepted.

If the non-Jewish trustee is not authorized to extend a loan, but he nevertheless lends the money in his care to a Jew, he is responsible for the money which he loaned out. In this case, the trustee is the lender, and Ribbis may be collected and passed on to the estate.[69]

42. A special dispensation for a trustee who manages the assets of a minor who has been orphaned has been discussed above; see Paragraphs 14-20.

If a trustee receives funds with the stipulation that they be used for investment, but he instead uses the funds for his own personal use, he is considered a thief. Here too, he is not obligated to reimburse the orphans for their lost income, but if he wishes to reimburse them, he is permitted to do so. However, this trustee should not be permitted to continue managing the orphans' funds, even if he intends to continue making these payments on a voluntary basis. This is because the orphans' income should not be subject to the voluntary donation of the trustee. Their funds should be invested in a manner which provides a regular income.[70]

---

69. *Rema* 168:21. Since he was not authorized to extend this loan, the non-Jewish trustee is responsible if the loan defaults. Whenever a non-Jew is responsible for the loan, he is considered the lender, and he may collect Ribbis and pass it on to the estate.

70. *Chasam Sofer* C.M. 48 advises that a Heter Iska be used to obligate the trustee to make these payments.

CHAPTER SIX

Buying on Credit

- ☐ Charging for credit (1)
- ☐ Late fees (2-3)
- ☐ Lease agreements (4)
- ☐ "Cash only" prices (5-10)
- ☐ Permissible forms of credit charges (11-14)
- ☐ Selling real estate (15-17)
- ☐ Service charges (18)
- ☐ Protecting against inflation (19)
- ☐ $2/10$ net 30 (20-22)
- ☐ Pressuring a customer to pay (23-24)
- ☐ Extending the due date (25)
- ☐ **Appendix I:**
  Heter Iska for credit purchases
- ☐ **Appendix II:**
  Heter Iska Klali for credit billing

Introduction

The prohibition of Ribbis is not limited to situations where cash changes hands. It also applies to purchases made on credit. In this case the customer has the status of a borrower and is prohibited from paying interest on the credit that he owes the seller.[1] He is also prohibited from giving gifts to or doing favors for the merchant during the entire period that the loan is outstanding.[2] In general, all of the laws which were outlined in the previous chapters apply here as well. In this chapter we will examine how these laws are applied to the contemporary marketplace.

The laws outlined in this chapter apply both when credit is extended to a customer on a retail level, and when it is extended to a business on a wholesale level.[3] These laws apply regardless of whether the seller is making a profit from the sale or not.

---

1. It should be noted that there is a major distinction between a loan (where cash is exchanged) and credit (where merchandise is taken on credit). The Biblical prohibition on Ribbis applies only to loans, where cash is passed from lender to borrower. Where debt is created by a purchase, the prohibitions apply, but only on the level of a Rabbinic prohibition (except as outlined below, Paragraph 11) (Rema 161:1).

There are numerous practical differences between Biblical Ribbis and Ribbis which is prohibited by Rabbinic law. Some of these differences are listed in Chapter 2, Note 1.

When credit for a purchase is due, and the creditor is paid to extend the credit for a longer period of time, this is considered Biblically prohibited Ribbis (Chavos Daas 166:4, S.A. Harav §4).

2. This is subject to the same rules which apply when cash is lent. If the merchant and customer are close friends, the customer may continue extending the same type of favors he had been extending before the loan was given (Y.D. 160:7). This leniency applies both to benefits which do not involve a financial expense (such as tutoring the lender) and to benefits which cause a loss (S.A. Harav §11).

This leniency may be practiced only under the following two conditions. First, the borrower may not give a gift or do a favor in a publicly noticeable manner (befarhesya). For example, the borrower may not allow the lender to live in his home. The borrower is also prohibited from purchasing an aliyah for the lender in the synagogue (Y.D. 160:7 and Shach 9). The second condition is that the lender may only use the borrower's utensils with his expressed permission (Y.D. 160:7). These halachos are discussed in greater detail in Chapter 1, Paragraphs 2-4.

3. The question of extending credit to a corporation is discussed in Chapter 5, Paragraph 27. (In situations where the creditor is a corporation, but the lender is an individual, the laws of Ribbis apply just as they do for two individuals.)

Where charities are involved, see Chapter 5, Paragraph 13.

Charging for Credit

1. A business may not charge its Jewish customers for credit extended to them. Therefore, if the customers do not pay on time, the business may not attach an additional charge for the additional time that the debt remains unpaid.

The business may pass on its billing costs to the customer. However, this fee may not exceed the actual cost to the business.[4]

Even if the customer's failure to pay on time causes the business to lose an opportunity to profit, the customer is prohibited from reimbursing the business for this loss.[5]

A Heter Iska may be used to permit the seller to be compensated for the time that his money is outstanding. This is especially appropriate when the customer is a business which uses the merchandise for profit. Appropriate Iska forms are found at the end of this chapter.[6]

Late Fees

2. A one-time late fee may be included in the credit agreement. This means that if payment is not made by a specific time, an additional penalty must be paid.

This is permitted only when merchandise was received as part of a business transaction and credit was extended.[7] In this case, a penalty

---

4. When expense payments are charged to the borrower, the bill should not combine the entire balance in a single total. Rather, the bill should contain a separate account of the debt and a separate account of expenses (*Bris Yehudah* 9:n13).

5. *Rashba* in Responsa 3:227, *Beis Yitzchok* 2:1, *Imrei Yosher* 1:149, *Bris Yehudah* 2:15. Cf. *Beis Hillel* Y.D. 170. See also *Har Tzvi* Y.D. 131.

When the failure to pay on time actually causes a financial loss (not just a failure to make a profit), this loss may be reimbursed by the debtor (*Bris Yehudah* 9:13, based on *Taz* 170:3).

6. Three Heter Iska forms appear at the end of this chapter. The first Iska form is suitable for a customer who uses the merchandise to make a profit. The second form is suitable for a customer who needs the merchandise for personal use. The third Iska form is for use by a business to permit it to profit from all outstanding credit. This is drawn to yield a 2% profit the first month and a 10% annual profit per year thereafter. The $^2/_{10}$ formula is used in this Iska because it is a common business formula. These figures may be changed to adapt to a specific agreement.

Before using any Heter Iska, it is important that both parties understand the concept of Heter Iska, as well as its limitations. This is explained at length in Chapter 22.

7. *Bris Yehudah* (4:n24, based on his comparison to the rules in Y.D. 163:3) extends this leniency to a case where merchandise is exchanged for a different type of merchandise.

clause may be added,[8] subject to the following conditions:

- ☐ The late fee must be a one-time payment. There may not be a requirement that the purchaser pay additional fees, based on the period of time that the debt is outstanding.[9]

- ☐ Payment of the penalty may not entitle the purchaser to any additional grace period for payment. The customer remains obligated to make payment immediately.[10]

The agreement may call for payment in the form of cash (or a different type of merchandise). If a late fee is charged, the penalty clause may not require the purchaser to return the same type of merchandise he purchased.[11]

3. When the purchase agreement calls for payments to be made in installments, a separate late fee may be charged for each installment.[12]

4. Lease agreements: This rule is not limited to credit which involves a sale. It also applies to business transactions such as lease or rental agreements. A lease may call for a penalty if rental payments are not made on time. The conditions that apply to credit for purchases apply here as well.[13] A lease agreement may therefore call for an additional late fee for each month's rent.

'Cash Only' Prices

5. A business may not set two prices for the same item, where one price is charged for cash payments and a higher price is charged when the

---

8. Y.D. 177:18 and *Shach* 38.

9. In a case involving a cash loan, a one-time late penalty is prohibited as *Haaramas Ribbis*, while a penalty which is structured to increase with time is a form of true Ribbis.

In our case, debt was created by a purchase. Because this does not involve a loan, we are more lenient (see Note 1) and allow the more lenient form of late penalty, involving a one-time payment. Penalties which are structured to increase with time remain prohibited.

10. *Chochmas Adam* 132:13. (See Chapter 9, Paragraph 5, and Note 10.)

11. When the purchaser is required to return the same type of merchandise, the transaction takes on the form of a loan rather than a sale. The entire basis of this leniency then falls away. (See *Chavos Daas* 167:1, that the penalty clause may not require that where payment is not made on time, a penalty is charged *and* the sale is dissolved.)

12. *Mishnas Ribbis* 11:n11 and 20:5. This is not considered a penalty which increases with time (which would be prohibited — see previous paragraph); rather, each is a separate one-time penalty for a separate payment.

13. *Mishnas Ribbis* 11:8.

item is purchased on credit. This is because someone who pays the higher price is actually paying an additional fee for credit. This is Ribbis.

A customer who is faced with this situation is permitted to make a cash purchase (at the lower price) but may not purchase on credit.[14]

Today, it is a common practice for gas stations in the United States to charge a higher price when payment is made by credit card. It is prohibited to buy gas on credit at the higher price from a station which is owned by a Jew.[15]

6. When the item which is being sold has a clear market value, some poskim hold that a two-tier price system is permitted, as long as the credit price is set at the fair market value. In this case, a lower sale price may be set for cash customers. The reason for this leniency is that the credit customer is not being charged for credit; it is the cash customer who is being rewarded for paying cash. According to some poskim, this is permitted.[16]

---

14. Y.D. 173:1, *Rema* 173:3.

15. *Bris Yehudah* 22:n18 regarding Israeli businesses which have similar arrangements. The gas-station owner does not receive payment from the card company until later. In the interim, he is actually the one who is extending credit to the customer.

Where the gas stations charge more for credit card purchases to offset the costs which they incur in connection with the processing of credit card slips, this is permitted. Unfortunately, the markup for credit purchases often exceeds the added cost to the company. This is prohibited.

[If a company pays a flat monthly fee for processing its credit card vouchers, it is not clear how to pass this fee on to its customers. In this case, the additional voucher which is generated by any one purchase does not add to the company's cost. One could therefore argue that there is no cost which may be passed on to any individual customer. However, where the fee for processing credit vouchers is based on the number of vouchers processed, the cost may certainly be passed on to the customer.]

16. *Chochmas Adam* 139:5, *Machneh Ephraim* §31. Where it is not absolutely clear that the higher price (charged for credit purposes) is the market price, all agree that the two-tier price system is prohibited.

Divrei Sofrim (173:*Emek Davar* 68), citing the comments of *Chochmas Adam* elsewhere (132:10), limits this leniency. He contends that *Chochmas Adam* permits a two-tier system, only when the seller stipulates that his credit price is set "at the fair market value." If a figure is posted, without explicitly stating that it represents the market value, *Chochmas Adam* would concede that it is prohibited.

[The price of most items tends to fluctuate greatly from merchant to merchant and from day to day. For example, the price of gasoline tends to fluctuate and it is usually impossible to know if the fair market price is the cash price or the credit price. It therefore remains prohibited to purchase on credit, at the higher price. (The fact that gas stations label the credit price as the regular price and the cash price as a discount may not truthfully represent the reality of the situation.)]

Other poskim disagree. According to this opinion, any time an item is available at a lower price for a cash payment, it is prohibited to pay a higher price for credit.

One should conduct himself according to the second opinion.[17]

7. Sale prices: Many businesses limit their sale prices to cash purchases.

As we have seen, this is prohibited because the credit customer is actually paying an additional fee for credit.[18] An acceptable method of running 'cash only' sales is to make the item unavailable on credit, at any price.[19]

8. A business may not offer discounts for cash purchases even when a discount is deducted from the final bill, and not on an item by item basis. For example, a business may not offer a 10% discount on all cash purchases. If this is offered, customers may accept a discount for cash purchases, but are prohibited from making a credit purchase at the regular price.[20]

9. Businesses may not add a surcharge for payments made by check, because these are also considered credit purchases. This arrangement is prohibited even when the check can be cashed immediately.[21]

10. These prohibitions are not limited to a store or business. Where an individual sells an item (for example, when selling a used car), it is also prohibited to quote different prices for cash and credit purchases.[22]

---

17. *Pischei Teshuvah* 173:5 quoting *Tiferes LeMoshe*, *Yad Avraham* to 173:1, *S.A. Harav* §18, *Mishneh LaMelech* to *Hil. Malveh* 8:1, *Maharam Shick* Y.D. 163, *Imrei Binah* in Responsa 2, *Imrei Yosher* 1:149, *Bris Yehudah* 22:7. This is the opinion of the majority of poskim. *Maharam Shick* also quotes *Ramban* as having ruled stringently in this situation.

18. *Mishnas Ribbis* 7:3, based on the halachah which was outlined in the previous paragraph.

19. When this is done, no credit is extended for purchases involving the sale item. When no credit is extended, there is no possibility of a Ribbis violation.

20. *Mishnas Ribbis* 7:3. [Unfortunately, this is not a well-known halachah. Even in Orthodox Jewish neighborhoods, many merchants offer discounts for purchases which are made on certain days, but limit the discount to cash purchases. One could argue that they are relying on the lenient ruling of *Chochmas Adam* (in Note 16, above). In truth, however, they are simply unaware that most poskim prohibit this arrangement under all circumstances.]

21. When a check is postdated, the customer is actually buying on credit. Even when a check is not postdated, a loan is being extended, since payment is not received until the check is cashed. Since there is no minimum time period which is used to define a loan, even this short period is enough for the rules of Ribbis to apply (*Bris Yehudah* 2:3).

22. This also applies to the sale of real estate; see Chapter 13, Paragraphs 1-4.

Permissible Forms of Credit Charges

11. The prohibition on raising prices for credit purchases is Rabbinic in nature,[23] and was prohibited because of its similarity to Ribbis Ketzutzah. The prohibition therefore applies only to situations where it is obvious that a charge is being added for credit. Where an item has no set market value,[24] a seller who knows that the purchase will be made on credit may quote a higher price to a customer.

This leniency has two conditions: 1) The seller may not say that the price is based on the fact that the purchase is being made on credit; and 2) a lower price may not be offered for a cash sale. This would make it obvious that the higher price includes a charge for credit.[25]

12. In this case, a higher price for credit is permitted only when the increase is nominal. When a very high price is requested for a credit purchase, it becomes obvious that the customer is overpaying because of his need for credit. For this reason, only an increase of up to 20% of the purchase price is permitted.[26]

13. When negotiating a price, the seller might assume that the sale will be made for cash, and quote a cash price. If, after the two sides have agreed on a purchase price, the buyer asks that the seller finance the sale

---

23. See Note 1.

24. An item has no set market value in any of the following situations:

   a) When the price of an item varies from store to store (*Bris Yehudah* 22:n4). Sale prices are not included in this determination. The price which is charged for a credit purchase may not go above the highest price in this range (*Mishnas Ribbis* 7:n11).

   b) Items which are appraised individually, such as precious stones, used cars, used machines and custom furniture (*Darkei Teshuvah* 173:5).

   c) When prices for a particular item fluctuate over a short period of time (*Chavos Daas* 173:3 in explanation of *Rema* 173:1).

   Today, most items fall within one of the categories outlined here.

25. Y.D. 173:1.

26. *Shach* 173:5, R' Akiva Eiger to *Shach*, *Pischei Teshuvah* 173:4, [This *Pischei Teshuvah* contains a printing error; it should read עוד שוה ה' בו'], *Shaar Deah* 173:2, *Chavos Daas* 173:3.

[The 20% figure is meant as a general rule. In fact, this would vary, depending on market conditions for each item (*Beis Yosef* 173, *Chavos Daas* 173:3). The primary consideration is that it not be obvious that a higher price is being charged because credit is being extended. Therefore, when the market value of an item varies within a limited range, the selling price must stay close to the top of this range (*Mishnas Ribbis* 7:n11).]

(or a portion of the sale), the seller may not ask for a higher price in exchange for the credit.

However, the seller may declare that he is withdrawing his previous offer.[27] He may then offer the item at a higher price, for either cash or credit. If the buyer agrees to this price, the sale would then be completed as a credit sale, at the higher price.[28]

14. A two-tier price agreement may be created in the following manner. First, a deal is concluded, setting a price for a purchase which will be made on credit. Then, a legal *kinyan* is made, to render the agreement binding.[29] The seller then offers a discount if payment is made immediately.[30] The buyer would then have the option to choose between the two prices, depending on his needs.[31]

If the original bill listed only one price, but the bill contains a provision which calls for a discount for prepayment, this is prohibited because it is considered that the original agreement is for a two-tier price arrangement.[32]

---

27. This is possible only when the agreement between the two sides (at the original price) is not legally binding. If a binding agreement was signed, it cannot be dissolved unilaterally. The initial offer can be withdrawn only if the original agreement is dissolved by mutual agreement (*Bris Yehudah* 22:n21).

[Even if the original agreement was not dissolved by both parties, the seller is not obligated to offer credit for the sale. If the buyer is unable to make the payments called for by the agreement, the sale would be dissolved by default.]

28. *Chavos Daas* 173:2, *Imrei Yosher* 2:192, *Bris Yehudah* 22:9. [This situation is most common in deals involving real estate, but the halachah is the same for any type of sale.]

29. *Rema* 173:3. A *kinyan* can be made in either of the following ways: 1) The buyer takes physical possession of the item being purchased by lifting it (or dragging it, if this is the normal way to transport the particular item). 2) The buyer gives his handkerchief (or another utensil or item of clothing) to the seller and stipulates that in exchange, he is receiving legal title to the item. The seller lifts the handkerchief to acquire it, thereby effecting the *kinyan*. The handkerchief is then returned to the buyer.

There is disagreement among contemporary poskim if the payment itself constitutes legal *kinyan* in this case (*Mishnas Ribbis* 7:n25).

30. Y.D. 173:3. The prohibition of offering two prices for an item has been explained in Paragraph 5. The prohibition is based on the assumption that the higher price, which must be paid for credit to be extended, actually includes a fee for credit.

When only one price is mentioned, this is the purchase price. After the agreement is concluded, a discount may be offered for prepayment. (This is even permitted in situations involving cash loans.) In this case, the higher price (which applies when the credit is used) is considered the true price, and does not include an added credit charge.

31. *Bris Yehudah* 22:10.

32. *Har Tzvi* Y.D. 131. It is common for the fine print on a bill to contain a provision allowing for a 2% discount for prepayment.

Selling Real Estate

15. These laws also apply to the sale of real estate. One may not offer two prices for a property, a lower one for a cash purchase and a higher one if the seller provides financing for the purchase.[33]

16. Real estate has no set market value. One may therefore charge a higher price when financing is included in the sale.[34] This is permitted even when the buyer realizes that the price has been raised because it includes financing.[35]

17. If a property was sold at a higher price because the deal included financing and the buyer later decided to prepay the debt, the seller is permitted to offer a discount in return for the prepayment. For example, a home was sold for $200,000, with the mortgage provided by the seller. The seller may later allow the buyer to satisfy the debt for $180,000.[36]

Service Charges

18. When an agreement calls for payment to be made in installments, a service charge may be added for each payment. However, this charge must be within the customary range of such charges.[37] This charge must be the same for each payment, regardless of the amount being paid. It also may not fluctuate based on the length of time that credit is being extended.[38]

---

33. *Shach* 173:2.

34. This is permitted, provided that a lower price (which does not include financing) is not mentioned. The restrictions here are identical to those for all sales (in Paragraph 11). However, the 20% limit mentioned earlier does not apply to real estate, since its price fluctuates in a much wider range. Still, if the price were obviously excessive, this would be prohibited (see *Shach* 173:2 and *Shaar Deah* 173:2).

Additional halachos which pertain to real estate sales and mortgages appear in Chapter 13, which deals exclusively with real estate issues.

35. *Magid Mishnah* to *Hil. Malveh* 8:1, *Shach* 173:2.

36. This is because a lender may offer to forgive part of a debt, on the condition that the borrower prepays the remainder (Y.D. 173:3, in a case involving merchandise which was sold on credit).

37. Insurance companies add a service charge when payment is made in installments. This is permitted as long as it is called a service charge and not a credit fee or interest (*Bris Yehudah* 22:n18; this refers to Jewish insurers).

[A seller may add a service charge even when his intent is to profit from his loan, as long as it is called a service charge and not a credit fee or interest. See *Imrei Yosher* 2:192, quoted in *Bris Yehudah* 22:n6 and n18.]

38. *Bris Yehudah* 22:n18, *Toras Ribbis* 8:n22, *Mishnas Ribbis* 7:15. A service charge is paid for service which is received. This is the same for any payment, regardless of its

Protection Against Inflation

19. During periods of inflation, a businessman who offers credit loses the real value of his money. For example, if he were to receive a $100 payment at the time of sale, he could use this money to buy a certain amount of merchandise. If he waits six months to receive payment, the $100 could no longer buy the same amount of merchandise. Even in this case, the buyer may not pay more than $100, since this constitutes Ribbis. Still, the businessman can protect himself against inflation in one of the following ways:

When the purchaser does not actually take possession of his purchase until a later date, the seller may stipulate that the price be based on the item's value at the time it is acquired by the buyer. If inflation drives up the cost of the item, the seller would receive a higher price.[39]

When the purchaser is taking immediate possession, the agreement may stipulate that the purchase price will be based on the value of the item at the time of payment. However, this may be done only if there is no explicit offer of a lower price for immediate payment.[40]

$^2/_{10}$ Net 30

20. In the United States, it is a common business practice to bill customers under terms known as $^2/_{10}$ net 30. This stipulation allows customers the option of deducting 2% from their bill if they pay within ten days. Otherwise, full payment is required at the end of thirty days.

---

terms. When a fee is based on the amount of money owed or to the period of time that it is outstanding, this is obviously a credit charge.

39. *Rema* 173:14. This applies whenever the item being sold is in the possession of the seller.

If the item is in the seller's possession, but the buyer has acquired legal title to it (via a proper *kinyan*), the same rule applies. In this case, the seller is not liable if the item becomes ruined while in his possession. Nevertheless, the price may be pegged to the item's value at the time it is delivered (*S.A. Harav* §22, *Avnei Nezer* 207:4).

[If the item's value were to drop during this interval, the seller would have to accept a lower price.]

40. *Shach* 173:3 permits this for all items; R' Akiva Eiger and *Chavos Daas* 173:1 limit this leniency to items which have no set market price.

One may rely on *Shach's* lenient ruling whenever the price is determined by a designated payment date. If the purchaser has an open-ended period of credit, with no designated date for payment, this is prohibited (*Avnei Nezer* 207:4, *Minchas Yitzchak* 7:65).

If an item has no set market value, this would be permitted even if the agreement allows for an open-ended period of credit, with no designated day of payment (ibid.).

This is actually a two-tier pricing system, which calls for a higher payment when credit is extended beyond ten days. This is similar to the agreement described in Paragraph 5, and is prohibited. A businessman may not use these terms when selling to other Jews, unless he uses a Heter Iska.[41]

---

41. *Har Tzvi* Y.D. 131, *Minchas Yitzchak* 1:20 and 21, *Bris Yehudah* 22:8 and *Mishnas Ribbis* 7:10 and 18. *Maharam Shick* Y.D. 164 and *Imrei Yosher* 1:149 discuss a similar method of billing (which was popular in their communities) and prohibit this.

Numerous arguments have been advanced to defend the widespread use of ²⁄₁₀ net 30. These include the following arguments and rebuttals:

- *Chochmas Adam* and *Machneh Ephraim* (quoted above, Note 16) hold that a two-tier price system is permitted when the higher price (which is charged when credit is extended) is the fair market price. According to this opinion, it stands to reason that when the thirty-day price is the fair market price, a 2% discount may be offered for prepayment.

    The difficulty with this argument is that most poskim do not accept the ruling of *Chochmas Adam* and *Machneh Ephraim* (see Note 16). Additionally, *Bris Yehudah* (22:n18) points out that in businesses where all billing is done based on ²⁄₁₀ net 30, the thirty-day price already includes a thirty-day credit arrangement. Thus, the price for the item itself is the ten-day price. Since, the thirty-day price includes a 2% credit fee it is prohibited.

- *Tzur Yaakov* (Responsa 124 and quoted by *Bris Yehudah* 22:n18) argues that ²⁄₁₀ net 30 should be permitted for the following reason. We have seen (in Paragraph 2) that a one-time late fee is permitted in business transactions. *Tzur Yaakov* argues that ²⁄₁₀ net 30 can be interpreted as a one-time 2% fee for payments which are made after the ten-day due date. According to this interpretation, this billing procedure is permitted.

    The problem with this argument is that this interpretation of ²⁄₁₀ net 30 is factually incorrect (in most cases). Most people understand the higher price to be the cost of the item and not the cost plus a late fee. This is indicated by the fact that when the business is asked to quote a price, the business quotes this price. It is difficult to argue that the price quoted is actually a lower price with a 2% fine attached.

    Additionally, *Mishnas Ribbis* 7:18 points out that payment of a one-time fine is permitted only when this payment does not entitle the buyer to an additional grace period, and payment remains due immediately (*Chochmas Adam* 132:13). Under ²⁄₁₀ net 30, the buyer has another twenty days to make payment, after the 2% fine is added. (*Tzur Yaakov* concedes that *Chochmas Adam* would prohibit this, but relies on other poskim who disagree with *Chochmas Adam*.)

- R' Samuel Zanvil HaCohen, Dayan of prewar Munkatch, Hungary, (quoted in *Imrei Yosher* 150) discusses a situation similar to ²⁄₁₀ net 30. He argues that this prohibition does not apply in all cases. In certain types of business it is the accepted practice to pay for merchandise thirty days after delivery. In this case, there is no obligation to pay within thirty days. This is analogous to a rental agreement in situations where it is customary to pay rent at the end of the rental period. *Shulchan Aruch* (Y.D. 176:6), in discussing such rental agreements, rules that a discount may

According to some poskim, it is permitted to bill a customer under $^2/_{10}$ net 30 if the customer is a corporation, even if it is owned by Jews.[42]

21. A customer who receives a bill containing these terms should be careful to pay within ten days. In this way he avoids paying the 2%

---

be offered for prepayment. This would apply here as well. *Mishnas Ribbis* 7:n28 applies this ruling to billing under the terms of $^2/_{10}$ net 30.

The difficulty with this argument is that it applies in very limited circumstances. Where merchandise is sold on a retail level, it is customary for the seller to require immediate payment. In this case, $^2/_{10}$ net 30 would still be prohibited.

When merchandise is sold on a wholesale level, businesses are customarily allowed thirty days to make payment. However, these sales are usually based on terms of $^2/_{10}$ net 30. While one could interpret this to mean that it is customary to allow thirty days for payment, this is not necessarily so. One could argue that payment is actually due within ten days. The customary business practice is to allow an additional twenty days, in exchange for a 2% fee. In fact, we have already seen that *Bris Yehudah* (quoted earlier in this note) defines the thirty-day price as the market price plus a credit charge.

It would therefore appear that $^2/_{10}$ net 30 would be permitted only in situations where it is customary to bill a flat price (without $^2/_{10}$ net 30) and allow thirty days for payment. Only in this case could an individual seller choose to use these billing terms.

An option: *Maharam Shick* Y.D. 164 allows use of an oral Heter Iska (when it is accepted in the presence of two qualified witnesses) under these circumstances, even if it is applied unilaterally. This ruling is the subject of controversy; see, for example, the comments of *Maharam Shick's* disciple in *Maharshag* Y.D. 5. Still, *Minchas Yitzchak* (1:21) rules that in case of necessity one may rely on the ruling of *Maharam Shick*, particularly in situations where the argument of R' Samuel Zanvil HaCohen would apply.

Another option would be to use the method outlined in Paragraph 14. This would require that bills be written for the regular thirty-day price (the fine print would not contain terms of $^2/_{10}$ net 30). Later, if a particular customer were to request a 2% discount for prepayment, this would be permitted. The drawback in using this method is that businesses prefer to encourage prepayment by notifying their customers of this option. There is also a potential halachic problem. If a particular customer were to pay the discounted price on a regular basis, this would become the understood agreement between him and the seller for any future sales. Thus, any new agreement would automatically contain the two-tiered price agreement, which is prohibited.

To sum up: The prevalent use of these billing terms is highly questionable. Since this problem could easily be resolved by use of a Heter Iska, businesses should be encouraged to do so.

42. *Igros Moshe* Y.D. 2:63 permits corporations to pay interest. According to this opinion, the prohibition on Ribbis is limited to situations where the borrower has personal liability for the debt. Other poskim dispute this leniency (see *Minchas Yitzchak* 1:3 and 4:16 and *Bris Yehudah* 7:n66). One may rely on this opinion here, since this is an issue of Rabbinically prohibited Ribbis. Still, wherever possible, a person should satisfy both opinions by using a Heter Iska. (See Chapter 5, Paragraphs 27-28.)

fee. Nevertheless, a person should refrain from agreeing to terms of $^2\!/_{10}$ net 30, even if he plans to pay within ten days.[43]

22. A Heter Iska may be used to allow a company to charge under these terms. An appropriate Heter Iska appears at the end of this chapter.[44]

Pressuring a Customer to Pay

23. A merchant who sells on credit may refuse to extend further credit to a customer whose account is overdue. Although he is actually demanding payment in exchange for credit, this is permitted because he is entitled to this payment.[45]

24. There is a dispute among the poskim if this applies when the customer has an outstanding balance which has not yet come due. In this case, some poskim prohibit the merchant from demanding payment in exchange for further credit; others permit this.[46]

Extending the Due Date

25. A customer whose debt has come due may not offer additional payments (or a gift) in exchange for an extension of the due date. This is a form of Ribbis Ketzutzah.[47]

---

43. *Mishnas Ribbis* 7:n28. See Chapter 2, Note 17, that many poskim rule that one may not agree to terms which call for Ribbis, even if the Ribbis will never be paid. (This is based on the Biblical verse *lo seseemoon alav neshech*, do not place a Ribbis obligation on him.) It is sometimes difficult to avoid these terms in business dealings. Since this prohibition is an issue of dispute, one who is billed under $^2\!/_{10}$ net 30 should write ד"ע 'היתר עוסקא on the bill, and be sure to pay within ten days (*Mishnas Ribbis* 7:n28, quoting the author of *Bris Yehudah*). [Writing this on the bill does not actually effect a Heter Iska, since a Heter Iska requires the agreement of both parties. Still, because it is not clear that the Ribbis prohibition applies in this situation, *Bris Yehudah* relies on the poskim who allow a Heter Iska clause to be incorporated unilaterally.]

44. Before using any Heter Iska, it is important that both parties understand the concept of Heter Iska, as well as its limitations. These are explained at length in Chapter 22.

45. *Mishnas Ribbis* 4:n18.

46. *Shaar Deah* 173:5 rules that one may make a loan conditional on the prepayment of prior loans. *Sheiris Chaim* (quoted in *Bris Yehudah* 11:n15) disagrees because the lender is demanding money to which he is not yet entitled. See *Bris Yehudah* (ibid.) who discusses this at length.

47. Ribbis which is paid for credit on a purchase is prohibited by Rabbinic law (see Note 1). But an extension on an existing loan is similar to a new loan, and payment is prohibited by Biblical law (*Chavos Daas* 166:4, *S.A. Harav* §4).

Other actions which formally change a purchase debt to a loan include the writing of a promissory note (*Rashi B.M.* 72a, *Teshuvos HaRashba* 1:1189), or the storekeeper's

Appendix I To Chapter Six:
Heter Iska for Credit Purchases
(see Paragraph 1)

Iska A: When Merchandise Is for Business Use

The following Heter Iska is suitable for use when a customer buys merchandise on credit and the seller charges him for the credit. Without a Heter Iska, this is prohibited.

When the customer uses the merchandise to make a profit, he may allow the seller to share in those profits by making him an investing partner in his business. The following Heter Iska does this, but uses the regular Heter Iska concept to establish the seller's share of the profit at a specific sum of money. The seller may set this at the amount he would have charged for credit if this were permitted.

Iska Contract[1]

I, the undersigned, hereby acknowledge receipt of merchandise valued at $_____ from _____ (hereafter referred to as the "Investor"), to be used for business purposes. I obligate myself to utilize this merchandise in a manner which I believe will generate profits. Any profits realized or losses sustained shall be shared equally between the investor and myself.

Any claim of loss must be verified through the testimony of two qualified witnesses in, and under conditions acceptable to, an Orthodox Jewish court of law. Any claim regarding the amount of profit generated by this merchandise shall be verified under solemn oath, before and under conditions acceptable to, an Orthodox Jewish court of law.

It is agreed that if I pay the investor the sum of $_____ (enter amount that is due) on or before _____ (enter date that payment is due) as payment of both the investment and his share of the profits which are generated, then I will not be required to make any further payment nor will I be required to make an oath.

Continued on next page

---

totaling of various purchases into a single bill (*Chavos Daas* 175:2; *Taz* 163:5 mentions that this is also true if the debtor totals the debt which he owes to the particular merchant).

1. Hebrew versions of a Heter Iska suitable for use in this situation appear in *Tam Ribbis* p. 307 and *Mishnas Ribbis* p. 256.

I have received one dollar from the investor as payment for my services during the term of our partnership.[2]

It is agreed that any dispute which may arise in connection with this agreement shall be submitted before _____.[3] Judgment rendered by the aforesaid authority may be entered in any court having jurisdiction thereof. This agreement shall follow the guidelines of Heter Iska as explained in *Sefer Bris Yehudah* and has been executed in a manner which effects a legal transfer and obligation, known as *kinyan sudar*.[4]

Signature of the Recipient _____

Dated _____

Signature of the Investor[5] _____

Dated _____

Witnesses[6]

In witness whereof the above-mentioned parties have entered into this Heter Iska agreement on this _____ day of _____.

Signature of Witness _____

Signature of Witness _____

Iska B: When Merchandise Is for Personal Use

When a customer buys merchandise for personal use, and not to generate a profit, the previous Heter Iska should not be used. This is because the merchandise does not generate profit in a direct way.

---

2. The purchaser should pay one dollar to the trader. The reason that this payment is necessary is explained in Chapter 22, Paragraph 29.

3. This part of the contract is optional.

4. The supplier gives a handkerchief (or another utensil or item of clothing) to the customer. In exchange, the customer obligates himself to the terms of the Heter Iska. This is *not* required when the Heter Iska is signed before the delivery of the merchandise. This is explained in Chapter 22, Note 67.

5. This is required only if there are legal documents which refer to this as a debt (see Chapter 22, Paragraph 43).

6. This part of the contract is optional, depending on whether the parties prefer to have witnesses attest to their agreement.

Still, since the customer does not immediately have to pay for the merchandise, he has more money available for other investments. In exchange for the merchandise, he may accept the seller as a partner in these investments and share their profits with him. The following Heter Iska accomplishes this.

Iska Contract[1]

I, the undersigned, hereby acknowledge receipt of merchandise valued at $ _____ from _____ (hereafter referred to as the "Investor"), subject to the following terms:

In exchange for the aforementioned merchandise, the investor shall acquire a share (in the value of the merchandise received) in any investment, real estate or business which I own.[2] This investment shall be owned jointly by the investor and myself. Any profits realized or losses sustained shall be shared equally between the investor and myself.

Any claim of loss must be verified through the testimony of two qualified witnesses in, and under conditions acceptable to, an Orthodox Jewish court of law. Any claim regarding the amount of profit generated by this investment shall be verified under solemn oath, before and under conditions acceptable to, an Orthodox Jewish court of law.

It is agreed that if I pay the investor the sum of $_____ (enter amount that is due) on or before _____ (enter date that payment is due) as payment of both the investment and the profits which are generated, then I will not be required to make any further payment nor will I be required to make an oath.

I have received one dollar from the investor as payment for my services during the term of our partnership.[3]

It is agreed that any dispute which may arise in connection with this agreement shall be submitted before _____.[4] Judgment

Continued on next page

---

1. Hebrew versions of a Heter Iska suitable for use in this situation appear in *Tam Ribbis* p. 307 and *Mishnas Ribbis* p. 257.

2. If the customer does not own any type of investment, this previous sentence should be replaced with the following: "In exchange for the aforementioned merchandise, the investor will acquire partnership in any future investment which I shall make. The investor appoints me as an agent to execute this investment (or investments), as I deem appropriate, on his behalf." [The investor should add his signature to the bottom of this document.]

3. The purchaser should pay one dollar to the trader. The reason that this payment is necessary is explained in Chapter 22, Paragraph 29.

4. This part of the contract is optional.

rendered by the aforesaid authority may be entered in any court having jurisdiction thereof. This agreement shall follow the guidelines of Heter Iska as explained in *Sefer Bris Yehudah* and has been executed in a manner which effects a legal transfer and obligation, known as *kinyan sudar*.[5]

Signature of the Recipient _____

Dated_____

Witnesses[6]

In witness whereof the above-mentioned parties have entered into this Heter Iska agreement on this _____ day of _____.

Signature of Witness _____

Signature of Witness _____

Appendix II To Chapter Six: Heter Iska Klali for Credit Billing
(see Paragraph 22)

The previous versions of Heter Iska are drawn for use by a person on an individual basis. The following Heter Iska is suitable for use by businesses which sell on credit. This would be used by a business to cover all its credit arrangements with Jews.

This would be used by a businessman who wishes to bill under the terms of ²/₁₀ net 30 but is prohibited from doing so by halachah. This agreement accomplishes the result of ²/₁₀ net 30, by arranging for the payment to be used as an investment.[1] Where this Heter Iska is used, this would be permitted.[2]

---

5. The supplier gives a handkerchief (or other object of value) to the customer. In exchange, the customer obligates himself to the terms of the Heter Iska. This is *not* required when the Heter Iska is signed before the delivery of the merchandise. This is explained in Chapter 22, Note 67.

6. This part of the contract is optional, depending on whether the parties prefer to have witnesses attest to their agreement.

1. When payment is not received by thirty days, this contract calls for a 10% per annum charge.

2. It should be noted that the appropriate manner of using this type of Heter Iska Klali is a subject of discussion among the poskim. It is always preferable to avoid charging for

Iska Contract[3]

I. Whereas ABC Inc. desires that all its transactions be in accordance with Orthodox Jewish Law, which prohibits the payment and acceptance of Ribbis on loans between Jews.

II. We hereby declare that all transactions involving Jewish customers will be made in accordance with the terms of Heter Iska, stating that:

III. In exchange for any goods or services received by the customer, ABC Inc. shall acquire financial partnership (in the value of goods or services received) in any present investment, real estate or business that the customer may presently have. If the customer has no present investment, real estate or business, ABC Inc. will assume partnership in any future investment that the customer will make. ABC Inc. hereby appoints the customer as its agent to enter into any such agreement which he feels will be worthwhile.

IV. Any profits realized or losses suffered as a result of the afore-mentioned investment(s), in the value of goods or services received, shall be allocated to ABC Inc., except that the customer shall retain 5% of profits for his efforts as manager of the investment(s). ABC Inc. accepts no liability in excess of the value of the funds invested on its behalf.

V. Any claim of loss by the customer must be verified through the testimony of two qualified witnesses in, and under conditions acceptable to, an Orthodox Jewish court of law. Any claim regarding the amount of profit generated by these investment(s) shall be verified by the customer, under solemn oath, before and under conditions acceptable to, an Orthodox Jewish court of law.

VI. However, in the event that the customer returns the invested funds within 10 days of time of delivery of goods or services, ABC Inc. shall waive receipt of profits to which it would otherwise be entitled.

Continued on next page

---

credit, even through use of a Heter Iska. This is discussed below in Chapter 23. [Where the customers are businesses which are incorporated, one may certainly rely on use of this Heter Iska.]

3. This is a Heter Iska Klali contract, which is held by the company and is not actually signed every time a sale is made. Bills which are sent to Jewish customers should contain the words 'subject to the terms of Heter Iska.' The concept of a Heter Iska Klali is explained in Chapter 23.

VII. Furthermore, if payment of said funds, with an additional 2% payment for profits generated, is made to ABC Inc., at any time after 10 days, the aforementioned oath shall not be required. (It is understood that the customer will have retained 5% of the profits, as outlined in IV above, furthering only the remaining 2% profit payment to ABC Inc.) Additional profits, if any, shall belong to the customer.

VIII. Furthermore, if payment of said funds, with an additional 10% per annum payment for profits generated, is made to ABC Inc., at any time after 30 days, the aforementioned oath shall not be required. (It is understood that the customer will have retained 5% of the profits, as outlined in IV above, furthering only the remaining 10% per annum profit payment to ABC Inc.) Additional profits, if any, shall belong to the customer.

IX. ABC Inc. shall be entitled to a presumption of credibility in any claim made regarding compliance with the terms of this agreement.

X. The customer is obligated to return the invested funds and profits as they are billed. If payment is not made by the due date, the terms of this Heter Iska shall remain in force.

XI. In the event of any conflict between the terms of this Heter Iska and any other agreement between the parties relating to the aforementioned funds, the terms of this agreement shall prevail.

XII. This agreement shall follow the guidelines of Heter Iska as explained in *Sefer Bris Yehudah*. Delivery of goods or services from ABC Inc., and its acceptance by the customer, are accepted as a means of effecting this legal transfer and obligation, as applicable under Orthodox Jewish Law.

CHAPTER SEVEN:

Discounts Which Require Prepayment

□ Discounts (1-2)

□ Deposits (3-4)

□ Corporations (5)

□ Exceptions to this prohibition (6-18)

□ Heter Iska (19)

□ When a discount was already given (20-21)

□ **Applications (22-28):**

□ Early registration (22)

□ Bus rides (23)

□ Mikvaos, swimming pools and athletic clubs (24)

□ Prepublication prices (25-27)

□ Newspaper and magazine subscription discounts (28)

□ **Appendix:**

Heter Iska for prepayment discounts

Introduction

The previous chapter dealt with the laws relating to credit purchases. In that situation, a customer receives merchandise at one time, and is obligated to pay at a later time. We have seen that since debt is created when the customer receives the merchandise, the laws of Ribbis apply.

In this chapter, we will deal with the reverse situation. This situation involves a customer who is required to make payment ahead of time for merchandise which he will receive at a later date. Here too, since debt is created when prepayment is made, the laws of Ribbis apply.

Businesses sometimes offer discounts to customers who make prepayment. These businesses actually have a two-tier price arrangement: a higher price for conventional customers, and a lower price for those who pay in advance. In many cases, this arrangement is prohibited as Ribbis.[1] In this chapter, we will examine the situations under which this arrangement is permitted.

Where prepayment is required for a rental discount see Chapter 11, Paragraphs 12-19; for services which are provided by a contractor, see Chapter 10, Paragraphs 23-26.

Discounts

1. A regular sale agreement requires a customer to make payment when he receives merchandise. When an agreement calls for money to be paid in advance, the money being paid is actually being extended as a loan. The seller is therefore prohibited from benefiting a customer who agrees to pay in advance.

Similarly, a business may not set up a two-tier price system in which a lower price is offered to those who pay in advance.[2]

2. Even when a business requires advance payments from all its customers (and no two-tier price system exists), it may not offer the customer a lower price because of this.[3]

---

1. This is similar to the situation in the previous chapter, where a two-tier situation was prohibited because it charged higher prices for credit sales.

2. Y.D. 173:7. This type of Ribbis is prohibited by Rabbinic law. Whenever Ribbis is part of a purchase agreement and not part of a conventional loan, it is not Biblically prohibited (*Rema* 161:1). [The fact that this is only a Rabbinic prohibition is significant in allowing certain leniencies; see Notes 7 and 8.]

3. The price must be consistent with the fair market price (Y.D. 173:7). When the price varies from merchant to merchant, it must stay within the range of prices offered. [One

Deposits

3. In many businesses, a deposit is required when a customer places a sale. The deposit is usually a nominal fee and it is generally clear that the seller's intent is not to secure advance payment, but to be assured that the customer will follow through with the purchase. The prohibition of Ribbis does not apply to this type of advance payment, since this is not seen as a form of loan.[4]

4. It is even permitted to offer a lower price to a customer who makes a deposit payment, as long as it does not appear to be a Ribbis payment. This means that the seller may not say anything which implies that he is requiring the deposit because of his need for advance funding. He is not permitted to say that he needs the money to enable him to purchase the merchandise or that he is offering the lower price to induce the customer to advance the deposit money. If he does say this, he is prohibited from offering a lower price for the purchase.[5] (When a fair market price is paid, these restrictions do not apply since no discount is being offered.)

Corporations

5. When the discount for prepayment is offered by a corporation, some poskim hold that these prohibitions do not apply. According to this view, a corporation may offer a discount for advance payment. For example, a publishing house which is incorporated is permitted to offer a lower prepublication price for books and a magazine publisher is permitted to offer lower rates to subscribers who prepay.[6]

---

would be prohibited from offering a price which is at the lower end of this range, unless this is his usual business practice (based on *Shach* 175:7).]

This prohibition applies even when the prepayment is not cited as the reason for the discount (*Rema* ibid.).

4. *Maharsham* in *Mishpat Shalom* (C.M. 209:25). *Bris Yehudah* 24:n2 is uncertain how to define a 'nominal payment.' [It would seem that this should depend on the normal business practice for each type of purchase, at that given time and place. Clearly, the primary consideration is that the payment be perceived as a deposit rather than an advance of funds. This determination would depend on the circumstances of each type of sale.]

5. *Bris Yehudah* 24:n2. This is because *Maharsham* bases his leniency on the fact that a deposit payment does not appear to be a form of loan. But when the seller says that he needs the advance funding, this is similar to a loan, and it would be prohibited to benefit the customer.

6. These issues are discussed at greater length in Paragraphs 25-27.

Other poskim disagree and maintain that Jewish-owned corporations have the same restrictions as individuals.[7]

Exceptions to This Prohibition

6. As a rule, discounts may not be offered for prepayment. However, there are three significant exceptions to this rule, as outlined below. It should be noted that even in these cases it may not be clearly stated that the advance funding is the reason for the discount. This means that a two-tier price system, which calls for regular prices for conventional payment and lower prices when advance payment is offered, is prohibited in virtually all cases. Still, there are numerous practical applications of these leniencies, as will be demonstrated below.

The three exceptions are:

☐ When the seller has the merchandise in stock at the time payment is advanced. This is known as *yesh lo*, lit., he has (the merchandise).

☐ When the item which is being ordered has no set market value.

☐ When the customer accepts liability at the time that he makes prepayment.

Each of these exceptions is explained below.

Exception A: Yesh Lo

7. When the customer pays for an item which the seller does not have in his possession, this is considered advance payment. However, if the seller has the merchandise in stock at the time payment is made, this is similar to a conventional sale, and a discount may be offered. This is true even in situations where the customer does not receive legal title to the merchandise after making payment, and where delivery is scheduled for a later date. Still, since the payment binds the seller to honor the sale agreement, it is considered a conventional payment for immediate purchase.

---

7. *Igros Moshe* (2:63) and *Maharshag* (in a letter published in the *Noam Journal*) rule that corporations are permitted to pay Ribbis. According to this opinion, the rules of Ribbis apply only when a borrower is personally responsible for the loan. When a corporation borrows money, liability is limited to company assets.

This ruling is the subject of dispute between contemporary poskim, as has been discussed in Chapter 5, Paragraph 27. Since the question here involves an issue of Rabbinic law, one cannot be faulted for relying on the lenient opinion.

In this case, a seller may intentionally charge a lower price because he is receiving payment in advance.[8]

8. There is no limit to the discount which may be offered. Therefore, even if the discount is clearly below the market price, this is permitted.[9] The seller is also permitted to benefit the customer by agreeing to absorb expenses which the customer would normally pay.[10] For example, he may agree to pay for delivery of the merchandise.

9. When is an item considered to be in the possession of the seller? The poskim present the following guidelines:

a) The merchandise must be complete and in a condition which is suitable for delivery. If additional assembly must be completed before delivery, the item is not considered in stock at the time of payment.[11] Similarly, if the merchandise must age or ripen before becoming suitable for delivery, it is not considered in stock, and these prohibitions apply.[12]

---

8. Y.D. 173:7. *Beis Yosef* explains the reason for this leniency. According to Biblical law, one who pays for an item acquires legal title at the time of payment, even if the item is still in the seller's physical possession. As explained in the Talmud (*Bava Metzia* 46b), the Rabbis decreed that payment is not sufficient to convey legal ownership. Still, once payment has been made, the buyer and seller are bound by a strong obligation (known as *mi shepara*) to complete their sale agreement. Where questions of Rabbinic law are concerned, this obligation is sufficient for us to consider the sale to be complete at the time of payment. The case under discussion involves only Rabbinic prohibitions (see Note 2), and the laws of Ribbis therefore do not apply.

[For additional explanation of the rationale for the rule of *yesh lo*, see *Chavos Daas* 163:2.]

9. *Chochmas Adam* 139:14, R' Akiva Eiger in Responsa 52. The seller may offer a discount, even if it is clearly excessive. In this case, no loan has taken place, so there can be no Ribbis violation.

10. *Bris Yehudah* 24:n41.

11. *Shach* 175:7.

If assembly is normally completed by the customer, an item is considered complete and ready for delivery as soon as the manufacturer's portion of the assembly is completed.

12. I.e., even if the merchandise will become suitable for delivery on its own and without any action on the part of its owner, it is still considered incomplete until it is actually ready for delivery. [This is similar to 173:10.] Where an item is useable in its present form, but improves or grows with time, see Chapter 18, Note 3.

Dried fruits are made by placing fruit in the sun to dry. Even if produce was already placed in the sun to dry, it is considered incomplete until it actually dries (*Bris Yehudah* 24:n17).

b) The seller must actually have the merchandise under his physical control.[13] Even if he is temporarily unable to gain access to the merchandise (for example, the key to the building was misplaced or is in the possession of a worker or relative), the merchandise is considered in stock.[14]

c) The seller must have sufficient stock for the quantity being sold.[15]

---

13. If the seller had allowed someone to take the merchandise with the stipulation that he return similar merchandise, the leniency of *yesh lo* begins only after the merchandise is actually delivered to the seller (Y.D. 173:7).

[Similarly, if the seller had ordered the merchandise from his supplier, but it had not yet been delivered, this is not considered *yesh lo* (*Bris Yehudah* 23:18). In this case, the sale may still be completed if the seller would arrange to act as an agent for his supplier. He could then sell the merchandise directly to the buyer and accept payment for the merchandise which is in the supplier's possession (based on *Tuv Tam Vodaas* 3:41). This may only be done with the knowledge of the supplier and only when the supplier is a Jew.]

14. This applies even if the merchandise is in another town (*S.A. Harav* §30, *Kreisi* 162:2). Others disagree and hold that the merchandise may not be in another town unless it is in a city which the purchaser frequents (*Machneh Ephraim* §29, quoted in *Mekor Mayim Chaim* 173:7; he argues that this is similar to merchandise which is incomplete and not ready for delivery).

If the merchandise is being stored in someone else's property, this is still considered *yesh lo* (*Shach* 173:18).

15. Y.D. 173:6, *Shach* 15. [See R' Akiva Eiger (to *Shach* 15) who quotes an innovative method of working around this restriction, under certain conditions. See also *Mishnas Ribbis* 8:n7 that some poskim limit its application.]

[The concept of *yesh lo* appears in three areas of the laws of Ribbis; here and again in Chapters 8 and 14. This definition of *yesh lo* holds true both here and in Chapter 8, but not in the case outlined in Chapter 14. See also Notes 14 and 18 there.]

We only require that the seller have sufficient merchandise for *each* sale. If he completes separate agreements with numerous individuals for sales involving the same merchandise, he does not have to possess enough merchandise for them all. A businessman may therefore make numerous sales for advance payment, relying on the same stock of merchandise for each sale. The reason for this is that the merchandise is never transferred to the legal title of any customer, even after payment is made. Since it remains the property of the seller, he may use it to effect further sales.

Chavos Daas 163:1 adds that the seller is even permitted to use the same merchandise to permit a second sale to the same customer, providing that it take place at a separate time and not immediately after the first sale. *Mishnas Ribbis* 8:n7 questions whether arrangements for the second sale may be made at the time of the first one.

10. Before making payment, the customer must be told that the seller has the merchandise in stock.[16] He may rely on the seller to verify this.[17]

11. *Yesh lo* is permitted only when advance payment is made in the form of cash (or merchandise). When previously owed moneys are counted as advance payment, there is a dispute among the poskim if *yesh lo* is permitted.[18]

12. In all cases of *yesh lo*, neither the buyer nor the seller may mention that a discount is being offered because of the advance payment.[19]

Exception B: Items With No Set Market Value

13. A discount may be offered for advance payment, if the item being purchased has no set market value. Common examples of items with no set market value are precious stones, used cars or machines, and custom furniture. These items are appraised individually and their value can fluctuate greatly. When these items are sold at a discount, it is not readily obvious that a discount is being offered. It is therefore permitted to offer a lower price, even if the seller knows that he is doing so only because payment is being offered in advance.[20]

---

16. *Chavos Daas* 163:1. Cf. *Binas Adam* 132:5 and *Pischei Teshuvah* 173:7 who disagree. One should follow the opinion of *Chavos Daas* and notify the customer. Still, if the sale was already completed and the customer was unaware that the merchandise was in stock, one may rely on the lenient opinions and deliver the merchandise at the discounted price (Rabbi Y.S. Eliyashev Shlita, quoted in *Ribbis LeOhr HaHalachah* 16:3).

17. *Rema* 173:7. The seller may not mislead the customer. If the customer realizes that he is being misled into believing that the seller has it in stock, he may not accept the discount in return for the advance payment. (*Taz* 173:end of 9, *Chochmas Adam* 134:12, *S.A. Harav* 23 and 46).

18. *Chochmas Adam* 134:12 and R' Akiva Eiger in Responsa 52 permit this. *Yad Avrohom* (to Y.D. 163:1) prohibits offering a discount when a previous debt is used as payment. This is also the opinion of *Pnei Yehoshua* 63a and *Chazon Ish* 76:2.

19. *Rema* 173:7.

20. *Rema* 173:7; Cf. *Taz* 12 who disputes this. Most poskim follow the ruling of the *Rema* (*Chochmas Adam* 139:14, *Bris Yehudah* 23:3; cf. *S.A. Harav* who does not mention this leniency).

Be'er HaGolah explains why this is permitted. The Rabbis prohibited sellers from offering discounts in return for advance payment because this arrangement appears similar to a Ribbis arrangement (*mechzei keRibbis*). However, when the item being sold has no set value, the discount is not obvious. In that case there is no concern that this would appear to be similar to a Ribbis arrangement.

14. The discounted price which is offered to someone who is paying in advance may not be so low that it is obvious that the discount is being offered because of the advance payment.[21]

15. Seasonal items which do not have a set market value at the time they are ordered, but will have a set market value at the time of delivery, are not included in this exception.[22] For example, esrogim have a market value only during the Yom Tov season. Someone who orders esrogim during the previous spring (for delivery during the season) may not receive a discount for paying in advance.

16. Where this leniency applies there may be no explicit mention of a discount for advance payment.[23]

Exception C: When the Buyer Accepts Liability

17. A discount may be offered for advance payment when a buyer is willing to accept financial risk at the time of payment. For example, a customer agrees to buy all the crops which a farmer will produce in a given field during the following year. The farmer may ask for a low price because there is a possibility that the field will produce less than anticipated; thus, it is not clear that a discount is being offered. The prohibition on offering prepayment discounts therefore does not apply.[24]

---

21. *Mishnas Ribbis* 8:13. The entire basis for permitting a discount in these cases is because it is not obvious that a discount is being offered. However, when the discount is obviously excessive, it is clear that it is being given because of the advance payment.

How large a discount is considered 'excessive'?

This depends on each item, and the degree to which the price tends to fluctuate. As a general rule, *Mishnas Ribbis*, citing 173:1, suggests limiting the discount to 20%.

22. *Be'er HaGolah* to 173:7, *Beis Meir*, *Tiferes LeMoshe*, *Chochmas Adam* 139:14 and *Binas Adam* 8, *Avnei Nezer* 210. If the item has a set value at the time of delivery, it is obvious that the low price paid by the customer included a discount for prepayment. This would appear to be Ribbis (*mechzei keRibbis*).

[We have seen in Note 20 that *Taz* disagrees with the entire ruling of *Rema*. The Talmudic basis for the Taz' objections are answered by adding this limitation.]

23. *Rema* 173:7.

24. Y.D. 173:9, in a similar case involving the purchase of all the milk which a particular animal will produce in the coming year. *Nesivos HaMishpat* 209:1 adds that this is permitted even when the seller is motivated by his need for advance funding (as long as he does not say so), because the prohibition on offering discounts is based on the fact that this would appear to be Ribbis (*mechzei keRibbis*). When it is not clear that a discount is being offered, there is no concern that this appears to be a Ribbis arrangement.

18. Here too, it may not be stated explicitly that the discount is being offered because of the advance payment.[25]

Using a Heter Iska

19. When none of these exceptions apply and a seller wishes to offer a discount for advance payment, a Heter Iska may be used. A suitable Heter Iska form appears at the end of this chapter. The standard Heter Iska form may also be used (see note below).[26]

When a Discount Was Already Given

20. If a buyer makes an advance payment in exchange for a discount and the parties later realize that this is prohibited, the sale does not automatically become negated. However, the provision of the agreement which is prohibited as Ribbis is not valid. This means that the discounted price may not be honored. In this case, the customer may either pay full price for the merchandise which he ordered or he may cancel the order entirely.[27]

21. If a customer received a discounted price for future delivery, this discounted price may not be honored. Even if the actual market price of the item dropped so that the market price at the time of delivery was the same as the discounted price, it is still prohibited to honor the original commitment.[28]

---

25. *Mishnas Ribbis* 8:n16; Cf., *Minchas Yitzchak* 4:99:1.

26. The standard form appears at the end of Chapter 23. The amount of money being advanced should be entered into the first space. The amount being discounted should be entered in the line: "$_____ for his share of profits." (For example, if a $1200 shipment of merchandise is being ordered and the customer is paying $1000, the amount of profit is $200.) A sentence should be added stating that payment will be in the form of the particular merchandise which is being offered.

Before using any Heter Iska, it is important that both parties understand the concept of Heter Iska, as well as its limitations. These are explained at length in Chapter 22.

27. Y.D. 175:8 rules that whenever an agreement contains a Ribbis provision, that provision must be canceled. In this case, it is the discount which is considered Ribbis. This must therefore be ignored and the full price must be paid for the merchandise. The customer (who is now required to pay a higher price) could argue that he never agreed to buy for that price. He therefore has the option of canceling the sale.

28. *Bris Yehudah* 23:n2, based on *Taz* 173:12. He also cites *Shaar Deah* 172:5 who rules that in this case the discounted price may be honored.

Applications

22. Discounts for early registration: It is common for hotels, schools and day camps to offer advance payment discounts. These 'early bird specials' offer savings for people who register in advance. When only a deposit is required to secure these low rates, this type of discounting is permitted.[29] However, when the discount is available only to those who pay a substantial portion of the fees (or tuition) in advance, this practice is highly questionable and should be avoided.[30]

Today, virtually all hotels, schools and day camps are set up as corporations. According to the view of *Igros Moshe*, corporations are not bound by the prohibitions of paying Ribbis. They would therefore be permitted to offer these discounts. This is not true according to the poskim who dispute the leniency of *Igros Moshe*.[31]

23. Discounts for multiple rides: Many bus and taxi companies offer discounts to customers who purchase cards entitling them to multiple rides. Since this discount is available only for advance payment, this would seem to be another example of the prohibition outlined in this chapter.

However, many poskim permit this. They explain that these discounts are generally offered because this is a more efficient manner of running the business and not because of the advance payment. Thus,

---

29. As explained above, Paragraphs 3-4.

30. These 'early bird specials' are examples of the prohibited type of discounts described in this chapter.

Some schools have no set tuition price; instead, tuition fees are negotiated separately with each set of parents. This would be permitted under 'exception b' ('items with no set market value'), as long as two prices, one for advance payment and another for regular payment, are not mentioned. Still, a parent would be permitted to state, at the beginning of his discussion with school officials, that it is his intention to pay in advance, with the hope that this would influence them to agree to a lower tuition price. However, he may not specifically request that they do so.

Regarding school tuition: R' Y.S. Eliyashev Shlita (quoted in *Toras Ribbis* 10:74 and *Mishnas Ribbis* 9:n40) permits early registration discounts on different grounds. He maintains that the rules for prepayment of merchandise do not apply to the case of school tuition. According to his view, school administrators are actually paid contractors who contract with the parents to provide the various requirements (teachers, classrooms, etc.) for the child's education. In this case, the rules which apply to the sale of merchandise do not apply. Instead, the rules of prepayment of wages are applicable. We will see (in Chapter 10, Paragraph 22) that workers who have already begun their job are permitted to offer discounts for advance payment. This applies here as well.

31. See Paragraph 5, above.

the discount is not being offered for the loan and the rules of Ribbis do not apply. One may rely on this opinion; however, if the company were to state that the discount is motivated by the fact that they receive advance funding, this would be prohibited.[32]

24. Mikvaos, swimming pools and athletic clubs: These facilities usually offer discounts to people who become members for a month or year at a time. This is a form of rental and is permitted.[33]

25. Prepublication prices: Publishers often offer books at significant savings when orders are received and paid for prior to publication. These offers generally constitute Ribbis and should be avoided.[34]

26. A prepublication discount may be offered if it is structured in the following manner:

---

32. *Bris Yehudah* 23:n21, *Toras Ribbis* 10:63, *Mishnas Ribbis* 9:31.

R' Y.S. Eliyashev Shlita (quoted in *Mishnas Ribbis*, ibid.) rules leniently for another reason. He views a bus service operator as a contractor who is paid to provide all of the necessary arrangements for transportation. In this case, discounts are permitted (as in Note 28, above).

Another argument is that the exception of *yesh lo* ('exception a,' above) should apply. Since rides are constantly available, all of the rides to which a person is entitled could, theoretically, be redeemed immediately (*Lehoros Nosson* 5:4). This argument seems inadequate, because even if we were to concede that *yesh lo* does apply, the company would still be prohibited from offering two price schedules, one for rides which are purchased individually and another for purchasing multiple-ride cards. This is a two-tiered price system and is prohibited in all cases.

33. In these cases, a customer does not pay for goods or services. Rather, he is paying for use of a certain area. This constitutes a rental and discounts are permitted (*Mishnas Ribbis* 9:32).

34. *Minchas Yitzchak* 4:99, Rabbi Y.S. Eliyashev Shlita, quoted in *Ribbis LeOhr HaHalachah* 17:19.

An argument in defense of the widespread practice of offering prepublication discounts is presented in *Minchas Yitzchak*. He explains that a publisher sets a price for a book, based on his own projections of the book's popularity. Often, his hopes do not materialize and he is forced to lower the price. This may cause the prepublication price to actually be higher than the book's postpublication price. Because of this possibility, anyone who pays in advance is actually taking a risk by agreeing to a set price. This would be permitted under 'exception c' ("when the buyer accepts liability"). *Minchas Yitzchak* concludes that "it is possible to defend the widespread custom, but in practice it is proper to be careful to do (business) in a manner which avoids the problem totally."

According to the ruling of *Igros Moshe* (quoted above, Paragraph 5), if the publishing company is a corporation, it is permitted to offer prepublication discounts. It would nevertheless be preferable for the discount to be structured in the manner described in the following paragraph.

The leniency of *yesh lo* permits a discount to be offered when the item being sold is in stock at the time of payment. Thus, if publication is anticipated by a specific date, for example May 1, the publisher may offer a discount for payments received on May 1 (since it is then in stock), even if delivery will be made at a later time.[35] In this case, the publisher may offer the discount for all orders placed (and paid for) between January 1 and May 1. Since the customer has the option of paying on May 1 and receiving the identical discount, he is not receiving any additional benefit by paying earlier. Therefore, payments which are received on January 1 would be the same as payments which are received on May 1, and are permitted.[36] This would be permitted even if the book is not available in stores on May 1, as long as the publisher has it in stock on that day.[37]

---

35. Even if the publisher will only have a limited number of copies available on May 1, he is permitted to accept numerous prepayments. The only restriction is that no *single* order be for more copies than he has in stock (as explained above, Note 15).

36. A possible objection to this proposal may be based on *Rema* 173:7, who rules that even where *yesh lo* applies, it is prohibited to explicitly offer two prices, a regular price for postpublication and a lower price for prepublication. Advertisements which offer prepublication specials usually display two prices, and it would seem that this is prohibited.

Although we have followed the stringent ruling of *Rema* (in Paragraph 12), one may rule leniently in the case outlined here. It should be noted that *Rema's* ruling is itself the subject of dispute (see *Tur* and *Beis Yosef* 173). We may assume that *Rema's* stringent ruling is limited to the case discussed by Rishonim and *Rema*, where *yesh lo* is used as a legal fiction. In that case, the delivery date is set for a later time. Although the merchandise may be in stock, it is not truly available to the customer. However in the case of prepublication prices, the book is truly available on May 1. One who pays the discounted price on that day should be permitted to do so even according to *Rema*, even if it will take a short while until the book is delivered.

To illustrate the point: This is similar to someone who orders groceries at a sale price from his local grocer. He pays the sale price, but arranges for delivery to be made to his home the next day, when the sale price is no longer available. In effect, he has actually secured the discount price by making advance payment. Still, it would be permitted for him to receive delivery, since the item was in stock at the time of payment. Although the grocer had advertised two prices (the regular price and the sale price), this should not matter because the items were truly available to him at the time of payment.

An additional point: It is not obvious that prepublication discounts are offered to raise funds in advance. Often, this is done as a marketing tool to encourage purchases or to help the publisher predict demand. As noted in Paragraph 23, this is itself a basis for permitting prepayment discounts.

If we also take into account the argument presented by *Minchas Yitzchak* (in Note 34), it is clear that there are enough contributing factors to rely on this leniency.

37. If publication were subsequently delayed, the publisher would be obligated to extend the discount, so that the discounted rate is available on the publication day.

27. When someone has no interest in a book, but orders it in advance because he wishes to benefit the author or publisher, there is no prohibition on accepting prepublication discounts.[38]

28. **Newspaper and magazine subscription discounts** are discussed in the next chapter.

Appendix to Chapter Seven:
Heter Iska for Prepayment Discounts
(see Paragraph 19)

The following Heter Iska is used when a customer orders merchandise for future delivery, if the seller offers a discount on the price of the merchandise, in exchange for the customer's advance payment. This is generally prohibited, unless a Heter Iska is used.

Iska Contract[1]

I, the undersigned, acknowledge receipt of the sum of $_____ from _____ (hereafter referred to as the "Investor"), to be used for business investment purposes. I obligate myself to utilize these funds in investments which I believe will generate profits. Any profits realized or losses sustained shall be shared equally between the investor and myself.

Any claim of loss must be verified through the testimony of two qualified witnesses in, and under conditions acceptable to, an Orthodox Jewish court of law. Any claim regarding the amount of profit generated by these investment(s) shall be verified under solemn oath, before and under conditions acceptable to, an Orthodox Jewish court of law;

It is agreed that if I deliver _____ (enter type and amount of merchandise) to the investor, on or before _____ (enter date of delivery) as payment of both the investment and the profits which are generated, then I will not be required to make any further payment nor will I be required to make an oath.

I have received one dollar from the investor as payment for my services during the term of our partnership.[2]

Continued on next page

---

38. Rabbi Y.S. Eliyashev Shlita, quoted in *Ribbis LeOhr HaHalachah* 17:19.

1. This Heter Iska is based on *Kitzur Shulchan Aruch* 66:8. For a Hebrew version of a Heter Iska suitable for this use, see *Mishnas Ribbis* p. 255.

2. The purchaser should pay one dollar to the trader, in addition to the moneys which are invested for the commodities. The reason that this payment is necessary is explained

It is agreed that any dispute which may arise in connection with this agreement shall be submitted before _____.[3] Judgment rendered by the aforesaid authority may be entered in any court having jurisdiction thereof. This agreement shall follow the guidelines of Heter Iska as explained in *Sefer Bris Yehudah* and has been executed in a manner which effects a legal transfer and obligation, known as *kinyan sudar*.

Signature of the Recipient_____

Dated_____

Witnesses[4]

In witness whereof the above-mentioned parties have entered into this Heter Iska agreement on this _____ day of _____.

Signature of Witness _____

Signature of Witness _____

---

below, Chapter 22, Paragraph 29.

3. This part of the contract is optional.

4. This part of the contract is optional, depending on whether the parties prefer to have witnesses attest to their agreement.

CHAPTER EIGHT

Guaranteed Low Prices

Introduction

In the previous chapter, we have learned that a customer may not be offered a discount in exchange for making a payment in advance. This is because advance payments are considered a form of loan. In this chapter, we will see that it is prohibited to extend other benefits to a customer because he is making payment in advance.

A customer who orders merchandise for future delivery may wish to lock in today's price for that merchandise. This protects him from future price increases. In general, a seller is permitted to guarantee a specific price for future delivery. However, when he offers to do so only if the customer makes payment in advance, this is prohibited. This is a Rabbinically prohibited form of Ribbis.[1]

1. Merchants may guarantee a price on an item which will be delivered at a future date. However, if this guarantee is provided only if the customer makes payment in advance, this is prohibited.[2]

For example, a manufacturer may wish to know, in advance, the price of the materials needed for future production. His supplier guarantees a price for a specific period of time, on the condition that payment is made in advance. This is prohibited (except where one of the exceptions, listed

---

1. Ordinarily, payment is due to a merchant only after the merchandise is delivered to the customer. When the merchant receives payment before delivery, he is actually receiving a loan. He is therefore prohibited from benefiting the customer in exchange for this loan.

Anytime money is advanced as part of a business transaction, the prohibitions which apply are only Rabbinic prohibitions (*Rema* 161:1).

Some exceptions to this prohibition:

- If the money is advanced to the merchant on the condition that he does not use it until delivery is made, no loan has taken place. Therefore, if a merchant requests advance payment only because he wants to be sure that the customer will not default on payment, he may stipulate that the customer deposit funds in escrow, pending delivery. He would be permitted to offer the customer a financial incentive (such as guaranteeing his low prices) for doing so.

- These prohibitions apply only where advance payment is *required*. When a merchant guarantees a price, and the customer makes advance payment on his own, this is permitted.

- According to *Igros Moshe* (2:63), whenever the seller is a corporation, these prohibitions do not apply (see previous chapter, Paragraph 5). However, since this ruling is a matter of dispute it is preferable that an agreement be designed to avoid this problem.

2. Y.D. 175:1.

below, applies). Therefore, if the market price of the materials were to rise before the time of delivery, the supplier would be prohibited from honoring his obligation to deliver at the lower price.

Similarly, purchase agreements that allow a consumer to 'lock in' a price by ordering (and paying) in advance are prohibited. Appliance stores, for example, frequently guarantee a price only if payment is made in advance.[3]

Deposits

2. Many businesses require a customer to pay a portion of the sale price when placing an order. The deposit is usually a nominal fee, and it is generally clear that the seller's intent is not to secure advance payment, but to be assured that the customer will follow through with the purchase. This is not seen as a form of loan, and the prohibition on guaranteeing a price does not apply to this type of advance payment.[4]

3. It is permitted to offer a lower price to a customer who makes a deposit payment. Still, one must avoid making this appear as a Ribbis payment. Therefore, the seller may not say anything which implies that he is requiring the deposit because of his need for advance funding. If he does say this, the seller is prohibited from guaranteeing the price of the purchase.[5]

Exceptions to This Prohibition

4. This rule prohibits the guaranteeing of prices when advance payment is required. However, there are three significant exceptions

---

3. Fortunately, many of these businesses are incorporated. According to the view of *Igros Moshe* (see Note 1), corporations are permitted to make these business deals. Still, since these businesses are constantly involved in these situations, it is preferable that they arrange to do business in a manner which is acceptable according to all opinions. Wherever possible, they should therefore structure their business dealings in a way that uses one of the exceptions (listed below).

4. *Maharsham* in *Mishpat Shalom* (C.M. 209:25). *Bris Yehudah* 24:n2 is uncertain how to define a 'nominal payment.' [It would seem that this should depend on the normal business practice for each type of purchase, at that given time and place. Clearly, the primary consideration is that the payment be perceived as a deposit rather than an advance of funds. This determination would depend on the circumstances of each sale.]

5. *Bris Yehudah* 24:n2. This is because *Maharsham* bases his leniency on the fact that a deposit payment does not resemble a form of loan. However, when the seller says that he needs the advance funding, it does resemble a form of loan, and it would be prohibited to benefit the customer.

to this rule, as outlined below. In modern times, most business transactions are covered by one of these exceptions.

The three exceptions are:

☐ When the seller has the merchandise in stock at the time payment is advanced. This is known as *yesh lo*, lit., he has (the merchandise).

☐ When the item being ordered has no set market value.

☐ When the item which is being ordered has a set market price and is readily available.

Each of these exceptions are explained below.

Exception A: Yesh Lo

5. When the customer pays for an item which the seller does not have in his possession, this is considered advance payment. However, if the seller has the merchandise in stock at the time that payment is made, this is similar to a conventional sale, and the seller is permitted to guarantee the price of the item.[6]

This is true even if the customer does not receive legal title to the merchandise when he makes payment, and even if the merchant does not plan to deliver the actual item of merchandise he has in stock.[7] Still, since the payment binds the seller to honor the sale agreement, this is considered a conventional payment for immediate purchase.

6. When is an item considered to be in the possession of the seller? The poskim present the following guidelines:

a) The seller must actually have the merchandise under his physical control.[8] Even if he is temporarily unable to gain access

---

6. Y.D. 175:4. [As far as the laws of Ribbis are concerned, we view the merchandise which is in stock as being sold; thus, the payment is not an advance of funds. In fact, the merchandise is not actually transferred to the customer's possession. If the merchandise were to be damaged, the seller would suffer the loss, because the merchandise is still his. Still, since we are dealing with a Rabbinic law, the consideration that the merchandise is sold is sufficient to remove the prohibition.]

7. *Teshuvos R' Akiva Eiger* 1:52, *S.A. Harav* §34, *Chazon Ish* 76:1.

8. If the seller ordered the merchandise from his supplier, but it had not yet been delivered, this is not considered *yesh lo* (*Bris Yehudah* 23:18).

[In this case, the sale may still be completed, if it is arranged in the following manner. The seller acts as an agent to sell the merchandise for his supplier. He may then sell the merchandise to the buyer and accept payment for the merchandise which is in the supplier's possession. Since the supplier has the merchandise in stock, this is considered

to the merchandise (for example, the key to the building was misplaced or is in the possession of a worker or relative), the merchandise is considered to be in stock.[9]

If the seller does not have the merchandise in stock, but a third party owes him the merchandise, there is a disagreement among the poskim if this is considered *yesh lo*.[10]

b) The manufacture of the item must be nearly complete and suitable for delivery. If only one or two changes are necessary to complete the item, this is considered complete. However, if three or more changes are necessary, the item is considered incomplete and its price may not be guaranteed.[11] This rule applies even if the seller is capable of easily completing the last steps of manufacture.[12]

---

yesh lo and arrangements may be made for a guaranteed price (based on *Tuv Tam Vodaas* 3:41). This may only be done with the knowledge of the supplier and only when the supplier is a Jew.]

9. This applies even if the merchandise is in another town (*S.A. Harav* §30, *Kreisi* 162:2, *Machneh Ephraim* §29; although *Machneh Ephraim* argued this point in Chapter 7, Note 14, he agrees in this case).

If the merchandise is being stored in someone else's property, it is still considered *yesh lo* (as in Y.D. 162:2 and *Shach* 173:18).

10. *Gedulei Terumah* 4:56 and *R' Akiva Eiger* to 162:2 (quoting *Toras Chaim*) rule that if others owe this merchandise to the seller, this is considered *yesh lo*, and the seller may guarantee the price of the merchandise for future delivery.

Maharam Alshikr in Responsa 34 and *Maharam Shif* to B.M. 63b rule that when the merchandise is owed to the seller, it is not considered *yesh lo*.

The concept of *yesh lo* also appears in the previous chapter, where we prohibit the merchant from discounting his price when payment is made in advance. There too, this is permitted under circumstances of *yesh lo*. In that case, all these poskim concede that the seller must actually possess the merchandise.

11. Y.D. 175:4. This is different than the rules of *yesh lo* as they appeared in the previous chapter. There, where a greater leniency is allowed (i.e., the price may be discounted), we require that the merchandise be complete at the time that payment is made.

12. *Shach* 175:8. [When assembly is normally completed by the customer, an item is considered complete and ready for delivery as soon as the manufacturer's portion of the assembly is completed.]

Bris Yehudah (24:n17) presents the following guidelines for defining the 'three needed changes' which make an item incomplete:

- **Delivery** is not considered a 'change' in the item. However, where it is necessary to place the item into an oven (or machine) in a manner which requires the expertise of a professional, this placement is considered a 'change.'
- When the item will change on its own, without the assistance of a person, it is considered a 'change.' For example, if wheat was put out in the sun to dry, but it has

c) The seller must have sufficient stock of the item, in the quantity being sold.[13]

7. Before making payment, the customer must be told that the seller has the merchandise in stock.[14] He may rely on the seller to verify this.[15]

8. The seller should not state explicitly that he is guaranteeing the price only because the money is being paid in advance.[16]

Exception B: Items With No Set Market Value

9. When payment is made in advance, a price may be guaranteed, if the item being purchased has no set market value. Common examples of items with no set market value are precious stones, used

---

not yet dried, this is a missing change. If two other changes are necessary before the wheat can be delivered (e.g., it must still be threshed and winnowed), the wheat is considered incomplete.

• Even where a machine is used to complete the item, and it would complete all three changes in a single motion, it is considered incomplete until the changes are actually made (*Darkei Teshuvah* 175:5).

13. Y.D. 175:4.

We require only that the seller have sufficient merchandise for *each* sale. If he makes separate agreements with numerous individuals for sales involving the same merchandise, he does not have to possess enough merchandise for them all. A businessman may therefore make numerous sales for advance payment, relying on the same stock of merchandise for each sale. The reason for this is that the merchandise is never transferred to the legal title of any customer, even after payment is made. Since it remains the property of the seller, he may use it to effect further sales.

Chavos Daas 163:1 adds that if the seller wants to make a second sale to the same customer, he is permitted to use the same merchandise, providing that the second sale take place at a separate time and not immediately after the first sale. *Mishnas Ribbis* 9:n2 questions whether arrangements for the second sale may be made at the time of the first one.

14. *Chavos Daas* 163:1. According to this opinion, if the customer was unaware (at the time of payment) that the seller had the item in stock, the seller may not honor his commitment to a particular price. If the market price of the item subsequently went up, the seller must charge the higher price. Cf. *Mishnas Ribbis* 9:n11 and the previous chapter, Note 16, that if the sale was already completed, one may rely on those who permit the commitment to be honored even if the customer was not aware that *yesh lo.*

15. *Rema* 173:7. The seller may not mislead the customer. If the customer realizes that he is being misled, this exception does not apply and he may not enter into this agreement (*Taz* 173: end of 9, *Chochmas Adam* 134:12, *S.A. Harav* 23 and 46).

16. This condition is not mentioned in *Shulchan Aruch*. Still, since Rishonim mention this, it is preferable that the seller refrain from making this statement (*Bris Yehudah* 24:n6, based on *Shitah Mikubetzes* and *Meiri* to B.M. 63b).

cars, used machines and custom furniture. These items are appraised individually and their value can fluctuate greatly. Since these items have no set market price, when a price is guaranteed this is not a clear benefit. This is therefore permitted.[17]

Exception C: Items Which Are Available at a Set Price

10. The third exception applies when there is a stable supply of the merchandise at a set market price. When this merchandise is sold, a seller is permitted to guarantee the market price, even if delivery will be made at a time when the price tends to be higher.[18]

An example of this involves the sale of fruits and vegetables. During the summer season, produce which is grown locally is abundantly available at stable prices. If a customer pays for winter delivery, the seller may guarantee the price at the summer rate (even though produce prices tend to rise during the winter). This is permitted even if the seller does not actually have produce in stock at the time payment is made.

In the contemporary marketplace, most products (with the exception of seasonal items) are readily available all year long, but their prices vary from merchant to merchant. Over time, though, these prices remain steady within a given range. Most poskim hold that this is considered an item which has a set market price, despite the disparity in price between merchants. A seller may therefore guarantee a price on these items.[19]

---

17. In this case, the seller is even permitted to offer a discounted price (*Rema* 173:7, *Chochmas Adam* 139:14, *Bris Yehudah* 23:3; this has been explained in the previous chapter, Note 20). See Paragraph 23, below, for additional details.

18. Y.D. 175:1.

The Talmud (B.M. 63b) explains that when a product is readily available, the customer does not really gain from the deal, since he could easily purchase the product himself and hold it for future use. By doing this, he would purchase the product at the current price. Thus, when the seller guarantees the price for future delivery, he is giving the customer something which he is capable of easily acquiring on his own. In the words of the Talmud, the customer could tell the seller, "Take your favor and throw it to the hogs! How have you helped me? If I hold the money in my hand, I could purchase this. . . ." This explanation is quoted by *Taz* 175:1.

Elsewhere, the Talmud (B.M. 72b) offers a different explanation. When an item is readily available, it is as if it was already in the person's possession. This is an extension of *yesh lo*, where a guarantee is permitted because merchandise was in the seller's possession at the time of payment.

Chavos Daas 163:3 and *S.A. Harav* §25 quote both reasons. (See also *Shach* 175:1 who seems to combine the two reasons as one.) *Shaar Deah* and *Mekor Mayim Chaim* (to 175:1) discuss why both reasons are needed. See also Note 21, below.

19. *Mishnas Ribbis* 9:9.

11. This exception applies only under the following conditions:

    a) Advance payment must be made in cash. When previously owed moneys are counted as advance payment, no guarantee may be made.[20] If the seller has other cash on hand, some poskim hold that even previously owed moneys may be used as payment.[21]

---

20. Y.D. 163:1.

This holds true when the moneys are owed due to a previous loan. Regarding debt which results from a previous purchase, the poskim present the following rules:

- When a customer paid for merchandise and did not receive it, and he wishes to accept payment of the debt of that merchandise with a different type of merchandise (for example, if the customer was owed a bushel of apples and he now wishes to transfer this debt so that he is owed a crate of oranges with the same value), this is permitted. He may be guaranteed the new merchandise at the present price, if it has a set market price (Y.D. 175:6).

- In this case, if the customer had set a dollar value for the merchandise he is owed, *Rema* (175:6) holds that it is considered a debt of money, and new merchandise may not be guaranteed at the present price (unless one of the other exceptions applies). *Chavos Daas* (175:2) adds that if the seller (rather than the customer) had set a dollar value for the merchandise, *Rema* would concede that this would not effect the halachah and a price may be guaranteed for different merchandise. Cf. *Machneh Ephraim* §28 and *Pischei Teshuvah* 175:2 who question the Rema's ruling.

- Once the seller's obligation is formally established as a financial obligation (for example, if it is billed as a debt of money), all would agree that this constitutes a debt which cannot be transferred onto merchandise for a guaranteed price (*Nemukei Yosef* quoted by *Beis Yosef*, see also *Bris Yehudah* 24:18).

21. *Taz* 163:4 permits this. We have seen (in the previous note) that this leniency applies only when the merchandise could easily have been purchased at the same time that payment was made. It is for this reason that we require that cash be used as payment. Where the seller had cash in hand, he could easily have purchased the merchandise even if the customer did not use cash as payment. He is therefore permitted to guarantee the price for future delivery.

Many poskim dispute this leniency (*Shach* 163:1 based on *Beis Yosef*, *Darkei Moshe*, and *Bach*; *Gra* 163:1, this also appears to be the ruling of *Chavos Daas* 163:3; cf. *Chasam Sofer* C.M. 170 who accepts the ruling of *Taz*). *Chavos Daas* maintains that this dispute is dependent on a dispute between Rishonim.

It is preferable that one follow the opinion of *Shach* and *Gra* who prohibit this.

[It appears that this dispute is linked to the two explanations which were quoted above, in Note 18.

The first explanation (quoted from B.M. 63b) held that the price may be guaranteed because the customer does not really have a gain, since he could have purchased the merchandise at the market value. According to this view, this leniency is based on the *customer's* ability to obtain the merchandise. The fact that the seller has cash on hand does not help the customer. This is therefore prohibited. This explains the opinion of *Shach* and *Gra*.

The second explanation (quoted from B.M. 72b) held that the price may be guaranteed because the seller could easily obtain the merchandise. This is therefore considered *yesh*

b) Some poskim require that the advance payment be for the full purchase price.[22]

c) The buyer may not stipulate that specific merchandise be delivered, unless that merchandise is available at the time of payment. For example, the customer might wish to stipulate that only the actual produce which will grow in the seller's field is to be used for delivery. This guarantee may not be made, even if similar produce is presently available in the marketplace.[23]

d) This leniency applies only to merchandise which would not spoil if it were purchased at the time of payment and held until the time of delivery.[24] If the merchandise would not spoil, but its weight would decrease for natural reasons (e.g., it would dry up over time), adjustments must be made to compensate the seller for this difference.[25]

12. Even when this exception applies, it is preferable not to explicitly state that the price guarantee is linked to the advance payment.[26]

---

lo. According to this view, this leniency is based on *the seller's* ability to obtain the merchandise. When he has cash in hand, this makes the merchandise available. This is therefore permitted. This explains the opinion of *Taz*.

Although this explanation seems to follow logically, this seems difficult in view of the fact that *Taz* (175:1) himself accepts the first explanation, and nevertheless rules leniently here.]

22. *Panim Me'iros* 2:8. This is also the simple translation of Y.D. 175:1. *Shaar Deah* 175:1 disagrees and maintains that full payment is not required.

Avnei Nezer Y.D. 214 rules that one may rely on the opinion of *Shaar Deah* whenever the merchant has sufficient cash of his own to make the purchase. When he does not have his own cash, full payment is required.

23. *Maharsham* 5:51, *Bris Yehudah* 24:10. This is because this exception applies only when the merchandise which is being paid for could have actually been bought at the time of payment.

24. *Bris Yehudah* 24:n43. Prices may be guaranteed because the merchandise could easily be purchased at today's price and held for future delivery. If the merchandise could not be held until the delivery date, this leniency does not apply.

25. Y.D. 175:5. Since the advance payment is viewed as a loan, the seller is prohibited from benefiting the buyer by absorbing a loss which the buyer would have incurred if he had accepted delivery at the time of payment. If the customer had purchased the produce on the open market, the produce would have decreased in weight by the date of delivery. It is therefore prohibited to deliver the greater amount of the product at the time of delivery.

26. *Bris Yehudah* 24:n6, based on the sources cited above in Note 16. Others add another condition; that the seller be entitled to deliver the merchandise at any time until the stipulated delivery date (see *Toras Ribbis* 10:23 and *Mishnas Ribbis* 9:16).

After the Agreement: If the Market Price Falls

13. Where this exception applies, the seller is permitted to guarantee a price for future delivery. If the price increases, the customer will have gained by receiving merchandise at the lower price.

If the price were to fall, the seller would still deliver the merchandise at the guaranteed price. In this case, the customer will have lost by entering into this agreement, since he will be paying more than the market price for the merchandise which he receives. The seller would be prohibited from delivering the merchandise at the lower current price.[27]

The customer may protect himself from this possibility, in the following manner. At the time of the original agreement (before payment), he may stipulate that the merchandise is to be delivered at whichever price is lower, the guaranteed price or the actual price at the time of delivery. When this is part of the original agreement, delivery may be made at the lower price.[28]

14. This rule applies in cases where the agreement called for delivery of a specific type of merchandise, but did not specify the actual piece of merchandise which is to be delivered.[29]

If the sale calls for the future delivery of specific merchandise which is in the seller's possession (for example, if a barrel of wine, which is aging in the seller's possession, is sold), this agreement restricts the seller from dealing with that merchandise. This is similar to an immediate sale, and the buyer must accept some degree of liability for this merchandise. If the market value of the merchandise fell after payment, the seller could not guarantee to honor the lower price, unless the buyer accepts some form of liability for the merchandise.

For example, if the buyer agrees to accept liability if the merchandise were to become ruined in the interim, he could be guaranteed that if the price falls, the sale would be based on the lower price. If the seller guarantees that the merchandise will not be ruined in the interim, the buyer would honor the sale price even if the value of the merchandise went down in the interim.[30]

---

27. Y.D. 175:7. The seller has received advance funds from the customer and he is therefore prohibited from benefiting the customer in any way.

28. Y.D. 175:7.

29. Even when a sale is based on *yesh lo*, the seller must have the item in possession at the time he accepts payment, but is permitted to subsequently sell that item.

30. Y.D. 173:13 as explained by *S.A. Harav* §34; *Bris Yehudah* 24:26. This follows the explanation of *Tosafos* (quoted by *Taz* 173:17 and 175:9; cf. *Shach* 24 who explains this

Delivery Charges

15. When a seller uses the leniency of 'exception c' (the item is readily available at a set price), he is prohibited from benefiting the customer in any way. Therefore, he may not absorb an expense which the customer usually pays for.[31] For example, if the customer would normally pay delivery charges, the seller may not pay these charges himself.

If the Customer Receives Cash

16. When one of these exceptions is used to guarantee a price for future delivery, it may turn out that the market value of the merchandise at the time of the scheduled delivery is more than the original payment. For example, if the customer paid $100 for a hundred pounds of produce, the produce may actually be worth $110 at the time of delivery.

In this case, some poskim hold that the customer may later accept cash in place of delivery of the merchandise. In this example, the customer will receive $110 for the merchandise which he is owed. Other poskim prohibit this.[32]

One may rely on the lenient opinion in cases where the merchant actually has the merchandise in his possession at the time that he is paying the customer.[33]

---

differently. *Chavos Daas* 173:18 notes that *Shach* is actually explaining an opinion which he himself may not accept as halachah).

31. Y.D. 173:5. This is because the seller accepted money from the customer, and is considered his borrower. This holds true whenever this exception ('exception c') applies.

However, in cases of *yesh lo* ('exception a'), the merchant is permitted to stipulate that he will absorb these expenses. The reason for this is that the merchant is even permitted to offer an outright discount when he has the merchandise in stock (*Bris Yehudah* 24:n41).

32. Y.D. 175:6 brings both opinions, and appears to favor the more stringent opinion. This is also the ruling of *S.A. Harav* §28, who explains that since the customer gave $100 and received $110 in return, this appears to be Ribbis (*mechzei keRibbis*) and is prohibited.

Gra 175:8 and *Shaar Deah* 175:2 accept the lenient opinion. According to this view, there is no difference if payment is made in cash or merchandise, since the customer is receiving the same value either way.

33. *Pnei Yehoshua* (B.M. 63a), quoted in *Bris Yehudah* 24:22.

Bris Yehudah (in Note 63) also quotes *Gedulei Terumah* 5:4 and *Beis David* 91 who rule that if one wishes to rely on the lenient opinion, he may do so in any case. [However, if the customer wishes to follow the stringent opinion, the merchant cannot compel him to accept the cash payment.]

17. Those poskim who allow the customer to receive cash permit this only if the original agreement called for the delivery of merchandise. However, if the original agreement called for the customer to receive the cash value of the merchandise, this agreement may not be honored.[34]

18. Those poskim who prohibit the customer from receiving cash nevertheless permit the payment to be made in any form of merchandise, even if this is not the merchandise which was originally ordered.[35]

Applications

19. Foreign Currency Trading: Each country has its own legal currency. Any foreign currency is considered a form of merchandise, to which the laws of purchase (as outlined in this chapter) apply. It is therefore prohibited to make advance payment as part of a deal which guarantees future delivery of a foreign currency at a given rate.

We have seen that when a product is readily available at a set market price, these prohibitions do not apply ('exception c'). Does this exception apply to foreign currencies?

It is clear that this exception does not apply. Although currencies are readily available, their exchange rates are constantly changing. Thus, no currency can be said to have a set value in relation to a second currency. These prohibitions therefore apply.[36]

---

34. *Bris Yehudah* 24:23 based on Rishonim. If the original agreement stipulated that the customer would receive either the merchandise or its cash value, this is permitted (according to the lenient opinion in Paragraph 16).

35. Y.D. 175:6. The value of the merchandise which is delivered must be equal to the present value (i.e., value at the time of payment) of the merchandise which was ordered.

It is not clear if this would be permitted in cases where this was part of the original agreement (i.e., where this called for delivery to be valued according to one form of merchandise, but actually delivered in the second form of merchandise). This depends on the two explanations offered by *Perishah* 175:27.

36. Many banks and financial institutions will set currency exchange rates in the morning for that entire business day. *Shevet HaLevi* 3:109 argues that this constitutes a set price. According to this view, the prohibition on guaranteeing a price for future delivery does not apply.

Others dispute this leniency. Rabbi Y.S. Eliyashev Shlita (quoted in *Ateres Yaakov* Y.D. 17 and *Mishnas Ribbis* 6:n12) rules that rates which constantly fluctuate from day to day are not considered set rates. *Kitzur Dinei Ribbis* 4:5 adds that even bank rates are only available for a number of hours and are therefore not even considered set rates for an entire day. One should follow this opinion.

If the seller actually has the foreign currency in his possession, the leniency of *yesh lo* ('exception a') would apply and any business deal which involves that amount of currency would be permitted.[37]

20. This is not limited to professional currency trades. This also applies when an individual loans money and requests payment in a foreign currency.

For example, a person in the United States lends someone ten American dollars at a time when they are worth twelve Canadian dollars. The lender is prohibited from stipulating that the borrower pay him back twelve Canadian dollars at a future time. If payment is made in Canadian dollars, the exchange rate which exists at the time of payment must be honored. The borrower is therefore only permitted to pay Canadian dollars which have a value of ten American dollars at the time of payment.[38]

Commodity Trading

21. The price of precious metals and other commodities on the world markets is constantly changing. It is therefore prohibited to guarantee future delivery at a given rate when advance payment is required.[39]

---

37. The trader may make numerous deals, providing that he has enough currency in hand for *any one* deal. He does not have to possess enough currency for all of the deals which he is making (Y.D. 175:4).

If the seller does not actually possess the currency, but others owe it to him, this would be subject to the dispute recorded above, Note 10.

38. *Bris Yehudah* 18:5.

If the loan takes place in the United States (using American dollars), and payment is made when the borrower and lender are in Canada (using Canadian dollars), it is not clear if this restriction would apply. See *Bris Yehudah* 18:n15, who expresses doubt regarding this case.

[In most situations there is no clear stipulation (at the time of the loan) that Canadian currency will be used when the debt is paid. In this case, if the rate has only changed slightly, one may be lenient and make payment in Canadian dollars, at the old rate. In this case, one may take into account the opinion of *Taz* 160:2 who holds that a slight overpayment is permitted if it is given without mentioning the fact that an over-payment has occurred. In addition, see *Minchas Yitzchak* 9:88 regarding a borrower who does not have exact change at the time he pays his loan. He rules that when there is a slight overpayment, for an amount that neither the borrower nor lender would consider significant (in that they would not search for it, if it had been lost), this is not prohibited. This ruling can be applied here as well.]

39. Here too, if the trader has the commodity in his possession at the time of payment (*yesh lo*), it is permitted.

22. This type of trading is permitted when a Heter Iska is used. An appropriate Heter Iska form appears at the end of this chapter.

Custom Furniture or Clothing

23. When ordering custom-made furniture or clothing, the seller may demand advance payment in exchange for a guarantee on his price. This is permitted because custom-made items have no set market price ('exception b,' above).

The bill for custom-made items often includes a separate charge for raw materials (such as the lumber or cloth being used). When advance payment is required, the price of these items may not be guaranteed. The charge for these items must be based on their value at the time of delivery.[40]

In practice, this restriction makes billing cumbersome, since different standards apply to different parts of the bill. The manufacturer can avoid this problem by taking possession of the raw materials before taking payment. Since the raw materials are in stock on the payment date, its price may be guaranteed, because this is considered *yesh lo* ('exception a,' above).[41]

Subscriptions

24. Newspaper and Magazine Subscriptions:[42] It is common for publishers of periodicals to offer long-term subscriptions at reduced rates. Subscribers pay in advance and are protected from rate increases during their subscription period. This advance payment presents a problem, since the reduced rate and the protection against rate increases are benefits which the customer receives because he advanced payment. Therefore, when a periodical is owned by Jews one may only subscribe under the conditions detailed in the note below.[43]

---

40. *Bris Yehudah* 24:n18. 'Exception b,' which allows a guarantee for custom-made items, does not apply to the raw materials. Still, where these materials are readily available at set market prices, it would be permitted to guarantee the price of the raw material (under 'exception c').

41. Although the material must be suitable for this customer, the manufacturer does not actually have to use it for him (based on the sources cited in Note 13).

42. This discussion applies only where the newspaper and magazine companies are owned by Jews. The laws of Ribbis do not apply when business is transacted with a non-Jew.

43. The issue of prepaid subscriptions is discussed in *Lehoros Nosson* 6:74, *Avnei Yashpei* Y.D. 158, *Toras Ribbis* 10:22BH, *Kitzur Dinei Ribbis* 5:2 and *Ribbis LeOhr*

According to some poskim, if a periodical is published by a corporation these benefits are permitted.[44]

25. Book subscriptions: Reduced-rate subscriptions are often offered by individuals who plan to publish a series of books. *Minchas Yitzchak* discusses the planned publication of a set of the Talmud. He maintains that someone who pays, in advance, for a complete set is actually taking a risk, since it is possible that the publisher's plans will

---

HaHalachah 17:10. All these contemporary poskim prohibit the offering of reduced payments and/or guaranteed prices when advance payment is required.

Bris Yehudah 23:7 also prohibits this, but he offers the following qualification. These prohibitions apply when a publisher is motivated by his need for advance funding. If a publisher is motivated by other considerations, this would be permitted. For example, a publisher may offer discounted subscription rates because this makes his publication more attractive to advertisers; because this guarantees him a certain number of sales; or because this keeps his billing costs down. When these are the sole motivations for the discount, subscriptions may be offered at a reduced rate. Still, the offering may not explicitly state that the discount is made for advance funding ('pay in advance and save 20%').

Mishnas Ribbis 9:n37 maintains that *Bris Yehudah's* ruling is acceptable only for allowing subscription discounts. If the price of the periodical increases during the subscription period, the subscribers could not be indemnified from the increase. In this case, a new subscriber who joins after the price increase is charged a higher price than the person who subscribed earlier. All of the outside motivations listed by *Bris Yehudah* apply to both subscribers. The only reason that those who subscribed earlier are protected from the increase is because they advanced funds at an earlier time. This benefit is prohibited.

A practical solution to this problem: The reason that subscription discounts present a Ribbis problem is because the publisher receives money in advance (this is considered a loan) in exchange for the benefits which he offers. This prohibition does not apply if a publisher offers discount subscriptions, but keeps the payments in escrow. Later, as each issue is published, the publisher could withdraw the appropriate charge. Since the publisher cannot use the prepayments, there is no Ribbis problem. (The publisher would be prohibited from earning interest on the money while it is held in escrow.)

This means that publishers can avoid Ribbis problems, according to all opinions, by using the following option. The publisher, in its offering, should offer customers the choice of paying in advance or having their payment placed in escrow. Since the customer receives the same deal whether payment is made to escrow or not, there is no additional benefit for advance payment. Thus, even if the customer elects to allow the publisher to use the money, this would be permitted.

Lehoros Nosson and *Toras Ribbis* recommend that a Heter Iska Klali be used when offering a subscription discount.

44. This is based on *Igros Moshe* 2:63, who rules that corporations may pay Ribbis. Although many poskim disagree (see Chapter 5, Paragraph 27), one may rely on the lenient opinion here, since the prohibition is itself a matter of dispute. Still, wherever possible one should try to satisfy all opinions, as outlined in the previous note.

not come to fruition. If this happens, the subscriber will have lost his investment. It is therefore permitted to offer reduced-rate subscriptions in this case.[45]

Trading Merchandise

26. According to many poskim, the restrictions which are outlined in this chapter are not limited to cases where cash is used for advance payment. When merchandise is traded, these restrictions are also in force.

This applies where someone delivers merchandise with the agreement that the payment will be made with other merchandise, at a later date. In this case, the value of the goods which are used as payment may not be set in advance. The amount of merchandise which is used for payment must be based on their value at that time.[46]

For example, a supplier and a manufacturer agree to a trade. The supplier will deliver $1000 worth of raw material on January 1st, with the stipulation that the manufacturer repay him by delivering $1000 worth of the final product on July 1st. This is permitted, provided that the final product is worth $1000 at the time of delivery. The manufacturer is not permitted to guarantee delivery of a specific

---

45. *Minchas Yitzchak* 4:99:4. This is based on Y.D. 175:9, where it is permitted to receive benefits for advance payment when there is a level of risk to the person who advances these funds. The possibility that a loss may be incurred must be real, not just theoretical. Where a major investment is required for the publication to be completed, the risk is especially real.

Bris Yehudah 24:n18 maintains that this ruling applies only where the subscriber agrees to accept a loss if the series is not completed. If he would be entitled to a refund, he is not taking a risk and this leniency does not apply.

Often, the subscription agreement entitles the subscriber to a refund if the books are not all published. Still, the subscriber realizes that if the project fails, it is unlikely that he will be repaid. *Bris Yehudah* maintains that in this case, the subscriber is not technically taking a risk, since the agreement calls for his money to be refunded. If the refund did not materialize, this is due to a subsequent act of thievery and is not part of the agreement. He therefore prohibits entering into this agreement. [Where there is an obvious possibility that the project will default, it seems that there is a clear risk in purchasing an advance subscription. In this case, one could cogently argue that this should be permitted. Still, *Bris Yehudah* seems to prohibit in any case where the agreement entitles subscribers to reimbursement if the project is not completed.]

46. *Chazon Ish* 72:5, *Bris Yehudah* 22:17. Cf. *Chavos Daas* 162:1, who permits this in cases where the value of the two items which are being traded are usually consistent with each other and it is unusual for the price of one to increase unless the other increases as well. See also *Bris Yehudah* 16:n18.

amount of the final product, since the product may turn out to be worth more than $1000 at the time of payment.

Payment in Foreign Currency

27. We have seen that foreign currency is a form of merchandise, with a fluctuating value. Therefore, when merchandise is delivered on credit, bills must be calculated in the local currency.[47] Later, at the time of payment, foreign currency may be used, provided that the exchange rate is calculated based on the currency's market value on the day of payment.

28. When payment is made in a foreign country, the bill may be established in that country's currency.[48]

29. A check which is drawn on a foreign bank, in that country's currency, may be used for payment, provided that the check is given at the time of delivery.[49]

If an Agreement Was Already Made

30. If an agreement was already made, where advance payment was given and a price was guaranteed for future delivery, and the parties later realize that this is prohibited, the sale does not automatically become negated. However, the provision of the agreement which is prohibited as Ribbis is not valid. This means that the guaranteed price may not be honored.

If the market price of the merchandise does not increase by the date of delivery, the sale may take place as agreed. However, if the market

---

47. *Bris Yehudah* 22:n33. Billing may not be established in a foreign currency because this is the same as guaranteeing a price for the currency.

For example, $100 worth of merchandise is delivered in the United States, on credit, at a time that this is worth $85 in Canadian currency. If the customer agrees to pay eighty-five Canadian dollars, at the end of thirty days, he is in effect guaranteeing the value of the Canadian dollar for that month. If, at the end of thirty days, $100 in American currency is only worth $84 in Canadian currency, the extra dollar is considered Ribbis and the customer would be prohibited from paying it.

Bris Yehudah adds that if the customer has this foreign currency in his possession at the time that he receives the merchandise, he may guarantee payment in that currency. (This is because of the exception of *yesh lo.*)

48. *Mishnas Ribbis* ibid.

49. *Mishnas Ribbis* ibid. If payment is mailed, but not yet received at the time of delivery, it is not clear if the check may be drawn on a foreign bank.

price does increase, the seller may not deliver the merchandise at the lower price. The customer would have the option of either paying full price for the merchandise or canceling the order entirely.[50]

In Conclusion

31. The laws outlined in the previous three chapters have one point in common. A routine purchase agreement provides for payment at the time of delivery. When payment is made in advance (as in this chapter and Chapter 7) or when credit is extended to allow for late payment (as in Chapter 6), these are seen as forms of loan. In both cases, payment may not be adjusted to benefit the person who extends cash (or credit) in advance.

Unfortunately, most businessmen (and most customers) are unaware of these prohibitions. Although people are cognizant of the laws of Ribbis when a loan is involved, this awareness is lacking in situations which involve purchases. In his day, *Chavos Daas* bemoaned this lack of awareness, and wrote: "Due to our many sins, most of the world is not careful regarding this...."[51]

In his last will, Rabbi Yaakov of Lisa, the author of *Chavos Daas*, instructed his children that if any of them become businessmen, they should constantly review these laws. All businessmen would do well to heed this advice.

Appendix to Chapter Eight: Heter Iska for Commodity Trading

The following Heter Iska is suitable for use when trading commodities. This form may be used by a businessman who wishes to guarantee delivery of a specific commodity at a future time, for a specific price. In exchange for this guarantee, he requires that the customer make

---

50. Y.D. 175:8 rules that whenever an agreement contains a Ribbis provision, that provision must be canceled. In this case, it is the price guarantee which is considered Ribbis. This must therefore be ignored and the price of the merchandise must be based on its value at the time of delivery.

If the price goes up in the interim, the customer would have to pay more. The customer could argue that he had never agreed to purchase the merchandise for that price. If he does not wish to pay the actual market price, he has the option of canceling the sale. His money would then be refunded (C.M. 208:1).

51. *Chavos Daas* in *Chidushim* 163:2.

payment in advance. This is generally prohibited. Where the following Heter Iska is used, this would be permitted.

Iska Contract

I, the undersigned, acknowledge receipt of the sum of $ _____ from _____ (hereafter referred to as the "Investor"), to be used for business investment purposes. I obligate myself to utilize these funds in investments which I believe will generate profits. Any profits realized or losses sustained shall be shared equally between the investor and myself.

Any claim of loss must be verified through the testimony of two qualified witnesses in, and under conditions acceptable to, an Orthodox Jewish court of law. Any claim regarding the amount of profit generated by these investment(s) shall be verified under solemn oath, before and under conditions acceptable to, an Orthodox Jewish court of law.

It is agreed that if I deliver _____ (enter type and amount of commodity) to the investor, as payment of both the investment and the profits which are generated, then I will not be required to make any further payment nor will I be required to make an oath.

I have received one dollar from the investor as payment for my services during the term of our partnership.[1]

This agreement shall follow the guidelines of Heter Iska as explained in *Sefer Bris Yehudah* and has been executed in a manner which effects a legal transfer and obligation, known as *kinyan sudar*.

Signature of the Recipient _____

Dated _____

Witnesses[2]

In witness whereof the above mentioned parties have entered into this Heter Iska agreement on this _____ day of _____ .

Signature of Witness _____

Signature of Witness _____

---

1. The purchaser should pay one dollar to the trader, in addition to the moneys which are invested for the commodities. The reason that this payment is necessary is explained below, Chapter 22, Paragraph 29.

2. This part of the contract is optional, depending on whether the parties prefer to have witnesses attest to their agreement.

Penalty Clauses

Introduction

The Biblical prohibition against paying Ribbis applies only when the lender charges interest for a loan or for postponing the payment date. We have already seen that any form of gift which is given in gratitude for a loan is prohibited as Ribbis DeRabbanan.

The following chapter deals with penalty clauses. A person who offers a loan is concerned that he be repaid on time. In an effort to compel the borrower to pay on time, the lender may wish to add a stipulation that if payment is not made by the due date, the borrower must pay a late fee. In this case, there is no intent to collect Ribbis, because the extra payment is not being made to procure a loan or an extension of the payment date.

Although these are payments which pass from borrower to lender, they are not interest payments, nor are they gratuities which are given in appreciation of the loan. Thus, these payments do not fall into the category of the regular Ribbis prohibitions. Still, because of its similarity to Ribbis, it is prohibited under a category of Ribbis, known as *haaramas Ribbis*.[1] The parameters of this prohibition, and significant exceptions to it, are explained below.

Prohibited Clauses

1. A borrower may not guarantee that he will pay a loan on time by agreeing to pay a fee for late payment. In some cases, this stipulation

---

1. Lit., *trick Ribbis*, i.e., a roundabout way of collecting Ribbis.

This prohibition is based on *Teshuvos HaRashba* 1:651 (1:221, in earlier prints). It should be noted that many Rishonim reject this prohibition and permit penalty clauses which call for a one-time late penalty. *Ginas Viradim* (6:1) suggests that even *Rashba* would agree, in principle, that this is permitted. *Rashba* prohibited this only because of his concern that the parties would deliberately set up a penalty clause as a way of evading the Ribbis prohibition, thereby allowing the borrower to make an additional payment to the lender. This is prohibited as *haaramas Ribbis*, a trick way of paying Ribbis. According to *Ginas Viradim*, if their intent was truly to ensure that payment is made on time, even *Rashba* would permit the penalty clause.

As a matter of halachah, penalty clauses are prohibited in all loan agreements, regardless of the intent of the parties involved. Still, this falls under the category of *haaramas Ribbis*, which is the most lenient form of Ribbis DeRabbanan. (This is the reason for some of the leniencies outlined below; see, for example, Paragraphs 2 and 3.)

[Regarding precise guidelines for determining which cases fall under the broader category of *haaramas Ribbis*, see *Bris Yehudah* 8:n3, that this category applies only to cases mentioned in the Gemara or in the earlier poskim.]

is prohibited by Rabbinic law.[2] However, where the agreement requires the borrower to make constant payments (e.g., weekly or monthly) for the period after the loan was to be repaid, it constitutes true Ribbis and is prohibited by Biblical law according to most poskim.[3]

One-Time Penalties

2. Although penalty clauses which call for a one-time late payment are prohibited, once it had already been agreed upon, many poskim hold that the penalty must be paid, and that it can be enforced in Beis Din.[4] This is an exception to the general rule of Ribbis that a clause calling for a Ribbis payment is null and void.[5]

3. After a one-time late payment has already been made, the lender has no obligation to return the payment. This is an exception to the general rule of Ribbis DeRabbanan, that a lender has a moral obligation ('latzeis yidei shamayim') to return Ribbis.[6]

4. A lender may not include a penalty clause as a way of compelling the borrower to make prompt payment, even if he has no intention

---

2. Y.D. 177:14. This is prohibited as *haaramas Ribbis*, which is the most lenient form of Ribbis. This is prohibited whenever the agreement calls for an additional payment to be made if the loan is not repaid on time. It does not matter if this is explicitly referred to as a penalty clause or not (*Bris Yehudah* 4:4, based on *Teshuvos HaRashba*).

If the original agreement did not call for a penalty fee, and the borrower wishes to voluntarily add a penalty payment because he is late, this is considered *Ribbis Me'ucheres* and is prohibited (*Bris Yehudah* 4:n5).

3. Y.D. 177:16 and *Shach* 33; see also Note 10. Some poskim consider this Rabbinically prohibited Ribbis; nevertheless they concede that it is more stringent than *haaramas Ribbis*.

Pischei Teshuvah 177:4 cites poskim who permit this clause to be written into loans which are made on behalf of orphans. This is based on the rule (*Rema* 160:18) that Rabbinically prohibited Ribbis may be collected by charities or the estate of young orphans (this was discussed at length in Chapter 5).

4. Y.D. 163:3, regarding another form of *haaramas Ribbis*. The language of the *Shulchan Aruch* implies that the same rule applies to all types of *haaramas Ribbis*. *Remah* cites a dissenting opinion, but the dissent is based on arguments which are unique to the particular case under discussion there. All would agree that penalty clauses, as well as other types of *haaramas Ribbis*, are enforceable (*Knessess Hagedolah* to *Tur* 163:11, *Chochmas Adam* 133:1 and 134:14, *Bris Yehudah* 8:1; cf. *Rivash* quoted in *Knessess Hagedolah* and *Divrei Sofrim* to 163:3).

5. Y.D. 161:11.

6. See Y.D. 177:14. This applies to one-time penalties which are imposed when a loan is not repaid on time. It does not apply to penalties which continue to accrue every week or month.

of actually collecting the late fee. Although he will never collect the fee, this is prohibited because many poskim maintain that entering into an agreement which calls for Ribbis is prohibited, even if it is never enforced.[7]

Permitted Penalty Clauses

5. Loans: A penalty clause may be added to a loan agreement only if it is drawn in the following manner:

☐ In the case of a cash loan, the agreement may call for a late penalty, requiring the borrower to pay the loan with merchandise [or services] which is worth more than the original loan. For example, a $100 loan was made. The agreement may stipulate that if payment is not made by a specific date, the borrower will be required to repay the loan by giving the lender $110 worth of produce.[8]

☐ This is permitted only if the merchandise is not given at the time of the loan. Therefore merchandise which was given as collateral (*mashkon*) for repayment may not be used to satisfy this condition.[9]

☐ The late fee must be a one-time payment. There may not be a requirement that the borrower pay an additional amount of merchandise if payment is delayed further.[10]

---

7. This is based on the verse, *And you shall not place neshech on him* (Ex. 22:24), which is understood by many poskim to prohibit the setting of Ribbis, regardless of whether it is ultimately paid (*Bach*, quoted by *Shaar Deah* 159:1 and 177:11, *Maharsham* 4:138 s.v. *u'ma sheshaal*, *Imrei Yosher* 1:149:3, *Igros Moshe* Y.D. 2:65). See Chapter 2, Note 17 where this was discussed at length.

8. *Rema* 177:14. *Bris Yehudah* (4:n24) explains that this is similar to a purchase agreement, where this type of arrangement is permitted (see Y.D. 163:3). For this reason, both the principal and penalty must be paid in the form of merchandise.

   Shach 30 maintains that the *Shulchan Aruch* would agree with this leniency. *Tiferes LeMoshe* and *Shaar Deah* disagree.

   As a matter of halachah, most poskim accept this leniency (*Gra* 177:36, *Kuntres HaSma* §21, *Chochmas Adam* 132:13, *S.A. Harav* §47, *Bris Yehudah* 4:8). *Sma* adds, "Although one could argue that this is permitted only if this (agreement) already happened, but that one should not lend in this manner in the first place, because he knows that repayment will not take place within thirty days, and that (the borrower) will have to pay with merchandise and he will have a profit; still it seems to me that even this is permitted, since it is formulated as a penalty."

9. Y.D. 177:17, *Chavos Daas* 177:16, *S.A. Harav* § 47. See Paragraphs 16-17 below.

10. This constitutes a more stringent form of Ribbis, as explained in Note 2. However, once the due date passes and the borrower is obligated to pay the penalty, the lender

□ Payment of the penalty may not entitle the borrower to a grace period for payment. The loan must remain due at the originally agreed time.[11]

6. When a purchase agreement calls for payments to be made in installments, a separate late fee may be charged for each installment. A lease agreement may therefore call for an additional late fee for each month's rent.[12]

7. Credit for purchases: Penalty clauses are prohibited because of their similarity to interest payments. However, this similarity exists only in cases involving loans, where the borrower receives cash and then pays a greater amount of cash because of the added late fee. Where credit is extended as part of a business transaction, a penalty clause may be used,[13] subject to the conditions outlined below in Paragraph 8.

This applies in either of the following two cases: 1) Where cash is paid in advance, with delivery of merchandise slated for a later time. A penalty clause may obligate the seller to deliver additional merchandise if delivery is delayed. 2) Where merchandise is given in advance, with cash payment due at a later time.[14] It is permitted to add a penalty if payment is not received on time.[15]

8. This is permitted only under the following guidelines:

□ The late fee must be a one-time payment. There may not be a requirement that the purchaser continue paying additional fees

---

may once again extend the due date and the borrower may then obligate himself to pay an additional penalty if he does not pay by that time. [However, this second penalty may not be part of the original agreement (*Divrei Sofrim* 177:94).]

11. *Bach*, quoted in *Shach* 177:32, *Chochmas Adam* 132:13, "...this would be true Ribbis, (for it is) payment for a delay." This is actually the subject of a dispute among the poskim. *Chavos Daas* 177:18 understands the *Shach* to be disputing this ruling. *Taz* 177:23, too, disagrees with the ruling of the *Bach*. Still, most poskim rule stringently (see *Be'er Heitev, S.A. Harav* §46, *Atzei Levonah* and *Shaar Deah* 177:10 who maintain that there is no dispute between the *Bach* and *Shach*).

This applies only to the due date of the loan. A later date may be set for payment of the additional penalty (*Chochmas Adam* ibid.).

12. *Mishnas Ribbis* 11:n11.

13. Y.D. 177:18 and *Shach* 38.

14. *Bris Yehudah* (4:n24, based on his comparison to the rules in Y.D. 163:3) extends this to a case where merchandise is exchanged for a different type of merchandise.

15. The first case is mentioned in Y.D. 177:18. *Radvaz* (1:493, cited by *Bris Yehudah* 4:7) applies this to the second case as well.

based on the period of time that the debt is outstanding.[16]

☐ Payment of the penalty may not entitle the purchaser to a grace period for payment. The debt must remain due at the time originally agreed upon.[17]

☐ The agreement may call for payment in the form of cash (or a different type of merchandise). If a late fee is charged, the penalty clause may not require the purchaser to return the same type of merchandise he purchased.[18]

☐ Some poskim require that the parties refer to their agreement as a 'sale.' According to this opinion, if the borrower originally requested a loan, he may not subsequently enter into this type of agreement. Although most poskim disagree with this stringency, it is certainly preferable that the parties satisfy both opinions by referring to their dealing as a sale arrangement.[19]

9. Lease agreements: A lease may call for a penalty if rental payments are not made on time. The conditions which apply to purchase credits apply here as well.[20]

10. When the purchase agreement calls for payments to be made in installments, a separate late fee may be charged for each installment. A lease agreement may therefore call for an additional late fee for each month's rent.[21]

Setting up a Penalty Clause

11. Asmachta: Agreements are binding only when they are entered into with the full consent of both parties. They are not binding when one party accepts an obligation to pay but believes it is within his

---

16. Late fees are permitted in business dealings only because they are a lenient form of Ribbis. This holds true whenever the fees are only prohibited (in regard to true loans) as *haaramas Ribbis*. When a late fee is structured to increase with time, this is a form of true Ribbis, and is not permitted (see Note 2).

17. *Chochmas Adam* 132:13. (See Note 11, above.)

18. In this case, the transaction takes on the form of a loan rather than a sale. The entire basis of this leniency then falls away. (See *Chavos Daas* 167:1, that the penalty clause may not serve to dissolve the sale.)

19. *Taz* 167:1 and 177:22 rules stringently. *Nekudos HaKesef* (to 167:1) disagrees.

20. *Mishnas Ribbis* 11:8.

21. *Mishnas Ribbis* 11:n11 and 20:5. This is not considered a penalty which increases with time (which would be prohibited — see Paragraph 8), but rather separate penalties for separate payments.

NO. **R75682**

PLEASE REFER TO
THIS NUMBER ON ALL
CORRESPONDENCE

PAID ($24.54) BY CHARGE: VISA # 4356024108085491 11/99
060999 005

NET INVOICE	SALES TAX	SHIPPING	PAY THIS AMOUNT ➡	TOTAL INVOICE
21.59	0.00	2.95		$24.54

Mesorah Publications ltd

Publishers of the ArtScroll Series®

4401 SECOND AVENUE / BROOKLYN, NEW YORK 11232 / (718) 921-9000 / FAX: (718) 680-1875

SOLD TO:

DR MYRON GRAFF
5522 GULF DRIVE
NEW PORT RCHY, FL 34652-4022

SHIP TO:

DR MYRON GRAFF
3734 HAYDON COURT
#201
PALM HARBOUR, FL 34685

CUSTOMER ORDER NO.	INVOICE NO.	INVOICE DATE	TERMS	CODE	SHIPPED VIA	CTNS.
79991	R75682	06/09/99	VIA CHARGE CARD	GRAF5522	UPS	

QUANTITY ORDERED	QUANTITY SHIPPED	ISBN 0-89906-	DESCRIPTION	LIST PRICE	DISC.	NET UNIT PRICE	EXTENSION
1	1	LORH	ARTSCROLL SHAVUA SEFER FRI. 6/4/99 - MON. 6/14/99 LAWS OF RIBBIS [R' Reisman] (H/C)	26.99	20%	21.59	21.59

power to avoid ever having to pay. This is known as *asmachta*. A penalty clause is a form of *asmachta*, because the individual may agree to this clause with the expectation that he will make his payments punctually, and never have to pay a late fee.[22]

Penalty clauses are therefore not binding (irrelevant of whether they constitute Ribbis), unless they are set up in a manner which makes them binding. This can be accomplished by entering into the agreement in the presence of a distinguished Beis Din, or if the contract states that the agreement was entered into in their presence (even if it did not actually take place).[23]

An alternative manner of avoiding this problem is to use a standard contract form (such as a lease agreement) which includes a penalty clause. Wherever the penalty clause is a standard for the particular transaction, the clause is binding.[24] (One must avoid contracts which call for late fees that increase with time.[25] Most standard lease forms contain this type of provision, and must be reworded to call for only a one-time late penalty.)

12. A penalty clause is not binding when it was written in a manner which is an *asmachta*. If this happens, may the purchaser honor the clause and pay the penalty anyhow? Or do we say that this voluntary payment is itself a prohibited gratuity which the purchaser is paying his creditor?

There is disagreement among the poskim regarding this issue. Some rule that the borrower may nevertheless voluntarily pay this penalty. According to this view, the problem of *asmachta* has no bearing on the laws of Ribbis, and since the penalty clause was written to satisfy the

---

22. *Rema* C.M. 207:14; see *Sma* 18.

23. *Rema* requires the presence of a *Beis Din Chashuv* (distinguished Beis Din). *S.A. Harav* §46 adds that the actual presence of the Beis Din is not required, as long as the two sides agree that the penalty clause is binding as if made in a *Beis Din Chashuv*. To do this, a contract should state that the obligation was entered into in the presence of a *Beis Din Chashuv*. (In this case, the phrase *'before a Beis Din Chashuv'* is used as a formula rather than as a statement of actual fact.)

A proper *kinyan* must be made at the time of this agreement. This can be accomplished by performing a *kinyan sudar*; a handkerchief (or another utensil or item of clothing) is given to the borrower in exchange for his agreement; after taking possession, the borrower returns it to its original owner.

24. *Chasam Sofer* (C.M. 66) rules that this is a valid *kinyan situmta*; see also *Aruch HaShulchan* (C.M. 201:3) that the rules of *asmachta* do not apply to contracts which are binding by secular law (*Mishnas Ribbis* 11:n11).

25. This type of late fee is always prohibited; see Paragraphs 5 and 6.

laws of Ribbis, it may be paid. Others hold that since there is no obligation to pay the penalty, this is not a penalty payment but an outright gift to the lender, which is prohibited as Ribbis.[26]

13. Oness: Where penalty clauses are permitted, if the purchaser was prepared to make payment, but was prevented from doing so due to circumstances beyond his control (oness), there is a question as to whether he is required to pay the late fee. If no obligation exists, voluntary payment may be prohibited as Ribbis, because it benefits the lender or merchant.

The parties can avoid this problem by stipulating at the time of the agreement, that the borrower is obligated to pay the late fee if payment is withheld due to *oness* circumstances.[27]

Voluntary Payment

14. When a borrower is unable to pay on time, he may wish to compensate the lender even though their agreement does not call for a penalty clause. Although he is prohibited from doing so at the time of payment, he is permitted to send the lender a gift at a later time (*Ribbis Me'ucheres*). However, the gift must be one of minimal value,[28] so that it is not obvious that it is being given in connection with the loan. Additionally, the borrower may not stipulate that the gift is being sent in connection with the loan.[29]

---

26. *Chasam Sofer* (in his essay on *asmachta*, page 82) permits payment as if there were no *asmachta* problem. *Bris Yehudah* 4:n5 cites numerous sources on both sides of this issue, without coming to a clear conclusion. One should therefore refrain from making payment.

27. *Bris Yehudah* (4:n5); see C.M. 207:15. If no such stipulation was made, and an *oness* occurred, the late fee may not be paid (ibid.).

28. This refers to a gift which 'many people routinely send to their friend' (*S.A. Harav* §7).

29. Y.D. 160:6 and *Shach* 8. Most poskim permit this even when the gift is being sent in gratitude for the loan, as long as this is not mentioned explicitly (see Chapter 2, Paragraph 23).

If a long period of time has elapsed since the loan was repaid, the borrower is permitted to send a large gift, provided that the loan is not mentioned in connection with the gift (*Shach* 160:10). *Chochmas Adam* 131:8 defines a longer period of time as 'many days.' It would appear that this depends on the relationship which exists between the borrower and lender. If they have other personal or business dealings, there would be no obvious connection between the gift and the loan even after a brief period of time. However, if they have no other relationship other than this loan, the connection would remain obvious for a very long time (see *Shevet HaLevi* 2:69).

Additional details regarding *Ribbis Me'ucheres* have been outlined in Chapter 2, Paragraphs 22-25.

15. If the borrower's failure to pay on time caused financial damage (not only a loss of profit) to the lender, this may be reimbursed.[30] However, if the lender was in need of funds and borrowed money from a bank, the interest costs which he incurred may not be reimbursed.[31]

Collateral

16. When collateral which is given for the loan is worth more than the loan itself, the borrower may not agree to surrender the collateral if he fails to pay on time. In this case the borrower would be paying more than he borrowed. This is also a form of penalty clause and is prohibited as *haaramas Ribbis*.[32]

17. Collateral may be used for payment, even if it is worth more than the loan, in the following two situations:

  □ **When the condition is added later:** If the collateral was given at the time of the loan, but no stipulation was made at that time, the borrower may later agree to surrender the collateral if payment is not made on time.[33]

---

30. *Bris Yehudah* 9:13, based on *Taz* 170:3. This is not meant to imply that the borrower is *obligated* to do so, only that he is permitted to reimburse the lender.

31. *Taz* 170:3.

32. Y.D. 177:17; *Shach* 35 points out that this contradicts the ruling in *Rema* 177:14 (quoted above, Paragraph 5) which permits penalty clauses when merchandise is used as payment. Here too, the collateral is merchandise which is being used as payment. Why is this prohibited?

Shach (as understood by *S.A. Harav* §47) suggests that there is a difference between merchandise that is given at the time of payment (which is permitted) and collateral that is given at the time of the loan (which is prohibited). When it is given at the time of the loan, it is most similar to Ribbis and is therefore prohibited.

Chavos Daas 177:16 offers a different explanation. (It appears that *Chavos Daas* understands this to be the intent of *Shach*.) If the collateral exists at the time that payment is due, the borrower has the option of selling the collateral and using a portion of the revenue to satisfy the debt. When he does not do this, and he instead chooses to give the collateral to the lender, he is giving him a gift, by giving him an item which is worth more than the loan itself. This is prohibited.

Bris Yehudah (4:n9) cites *S.A. Harav's* explanation, apparently accepting this as halachah (Cf. *Gra* 177:39).

33. *Shach* 177:34, *S.A. Harav* §47. [At the time of the loan, the creditor was only permitted to use the collateral to collect the exact amount owed. It was only later that the borrower decided to pay the loan with the additional value of the collateral.] This leniency applies only when collateral is used for payment. A person may not obligate himself to pay a cash penalty, even if he does so after receiving the loan.

□ **When real estate is used as collateral:** Real estate has no set value, since the price which is paid for real estate varies greatly, depending on the situation. One may therefore agree to surrender this collateral if payment is not made on time.[34]

Gifts

18. A person who obligates himself to give a gift may stipulate that if he is late in delivering the gift he will pay an additional penalty. This is permitted because the obligation to pay a penalty is not connected to a debt obligation. (When no debt is involved, the laws of Ribbis do not apply.) In this case, there is no difference if the penalty clause calls for a one-time penalty or if the penalty increases with time.[35]

---

34. *Shach* 177:35 and *S.A. Harav* ibid., as explained by *Chavos Daas* 177:16 and *Yad Avraham*. The borrower must retain the right to sell the property to someone else if he desires to do so at any time prior to the payment date. He may not guarantee the lender that if he sells the property, it will be to him (*S.A. Harav*, based on *Shulchan Aruch* 177:17).

35. Y.D. 177:15, *Rema* 176:6, in discussing the dowry which a parent promises his children. The parent may stipulate that as long as the dowry remains in his possession, he will add a certain amount to the payment.

The obligation to pay a dowry is binding from the time a contract which includes this obligation (known as a *Tanaim*) is written and formalized by a *kinyan*, even if the marriage has not yet taken place (*Chasam Sofer* E.H. 135; *Maharsham* 2:266 contends that this is not binding until the customary second *Tanaim* contract is written, immediately before the wedding ceremony; cf. *Bris Yehudah* 2:n30 that *Maharsham* later consented to the aforementioned ruling of *Chasam Sofer*). Once this obligation is formalized, a penalty clause may no longer be added (*Taz*, quoted in the note which follows; see also *Avnei Nezer* Y.D. 132).

When settling a claim: *Bris Yehudah* (2:n29) deals with the following situation. Reuven caused damage to Shimon in a manner which makes the cost of the damage difficult to calculate. Since the value of the loss is unclear, they negotiate a settlement. May Reuven obligate himself to pay a certain sum, with the stipulation that if he is late in paying, he will add to the payment?

One could argue that this should be permitted, since Reuven is voluntarily obligating himself to pay. This is therefore similar to a gift. In addition, Reuven could have originally obligated himself to pay the greater amount. He should therefore be permitted to obligate himself to pay that amount under certain conditions. On the other hand, this is not entirely similar to a gift situation, since Reuven certainly owed *something* to Shimon, and he is now obligating himself to pay a penalty in connection with that obligation.

Bris Yehudah does not come to a clear conclusion. However, it is clear that in situations where it is not certain that Shimon owes *anything* to Reuven, the entire payment would have the status of a gift. In this case, it would be permitted to add a penalty clause if payment is delayed.

This is true only when the penalty is part of the original obligation. If someone had already obligated himself to give a gift, he may not later agree to pay an additional penalty if the gift is delivered late. This is because the original agreement created a debt, since it created a commitment to give a gift. A penalty clause may not be attached to a debt obligation.[36]

19. **A will** may contain a provision which penalizes any heir who causes a delay in the execution of the will. For example, if the will grants a gift to a friend, it may also stipulate that if the relatives delay payment of the gift, the friend would receive an additional 10%.[37]

---

36. *Taz* 176:9, in explanation of *Rema*. This would be Ribbis Ketzutzah (*S.A. Harav* §17).

37. *Maharsham* 3:109, *Bris Yehudah* 2:n30.

It should be noted that a will which instructs the children to give a gift to a non-heir may not be enforceable in Beis Din (see R' Akiva Eiger in Responsa 1:68 s.v. *vehinei*). A competent Rav should be consulted for instructions on how to include a gift in a will.

CHAPTER TEN

Wages

The obligation to pay promptly (1-11):

- ☐ The obligation (1)
- ☐ Short-term employment (2-3)
- ☐ Long-term employment (4)
- ☐ Contractors (5)
- ☐ Exceptions (6-11):

Ribbis problems (12-30):

- ☐ When wages are not paid on time (12-13)
- ☐ Negotiating a contract (14)
- ☐ Late penalties (15-16)
- ☐ Advance payment (17-19)
- ☐ Advancing a deposit (20)
- ☐ Exceptions (21)
- ☐ When employment begins (22-23)
- ☐ A contractor (24-27)
- ☐ Labor with no set pay scale (28)
- ☐ Additional leniencies (29-30)
- ☐ Vacation days (31)

Introduction

The rules of Ribbis apply any time a debt is created. In the previous chapters, we have seen that these laws are not limited to debt which results from a loan, but that they apply to situations involving purchases as well. In this chapter, we examine the laws regarding financial obligations which are the result of employment, and how these obligations are affected by the laws of Ribbis.

The Obligation to Pay Promptly

1. An employer is obligated to pay his workers promptly. When he has funds available but refuses to pay his workers on the day that their wages are due, the employer is in violation of numerous Biblical commandments.[1]

An employer is obligated to pay the full wage on the day it comes due. Someone who pays only a part of the wage remains in violation of these commandments.[2]

---

1. The Torah requires that an employee be paid on time, as it states (*Lev.* 19:13), *Do not withhold the wages of your employee overnight.* Elsewhere, we find an additional admonition (*Deut.* 24:15), *On that day pay his wage and do not allow the sun to set on him (without first making payment).*

The Talmud views this transgression with particular severity and teaches that when a man delays payment of wages or fails to pay his employee at all, his own wealth becomes jeopardized (*Succah* 29b).

The *Chofetz Chaim*, writing in *Ahavas Chessed* 1:9, comments: "In our many sins, it is the common practice of many people that their employee knocks on their door day and night (seeking payment) and nobody pays attention; and it is especially so when the worker performed a minor job. People are not aware that the laws of the Torah make no distinction between cases involving a penny and cases involving hundreds of dollars. Many of these (employers) are otherwise straight people of good character who perform other Biblical commandments properly. This particular commandment, of paying wages on time, is weak in their hands. I realize that this comes from a lack of knowledge regarding this law ... therefore, I have taken this to heart, thought about this with the help of G-d Who gives man wisdom, and gathered all the common practical laws, so that (by studying these laws) each person would be more careful in performing them properly."

The *Chofetz Chaim* therefore included a synopsis of these laws in *Ahavas Chessed*, his sefer on the laws of philanthropy. We have followed his example and present a brief synopsis of these laws, drawn primarily from *Ahavas Chessed*.

2. *Ahavas Chessed* 1:9:10. If the employer has only enough funds to make partial payment, he is obligated to do so (ibid.).

Short-Term Employment

2. Where someone is hired to perform a particular job (such as a baby-sitter, repairman or cleaning lady), and the job is completed during the day, payment must be made before sunset. When the job is completed during the night, payment is due before sunrise.

If the work is actually completed at the *very end* of the day, the employer has until the end of the following night to make payment; if completed at the *very end* of the night, he has until the end of the following day.[3]

3. These laws are not limited to cases involving major or meaningful employment. When a person promises payment for a small favor, even if he promises a child a candy for delivering a message, the obligation to pay promptly applies.[4]

Long-Term Employment

4. When someone is paid by the week, month or year (depending on the terms of the agreement), these laws apply on the last day of work, before the wages are due. For example, if an employee's wages are due on the first of the month and he completes work during that day, the employer is obligated to pay him before sunset of that day; if his work is completed during the night, the pay is due before sunrise.[5]

---

3. *Bava Metzia* 110b. The verses quoted in Note 1 appear to contradict one another. One verse requires payment 'overnight,' while the other requires that payment be made before 'the sun set.' The Talmud resolves this by explaining that there is a distinction between when wages are due to a worker who completes his work during the day and one who completes his work at night, as explained above.

4. *Ahavas Chessed* 1:9:n16. All laws of the Torah apply equally in all cases, no matter how much money is involved. In cases of employment too, this applies to situations involving any amount of work. "Even if he hired him to pick a single cluster of grapes. . ." (*Bava Metzia* ibid.).

[When a minor is hired to do a job, there is actually an added stringency to the obligation to pay on time, as follows. An employee is entitled to be paid on time. However, if he chooses, he can forgo this right. This is known as *mechilah*, and this absolves the employer from paying his employee on time.

The option of *mechilah* is limited to adults; only an adult can elect to forgo his right to be paid. A minor lacks full mental maturity and his decision to forgo a right (*mechilah*) is not a valid decision. Thus, even if he tells his employer that he is willing to wait until the next day to receive payment, the employer is still obligated to pay him that day.

If a minor was originally hired with the understanding that he would not be paid that day, the employer is absolved of the obligation to pay immediately.]

5. C.M. 339:5.

Contractors

5. A contractor is someone who is paid by the job and not by the hour.
His wages are due when the job is completed. When an item is given
for repair (for example, when a tailor takes a suit to make alterations, or
a mechanic takes a car for repair), wages are not due until the repaired
article is returned to its owner. Even if the work is completed and the
owner is asked to pick up his article, he does not violate these Biblical
prohibitions by delaying in picking up his repaired item. However, once
he takes possession, the wages are due before sunset of that day (or
before sunrise, if it was picked up during the night). At that point, one
who delays making payment violates these prohibitions.[6]

Exceptions to This Prohibition

6. If the employer does not have money with which to make payment, he is not in violation of these Biblical commandments when
the wages are not paid. However, he is obligated to exert himself to
procure funds for payment. If he has moneys on deposit at a bank or on
loan to an individual, he must withdraw these funds to make payment.[7]

If he has no funds at all, some poskim require the employer to borrow
money so that he can fulfill his Biblical obligation to pay promptly.[7]

7. If the employer has limited funds, and he has to choose between
paying his employee and performing another mitzvah, such as
purchasing food for Shabbos, he should pay the employee. Payment
takes precedence because it fulfills two Biblical commandments (*asei*

---

6. *Ahavas Chessed* 1:10:1. A ramification of this law on the laws of Ribbis appears below,
Paragraph 29.

If the repairman brings the repaired item to the home of its owner and the owner
cannot spare the funds for payment on that day, the owner may refuse to accept it. By
doing this, the owner avoids transgressing the prohibition on delayed payment (*Bi'ur
Halachah* 242:1, s.v. *lechivode*).

Regarding charging for this delay, see Paragraph 29.

7. *Ahavas Chessed* 1:9:7.

Cf. *S.A. Harav*, quoted in *Pischei Teshuvah* (C.M. 339:8), who holds that a righteous
person should take a loan to pay his employees ('*midas chassidus*') but that this is not
obligatory.

If the employer is unable to secure a free loan, it would appear that all agree that he
is not obligated to procure a loan which would require interest payments. This is based
on *Sefer HaChinuch*, quoted by R' Akiva Eiger (to C.M. 339:10), who rules that where
great loss is involved, the obligation to pay on time does not apply. For this reason too,
if an employer would incur a significant penalty for withdrawing a bank deposit so that
he can pay his employee, he would not be obligated to do so.

velo sasei), while *Oneg Shabbos* (enjoying the Shabbos) fulfills only a single commandment.[8]

8. If an employer owes wages to two employees, but only has enough funds to pay one of them, it is preferable that he pay each worker half of what he owes him, rather than to pay one worker his entire wage, while leaving the second worker without pay.[9]

9. This obligation applies only where the employee requests payment.

If an employee does not approach his employer to request payment, the employer may assume that he is willing to forgo prompt payment and he is not obligated to seek him out so that he can make payment.[10] Still, if the employer seeks out his worker and pays him, even when he was not asked to do so, he fulfills the Biblical mitzvah of *On that day pay his wage* (*Deut.* 24:15).[11]

10. An employer who fears that he may be unable to pay his employees on time should say so when he hires the employee. If he stipulates that he is hiring the employee with the understanding that payment may be delayed, the Biblical prohibition is removed.[12]

11. These laws are not limited to payments which are due for wages.

Payment of rental fees for use of utensils or animals are also covered by these laws.[13] There is a dispute if this also applies to rentals of real estate.[14]

---

8. *Bi'ur Halachah* 242:1.

9. *Ahavas Chessed* 1:9:8. He adds that even if only one worker requests payment, the employer should assume that the second worker will also request payment on that day. The employer should give him half his money, and set the rest aside for the second worker. [This implies that if the employer knows that the second worker will not request payment, he should pay the first person his entire wage.]

10. C.M. 339:10. The employee need not verbally request payment. If his behavior suggests that he is awaiting payment, the obligation exists. [This is especially common in the case of teenage baby-sitters who obviously expect payment when the baby's parents return, but are often too shy to request it.] (*Ahavas Chessed* 1:9:n29).

11. *Ahavas Chessed* 1:9:11; see *Shaar Mishpat* 339 and *Pischei Teshuvah* 339:7 who cite the ruling of the *Zohar* that one is strictly obligated to make payment, even when the employee does not request it. This is also implied by the Talmud (*Bava Metzia* 111a — see *Pischei Teshuvah*).

12. *Shach* C.M. 339:2, *Sefer HaChassidim* §1071.

13. C.M. 339:1.

14. C.M. ibid.; see also comments of *Gra*, *Kitzos HaChoshen* and *Pischei Teshuvah*.

Rabbi Avrohom Pam Shlita points out that this discussion is not germane to the common rental situations today, for the following reason. In Talmudic times, rental fees

When Wages Are Not Paid on Time

12. It sometimes happens that an employer is unable to pay his employee's wages on time. When this happens, the employer may not offer his workers additional payment to induce them to agree to a delay in receiving their pay.[15]

This prohibition is not limited to situations involving formal employment. When a youngster is hired to clean a yard or to baby-sit, the employer is also prohibited from compensating him (even by giving a simple gift such as a candy) for being late with payment.[16]

---

were due at *the end* of the month (or other rental period). The Talmud therefore has a rule that *'rentals are not paid until the end.'* When payment is delayed past this day, some poskim maintain that these prohibitions apply.

Today, in most countries, rental agreements routinely require payment on the first of the month. The Biblical prohibitions on delaying payment apply only when payment is required due to employment or a rental. Whenever payment is required because of an agreement between the parties, that agreement must be honored, but these particular prohibitions do not apply. When rent comes due on the first of a month, this obligation is a result of a prior agreement and not the result of a rental that has already occurred. Thus, according to all opinions, this payment does not fall under the prohibitions outlined here.

15. Y.D. 173:12 and *Chavos Daas* 16. If the employer offers to pay his workers for waiting, this may constitute Ribbis Ketzutzah (*Bris Yehudah* 26:n15. This is based on *Beis Yosef* 176, discussing a similar situation, who raises the possibility that this is a Biblical prohibition).

Shulchan Aruch allows for an exception to this prohibition. This exception, as explained by *Be'er HaGoleh*, is limited to the following situation:

When a person is paid by the job and not by the hour, he is a contractor, and his wages are not due until the job is completed (see Paragraph 5). In this case, if an employer sees that he will be unable to make payment on time, he has the option of extending the actual job, so that it is not completed until later. When this happens, the wages do not come due until a later time.

For example, a watchman is hired to guard a field of produce until the harvest is completed. When the harvest is finished, his wages become due. If he realizes that he will be unable to pay at that time, the employer may extend the worker's job to include participation in the threshing process. (These arrangements must be made before the wages come due.) In this case, the employee's wages are not due until later, when the threshing is completed. Later, when the threshing is completed, the employer is permitted to add to his employee's wages to compensate him for the delay in receiving payment. The reason that this is permitted is that these wages are being paid at the time they are legally due. Since payment of the wages was never delayed, debt never existed. The rules of Ribbis therefore do not apply.

[It should be noted that the employee's term of employment can only be extended with his consent.]

16. Halachah allows for no distinction between situations involving large sums of money or those involving smaller payments. Similarly, there is no difference between an older employee or a youngster.

13. An employer who issued his paychecks late is permitted to compensate his employees by issuing paychecks ahead of schedule in subsequent months. For example, if the January check was distributed late, the February check may be paid earlier. However, the employer may not explicitly mention his previous late payment in connection with his early payments.[17]

Negotiating a Contract

14. When negotiating a contract, an employee may request a higher wage because he knows that the employer tends to be late in paying. However, this is permitted only if the employee's intent is not obvious. Therefore, he may not request a wage which is obviously greater than the norm, nor may he explicitly tell his employer that he is requesting a higher wage because the employer tends to be late with his payments.[18]

Late Penalties

15. Late penalties are sometimes included in a contract. This calls for the employer to be penalized a specific sum of money if he is late in paying his employees. This type of clause may be included in a contract,[19] subject to the following conditions:

---

17. This is a form of *Ribbis Me'ucheres*, Ribbis which is given after a loan has been repaid. Most poskim permit this type of benefit, as long as the previous loan is not mentioned in connection with it. Although *S.A. Harav* §7 rules that it is preferable to refrain from paying *Ribbis Me'ucheres*, this applies only when the lender receives cash or other direct financial benefits. In our case, the benefit is in the form of a prepayment and is permitted (*Mishnas Ribbis* 4:n13 based on *S.A. Harav* §16, *Kitzur Shulchan Aruch* 65:7 and *Ben Ish Chai V'eschanan* 7).

18. *Chavos Daas* 173:16 compares this to the laws of selling on credit. There, a higher price may be requested for an item which has no set market value. Here too, if the employee's request stays within the normal range for such employment, this is permitted. In this case, the contract may be drawn to permit late payments.

[*Chavos Daas* is discussing a case of an employee who agrees to a delay in payment as part of his deal with the employer. In cases where the contract requires prompt payment, but the employee knows of the employer's tardiness or inability to pay on time, it would appear that he may explicitly state that this is his reason for requesting a higher wage. Since the employer is still required to pay on time, no loan has taken place and the laws of Ribbis do not apply.]

19. A penalty clause may not be included in a loan agreement. This is prohibited because of its similarity to interest payments. However, this similarity exists only in cases involving loans, where the borrower receives cash and then pays a greater amount of cash because of the added late fee. In Y.D. 177:18, we find that when merchandise is offered, this similarity does not exist, and a late fee may be charged. The same rules apply to wages.

□ The late fee must be a one-time payment. There may not be a requirement that the employer continue paying additional fees based on the period of time that the debt is outstanding.[20]

□ Payment of the penalty may not entitle the employer to a grace period for payment. The wages must remain due at the time originally agreed upon.[21]

16. Late penalties that require the employer to pay interest for the time that wages are delayed are prohibited. It is prohibited to include this clause in a contract even if the employee is honest and has no intention of ever collecting such interest. Still, the employee would prefer to include this clause in his contract as a way of inducing the employer to make payment on time. This is prohibited because the laws of Ribbis include a specific prohibition on signing an agreement which calls for a Ribbis payment.[22]

Advance Payment

17. An employee is not legally entitled to his wages until he begins to work. If an employer agrees to pay him in advance, this has the status of a loan. The employee would not be permitted to benefit the employer in exchange for this advance payment. Therefore, an employee may not agree to accept a lower wage because his salary is paid in advance.[23]

18. A two-tiered wage scale, stipulating one wage for conventional payment and a lower wage if payment is made in advance, is prohibited. Wherever such an agreement is made, only the conventional payment scale may be used.[24]

---

20. Late fees are permitted in business dealings only because they are a lenient form of Ribbis. This holds true whenever the fees are only prohibited (in regard to true loans) as *haaramas Ribbis.* When a late fee is structured to increase with time, this is a form of true Ribbis, and is not permitted.

When a purchase agreement calls for payments to be made in installments, a separate late fee may be charged for each installment. A lease agreement may therefore call for an additional late fee for each month's rent (*Mishnas Ribbis* 11:n11).

21. *Chochmas Adam* 132:13, in regard to penalties for purchase payments. (See Chapter 9, Paragraph 5, and Note 11.)

22. See Chapter 9, Paragraph 4. This applies to Rabbinically prohibited forms of Ribbis as well (*Beis Meir* to *Taz* 170:5).

23. *Bava Basra* 86b-87a. This is a Rabbinic prohibition (ibid.).

We have already seen (in Chapter 7) that when merchandise is sold, one may not benefit a customer who pays in advance. Here we see a similar ruling in regard to wages.

24. *S.A. Harav* §15.

19. Similarly, an employee may not guarantee that he will work at today's wage scale in the future if this agreement is contingent on receiving payment in advance.[25]

Advancing a Deposit

20. Where the employee requests an advance on part of his salary, these prohibitions also apply. However, this is permitted if the advance is a nominal payment and it is clear that the intent is not to secure advance moneys, but to assure the employee that the employer is serious about following through with his commitment. Since this is not a loan, the Ribbis prohibitions do not apply.[26]

Exceptions to This Prohibition

21. As a rule, discounts may not be offered for prepayment. However, there are three significant exceptions to this rule, as outlined below.

a) When employment begins immediately after payment;

b) When a contractor formally obligates himself (via a *kinyan*, at the time of payment) to complete the job;

c) Where there is no set pay scale for this type of employment.

Each of these exceptions is explained below.

---

25. Y.D. 176:8.

Bris Yehudah 26:n13 points out that in the case under discussion (both in the Talmud and *Shulchan Aruch*), it was customary for wages to increase from the time the agreement is made until the actual employment begins. This is because the discussion was about seasonal work which is scheduled for a period of increased demand. During the off-season, the employee accepts advance payment for work which he will perform during the coming season. If he agrees to do the work at the off-season wage scale, this is an obvious financial benefit to the employer. Since this agreement is tied to a commitment to make advance payment, this is prohibited as Ribbis. Today, in most situations where an employee agrees to future work for a salary which is set at today's wage scale, it is not certain that the pay scale will rise in the interim. In this case, it is not clear that this prohibition applies. This is also the opinion of *Divrei Sofrim* in *Emek Davar* 176:104.

[Numerous Rishonim compare the issue of prepayment of wages to the laws of prepayment when purchasing merchandise. The prohibition, in cases involving purchases, applies even where a price increase is only a possibility. This comparison would indicate that this is true here as well.]

26. This is based on an identical ruling in regard to deposits which are given for purchases (*Maharsham* in *Mishpat Shalom* C.M. 209:25, *Bris Yehudah* 24:n2).

Exception A: When Employment Begins

22. If an employee is hired for work beginning immediately after a contract is made, the employee may offer a two-tier wage proposal, allowing for lower wages in exchange for prepayment of his salary.[27]

23. The agreement to work for a reduced wage may only apply to labor which runs continuously from the day of payment. If the work will be done at intervals, advance payment may only be made for the first segment. For example, if the employee is committed to work during January and March, advance payment which is given on January 1st may only include the salary for January work.[28]

Exception B: A Contractor Who Obligates Himself

24. A person who is paid by the job (not by the hour) is considered a contractor (*kablan*) rather than an employee. If he formally obligates himself (by making a *kinyan*) to complete a specific job, he may offer a discounted rate in exchange for advance payment. This is because a contractor (unlike regular employees) is not legally entitled to back out of this type of obligation.[29] The employment obligation begins at the time of the *kinyan* and payment may then be made. This is similar

---

27. Y.D. 176:8. (Rishonim offer numerous explanations for this leniency; see *Rashbam*, *Rashba* and *Shitah Mikubetzes* to *Bava Basra* 87a.)

This work must begin immediately. If moneys are advanced in the morning, it is not sufficient for work to begin in the evening (*Bris Yehudah* 26:n7, based on *S.A. Harav* §15).

28. *Bris Yehudah* 26:n13; cf. *Chelkas Yaakov* 3:204 and 205. [The agreement to accept a lower wage may apply to the March work as well, provided that the March salary is not advanced until March 1st, when that period of work begins.]

For work to 'run continuously,' the employee must work in the normal manner. He may stop working for lunch, illness or regular holidays and he may go home at night. (See *Bris Yehudah* 26:n7 that overnight breaks are permitted because it is the normal practice, and it does not cause the advance in salary to appear as a loan. This applies to these other examples as well.)

[Doctors, such as chiropractors, often offer a reduced rate if a patient makes prepayment for numerous office visits. This is prohibited, since this does not constitute continuous employment.

Obstetricians may be permitted to offer a reduced rate for prepayment. Although an obstetrician also provides numerous visits over an extended period, he is not paid per visit. Instead, he is paid a set salary for the medical care of a woman throughout her pregnancy. This is a continuous employment, for which discounts may be offered (heard from the author of *Mishnas Ribbis*).]

29. This halachah appears in C.M. 333:1.

to the case involving real estate rentals, where discounted rental rates may be offered for advance payment at the time of *kinyan*.[30]

25. A *kinyan* (to formally obligate a contractor) is done in the following manner. The employer takes his handkerchief (or another utensil or article of clothing which has value) in his hand and says to the contractor, "By accepting this handkerchief from me, you obligate yourself to the terms of our agreement."

The contractor verbally agrees and then takes possession of the handkerchief by lifting it at least four inches. This is known as *kinyan sudar* and serves to obligate the contractor to his agreement.[31]

26. This leniency applies to a case of a contractor who is personally involved with the actual labor. However, if he is paid to provide laborers but does not work himself, it is questionable if this leniency applies.[32]

27. [When a contractor agrees to repair a utensil or an article of clothing, he obligates himself to complete the job by taking possession of the utensil.[33] Therefore, a mechanic who takes a car for repair, or a dry cleaner who accepts an article of clothing, may offer a discount for prepayment, even if he does not immediately begin working on the job.]

Exception C: Labor With No Set Pay Scale

28. The third exception applies to specific forms of labor, such as the services of a *chazzan* (cantor) or professional entertainer. These

---

30. *Nemukei Yosef* to *Bava Basra* 86b; *Chelkas Yaakov* 3:204, *Bris Yehudah* 26:n7, *Shevet HaLevi* 3:110. See also *S.A. Harav* §15 for an earlier source which links this prohibition to an employee's right to back out of a labor agreement.

'Exception a' also applies to a contractor. Therefore, even if he does not make a formal *kinyan*, he is permitted to accept advance payment at the time he begins work (*S.A. Harav* §15, *Bris Yehudah* ibid.). In this case, the contractor may accept the complete payment in advance, and agree to a lower rate, even if he will not be working on this project for continuous days (*Bris Yehudah* 26:n13).

31. *Shach* C.M. 333:4. The transfer of a signed contract may also serve as a *kinyan* to obligate a contractor; see *Noda BeYehudah* quoted by *Pischei Teshuvah* C.M.333:2.

32. *Bris Yehudah* 26:n7 expresses uncertainty in this case. He argues that when a contractor is providing employees and not labor, we should apply the laws of prepayment for sales and not the laws for prepayment of labor.

Rabbi Y.S. Eliyashev Shlita (quoted in *Mishnas Ribbis* 9:n40) rejects this argument and rules leniently. He argues that every contractor obligates himself to complete a specific job. The manner in which the job is completed (whether he himself works or hires others) is his own affair and is not relevant to the customer.

33. C.M. 333:1.

services have no wage scale at all, since their value varies greatly from individual to individual. In this case, an employee may offer to work for a lower salary because he is receiving payment in advance. However, he may not explicitly state that he is offering the lower salary because of the advance payment.[34]

Additional Leniencies

29. A worker is entitled to his wages when he completes his work. We have seen (in Paragraph 5) that if a contractor takes possession of an item (for example, when a tailor takes a suit to make alterations, or a mechanic takes a car for repair), wages are not due until the repaired article is returned to its owner. Even if the work is completed and the owner is asked to pick up his article, payment is not due until it is actually picked up. The contractor is therefore permitted to charge more if the owner delays in picking up the item. Since the money is being paid when it comes due, no loan has taken place and Ribbis is not prohibited.[35]

30. If an employee (or contractor) provides material to the employer, he may offer a discount for prepayment of the charge for the material, based on the laws for prepayment of merchandise (Chapters 7 and 8).[36]

Vacation Days

31. Most contracts entitle an employee to a specific number of paid vacation days. If an employee does not use all of his vacation

---

34. The prohibitions outlined in this chapter are Rabbinically prohibited forms of Ribbis. These prohibitions apply only to cases where it is obvious that a discount is being offered. This is a leniency which we have seen earlier in regard to prepayment for merchandise (based on Y.D. 173:1). The discount may not be so great that it would be obvious that the employer is not receiving his full salary. (A 20% cap on discounts is mentioned elsewhere; see R' Akiva Eiger to *Shach* 173:5, *Pischei Teshuvah* 173:4 and *Shaar Deah* 173:2; see also Chapter 6, Note 26.)

35. *Bris Yehudah* 26:*hashmatos*, *Toras Ribbis* 14:23, *Mishnas Ribbis* 10:10, based on *Shach* C.M. 306:3.

[This means that there is no Ribbis prohibition when this charge is added. Still, the customer may not be compelled to pay this added fee, unless this was part of the original stipulation or if this is the normal business practice in that particular place. Where this is not the case, these charges could not be imposed because it is not possible for a charge to be imposed unilaterally by one partner to an agreement.]

36. *Mishnas Ribbis* 10:n2. If the employee has the material in stock, he may offer a discount if the employer pays in advance, even if delivery is scheduled for a later date (this is known as *yesh lo*). See *Bris Yehudah* 26:n7, regarding a contractor who offers a single price which includes both labor and material.

days in a given year, he may wish to carry these days over to the next year.

Bris Yehudah suggests that this presents a Ribbis problem for the following reason. Often, the employee receives a raise from year to year. Thus, his daily salary will have gone up. In the previous year, he would have been entitled to a certain payment for the vacation day.[37] By carrying over the vacation day, he is receiving more money for that day, only because he is taking it at a later time. In effect, then, he is being paid for collecting at a later time.

Because of this argument, *Bris Yehudah* draws the following distinction. If an employee's original contract entitles him to carry over vacation days, he may do so, even if he receives a raise in the interim.[38]

However, if the contract does not contain such a provision, and the employee requested special permission to carry over the vacation day, he may only be paid for that day, based on his previous year's salary.[39]

---

37. [In many businesses, if an employee does not take a vacation day he does not receive compensation; either he takes it or he loses it. Still, since the contract calls for him to receive a salary based on a certain number of days, each day has a set value. The fact that he gets paid his full salary even when taking vacation means that even vacation days have that value.]

38. In this case, the vacation days were never set at the first year's salary, since the original agreement gives the employee the right to take his vacation days during subsequent years (*Bris Yehudah*).

39. *Bris Yehudah* 26:n13.

[This ruling can be challenged, as follows. An employee contracts to receive a certain wage for a year's work. For example, his contract may call for a salary which comes to $100 per day. He receives this amount of money for each of the days of the year, whether he works every day or takes some days off for vacation. There is no separate wage for vacation days. When he fails to take all of the vacation days to which he is entitled, no true loan has occurred because he has received his full salary. The following year, his salary may come to $105 per day. This salary, too, remains the same whether he works or takes vacation days. When the worker transfers a vacation day from one year to the next, he does not receive additional payment. This should be permitted in all cases for two reasons; first, because there is no loan taking place, and second, because there is no financial benefit to the worker.

Perhaps *Bris Yehudah* was referring to a vacation system which works in a different manner.]

CHAPTER ELEVEN

Rentals

- ☐ Renting objects which decrease in value when used (1-3)
- ☐ Renting objects which do not decrease in value when used (4-5)
- ☐ **Applications (6-26):**
- ☐ Borrowing a car (6)
- ☐ Renting cash (7-9)
- ☐ Transferring bank accounts (10-11)
- ☐ Setting rental charges (12-19)
- ☐ Late penalties (20)
- ☐ Prepaying for future rentals (21-22)
- ☐ Trading rentals (23)
- ☐ Borrowing a utensil (24-26)

Introduction

The laws of Ribbis are not limited to cash loans; they also apply to loans involving merchandise or utensils. Thus, someone who borrows cooking ingredients from a neighbor may not offer a gift when returning the ingredients.

Rental fees are permitted. Thus, someone who borrows a utensil from a neighbor is permitted to pay an additional fee or offer a gift as a rental fee for use of the utensil.

This leads to an obvious question: If utensils may be rented, why is it not permitted to pay a rental fee for cooking ingredients which are borrowed from a neighbor?

The Talmud relates that one *Amora* took this a step further. Rav Chama would rent money, charging a per day 'rental fee' for cash! Rav Chama erroneously held that this is permitted: "Why is this different than (renting) a shovel (which is permitted)?"[1]

In this chapter we will examine the response to this question and distinguish between rental agreements (for which payment is permitted) and loans (for which payment may not be offered). We will also examine other aspects of the Ribbis laws which pertain to rentals.

Objects Which Decrease in Value as They Are Used

1. None of the Ribbis prohibitions apply to rental agreements. However, an agreement can be defined as a rental only when the owner

---

1. *Bava Metzia* 69b. The Talmud concludes that there are two basic differences between rentals and loans. First, rented objects are returned as is. When a tool or utensil (such as a hammer or a pot) is borrowed, the very same tool is returned to its owner after it is used by the borrower. This is not true of borrowed money. The borrower spends the money which he receives, and he pays back with other moneys. The same is true of borrowed cooking ingredients. In these cases, Ribbis is prohibited.

Secondly, a rented utensil constantly decreases in value due to normal wear and tear. This loss is absorbed by the owner. Appliances, clothing, tools and mechanical instruments are examples of items that decrease in value as they are used. The owner is therefore entitled to payment. This is not true of cash loans.

Some Rishonim understand that the Talmud requires *both* these conditions to permit rental fees. According to this opinion, items which do not decrease in value, such as jewelry, precious stones and rare coins, may not be rented. *Tosafos* disagree, maintaining that rentals are permitted when any one of these two conditions are present. *Shulchan Aruch* follows this opinion.

Items which do not decrease in value as they are used may be rented, but only under the conditions outlined below, Paragraph 4.

of an object risks some financial loss by renting out his object. He is entitled to payment only when he risks or absorbs loss as part of the arrangement. Appliances, vehicles, tools and clothing are examples of items which decrease in value as they are used. Because the owner is prepared to absorb this loss, he may charge rent for use of these items.[2]

2. Liability: The owner of the rented item is required to absorb all losses which are a result of the normal use of the item.[3] This is not limited to the normal wear and tear of the rented item. Price fluctuations which are a result of market conditions must also be absorbed by the owner; for example, electronic devices such as calculators, fax machines or computers decrease in value as updated models are introduced. The renter may not obligate himself to reimburse the owner for this loss.[4]

The renter is permitted to accept responsibility for any other loss to the rented item.[5]

---

2. Y.D. 176:2 and *Taz* 1.

3. *Beis Yosef*, *Chavos Daas* 176:3.

4. *Shach* 176:4, *Chavos Daas* 177:1.

5. Y.D. 176:3-4 and *Shach* 176:4. This is not to say that he must accept all responsibility. The Torah delineates rules of liability for rental agreements. These rules assign limited liability for damages which occur to a rented object (these rules are outlined below, in Note 8). Still, individuals are free to draw their own agreements. If the rental agreement specifically obligates the renter to accept liability for *all* damages, this is binding. The laws of Ribbis do not apply here, since the owner still absorbs the decrease in the value of the rented item. Therefore, a rental fee may be charged.

If the item were to become damaged or ruined, but not due to normal use, the renter may be obligated to replace the item. In such cases, the renter may only obligate himself to pay the item's value at the time of the damage (and not its value at the time of rental). This is because the renter may not accept responsibility to restore the loss in value which results from the normal use of the item, even if this responsibility is limited to cases where the item suffers additional damage (*Rema* 176:3, *S.A. Harav* §35; cf. *Shulchan Aruch* 176:3-4 who apparently disagrees; see also *Machneh Ephraim* §32).

If a rental agreement requires the renter to pay the item's original value, this constitutes Ribbis. Any part of an agreement that violates the laws of Ribbis may not be honored. Here too, if the item later became ruined, the owner may not be reimbursed based on its value at the time of rental.

Chavos Daas 176:4 rules that the owner has two options. He may accept payment, based on the item's value at the time it became ruined. Or, he may refund the rental payment and collect the full value of the item, based on the time of rental. By returning the rental fee, the rental portion of the agreement is nullified, and the owner may be reimbursed the full value of the item.

If the item increased in value before it became ruined, the renter would be obligated to pay its full value. This is because the item remains the property of its owner, even while it is in the renter's possession. The increased value therefore belongs to the owner (*Divrei Sofrim* 176:23, based on *Levush* 176:4 and *S.A. Harav* §35; cf. *Machneh Ephraim* §32).

3. When items which decrease in value are rented, the renter need not be required to return the very same object which he rented. He may be given the option of returning another object of the same type, even if it is new.[6]

Objects Which Do Not Decrease in Value When Used

4. Items such as jewelry, precious stones, rare coins and rare stamps do not decrease in value. Fees may be charged for renting these items only under the following two conditions:

  a) They may be rented only where the same object which is rented is returned. If the renter has the option of returning another object of the same type, the transaction is a loan rather than a rental, and no fee may be charged.[7]

  b) The owner must accept a level of risk of loss if the item were to become damaged or lost. This means that the renter may not accept liability for damage or theft beyond those obligations which are placed on him by Biblical law.[8]

---

6. Y.D. 176:2. This is not permitted when renting utensils that do not decrease in value (*Chavos Daas* 176:3).

If the renter exercises this option and returns a new object, the owner will not have suffered from devaluation of the item due to its use. Still, the owner may charge rent because he has accepted a risk of loss, since the renter had the option of returning the actual item which was borrowed (*Tosafos* and *Rosh* to *Bava Metzia* 69b).

[This would appear to contradict *Rema's* ruling (in the previous note) which prohibits the renter from paying the full value of the object if it becomes damaged. There too, it should suffice that the owner agreed to absorb the item's devaluation if the renter were to return the actual item. See *Perishah* 176:2 who draws a distinction between these cases. See also *Machneh Ephraim* §32.]

7. *Chavos Daas* 176:3. If the renter were entitled to return a different item, both of the Talmud's criterion for defining a rental (quoted above, Note 1) would be missing. It would therefore have the status of a loan, and a rental fee would be prohibited.

8. Y.D. and *Rema* 176:1. The Torah delineates specific rules of liability for situations involving rentals and guardianship. These rules apply when no specific agreement was made between the parties. In general, the Torah does permit agreements which deviate from the Biblical guidelines for liability. For example, a guardian has only limited liability for the item he is guarding. If he agrees, he may accept full liability. This is known as *masneh shomer chinom lehiyos keshoel*, lit., a guardian may contract (to be liable) as (if he were) a borrower. This principle does not apply to situations involving loans, where the laws of Ribbis would be violated by the agreement.

The Biblical rules of liability hold a renter responsible for all forms of avoidable loss (*geneivah v'aveidah*), even in situations where no negligence is involved. He is not responsible for unavoidable (and unpredictable) types of loss (*oness*). In these cases, the owner would absorb the loss. It is only because the owner takes responsibility for these

5. The owner may protect himself by insuring the rented object against loss. This does not affect the status of the rental agreement.[9] However, the renter himself may not act as insurer for the item.[10]

Applications

6. Borrowing a car: One who borrows a car may benefit its owner (for example, by making repairs or filling the gas tank) before returning the car. Since the borrower intends to return the same car which he borrowed,[11] the laws of Ribbis do not apply.[12]

Renting Cash

7. If cash is needed for non-spending purposes (for display or to make oneself appear wealthy), it is permitted to rent moneys, as long as the owner stipulates that the same cash must be returned.[13]

---

potential losses that he may demand rental payments. If the renter were to accept these responsibilities on himself, the transaction would have the status of a loan and a rental fee would be prohibited.

It should be noted that when an object is lost due to unavoidable and unpredictable causes, it is the renter's obligation to prove that this took place. It is likely that he will be unable to present witnesses with firsthand knowledge of the loss. In this case, the owner may require that he swear, in Beis Din, that the damage or loss was unavoidable. Traditionally, G-d-fearing Jews are reluctant to swear in Beis Din, even when failure to do so would obligate them to pay for the lost object. Therefore, as a practical matter, the owner rarely suffers a loss.

9. *Minchas Yitzchak* 4:20:13, *Bris Yehudah* 29:n7. *Minchas Yitzchak* permits the cost of the insurance to be added to the rental fee.

10. *Bris Yehudah* ibid.

11. One could argue that this is different, in that the person who borrows a car is also borrowing the gas which is in the gas tank. When he refills the tank, he is returning something which was consumed. We have seen that Ribbis prohibitions do apply when the borrowed item is consumed and replaced with another item of the same type. Still, this is permitted because it is apparent that the extra payment is given in gratitude for use of the car, not for the loan of the original gasoline (*Mishnas Ribbis* 6:n5; cf. *Chayei HaLevi* 2:53 who requires that the borrower state explicitly that the extra gas is in gratitude for use of the car. When the car owner did not require that the gas be returned, he concedes that it is not necessary to make this statement.)

12. Since the car decreases in value as it is used, the owner does suffer a loss. For this reason, the renter is permitted to accept liability for all other damages which may occur (as in Paragraph 2).

13. Y.D. 176:1. The rental agreement would have to be consistent with the rules regarding liability which were outlined in Paragraphs 4 and 5.

A person may rent cash only when the very same cash is returned. If it is deposited

8. When cash was rented properly (with the agreement that the same cash will be returned), but the renter violated the agreement by spending the money, he is prohibited from paying the rental fee.[14]

Once the renter spends the cash, he has the status of a borrower. He is then prohibited from paying any rental fee for the money, even for the time before the money was spent. For example, if the renter held the cash for one month and then spent it during the second month, he is prohibited from paying the rental fee for the first month as well.[15]

9. If the agreement allows the cash to be spent, but the borrower did not use the money and he returned the very same cash which he borrowed, this transaction still has the status of a loan. This is because the agreement did not require the borrower to return the same cash.[16] If Ribbis is paid for this loan, it is Rabbinically prohibited.[17]

---

in a bank account and other moneys are being returned, the transaction has the status of a loan, not a rental.

14. *Beis Yosef* 176, *Shach* 176:1.

A similar question involves a guardian or trustee who is not authorized to borrow the money which is under his care. If he takes an unauthorized loan, and profits from an investment which he made with this money, the *Shulchan Aruch* (Y.D. 177:19) rules that the trustee is permitted (but not obligated) to share these profits with the fund from which he took the money. [This ruling has been presented in Chapter 5, Paragraph 40.]

Shaar Deah 176:1 points out that this ruling seems to contradict the ruling of *Beis Yosef* here. Here too, money was used without authorization. Yet, the borrower is prohibited from making the rental payments because he would be benefiting the person whose funds he used.

Mekor Mayim Chaim (to 176:1) resolves this contradiction in the following manner. In the case discussed here by *Beis Yosef*, the moneys were originally given as part of a rental agreement which called for rental payments. Where the original agreement required payment, this payment is prohibited if the money was used as a loan. These payments would appear to be Ribbis (*mechzei keRibbis*).

In the case discussed in Y.D. 177:19, the original agreement was for a guardianship. That agreement did not call for any payments to be made to the owner of the money. In that case, if the trustee does make a voluntary payment this would appear to be a gift rather than Ribbis. This is therefore permitted.

See also *Atzei Levonah* 176:1 and *Bris Yehudah* 29:n6 for additional resolutions of the question posed by *Shaar Deah*.

15. *Chavos Daas* 176:1. [If the rent for the first month was paid at the end of that month, this rental fee need not be returned, even if the renter subsequently used the moneys. In this case, there is no appearance of Ribbis since the payment was made before the money was used.]

16. *Taz* 176:1, *Shach* 176:1.

17. *Bris Yehudah* 29:n2 citing *Nachal Yitzchak* 81:32:6. [Cf. the language of *Bris Yehudah* 29:4 which can be misleading because it implies that if the borrower accepts

Transferring Bank Accounts

10. Reuven needs to have a large sum of money in his bank account (e.g., for credit purposes). He asks Shimon to transfer his savings account to Reuven's name.[18] If Shimon does this, interest which subsequently accrues to the account belongs to Reuven. Since a loan (and not a rental)[19] has taken place, Reuven may not pass this interest on to Shimon. He is permitted to return only the amount of money he actually borrowed.

Reuven may pass the interest on to Shimon when the transfer is structured in the following manner. Before transferring the funds, Shimon would designate Reuven as his agent to open a bank account for Shimon. Shimon would also accept liability for the funds deposited in this account. This account would be considered Shimon's (even if it were opened in Reuven's name) and the interest would accrue to Shimon.[20]

11. Bank accounts are sometimes transferred to other people's names for various reasons (for example, to avoid estate taxes when the owner of the funds passes away). In these cases too, the interest belongs to the account's owner of record. He is permitted to give the interest to the owner of the money, only if the account was originally set up in the manner described in the previous paragraph.[20]

Setting Rental Charges

12. When businesses offer goods for sale, they are prohibited from having a two-tier price system, with a lower price for cash payments

---

full liability for loss this would be Biblically prohibited Ribbis. *Nachal Yitzchak* clearly considers this Rabbinically prohibited Ribbis.]

18. This is permitted only where Reuven is not misrepresenting himself. If the transfer of funds would cause a misrepresentation, this is prohibited as *geneivas daas*. There is no difference if a Jew or non-Jew were being misled. In either case, this is prohibited.

19. Although a person may rent money if it is being used to make him look wealthy, he may only do so if he returns the very same cash. When he places the money in a bank account and pays the loan with other moneys it is considered a loan, not a rental.

20. *Mishnas Ribbis* 12:n8, based on Y.D. 168:13.

[If the money was already transferred to Reuven, and the account was not set up in this manner, all interest which is earned belongs to Reuven. Still, this can be corrected for future interest. Shimon would reacquire the funds by taking legal possession through a *kinyan*. He would then give the funds back to Reuven and direct him to open an account for Shimon, as explained above. Interest credited to the new account would then belong to Shimon.]

and a higher price for extending credit. This higher price is viewed as a charge for credit.

When items are offered for rent, it is often permissible for a two-tier price system to be used, as explained in the following paragraphs.[21]

13. Rental agreements are divided into two categories:

a) Agreements which call for payment at the *end* of the month (or other rental period). Most car rental agreements fall under this category, since payment is made at the end of the rental period.

b) Agreements which call for payment at the *beginning* of the month (or other rental period). In the United States, most real estate rentals call for payment at the beginning of each month.

The laws of Ribbis draw a distinction between these two categories.[22] The laws which pertain to each of these categories are explained below.

A. When Rent Is Normally Due at the End of a Rental Period

14. When a rental agreement calls for payment at the end of the rental period, a two-tier price system may be used. The rental fee may be set at one price, with a discounted price for those who pay at the time of rental. For example, a business may charge $100 per month for a rental when payment is made in the regular manner, but charge only $95 if payment is advanced. The business may also add an option allowing a customer to receive twelve months of rental for $1000 if payment for the entire year is made in advance.[23]

---

21. The Talmud (B.M. 65a) teaches, "(When payment is delayed) we may add to rental fees, but we may not add to purchase fees."

Of course, this is not to say that interest may be paid in all cases where credit stems from a rental agreement. Rather, this refers to the one specific case of a renter who wishes to make payment at the end of his rental period, rather than at the time of rental. He may be charged for this delay in payment, as explained in the paragraphs which follow.

This is a major difference between the laws regarding sales and the laws regarding rentals.

22. This follows *Chochmas Adam* 136:10 and *Imrei Yosher* 1:150; cf. *Machneh Ephraim* §31.

23. Y.D. 176:6. *Shulchan Aruch* refers to real estate rentals in an era when it was customary to pay rent at the end of the month. These laws apply to the rental of utensils as well (*S.A. Harav* §16, *Shaar Deah* 176:2).

The reason that this is permitted is because no loan or delay in payment is taking place. The customer can choose either of two options. If he chooses to pay in advance, no Ribbis is being paid since he is paying the lower fee. (A customer is permitted to choose the

15. This offer may be made at any time until a final rental agreement has been reached. However, once the two sides have concluded a binding rental agreement[24] at a lower rate, they may not switch to the later payment schedule at the higher rate.[25]

16. If the renter is offered different payment options, he is not required to choose one before committing himself to the rental. He may agree to the rental and later choose between the two options.[26]

---

lower price, even where two prices are offered for a purchase; see Chapter 6, Paragraph 5.) If the customer chooses to pay at the end of the rental period, he is making payment at the time that it is actually due. Since his payment is not being delayed, this is not considered a loan and it is permitted to pay the higher price (*Taz* 176:7).

[**A difficulty:** When selling an item, a merchant may not offer a discount which requires payment to be made in advance (Y.D. 173:7; these laws have been outlined in Chapter 7). This is because the advance payment is seen as a loan to the merchant, which is given in exchange for the discount. If so, it should similarly be prohibited to offer a discount for advance rental payment, since this prepayment should be viewed as a loan which is given in exchange for a discount.

Kehilos Yaakov (to B.M. §37; *Bris Yehudah* 26:n2 suggests a similar answer) explains that this is permitted because it is not a true prepayment. Although the rental agreement would normally call for payment at the end of the rental period, someone who makes payment earlier is actually purchasing the rights to use the rented item. By agreeing to prepayment, the customer is structuring the agreement as a purchase agreement. Payment on this agreement is being made on time and not in advance. There is therefore no concern that Ribbis is being paid. This is not similar to the case of someone who pays in advance for an item which will be delivered at a later time. There, the payment is truly an advance of funds, and the buyer may not receive benefit for this. (See *Kehilos Yaakov* for further elaboration. See also *Chasam Sofer* to B.M. 65a and *Kovetz Haaros* Chapter 53.)

A practical result of this explanation would be to limit discounts to rental agreements which call for payment at the time that the owner commits himself to the rental. If the agreement provided a discount but required payment to be made before the commitment, this would be prohibited.]

24. Once an agreement is reached, it is considered binding if a contract is signed *or* if a formal *kinyan* has taken place between the parties or if the tenant has moved into the property (or taken possession of the rented object).

25. *Rema* 176:6. This is because a two-tier system is permitted only when rentals are due at the end of the month. Once a binding agreement is reached, payment is due on the date established by the agreement. An increase which is offered to change a payment schedule is considered a Ribbis payment.

Darkei Teshuvah 176:13 suggests a way of changing the payment schedule after a binding agreement has been reached. Both parties may agree to nullify their previous agreement and enter into a new rental agreement for the future. This would not change the rental fees for the period which already passed, but it can be used to change the future rates and payment schedule. (*Bris Yehudah* 26:n4 cites this *Darkei Teshuvah* and appears to concur with this ruling.)

26. *Machneh Ephraim* §31.

B. When Rent Is Normally Due at the Beginning of the Rental Period

17. When rent is normally due at the beginning of the rental period, this leniency does not apply. In our example, if a business were to charge $95 per month for a rental when payment is made in the regular manner (at the beginning of the month), but charge $100 if payment is delayed, the additional five dollars constitutes Ribbis, since it is being paid to delay the payment schedule.[27]

This also applies to real estate rentals in countries where it is customary to pay rent at the beginning of the month.[28]

18. Even in this case, the following discount option is permitted. The customer may be offered the choice of a $95 per month rental, with rent due at the first of each month or $1000 per year, with payment for the entire year due in advance.[29] [In communities where it is normal to pay a full year's rental at the beginning of the year, this too would be prohibited.]

19. To summarize: The laws of prepayment for rentals allow a lower price for payment which is made prior to the conventional payment

---

27. *Chochmas Adam* 136:10. This is prohibited even when the renter must advance part of the payment in order to secure the discount. However, this is permitted where only a small deposit fee is required, and remaining payments are made according to the regular monthly schedule (*Mishnas Ribbis* 11:n7; regarding deposit fees, see Chapter 8, Paragraph 2).

[If a two-tiered rate was offered, the customer should be permitted to choose the cheaper option, which calls for payment at the beginning of the rental period. See, however, the language of *Chochmas Adam* which is unclear on this point.]

28. In Talmudic times, as well as during the period of the Rishonim, the prevalent custom was to pay rent for real estate at the end of each month. For this reason, the poskim permitted two-tiered rent offerings for real estate rentals.

Today, most rental agreements involving real estate call for payment to be made at the beginning of each month. Halachah recognizes the prevalent business practice as binding. Therefore, the leniency mentioned by these poskim does not apply to real estate rentals, and a two-tiered system may not be used (*Chochmas Adam* 136:10 and *Imrei Yosher* 150; *Machneh Ephraim* §31 disagrees, see also *Toras Ribbis* 14:17; Rabbi Y.S. Eliyashev Shlita, quoted in *Mishnas Ribbis* 11:n1, rules in accordance with the opinion of *Chochmas Adam*).

29. This is permitted because a discount is being offered for early payment. This case is identical to that in Paragraph 14, where a two-tiered system is permitted because the later payment is made at the normal time, and a discount is offered for prepayment. Here too, the option of paying at the later time (the first of each month) does not allow for a delay beyond what is the normal payment time.

time. When higher rates are offered to permit payment later than the conventional time, this is prohibited.

Late Penalties

20. Many standard rental leases call for penalties if rent is received late. This is a form of Rabbinically prohibited Ribbis and is prohibited. A lease may call for a one-time penalty if rental payments are not made on time.[30]

Prepaying for Future Rentals

21. Rental agreements are often concluded well in advance of the actual rental. For example, an agreement calling for a July rental may be made in January. A discount may be offered if payment is made in advance, even if the agreement requires that payment be made in January. This is permitted even though the renter will not move into the property until a later time.[31] However, this is only permitted if a lease is signed in January to formally commit both sides to the rental agreement.[32]

---

30. *Mishnas Ribbis* 11:8. This must be consistent with the laws of penalty payments for purchase agreements, as outlined in Chapter 9. As we have seen there, payment of the penalty may not entitle the purchaser to a grace period for payment. The debt must remain due at the time originally agreed upon (*Chochmas Adam* 132:13). When a purchase agreement calls for payments to be made in installments, a separate late fee may be charged for each installment. A lease agreement may therefore call for an additional late fee for each month's rent (providing that no one payment has two penalties attached to it) (*Mishnas Ribbis* 11:n11).

31. This is the subject of a disagreement between two Rishonim who are (coincidentally) both known by the acronym *Rashba*. R' Shlomo ben Avraham (the Tosafist known as *Rashba*) requires that the rental begin at the time of payment. R' Shlomo ben Aderes (the author of *Chidushei HaRashba* and *Teshuvos HaRashba*) disagrees. Although the poskim quote both opinions, it is clear that they favor the latter (lenient) opinion of R' Shlomo ben Aderes. This is also the ruling of *Be'er HaGolah* 176:16, *Chavos Daas* in *Chidushim* 176:8, *S.A. Harav* §16, *Shaar Deah* 176:2 ["...we may be lenient since this is a (question of) a Rabbinic prohibition."] and *Bris Yehudah* 26:1.

Although Rishonim discuss this in reference to the renting of real estate, this is also true in regard to the renting of animals or utensils. These rental agreements are considered binding from the time the renter pulls [or, for small utensils, when he lifts up] the rented item to take it for himself (*S.A. Harav* §16).

32. The reason a discount is permitted for advance payment is that the rental agreement becomes binding at that time. The renter therefore receives something (namely, the commitment on the part of the owner) at the time of payment. The payment is therefore not considered an advance payment, but rather a payment at the proper time. This is the

22. Some poskim require that the rental property be physically fit for use at the time that payment is advanced. This means that if a home or bungalow is being renovated at the time of payment, it would be prohibited to offer a prepayment discount.[33]

Trading Rentals

23. It is permitted for two people to trade rentals. For example, two people may trade apartments.

However, if one person allows another to use his home for a month, on the condition that he is then allowed to use the other's home for a month, at a later time, they may do so only if the rental value of the two homes is equal (or if the second home is worth less). If the value of the second rental is greater,[34] this is considered Ribbis.[35]

Borrowing a Utensil

24. Someone who borrows a utensil (and does not obligate himself to pay rent or to otherwise benefit the owner in exchange for its use) has greater liability for damage than a renter. He is responsible even for

---

ruling of *S.A. Harav* §16 and is implied by *Rashba* (quoted by *Taz* and *Nekudos HaKesef*, ibid.).

When is a rental agreement considered to be binding?

A *kinyan* is required to finalize any financial agreement. A common form of *kinyan* is *shtar* (a contract). If the parties sign and exchange lease agreements, this *kinyan* is accomplished (C.M. 195:9 and *Pischei Teshuvah* 333:2).

Another *kinyan* which is valid for real estate is *kesef* (payment). *Rema* C.M. 195:9 rules that this is a valid *kinyan* for rentals. *Aruch HaShulchan* C.M. 195:13 maintains that wherever it is the common business practice to sign a lease, payment alone may not be a valid *kinyan*.

Checks may not be used for this *kinyan* (see *Tam Ribbis* p. 306 and *Mishnas Ribbis* 10:n3).

[The crucial point here is that the agreement is made binding on the owner, so that the renter receives something (i.e., the commitment) in exchange for his payment. It would therefore seem that if the renter is allowed the option of canceling the agreement, this would still be valid. Cf. *S.A. Harav* §16 who mentions that the agreement should be binding on both sides. We have followed this opinion.]

33. R' Akiva Eiger (to B.M. 72b) requires that the property be suitable for use. None of the other poskim mention this requirement.

34. For example, if the second apartment was bigger, or if the second person was allowed a longer use of the apartment.

35. *Bris Yehudah* 11:n2; cf. *Avnei Nezer* Y.D. 148 who discusses this without coming to a clear conclusion.

unavoidable or unpredictable types of loss (oness).[36] Someone who borrows a utensil may obligate himself to pay an extra fee in case the utensil is damaged or ruined.[37]

25. Someone who borrows a utensil is not obligated to pay the owner if the utensil becomes damaged or ruined in the normal course of use. Still, if he wishes, the borrower may voluntarily replace the item which became ruined.[38]

26. Someone who borrows an item may not obligate himself to return the favor and later lend a utensil (to the person who is now lending to him) unless the value of the second item is equal to, or less than, the value of the first item. If the second item is worth more, or if it is loaned for a longer period of time, it constitutes Ribbis.[39]

---

36. In contradistinction to a renter who is not obligated to pay the owner if the item is damaged for this reason (see Note 8).

37. *Chavos Daas* 161:1.

38. *Bris Yehudah* 29:11.

39. *Bris Yehudah* 11:n2, based on *Tosefta* B.M. 6:5. It is not clear why the *Shulchan Aruch* omitted this. *Bris Yehudah* adds that when neighbors allow each other to use their utensils, this is permitted. Even if they promise to allow each other use of their utensils, they do not mean it as a binding agreement, but only as part of a friendly relationship.

[This type of trading does not fall under the category of *halveini v'elveh loch* (see Chapter 3, Paragraph 20), since the item which is being loaned is returned; *halveini v'elveh loch* applies when an item is taken to be consumed or spent.]

CHAPTER TWELVE

Promissory Notes, Checks and Bonds

Rules (1-19):

- ☐ Selling promissory notes and debts (1-5)
- ☐ Methods of protecting the buyer (6-8)
- ☐ Voluntary reimbursement (9)
- ☐ Using a Heter Iska (10)
- ☐ Notes which are written to create debt (11-12)
- ☐ How debt is sold (13-14)
- ☐ Purchasing debt from a non-Jew (15-17)
- ☐ A non-Jew's promissory notes (18-19)

Applications (20-39):

- ☐ Mortgages (20)
- ☐ Heter Iska agreements (21)
- ☐ Transferring bank accounts (22-23)
- ☐ Purchase notes (24)
- ☐ Bank checks and money orders (25)
- ☐ Cashing checks (26-29)
- ☐ Offering one's own check at a discount (30-31)
- ☐ Checks drawn on U.S. banks (32)
- ☐ Foreign currency checks (33)
- ☐ Charging for expenses (34)
- ☐ Selling one's own promissory note (35)
- ☐ Stocks and bonds (36-38)
- ☐ Trading bonds (39-40)
- ☐ Prepaying a debt (41)

Appendix I: Heter Iska form for sale of debt
Appendix II: Heter Iska Klali for sale of notes
Appendix III: An analysis of the legal status of checks.

Introduction

A promissory note is a note which promises payment at a future time. These notes may be written for many reasons; most often, they are written by a borrower in return for a loan or by a customer who receives delivery of merchandise on credit. The reason that the note was written does not affect the laws outlined in this chapter.

There is a market for the buying and selling of promissory notes. When a promissory note is sold, the debt is transferred, so that it must be paid to the person who buys the note. For example, Reuven owes Shimon $1000, and he writes a note of debt which calls for payment in six months. Shimon needs cash immediately and is willing to sell the note now to Levi for $900. Levi will make a $100 profit when he redeems the note, six months later.

This is similar to interest on a loan, because Levi is profiting from his ability to advance cash to Shimon. **Rambam** describes this as "something which is similar to Ribbis and is (nevertheless) permitted."[1]

The conditions under which this is permitted are outlined in this chapter.

Selling Promissory Notes and Debts[2]

1. A lender is permitted to sell a loan at a discount. For example, if someone owes him $1000, due in six months, he is permitted to sell the debt for $900 cash. This is true both when he is selling a written promissory note and when he is selling debt for which there is no written note. In either case, the loan may be sold at less than its face value, provided that the following conditions are met.[3]

---

1. *Rambam, Hil. Malveh* 5:14. *Rambam* implies that this is permitted because no loan has actually taken place. Promissory notes are financial instruments with a true market value. They are sold because of their present value. The person buying the note is not lending money to anyone; he is simply making a purchase. The fact that the buyer realizes a profit is not problematic, because "the Torah prohibits only Ribbis which passes from borrower to lender" (*Bris Yehudah* 15:n3).

2. The discussion in this section concerns the sale of a promissory note which was issued by a third party. In our earlier example of Shimon selling a note to Levi, the note reflects Reuven's indebtedness. If Shimon were to write his own note of indebtedness, he may not sell it at a discount (see Paragraph 35).

Regarding situations where the original loan involved the use of a Heter Iska, see Paragraph 21.

3. Y.D. 173:4.

2. A debt may be sold only if the buyer accepts liability. This means that if the borrower becomes unable (or unwilling) to pay, the buyer would take the loss. The seller may not guarantee that the note will be paid.

This is because ownership of a debt is defined by the potential for liability in case of non-payment. The owner of the promissory note is the person who stands to lose if its value decreases. When someone pays $900 for a $1000 note but accepts no risk (i.e., the seller guarantees that payment will be made), he has not truly purchased the note. In this case, the seller still owns the note, since he stands to lose if it is not paid. He has actually received $900 as a loan from the 'buyer,' passing the note as collateral for the loan. The 'buyer' is therefore prohibited from receiving more than his original $900.[4]

3. Although the buyer must accept liability, this obligation may be limited. He is required to accept liability for a loss which is due to the borrower's failure to pay, but he is *not* required to accept liability for loss due to other factors, such as the note proving to be a forgery, or the discovery that the debt had already been collected[5] or cannot be

---

4. Y.D. ibid., as explained by *Taz* 3. This holds true even when the seller guarantees only the purchase price ($900, in our example), and not the full debt ($1000) (*Shach* 173:9).

If the seller guarantees the full value of the note, some poskim hold that this is a Biblically prohibited form of Ribbis (*Maharit* Y.D. 39). Others maintain that this is only a Rabbinic prohibition (*Sefer HaTerumos* 4:13, *Maharshag* Y.D. 2; see *Bris Yehudah* 15:n10).

[It would appear that this dispute depends on how the prohibition is understood. According to the explanation offered above, when a note is guaranteed by the seller, no sale has truly taken place. This is actually a loan, for which collateral was offered. According to this understanding, the prohibition is Biblical.

Sefer HaTerumos understands it differently. He explains that a sale has taken place. It is only later, when the borrower fails to pay and the person who sold the note fulfills his guarantee by paying the debt, that the sale is nullified. When the note was sold, it was not certain that this would happen. Therefore, according to *Sefer HaTerumos*, the prohibition is only Rabbinic.

Levush 173:4, *Taz* 173:3 and *S.A. Harav* §57 all accept the first explanation of this prohibition. It would therefore appear that they hold this prohibition to be a Biblical one, in line with the ruling of *Maharit*. This opinion should therefore be accepted as halachah. See Chapter 2, Note 1, for a list of practical differences between Biblical and Rabbinic forms of Ribbis.]

5. Y.D. 173:4. If the note proves to be a forgery, the seller would be obligated to reimburse the buyer even if he had not explicitly guaranteed to do so at the time of the sale. This is because the original sale was a *mekach ta'us*, an erroneous sale. The rules of *mekach ta'us* protect a buyer who receives damaged or unusable merchandise; see C.M. 66:34. [This holds true even if, at the time of sale, the seller was not aware that it was a forgery.]

collected for other legal reasons.[6]

4. When a sale is nullified because the debt had already been collected, the seller is only obligated to refund the purchase price of the note ($900, in our example) to the buyer.[7]

5. Once the promissory note was sold, the seller may not collect the debt from the borrower. If the seller later cheated the buyer by collecting the debt from the borrower, he is obligated to pay the buyer the full value of the promissory note.[8]

Methods of Protecting the Buyer

6. When purchasing a promissory note, a person typically wants to be protected from losing his money if the borrower fails to pay. We have already seen that the person selling the note may not guarantee that the buyer will receive payment. Still, there are ways in which the buyer can protect himself against loss. These include the following:

□ The buyer may demand collateral from the borrower. If the person selling the note had originally taken collateral from the borrower, he may transfer it to the buyer.[9]

□ An outside party (other than the seller) may guarantee the note. If the borrower fails to pay his debt, this guarantor would pay the buyer.[10]

---

6. For example, if the note had been designated as collateral for a previous loan (Y.D. 173:4) or if the government abolished all debts (*Beis Yosef* 173 from *Teshuvos HaRashba*, *Shach* 173:10; cf. *Chochmas Adam* 139:8). [In the case of a government decree, the seller would not be obligated to reimburse the buyer unless he had specifically obligated himself to do so (C.M. 66:34).]

7. *Bris Yehudah* 15:n12 based on *Shach* C.M. 66:111.

This refers to cases where the seller did not explicitly guarantee the note. If the seller does specifically guarantee the note for its full value, some poskim hold that he is obligated to pay the full face value ($1000) if it proves to be a forgery (*S.A. Harav* §57; see also *Maharam Shick* Y.D. 162, s.v. *u'lichora*, who explains the *Shulchan Aruch* this way, although he does not come to a clear decision).

Bris Yehudah maintains that this is also prohibited (except in the case outlined in the following paragraph). Additionally, *Bris Yehudah* 15:7 rules that anytime the sale of debt is invalidated as *mekach ta'us*, the seller may only refund the purchase price. This also appears to be the opinion of *Chochmas Adam* 139:9.

8. *Bris Yehudah* ibid.

9. Y.D. 173:4.

10. Y.D. ibid.

7. Later poskim suggest another method of guaranteeing the promissory note.[11] When buying the note, the buyer may add the following provision to the terms of sale: "If the borrower is presently too poor to repay the loan, this sale is null and void."

If it is later discovered that the borrower was too poor to pay, the sale would be nullified and the buyer would be entitled to a refund of his purchase moneys.[12]

This method would only protect the buyer if the borrower was a poor man at the time the note was purchased. If he was capable of repaying the loan at that time, but subsequently suffered financial losses which make him unable to pay, the buyer would suffer the loss.

8. An alternative form of this provision would state: "This purchase is made on the understanding that the borrower is not a credit risk. If the borrower is presently a credit risk, to the degree that he would have difficulty obtaining a loan, this sale is null and void."

This phrase offers the buyer better protection than the previous form.[13] Still, if the borrower is not a credit risk at the time of the loan, the buyer is not protected if the borrower later fails to make payment.

Voluntary Reimbursement

9. When a promissory note is sold properly, the buyer accepts liability.

Later, if the borrower fails to pay, the seller is permitted to refund the buyer's money or even to pay him the entire value of the promissory

---

11. This is based on *Ksav Sofer* Y.D. 85. *Chasam Sofer* (6:26) suggested still another method of guaranteeing a note, see Paragraph 15, below.

12. By making this a condition of the sale, the buyer is guaranteed that the borrower is capable of repaying the loan. If it should turn out that he was unable to pay at the time he purchased the note, the sale of the note would become invalidated as a *mekach ta'us*, an erroneous sale, since the purchase was made under the false assumption that the borrower was then capable of paying the loan. (This condition may not be drawn to guarantee that the borrower would not become poor, in the future.)

In this case, the seller would refund the purchase price of the note ($900, in our example), but not its full face value ($1000).

13. Based on *Maharam Shick* Y.D. 161-2. Since the definition of 'credit risk' can be contested, it is preferable that a clear definition be included. For example, the sale could be made contingent on the borrower's credit rating at a specific financial institution.

The advantage in using this language is that the buyer is protected even if the borrower is wealthy enough to repay the loan, but is a credit risk because of his dishonesty.

note. Since he is not obligated to do this, it does not nullify the original sale.[14]

Using a Heter Iska

10. If a proper Heter Iska is used, the seller may guarantee that the loan will be repaid. It should be noted that the standard Heter Iska form is not appropriate for use in this case. An appropriate form appears at the end of this chapter.

Notes Which Are Written to Create Debt

11. These rules even apply to a promissory note which was written when no loan or credit has taken place.

For example, Reuven is in need of funds. His friend, Shimon, would like to lend him money but does not have the available funds. Shimon may write a promissory note, obligating himself to give Reuven $1000 in six months.[15] Reuven could now sell this note to a third person for $900 cash. At the end of the six months, Shimon would pay $1000 to the person holding the note, and Reuven would owe him this amount of money. This is permitted under the conditions outlined above for the sale of promissory notes.[16]

This is permitted despite the fact that the note was written for the specific purpose of raising money by selling it for a discount.[17] However, Shimon must understand that when he writes the note to Reuven, he

---

14. *Bris Yehudah* 15:n25, *Mishnas Ribbis* 13:n2. Whenever the sale transaction remains valid, none of the laws of Ribbis apply. It is not clear if this holds true in cases where no *kinyan* was made at the time that the promissory note was originally sold — see Paragraph 13. (See also Paragraph 14 for a list of appropriate *kinyanim*.)

15. This note is given to Reuven as a loan, in place of cash. In exchange for this note, Reuven owes Shimon $1000.

16. *Kuntres HaSma* 18; this is permitted only when the person buying the promissory note did not set up this situation by suggesting that Shimon write this note for Reuven. *Sma* also requires that at the end of the six months, the third person collect the debt from Shimon, not Reuven. [The provision outlined above in Paragraph 9, allowing voluntary payment (by the person selling the note), does not apply in this case (*Bris Yehudah* 15:n25).]

17. Y.D. 173:5 discusses a case of a community doing this to raise funds for community needs. In this case, the community presells certain rights which it holds (the example used involves a community that distributes licenses to sell wine; contemporary examples might include selling the right to use an organization's catering hall or preselling certain honors which are traditionally sold in the synagogue) and receives promissory notes in return. These notes are then sold at discount, for the purpose of raising cash.

has truly obligated himself to pay Reuven these funds at the designated time, even if Reuven does not sell the note.[18]

12. The rules outlined above also apply to a promissory note which was written as part of a business transaction. For example, a customer received goods and issued a promissory note in lieu of payment. The note may be sold at discount, only under the conditions outlined above.

How Debt Is Sold

13. Financial transactions are not binding when they are concluded by oral agreement alone.[19] Unless a formal *kinyan* is performed, either side may withdraw from the agreement.

There is considerable disagreement as to how this affects the laws of Ribbis. Some poskim maintain that debt may be sold at a discount only if a formal *kinyan* takes place. This is because a legal transfer of the debt must take place at the time that the debt is sold.[20] Others disagree and maintain that no *kinyan* is required. According to this view, a sale is valid even if no *kinyan* has taken place, as long as neither side withdraws from the agreement.[21]

Since this is a subject of dispute, a *kinyan* should be performed to validate the sale.

14. A *kinyan* may be performed in any one of the following ways:

a) *Maamad Shiloshton* (a meeting of the three): The borrower, seller and buyer come together and the seller tells the borrower,

---

18. *S.A. Harav*, quoted by his grandson in *Tzemach Tzedek* (*Piskei Dinim* to 173), *Bris Yehudah* 15:n23.

19. Oral agreements are not enforceable in Beis Din. Still, a person who is meticulous in performing mitzvos should consider his oral commitments as binding (*Bava Metzia* 49a; see *Rema* C.M. 204:11 and *Shach* 5).

Even where there was no oral commitment, if a person has made a firm decision in his own mind to commit to an agreement, it is preferable that he follow through with this decision (*Igros Moshe* C.M. 1:58). Others disagree and hold that a mental decision to buy or sell does not create a moral commitment to follow through with his decision (*Pri Yitzchak* 1:51).

20. *Shach* 173:8, *Chochmas Adam* 139:8, *S.A. Harav* §57, *Shealas Yaavetz* 39, *Teshuvos Maharam Alshich* 100, *Ben Ish Chai* to *V'eschanan* 21. According to this opinion, the transfer of debt is only viewed as a sale in cases where the sale is legally binding.

21. *Chavos Daas* 173:4, *Machneh Ephraim* §33. This opinion is supported by the fact that *Shulchan Aruch* mentions no requirement regarding a *kinyan* (*Machneh Ephraim*).

Even according to this opinion, this sale would be permitted only if the individuals involved referred to the transaction as a sale and not as a loan.

"The debt which is owed to me because of this loan should be paid to the buyer."[22]

This method is valid both where a promissory note has been written for the debt and where no such note exists.[23]

b) *Shtar* (contract): A postscript may be added to the promissory note, stating that the debt is being transferred, in its entirety, to the buyer.[24] The seller then hands this note to the buyer. When a note is payable to the bearer, no postscript is necessary.[25]

c) All other *kinyanim* which are routinely accepted by merchants in a community as binding for the sale of promissory notes, and which are enforceable by law, are also valid *kinyanim* according to most poskim.[26] This is known as *kinyan situmta*.

Purchasing Debt From a Non-Jew

15. **Non-interest-bearing notes:** A promissory note (even one which was written from one Jew to another) may be sold to a non-Jew, even if the seller guarantees the note. Later, the non-Jew would be permitted to sell the note to another Jew, even if he also guarantees the note.

Earlier, we had seen that if the seller guarantees the note, one Jew may not purchase a note from another Jew. However, in the case of a Jew purchasing a note from a non-Jew, it is the non-Jew who is guaranteeing the note to the Jewish buyer, and this is permitted.

Chasam Sofer suggested using this mechanism to sell notes between Jews, using non-Jewish buyers as intermediaries, so that the bond may

---

22. *Chochmas Adam* 139:8, based on *Shach* 173:8.

23. *Mishnas Ribbis* 13:n7, based on *Choshen Mishpat* 126:1 and *Shach* 126:2. [Cf. the language of *Shach* 173:8 and *Chochmas Adam* 139:8 which implies that a *kinyan* is valid only where no note had been written for the debt. However, this language must be explained differently, because it is clear from *Choshen Mishpat* that this *kinyan* is valid even where a note exists.]

24. *Shach* 173:8.

25. *Chochmas Adam* 139:8.

26. *Ben Ish Chai* to *V'eschanan* 23-24, *Mishnas Ribbis* 13:6.

Nesivos HaMishpat (201:1) holds that this type of *kinyan* is not valid for the sale of contracts. Most poskim, however, do not accept this opinion (*Maharsham* in *Mishpat Shalom* 201:2, *Aruch HaShulchan* 201:3, *Pischei Choshen* to *Halvaah* 10:19).

[Although *Nesivos HaMishpat* holds that this *kinyan* is not valid, it should be noted that the author of *Nesivos HaMishpat* himself, in *Chavos Daas* 173:4 (quoted in Note 21, above), does not require that a *kinyan* be made at all.]

be guaranteed. This is permitted, provided that the Jewish customer pursues the non-Jew should he need to fulfill the guarantee.[27] (The non-Jew would then collect from the Jew from whom he had purchased the note.)

16. Interest-bearing notes: A Jew is permitted to write a promissory note to a non-Jew, even if interest payments are required. If the non-Jew were then to sell this note to a Jew, the status of the loan would change; it now becomes a loan between two Jews, and interest may not be paid for the period that the debt is the property of the Jewish purchaser.[28]

17. In the case discussed in the previous paragraph, we have seen that a Jew who purchases an interest-bearing note cannot collect the interest which accrues after the sale. Still, where the non-Jew has an interest-bearing note, and he borrows money from a Jew, the lender may accept this note as collateral for the loan. Since the non-Jew is borrowing money (and not selling the debt), the interest is paid by him and not by the Jew who issued the note.

---

27. *Chasam Sofer* in Responsa 6:26, *Daas Torah* 173:4 s.v. *v'ayin Chasam Sofer, Tam Ribbis* 168:3. [To induce him to participate, the non-Jew would be offered a profit when reselling the note. For example, if the non-Jew purchased a $1000 note for $900, he would sell it to another Jew for $910.]

Chasam Sofer requires that the Jewish buyer agree that he will not pursue the Jewish seller for payment. The note should therefore be written in the name of the non-Jew.

If the Jewish buyer made a serious effort to collect from the non-Jew (for e.g., he sued him in court), but found that the non-Jewish seller is unwilling or unable to pay, he would then be permitted to collect from the original seller.

[This is permitted because a Jew may serve as an *areiv stam*, a regular guarantor, for a non-Jew (*Rema* 170:2; the concept of *areiv stam* is explained in the introduction to Chapter 15). The original seller may therefore back up the non-Jew's guarantee, with a guarantee of his own.]

28. Interest which had accrued prior to the sale may be paid. This is true even if provisions of the sale call for these payments to be made to the Jewish purchaser of the debt. [This is a subject of dispute between *Taz* 168:12 and *Shach* in *Nekudos HaKesef* ibid. The opinion quoted here is that of the *Taz*. This opinion is accepted by the later poskim (*Gra* 168:25, *Chavos Daas* 168: *Chidushim* 20, *Chochmas Adam* 137:11, *Divrei Chaim* Y.D. 2:56, *Avnei Nezer* 194:16; see also *Bris Yehudah* 31:10).]

If the promissory note is written in a manner which does not allow for prepayment of the debt, a Jew may purchase the note and continue to collect interest until the date that the note is due (*Rema* 168:20; in this case the entire interest charge already existed when the non-Jew owned the note).

[In this case, the purchaser would be limited to collecting the interest which is included in the original agreement. If the payments were not made on time, no additional interest charges could be added.]

Later if the non-Jew were to fail to make payment, the money he owes could be collected from the collateral. However, the Jewish lender may not collect any of the interest which accrued after the debt was designated as collateral directly from the Jewish borrower. This money could only be collected by the non-Jew (and then passed on to the lender).[29]

A Non-Jew's Promissory Notes

18. A Jew who owns the promissory note of a non-Jew may sell it to another Jew under the conditions outlined above, Paragraphs 1-3. This is permitted even if the note earns interest while it is being held.[30]

19. We have seen that many poskim require that a proper *kinyan* be made when a note is sold. When the promissory note is for the debt of a non-Jew, there is disagreement among the poskim regarding the proper *kinyan* which should be made.[31] It is preferable that a *kinyan situmta* be used to transfer the debt to the buyer.[32]

---

29. *Mishnas Ribbis* 17:n13 based on *Taz* 168:12. This is because of the concern that if the Jewish lender were to collect this money from the Jewish borrower it would seem to be interest which accrued to him. This is not a question of Ribbis Ketzutzah.

30. *Rema* 168:end of 18. When the note earns interest, the buyer must accept liability even if he is not buying it at a discount (*Mishnas Ribbis* 13:n9).

31. *Shach* 168:60 and 173:8 maintains that a non-Jew's debt cannot be transferred by *kinyan*. He rules that the debt could effectively be sold only in the following manner. The seller tells the person who is buying the debt, "In exchange for these moneys, I hereby forgive the debt which is owed to me by the non-Jew, but I will not notify him of this. If he gives me money because of this debt, I will not acquire it for myself. Instead, I will pass these moneys on to you."

Chochmas Adam adds the following: "Any moneys which you receive directly from the non-Jew are yours." (See Y.D. 168:16.)

In this case, the original lender forgives the debt only as a legal fiction. This enables the buyer to receive the debt payment in a manner which excludes the seller from the transaction.

Chochmas Adam 137:26 and *S.A. Harav* §69 accept the *Shach's* ruling.

Other poskim disagree and maintain that any of the three *kinyanim* mentioned above (Paragraph 14) can be used to transfer the debt of a non-Jew (*Pischei Teshuvah* 168:6, *Shaar Deah* 168:8, *Beis Shlomo* C.M. 21).

32. *Ben Ish Chai* to *V'eschanan* 23, maintains that even if other *kinyanim* are not valid, *kinyan situmta* is valid. It is possible that *Shach* would concede this point, as he explicitly rules out only other *kinyanim*.

Many contemporary poskim rule that one may rely on this opinion (*Mishnas Ribbis* 13:n11; we may accept this opinion because many poskim hold that no *kinyan* is required at all — see Paragraph 13, above).

[If one prefers, he may certainly follow *Shach's* opinion, quoted in the previous note.]

Applications

20. Mortgages are promissory notes. A Jew who extended a mortgage to a non-Jew (and is receiving interest payments) may later sell that mortgage to another Jew provided that the purchaser accepts liability, so that if the borrower were to become unable (or unwilling) to pay his debt, the purchaser would suffer the loss.[33]

If a non-Jew owns the mortgage of a Jew and he wishes to sell it to another Jew, see Chapter 13, Paragraphs 45-47.

21. Heter Iska agreements: When a lender uses a Heter Iska, he creates a partnership with the person in need of the funds. A Heter Iska is not a promissory note. It is a business agreement which gives the investor (the lender) a share in the investments of the person receiving the funds. Still, it does contain conditions for payment, and may be sold in the same manner as a promissory note, as outlined in the beginning of this chapter.[34]

---

33. Y.D. 168:18, *Shach* 173:8. This is because the seller may not serve as a guarantor for the mortgage, just as a Jew may not guarantee any loan which calls for Ribbis payments to be paid to another Jew. This is true even if the seller guarantees only the principal and not the interest (see *S.A. Harav* §69).

Although the buyer must accept liability, this obligation may be limited. He must be liable only for loss which is caused by the borrower's failure to pay. He is not required to accept liability for loss caused by other factors, as explained above in Paragraphs 2-8.

34. *Mishnas Ribbis* 13:20. The buyer of a promissory note must accept liability for loss only when he buys it for a discount. The buyer of an Iska, though, must accept liability whether he buys it for a discount or at full value. Since the buyer receives profits during the term of the Iska, he must be its true owner. This requires that he be liable for loss.

We have seen (in Paragraph 13) that most poskim require that a proper *kinyan* be made when a promissory note is sold. This also applies to the sale of a Heter Iska.

Kitzos HaChoshen (66:35) discusses the proper *kinyan* for the sale of an Iska. The various forms of *kinyan* mentioned earlier are appropriate for the sale of debt. When an investment is sold, these *kinyanim* may not work to transfer ownership. *Kitzos HaChoshen* therefore rules that *kinyan agav* be used. This is accomplished in the following manner. The person selling the Iska should also sell a small portion of his house (or other real estate) to the buyer. The buyer should pay him for this and for the Iska simultaneously, thereby taking ownership of both the property and the Iska with one payment. We will see in Chapter 23 that there are two types of Heter Iska; this works for both the *kulo pikadon* and *palga pikadon* Iska forms. (The seller may subsequently repurchase the real estate which he had sold. This does not effect the sale of the Heter Iska.)

[Of the forms of *kinyan* mentioned earlier (in regard to the sale of promissory notes), it is clear that *maamad shiloshton* is appropriate only for the transfer of debt, not for the sale of investments (see *Bris Yehudah* 35:n65).

Kitzos HaChoshen discusses whether *shtar* is a proper *kinyan* for an Iska. *Maharit* 2:21 (quoted by *Kitzos HaChoshen* and by *Nesivos HaMishpat* 66:38) maintains that

22. Transferring bank accounts: A bank account is actually a statement of debt which the bank owes the depositor. A person may sell an account only if the buyer accepts liability, as outlined in this chapter. A proper *kinyan* is also required.[35]

23. A person who has moneys in a term account or a certificate of deposit may suddenly find himself in need of cash. If he were to withdraw these funds, he would incur a substantial penalty. He may therefore ask another person to advance the same amount of cash that is in the account. In exchange, the depositor conveys ownership of the bank deposit to the other person, stipulating that any interest which accrues for the remainder of the term of deposit would belong to the other person.[36]

This arrangement is permitted only if the other person accepts liability, so that he would take the loss if the deposit became uncollectible. Although most poskim require that a *kinyan* take place when debt is transferred, it is not clear what type of *kinyan* would be valid for this type of transfer (see note below).[37]

A Heter Iska may also be used to facilitate this arrangement.

Purchase Notes

24. In many industries, it is common for payment to be made in the form of a note. Many businesses do not actually wait and redeem the note. Instead, they sell it at a discount. One Jew may sell a note to another only if the purchaser accepts liability (in the manner described

---

investments may not be sold by *shtar*. (This would certainly preclude use of *kinyan shtar* when a *kulo pikadon* type of Iska is used, and may also disqualify a *shtar* for the investment portion of a *palga pikadon* type of Heter Iska.) See also *Maharshag* Y.D. 3 and *Bris Yehudah* 35:19.

However, it is not clear why *kinyan situmta* is not mentioned as an acceptable method of transferring investments.]

35. *Mishnas Ribbis* 13:8. Regarding the proper *kinyan*, see Note 37.

36. [This arrangement is not a loan, but a sale of the bank deposit. The parties involved should refer to this transaction as a sale rather than a loan.]

37. If arrangements could be made for the bank to transfer the deposit to the name of the lender, this would certainly be a valid *kinyan*. Other legal means of transfer (such as conveying a contract which assigns the debt to the lender) would also be valid, if they were recognized by the bank. These are not practical options. In fact, banks do not allow any transfer of time deposits or CDs unless the old account is closed and a new account is opened. This would incur the penalty which the depositor is seeking to avoid.

Therefore, the only viable method for transfer would be the *Shach's* method, outlined above in Note 31. An alternative option would be to use a Heter Iska.

in Paragraphs 2 and 3) and a *kinyan* is made. If the seller signs his name to the note and hands it to the buyer, this is a valid *kinyan*.[38]

The seller may not guarantee the note (as in Paragraph 2, above). Therefore, a business which does sell notes in this manner should use a Heter Iska. It is not necessary to draw a separate Heter Iska for each note which is cashed. It would be sufficient to use a Heter Iska Klali which covers all transactions between the business and its factor. An appropriate Heter Iska Klali appears in Appendix II to Chapter 12.

Bank Checks and Money Orders

25. Bank checks and money orders are promissory notes, written by a bank. These may be sold, for a discount, in the same manner as all promissory notes.[39]

Cashing Checks

26. May checks be cashed at a discount?

This issue is a complex one, and is dependent on an accurate interpretation of secular banking laws. There is a major difference between European law and American law in this regard. In Paragraphs 27-31, the published opinion of contemporary poskim is presented. These poskim were dealing with cases involving checks which were drawn on British or Israeli banks. In Paragraph 32, we have presented the halachah regarding checks which are drawn on banks in the United States.

27. Checks issued by a third party: A check represents a debt which the bank owes its customer. When Reuven issues a check, payable

---

38. This is a *kinyan shtar*. If the note is payable to bearer, no notation is necessary; it would suffice to simply hand the note to the buyer (*Chochmas Adam* 139:8, based on *Rema* C.M. 66:1).

[Unfortunately, the practice of discounting notes is widespread in many industries, even where the seller guarantees the debt. Perhaps this is because businesses rely on the ruling of *Igros Moshe* (2:63) who holds that corporations are permitted to pay Ribbis. According to this opinion, a corporation is permitted to sell a bond on discount (providing that there are no personal guarantees on the bond). This ruling is the subject of dispute among contemporary poskim. To avoid this problem, it is certainly preferable to use a Heter Iska.

It should be noted that according to *Igros Moshe*, this leniency would only apply where the note is sold by a corporation. If a note was issued by a corporation, to an individual, even *Igros Moshe* would concede that the individual would not be permitted to sell the note at a discount.]

39. *Mishnas Ribbis* 13:n15.

to Shimon, the bank's debt is transferred to Shimon.[40] If Shimon then asks Levi to cash the check for him, the debt is transferred to Levi at the time that he pays cash for it. The bank now owes Levi the money which is on deposit.[41]

Therefore, in regard to the laws of Ribbis, a check has the same status as a promissory note. Levi may be offered a discount for cashing the check, but only if he accepts liability. If payment is later refused, he would suffer the loss.[42]

---

40. This is the opinion of the poskim cited in Notes 41 and 42. **Please note** that this does *not* apply to checks drawn on American banks. The law regarding these checks is presented separately, in Paragraph 32.

41. **An important question:** The transaction between Shimon and Levi, where Shimon sells Levi this check, can be viewed in two different ways:

One could say that this is a transaction involving the bank's debt to Reuven. Originally, when Reuven gave Shimon the check, he transferred the bank's debt to Shimon. When Shimon asks Levi to cash the check, he is transferring the bank's debt to Levi. This is how the transaction is understood by *Minchas Yitzchak* (7:beginning of 64), and this is how it has been presented here. According to this explanation, the sale involves the bank's debt.

One could argue that Shimon is actually selling the debt which Reuven owes him as a result of their previous transaction. The check is only a means of collecting this debt. According to this explanation, it is Reuven's debt, and not the bank's debt, which is being sold.

A practical difference between these explanations: We have seen that debt may be sold at a discount only when the buyer accepts liability if the borrower fails to pay. The seller may accept other liabilities, but not the liability for loss which is caused by the borrower. In our case, who is the borrower?

According to the first explanation, the bank is the borrower, and its debt is being sold. The buyer would have to accept the risk that the bank will fail and be unable to pay its obligations. If this happens, he would suffer the loss. However, if the check were to bounce due to Reuven's negligence (for example, if there were insufficient funds), the agreement may call for the seller to be liable.

According to the second explanation, Reuven is the borrower and his debt is being sold to Levi. The buyer would have to accept liability if the check were returned due to Reuven's negligence. This includes the risk that there are insufficient funds to cover payment.

This is a major difference; most people would be willing to accept the risk of bank failure, but would be reluctant to accept the risk that the check may bounce. We have followed the opinion of *Minchas Yitzchak* who rules that the seller (Shimon) may accept liability if the check is returned due to insufficient funds. The buyer is only obligated to accept liability for lack of payment which is caused by the bank itself.

Minchas Yitzchak's ruling was written in Israel. The law regarding checks drawn on American banks is presented separately below, see Paragraph 32.

42. *Bris Yehudah* 15:16.

This ruling is a matter of dispute among contemporary poskim: A check is not actually a promissory note (even under Israeli law). It is an order of payment which

28. Liability: How much liability must the buyer accept?

The buyer is not liable if the check proved to be a forgery[43] or if the check was drawn on an account which no longer exists.[44] The buyer may also stipulate that the seller is liable if the check bounces because there are not sufficient funds in the account.[45] The buyer must only be liable for loss which is caused by the bank's failure to pay (for example, bank failure or a bank error).

---

instructs the bank to release funds to a particular individual. For this reason, some poskim maintain that a check may not be cashed at a discount, even if the person who is receiving the check is willing to accept liability. This would be based on the fact that debt cannot be transferred without a *kinyan*. Since the check is not a promissory note, its transfer does not effect a transfer of the debt (*Birchas Shamayim* Y.D. 44, *Ribbis LeOhr HaHalachah* 13:5, R' Moshe Shaul Klein Shlita, writing in *Am HaTorah* 5753).

Bris Yehudah (15:n37) agrees that a check is not actually a promissory note, but nevertheless rejects the argument that it cannot be sold. He points out that debt can be transferred by *kinyan* even if no note was written for it. We have seen that any *kinyan* which merchants accept as binding and is enforceable by law is a valid *kinyan* (this is known as *kinyan situmta*). This applies whenever a check is endorsed and given to another person. Since this is a valid *kinyan*, a check may be cashed at a discount under the guidelines for selling debt which are outlined in this chapter.

This is also the opinion of *Minchas Yitzchak* 7:64, *Keren HaTorah* 173:33, *Toras Ribbis* 18:18 and *Divrei Sofrim* in B.H. to 173:4. One may rely on this opinion.

43. C.M. 66:34.

44. This is similar to someone who sells a promissory note which was already paid (Y.D. 173:4).

45. *Minchas Yitzchak* ibid., as explained in Note 41. [In this case, there is no difference if the account did not have sufficient funds at the time the check was sold or if its funds were withdrawn later.]

According to the second explanation, mentioned in Note 41, the buyer must be liable if the check were to bounce. [If the bank returned the check because there were insufficient funds to cover it, Levi may pursue Reuven (who issued the check) to demand payment, but he may not pursue Shimon (who issued the check) (*Mishnas Ribbis* 13:n15).]

One who wishes to satisfy this opinion could still protect himself against loss if the check should bounce. He could accept liability in a limited way by making the following stipulation when cashing the check: "I accept this check with the understanding that there are presently sufficient funds in the account to cover the check. If there are not sufficient funds at this time, the sale of this check is null and void."

This stipulation (which may be made orally or in writing) protects the person who is paying for the check, but not completely. If the account had sufficient funds when the stipulation was made, but the funds were subsequently withdrawn, he would remain liable. Still, where he can cash the check promptly, this is a practical solution, since the level of risk would be acceptable to most people (based on *Maharam Shick* Y.D. 161-2, quoted above, Paragraph 8, and *Bris Yehudah* 15:n18; *Mishnas Ribbis* 15:n16 recommends that check-cashing establishments display a declaration stating that all transactions are done based on this clause of *Maharam Shick*).

29. When a check is sold at a discount, a *kinyan* should be made by having the seller endorse the check and hand it to the buyer. If the check is made to 'cash,' no endorsement is necessary.[46]

Offering One's Own Check at a Discount

30. According to many poskim, a person who has money in his checking account may write a check and sell it to someone else at a discount. For example, someone who is in need of cash and is unable to go to a bank may write a $100 check and cash it for $90. The person selling the check may guarantee that there are funds in his account. The person buying the check would have to accept liability if the check could not be cashed for other reasons (for example, if the bank failed).[47]

31. A person may not sell his check at a discount, in the following cases:

☐ If he has no funds in the account, he may not sell a check written on the account (even if he has overdraft privileges). In this case, the bank owes him no money, and he would not be selling a debt.[48]

☐ If there are funds in the account, but the individual already issued checks (which did not yet clear the bank) for those moneys, he may not issue another check on the same moneys.[49]

☐ If the check is postdated, even if there are funds in the account, the check may not be sold at a discount.[50]

---

46. This is based on *Bris Yehudah*, who rules that the check must be transferred in the normal manner of businessmen. When instruments are payable to bearer, a *kinyan* can be made without the signature of the seller (*Chochmas Adam* 139:8, based on *Rema* 66:1).

47. *Bris Yehudah* 15:17, based on the reasoning outlined in the previous paragraph. Those who disagree with that ruling would disagree here as well. (See also the added objections of *Divrei Sofrim* in B.H. to 173:4.)

The person writing the check may not subsequently withdraw the funds which are needed to cover the check from the account (or write other checks on those moneys). The person buying the check does not have to accept liability for this (*Bris Yehudah* 15:n38).

48. *Bris Yehudah* 15:17. This is similar to a person who sells his own promissory note; see Paragraph 35, below.

49. *Bris Yehudah* 15:n39 expresses uncertainty regarding the halachah in both these cases.

50. *Divrei Sofrim* in B.H. to 173:4.

Checks Drawn on U.S. Banks

32. The poskim quoted in Paragraphs 27-31 were discussing checks which are drawn on Israeli banks. They permit checks to be sold at a discount (under the conditions outlined above), because the bank's debt is transferred when a check is written. It is clear that this is not true in the United States, under present banking regulations. Under U.S. law, debt is not transferred when a check is written. Since debt is not being sold, offering a check at a discount (if it is drawn on a U.S. bank) is prohibited as Ribbis.[51]

Foreign Currency Checks

33. Checks drawn on foreign currencies may be sold in the manner outlined in Paragraphs 27-31. This also applies in the United States if the checks were drawn on European or Israeli banks.[52]

---

51. Under U.S. law, an individual who passes a check is entitled to subsequently go to his bank and issue a stop payment order, which prevents the bank from honoring the check. Thus, the depositor retains legal rights to the money even after selling the check. This makes it clear that the bank's obligation is not truly sold to the buyer. A lengthier analysis of these laws appears as an appendix to this chapter (Appendix III).

Mishnas Ribbis (13:n14) suggests that the ruling of *Bris Yehudah* applies only in Israel, where bank laws require that cause be shown before a stop order is issued. Israeli law is based on British law, where it is a crime to stop payment on a check without good cause.

This is a compelling argument. Since this is a question of Ribbis Ketzutzah, one should be careful to refrain from this practice.

52. The issue of checks which are drawn on foreign currencies is discussed by many contemporary poskim; see *Minchas Yitzchak* 7:64, *Bris Yehudah* 15:n18, *Toras Ribbis* 19:n52 and *Mishnas Ribbis* 13:n15.

A question: When the purchaser is unable to cash a check because the check is a forgery or for legal reasons, the person who sold the note or check must refund the money which he received. We have already seen (in Paragraph 4) that he may only return the amount of money which he originally received. Where the check was for foreign currency, there is an additional complication. For example, a check for 10,000 *yen* was sold (at a 10% discount) for $90, at a time that 100 *yen* were worth $1 (the 10,000-*yen* check was therefore worth $100). Later, it was discovered that the check was forged and the purchaser asks that his payment be refunded. However, in the interim the value of the *yen* went up, so that the 10,000-*yen* check is now worth 10% more, or $110. The purchaser therefore requests a refund of $99 to reflect the 10% increase of the check while it was in his possession.

Bris Yehudah (ibid.) forbids this. He rules that the person selling the check may only return the original payment in the local currency. (Where the original payment was made in a foreign currency, the seller would repay this money based on its value in the local currency at the time of payment.)

Minchas Yitzchak disagrees. He holds that the payment may include the additional

Charging for Expenses

34. When someone does not accept liability, he may only cash a check for its face value. He is permitted to deduct a fee for his exertion or for the expenses incurred when cashing the check.[53] This fee must be fair, commensurate to the exertion and expense which is involved. Where checks are drawn on local banks, this fee would be nominal. However, where foreign checks or instruments of credit are involved, there may be a greater amount of difficulty and expense involved. In this case, a significant fee would be permitted.[54]

Selling One's Own Promissory Note

35. A person may not sell his own promissory note (i.e., a note which he writes, obligating himself to make a payment to the bearer of the note) under any condition. In this case, the note does not represent an obligation to pay while it is in the seller's hand. When this note is passed to a 'buyer,' new debt is created. This is not considered a sale of a financial instrument.

When receiving funds in exchange for this note, a person is borrowing money. If a $1000 note were sold for $900, this would constitute Biblically prohibited Ribbis.[55]

---

value of the foreign currency. However, he limits this to the increase in value at the time that the two parties realized that the check could not be cashed. If the currency continued to increase afterwards, even if payment was not yet made, it would be prohibited to forward this additional money.

53. *Minchas Yitzchak* 7:64.

54. *Mishnas Ribbis* 13:n18, quoting the author of *Bris Yehudah*. There is a greater risk of being defrauded when cashing foreign checks. One may charge for accepting this risk (ibid.). [The case discussed by *Minchas Yitzchak* also involved a foreign check.]

Since expense charges must reflect the true expense of processing a check, these charges should be a flat fee, regardless of the amount of the check. Charges which are based on a percentage of the check's face value do not accurately reflect expense costs, since these expenses do not rise in proportion to the check's value. (See *Ribbis L'Ohr HaHalachah* 13:9, *Mishnas Ribbis* 13:13; a collection of opinions on this matter appears in *Kovetz Beis Talmud Lehoraah* 4:71.)

Where foreign checks are involved, a charge which is based on a percentage of the check's value is appropriate. This is because the primary expense in dealing with foreign checks is the possibility of loss due to the difficulties in collection. The cost associated with this risk is based on the value of the check (*Mishnas Ribbis* 13:n18, quoting the author of *Bris Yehudah*; this is also the opinion of *Minchas Yitzchak* ibid.).

55. *Chochmas Adam* 143:8, *Nachalas David* Responsa 5, quoting Rabbi Chaim of Volozhin, *Bris Yehudah* 15:15. This is prohibited, even when the owner of the note sells it through an agent (*Nachalas David*, ibid.).

Stocks and Bonds

36. Two common ways for a business to raise capital are by selling shares in their business or by issuing bonds.

When someone buys a share in a company, he becomes a partner in the company, and has a share in its profits and the losses. This is an investment and not a loan. The laws of Ribbis do not apply.

37. Bonds are actually interest-paying loans which are guaranteed by the institution issuing them. One should not purchase a bond from a Jewish-owned business, unless a Heter Iska is used.[56]

38. Bonds issued by non-Jewish businesses may be purchased. If a business is owned by both Jews and non-Jews, it is considered a non-Jewish business if a majority of the shares are owned by non-Jews[57] and these non-Jews actually run the business.[58]

---

56. The standard Heter Iska form may be used.

Igros Moshe (Y.D. 2:63) maintains that a corporation is permitted to pay Ribbis for loans that it takes. According to this opinion, a person is permitted to purchase bonds from a Jewish business, provided that the loan is guaranteed by the business and not by the individuals who own the business. However, we have seen (Chapter 5, Paragraph 27) that this ruling is a subject of dispute among contemporary poskim. The sale of bonds involves questions of Biblically prohibited Ribbis. One should therefore follow the stringent opinions and use a Heter Iska when purchasing these bonds.

Israeli Government Bonds: The Israeli Government uses a Heter Iska to permit the sale of its bonds. *Bris Yehudah* (7:n68) questions whether it is appropriate for a government to use a Heter Iska. A Heter Iska is valid because of the possibility that profits will be generated by the investment. Since the government is not involved in generating profits, this would seem inappropriate. He nevertheless concedes that one who wishes to rely on the lenient opinions who permit this may do so. According to *Igros Moshe* (ibid.) a Heter Iska is not required; this is also the opinion of *Har Tzvi* Y.D. 126.

Israeli Government Loans: The Israeli government offers loans to new immigrants, at low-interest rates. One may not pay Ribbis to any Jewish institution, including the Israeli government. A Heter Iska should therefore be used (*Vechai Achicha Imach* §101).

57. *Bris Yehudah* 30:n43, based on *Shoel U'Meishiv* 1:3:31, *Shaarei Tzedek* 124, *Maharam Shick* 158 and *Maharsham* 1:20; see also the index page, Note 31. See also *Teshuvos Vehanhagos* 2:421, quoting Rabbi Yisroel Salanter.

58. If Jews own a significant share of the business, to the extent that their opinion carries weight in policy decisions, this is considered a Jewish company, in regard to the laws of Ribbis (R' Moshe Feinstein zt"l, quoted in *Mishnas Ribbis* 2:n7). This is also the opinion of R' Yecheskeil Roth Shlita (also quoted in *Mishnas Ribbis*); cf. *Bris Yehudah* ibid.

[This does not refer to situations where Jewish employees who are at management level own some company shares. In this situation, these people make decisions as employees not as owners, and this does not effect the status of the company. Rather, the reference here is to situations where Jews make management decisions because of their extensive degree of ownership.]

Trading Bonds

39. Bonds are a form of promissory note. A person is therefore permitted to sell a bond for a discount, in the same manner that promissory notes may be sold (i.e., where the buyer accepts liability, and when a proper *kinyan* is performed).[59]

40. **Non-transferable bonds** may not be sold (from one Jew to another) even when they were issued by non-Jewish institutions.[60]

Prepaying a Debt

41. A person is permitted to purchase his own promissory note, at a discount. For example, if Reuven owes Shimon $1000, payable in six months, he may offer Shimon $900 cash as full payment for the loan.[61]

Appendix I To Chapter Twelve: Heter Iska for Sale of Debt

(see Paragraph 10)

The following Heter Iska is suitable for use when selling a promissory note. If no Heter Iska is used when the note is sold, the person buying the note would have to accept the risk that the debtor will be unable or unwilling to pay, as explained in the beginning of this chapter. Most people would not be willing to accept this risk. But when the following Heter Iska is used, the person who purchases the note is actually investing in the seller's business or investments. He receives the note as payment for profits which are generated by this investment. If the note would later become worthless, the seller would still be obligated to pay the full face value of the note under the terms of this Iska.

---

59. *Bris Yehudah* 15:18. The transfer must be accomplished in a legally binding manner. Where bonds are held on account at a financial institution, the account must be transferred at that institution (ibid.).

60. *Bris Yehudah* 15:18. When a bond is non-transferable, it remains the property of its original owner. If he were to give it to a third party in exchange for money, this is not actually a sale, but rather collateral for a loan. Therefore, the person holding the bond could not sell it at a discount; he would even be prohibited from selling it for face value. This is because the interest which accrues after the sale actually belongs to the bond's original owner. Since the person 'buying' the bond is actually lending money, he is prohibited from accepting these interest payments.

61. Y.D. 173:4.

Iska Contract[1]

I, the undersigned, have extended the sum of $ _____ to _____ (hereafter referred to as the 'Managing Partner'), to be used for business investment purposes. The Managing Partner has obligated himself to utilize these funds in investments which he believes will generate profits. Any profits realized or losses sustained shall be shared equally between the Managing Partner and myself;

Any claim of loss, by the Managing Partner, must be verified through the testimony of two qualified witnesses in, and under conditions acceptable to, an Orthodox Jewish court of law. Any claim regarding the amount of profit generated by these investment(s) shall be verified under solemn oath, before and under conditions acceptable to, an Orthodox Jewish court of law.

It is agreed that if the Managing Partner will pay $ _____ (enter face value of the promissory note) to me, as payment of both the investment and the profits which are generated, then he will not be required to make any further payment nor will he be required to make an oath. I hereby acknowledge that I have received, from the Managing Partner, _____ (enter a description of the promissory note), to guarantee the aforementioned payment. In the event that the investments do not generate profits equal to this note, the Managing Partner shall have the option of verifying this in the manner described in the previous paragraph. In the event that he does so, I will return the aforementioned note to him, in return for the principal and/or profits to which I am entitled as a result of these investments. If the Managing Partner does not exercise this option by _____ (enter date on which the note is due), I shall have the option of using this note to collect payment.

I have paid one dollar to the Managing Partner as payment for his services during the term of our partnership.[2]

Continued on next page

---

1. This Heter Iska is based on a Heter Iska which was printed by *Chasam Sofer*, in the name of his teacher, Rabbi Nosson Adler. A brief Hebrew version appears in *Bris Yehudah* 41:6.

A traditional Heter Iska is given to an investor in exchange for funds. This Heter Iska is different in that it is given to the person receiving the money. This is because the tradional Heter Iska is given in exchange for cash which is advanced. In our case, the Heter Iska is given to acknowledge receipt of the promissory note.

2. The investor should pay one dollar to the Managing Partner, in addition to the

It is agreed that any dispute which may arise in connection with this agreement shall be submitted before _____ .[3] Judgment rendered by the aforesaid authority may be entered in any court having jurisdiction thereof. This agreement shall follow the guidelines of Heter Iska as explained in *Sefer Bris Yehudah* and has been executed in a manner which effects a legal transfer and obligation, known as *kinyan sudar*.

Signature of the Investor _____

Dated _____

Witnesses[4]

In witness whereof the above-mentioned parties have entered into this Heter Iska agreement on this _____ day of _____ .

Signature of Witness _____

Signature of Witness _____

Appendix II to Chapter Twelve: Heter Iska Klali for Sale of Notes

(see Paragraph 24)

The following Heter Iska is suitable for use when a person cashes a business's promissory notes at a discount. If no Heter Iska is used when the note is sold, the person buying the note would have to accept a loss if the debtor will be unable or unwilling to pay, as explained in the beginning of this chapter. Most people are not willing to accept this risk. When the previous Heter Iska is used, a new Heter Iska contract would have to be used every time a promissory note is cashed. The following Heter Iska addresses all transactions between a business and the individual who cashes its promissory notes. When this is used, additional Iska forms do not have to be used for each transaction.

---

moneys which he has paid for the note. The reason that this payment is necessary is explained below, in Chapter 22, Paragraph 29.

3. This part of the contract is optional.

4. This part of the contract is optional, depending on whether the parties prefer to have witnesses attest to their agreement.

However, the Heter Iska Klali should be mentioned each time a transaction takes place.

Iska Contract[1]

I. Whereas ABC Inc.[2] and Mr. XYZ desire that all their transactions be in accordance with Orthodox Jewish Law, which prohibits the payment and acceptance of Ribbis on loans between Jews;

II. We hereby declare that all transactions between us which involve the transfer of promissory notes or any other debt instrument is made in accordance with the terms of Heter Iska, stating that:

III. In exchange for funds received from Mr. XYZ, ABC Inc. shall transfer financial partnership (in the value of funds received) in any present investment, real estate or business that it may presently have to Mr. XYZ;

IV. Any profits realized or losses suffered as a result of the aforementioned investment(s), in the value of money received, shall be allocated to Mr. XYZ, except that ABC Inc. shall retain 5% of profits for his efforts as manager of the investment(s). Mr. XYZ accepts no liability in excess of the value of the funds invested on its behalf;

V. Any claim of loss by ABC Inc. must be verified through the testimony of two qualified witnesses in, and under conditions acceptable to, an Orthodox Jewish court of law. Any claim regarding the amount of profit generated by these investment(s) shall be verified by the owners of ABC Inc., under solemn oath, before and under conditions acceptable to, an Orthodox Jewish court of law;

VI. Whenever funds are advanced by Mr. XYZ, he shall receive a promissory note in the value of his investment plus anticipated profits. This promissory note may be drawn by a third party. It is agreed that in the event that Mr. XYZ receives the face value of this

Continued on next page

---

1. This Heter Iska is based on a Heter Iska which was printed by *Chasam Sofer*, in the name of his teacher, Rabbi Nosson Adler. That Iska is adapted here as a Heter Iska Klali contract, which is held by the company and is not actually signed every time a sale is made.

2. Wherever this contract refers to 'ABC Inc.,' enter the name of the company which receives cash for its notes. Wherever it refers to 'Mr. XYZ,' enter the name of the person or company which accepts the notes at discount.

note (whether by cashing it or by direct payment from ABC Inc.) he shall waive receipt of any additional profits. Additional profits, if any, shall belong to ABC Inc.;

VII. In the event that the investments do not generate profits equal to the aforementioned note, ABC Inc. shall have the option of verifying this in the manner described in Paragraph V. In the event that he does so, Mr. XYZ will return the aforementioned note to ABC Inc., in return for the principal and/or profits to which he is entitled as a result of these investments. If ABC Inc. does not exercise this option by the date on which the note is due, Mr. XYZ shall have the option of using this note to collect payment;

VII. Mr. XYZ shall be entitled to a presumption of credibility in any claim made regarding compliance with the terms of this agreement;

IX. ABC Inc. is obligated to return the invested funds and profits on the date stipulated by the promissory note. Mr. XYZ accepts no liability if the payee of the note fails to make payment. ABC Inc. shall remain obligated to make this payment in full;

X. In the event of any conflict between the terms of this Heter Iska and any other agreement between the parties relating to the aforementioned funds, the terms of this agreement shall prevail;

XI. This agreement shall follow the guidelines of Heter Iska as explained in *Sefer Bris Yehudah*. Payment by Mr. XYZ and its acceptance by ABC Inc. are accepted as a means of effecting this legal transfer and obligation, as applicable under Orthodox Jewish Law.

_____

Mr. XYZ

_____

ABC Inc.

Appendix III to Chapter Twelve:
An Analysis of the Legal Status of Checks

What is a check? A check is not actually a promissory note. It is an order of payment which instructs the bank to release funds to a particular individual. Although a check is not a note of debt, it is accurate to say that **a check represents the debt which the bank owes its depositor.**

What happens when a check is passed between individuals?[1] There are two ways that this can be viewed. On the one hand, this can be seen as a sale of debt. According to this understanding, when someone passes a check, he is selling the debt which the bank owes him. On the other hand, one could argue that no sale is actually taking place. According to this understanding, the check is an instrument of collection by which the bank is instructed to pay the holder. But this does not effect the bank's debt, which is still owed to the depositor.

For example: Reuven writes a check to Shimon. Shimon then sells this check to Levi. This transaction can be viewed in two ways:

1) One could say that the bank's debt to Reuven is being sold. Originally, Reuven transferred the bank's debt to Shimon, when he gave him the check. When Shimon asks Levi to cash the check, he is transferring the bank's debt to Levi. According to this explanation, the sale involves the bank's debt.

2) One could argue that Shimon is actually selling the debt which Reuven owes him as a result of their previous transaction. The check is only a means of collecting this debt. According to this explanation, it is Reuven's debt, and not the bank's debt, which is being sold.

Which of these analyses is correct? The answer to this question is crucial in applying the laws of Ribbis.[2]

---

1. This refers both to a case where two people are selling a check which was written by someone else and to the case of someone who writes his own check, and offers it at discount. (The limitations on this type of transfer have been outlined above, Paragraphs 30 and 31.)

2. **A practical difference between these explanations:** We have seen that debt may be sold at a discount only when the buyer accepts liability if the borrower fails to pay. The

A study of the Uniform Commercial Code (U.C.C.) should help us answer this question. Yet, this code offers contradictory guidelines in dealing with this determination.

Indications That Debt Is Not Sold

Stop payment orders: A way of knowing if the debt is sold is to determine whether the depositor has the right to order the bank to stop payment. If we were to say that the bank's debt to Reuven has been sold to Shimon, the bank now owes this money to Shimon. Reuven, the bank's depositor, should not be permitted to order the bank to stop payment. Yet, we know that a customer may order the bank to stop payment, without showing cause [Section 4-403 (1)].

Why is the depositor entitled to do this? Is this because the debt has not been transferred? Or perhaps the debt has been transferred, but the law allows a bank to accept a depositor's stop payment order so that banks would not have the burden of verifying that each stop order is for good cause. Perhaps this is why banks are permitted to accept every stop order as if it were for good cause.

§3-409 (1) explains that the right to stop payment is consistent with the concept that a check "does not itself operate as an assignment of any funds in the hands of the drawee [bank] available for its payment and [that] the drawee is not liable on the instrument until he accepts it."

Comment 8 to 4-403 adds: "It has sometimes been said that payment cannot be stopped against a holder in due course, but the statement is

---

seller may accept other liabilities, but not the liability for loss which is caused by the borrower. In our case, who is the borrower?

According to the first explanation, the bank is the borrower, and its debt is being sold. The buyer would have to accept the risk that the bank will fail and be unable to pay its obligations. If this happens, he would suffer the loss. However, if the check were to bounce due to Reuven's negligence (for example, if there were insufficient funds), the agreement may call for the seller to be liable.

According to the second explanation, Reuven is the borrower and his debt is being sold to Levi. The buyer would have to accept liability if the check were returned due to Reuven's negligence. This includes the risk that there are insufficient funds to cover payment.

This is a major difference; most people would be willing to accept the risk of bank failure, but would be reluctant to accept the risk that the check may bounce. Above, we have presented the opinion of *Minchas Yitzchak* who rules that the seller (Shimon) may accept liability if the check is returned due to insufficient funds. Although this may hold true in Israel, where depositors are not entitled to stop payment without cause, it is the purpose of this presentation to demonstrate that this is not true in regard to checks which are drawn on U.S. banks.

inaccurate. The payment can be stopped but the drawer[3] remains liable on the instrument to the holder in due course (Sec. 3-305, 3-413)."

The law therefore seems clear; the bank apparently has no relationship with the holder of the check. Its debt is to its depositor until it accepts the check for payment.

In addition: In case of the depositor's death the bank may continue cashing his checks for a limited period of time [Section 4-405(2) allows for ten days from the day of death]. Even during this time, any "person claiming an interest in the account" may order the bank to cease payment.

In explaining this law, White and Summers (U.C.C., 3rd Ed. Vol. 1, Ch. 18) offer a fascinating application. They cite sec. 4-405 Comment 4 to indicate that the bank "is under no duty to determine the validity of the claim or whether it is colorable." The conclusion is drawn that creditors of the deceased may order the bank to stop payment so that their competitors would not "gain priority by promptly cashing decedent's checks." This means that the law allows for checks to be stopped by individuals who claim no direct right to the funds! These parties clearly desire to stop checks which were written under legitimate circumstances.

Above, we theorized that the intent of the law is only to allow stop orders in cases where the drawers are not holders in due course, and that all stop orders are permitted only because determining due course is too onerous a task to be assigned the bank. If this were true, creditors would not be allowed the power to issue a stop order. Since the law does allow

---

3. I.e., Reuven being the drawer and Shimon (and subsequently Levi) being the holder in due course. Section 3-302(1) explicitly defines a holder in due course as anyone who takes the check "(a) for value; and (b) in good faith; and (c) without notice that it is overdue or has been dishonored."

3-301(2) adds, "A payee may [also] be a holder in due course."

The Official Uniform Comment explains this provision: "The position here taken is that the payee may become a holder in due course to the same extent and under the same circumstances as any other holder. This is true whether he takes the instrument *by purchase from a third person* [emphasis mine] or directly from the obligor."

The Official Uniform Comment sets examples of cases to which this applies. The first example: "A remitter, purchasing goods from P, obtains a bank draft payable to P and forwards it to P, who takes it in good faith and without notice as required by this section."

[It should be noted that someone who receives a check as an outright gift is apparently not accorded the status of a holder in due course, since he has not received the check "for value." This would support the position that debt is not transferred when a check changes hands.]

Levi's status is covered by Section 3-201 on Transfer, which states that when a prior holder is himself a holder in due course, the purchaser succeeds to that status.

for this, the indication is that the bank's debt is not transferred when the check is sold.

Indications That Debt Is Sold

What happens when a bank cashes a check over the depositor's stop order? Most depositors would assume that the bank is fully liable and that the account would be recredited. Although this is sometimes true in cases where checks were stolen and fraudulently deposited, this is not the case under discussion here. We are dealing with a situation where a check was issued properly, in exchange for cash, merchandise or services. In this case, a bank which cashes a check over a stop order is not liable at all!

The law regarding these situations is outlined in Section 4-407, which states that when a bank pays an item over a stop order, "the payor bank shall be subrogated to the rights of any holder in due course on the item. . . ."[4]

The law, in 4-403(3), provides even greater protection for the banks, by providing that: "The burden of establishing the fact and amount of loss resulting from the payment of an item contrary to a binding stop payment order is on the customer."

This presents a different picture than the one we had before. The laws of liability allow the bank to say, post facto, that the payment of the check was justified. This means that the bank's debt has been effectively transferred when the check is given. This further indicates that the bank's role in obeying a stop payment order is more as a service to its customer (i.e., its depositor) than a reflection of the bank's role based on the particular transaction.

The laws of liability do therefore indicate that when a check is passed, the bank's debt is (in effect, even if not by explicit declaration) passed with it.

---

4. White and Summers (18-6) use the following example to explain this law. "R, the buyer of a valuable painting, gives his personal check in the amount of $30,000 to seller, C. Subsequently, R has second thoughts about the purchase, properly orders payment stopped, but his bank fails to follow the stop order. R instructs his bank to recredit his account, and bank responds as follows: . . .Since payee C had a good claim against you which he could have asserted for $30,000, we are subrogated to that right and can assert it in a defense in any suit you have against us for our failure to follow the stop order. Furthermore, the check was presented for payment to us, not by C, but by the depositary bank which was a holder in due course; therefore, even if you have a defense against C, it is not one you can assert against us for we are subrogated not just to C's rights but also to the rights of the presenting bank who was a holder in due course and who takes free of such defenses. In such case, the payor bank wins; seller C and buyer R get just what they deserve, $30,000 and the painting, respectively."

To sum up: The commercial code has a two-pronged approach to the transfer of checks. To borrow Talmudic terms, the law contains *lechatchilah* provisions and *bedi'avad* provisions. *Lechatchilah*, the bank is instructed to allow the depositor to continue controlling his funds, even after a check has been passed. For this reason, the bank is instructed to obey his stop order. This indicates that the debt has not been transferred. *Bedi'avad*, if the bank has neglected to obey the stop order, the law treats the transfer of a check as a transfer of debt.

Resolving the contradiction: In Talmudic tradition, contradictions are resolved by understanding the underlying concept of the law. An accurate understanding of the rationale behind the law yields an appreciation of its different facets. It would appear that this method would not work in regard to understanding U.C.C. This is because it appears that the primary concern of the drafters of these laws was not the establishing of a consistent rationale. Rather, the concern was to be fair to both the bankers and the consumer groups who lobbied for their respective interests when the laws were drafted.[5]

Still, logic would dictate that the *lechatchilah* provision is the most defining aspect of a law. Indeed, the opinion of legal experts whom I have contacted is that the first interpretation is accurate; debt is not transferred when a check is written. One of the legal textbooks refers to a check as "nothing more than an unfilled promise."

In conclusion: In this chapter we have seen that promissory notes may be sold at a discount. We have also seen that *Minchas Yitzchak* and *Bris Yehudah* extend this leniency to checks, which they view as promissory notes. This leniency should not be extended to checks which are drawn on U.S. banks. In the United States, when a person sells a $100 check for $90, he is not transferring debt. He is actually borrowing $90, with the check used as a means of payment. The check may therefore not be written for more than the $90 which was borrowed.

---

5. See, for example, White and Summers' explanation of Section 403 (3), quoted above: "Mr. Malcolm, an article four draftsman, tells us that subsection 4-403 (3) was inserted as a trade-off for the banks when the drafters decided to allow customers to give oral stop orders."

Even more revealing is Mr. Malcolm's testimony before the N.Y.S. Law Revision Commission (quoted in a note on p. 910) that this provision was actually inserted after the laws had been voted down at the legislature, in response to a comment from the floor. The draftsmen of the code "responded very quickly that they thought that would be a fair proposition, and it was acquiesced in."

One cannot help but wonder if the insertion of the law was a matter of expediency or a matter of consistency with the rationale of the law.

CHAPTER THIRTEEN

Buying Real Estate

Introduction

The potential for serious Ribbis problems exists whenever a complex business deal is negotiated. For many people, the first experience of this sort occurs when they purchase a home. The variety of possible financing arrangements and the complexities of the actual contract agreement combine to cause various Ribbis problems of which buyer and seller are often unaware.

In this chapter, we will examine many of the common problems, and (wherever possible) suggest remedies to accomplish a contract's aim without violating the laws of Ribbis.

It should be stressed that many problems can be easily avoided by having a competent Rabbi review a contract prior to closing. Once a sale has been completed, it becomes more difficult to redress Ribbis problems.

Even worse, provisions of a contract that violate the laws of Ribbis are not enforceable, even when both sides wish to abide by those provisions.[1] This means that if one of the parties later realizes that the contract has provisions which are prohibited as Ribbis, he will be left in the uncomfortable position of being unable to keep his part of the agreement. Unfortunately, this is a common problem. These situations would be avoided if action were taken prior to closing to ensure that a contract is free of Ribbis problems.

Setting a Price

1. A seller may not quote two prices for his home: a lower price which is offered if payment is advanced at an earlier time, and a higher price if payment is made at closing. In this case, the discounted price is clearly an inducement to the buyer to advance funds before they are due. This constitutes Ribbis DeRabbanan.[2]

---

1. When an agreement calls for Ribbis payments, even if only for Rabbinically prohibited Ribbis, that provision is not binding. This is true even if a *kinyan* was made to validate the agreement. However, this applies only to the Ribbis provision. The rest of the contract remains valid; only the provisions calling for Ribbis are nullified (Y.D. 161:11). For additional details, see Paragraph 49.

2. *Rema* 173:7. A seller is entitled to be paid only when the real estate changes hands. A prepayment can easily be viewed as a form of loan, in that money is being advanced for the seller's use. Therefore, one may not explicitly offer financial benefit in exchange for prepayment.

   This prohibition applies to prepayment in the sale of merchandise as well.

   The status of deposits is discussed below.

2. However, a seller may originally quote a low price to a customer, because he is sure that the customer will advance funds to him. However, he may not explicitly state that the discount is being offered for this reason.[3]

3. A seller may offer a discount to induce the buyer to make a larger down payment if the moneys are held in escrow. However, he may not derive benefit (for example, earn interest) from that additional amount of money.[4]

4. A Heter Iska may be used to permit a discount in exchange for the advancing of funds.[5]

Between Contract and Closing: Escrow Funds

5. When two sides draw up a contract for a real estate purchase, the money which is advanced as a deposit is usually held in an escrow account, by one (or both) of the attorneys. The seller may request that he be allowed to use this money prior to closing. However, he may not pay the interest which the money would have earned in the escrow account.[6]

---

3. The basic rules regarding prepayment allow for a discount to be offered for prepayment when the seller is in possession of the item being sold (Y.D. 173:7). This is because the buyer's prepayment acquires for him a certain degree of ownership in the item which is in the seller's possession. Thus, this constitutes a purchase rather than a prepayment (*Taz* 10).

The only restriction on this type of deal is that there may be no explicit mention of the discount in connection with the advance of funds, because this would convey an impression of a Ribbis payment (*Rema* 173:7). This is the basis for the prohibition in the previous paragraphs.

[If the discount is so excessive that it is obvious that it is being offered in consideration of the advance, this would be prohibited. However, since it is the nature of real estate prices to fluctuate within a very wide range, depending on individual circumstances, it is rare that a discount would fall so far below regular market prices so as to be obviously excessive (see *Shach* 173:2) .]

4. *Minchas Elazar* 5:19, s.v. *henei*; *Mishnas Ribbis* 18:3.

5. The standard Heter Iska form (see Chapter 23) and procedure may be used. Where there is a blank for the insertion of the payment amount (after the words "the undersigned pays to the investor the sum of . . .") it should be amended to read "the undersigned provides the investor with a home at . . . . . . for $. . . . . ."

6. This prohibition also applies to a lawyer who is given permission to use escrow funds. The laws of Ribbis prohibit reimbursing a lender for money he could have earned by lending the money to a non-Jew or leaving it in a bank. *Rashba* (in Responsa 3:227) prohibits such reimbursements and adds that if this were permitted, "all Ribbis would be permitted, for every loan causes loss since (the lender) is unable to profit by other investments during the time (that the money is outstanding)." *Bris Yehudah* 3:n4 calls this a common problem, since "people don't realize" that this can be Ribbis Ketzutzah.

In addition, the seller may not offer a discount in the purchase price to induce the buyer to agree to release these funds.[7]

A seller who wishes to use the escrow funds may make this a condition of his sale. He would then be entitled to use this money.[8]

6. When a contract is signed, and a deposit payment is placed in escrow, there are no restrictions on the relationship between the buyer and seller. Since no loan has taken place, there are no Ribbis problems if favors or gifts are exchanged between buyer and seller. For this reason, the seller may allow the buyer to move into the home before the time of closing.[9]

However, if the seller has the right to use the deposit funds, the rules are different. In this case he is actually a borrower, since he is using the purchaser's funds. He is therefore prohibited from benefiting the buyer in any way, and may not allow the buyer to move into the property before closing. If the buyer pays a fair rental price for use of the home until closing, he would be permitted to move in.[10]

Moving Into the Home Before Closing

7. If the buyer plans to allow the seller to use the deposit money and he also wants to move into the home before closing, he may include this

---

7. *Rema* 173:7. This is similar to the case mentioned above, in Paragraph 1.

8. *Vechai Achicha Imach* 2:19. [This is a common demand in the case of a seller who needs the funds to make a down payment on another home.]

In this case, the seller is agreeing to sell the property on the condition that the deposit moneys are loaned to him. Although this would seem to be Ribbis because the buyer is given access to the purchase in exchange for a loan (*tovas hanaah*), it is permitted because of the general rule (outlined above, Chapter 7, Paragraph 7) which allows discounts for prepayment in cases where the item which is being sold is already in possession of the seller (this is known as *yesh lo*).

9. If interest on the escrow account belongs to the seller, this is considered a use of the funds by the seller, and the rules of Ribbis would apply, as explained in the following paragraph.

10. *Mishnas Ribbis* 18:6. This applies when the buyer agrees to allow the seller to use these funds.

Where the agreement calls for the deposit to be put into an escrow account and the lawyer (without the knowledge of the buyer) allows the seller to use the funds, provided that he pays the interest which would have been earned in the escrow account, this too is prohibited. In addition to the question of *geneivah* (thievery), which prohibits the use of an individual's money without his consent, the interest which is paid is Ribbis Ketzutzah. By allowing the seller to use the money, the Jewish lawyer is responsible for the return of these funds to the buyer. Since he is responsible for this money, he has the

as a provision of the purchase contract. He should stipulate that the purchase price includes a rental fee for a specific number of months. If the buyer did move into the home, and the sale was later canceled, he would still be obligated to pay this rental fee.[11]

If the closing date was later postponed, an additional rental fee would be required for the additional time that the buyer is living in the seller's home.[12]

8. **A second option:** A Heter Iska may be used to permit the buyer to move into the home prior to closing. The Iska should be signed at the time of contract, when the buyer advances his deposit payment to the seller (see note below for details).[13]

9. If the Heter Iska was not used at the time of contract, an expert in the laws of Ribbis should be consulted as to whether it may be used afterwards, to permit the buyer to move into his home.[14]

---

status of a lender. Any interest which the seller adds when returning these funds constitutes Ribbis. This prohibition does not apply if the lawyer is not Jewish, and the money is being loaned without the knowledge of the Jewish buyer (*Vechai Achicha Imach* 2:17).

11. *Mishnas Ribbis* ibid.; see *Toras Ribbis* 12:13.

12. *Mishnas Ribbis* 18:n8.

13. The deposit money is given to the seller under the terms of a Heter Iska. The standard form, which appears at the end of Chapter 23, may be used, with the following amendment: Where the Heter Iska reads, "an additional. . . . . .for his share of the profits," this should be replaced with the following words, "use of his home for . . . months in exchange for his share of the profits."

The option of using a Heter Iska in this manner applies only when the purchaser is entitled to use the deposit moneys (or a portion of the deposit moneys) in any way he chooses. If he is required to keep the funds in a specific investment (e.g., in an escrow account from which he will draw interest), the option of using a Heter Iska is not viable. [As we will see in Chapter 22, a Heter Iska is valid only when the person receiving the funds could be required to verify, under oath, the amount of profit which was earned by the advanced funds. In our case, the person giving the funds is aware of the amount of profit being generated by his investment. Since the profit is known, no oath can be required, and the Heter Iska would not be valid (*Igros Moshe* Y.D. 2:62 and 63, *Bris Yehudah* quoting *Panim Me'iros* 2:36, *Tuv Taam Vodaas* 3:2:40 and *Divrei Chaim hashmatos* to 2:16).]

14. [This could be accomplished by having the seller return the deposit moneys to the buyer, who would then return these funds to the seller under the terms of a Heter Iska. Since it is not usually easy to actually hand over such a large a sum of money, a Rabbi would devise another form of *kinyan* to transfer the funds (for example, part of the seller's real estate holdings would be transferred to the buyer by *kinyan chalipin*) to the buyer, who would then reinvest it (by performing a *kinyan* to return the funds) under the terms of a Heter Iska. Since this is a complicated procedure, a competent Rabbi

10. A third option: The advanced funds may be held in an escrow account which earns interest. An arrangement may be made whereby the interest is used as a rental fee for the purchaser's use of the home. The seller would therefore acquire that interest.

Naturally, this option is limited to situations where the interest earned is the equivalent of a fair rental price for the period the property will be used prior to closing.

After Closing: Must the Seller Vacate?

11. At closing, the buyer pays for the property and becomes its legal owner. He may choose to allow the seller to continue living in the home or he may order that the premises be vacated.

The buyer has complete legal ownership only after paying the seller in full at the closing. If the buyer does not make full payment at that time, and the seller offers a credit arrangement to allow the closing to be completed, a lender-borrower relationship is created. Therefore, the seller may insist that the buyer not move into the property until payment is completed. However, the seller may not continue living in the home after closing, unless he pays a fair rental to the buyer.[15]

12. Income which is generated by the property after closing (for example, rental income) belongs to the buyer. An arrangement which allows the seller to continue collecting the income until the full purchase payment is made is prohibited as Ribbis.[16]

Methods of Avoiding This Problem

13. After closing, the seller who extended credit to the buyer may wish to continue living in his home until payment is completed. He may do so only if the contract of sale is drawn with the expressed

---

should be consulted to help facilitate this procedure. If the Rabbi chooses to return the deposit money by transferring real estate holdings (as in the parenthesis above), he may require that a *kinyan shtar* be used as well as *kinyan chalipin* — see *Pischei Teshuvah* to C.M. 190:1.]

15. *Rema* 174:1, *Shach* 3. In this case, the buyer took full title to the property without having made full payment, only because the seller was willing to extend credit to him. Thus, a lender-borrower relationship exists. If the buyer were then to benefit the seller, this would constitute Ribbis.

16. Ibid. [The income may be given to the seller if it is counted as payment towards the outstanding balance which he is owed. In this case, the income may even be paid directly to the seller.]

stipulation that the seller is permitted to live in the house after closing. When this is done, the seller actually owns the right to continue occupying the house. Since this is part of the purchase agreement and is not dependent on the credit which was extended, it is not a form of Ribbis.[17]

This is permitted even if the contract also calls for the seller to extend credit to the buyer, as long as the language of the contract does not limit the seller to living in the house only if credit is extended.[18]

14. A drawback to this method is that the seller may live in the house only for the time stipulated in the contract. After this period of time has elapsed, he would be required to move out (or pay a rental fee) even if the buyer had not completed payment.[19]

15. A second option: When transferring title, the buyer and seller may clearly stipulate that the transfer of ownership will take effect only when the payment is completed. In this case, the seller retains legal ownership of the house and may continue to live there and to collect any income generated by the property, as if he had never gone to closing.[20]

In this case, the seller would also be liable for any losses (by fire, vandalism, theft or legal suit) sustained by the property.[21]

---

17. *Bris Yehudah*, *hashmatos* to 28:n53. *Bris Yehudah* requires that this stipulation be entered into the contract at the time that the purchase price is agreed upon. It is also preferable that the contract state, "In consideration of the purchase price, the seller is to be permitted to remain in the home after closing. . ." (This language clearly links the stipulation to the purchase rather than to the extension of credit.)

18. Ibid. [If the contract did not contain a stipulation which allows the seller to continue living in the home, this provision may not be added later when it becomes apparent that the seller will be extending credit at the time of closing. However, if the contract is subsequently redrawn because other changes (not involving credit) are being made to benefit the buyer, the stipulation that allows the seller to continue living in the home may be added as well. For example, if the seller later agrees to leave furniture, fixtures or floor coverings in the home, he may then ask that, in exchange, he be permitted to live in the home after closing. This should then be added to the contract.]

19. Ibid., *Mishnas Ribbis* 14:n19.

20. Y.D. 174:6. In this case, the buyer would be prohibited from living in the property without paying a rental fee to the seller. This is because he has advanced funds prior to taking title, as in Paragraph 7, above.

21. Adequate insurance coverage should be arranged so that the seller would not be hesitant to use this option. [The buyer may make the insurance payments to induce the seller to agree to this arrangement. In this situation, the buyer is not receiving a loan from the seller and is therefore permitted to benefit him.]

16. **A third option:** A Heter Iska may be used at the time of closing, to permit the seller to continue living in the home (or to continue collecting the rental income).[22]

Escape Clauses

17. Someone selling a home is permitted to add an escape clause to the contract. This provision allows him to regain title to the home by returning the purchase price to the buyer by a specific date. People who sell their home due to financial hardship will often add this clause with the hope that they will later acquire funds to regain their home.[23]

If the seller does later acquire the necessary funding to repay the buyer, and he exercises this clause to regain his home, he is dissolving the original sale. The moneys which he had received and used in the interim are now seen as loan funds, for which the house served as collateral. The buyer, who (as it turned out) was actually a lender, may not receive a financial benefit when the escape clause is exercised. This means that the escape clause may not stipulate that the reimbursement will be for an amount greater than the original purchase price. For example, if a home was sold for $400,000 and the seller exercises an escape clause two years later, he may return only the original $400,000 which he received as payment.

Additionally, if the buyer had profited from holding the property (for example, if he had collected rental fees), he must return these fees to the property's original owner.[24] He is entitled only to reimbursement for expenses incurred as a result of the transaction.[25]

---

22. The standard Heter Iska form and procedure may be used. The amount of credit which is being extended should be filled in to the Iska contract. (The buyer actually receives these funds in the form of real estate which is being transferred to him.) Where the contract reads, "pays to the investor the sum of $ _____ ," it should be amended to read, "provides the investor with a home at _____ for his use."

23. Y.D. 174:1. The example mentioned above is the most common form of escape clause, and is mentioned in *Shulchan Aruch*. However, the laws outlined here apply to any clause which would serve to retroactively invalidate a sale (see *S.A. Harav* §56 and *Chavos Daas* 174:1).

24. Y.D. 174:1 and R' Akiva Eiger; C.M. 207:6. (Whether this constitutes Ribbis Ketzutzah or Rabbinically prohibited Ribbis is an issue of dispute; see comments of *Shach, Taz* and R' Akiva Eiger to Y.D.)

R' Akiva Eiger points out that the sale is nullified only *after* the buyer is reimbursed the purchase price. The seller could not argue that the rental fees or other profits which the buyer received should be counted towards this reimbursement, since the sale of the property remains valid until a reimbursement is actually paid to the buyer. Only subsequent to the reimbursement is he required to refund the accumulated profits.

25. Ribbis laws prohibit profiting from a loan; they do not prohibit reimbursements

18. An escape clause is sometimes drawn to allow the *buyer* to back out by a specific date (or under specific circumstances). When the purchaser exercises this option, the sale is invalidated and the buyer is refunded his purchase price. The restrictions outlined in the previous paragraph apply here as well. Here too, the seller may not be required to return more than the original funds which he received. All profits generated by the property while it was under the control of the buyer must be returned to the seller.[26]

19. When an escape clause is included in a purchase agreement, the buyer may not move into the property which he purchased until the time stipulated in the clause has passed, thus finalizing the sale.[27]

The buyer may occupy the property if he agrees to pay a fair rental to the seller in the event that the sale is invalidated. Later, when (and if) the seller elects to recover his property and return the purchase price to the buyer, the rental fee would be deducted from this reimbursement.[28]

20. If a sale was completed without any provision for an escape clause, and both parties later agreed to add this clause to the terms of the sale, this does not present a Ribbis problem.[29]

---

for expenses which were caused by a loan. This has been discussed in Chapter 4, Paragraphs 1-10.

(Reimbursement of expenses is permitted. This is not to say that the seller is *required* to reimburse all expenses; this would depend on the particulars of the agreement. If the agreement does not address this issue, the buyer could compel reimbursement only if he could establish that this is the accepted business practice in that particular community.)

26. *S.A. Harav* §55, *Minchas Elazar* 1:46, *Bris Yehudah* 28:4.

27. Y.D. 174:1. The buyer may not move into the home for the following reason. If the escape clause is subsequently exercised, the sale will have become invalidated retroactively. We have seen (in the previous paragraphs) that this changes the purchase payment to a loan, which the seller must now return to the buyer. The buyer will have received a benefit from the seller (i.e., free use of his property in the interim) as part of this transaction. This constitutes Ribbis.

Is this Ribbis Ketzutzah? This type of Ribbis is known as *tzad echad beRibbis*, because under the terms of the original purchase agreement, the residency in the house would constitute Ribbis only if the seller exercised his rights under the escape clause. The status of this type of Ribbis is a subject of dispute; see Chapter 2, Paragraph 13.

28. Y.D. 174:5. The rental fee must be a fair one, based on market conditions for that particular property (*Bris Yehudah* 28:n4). The agreement must be phrased in a manner which permits the seller to deduct the rental fees from the reimbursement of the original purchase price (*Rema* 174:5).

29. Y.D. 174:2. Since the sale had been completed unconditionally, it cannot be invalidated later. The subsequent agreement, no matter how it is worded, actually calls for a new sale (i.e., it allows the original owner to repurchase the property) and not for a cancellation of the previous sale.

21. According to many poskim, these restrictions are not limited to the sale of real estate. They also apply to the sale of merchandise (or financial instruments, such as stocks and bonds);[30] see Chapter 1, Paragraph 15.

Methods of Avoiding Problems With Escape Clauses

22. The problem with an escape clause lies in the fact that it invalidates a sale retroactively. When this happens, the result is that the moneys which were paid for the purchase were actually on loan to the seller. This creates a borrower-lender situation to which the Ribbis restrictions apply.

The entire problem can be avoided if the escape clause is originally drawn up in a manner which does not invalidate the sale retroactively. Instead it calls for the buyer to sell the property back to the original seller if either of the original parties demands it within the time specified. This accomplishes the objectives of an escape clause, without creating Ribbis problems.[31]

The escape clause should be worded as follows:

"This sale is valid, subject to the following condition: If within (insert

---

30. *S.A. Harav* §54, *Chikrei Lev* Y.D. 18, *Bris Yehudah* 28:n8. Regarding stocks which are sold in this manner, see *Levushei Mordechai* 2:Y.D. 72 and *Bris Yehudah* 28:n11.

31. *Machneh Ephraim* §13, *Chavos Daas* 174:1, *Noda BeYehudah* 2:75, *Kreisi* 168:10 and 169:18, *Bris Yehudah* 28:8. This language calls for a new sale rather than for return of the property. Cf. *Har Tzvi* 139.

Chavos Daas takes an even more lenient approach, permitting language which is phrased as follows: "The sale is made on the condition that the buyer return the property to the seller if he so requests by such and such a time."

Chavos Daas takes this approach because he maintains that when the language of a contract makes a sale conditional to an obligation to return the property on request, it is considered a *mechirah al minas lehachzir*, a sale which is made with the stipulation that the property be returned. He maintains that in this case the original sale is not invalidated when the property is later returned. (On the contrary, if the property were *not* returned upon request, this would invalidate the sale since the conditions of sale were not honored!) When the property is returned, the original sale stands and the return is viewed as a new sale.

Thus, while *Chavos Daas* concedes that there is a Ribbis problem when an escape clause states simply that the seller has a right to demand return of his property, this problem is alleviated when the sale is made *conditional to* the right of the seller to regain the property. This phrase ('conditional to') is crucial because it implies that the present sale is final if the condition is met.

Machneh Ephraim §13 apparently concurs with this ruling. Cf. *Daas Torah* 174:1 who cites *Ritva* and *Shitah Mekubetzes* (to B.M.), who rule that this is prohibited. *Bris Yehudah* 28:n22 follows this opinion.

number) days, the buyer/seller shall so request, the buyer shall resell the property to the seller for (insert price)."

It is preferable that the following sentence be added as well:[32]

"The buyer/seller shall not have the right to demand such a resale until a minimum of (insert number) days have passed."[33]

A Non-Binding Pledge to Return Property

23. A buyer may assure the seller that he would be willing to return the property to him at a later time, if the seller so requests, as long as the assurance is clearly not legally binding and not a condition of sale.[34]

Using a Mortgage Broker

24. When a Jewish broker arranges a mortgage loan through a non-Jewish bank (or individual), the prohibitions of Ribbis do not apply. In this case the broker is neither a lender nor a guarantor.[35] He

---

32. There are some poskim who disagree with the leniency outlined previously (see *Chikrei Lev* Y.D. 18, quoted in *Bris Yehudah* 28:8). To satisfy this opinion, one should add the sentence recommended here. Adding this sentence gives the sale a greater sense of authenticity, in that it is irrevocable for a period of time (see Note 31). The escape clause which was challenged by *Chikrei Lev* allowed the *seller* to demand a resale. Where the escape clause permits the *buyer* to do so, it is not clear that these objections would apply (see *Bris Yehudah* ibid.). Still, it is preferable to add this sentence to the contract.

33. *Sma* (C.M. 207:11) maintains that this condition makes it clear that the sale is a final one. In this case, the buyer has irrevocable control of the house for a specified period of time. This makes it clear that the property has become his. Any subsequent transaction would therefore be seen as a new sale. Many poskim maintain that this condition alone would be sufficient to remove the Ribbis problems which are caused by an escape clause. (This opinion is accepted by *Machneh Ephraim* §13 and *Tiferes LeMoshe* to *Shach* 168:57. *Bris Yehudah* 28:6 refers to this as a majority opinion.)

Still, since *Chavos Daas* 174:1 and *S.A. Harav* §54 reject this leniency, it is preferable to combine this language with the version of the escape clause outlined previously. The combined language should be acceptable according to all poskim.

[Even according to *Sma*, this wording would suffice to permit a repurchase at the original price. This would not allow a repurchase at a higher price, since this would appear to be Ribbis (*Tiferes LeMoshe* ibid.).]

34. Y.D. 174:1. It must be clear that the seller does not consider this pledge to be a binding one.

35. Y.D. 168:23 and 24 discusses the case of a Jew who is authorized to make loans with a non-Jew's money. *Shulchan Aruch* raises the concern that it might appear to outsiders that the Jewish broker is actually lending his own money for interest. (This is known as *maris ayin*.) This would seem to be grounds for prohibiting this arrangement. *Rema* (168:23) and *Shach* (71) maintain that this concern does not apply when the Jewish

is simply providing a service, for which he is entitled to a fee.[36]

25. Mortgage companies do not hold on to their mortgages for a long period of time. They sell their mortgages to other banks or institutions. Between the time that a company lends the money and sells the mortgage, the company is lending its own money to the borrower. Therefore, if the lending company is owned by Jews, the laws of Ribbis would prohibit the payment of interest during this period.[37]

In fact, many mortgage companies are owned by Jews, including some of the well-known national chains.[38] Halachah prohibits a Jew from securing a loan through these institutions unless a Heter Iska is used.[39]

---

middleman is a professional broker, because it is apparent to all that he is not lending his own money. This ruling is accepted by the later poskim (*Chochmas Adam* 137:33 and *S.A. Harav* §74). *Bris Yehudah* (31:n5, based on *Meiri*) adds that when the loan is for a sum of money which is so great that the broker obviously could not lend it on his own, there is no concern that it would appear that he is lending his own private funds. A broker could therefore arrange a loan in either of these situations; where he is a professional broker or where the loan is for a large sum of money. (This is discussed in greater detail in Chapter 17, Paragraph 2.)

[In the case of a mortgage broker, it would seem that this should be permitted on entirely different grounds. Y.D. 168:23 and 24 discusses the situation of a Jew who is an agent for a non-Jew to lend his money. It is there that we find the concern regarding *maris ayin*. A mortgage broker, however, is the agent of the borrower (who pays his fee) and not of the lender. This is similar to the case in Y.D. 168:17, where a Jew asks his friend to arrange a loan for him through a non-Jew. In that case, no concern for *maris ayin* is mentioned (*Bris Yehudah* 31:n14 citing *Darkei Moshe* 168:22). It would therefore seem that in the prevalent situation today, where brokers are agents of the borrower, that this is permitted even if the broker does not regularly arrange loans, and even if the mortgage is for a smaller amount of money.]

36. It should be stressed that a broker, as any other employee, is entitled to the fee for which he worked. There is a misconception that because there are no out of the pocket expenses involved in providing information, the broker is not truly entitled to a fee. Those who cheat brokers (mortgage brokers, real estate brokers or *shadchanim*) out of their fee, by taking the information provided by the broker and then dealing directly with the lender (or seller), are guilty of *geneivah*.

37. *Mishnas Ribbis* 18:n13.

38. Some of these companies are owned solely by Jews, others are partnerships. The status of businesses which are owned jointly by Jewish and non-Jewish partners has been discussed above, in Chapter 5, Paragraph 26. We have also seen (Chapter 5, Paragraph 27) that *Igros Moshe* Y.D. 2:63 rules that Jewish owned corporations are permitted to pay Ribbis when taking a loan. It should be noted that this ruling applies only where a corporation is *borrowing* money and not when a corporation is *lending* money to an individual. In this case, the prohibitions of Ribbis apply.

39. The method of using a Heter Iska is outlined later in this chapter. [There are some brokerages in the New York-New Jersey area which have Orthodox Jewish owners

Unfortunately, many of these firms refuse to accommodate their Orthodox Jewish customers by using a Heter Iska. Since a borrower cannot use a Heter Iska without the consent of the lender,[40] those who wish to avoid Ribbis may not borrow from these institutions. It is the consumer's responsibility to research the ownership of the institution with which he is dealing or to consult a Rabbi who is familiar with the status of the lending companies in the area.

26. If the seller is a Jew, and he offers the buyer a personal mortgage, whereby he allows a portion of the payment to be made after the closing date, he too is prohibited from taking interest for the credit which he is extending, regardless of the length (or brevity) of time for which he extends credit. Here too, a Heter Iska may be used to facilitate this loan.[41]

The Mortgage

27. A mortgage is a loan which is secured by the real estate which is being purchased. All of the prohibitions of Ribbis apply to this type of loan, as to any other loan. Therefore, when purchasing a home, the buyer is prohibited from taking a mortgage from another Jew (or from a lending institution owned by Jews), since he would be paying him Ribbis.[42]

Methods of Avoiding This Problem

28. A Heter Iska may be used to permit a mortgage arrangement.[43] The proper forms appear at the end of Chapter 23. See Chapter 22, Paragraphs 31-35 for instructions regarding which Heter Iska form to use (this depends on circumstances, as explained there).

29. When a Heter Iska is used, the parties are permitted to sign legal documents which ignore the Heter Iska and refer to the deal as a conventional loan or mortgage. In this case, the following clause must be inserted into the Heter Iska:

---

who use a Heter Iska Klali for all the loans which they make to Jews. As we will see below, Chapter 23, Paragraphs 12-16, this is an acceptable manner of avoiding Ribbis problems.]

40. See Chapter 23, Note 2.

41. This is identical to the situation discussed earlier, in Paragraphs 11-16 of this chapter.

42. A Heter Iska may be used to facilitate this mortgage, as outlined below.

43. When points are paid to the lender, this must also be included in the Heter Iska (*Mishnas Ribbis* 22:n34).

"In the event of any conflict between the terms of this Iska agreement and the terms of any other agreement signed by the two parties relating to the above-mentioned funds, the terms of this agreement shall prevail."[44]

30. A second option: R' Moshe Feinstein zt'l suggests another method of redrawing a mortgage when purchasing a home.[45] He recommends that a sale-lease agreement be used.

In his example, a home is purchased for $20,000, with half paid at closing and the other half to be paid over time. The seller wishes to receive interest for the time that he is extending $10,000 of credit. However, he is not permitted to receive interest. R' Feinstein suggests that the seller retain ownership of 50% of his home. He would sell only half his home for the $10,000 cash which he receives. Over time, the buyer makes monthly payments to him, until these payments total $10,000. With each payment, the buyer acquires additional ownership in the property, until he has paid the full $10,000 and becomes its sole owner.

In the interim, the buyer is living in a home which is only partially his. The seller is allowing the buyer to live in a home in which he has partial ownership, and he is entitled to a rental fee from him. Thus, each month, the buyer makes a payment to the seller which contains two parts; a payment of principal towards ownership of the house, and a rental payment for its use. This fee can be set at an amount equal to the interest rate which the seller desired. For example, if there is a prevailing interest rate of 8½ % (or $850 per $10,000 loaned), the seller may charge $850 per year as rental for his portion of the home (see note below for additional points regarding these payments). In this manner, the seller receives his desired revenue without actually making any sort of loan.[46]

---

44. *Kol Kisvei R' Henkin* 2:50:3, *Igros Moshe* (Y.D. 2:62 and 3:38). The purpose of signing a legal document is to expedite legal redress in the event that the terms of the Heter Iska are violated (ibid.).

Chochmas Adam (142:13) and *Kitzur Shulchan Aruch* (66:9) rule that in this case it is not permissible to leave the Heter Iska in the hands of the investing partner. This is because of the possibility that the investor will hide the Heter Iska and demand payment based on the note of debt. For this reason, a duplicate Heter Iska must be signed by the investor and given to the managing partner. Alternatively, the Heter Iska may be entrusted to a third party. See Chapter 23, Note 7, where this is discussed at length.

45. *Igros Moshe* (2:62). A contract suitable for use when buying a home appears at the end of this chapter.

46. A practical method of expediting this procedure would be to secure a schedule of payments (the type used by all banks in scheduling mortgage payments) for, in our example, a $10,000 loan. This schedule of payments contains two columns: One which

This sale-lease agreement can be used both when the seller finances the purchase (as in the aforementioned example) and when a third party extends funds for the purchase. The sale-lease agreement which appears at the end of this chapter is suitable for use in either case. (The introductory footnote, there, explains how this works in cases where a third party extends funds.)

31. The advantages of using this method: There are poskim who are opposed to the use of a Heter Iska when the money is not actually used in a business or other revenue-producing investment.[47] These objections do not apply to R' Moshe Feinstein's method.

---

calculates the monthly interest payment, and the other which calculates the monthly payment of principal. Although the total payment for each month is identical, the portion which is paid towards principal and the portion paid for interest change gradually. Each month, the principal portion increases while the interest portion decreases (since the amount of outstanding principal decreases every month, the amount of interest also decreases). This is true of all routine payment schedules.

This schedule should be incorporated into the sale-lease agreement, but the interest fees should be relabeled as rental charges. Thus, every month the buyer pays a set sum, identical to the sum he would pay if he had actually taken a loan. The portion labeled 'principal' is used to acquire additional ownership in the home, until the entire $10,000 is paid and he acquires complete ownership. The portion labeled 'rental charges' is due to the seller because the buyer is using his portion of the home. As each month passes, the buyer owns an increasingly greater percentage of the home, and rents a smaller percentage. It is therefore appropriate that the amount of money paid as rental charges decreases each month, as shown in the schedule of payments.

A contract based on this concept, but with some variations, appears in R' J. David Bleich's *Contemporary Halachah*, Appendix to Volume 2.

47. See *S.A. Harav* §42, who maintains that a Heter Iska may not be used to finance the purchase of a home, because this is not a revenue-producing investment. A Heter Iska may be used only where there is a potential for profits to be realized by the investment. (See Chapter 22, Paragraphs 31-33, where this is discussed at greater length.)

Tam Ribbis (*kuntres acharon* §23) points out that in the time and place that the ruling of *S.A. Harav* was written (Eastern Europe, circa 1750), real estate prices did not fluctuate greatly. In situations where the market is such that the value of real estate may significantly increase in price, the purchase of real estate is actually an investment. Therefore, when there is potential for the profit margin stipulated in the Heter Iska to be realized, the objections of *S.A. Harav* would not apply.

Still, the *Chazon Ish* (quoted in *Tam Ribbis*) ruled that if a Heter Iska is used, and the lender is certain that the value of the real estate did not increase, he may not collect the profit to which he would be entitled under the terms of the Heter Iska.

Maharsham (2:216) points out that when a property has rental income, it is considered a revenue-producing investment even if there is no prospect for an increase in the value of the property. In this case, a Heter Iska may be used.

In addition, when this method is used, no loan takes place at all. Prohibitions on benefiting a lender therefore do not apply. This may prove important if the buyer and seller have additional details to resolve and the buyer is willing to concede these details in the seller's favor. If no loan has occurred, he would not be prohibited from doing so.

When a standard Heter Iska is used, most poskim hold that the buyer and seller have a borrower-lender relationship, and the buyer is prohibited from benefiting the seller in any manner not explicitly mentioned in the Iska.[48] By using R' Moshe Feinstein's method, the buyer is permitted to benefit the seller in any way he chooses.

32. The disadvantage of this method: When a sale-lease agreement is used, the seller retains partial ownership in the property. This means that if the home is damaged (for example, by fire or vandalism) he would be partially liable. Most sellers would be reluctant to accept this liability.

However, this problem can be avoided if the sale-lease contract requires the buyer to maintain adequate insurance coverage for the property and holds him fully liable for any failure to do so.[49] The buyer himself is prohibited from insuring or guaranteeing the property.[50]

33. A third option: Still another method of redressing a mortgage is mentioned by contemporary poskim. A seller may offer his home for sale, deliberately charging a higher price because he is offering credit. For example, if the seller was contemplating selling his home for $100,000 on a cash sale, he may instead offer it for sale for $140,000

---

48. *S.A. Harav* §39, *Maharsham* 4:95, *Tuv Tam Vodaas* 3:35, *Mishnas Ribbis* p. 64; cf. *Bris Yehudah* 10:n7. (See also *Chavos Daas* 166:1.) The discussion here applies only to the standard Heter Iska form, known as *chetzyo milveh vechetzyo pikadon*. The mechanism of this type of Iska form does not completely eliminate the borrower-lender relationship between the parties; it only allows a specific amount of profit to be passed to the investor by the person using the funds. Where the *kulo pikadon* form is used, no loan whatsoever has taken place and the buyer is not prohibited from benefiting the seller (*Mishnas Ribbis* ibid.). [Both types of Heter Iska forms appear in Chapter 23; the difference between them is explained there at greater length, in Paragraphs 8-11.]

49. The buyer may be required to pay the insurance costs as part of the rental charges. This requirement should be incorporated in the text of the contract.

50. This is based on the laws relating to rentals, which were discussed in Chapter 11. There, in Paragraphs 4 and 5, we have seen that rental fees may be charged only in situations where the owner of the rental property (or item) bears some liability for the property.

payable over five years. A purchaser would naturally be willing to pay a higher price because of the financing built into the agreement. This is permitted, provided that there is no explicit linkage (neither oral nor written) of the price to the credit arrangement.[51] It is therefore prohibited to offer the purchaser a choice of paying $100,000 cash or $140,000 with the financing package.[52]

34. This option is generally suitable only for sales involving short-term financing. When a mortgage runs for twenty or twenty-five years, the total interest cost which would have to be incorporated into the purchase price is enormous. The purchase price would be so high that it would be obvious that the price is linked to the credit terms. This type of agreement is therefore prohibited.

35. A disadvantage of this method: If the buyer is later unwilling or unable to complete payment on schedule, the seller may not charge him for the additional time that the payment is delayed.[53] (When the previous two options are used, their terms automatically continue until payment is completed.)

Assuming a Mortgage

36. Someone purchasing a home may wish to assume the mortgage which the seller had secured from a bank. When the bank is willing

---

51. *Igros Moshe* Y.D. 3:38 and *Kol Kisvei R' Henkin* 2:50. This is based on Y.D. 173:1 and *Shach* 2. The text of a contract employing this method appears in *Igros Moshe*. The reason this is permitted is that the prohibition on Ribbis as part of a purchase is only Rabbinic in nature. The Rabbis limited this prohibition to cases where it is obvious that the higher price is being paid for the credit arrangement. Real estate, however, has no firm market value, in that people who desire a particular property will often overpay to acquire it. Consequently, when a seller asks a higher price, it is not obvious that it is linked to the credit terms.

There are two situations where this is prohibited. When a lower cash price is offered as an alternative, it becomes obvious that the higher price actually contains a finance charge. Additionally, when the price is so high that it is obviously excessive, even for real estate, the fact that the price contains a finance charge is also obvious (see Chapter 6, Paragraph 12). In these two situations this option may not be used.

52. *Shach* 173:2. This is identical to the case described in Paragraph 1 of this chapter.

53. *Igros Moshe* addresses this problem by incorporating into the contract a clause which allows the seller to repossess the house in the event that payment is not completed on time. This is not always a practical option. It would therefore be advisable to use this method only when the seller is reasonably sure that this problem will not develop, or where other collateral is offered to insure payment.

to switch the mortgage to the name of the buyer, the buyer may assume the mortgage.[54]

37. When the seller remains responsible for the loan (for example, the bank is unaware of the sale of the property, or the bank requires that the seller remain a coborrower of the loan),[55] assuming a loan is prohibited. This is true even if the buyer makes mortgage payments directly to the bank.[56] A Rabbi should be consulted on how to use a Heter Iska to permit this arrangement.

Buying a House in Someone Else's Name

38. A person seeking to purchase a home may be unable to secure a mortgage for financial reasons (e.g., the bank considers him a credit risk because of past credit problems or because he lacks adequate income to cover the mortgage). A friend may be willing to allow him to purchase the home in his (i.e., the friend's) name and to take out a mortgage for him, based on the friend's credit standing. In this case, the friend becomes the legal owner of the home and borrower of funds. A separate agreement between them states that the home actually belongs to the first individual and that he accepts the responsibility of making prompt mortgage payments to the bank. This arrangement is prohibited as a form of Ribbis.[57]

---

54. In this case, the seller's original loan is terminated, and a new loan is issued to the buyer. Because no loan passes between the buyer and seller, there is no problem of Ribbis.

In a similar case, *Shulchan Aruch* (Y.D. 168:1) rules that a Jew is prohibited from passing a non-Jew's money to a Jewish borrower (who will pay interest on the loan), because it might appear that he himself had made an interest bearing loan. This would seem to contradict the ruling offered here. However, *Chelkas Yaakov* (3:196:note 3) maintains that this does not apply in the case of a transferred mortgage. This is also the ruling of R' Yecheskeil Roth Shlita (in his introduction to *Keren HaTorah*). *Bris Yehudah* (31:n18) also permits a mortgage to be assumed, providing that both the loan and the home are recorded in the name of the purchaser. *Mishnas Ribbis* (18:n14) reports that this leniency is accepted by contemporary poskim. (See also *Teshuvos R' Yonasan Shteif* §25.)

55. *Mishnas Ribbis* 18:n14. For a ruling in a case where the seller is not a coborrower, but remains as a guarantor, see *Chelkas Yaakov* ibid.

56. *Teshuvos R' Yonasan Shteif* §25, *Bris Yehudah* 31:5 and Note 18, based on Y.D. 168:1. This is prohibited because the seller is still the borrower of record and is actually lending these funds to the buyer. When the buyer makes a mortgage payment to the bank, he is satisfying the seller's debt. This is actually a payment to the seller.

57. Based on Y.D. 168:17; *Bris Yehudah* quoted in *Mishnas Ribbis* 17:n10, *Shevet HaLevi* 7:141. (See also *Igros Moshe* Y.D. 3:42, who rules this way in a similar situation.) In this case, two loans have actually taken place. The first, between the bank and the mortgage's

If a Heter Iska is used, this arrangement is permitted.[58]

39. This arrangement would be permitted (even without use of a Heter Iska) if the bank would provide a mortgage which does not assign personal responsibility to the borrower and relies solely on the property as collateral for collection.[59]

A Mortgage Guarantor

40. A Jew is generally prohibited from guaranteeing a loan, such as a mortgage, because the loan calls for interest payments. It is common

---

legal owner (i.e., the friend), is not a Ribbis problem. The second loan occurs when the property is transferred to another individual (the person who actually wishes to purchase the home) who agrees to pay the mortgage. The person paying the mortgage is actually borrowing these funds from his friend when he takes the property. He is repaying this loan, with interest, when he satisfies his friend's obligation to the bank.

This prohibition applies despite the fact that the bank uses the property as collateral for the loan (see Note 59).

Please note: When complex financial arrangements are made, it is common for this to lead to misunderstandings. Experience has shown that it is wise for the arrangement to be spelled out in writing, so as to avoid future disputes. (For example, where the person in whose name the property is held would die or become incapable of communicating, his relatives might assume that the property is truly his.) It is therefore highly recommended that a contract be signed to establish the true owner of the property and his obligations (if any) to the person who has taken the property in his own name. Such a contract appears at the end of this chapter.

58. The author of *Bris Yehudah*, quoted in *Mishnas Ribbis* 17:n10. This is done in the following manner: The friend (in whose name the mortgage is issued) buys the house. Once it has become his, he sells it to the first individual, using any of the three methods outlined above (Paragraphs 28-34) for selling a house on credit.

59. *Mishnas Ribbis* 17:n10, based on *Shach* 168:51 and 52, who permits this arrangement when the collateral has sufficient value (to cover both principal and interest). See also Chapter 17, Paragraph 13, where these laws are discussed.

At present, in the U.S.A., mortgage agreements assign personal liability to the borrower of record. If he fails to pay, the bank collects from the property only because this is the easiest method of collection. However, since the bank is entitled to collect from the individual who applied for the loan, he has the status of a borrower. If he arranges a loan, which uses the property as collateral and indemnifies him from personal responsibility to repay, it is permitted. (This type of loan may be available for commercial properties.) In this case, since the property belongs to the same individual who is paying the interest, this is considered a direct loan from the bank to that person and is permitted.

[The individual who arranges the loan could serve as a guarantor for the mortgage provided that his commitment falls within the guidelines of guarantors for any loan between Jew and non-Jew, as outlined in Chapter 15, Paragraphs 19-20 (*Shach* 52, *Chavos Daas* 170:8, *S.A. Harav* §66, *Avnei Nezer* 135; this is applied to our situation by *Shevet HaLevi* ibid.).]

for a young couple purchasing a home to have difficulty getting a mortgage. Even if close relatives are willing to cosign the mortgage, they are prohibited from doing so.[60]

This prohibition applies even when the borrower puts up collateral for the debt.[61] However, if it is known that the lender will pursue the collateral rather than the guarantor, a Jew may guarantee the loan. When a mortgage loan is issued, the property which is being purchased serves as collateral for the loan. Therefore, wherever it is the common practice for a bank to foreclose on a home rather than to pursue the guarantor, one may serve as a guarantor (*areiv kablan*) for a mortgage.[62]

Partners in a Purchase

41. When a partnership takes a loan or mortgage in the name of one of its partners, with the partnership making payments, a Heter Iska is required.[63]

42. When a bank issues a joint loan, with the mortgage in both names, each individual is legally responsible for the entire loan. In Chapter 16, Paragraphs 1-7 we will see that partners are generally prohibited from taking this type of loan (see Chapter 16 for additional details).[64]

---

60. Y.D. 170:1. This applies to situations where the lender is entitled to pursue the guarantor directly, and is not required to first sue the borrower for payment. This is known as an *areiv kablan*, a guarantor who accepts (responsibility for the loan). [These rules are outlined in Chapter 15, Paragraphs 9-13.]

However, if the bank is required to first sue the borrower, another Jew may serve as his guarantor. This is known as an *areiv stam*, an ordinary guarantor.

61. *Chavos Daas* 170:8.

62. *Minchas Yitzchak* 4:19:12. This guarantor has the status of an *areiv stam* since it is known that the bank will pursue the borrower first. See also *Mishnas Ribbis* 15:8 where this is discussed at length.

63. This is similar to the case in Paragraph 38, where an individual's credit line is being secured to arrange a loan for someone else. Here too, the individual's credit line is being used by his partners to arrange a loan, which is then used by all the partners jointly. All of the partners are joining to repay the loan, and are making the interest payments which the individual is personally obligated to make. This is prohibited (*Mishnas Ribbis* 18:13).

There are exceptions to this, in situations where a business invests in a purchase. For details, see Chapter 15, Paragraphs 17-18.

64. Since each person has actually borrowed only half the money, they are serving as guarantors for each other. This is prohibited, as explained in Paragraph 40. In situations (described there), where one is permitted to act as a guarantor, this too would be permitted (*Taz* 170:3, *Chavos Daas* 170:1, *S.A. Harav* §64).

A joint loan would be permitted if the terms of the agreement required the bank to

Buying or Selling Mortgages

43. A Jew is permitted to extend a mortgage to a non-Jew and receive interest payments. He may later wish to sell that mortgage to another Jew. This is permitted, provided that the purchaser accepts liability, so that if the borrower were to become unable (or unwilling) to pay the debt, the purchaser would suffer the loss.[65]

44. When the mortgage is sold, a proper *kinyan* must be made to transfer ownership to the purchaser. There is disagreement among the poskim as to which *kinyan* is required when a non-Jew's debt obligation is sold.[66] One may rely on the opinion that a *kinyan* which is accepted by businessmen in the local community as binding and is enforceable by law is a valid means of transferring ownership. This is known as *kinyan situmta*.[67] (In many communities, the transfer of a legally binding document serves this purpose.)

Purchasing a Jew's Mortgage

45. A Jew is permitted to borrow money from a non-Jew under terms which require interest payments. If the non-Jew were then to sell this debt obligation to a Jew, the status of the loan would change. This

---

pursue each of the borrowers in court, for his portion of the loan. In this case, each partner would be an *areiv stam* for his friend's portion of the loan.

65. Y.D. 168:18, *Shach* 173:8. This is because the seller may not serve as a guarantor for the mortgage, just as a Jew may not guarantee any loan which calls for Ribbis payments to be paid to another Jew. This is true even if the seller guarantees only the principal and not the interest (see *S.A. Harav* §69).

Although the buyer must accept liability, this obligation may be limited. He must be liable only for loss which is caused by the borrower's failure to pay. He is *not* required to accept liability for loss caused by other factors, such as if the note turns out to be a forgery, if the debt had already been collected (Y.D. 173:4) or if the debt cannot be collected for other legal reasons [for example, if the note had been designated as collateral for a previous loan (Y.D. 173:4) or if the government abolished all debts (*Beis Yosef* 173 from *Teshuvos HaRashba*, *Shach* 173:10; cf. *Chochmas Adam* 139:8)].

66. *Shach* 168:60 and 173:8, *Chochmas Adam* 137:26 and *S.A. Harav* §69 maintain that standard *kinyanim* are not valid for the transfer of a non-Jew's debt. Cf. *Pischei Teshuvah* 168:6, *Shaar Deah* 168:8 and *Beis Shlomo* C.M. 21 who disagree. This has been discussed at length in Chapter 12, Paragraph 19. See also *Bris Yehudah* 33:24.

67. *Ben Ish Chai* (to *V'eschanan*, 23) maintains that all poskim would agree that this is a valid *kinyan* (see Chapter 12, Paragraph 18). An alternative method of transfer is outlined in *Shach* 173:8 and *S.A. Harav* §69.

now becomes a loan between two Jews and interest may not be paid for the period that the debt is the property of the Jewish purchaser.[68]

46. Interest which had accrued prior to the sale may be paid. This is true even if provisions of the sale call for these payments to be made to the Jewish purchaser of the debt.[69]

47. An exception to this prohibition: If the debt being sold is a mortgage agreement which does not give the borrower the option of prepaying the mortgage, this sale would be permitted, and interest could be paid to the Jewish purchaser. This is because the entire debt obligation (for the entire life of the mortgage) already existed when the loan was still in the non-Jew's possession, and no additional interest is charged while it is in the possession of the Jewish purchaser.[70]

Ginnie Mae

48. Ginnie Mae (Government National Mortgage Association) is a government agency which issues mortgages to homebuyers. These mortgages are funded by investors, who invest their money with Ginnie Mae. This money is passed on to homebuyers in the form of mortgages, with the interest paid to Ginnie Mae and then forwarded to the investors. It is permitted to invest in a Ginnie Mae fund.[71]

---

68. *Taz* 168:12, *Bris Yehudah* 31:10. This prohibition applies even if the non-Jew actually collects the money, and then passes it on to the purchaser.

69. This is a subject of dispute between *Taz* 168:12 and *Shach* in *Nekudas HaKesef* ibid. The opinion quoted here is that of the *Taz*. This opinion is accepted by the later poskim (*Gra* 168:25, *Chavos Daas* 168: *Chidushim* 20, *Chochmas Adam* 137:11, *Divrei Chaim* Y.D. 2:56, *Avnei Nezer* 194:16; see also *Bris Yehudah* 31:10). *Chavos Daas* 168:20 notes that any question of Ribbis in situations involving the sale of debt is a question of Rabbinically prohibited Ribbis. In light of this, one need not hesitate to rely on the lenient ruling of the *Taz*.

70. *Rema* 168:20. (The purchaser would be limited to collecting the interest which is included in the original agreement. If the mortgage payments were not made on time, no additional finance charges may be added.)

71. *Vechai Achicha Imach* 8:97.

It is certain that Jews are among those who borrow from Ginnie Mae, and pay interest on their loan. The Jewish investor does receive a portion of these interest payments, as his interest from the Ginnie Mae Fund. *Vechai Achicha Imach* nevertheless offers numerous reasons to permit investment in a Ginnie Mae. A major point is that it is not clear that investors actually receive legal title to the mortgages. Since the government guarantees Ginnie Mae mortgages, it is they who act as owners of the mortgage to initiate foreclosure proceedings in case of delinquency. From a legal standpoint, the technical issue of actual ownership of the mortgages is therefore difficult to verify.

[An additional reason to permit this is because the investor does not purchase any

When a Ribis Deal Was Already Made

49. Often, a contract which calls for Ribbis payments has already been signed before a Rabbi is consulted. It is only later that the parties involved realize that their agreement is prohibited, and wish to correct the problem. As a rule of thumb, only the clause which calls for Ribbis payments is invalid; the rest of the contract remains valid, with only the portion calling for Ribbis nullified.[72]

In many cases, a seller could cogently argue that he would never have agreed to the contract if the Ribbis provision were not included. For example, a seller may concede to certain provisions only because he is receiving financial benefits or payments in return. If those benefits or payments were later shown to be violations of Ribbis, the seller would be left with a contract containing concessions to which he would never have agreed.[73] In this case, the seller could demand that either the concessions be struck from the agreement or that the entire agreement be nullified. The buyer would choose between these two options.[74]

50. If both sides agree, a Heter Iska may be incorporated into the agreement at any time. However, since the sale had already been completed, the portion of the sale which calls for Ribbis payments must be undone before the Heter Iska may be used.

This is accomplished in the following manner: Suppose a $200,000 home was sold for $150,000 cash,[75] and a private mortgage was offered by the seller for the remaining $50,000 at an annual interest rate of 8%. Two months later, before any payments are made, both sides realize that their agreement is prohibited because it calls for Ribbis payments. They go to a Rabbi, who advises them to enter into a Heter Iska agreement. To do so, the buyer first returns $50,000 to the seller. This may be done

---

individual mortgage, and he receives payment from the pool of Ginnie Mae mortgages. This is a pool of mortgages of which a majority of borrowers are non-Jews. This would be similar to a loan which is issued to a partnership, where interest may be collected if a majority of partners are non-Jews (as we have seen in Chapter 5, Paragraph 26).]

72. Y.D. 175:8.

73. For example, where the seller sold a $200,000 home for $150,000 cash and offered the buyer a private mortgage on the remaining $50,000, he could certainly argue that he would not have agreed to the sale if he had known that he would not be permitted to collect interest on the credit.

74. C.M. 208:1.

75. The halachah would be the same if a bank loan was used to pay all or part of this $150,000.

by using a *kinyan sudar* to transfer ownership of $50,000 worth of the home back to the seller. The seller then invests the $50,000 with the buyer, by returning it to him under the terms of a Heter Iska. The seller may return the $50,000 in the same manner as he received it, by use of a *kinyan sudar*.

51. The viability of the aforementioned arrangement depends on the proper execution of a *kinyan sudar*. Because technical errors may be made in the execution of a *kinyan sudar*, it is advisable to also employ a second form of *kinyan* to transfer the $50,000 worth of real estate. This can be done most easily by using *kinyan shtar*: The person returning the property signs a document which states simply that he "does hereby transfer to (name of receiver) $50,000 worth of the property located at (address)."

This document is then handed to the receiver of the property in the presence of two witnesses.

See the note below for an additional reason to use *kinyan shtar*.[76]

If Ribbis Payments Were Already Made

52. If interest payments had already been made before the parties realized that their agreement involves Ribbis, this too must be corrected.

For example, there is a $200,000 mortgage which calls for monthly payments of $1,000 towards principal and an additional $1,000 for interest.[77] Three months elapse before the parties realize that their agreement is prohibited. Six thousand dollars has been paid; according to their agreement half of this was Ribbis. This means that $197,000 of principal remains outstanding. To correct the Ribbis problem, they should calculate the entire $6,000 as payment of principal, leaving a balance of $194,000. This redresses the Ribbis violation, since the $3,000 which was paid as Ribbis is being reckoned as a payment of principal. A Heter Iska is subsequently drawn between the parties, based on a $194,000 debt, in the method outlined in Paragraph 49.[78]

---

76. In most places, it is the common business practice to draw up a contract when selling real estate. Some poskim maintain that in places where it is unusual to sell real estate without writing a contract, the contract is required as part of the *kinyan* (see *Pischei Teshuvah* to C.M. 190:1).

77. Actual mortgage schedules call for an accelerated schedule of principal payments and a descending schedule of interest payments. The example here was chosen for clarity, and can be applied to any schedule of payments.

78. Based on *Rema* 166:3. *Igros Moshe* (Y.D. 3:notes to Ribbis 161:23) explains that as long as the principal has not been fully repaid, all interest payments are automatically credited

Appendix I To Chapter Thirteen:
Sale-Lease Contract

(For use in place of a private mortgage[1] — see Paragraph 30)

This agreement is drawn between _____ ,[2] hereafter referred to as the buyer, and _____ ,[3] hereafter referred to as the partner, in regard to the real estate property located at _____ , in the city of _____ .

The aforementioned property is registered in legal documents and/or at the office of the County Clerk as belonging to the buyer. The partner has actually advanced $ _____[4] and has attained ownership of the property in a value equal to this amount. The buyer and partner have entered into this arrangement, subject to the sale agreement and lease agreement which appear below. Neither party may terminate these agreements without the consent of the second party.

SALE AGREEMENT: The partner has agreed to sell his portion of the property to the buyer, under the terms described herein. The buyer has committed himself to purchase the partner's portion of the property in

Continued on next page

---

towards that balance. In our example, all $6,000 are considered payment on principal. This is true even if the payments were clearly labeled as interest. Even if the buyer were willing to forgive the $3,000 paid as interest (something he would be allowed to do if Ribbis payments had already been made) and pay the $197,000 balance, he would be prohibited from doing so. Since the true balance is $194,000, the extra $3,000 would constitute Ribbis. (See also *Machneh Ephraim* Ribbis:3, who concurs with this ruling, but for a different reason; see also *Pischei Teshuvah* 161:6, and below Chapter 20, Note 7.)

1. This contract is recommended for use when an individual lends his friend money to purchase real estate (or where the seller offers a private mortgage). This contract is based on *Igros Moshe* Y.D. 2:62, and is used in place of a Heter Iska. (The advantages of this method are outlined above, Paragraphs 30-31.) A brief explanation of this agreement appears below (at the end of the contract).

2. Enter name of the person (or persons) in whose name the real estate is recorded.

3. Enter name of the person who is advancing funds for the purchase, but does not wish to retain permanent ownership in the property.

4. Enter amount advanced by the partner. Where the previous owner of the property desires to offer a private mortgage for a portion of the sale price, this contract may be used. However, this sentence must be changed to read, "The partner has retained ownership of the property, in the value of $ _____ ."

monthly increments, over the next _____⁵ months, for a total price of $ _____ .⁶ The attached 'schedule of payments' contains a column labeled 'principal.' The monthly payment listed thereunder shall constitute a purchase payment for a portion of this real estate, in the value of that payment. This portion of the real estate shall be sold to the buyer when payment is made. The buyer may, at any time, validate this transfer by means of a legal *kinyan* of his choice.

LEASE AGREEMENT: The buyer has agreed to lease the partner's portion of the property for the next _____⁵ months. As rental for this portion of the property, the buyer shall pay all sewer and water charges, taxes, fines, insurance and other costs associated with the property. In addition, a cash rental fee will be paid to the partner every month. The attached 'schedule of payments' contains a column labeled 'rental charges.' The monthly payment listed thereunder shall constitute this rental payment.

The buyer obligates himself to keep the property in good condition and to pay for its normal upkeep. He also obligates himself to keep adequate insurance, so that he and the partner would suffer no loss in case of suit or damage to the property. Any costs or reduction in property value, which result from the buyer's failure to honor these terms, shall be borne by the buyer alone.

In the event of any conflict between the terms of this agreement and those of any other agreement regarding these funds, the terms of this agreement shall prevail.

This agreement shall follow the guidelines established in *Igros Moshe* Y.D. 2:62. It is agreed that any dispute which may arise in connection with this agreement shall be submitted before _____ .⁷ Judgment rendered by the aforesaid authority may be entered in any court having jurisdiction thereof.

Signature of the Buyer _____

Dated _____

Signature of the Partner _____

Dated _____

Continued on next page

---

5. Enter the number of months on the schedule of payment.

6. Enter same figure as was entered above (at Note 4).

7. This part of the contract is optional. However, it is strongly recommended that the parties choose the name of a mutually acceptable Rabbi or Beis Din to arbitrate disputes which may arise.

Attach to this contract: A schedule of payments. This schedule may be set up in the following manner. The partner is extending a fixed sum of money, for a fixed period; for example, $25,000 for sixty months. If he would have been permitted to loan this money for interest, he would have requested a rate of return, for example, 8% per annum. The partner may acquire a computerized schedule of payments for this type of loan (in our example, for a $25,000 loan for 60 months, at 8%). [This type of schedule is easily obtained from anyone in the financing industry.] This schedule should be relabeled, so that the column which reads 'interest' should instead read 'rental payments.' The rationale for use of this schedule is explained below.

Understanding this contract: This contract is recommended for use when an individual lends his friend money to purchase real estate (or where the seller offers a private mortgage). Someone offering a loan is not permitted to receive interest. Still, the individual may not be willing to extend these funds unless he can benefit from the transaction. *Igros Moshe* suggests that the friend who is laying out money on behalf of the buyer should not issue a loan. Instead, he should purchase a portion of the real estate, in the value of the funds which he is advancing. (For example, if he was willing to lend $25,000 to the buyer, he should instead purchase $25,000 worth of the equity of the real estate. This makes him a partner with the buyer, in the property.) It is not necessary for the deed to actually record this ownership.

Every month, the buyer makes monthly payments to his friend, until these payments total the funds which were laid out. With each payment, the buyer acquires a portion of his friend's ownership in the property, until he has paid the full amount and becomes its sole owner.

In the interim, the buyer is living in a home which is only partially his. The friend, who owns a portion of the home, is entitled to a rental fee

---

8. This part of the contract is optional, depending on whether the parties prefer to have witnesses attest to their agreement.

from him. Thus, each month, the buyer makes a payment to the seller which contains two parts: the payment of principal towards ownership of the house (as mentioned in the previous paragraph), and a rental payment for its use. This fee can be set at an amount equal to the interest rate which the friend would have desired if a loan had been issued.

The parties to this agreement should obtain a regular computerized schedule of payments (the type used by all banks in scheduling mortgage payments) for a loan in the amount being extended. This schedule of payments contains two columns, one which calculates the monthly interest payment, and the other which calculates the monthly payment of principal. [Although the total payment for each month is identical, the portion which is paid towards principal and the part paid for interest change gradually. Each month, the principal portion increases while the interest paid decreases (since the amount of outstanding principal decreases every month, the amount of interest also decreases). This is true of all routine payment schedules.]

This schedule should be attached to the sale-lease agreement, but since no loan has taken place, the interest fees should be relabeled as rental charges. Thus, every month the buyer pays a set sum, identical to the sum he would have paid if he had actually taken a loan. The portion labeled 'principal' is used to acquire additional ownership in the home, until the entire amount is paid and the buyer acquires complete ownership. The portion labeled 'rental charges' is due to the friend because the buyer is using his portion of the home. As each month passes, the buyer owns an increasingly greater percentage of the home. He is therefore renting a smaller and smaller portion from the friend. It is therefore appropriate that the amount of money paid as rental charges decreases each month, as shown in the schedule of payments.

Appendix II To Chapter Thirteen:
Contract To Establish Proper Ownership

(See Note 57)

I, the undersigned _____ who resides at _____, does hereby attest, of my own free will, that the information recorded below is true. My signature, affixed below, testifies to the accuracy of this information and may be used as evidence to this effect.

The property located at _____ in the city of _____ is registered in legal documents and/or at the office of the County Clerk as belonging to me. I do hereby admit that despite this fact, these properties do not belong to me at all, and that neither I nor my heirs after me have a right to this property or to any structure built upon it. In fact, this property belongs to _____, who resides at _____. This property was recorded in my name for reasons known to us, but not to give me any financial stake in the property in any way. _____ shall have the sole right to sell, lease, build, demolish or otherwise use the property in the manner of an owner dealing with his own property. I shall not have the authority to prevent him from doing so.

Furthermore, I do hereby obligate myself unconditionally, to transfer the property to the name of _____, or to the name of anyone designated by him, at such time as he shall see fit. I shall fulfill this obligation promptly, without charge, and I shall sign all documents necessary for this transfer. I shall make myself available for any other proceedings needed to facilitate this transfer. However, I shall *not* be obligated to pay any of the charges, such as legal fees or filing costs, which may be needed to accomplish this transfer.

All the obligations outlined herein apply equally to me and to my heirs after me. I have made a *kinyan* to formally obligate myself to honor that which is outlined in this document.

_____, the property's true owner, obligates himself to pay all costs incurred by the property, including but not limited to taxes, fines, or decisions rendered against the property due to litigation. If a mortgage was taken to secure purchase of the property, whether in my name or his, he accepts responsibility to make payment, and to settle this debt before selling the property. He has formalized this

Continued on next page

obligation by use of a *kinyan sudar* and has affixed his signature below to attest to this.

This document is binding from the moment of signature, having been validated by *kinyan sudar,* and shall be applied according to the laws of the Torah. I accept upon myself to follow the ruling of the Rabbis (even if he be an individual Rabbi) who accept this document as binding.

To this I willingly affix my signature, with a clear mind and of my own free will, without any conditions (*bli asmachta*). I declare that any statements to the contrary (*modaos*), even if attributed to me, are null and void, and that any witnesses who claim that there was coercion of any type (*modaos or modaos demodaos*) shall not be accepted to testify in this regard.

I affix my signature on this _____ day of _____ , in the year _____ .

_____
(Owner of record signs here)

_____
(Actual Owner Signs Here)

Please note: This document is drawn to establish proper ownership of the property in question, and to protect the rights of both parties. It is highly recommended that a lawyer be consulted before a document such as this is signed. The author takes no responsibility for the enforceability of this contract in any way. This is simply being provided for the convenience of those who would otherwise not use any document at all.

Borrowing Merchandise[1]

---

1. This refers to situations where goods are borrowed and sold or used, with different goods of the same type used as repayment. The laws in this chapter do not refer to situations where an item (for example, a shovel or car) is borrowed and used and then returned; the laws regarding this type of borrowing have been discussed in Chapter 11.

Introduction

We have already seen that Ribbis is prohibited in all types of loans, regardless of whether the loan consists of cash, merchandise or services. Whenever a debt is established, payment must be limited to the amount which was borrowed.

All merchandise is assessed at its market value. Thus, if someone borrows a bushel of apples at a time that it is worth $100, he owes the lender $100. If he were to return a bushel of apples to the lender at a time that they are worth $110, he would be benefiting the lender. Although the lender is receiving the same amount of apples as he loaned, he is receiving something of greater financial value. This is Ribbis. For this reason, Chazal forbade the trading of merchandise. This means that a person who borrows a bushel of apples may not commit himself to return a bushel of apples, since their price may rise in the interim. This prohibition is known as *seah beseah*[2] (a *seah* is a measure of volume; this term refers to the trading of merchandise — 'a measure for a measure'). It requires payment to be set by the cash value of the merchandise on loan.

The Prohibition of Seah Beseah

1. A person may not borrow goods and agree to pay by returning the same amount of goods at a later time, because it is possible that the value of the goods will increase by the time of payment. This applies to all types of merchandise.[3] Only local currency may be traded in this manner.[4]

---

2. This is a form of Ribbis DeRabbanan (*Beis Yosef* 162, quoting numerous Rishonim).

3. Y.D. 162:1. [Rare coins are considered merchandise in regard to these laws.]

Foreign currency: Each country has its own legal currency. Any foreign currency is considered a commodity, to which the laws of trading, as outlined in this chapter, apply (see Paragraph 14). We have seen that this rule applies in other areas of the laws of Ribbis as well (see Chapter 8, Paragraph 19). Thus, debt may not be set according to the value of a foreign currency. See Chapter 1, Paragraph 20, regarding the halachah of lending foreign currency.

When the same item is returned: The laws outlined in this chapter apply to items which are borrowed to be consumed (or sold), with similar goods used to repay the loan. When the very item which is borrowed is to be returned (such as when someone borrows a car), this prohibition does not apply. The laws relating to this case appear in Chapter 11.

4. Y.D. ibid. The local currency is always considered to have a constant value. Any price changes are attributed to fluctuations in the value of the merchandise, and not to changes

2. Borrowing merchandise is permitted when the debt is established by the cash value of the merchandise. For example, if a caterer borrows a case of chickens worth $100, he now owes $100 to the lender. Later, when paying, he may return either $100 cash or $100 worth of chickens, based on their value at that time.[5] If the price of poultry were to decrease, the caterer would return $100 worth of chickens. This means that he would end up returning more chickens than he had borrowed. This is not Ribbis, because the value of the payment is equal to the value of the loan.[6]

---

in the value of the currency. This is true even where economic conditions are clearly the reason for the price change (e.g., where the price of a foreign-made car increases due to changes in the exchange rate of the country's currency). See *Igros Moshe* Y.D. 2:114 where this is explained.

Today, currency values are no longer tied to the value of gold or silver. Coins and bills have little intrinsic value; their value is linked to the strength of the government which stands behind them. It is not clear that the Talmud's designation of currency as an unchanging value would apply today.

Chasam Sofer Y.D. 134 (s.v. *aval*) and *Igros Moshe* Y.D. 2:114 rule that our coins and bills are considered currency (*Igros Moshe* is refering specifically to the laws of Ribbis). They base this on the concept of *dina d'malchusa dina*, which recognizes the law of the land in establishing coins and bills as currency.

In a similar vein, *Chazon Ish* Y.D. 72:2 writes, "The concept of currency applies to anything which the citizens of a country agree to use for selling, purchasing and to establish values for all market items, as is the custom [with the currencies] of our countries."

[*Igros Moshe* draws a distinction between the laws of Ribbis (to which the concept of *dina d'malchusa dina* applies) and the laws of *maaser kisafim*, tithing (where these rules do not apply, since this is not an area governed by secular law). He rules that currency does not have an unchanging value, where the laws of *maaser kisafim* are concerned. *Igros Moshe* applies this ruling to the case of someone who purchased a home for $1000, and sold it ten years later for $2000. In calculating his profit (for tithing purposes), the person may compute the rate of inflation to establish his margin of profit. Thus if inflation has caused $1000 to be worth $1800 ten years later, the person must pay *maaser* only on a profit of $200. It appears that *Chazon Ish* would not concur with this ruling, since he views our money as true currency.]

The status of paper currency has been discussed by numerous poskim in regard to other areas of halachah; see *Chasam Sofer* Y.D. 134, E.H. 1:126 and C.M. 65, *Beis Shlomo* C.M. 71, *Oneg Yom Tov* 1:102, *Maharsham* 2:100, *Imrei Yosher* 2:151, *Nachal Yitzchak* 66:1-3, *Oruch HaShulchan* Y.D. 305:18, *Har Tzvi* Y.D. 244, *Bris Yehudah* 18:n10 and *Lehoros Nosson* 8:105-107.

5. If the parties choose to do so, their agreement may *require* that payment be made in the form of merchandise (in this case, by delivering chickens) providing that the value is set at $100 (*Bris Yehudah* 17:3).

6. *Chavos Daas* 165:1, *Machneh Ephraim* 27, *Chazon Ish* 72:6, *Bris Yehudah* 17:3.

3. When lending merchandise, the borrower may not benefit the lender in any way. This restriction is identical for both cash loans and merchandise loans.

In addition, when businessmen lend each other merchandise, they may not do so with the condition that if the lender will need to borrow merchandise at a later time, the borrower will lend it to him.[7]

Exceptions to This Prohibition

4. There are three significant exceptions to this prohibition of borrowing merchandise. In each of these three cases, goods may be lent with the stipulation that payment will be made, using other goods. Even if the value of the merchandise does go up in the interval, payment would still be permitted.[8]

The three exceptions are:

a) when small amounts of an item are borrowed by friends or neighbors;

b) when the borrower has a small amount of the merchandise in stock at the time that he borrows additional goods. This is known as *yesh lo*, lit., he has (the merchandise);[9]

c) when the item which is being traded has a set market price and is readily available.

Each of these exceptions is explained below.

---

7. *Mishnas Ribbis* 6:21. Trading loans (*'halveini v'elveh loch'*) is prohibited, as explained in Chapter 3, Paragraph 20.

8. Sometimes, it is known from the outset that the value of the merchandise will certainly go up by the time of payment. For example, if seasonal fruits are borrowed in the summer, with the stipulation that the same type of fruit be returned in the winter, we know that the value of the payment will exceed the value of the loan. Do these exceptions apply even in this case?

• When 'exception a' (neighbors borrowing small amounts) applies, this is permitted (*Mishnah Berurah* in *Shaar Hatziyun* 450:4).

• When 'exception b' (*yesh lo*) applies, this is also permitted (*Shach* 162:11, *S.A. Harav* §31).

• However, when 'exception c' (the item has a set market price) applies, the borrower must have the option of paying at any time. The agreement may not require that payment be made only after a certain time (*Rema* 162:3).

9. *'Yesh lo'* has already been introduced as an exception to other Rabbinic Ribbis prohibitions, in Chapters 7 and 8. The concept is a bit different here. In those cases, we required that the seller have sufficient quantity of the item in stock, to cover the entire transaction. As we shall see below (Paragraph 7), this is not necessary here.

Exception A: Neighbors Borrowing Small Amounts

5. This prohibition does not apply to neighbors or friends who borrow small amounts of merchandise from each other. For example, a neighbor who borrowed a five-pound bag of sugar may later return a five-pound bag of sugar, even if the price of sugar had gone up in the interim.[10]

Exception B: Yesh Lo

6. If the person borrowing the merchandise already has some of this type of merchandise in his possession, this prohibition does not apply. He may borrow additional merchandise and pledge to make payment, at a later time, with identical merchandise.[11]

This is permitted even if the borrower does not receive legal title to the borrowed merchandise after he makes payment, and even if the borrower

---

10. *Rema* 162:1.

Mishnah Berurah (450:2) explains that this is permitted because prices tend to fluctuate by small amounts, and people generally ignore this small difference (unlike businessmen, who do take notice of small price fluctuations). The Rabbinic prohibition of *seah beseah* applies only because of the similarity to Ribbis. Therefore, when people do not notice the difference, this prohibition does not apply.

[*Mishnah Berurah* implies that even if there is a great fluctuation in the price, this would still be permitted. Since prices generally tend to fluctuate only slightly, people pay no attention to the market value of the items they borrow from each other (see *Divrei Sofrim* 162:19).]

Returning more than was borrowed: Although neighbors may borrow goods without regard to their market value, this does not mean that they may return a greater amount of the item which was borrowed. When the item is returned, only the amount which was actually borrowed should be returned. If anything were added to the payment, this would constitute Ribbis (*Bris Yehudah* 17:n6, based on Y.D. 160:17).

If someone borrowed a loaf of bread, he may purchase another loaf and use it to repay his neighbor, without paying attention to the exact size of the new loaf. Even if this loaf is actually a bit larger, this would not matter, as long as the difference in size is generally insignificant to people. Additional aspects of this law have been presented in Chapter 1, Paragraphs 5-8.

11. Y.D. 162:2.

[As regards the laws of Ribbis, we view this as if the actual pieces of merchandise which the borrower has in stock are being given to the lender. This explains why there is no Ribbis prohibition; merchandise of equal value is being traded.

Does this mean that the lender actually owns the merchandise? No. In fact, the merchandise is not actually transferred to the lender's possession. If the merchandise were to be damaged, the borrower would suffer the loss, because the merchandise is still his. Still, as regards the laws of Ribbis DeRabbanan, the fact that the merchandise already exists and is available for payment is sufficient to remove the prohibition.]

does not plan to deliver the same piece of merchandise which he has in stock.

7. When is an item considered to be in the possession of the borrower?[12] The poskim present the following guidelines:

a) The merchandise must be complete and in a condition suitable for delivery. For example, a flour merchant who wishes to borrow flour must actually have flour in his possession.[13] If he has wheat which he plans to grind into flour, it is not considered *yesh lo*.[14]

b) The borrower must have the merchandise under his physical control.[15] Even if he is temporarily unable to gain access to the merchandise (for example, the key to the building is misplaced

---

12. ***Taz's* leniency:** *Taz* 166:2, citing *Terumas HaDeshen*, maintains that the borrower does not actually have to possess any of the merchandise. If he has cash with which to buy the merchandise, this is sufficient to be considered *yesh lo*. In addition, even if he does not actually have cash, but he does own other articles which he could sell to receive cash, this too is sufficient to be considered *yesh lo* (even if he does not plan to sell those items).

On a practical level, this extraordinary leniency would effectively abolish the entire prohibition of *seah beseah*. It is rare that a person does not have a single penny with which he could buy a small amount of merchandise. It is even more unusual to find someone who does not own a single article of clothing which could be sold. [In addition, it would certainly be highly unusual for anyone to extend a loan to any person in such financial difficulty.]

Most poskim reject the leniency of *Taz* (*Shach* 162:5, R' Akiva Eiger and *Beis Lechem Yehudah* to *Taz*; the later poskim do not quote the *Taz's* leniency).

13. **Merchandise of a different type:** If he has flour, but it is a different type of flour, it is considered *yesh lo*, providing that payment could be made with that flour as well (*Maharsham* 2:170).

14. **If only one or two changes are still necessary to complete the item:** In Chapter 7, we have seen that an item must be complete and ready for delivery to be considered *yesh lo*. In Chapter 8, where the exception of *yesh lo* appeared again, the rules were different. There, the *Shulchan Aruch* (175:4) ruled that if only one or two changes are still necessary to complete the item, it is considered complete. (However, if three or more changes are necessary, the item is considered incomplete, even in regard to those halachos.)

In regard to the laws of *seah beseah*, the *Shulchan Aruch* makes no distinction, and therefore implies that the item must be complete. This is also the ruling of *Shaar Deah* 162:2 (cf. *Meiri*, cited in *Bris Yehudah* 17:32, who rules leniently).

15. If the merchandise is being stored in someone else's property, it is still considered *yesh lo*, since the owner has access to the merchandise. However, if the borrower had allowed someone to take the merchandise, with the stipulation that he return similar merchandise, it is only considered *yesh lo* after that person returns the merchandise to the borrower (*Rema* 162:2; this is similar to Y.D. 173:7).

or it is in the possession of a worker or relative), the merchandise is considered to be in stock.[16]

c) The merchandise must be in that city. If it is in another city it is not considered *yesh lo* unless that city is frequented by the lender. If it is frequented by the lender, this suffices to be considered *yesh lo*.[17]

d) The borrower need not have sufficient stock for the quantity being borrowed. Even if he has only a single kernel of wheat, he may borrow many bushels of wheat.[18]

8. Before entering into this agreement, the borrower must inform the lender that he has the merchandise in stock. However, even if he does not inform the lender, the agreement is nevertheless valid.[19]

Creating Yesh Lo

9. If a borrower and lender wish to trade merchandise, and none of these exceptions apply, they may create the exception of *yesh lo* in the following manner. The lender first gives the borrower a small amount of the merchandise as an outright gift or sells it to him. Since the borrower now possesses this merchandise, the lender may now lend him additional merchandise, with the stipulation that payment also be made in the form of merchandise.[20]

---

16. Y.D. 162:2.

17. *Rema* 172:2. This implies that if the merchandise is in a city which is frequented by the borrower, but not by the lender, this is not considered *yesh lo*, since the merchandise must be readily available to the lender, as payment. This is the ruling of *Bris Yehudah* 7:n70.

Others disagree. They maintain that if the borrower frequents the city, this is sufficient since he could easily transport the merchandise back home to the lender. They understand that *Rema* meant to tell us that it is sufficient even if it is only the lender who travels there (*Divrei Sofrim* in *birur halachah* to 162:2, *Toras Ribbis* 7:10).

18. Y.D. 162:2.

The concept of *yesh lo* appears in three areas of the laws of Ribbis; in Chapters 7 and 8 and again here. In the earlier cases, it was necessary to have a sufficient stock for the quantity involved. Here, this is not required. See *Taz* 163:2 who explains the reason for this distinction.

19. *Beis Yosef*, quoted by *Shach* 162:9.

20. Y.D. 162:2. *Shach* 162:8 adds that a small amount of the item may be sold to the borrower.

Another option mentioned by the *Shulchan Aruch* is for the lender to first lend a small amount of merchandise, with payment set at its cash value. Once the borrower has this

10. When the lender offers a gift to the borrower, to create a *yesh lo* situation, the borrower must agree to receive the gift. This gift cannot be given without the knowledge of the borrower, even if another party makes a proper *kinyan* on his behalf.[21]

Exception C: Items Which Are Available at a Set Price

11. The third exception applies when the merchandise being borrowed is readily available in the marketplace, at a set price.[22] An example of this involves trading seasonal fruits and vegetables. During the summer season, locally grown produce is abundantly available at stable prices. This produce may be borrowed, even if the borrower does not actually have produce in stock at the time that he receives produce from the lender. During the winter season, many types of fruits and vegetables are not readily available, and their price (when available) tends to fluctuate greatly. At this time, the produce may not be borrowed with the stipulation that an identical quantity of produce will be returned.

In the contemporary marketplace, most products (with the exception of seasonal items) are readily available all year long, but their price tends to fluctuate from merchant to merchant. Over time, though, these prices remain steady within a given range. Most poskim hold that these are considered items which have set market prices, despite the disparity in price between merchants.[23]

---

small amount of merchandise, the lender could lend him an additional amount as part of a trade agreement. Most poskim reject this method (*Bach*, *Levush*, *Taz* 162:4, *Shach* 162:8; *Chavos Daas* 166:4 also quotes *Shitah Mikubetzes* who explains why this method is not valid).

21. *Rema* 162:5. The principle of *zochin l'adam shelo befanav*, which permits transfer of a gift to a person even without his knowledge, does not apply here. This principle holds true because of the assumption that the person receiving the gift is happy to receive it. This does not apply here, since the gift is being given to the detriment of the receiver, by allowing the lender to demand payment in the value of the merchandise, even if its value is greater at the time of payment than at the time of the loan. This gift can therefore be given only with the consent of the borrower.

22. Y.D. 162:3. An identical exception is found in regard to prepayment for merchandise, in Y.D. 175:1, where a price may be guaranteed if the merchandise is available at a set market price. *Rema* (162:3) adds that the rules regarding this exception for *seah beseah* are identical to those which are set there. For this reason, many of the rules which apply here also appear in Chapter 8, regarding the laws of prepayment for merchandise.

23. *Mishnas Ribbis* 6:11 and 9:9.

12. When an item is available at a stable price, the borrower must have the option of paying at any time. The agreement may not require that payment be made only after a certain time.[24]

13. Before entering into this agreement, both the borrower and lender should know that the merchandise is available at a set price.[25] However, even if they do not know, the agreement is nevertheless valid.[26]

14. Foreign currency: When lending foreign currency, the borrower may not commit himself to pay back the same amount of identical currency because it is considered a commodity and may not be traded. If the amount owed would be set at the local currency, or if the borrower actually owns some of that currency (this would qualify under the exception of *yesh lo*), this is permitted.

Today, foreign currencies are readily available on world markets. Does 'exception c' apply to foreign currencies?

It appears that 'exception c' does not apply. Although currencies are readily available, their exchange rates are constantly changing. Thus, no currency can be said to have a set value in relation to a second currency. The prohibition of *seah beseah* therefore applies.[27]

Rules for Setting Payment

15. Where these exceptions apply, *seah beseah* is permitted. This means that when merchandise is loaned, payment may be set in one of two ways: according to the cash value of the merchandise being borrowed, or the agreement may stipulate that the same amount of identical merchandise be returned.

The lender is not permitted to set payment by stipulating that if the value of the merchandise increases, he would receive the same amount

---

24. *Rema* 162:3.

25. Y.D. 162:3. Although they should be aware that there is a set price, they do not have to know what that price is (*Shach* 162:9).

26. *Shach* 162:9, *Binas Adam* 132:5; cf. *Taz* 162:3.

27. Many banks and financial institutions will set currency exchange rates in the morning, for that entire business day. *Shevet HaLevi* 3:109 argues that this constitutes a set price. According to this view, trading would be permitted.

Others dispute this leniency. Rabbi Y.S. Eliyashev Shlita (quoted in *Ateres Yaakov* Y.D. 17 and *Mishnas Ribbis* 6:n12) rules that rates which constantly fluctuate from day to day are not considered set rates. *Kitzur Dinei Ribbis* 4:5 adds that even bank rates are only available for a number of hours and are therefore not considered set rates for an entire day. One should follow this opinion.

of identical merchandise as payment, but if the value decreased, he would receive its cash value at the time of the loan. This stipulation unfairly benefits the lender and is prohibited.[28]

16. When a person borrows merchandise and agrees to pay the loan with identical merchandise under any of these exceptions, and the value of the merchandise falls at the time of payment, the borrower may only return the same amount he borrowed. He is prohibited from adding to the payment to compensate the lender for his lost value.[29]

17. When merchandise was traded with the stipulation that payment be made in the form of merchandise, under any of these exceptions, the parties may later agree to make payment in cash. The amount of the payment would be set according to the value of the merchandise at the time of payment. If the value of the merchandise had gone up, this would mean that the lender would actually receive more than the cash value of the goods at the time of the loan. This is permitted.[30]

If Payment Is Unfairly Delayed

18. When stipulating that payment be made in the form of merchandise, under any of these exceptions, the lender is owed a set amount of merchandise. As with any loan, the lender is entitled to payment at the time the loan comes due. If he asks for payment at that time, but does not receive it, and the value of the merchandise subsequently decreases, he would suffer a loss, since the merchandise which he receives is now worth less.

Most poskim hold that the borrower is required to reimburse the lender for this loss, by returning the amount of merchandise which would have been due if payment had been made on time.[31]

---

28. *Rema* 162:2.

29. *S.A. Harav* §33, *Beis Ephraim* Y.D. 43, *Bris Yehudah* 17:5 based on *Ritva* and *Rivash* 396; cf. *Machneh Ephraim* 27, who permits the borrower to reimburse the lender for the loss in value.

30. *Beis Yosef* 162 (s.v. *im*), *Chavos Daas* 163:5, *S.A. Harav* §30.
   If the lender wants payment in merchandise: When payment is made in cash, this does not violate the laws of Ribbis. However, the laws regarding payment of loans require that payment be made with the same type of merchandise that was loaned, unless the lender agrees to accept a cash payment in its place (*Nesivos HaMishpat* 107:4, *Chazon Ish* Y.D. 72:5, *Bris Yehudah* 17:n26). If the borrower does not possess the merchandise, he may also make payment in cash (*S.A. Harav* §30, *Chazon Ish* ibid.).

31. *Radvaz* 3:1249, *Machneh Ephraim* 40, *Shaar HaMishpat* 74:5, *Maharil Diskin pisakim* 20, *Bris Yehudah* 17:26; cf. *Bigdei Sheish*, quoted by *Darkei Teshuvah* 162:31

19. If the value of the merchandise increased between the due date and the actual time of payment, the lender would be entitled to the full amount of merchandise which he is owed. This means that he would gain by the delay.[32]

When Payment Takes Place in a Different Country

20. When stipulating that payment be made in the form of merchandise, under any of these exceptions, the borrower makes payment by returning the same amount of merchandise. If payment takes place in a different city or country, where the merchandise is worth more than in the place where it was borrowed, the borrower may not return the full amount of merchandise. The value of his payment should be based on the value of the merchandise in the place where the loan took place.[33]

21. When this was part of the original agreement: Sometimes, a stipulation is made that payment be in a different country. For example, businessmen in the United States borrow merchandise with the stipulation that payment will be made in Israel. In many cases, the merchandise is worth more in Israel than it is in the United States, where it was borrowed. Where this is part of the original agreement, is it permitted to return the same amount of merchandise in a place where it is worth more?

In general, this is prohibited. However, it is permitted where all three of the following conditions apply:

☐ This must be a case of *yesh lo*, where the borrower had merchandise in the second city or country at the time of the loan. In this case, he must have had the full amount of that merchandise; it is not enough for him to have owned a small amount.[34]

---

who prohibits this.

This applies only if the lender requested payment. If the due date passed, but payment was not requested, this reimbursement would not be permitted (*Bris Yehudah* 17:n63, based on the language of the aforementioned poskim; cf. *Toras Ribbis* 7:24).

32. *Bris Yehudah* 17:26.

33. Y.D. 162:5. For example, if payment is made in a place where the merchandise is worth twice as much, only half of the amount of merchandise should be returned.

[This certainly applies in the case of 'exception b' and 'c.' In cases involving 'exception a' (for example, if friends visiting Europe borrowed film from each other, and they wish to return the film after returning to the United States), it would seem that this does not apply (unless there is a great difference in the price of the item).]

34. Y.D. 173:17.

□ This must be a city which is frequented by the lender.[35]

□ Many poskim require that this deal be phrased as a sale ("Give me the merchandise here. . ."), rather than as a loan ("Lend me the merchandise here. . .").[36]

Making Payment With Different Merchandise

22. According to many poskim, the exceptions which are outlined in this chapter are limited to cases where payment involves identical merchandise (e.g., flour for flour, or meat for meat). When a different type of merchandise is used for payment, these leniencies do not apply.[37]

Throughout this chapter, we have been discussing situations where goods are borrowed with payment made using identical goods. A similar situation involves the sale of goods with payment made at a later time, in the form of merchandise. When payment is made in the form of other merchandise, the value of the goods which are used as payment may not be set in advance. The amount of merchandise which is used for payment must be based on their value at the time of payment.[38]

For example, a supplier and a manufacturer agree to a deal. The supplier would deliver $1000 worth of raw material on January 1, with the stipulation that the manufacturer will repay him by delivering $1000 worth of the final product on July 1. This is permitted, provided that the final product is worth $1000 at the time of delivery. The manufacturer may not guarantee delivery of a specific amount of the finished product, since the product may turn out to be worth more than $1000 at the time of payment.

23. When stipulating that payment be made in the form of a different type of merchandise, this is considered a sale rather than a loan. Naturally, the exceptions which apply to cases of prepayment for merchandise (in Chapter 8) also apply here. However, this applies only if the people involved refer to their deal as a sale agreement rather than a loan agreement.[39]

---

35. *Bris Yehudah* 23:n35.

36. *Bris Yehudah* 23:n33.

37. *Rema* 162:5.

38. *Chazon Ish* 72:5, *Bris Yehudah* 22:17. Cf. *Chavos Daas* 162:1, who permits this in cases where the value of the two items which are being traded are usually consistent with each other and it is unusual for the price of one to increase unless the other increases as well. See also *Bris Yehudah* 16:n18.

39. *Shach* 173:16.

CHAPTER FIFTEEN

Guaranteeing a Loan

A. When a loan is passed between Jews (1-8)

B. When a non-Jew lends money to a Jew (9-20)

C. When a Jew lends money to a non-Jew (21-28)

D. When a loan passes between non-Jews (29)

Introduction

When a loan takes place, money passes between a borrower and a lender. As we have seen, when they are both Jews, their transaction is governed by the laws of Ribbis. In this chapter we will examine the involvement of a third party in a loan transaction: a person who neither gives nor receives funds when the loan is made, but who acts as a guarantor for the loan.

A lender is sometimes reluctant to extend a loan because he is afraid that the borrower will be unable (or unwilling) to repay it. In this case, he will ask the borrower to bring a friend or relative who is willing to cosign the loan. This person is known as an *areiv*, or guarantor.

To properly understand these laws, we must first be acquainted with the various forms of guarantor agreements. Depending on the nature of the agreement, a guarantor can fall under any one of the following three categories of *areiv*:

- ☐ *Areiv Stam* [lit., an ordinary guarantor]: The cosigner stipulates that the lender may not come to him, first, to demand payment. Instead, the lender must first attempt to collect payment from the borrower, even to the extent of taking him to court or seizing his assets.[1] The guarantor is willing to repay the loan only if the borrower is unable or unwilling to make payment. Of the three types of guarantors, an *areiv stam* accepts *the least* amount of risk.

- ☐ *Areiv Kablan* [lit., a guarantor who accepts (additional responsibility)]: The lender has the right to demand payment from either the borrower or guarantor, whichever he chooses. If he decides to first ask the guarantor for payment, the guarantor must repay the loan, even if the borrower is able to make payment.[2]

---

1. Under the terms of an *areiv stam* agreement, the lender must actually pursue the borrower (by taking him to court and/or seizing his assets) to seek payment. If the agreement only requires that the lender request payment from the borrower but does not require that he actually pursue him to receive payment before demanding payment from the guarantor, this guarantor would have the status of an *areiv kablan*.

2. The borrower would then be obligated to repay the *areiv*. (This is true in all cases where a guarantor makes payment for a borrower.)

☐ *Areiv Shilof Dotz* [lit., a guarantor who removes (the debt from the borrower, and) places (it on himself)[3]]: This lender collects the debt only from the guarantor. The borrower is not required to pay the lender, even if the lender requests payment and the borrower has the funds with which to pay.[4] Of the three types of guarantors, the *areiv shilof dotz* accepts *the greatest* amount of responsibility for the loan; in fact, he takes on all the obligations of a borrower.[5] For this reason, the laws of Ribbis are applied to an *areiv shilof dotz* as they would be applied to a borrower.

A person might serve as a guarantor in any one of the following four situations: 1) where a Jew lends money to another Jew; 2) where a non-Jew lends money to a Jew; 3) where a Jew lends money to a non-Jew; or 4) where a non-Jew lends money to a non-Jew. In this chapter, we will examine the laws of an *areiv* as it applies to each of the cases.

A. Guaranteeing A Loan Between Jews

1. A loan which involves Ribbis: When two Jews agree to a loan which calls for Ribbis, they are transgressing numerous Biblical prohibitions. Anyone who assists in arranging or expediting this loan is also

---

3.This is the interpretation of *Magid Mishnah*. A note, printed in Y.D. 170:1, defines *shilof dotz* as a type of herb used to clean the hands. In this context, it refers to the *areiv* who cleanses the borrower of his obligation to the lender.

4. Under the terms of an *areiv shilof dotz* agreement, the lender must first demand payment from the guarantor. If the lender then finds that the *areiv shilof dotz* is unable or unwilling to make payment, most Rishonim maintain that the lender would be entitled to demand that the borrower repay the loan. *Rashba* disagrees and maintains that under an *areiv shilof dotz* agreement, the lender can never require the borrower to make payment (*Avnei Nezer* 196:9). (See Note 24, below, for additional ramifications of this dispute.)

In practice, an agreement can be drawn either way. The two sides may agree to explicitly permit or to prohibit the lender from demanding that the borrower repay the loan. Regarding the laws of Ribbis, there is no difference which way the agreement is worded. Whenever the lender is required to first approach the *areiv* for payment, the guarantor is considered an *areiv shilof dotz*.

5. For halachic purposes, an *areiv shilof dotz* is actually considered to be the borrower. Even if the borrower were later to repay the loan directly to the lender, we would view this as if he were repaying someone else's (i.e., the *areiv shilof dotz's*) loan (*Ohr Someach* to *Hil. Malveh* 5:5).

in violation of a Biblical prohibition.[6] Therefore, one may not act as a guarantor (in any of the three categories mentioned above)[7] for this loan.

2. This prohibition applies even if the *areiv* guarantees only the principal and not the Ribbis payments.[8]

---

6. Y.D. 160:1. Someone who guarantees this type of loan violates two Biblical prohibitions. First, he transgresses the Biblical prohibition (*Exodus* 22:24): *Do not place neshech on him* (*Bava Metzia* 75b). This applies to all forms of guarantor, even to an *areiv stam* (*Bris Yehudah* 1:n22, citing *Ritva*).

Additionally, there is a Biblical prohibition (Leviticus 19:14): *Lifnei iver lo setain michshol* (lit., before a blind person do not place a stumbling block). This is a general prohibition against causing another person to violate any Biblical law. This applies when someone causes a violation of the laws of Ribbis as well (Y.D. 160:1).

In situations involving a guarantor, where the loan would have been extended even if no *areiv* were found, the prohibition of *Lifnei iver* does not apply (*S.A. Harav* §3). However, in most situations involving a guarantor, the loan would not have been extended if the *areiv* had not guaranteed payment. In these cases, the *areiv* is also violating this prohibition.

[This certainly holds true in situations where the *areiv* was the only individual willing to act as guarantor. In this case, the Ribbis-bearing loan would not have been passed if he had not guaranteed the loan. Since he has caused this loan to pass, he is guilty of *Lifnei iver*.

Sometimes, there is another individual who would have been willing to serve as *areiv* if the actual *areiv* had refused to sign. One might argue that in this case the guarantor is not in violation of *Lifnei iver* since the loan would have taken place even without his participation. The guarantor is therefore not causing the transgression to take place. *Mishneh LaMelech* (to *Hil. Malveh* 4:2, also quoted in *Pischei Teshuvah* 151:2 and 160:1) rules that this is not accurate. According to *Mishneh LaMelech*, the prohibition of *Lifnei iver* falls away only where the violation would have occurred without the help of any outsider (for example, if the loan would have been given even if there were no *areiv*). In our case, the loan would not have taken place unless someone served as guarantor. Therefore, whoever serves as guarantor is guilty of *Lifnei iver*. See *Ksav Sofer* Y.D. 83 and *Minchas Elazar* 1:53:n3 who question *Mishnah LaMelech's* ruling. Still, most poskim appear to accept his opinion (*Chavos Daas* 160:1, *Ben Ish Chai* to *V'eschanan* §2, *Minchas Yitzchak* 2:106:11; see also sources cited in *Sdei Chemed* Vol. 8, p. 303).

However, if the borrower had a non-Jew who was willing to act as guarantor, even *Mishnah LaMelech* concedes that the Jew who actually does serve as guarantor is not in violation of *Lifnei iver*, since the loan would have taken place without the help of a Jewish guarantor (see *Pischei Teshuvah* 151:2 and *Sdei Chemed* ibid., this is also implied by *Ben Ish Chai*, ibid.; see also Note 8).]

7. An *areiv shilof dotz* takes on the legal status of a borrower (see Paragraph 10, below). In addition to the two prohibitions cited above, he is in violation of the various Ribbis prohibitions which apply to a borrower. There is a dispute as to whether these additional prohibitions apply to an *areiv kablan* as well (*Bris Yehudah* 1:n22).

8. *S.A. Harav* §3 and *Ben Ish Chai* ibid. rule that the prohibition of *Lifnei iver* (see Note 6) applies in this case. This implies that the additional prohibition of *Do not place*

Similarly, this is prohibited when the *areiv* guarantees the Ribbis payments, even if he is not guaranteeing the principal. There are situations where a third party is permitted to pay the lender for offering a loan. See Chapter 4, Paragraphs 1-4, where this has been explained.

3. A loan which involves Ribbis DeRabbanan: One may not serve as a guarantor for a loan which involves Rabbinically prohibited Ribbis.[9] See the note below, regarding situations where the loan would

---

neshech on him does not apply except where the *areiv* guarantees the Ribbis as well (*Bris Yehudah* ibid.).

Since the guarantor is violating only the prohibition of *Lifnei iver*, it would follow that when this prohibition does not apply, the *areiv* is not in violation of any Biblical prohibition when he guarantees only the principal. An example of this would be where a non-Jewish guarantor is also available to guarantee the loan. We have seen (in Note 6) that in this case the Jewish *areiv* is not violating *Lifnei iver* by guaranteeing the loan. Although no Biblical prohibition exists in this case, a Rabbinic prohibition does apply because the loan is in fact being facilitated by the participation of the Jewish *areiv*. This is known as *mesayei'a ovrei aveirah*, aiding sinners (*S.A. Harav* and *Ben Ish Chai* in loc. cited).

There are numerous situations where the laws of *mesayei'a ovrei aveirah* allow for leniencies which would not apply if *Lifnei iver* were involved. See Chapter 2, Note 25, where this was discussed regarding lawyers and employees who are hired to collect Ribbis payments.

[When the loan would have taken place even if no guarantor had been found, *Lifnei iver* does not apply. In this case it is not even clear that a Rabbinic prohibition applies, since the guarantor is not facilitating the loan. The Rabbinic prohibition of *mesayei'a ovrei aveirah* applies wherever one person helps another commit a sin. In this case, the guarantor's participation is not helping the establishment of the loan; his action is independent of the agreement to pay Ribbis, and should be permitted. Still, *S.A. Harav* and *Ben Ish Chai* imply that this is prohibited. One should therefore not rely on this leniency.]

9. We have seen (in Note 6) that one who guarantees a loan involving Biblically prohibited Ribbis violates two prohibitions: *Do not place neshech* and *Lifnei iver*. Where Rabbinically prohibited Ribbis is involved, the prohibition of *Lifnei iver* also exists, albeit on a Rabbinic level (*Rema* 160:1).

However, there is a dispute regarding the prohibition of *Do not place neshech*. *Chavos Daas* (160:1, quoted in *Pischei Teshuvah* 160:2), maintains that on a Rabbinic level this prohibition applies only on the lender, and not on those who help facilitate the loan. (Although *Chavos Daas* only discusses the status of the witnesses to the loan, his logic should apply equally to the status of an *areiv*; *Bris Yehudah* 1:27.) According to this opinion, only the prohibition of *Lifnei iver* applies.

Some poskim dispute the ruling of *Chavos Daas* (*Mishnah LaMelech* cited by *Bris Yehudah* 1:27, *Divrei Sofrim* 160:8). According to this opinion, the guarantor also transgresses *Do not place neshech* when guaranteeing such a loan (see note which follows).

have taken place without the participation of a guarantor.[10]

4. A loan which is sold at discount: The prohibition on serving as a guarantor applies in the following case, even though this involves a loan which does not call for Ribbis payments at all.

Where a businessman is owed money, payable at a later time, he is permitted to sell the loan to another Jew at a discount. Suppose a businessman is owed $1000, payable in six months, and he chooses to sell the debt for $900 cash. The buyer would then have to wait until the debt comes due before he can collect its full value. In this case, the seller is prohibited from guaranteeing the loan, even though it does not call for Ribbis payment. If the borrower later defaults on payment, the loss would be the buyer's.[11]

However, a third party is permitted to serve as guarantor for this loan.[12]

---

10. According to the opinion of *Chavos Daas*, only the prohibition of *Lifnei iver* applies when an *areiv* guarantees a loan involving Rabbinically prohibited Ribbis. Even those who dispute this ruling would concede that when the *areiv* guarantees only the principal and not the Ribbis, only the prohibition of *Lifnei iver* applies.

We have seen (in Note 8) that in situations where the loan would have been made even without the participation of the *areiv*, the prohibition of *Lifnei iver* does not apply. Consequently, the question of whether it would be permitted to serve as an *areiv* in this case would depend on whether the Rabbinic prohibition of *mesayei'a ovrei aveirah* applies to an *areiv*. This is highly questionable, as has been explained in Note 8. In this case, where Ribbis DeRabbanan is involved, there is an additional factor which would be grounds for leniency. *Pri Megadim* (O.C. 163:2, cited by *Mishnah Berurah* 163:12) questions whether the prohibition of *mesayei'a ovrei aveirah* applies where someone is aiding the transgression of a Rabbinic law. This question is discussed by many poskim (see *Beis Yehudah* Y.D. 1:17 who rules leniently; see also *Tuv Tam Vodaas* 3:2:31, *Sdei Chemed* Vol. 2 and Vol. 6 and *Yechaveh Daas* 3:67). Additionally, when the borrower and lender are deliberately violating the law, many poskim hold that the prohibition of *mesayei'a ovrei aveirah* does not apply (see *Shach* 151:6 and *Dagul MeiRivavah*).

As a matter of halachah, when all of these factors are present (i.e., the loan involves Ribbis DeRabbanan, it would have taken place even without an *areiv*, and the principals are knowingly violating the laws of Ribbis), one may serve as an *areiv stam* for the loan.

11. Y.D. 173:4. The seller may guarantee the loan against loss caused by other factors, such as the discovery that the note turned out to be a forgery, that the debt had already been collected or that the debt cannot be collected for other legal reasons (Y.D. ibid.). If the seller later cheated the buyer by collecting the debt directly from the borrower, he would be obligated to pay the buyer the full value of the promissory note (*Bris Yehudah* 15:n12).

There are methods by which the buyer can protect himself against losing money. These laws have been discussed in detail in the beginning of Chapter 12.

12. Y.D. ibid.

Guaranteeing a Heter Iska

5. When two Jews enter into a Heter Iska agreement, a third Jew may guarantee the principal. If he wishes to guarantee the profit payments as well, he may do so,[13] as long as he obligates himself by making a *kinyan*.[14]

Being Paid to Act as Guarantor

6. When a loan does not call for Ribbis payments, one may certainly serve as an *areiv* for the loan. An *areiv stam* and an *areiv kablan* may be paid for providing this service.[15]

An *areiv shilof dotz* may not be paid for his services.[16]

7. A businessman who does not have a good credit standing might ask a friend to sign a letter of debt so that he can use it to order merchandise. The friend now becomes an *areiv shilof dotz*, and he may not be paid for his service.[17] If the letter of debt is signed by both the businessman and the guarantor, this would be a case of *areiv kablan*, and he may be paid.[18]

---

13. *Shoel U'Meishiv* 2:4:114, *Bris Yehudah* 38:7. This refers to both an *areiv stam* and an *areiv kablan*.

The *areiv* would be required to pay only under the same conditions that the managing partner would be obligated to pay. Thus, if the managing partner were absolved from paying because he satisfied the terms of the Heter Iska (by bringing witnesses to attest to a loss, or by swearing that there was no profit), the *areiv* would also not pay.

[It is preferable to attach the guarantee to the Heter Iska document, and that the guarantor state explicitly that he is appointing the managing partner to be in charge of the funds and that his oath would be believed in regard to profits; see Chapter 22, Note 43.]

14. *Shach* to C.M. 129:12. Although *Ketzos HaChoshen* 129:2 disagrees, see *Nesivos HaMishpat* who defends the need for a *kinyan*.

15. *Taz* (170:3), *Nekudos HaKesef*, *Chochmas Adam* 132:7, *S.A. Harav* §63.

16. An *areiv shilof dotz* repays the loan to the lender. The person who borrowed the money is obligated to pay the *areiv shilof dotz*. Because their relationship is that of borrower and lender, the *areiv shilof dotz* may not accept payment from the borrower. This would be similar to Ribbis, and is prohibited (*Taz* 170:3, *Chochmas Adam* 132:7 citing *Ritva*; cf. *Nekudos HaKesef* who rules that this is permitted since the money is being paid for the service and not for the loan. *Chochmas Adam* refutes this, explaining that the reason this is prohibited is that it is similar to Ribbis, and not that it is actually Ribbis).

17. *Taz* 170:3.

18. *S.A. Harav* §63, *Bris Yehudah* 9:20. This is permitted even though the supplier is relying primarily on the guarantor and intends to collect directly from him (ibid.). *Mishnas Ribbis* 15:n17 adds that this is permitted only where the businessman intends to pay the bill himself, and the friend's signature is only being used to assure the seller that

8. Someone who provides collateral for another person's loan may be paid for this service.[19]

B. When a Non-Jew Lends Money to a Jew

9. An *Areiv stam*: When a Jew borrows money from a non-Jew, he may obligate himself to pay Ribbis. Another Jew may guarantee this loan as an *areiv stam*.[20] If the borrower is not able to pay the loan, the *areiv stam* would pay the entire debt (both principal and interest) to the non-Jew when it becomes due. The borrower would be obligated to reimburse the *areiv stam* for this, and would repay him for both the principal and the interest which he paid to the non-Jew.[21]

Once the *areiv* paid the non-Jew, he is entitled to immediate reimbursement from the borrower. However, even if he is not paid, the *areiv stam* may not charge interest for the money which he is owed.[22]

10. An *Areiv shilof dotz*: A Jew may not serve as an *areiv shilof dotz* for this loan. This is because an *areiv shilof dotz* takes on all of the responsibility for the debt; he has, in effect, become the borrower. Halachah views this arrangement as if the *areiv* had borrowed the money from the non-Jew and then passed it on to the Jewish borrower. The *areiv shilof dotz* is therefore considered a lender to a Jewish borrower. Since the loan has passed from the *areiv shilof dotz* to another Jew, Ribbis may not pass between them.[23]

---

he will be paid. However, if their intention is to make payment with the friend's letter of debt, it is a true loan and no fee may be paid.

[Where the businessman originally intended to pay the supplier himself, he is permitted to pay a service fee. If he was later unable to pay the bill, and the supplier collected from the friend's letter of debt, the two friends would then have a borrower-lender relationship. Still, since this relationship did not exist when the fee was paid, the guarantor does not have to return this fee.]

19. *Avnei Nezer* Y.D. 200, *Bris Yehudah* 9:21. The money which is paid is actually a fee for use of the collateral. This is similar to a fee for serving as a guarantor, which is permitted.

20. Y.D. 170:1. This is permitted both where a flat fee is charged for the loan and where the interest is a per month fee for the period that the loan is outstanding (*Shach* 170:1).

21. *Rashi* to B.M. 71b, s.v. *ladon*, quoted by *Prishah* 170:1.

22. (I.e., he may be reimbursed for the interest he paid the non-Jew, but he may not charge additional interest for the time that he is owed the money.) *Bris Yehudah* 34:n4.

23. Y.D. 170:1. The Jewish borrower is prohibited from paying interest to the *areiv* for this loan. This is prohibited even if the borrower intends to pay the non-Jewish lender

11. If an agreement was already made: Often, a person will cosign a loan, agreeing to serve as an *areiv shilof dotz,* and later realize that this is prohibited. In this case, the borrower should not make any interest payments for the loan.[24] All interest should be paid to the lender by the *areiv shilof dotz.* The *areiv* may not subsequently accept reimbursement from the borrower for the interest payments.

If the *areiv* already paid the debt to the non-Jewish lender, the borrower would be obligated to reimburse him for paying the principal, but may not reimburse him for the interest which he paid.[25]

---

directly so that the *areiv shilof dotz* will not actually receive any payment.

[*Nekudos HaKesef* to *Taz* 170:5 maintains that when the *areiv* does not actually pay the debt, no transgression has occurred. Most poskim, however, prohibit this arrangement even if the *areiv* never actually makes a payment (*Taz* 170:2, *Beis Meir, Shaar Deah* 170:5, *Maharsham* 4:95, *Bris Yehudah* 34:n7).]

An exception: When someone who holds a public position takes a loan from a non-Jew for communal expenditures, he may be permitted to serve as an *areiv shilof dotz* and still be reimbursed for interest expenses; see *Chasam Sofer* Y.D. 135.

24. May the borrower make these payments directly to the non-Jewish lender?

This is the subject of considerable discussion among the poskim. *Ohr Someach* (to *Hil. Malveh* 5:5) cites *Rashba* who prohibits this. *Shaar Deah* 170:3 quotes Rishonim who permit it (although it is not clear that *Shaar Deah* is referring to a situation involving an *areiv shilof dotz*).

Avnei Nezer 196:9 explains that *Rashba* and the other Rishonim actually disagree in their basic understanding of the obligation of an *areiv shilof dotz*. When an *areiv shilof dotz* is unable to repay a loan, most Rishonim maintain that the borrower is obligated to make payment. *Rashba* disagrees and maintains that under an *areiv shilof dotz* agreement, the borrower can never be required to make payment.

This gives us an insight into the dispute regarding interest payments.

Those Rishonim who hold that the borrower has a direct obligation to the lender would permit him to fulfill this obligation by paying the lender directly. Since interest payments are part of his obligation to the non-Jewish lender, the borrower may make these payments to him.

Rashba disagrees because he holds that the borrower and lender have no relationship; only the *areiv shilof dotz* is obligated to pay the lender. According to this opinion, if the borrower were to make payment to the lender, he would be satisfying the *areiv's* debt. The borrower could pay the principal directly to the lender, since this is money which he borrowed from the *areiv*. However, if he makes an interest payment, he is paying more than he borrowed from the *areiv,* and this constitutes Ribbis.

As a matter of practical halachah there really is no dispute; each case depends on the way the agreement is drawn up. Anytime an agreement does not permit the lender to pursue the borrower (even if the guarantor is unable to pay), all would agree that the borrower is prohibited from paying interest to the lender. If the agreement allows the lender to pursue the borrower (when the *areiv* is unable to pay), the borrower would be permitted to pay interest directly to the lender.

[This note is based on an explanation heard from the author of *Mishnas Ribbis.*]

25. *Rema* 170:1.

If the borrower already reimbursed the *areiv* for the interest which he had paid, the *areiv* is obligated to return this money.[26]

12. An *Areiv kablan*: There is a dispute among Rishonim regarding the status of an *areiv kablan*. *Rashi* holds that an *areiv kablan* has the same status as an *areiv shilof dotz*. According to this opinion, a Jew may not serve as an *areiv kablan*, even for a loan from a non-Jew. *Rashba* holds that an *areiv kablan* has the same status as an *areiv stam*, and that this is permitted.[27]

Beis Yosef rules that one should follow the stringent opinion of *Rashi*, and refrain from serving as an *areiv kablan* for another Jew's loan, even where money is being borrowed from a non-Jew (where interest is involved). This ruling is accepted by virtually all poskim.[28]

13. If an agreement was already made: Often, a person will cosign a loan, agreeing to serve as an *areiv kablan*, and later realize that this is prohibited. When this happens, the borrower should be careful to make all of the payments (both for principal and for interest) to the non-Jewish lender, so that the *areiv* will not be asked to honor his pledge.

If the *areiv* already paid the debt to the non-Jewish lender, the borrower would be obligated to reimburse him for paying the principal,

---

26. *Taz* 170:2, *Shach* 170:2 based on *Beis Yosef*, *Gra* 170:5; cf. *Rema* 170:1 who apparently rules that it is not necessary to return this money.

[According to *Rema*, this constitutes only Rabbinically prohibited Ribbis, and the borrower therefore cannot be obligated to return the Ribbis. Still, as in all cases of Ribbis DeRabbanan, he should return the Ribbis *latzeis yidei shamayim* (see Chapter 20, Paragraph 19).]

27. The reason for *Rashba's* leniency is explained below, Note 45.

28. Y.D. 170:1 quotes *Rashi* as the primary opinion. Both *Taz* and *Shach* quote the *Beis Yosef* cited above. *Chochmas Adam*, *S.A. Harav* and *Kitzur S.A.* all cite only *Rashi's* opinion. [Cf. *Maharam Shick* 160 and *Avnei Nezer* 197 who defend the practice of those who rely on the opinion of *Rashba*. *Minchas Elazar* 2:33 expresses amazement at the lenient view of *Maharam Shick* and stresses that one should not rely on this view even in case of need. See also *Mishnas Ribbis* 15:n12.]

Some poskim hold that when the *areiv kablan* has only limited liability, *Rashi* would agree that this is permitted. According to this opinion, when the guarantor's liability is limited to a bond or property which he puts up to guarantee the loan, he could serve as *areiv kablan*. *Vechai Achicha Imach* §13 reports that this is a subject of dispute among contemporary poskim. See also *Mishnas Ribbis* 15:6 and 15.

[In an article in the *Hamesifta* journal (in the 5754 issue), the author of *Mishnas Ribbis* maintains that whenever the bank or lending institution is first required to ask the borrower for payment (even if they are not required to pursue him in court), one may serve as an *areiv kablan* when his liability is limited to a specific bond or property.]

but may not reimburse him for the interest which he paid.[29]

If the borrower already reimbursed the *areiv* for the interest which he had paid, the *areiv* is not obligated to return this money.[30]

Being Paid to Act as Guarantor

14. When one is permitted to act as a guarantor for the non-Jewish lender (i.e., as an *areiv stam*), he is also permitted to charge for this service.[31]

Practical Applications

15. Guaranteeing A Bank Loan: Someone who cosigns on a bank loan has the status of an *areiv kablan*. This is because, at the present time, most loan agreements allow the bank to demand payment from the cosigner without obligating them to pursue the borrower first. Often, an agreement requires the bank to first request payment from the borrower, but does not require the bank to foreclose on his property or to sue him in court. When the borrower fails to pay, the bank may immediately request payment from the guarantor. In this situation, the cosigner has the status of an *areiv kablan*.[32]

One would therefore be prohibited from cosigning a loan which a non-Jewish bank extends to a Jew.

16. Joint loans: When two Jews take a joint loan from a bank, each person actually borrows only half the money. Still, because it is a joint loan, each of them is liable for the entire loan. Since each of them is also responsible for his friend's portion of the loan, each is a guarantor for the other. Since the bank may go directly to either of them and demand full payment, they have the status of an *areiv kablan* to each other. This type of arrangement is therefore prohibited.[33]

---

29. *Rema* 170:1, based on the opinion of *Rashi*, quoted above.

30. Once the money was paid, one may rely on the opinion of *Rashba* (quoted in the previous paragraph), who maintains that an *areiv kablan* is permitted to make interest payments and be reimbursed by the borrower (*Beis Yosef* 170, *Shach* 170:2).

31. *Minchas Elazar* 2:33, *Bris Yehudah* 9:n42.

32. *Keren HaTorah* (Introduction, Paragraph 20); R' Shlomo Zalman Auerbach zt"l, quoted in *Toras Ribbis* 17:43; Rav Yosef Eliyashev Shlita, quoted in *Mishnas Ribbis* 15:n3. See also *S.A. Harav* §64.

33. *Chavos Daas* 170:1, *S.A. Harav* §64, *Ben Ish Chai* to *Eikev* §13, *Chidushei Rav Aryeh Leib Tzinz* 170:4, *Mishnas Ribbis* 15:5. This is a common problem. A joint loan is permitted only if the terms of the agreement require the bank to pursue each of the borrowers in court for his portion of the loan. In this case, each partner would be an *areiv stam* for the loan.

17. Partnerships: When a loan is issued to a business which has two Jewish partners, some poskim hold that the same restriction applies.[34] According to this opinion, neither of the partners is permitted to guarantee the entire loan. Others hold that if the loan will be repaid from business moneys, it is permitted.[35]

18. When there is one active partner who runs the business, Taz rules that he is permitted to borrow money for the business and to repay it, with interest, from business funds.

There is a dispute regarding the extent of this leniency. Some poskim permit any business funds to be used to pay the interest, even if it means drawing on capital.[36] Other poskim hold that only profits which are generated *after the loan is received* may be used to pay the interest.[37]

19. Guaranteeing a mortgage loan: The prohibition against guaranteeing a loan as an *areiv kablan* applies even when the borrower puts up collateral for the debt.[38] However, if it is known that the lender will pursue the collateral rather than the guarantor, this is permitted. When a mortgage loan is issued, the property which is being purchased serves as collateral for the loan. Therefore, wherever it is the common practice for a bank to foreclose on a home rather than to pursue the guarantor, one may serve as an *areiv kablan* for a mortgage.[39]

20. A Heter Iska may be used to permit a guarantor to cosign a loan.[40] The Heter Iska should be drawn between the borrower and

---

34. *Taz* 170:3 as understood by *Chavos Daas* 170:1.

35. *Darkei Teshuvah* 170:9, quoting *Chidushei Rav Aryeh Leib Tzinz* 170:4. See also *Minchas Yitzchak* 4:19:13 and *Mishnas Ribbis* 16:n2.

Where a business is incorporated, and the individuals have no personal liability for the loan, one may certainly rely on this lenient opinion. According to *Igros Moshe* (Y.D. 2:63), Ribbis restrictions apply only where there is a borrower with personal liability for the loan. When corporations borrow, they are permitted to pay Ribbis. See Chapter 5, Paragraph 26.

36. *Divrei Chaim* C.M. 29, *Maharsham* 7:63. [It should be noted that these poskim discuss situations where a loan was taken in a manner which obligates both parties, equally, to repay the loan. Where only the person who takes the loan has personal responsiblity for payment, they would concede that this is prohibited.]

37. *Chochmas Adam* 132:8, *S.A. Harav* §64, *Chavos Daas* 170:1. See also *Bris Yehudah* 6:n71.

38. *Chavos Daas* 170:8.

39. *Minchas Yitzchak* 4:19:12. This guarantor has the status of an *areiv stam* since it is known that the bank will pursue the borrower first. See also *Mishnas Ribbis* 15:8 where this is discussed at length.

40. *Mishnas Ribbis* 15:n9, quoting numerous contemporary poskim, including the author of *Bris Yehudah*.

guarantor, in the same manner that would be used if the guarantor had actually loaned his own money.[41]

C. When a Jew Lends Money to a Non-Jew

21. An *Areiv stam*: When a Jew lends money to a non-Jew, he may charge Ribbis. Another Jew may guarantee this loan as an *areiv stam*.[42] If the borrower is not able to pay the loan, the *areiv* would pay the entire debt (both principal and interest) to the Jewish lender when it becomes due. The borrower would be obligated to reimburse the guarantor for this payment.

The guarantor would be permitted to charge interest for the period that the reimbursement was not made.[43]

22. An *Areiv kablan* or *Areiv shilof dotz*: A Jew is prohibited from serving either as an *areiv kablan* or as an *areiv shilof dotz* for such a loan.[44] Although *Rashba* holds that one may serve as an *areiv kablan* when a non-Jew lends money to a Jew (in Paragraph 10), he concedes that this is prohibited when a Jew is lending money.[45]

23. If an agreement was already made: Often, a person will cosign a loan, agreeing to serve as an *areiv kablan* or *areiv shilof dotz*, and

---

41. In Chapter 23 we will see that there are two types of Heter Iska forms. Here, it is preferable that the *kulo pikadon* form be used (*Mishnas Ribbis* ibid.).

42. *Rema* 170:2. This is permitted both where a flat fee is charged for the loan and where the interest is a per-month fee for the period that the loan is outstanding (as in Note 20).

43. Once the guarantor pays the original lender, this becomes a loan between the guarantor and the non-Jewish borrower, and interest may be charged.

44. Y.D. 170:2.

45. This follows the opinion of *Ran*, quoted by *Shach* 170:3. This is also the opinion of the *Shulchan Aruch*, where the *Rashba's* opinion is quoted only in the previous case (involving a Jewish borrower) and not in this case (involving a non-Jewish borrower). Cf. *Bris Yehudah* 34:n19.

The reason for this distinction is as follows. In the previous case, *Rashba* held that one is permitted to serve as an *areiv kablan* for a Jewish borrower. According to this opinion, the interest which accrues during the period that the loan is outstanding is not prohibited, because it accrues (from the borrower) to the lender, who is a non-Jew. The two Jews who are involved are the borrower and *areiv kablan*, and they have no financial relationship until the time that the *areiv* pays the loan.

The case here is different, in that the lender is a Jew. The *areiv kablan's* debt obligation to him begins immediately, and grows as interest accrues. This increasing debt constitutes Ribbis between Jews (*Shach* 170:3).

later realize that this is prohibited. In this case, the *areiv* may not honor his commitment to guarantee the interest payments.

If the *areiv* already paid the debt to the Jewish lender: If the guarantor was an *areiv shilof dotz*, the lender must return the interest portion to him.[46] In the case of an *areiv kablan*, the lender could not be forced to return the interest to the guarantor.[47]

24. A loan which is sold at discount: The prohibition of serving as a guarantor applies when a non-Jew's debt is sold at a discount.

For example, a businessman is owed $1000, payable in six months, and he sells the debt for $900 cash. The buyer would then have to wait until the debt comes due before he can collect its full value. In this case, the seller is prohibited from guaranteeing the loan. If the borrower later defaults on payment, the loss would be the buyer's.

When the debt is passed on at its full value (for $1000), the seller would be permitted to guarantee the loan. However, if the debt earns interest as it is being held, this too would be prohibited.[48]

Exceptions to This Prohibition

25. One may serve as *areiv kablan* or *areiv shilof dotz* for the principal, as long as he is not responsible for the interest.[49]

26. Similarly, an *areiv kablan* or *areiv shilof dotz* may guarantee the interest, as long as they are not responsible for the principal.[50] However, in this case there is an added restriction. The *areiv* may not actually

---

46. *Chochmas Adam* 138:3 rules that this constitutes Ribbis Ketzutzah. Whenever Ribbis Ketzutzah is paid, it must be returned.

47. *Bris Yehudah* 34:5 and Note 19 maintains that this is only Ribbis DeRabbanan. Whenever Ribbis DeRabbanan is paid, the lender cannot be compelled to return the Ribbis, although it is recommended that he do so *latzeis yidei shamayim* (see Chapter 20, Paragraph 19).

48. See Chapter 12, Paragraph 18.

49. *Rema* 170:2, apparently referring to both *areiv kablan* and *areiv shilof dotz*. *Chochmas Adam* 138:4 mentions explicitly that this is permitted even in the case of an *areiv shilof dotz*.

50. *Rema* ibid. This is permitted only when the *areiv* guarantees a flat fee as interest. He would also be permitted to guarantee the interest on a per-month basis if it were limited to a specific period of time, such as a year or two. However it would be prohibited to guarantee interest which runs until the time that the loan is repaid. (*Levush* 170:2, *Taz* 170:6, *Chavos Daas* 160: *Chidushim* 11; cf. *Chavos Daas* 170:7 for an exception to this prohibition). This is similar to the ruling of the *Taz* 160:6, see Chapter 4, Paragraph 16.

take the loan from the lender and pass it on to the borrower, because this would give the impression that he is lending the principal.[51]

27. Collateral: When the non-Jewish borrower puts up collateral adequate to cover both principal and interest, a Jew is permitted to serve as *areiv kablan*.[52]

Guaranteeing a Promissory Note

28. When selling a promissory note:[53] If a non-Jew owns a promissory note (which was written by a Jew),[54] he may sell it to another Jew. The non-Jew is permitted to guarantee the note, so that he would pay the debt if the original borrower failed to do so.

---

51. *Rema* ibid. Where the *areiv* guarantees only the principal, *Shach* (170:6) rules that this restriction does not apply. *Shaar Deah*, though, maintains that most poskim would prohibit this even when the *areiv* guarantees only the principal.

If the guarantor is entitled to use the money while it is in his hands, this would be prohibited according to all opinions (*Mishnas Ribbis* 15:n14).

An *areiv stam* would be permitted to pass the loan to the borrower (*Shaar Deah* 170:5). *Shach* 170:6 appears to prohibit this even when the Jew is not an *areiv* at all. However, *Chavos Daas* 170:6 explains that *Shach's* ruling does not apply when the Jew explicitly mentions that he is taking the loan for a non-Jew.

52. *Rema* 170:2. *Chavos Daas* 170:8 explains that this is permitted because the Jewish lender will certainly seek to collect from the collateral before asking the guarantor for payment. (This gives the guarantor the status of an *areiv stam* and serves to permit the guarantee.)

[Where the lender is not an Orthodox Jew, and he therefore has no hesitation in first approaching the guarantor for payment, this leniency may not apply. Still, if the common business practice is to first seize the collateral, this would be permitted (as in Paragraph 19, above).]

When the collateral is adequate to cover the payment of principal, but not interest, this would be prohibited (*Shach* 170:8, as explained by *Chavos Daas* 170:8).

53. Promissory notes (or IOUs) are notes of debt which call for payment at a future time. There is a market for the sale of these notes. When these notes are sold, the debt is transferred, so that it must be paid to the person who buys the note. For example, someone owes a non-Jew $1000, and he writes a note of debt which calls for payment in six months. The non-Jewish lender might need the cash before the six months are up. He would therefore be willing to sell the note on the open market for $900. Investors would make a $100 profit when redeeming the note at the end of the six months.

Other laws pertaining to the sale of these notes have been discussed in Chapter 12.

54. This discussion pertains to promissory notes which are not interest bearing. If a non-Jew who holds a promissory note written by a Jew sells it to another Jew, the Jewish buyer would be prohibited from collecting interest which accrues after the purchase. This has been discussed in Chapter 12, Paragraphs 15 and 16.

If a promissory note is written from one Jew to another Jew, its owner may sell it to a non-Jew and he may guarantee it too. In this case, the non-Jew may also sell the note to another Jew, and guarantee that it will be paid. However, if the Jewish customer relies on the guarantee of the original seller, this would be prohibited.[55]

D. When a Loan Passes Between Non-Jews

29. When a loan passes between non-Jews, a Jew may serve as guarantor in any form or manner. This is because Ribbis restrictions apply only where there is financial interaction between two Jews.

---

55. *Chasam Sofer* 6:26. The Jewish seller may serve as an *areiv stam* for this sale, but not as an *areiv kablan* or *areiv shilof dotz.*

CHAPTER SIXTEEN

Business Partners

A. Businesses which are owned by Jewish partners (1-14):

- ☐ Personal loans (1-2)
- ☐ Business loans (3)
- ☐ Individual loans (4-6)
- ☐ Using a Heter Iska (7-10)
- ☐ Lending personal money (11)
- ☐ Buying merchandise (12)
- ☐ Dividing profits (13-14)

B. Businesses that are owned by Jewish and non-Jewish Partners (15-25):

- ☐ Small Businesses (15-16)
- ☐ Paying Ribbis to Jews (17-18)
- ☐ Collecting Ribbis from Jews (19-20)
- ☐ Setting up a partnership (21)
- ☐ Large companies and corporations (22-23)

Appendix: Contract for use in establishing partnerships between Jews and non-Jews

Introduction

The laws of Ribbis apply to a Jewish business, just as they apply to an individual. A business may not borrow or lend for Ribbis just as an individual may not do so. Thus, all of the laws which have been outlined in the earlier chapters apply here as well. In this chapter we will deal with issues that are unique to business partners.

A. Businesses Which Are Owned by Jewish Partners

Personal Loan

1. Personal Loans: Two Jewish partners may take a joint loan from a bank (or from a non-Jewish individual), and agree to pay Ribbis. However, when this is done, each partner may only be liable for half the loan.[1] The loan agreement may not hold them jointly responsible for the entire loan.[2]

2. One partner may not serve as a cosigner for the other partner's portion of the loan. Since the lender may choose to collect from the cosigner, the partner is, in effect, responsible for the entire loan.

---

1. This assumes that they are equal partners. If one partner owns 60% of the business, he would have to be liable for 60% of the loan, while his partner would only be liable for the remaining 40%. Similarly, if there were three equal partners, each would only be liable for one third of the loan. (The reason for this is explained in the note which follows.)

2. *Chavos Daas* 170:1, *S.A. Harav* §64, *Ben Ish Chai to Eikev* §13, *Mishnas Ribbis* 16:1; cf. *Darkei Teshuvah* 170:9.

When a business receives a loan, each of the partners is technically receiving a portion of that money. Since the money is being invested in the business, each partner's share in the borrowed money is equal to his share in the business. (This is why each partner's share in the liability must be equal to his share in the business.)

Thus, when two partners take a joint loan from a bank, each has actually borrowed only half the money. Still, the terms of a joint loan typically hold each partner liable for the entire loan. Since each of them is also responsible for his friend's portion of the loan, they are actually serving as guarantors for each other. Jews are prohibited from serving as guarantors for a Ribbis loan (Y.D. 170:1), except as outlined in the note which follows.

However, if the agreement requires the lender to pursue the borrower in court first, one partner may cosign for the other.[3]

Business Loan

3. A Jewish business may take a loan from a non-Jewish source and agree to pay Ribbis. However, this is permitted only if the partners do not issue personal guarantees for the loan.[4]

Individual Loan

4. If one of the partners takes a personal loan and invests the funds in the business, he may not use business funds to pay interest on the loan. Only the principal may be repaid by the business.[5]

---

3. A Jew is permitted to serve as a guarantor when the terms of the loan require the lender to pursue the borrower before requesting payment from the guarantor (Y.D. 170:1). (This type of guarantor is known as an *areiv stam* — see Introduction to Chapter 15 for an explanation of the different categories of guarantor.) Today, the terms of a routine cosigner agreement permit the lender to pursue the cosigner, without first taking the borrower to court. This is prohibited. (This type of guarantor is known as an *areiv kablan*.)

It should be noted that one opinion in *Shulchan Aruch* (ibid.) permits a Jew to serve as cosigner (even as an *areiv kablan*) for another Jew's loan, despite the fact that the non-Jewish lender will collect Ribbis. We have followed the opinion of virtually all poskim (including *Shach, Taz, Chochmas Adam, S.A. Harav* and *Kitzur Shulchan Aruch*) who prohibit this. Still, the fact that there is a more lenient opinion is significant because this may be taken into account when making halachic determinations in more complex situations (as in Paragraph 5, below).

A notable exception: *Maharam Shick* 160 and *Avnei Nezer* Y.D. 197 defend the practice of those who rely on the lenient opinion. While this may serve as a source to justify the common practice of partners who do take joint loans (particularly when the loans are actually repaid from the business, and not by the individuals; see *Darkei Teshuvah* 177:9), it is clearly contrary to the opinion of virtually all poskim. See, for example, *Minchas Elazar* 2:33, who expresses amazement at the lenient view of *Maharam Shick* and stresses that one should not rely on this view even in case of need. Therefore, partners who must take loans in this manner should satisfy both opinions by using a Heter Iska, as explained below, Paragraph 7.

4. When a loan is backed by a personal guarantee, it has the status of a personal loan. We have already seen that one partner may not guarantee the other partner's portion.

However, if the agreement does not permit the lender to collect from the guarantors unless he first pursues the business (in court) for payment, the partners are permitted to personally guarantee the entire loan (*Mishnas Ribbis* 16:n3, quoting the author of *Bris Yehudah*).

5. In this case, one partner has taken a personal loan and then lent the funds to the business. Although he is obligated to pay Ribbis to the non-Jewish lender, he is

5. An exception to this prohibition: Sometimes, a business has two owners, but only one is an active partner who manages the business. In this situation, the managing partner is permitted to take a personal loan from a non-Jew for use in the business, and to repay it, with interest, from business funds.[6]

There is a dispute regarding the extent of this leniency. Some poskim permit the borrower to pay the interest from any business funds, even if this means drawing on capital.[7] Other poskim hold that the borrower may pay the interest only from profits which are generated *after the loan is received*.[8]

6. Another option is for one of the partners to take a loan, but to pay the interest using business funds, *at the time that the loan is received.*

---

prohibited from charging Ribbis to the Jewish company which borrowed the funds from him. (Although a lender is permitted to charge his borrower for expenses which were incurred due to the loan, this does not apply to interest expenses — see Chapter 5, Paragraph 5.)

6. *Taz* 170:3. *Taz* explains that when a managing partner takes funds from a non-Jew for use in the business, this is considered an investment rather than a loan because the non-Jew's moneys are being used to generate profits for the business. Thus, when interest is paid to the lender, it is considered a business expense, not interest, and is permitted.

The role of an investing ('silent') partner is only to contribute funds to the partnership. Any expense he incurs is not considered a business expense. Thus, if he were to borrow money from a non-Jew, it is considered a loan, which he has taken in order to satisfy his obligation to the partnership. This is permitted only when the loan is extended privately to the investing partner (and the business carries no liability for it) and the interest is paid by him.

S.A. Harav §64 adds that this is also permitted when both partners are active in the business. They may take a joint loan, provided that interest will be paid only from the profits of the business.

7. *Divrei Chayim* C.M. 29 permits this because he views the interest payments as a business expense. *Maharsham* (7:45 and 63) also rules that this is permitted, but for a different reason. *Maharsham* maintains that when the managing partner commits to a loan, he has the authority to sign for the silent partner as well. The partner is therefore bound by his commitment. Contemporary poskim question whether the managing partner truly has this kind of authority.

It should be noted that these poskim concede that if the business were to lose all its funds, the partner could not be obligated to repay the loan from his personal funds. However, if he desires to pay the debt from his own moneys, he may do so. If the second partner (who did not take the loan) wishes to pay the entire debt, it is not clear if this would be permitted (*Mishnas Ribbis* 16:n5).

8. *Chochmas Adam* 132:8, *S.A. Harav* §64. See also *Bris Yehudah* 6:n71. *Chavos Daas* 170:1 also permits this (based on different reasoning). See *Bris Yehudah* 6:n60.

this is considered a business expense for the purpose of securing the loan. The business would then repay the principal when it comes due.[9] This option may be used by either an active partner or a silent partner.[10]

Using A Heter Iska

7. A business that is unable to raise capital because of the prohibition against paying Ribbis may use a Heter Iska to allow an investor to extend money and earn a profit. The standard Heter Iska form (which appears in Chapter 23) would be used. In this case, the Heter Iska should list both partners (or the business name) as receiving the funds.

8. It may happen that one of the partners borrows money by using a Heter Iska, and he accepts liability by signing his own name (and not the business name) to the Iska. If he then advances these funds to the business, it is considered his personal investment in the business. Still, if the business generates profits which are equal to (or greater than) the amount promised in the Heter Iska,[11] the business profits could be used to pay the investor who advanced the funds.[12]

---

9. *S.A. Harav* §65, *Beis Lechem Yehudah* to 168:17, *Bris Yehudah* 6:31. This is permitted only if the interest is paid before the loan money is advanced (*Bris Yehudah*, Note 72, quoting *Maharsham*). It is preferable that this interest payment be made with cash, or, if a check is used, that it clear the bank before the loan is given (see *Mishnas Ribbis* 16:n8).

The drawback to this arrangement is that only the original payment may be made using business funds. If the business were to hold the funds for a longer period of time than originally anticipated, the additional interest charges could only be paid by the partner who took responsibility for the loan.

10. *Bris Yehudah* 6:end of n72.

11. If there are profits, but they are less than the amount called for in the Heter Iska, it is not clear if the business may pay the investor (see *Bris Yehudah* 6:30 who records a dispute, but does not come to a conclusion).

12. *Taz* 170:3, *Chochmas Adam* 132:8; *Taz* explains that when money is borrowed, using a Heter Iska, it is understood that the funds are being advanced to the business under the same terms as the Heter Iska. If the funds generate a profit, they are paid in consistence with the Iska agreement. If the funds do not generate profits, the partner may not charge the business, despite the fact that he will end up paying the person who advanced the moneys.

Earlier (in Paragraph 5), there was a dispute among the poskim regarding the use of other business funds to repay a loan which was taken by the managing partner. Where a Heter Iska was used, the business's obligation is limited to the use of profits. (It is difficult to interpret the *Taz* differently. *Maharsham* concedes this, but it is not clear that *Divrei Chaim* would agree; see *Bris Yehudah* 6:end of n69.)

This ruling applies both when the Iska is arranged by the managing partner and when it is arranged by the silent partner (*Bris Yehudah* 6:60, based on *Chochmas Adam* 132:8).

9. This applies even when the partner originally borrowed the moneys (using a Heter Iska) for his own use. If he later decided to use these funds in the business and he told the partner that he acquired these funds under the terms of a Heter Iska, business profits should be used to pay the investor who advanced the funds.[13]

10. This ruling applies both when the Iska is arranged by the managing partner and when it is arranged by the silent partner.[14]

Lending Personal Money

11. If one of the partners wishes to lend his own money to the business, he may not charge interest. He may use a Heter Iska to facilitate the loan.[15]

Buying Merchandise

12. If a partner was sent to purchase merchandise for the business, and he discovered that he had to borrow money to facilitate the purchase, he may not charge the business for the interest which he paid. However, he is permitted to charge the business a higher price for the merchandise, so that he can recover this interest expense.[16]

---

13. *Maharsham* 4:109.

14. *Bris Yehudah* 6:27, based on *Chochmas Adam* 132:8.

15. *Chochmas Adam* 132:8, *Maharsham* 7:45.

In this case, a Heter Iska can be drawn in one of two ways:

   a) **Using the standard Iska form** (Chapter 23, Form A or D): The money may be given to the business, with the business acting as the party to the Heter Iska. In this case, the money which is extended is used to purchase a portion in the business. The Heter Iska works by paying a specified sum in lieu of profits which are generated by the invested funds. The drawback to this method is that it is possible that the business will not generate any profits and that the person investing the money will have first-hand knowledge of this. In this case, many poskim hold that a Heter Iska cannot be used to collect payment (*Igros Moshe* Y.D. 2:63).

   b) **Using the 'personal loan' Iska form** (Chapter 23, Form B): The money may be given to the second partner, who would be the party to the Heter Iska. (He would sign for only 50% of the money, so that each partner would be equally liable.) In this case, the money is used to purchase a share in any other investment which the partner owns. The advantage to this method is that the person investing the money would not usually have first-hand knowledge of the success or failure of the other person's investments. The Heter Iska would therefore work to permit him to collect his profit in any event. (This is an advantage to the investor; the partner would see this as a disadvantage to him and may not be willing to enter into this agreement.)

16. *Bris Yehudah* 6:25, quoting *Teshuvos Pnei Moshe* 2:22. [The partner should have in mind to first take the merchandise as his own, and later sell it to the business. If he did

Dividing Profits

13. When one partner invests funds and the other manages the business, this is known as an Iska partnership. The partners may agree to divide the profits in any manner they choose, provided that losses are divided in the same manner. Thus, if profits are divided evenly, losses must also be divided equally.[17] Additional details regarding an Iska partnership (and methods by which the investor can protect his principal) appear in the first section of Chapter 22.

14. When one partner invests more funds than the other, the original agreement should stipulate clearly how the profits are to be divided. The agreement may call for profits to be divided by a percentage or by time (i.e., one partner receives the profits of one month, and his partner receives the profits of the next month). If they wish, the parties may agree to divide the profits equally.

However, the agreement may not call for the person with the greater investment to receive a specific sum of profit, with the remaining profit divided equally. This sum would constitute a Ribbis payment for the extra funds.[18]

B. Businesses That Are Owned by Jewish and Non-Jewish Partners

Small Businesses

15. Businesses that are owned by two (or more) Jewish partners are bound by the restrictions outlined above, even if there are also non-Jewish partners.[19]

---

not do this, the interest expense (as well as any other legitimate expense) may be included in the merchandise price.]

17. The crucial factor here is the investing partner's share. The percentage of profits which he receives may not be greater than the percentage of losses for which he is liable. [This is because the investor is considered a lender, as explained in Chapter 22.] However, if both partners agree, the managing partner may receive a greater share of profits.

18. *Bris Yehudah* 35:24, based on *Maharshach* 3:115, *Rashdam* Y.D. 61, *Maharsham* 7:140. This is a question of Ribbis Ketzutzah.

19. These restrictions are based on the fact that when partners take a loan, each of them is actually borrowing a portion of the money. When they are all liable for the entire loan, each of them is serving as a guarantor for his partner's portion of the loan (as explained above, Note 2). This does not change when there are also non-Jewish partners involved. The Jewish partners are still guaranteeing the entire loan, including the portions which apply to each other.

16. A business owned by one Jewish and one (or more) non-Jewish owner is permitted to pay Ribbis for loans taken from non-Jewish sources.[20]

Paying Ribbis to Jews

17. Borrowing money from Jews: A business which is owned by Jewish and non-Jewish partners may not borrow money from Jews under terms which call for Ribbis payments.[21]

18. However, the business may take this loan in the following manner.

The non-Jewish partner would borrow the funds and he would accept personal responsibility for the entire loan. It should be specifically understood that the non-Jew is acting on his own behalf, and not as an agent of the Jewish partner.

The non-Jewish partner would then lend the money to the business, under the same terms. Since the business is receiving the loan from a non-Jew, this is permitted.[22]

Collecting Ribbis From Jews

19. Lending money to a Jew: A business which is owned by Jewish and non-Jewish partners may not lend money to Jews under terms which call for Ribbis payments.[23] This type of loan is considered Ribbis Ketzutzah.[24]

---

20. This is permitted even if the two partners guarantee the entire loan, since a Jew is permitted to serve as guarantor for a loan between two non-Jews.

21. *Melamed Lehoel* 2:59. [If a majority of the business is owned by non-Jews, most poskim consider it to be a non-Jewish entity, providing that the Jewish minority is not actually running the firm (*Mishnas Ribbis* 2:n7, quoting R' Moshe Feinstein zt"l; see Chapter 5, Paragraph 26).]

22. Ibid. In this case, two loans actually take place. The first is between the Jewish lender and the non-Jewish partner. This lender would only be permitted to demand payment from the non-Jew. The second loan is from the non-Jew to the business. Each of these loans is permitted.

[It would seem that the business would be permitted to make its payments directly to the Jewish lender, to satisfy the loan which was extended to the non-Jewish partner. See, however, *Melamed Lehoel* (at the end of the Responsa, in a slightly different context) that the Jewish partner not be the one to actually make these payments.]

23. *Kitzur Shulchan Aruch* 65:28.

24. This holds true whenever a non-Jew lends out a Jew's money for Ribbis; see Y.D. 168:21 and 24, *Taz* 32 and *Shach* 73. (Regarding the guidelines for Ribbis Ketzutzah, see *Chavos Daas* 160:10 who explains that this prohibition applies even when the Jewish partner is unaware that his funds are being loaned for Ribbis.)

The business is also prohibited from charging interest for overdue accounts of Jewish customers.[25]

20. An exception: This business is permitted to collect Ribbis if the non-Jewish partner (or partners) accepted responsibility for the loan, so that in case the borrower defaults he would suffer the loss. In this case, the business could even lend funds which belong to the Jewish partner, and he could share in the interest which is earned.[26]

Setting Up a Partnership

21. Setting up a partnership to avoid these problems: Some poskim rule that when a Jew and non-Jew enter into a partnership, they can avoid these Ribbis problems by drawing up a special agreement which eliminates these concerns. Terms of this agreement and an explanation appear at the end of this chapter. It should be stressed that this agreement may be used only in cases of great need, and under the direction of a competent Rabbi.[27]

Large Companies

22. Some poskim hold that these rules also apply to large companies which have Jewish shareholders, even if these shareholders do not

---

25. A Jew is prohibited from charging for an extension of credit, as was explained above in Chapter 6. However, services fees which accurately reflect billing costs may be charged (*Bris Yehudah* 22:n18).

26. *Melamed Lehoel* 2:59. This is based on a principle which applies in numerous situations (see, for example, Chapter 17, Paragraph 7), that the person liable for funds is its true owner. Here too, the non-Jew who accepts responsibility for the loan is the true lender.

See also Y.D. 168:21, that when a non-Jew receives a Jew's money for safekeeping (*pikadon*) he may lend it for interest to another Jew. Since the non-Jew is responsible for the loss of this money, he is considered its true owner.

Maharit 1:116 (cited by R' Akiva Eiger to 168:21) also permits this in a case of a Jew who invested his money in a non-Jewish business, with the stipulation that the non-Jewish partner be entitled to make all business decisions on his own. If the non-Jewish partner subsequently decides to make interest-bearing loans to Jewish borrowers, the Jewish investor may profit from his share of the interest.

This is permitted even if the Jew is aware that his money is being lent in this manner (*Maharit*).

27. *Melamed Lehoel* 2:59 (also quoted in *Shearim HaMitzuyanim BeHalachah* 65:15). *Minchas Yitzchak* 6:77 (at the end) also mentions this method. An explanation of this agreement appears in footnotes to the Appendix.

actually run the business.[28] Others dispute this.[29]

When a majority of the shares in a particular company are owned by Jews, one should follow the stringent opinion and consider this a Jewish entity. However, when most are non-Jews, one may follow the lenient opinion,[30] provided that the Jewish minority are not actually running the firm.[31]

23. Corporations: In this chapter, we have not drawn a distinction between businesses which are incorporated and those which are not. The status of a corporation is a subject of dispute, as seen above, Chapter 5, Paragraph 27. It should be noted that this dispute involves a corporation which receives a loan. When a corporation lends money to an individual, all of the rules of Ribbis apply, according to both opinions.

Appendix to Chapter Sixteen: Partnership Agreement Between Jews and Non-Jews[1]

A. **Setting up a partnership to avoid Ribbis problems:** Some poskim rule that when a Jew and non-Jew enter into a partnership, they can avoid the problems which are caused when the

---

28. *Kitzur Shulchan Aruch* 65:28.

29. This is the subject of extensive debate among 19th century poskim. See *Shoel U'Meishiv* 1:3:31 and *Maharam Shick* (Y.D. 158) who both dispute the ruling of *Kitzur Shulchan Aruch*, albeit for different reasons. See also *Maharshag* (Y.D. 3), *Maharsham* (1:20) and *Minchas Elazar* 2:22.

30. *Shaarei Tzedek* (124), *Maharam Shick* (158) quoted by *Maharsham* (1:20; see also the index page, Note 31), Rabbi Yisroel Salanter, quoted in *Teshuvos Vehanhagos* 2:421. *Bris Yehudah* (ibid.) accepts this as the opinion of most poskim. Cf. *Minchas Yitzchak* 3:1 and 6:77. [Wherever possible, a Heter Iska should be used as a way of satisfying all opinions.]

31. Although *Bris Yehudah* rules leniently even in this case, we have followed the opinion of R' Moshe Feinstein zt''l, quoted in *Mishnas Ribbis* 2:n7, who ruled that when a Jewish minority shareholder has a significant holding in the company, so that his opinion carries weight in management decisions, the Ribbis prohibitions do apply. This is also the opinion of R' Yecheskeil Roth Shlita (also quoted in *Mishnas Ribbis*, ibid.).

[This does not refer to situations where Jewish employees, who are at management level, own some company shares. In this situation, these people make decisions as employees not as owners, and this does not effect the status of the company. Rather, the reference here is to situations where Jews make management decisions because of their extensive level of ownership.]

1. This contract is drawn for use in businesses which borrow and/or lend money to or from Jews. A Jewish partner is not permitted to collect or to pay interest in relation to these loans

business either borrows or lends funds for Ribbis. These poskim have drawn up a special partnership agreement which eliminates Ribbis concerns. It should be stressed that this agreement should be used only in cases of great need, and under the direction of a competent Rabbi. The partners would agree to the following stipulations:[2]

I. Both partners agree that any interest bearing loans taken from Jews, are being loaned solely to the non-Jewish partner. Loans with an equal amount of interest which are taken from non-Jews are being loaned solely to the Jewish partner. All remaining loans are the responsibility of both partners equally.

II. Both partners further agree that any interest which is earned from loans which are made to Jews belongs entirely to the non-Jewish partner. An equal amount of interest which is earned from non-Jews belongs entirely to the Jewish partner. Any remaining interest income is to be shared equally (a third clause should also be added; see note below[3]).

---

as explained in this chapter. This contract effectively allows the business to be involved in these loans, under the guidelines explained below. This method appears in *Melamed Lehoel* 2:59 and is also quoted in *Shearim HaMitzuyanim BeHalachah* 65:15. *Minchas Yitzchak* 6:77 (at the end of the responsa) also mentions this method. It should be stressed that this method is a subject of dispute and should be used only in cases of great need, and under the guidance and advice of a Rabbi who is proficient in the laws of Ribbis.

2. This agreement is presented here as it appears in *Melamed Lehoel*.

Clause I is used if the business anticipates borrowing money from Jewish lenders. Clause II is used when the business anticipates lending money to Jewish borrowers. (If a business anticipates that it will need only one of the clauses, that clause may be used alone.)

Under the terms of this agreement, the partners have traded revenues of equal value. They may divide profits equally, just as they would have done if they had never entered into this agreement. Still, this agreement works because it designates all Ribbis revenue to the non-Jew. This agreement is patterned after a similar agreement which is used by Jewish and non-Jewish partners of a business which is open on Shabbos. There too, the Jewish partner surrenders his portion of the business which is generated on Shabbos, in exchange for an equal portion of the business which is generated during the week.

3. Clause II prevents the Jewish partner from receiving interest revenue from this loan. Still, the business funds which are being loaned include his money. *Shulchan Aruch* (Y.D. 160:14) clearly forbids a Jew from lending his money on the condition that interest payments are made to a third party, even when the third party is not Jewish. This transaction should therefore be forbidden even when this clause is used. It is not clear why *Melamed Lehoel* did not address this problem.

However, this problem can be rectified by adding another clause to the agreement:

III. Both partners further agree that any funds which are given as loans to Jews shall

B. After entering into this agreement, the Jewish partner should refrain from being personally involved in any Ribbis payments. These payments must be passed exclusively to or from the non-Jewish partner.[4]

C. This agreement is suitable for use only under the following business conditions:[5]

☐ Clause I is suitable only when interest which the business pays to Jewish lenders is not more than 50% of the total interest paid by the business.[6]

☐ Clause II is suitable only when interest which the business earns from Jewish borrowers is not more than 50% of the total interest earned by the business.[7]

---

come exclusively from the non-Jew's portion of the business. He alone shall be responsible for securing payment from the Jewish borrower. The Jewish partner agrees to serve as guarantor for 50% of any such loans, so that if the Jewish borrower defaults on payment, *and* the non-Jewish partner is unable to secure payment even after pursuing it in court, the Jewish partner will absorb half the loss.

4. *Melamed Lehoel*, ibid. [The Jewish partner may personally accept the loan money, despite the fact that someone else is paying interest for it (as in Y.D. 160:13). However, he should not be the one who tells the borrower that this payment will be made (as in Y.D. 160:13; see also Chapter 4, Note 23 that this is a subject of dispute among the poskim).]

5. The figures mentioned here apply when a Jew (or Jews) owns 50% of the business. If Jewish ownership is more (for example, 75%) or less (for example, 25%), substitute the appropriate percentage in the sentences here.

6. This means that the *average* of all the interest which is paid to Jewish lenders may not exceed 50% of the total interest costs. (If the interest exceeds 50% during any one month it may be offset by interest paid to non-Jews during the following month.)

This is because all interest which is due to Jewish lenders is charged to the non-Jewish partner. This is balanced by charging interest, which is due to other lenders, to the Jewish partner. If the interest which is owed to Jewish lenders is greater, there would not be sufficient charges from the other sources to balance it out. In this case, the clause may still be used, but the amount of added cost which is paid to Jewish lenders may only be paid by the non-Jewish partner.

7. This means that the *average* of all the interest which is paid by Jewish borrowers may not exceed 50% of the total interest which accrued. (If the interest exceeds 50% during any one month, it may be offset by interest earned from non-Jews during the following month.)

This is because the interest which accrues from Jewish borrowers is given to the non-Jewish partner. This is balanced by giving interest from other loans to the Jewish partner. If the interest from Jewish borrowers is greater, there would not be sufficient funds from the other sources to balance it out. In this case, the clause may still be used, but the amount of added revenue which comes from Jewish lenders would belong to the non-Jewish partner.

CHAPTER SEVENTEEN

Money Managers and Loan Brokers

☐ Managing a non-Jew's money (1-5)

☐ A non-Jew managing the funds of a Jew (6-8)

☐ A trustee (9-10)

☐ Loan brokers (11-13)

☐ Mortgage brokers (14)

☐ Borrowing a credit card (15-16)

☐ Passing a loan on to someone else (17-20)

☐ Assuming a mortgage (21)

☐ Purchasing debt (22-23)

☐ Charitable Remainder Trust (24)

☐ Charitable Lead Trust (25)

Introduction

The laws of Ribbis apply only to debts between Jews. Thus, Jews are permitted to receive, as well as to pay, Ribbis to a non-Jew.[1] Yet, there are situations where a Jew who is dealing with the funds of a non-Jew might violate the laws of Ribbis.

We have already seen one example of this (in Chapter 15), in situations involving guarantors. In this chapter we will examine other situations: where a Jew manages the funds of a non-Jew, and where a non-Jew manages the funds of a Jew.

Money Managers

A. Managing a Non-Jew's Money

1. The Biblical prohibition of Ribbis applies only where two Jews are involved as borrower and lender in a loan for Ribbis. Someone who manages a non-Jew's funds is simply an agent of the owner of the funds, and is not considered a lender. Thus, when a Jewish money manager lends a non-Jew's money to another Jew and charges interest, he does not violate a Biblical prohibition, provided that the money manager does not guarantee his client's investment.[2]

Still, this was prohibited by Rabbinic law (except in the circumstances listed below), because it may appear to others that the Jew is lending his own money for interest (*maris ayin*).[3] This is prohibited even if the Jewish recipient (and any other Jews who witness the loan) is told explicitly that the funds belong to a non-Jew.[4]

2. There are certain exceptions to this rule: situations where the concern of *maris ayin* does not apply, and a Jew is permitted to lend a non-Jew's money for Ribbis. This includes the following cases:

---

1. This has already been discussed in the beginning of Chapter 5.

2. See Paragraph 3, below.

3. Y.D. 168:23.

4. *Shach* 168:71, *Chochmas Adam* 137:33 and *S.A. Harav* §74. (See *Beis Yosef* 168 who discusses this question but does not come to a definite conclusion.) *Divrei Sofrim* 168:190 points out that this is also apparently the opinion of *Rema* 168:23, who permits this loan when 'it is well known to the public' that the Jew is managing the affairs of a non-Jew. This implies that it is not sufficient to simply notify the individuals who are present when the loan is made. Cf. *Keren HaTorah* 168:131 who questions this ruling.

□ When a Jew manages the entire estate of a non-Jew, he is permitted to lend these moneys to other Jews and charge interest for the loan. (The interest would accrue to the non-Jew's estate.) In this case, people would understand that the loan is made from the money which is being managed for a non-Jew, and there is no concern of *maris ayin.*[5]

□ A professional money manager may lend a non-Jew's money for Ribbis. We are not concerned that people would think that he is lending his own money for Ribbis, because it is known that a professional deals with money which belongs to other people.[6] This applies to professional mortgage brokers as well. These brokers are permitted to arrange mortgages for other Jews through third party (non-Jewish) lenders.[7]

□ A money manager may lend the funds of a non-Jew in the presence of the non-Jew because there is no fear that it would appear as a loan between Jews.[8]

□ Some contemporary poskim permit this in additional situations: When the loan is made in the non-Jew's home (or business), even if he is not present, people would understand that the non-Jew's funds are being loaned, and there is no concern of *maris ayin.*[9] Similarly, if a check bearing the non-Jew's name is issued for the loan, this would be permitted.[10]

---

5. Y.D. 168:24. *Bris Yehudah* (31:2 and Note 3) explains that this is permitted whenever it is well known that the Jew makes investments for a non-Jew. If the entire assets of a non-Jew are managed by a Jew, he is permitted to make interest-bearing loans with these funds in all cases, even if it is not well known that he is managing a non-Jew's moneys. [This applies only where the Jewish manager is not liable for losses caused by the loan, as explained in Paragraph 3.]

6. *Rema* 168:23, *Shach* 71, *Chochmas Adam* 137:33. A 'professional money manager' is someone who earns his livelihood by investing other people's moneys (*Bris Yehudah* 31:n5, based on *Shach* 71).

This is permitted even if the money manager has both Jewish and non-Jewish clients, and even if he often invests some of his own funds as well. In these cases we assume that someone observing that a Ribbis transaction is taking place would understand that it is only the non-Jew's funds which are being invested in this manner, and the concern of *maris ayin* does not apply (*Beis Yosef* 168 s.v. *kasav HaRashba*, *Yad Ephraim* to O.C. 551:5, *Daas Torah* 168:22).

7. See Chapter 13, Paragraph 24.

8. *Chavos Daas* 168:end of 4, based on *Taz.*

9. *Bris Yehudah* 31:n5. (The source for allowing this is not clear; see the note which follows.)

10. *Mishnas Ribbis* 17:n5.

[The source for permitting this is not clear, because in the exceptions mentioned in the

3. Even in these cases, when a Jew is permitted to facilitate an interest-bearing loan, he may not guarantee the investment.[11] He is permitted to guarantee the safety of the funds during the period that they are in his possession (or when they are loaned to non-Jews).[12]

4. There are situations where a Jew may serve as guarantor for a loan (between Jew and non-Jew) which involves Ribbis. The conditions under which this is permitted are outlined above, in Chapter 15. While those conditions are stated in regard to a routine guarantor, they also apply to a manager who guarantees this type of loan.[13]

5. When a Jew is permitted to arrange a loan calling for Ribbis payments, he may do so even if he is reimbursed for his time and effort, and even if the funds for his salary are drawn from the interest payments.[14]

B. A Non-Jew Managing the Funds of a Jew

6. The laws of Ribbis apply to all loans between Jews. Even if the loan is arranged by a non-Jewish investor or broker (and even if he is the one who actually handles the funds), the money of one Jew may not be lent to another Jew for Ribbis. This prohibition applies even if the

---

Shulchan Aruch it is *constantly* apparent that a non-Jew's funds are being loaned. However, in the two cases mentioned here, it is only made clear *at the time of the loan* that a non-Jew's funds are being lent. Once the loan is made, all subsequent dealings involving the loan might still appear to involve Ribbis between Jews. Furthermore, these two situations are similar (although not identical) to a situation where those present when the loan is given are told that the funds belong to a non-Jew. We have already seen that this is not permitted (see Paragraph 1; the words of *Rema*, as explained in Note 4, above, also seem to preclude these two leniencies)].

11. Y.D. 168:22. This means that the money manager may not tell the non-Jewish lender that he accepts responsibility for repaying the loan (*Shach* 69; he is permitted to serve as a simple guarantor, as outlined in the following paragraph. However, he may not be the lender's first source of repayment). If the Jew does accept full responsibility to repay the loan (even if he does not guarantee the interest), he is considered a lender. This is because halachah views the individual who is liable if a loan were to default as a lender.

   This constitutes Ribbis Ketzutzah (*Chavos Daas* 168:*Chidushim* 56).

12. *Shach* 168:69.

13. *Taz* 168:33, *Shach* 168:69.

14. This is not considered Ribbis, because he is receiving payment for his efforts and not for his funds (*Rambam*, quoted by *Tur* and *Shach* 168:70). Although other Rishonim (also cited by *Tur* and *Shach*) disagree, *Gra* (168:76) appears to accept the lenient opinion.

non-Jew receives a portion of the Ribbis as his payment. This type of loan is considered Ribbis Ketzutzah.[15]

7. If the non-Jewish investor guarantees the loan, telling the Jewish lender that he could come directly to him when he wishes to be repaid, this is permitted. In this case, the non-Jew is considered to have borrowed the funds from the lender, leaving the non-Jew with the status of lender in the subsequent Ribbis transaction.[16] However, this is permitted only if the non-Jewish investor arranged the Ribbis loan on his own. If the Jewish lender directed the non-Jew to lend his money to another Jew for Ribbis, it is prohibited even if the non-Jew guarantees the loan.[17]

8. A Jew is permitted to invest funds in a non-Jewish bank or lending company, despite the fact that they extend interest-bearing loans to Jews. In this situation, the company is considered a non-Jewish entity since most of its stockholders are non-Jews, and the rules of Ribbis do not apply.[18]

A Jew is *not* permitted to invest funds in a Jewish-owned company which offers interest-bearing loans to Jews. If the company makes these loans through use of a Heter Iska, it is permitted to invest.[19]

C. A Trustee

9. This prohibition also applies when a court-appointed trustee deals with the funds of a Jew.[20] This is also an example of a non-Jew

---

15. Y.D. 168:21 and 24, *Taz* 32 and *Shach* 73. (See *Chavos Daas* 160:10 that the prohibition of Ribbis Ketzutzah applies even when the lender is unaware that his funds are being loaned for Ribbis.)

16. Y.D. 168:21 and 24. *Avnei Nezer* (Y.D. 190) rules that if the non-Jew does not have assets (outside of Ribbis loans extended to Jews) to back his guarantee, this would be prohibited (*Bris Yehudah* 33:n8).

17. *Shach* 168:12, *Chavos Daas* 168:7, *Shaar Mishpat* 168:2, *Chochmas Adam* 137:7; cf. R' Akiva Eiger to *Shach* 12 and *Atzei Levonah* who question if this is permitted even when the investor did not direct that the funds be lent to a Jew.

18. The status of corporations and partnerships has been discussed in Chapter 5, Paragraphs 26-28. R' Moshe Feinstein zt"l (quoted in *Mishnas Ribbis* 2:n7) ruled that if a Jewish stockholder has a significant holding in the company, to the extent that he influences the decisions made by the company, this leniency does not apply (cf. *Bris Yehudah* 30:n43).

19. Many Jewish-owned banks use a Heter Iska Klali for all their dealings with other Jews. A copy of a Heter Iska Klali appears in Chapter 23.

20. *Bris Yehudah* 33:n10. Neither the courts nor the trustee is liable if the borrower were to default on the loan. (By law, a trustee is liable only for "gross negligence or willful misconduct.") It is therefore considered the Jew's loan.

managing the funds of a Jew, and the Ribbis restrictions apply.

If a trustee is not authorized to extend a loan, but he does nevertheless lend the money in his care to a Jew, he is responsible for the money which he lent. The Ribbis may therefore be collected and passed on to the estate.[21]

10. Where an estate is being managed for young orphans, loans which involve Rabbinically prohibited Ribbis may be offered by the trustee (even if the trustee is a Jew), but loans involving Ribbis Ketzutzah remain prohibited.[22]

Loan Brokers

11. A Jewish loan broker is permitted to arrange for a non-Jew to lend money to his Jewish client, even if the loan involves Ribbis. This is because the loan is strictly between the Jewish borrower and non-Jewish lender; the broker making arrangements is not a party to the actual loan.[23]

12. The loan broker may not assume responsibility to repay the loan (nor may he provide collateral to guarantee repayment).[24] He must make it clear to the lender that he is acting only as a broker, and that the borrower is responsible to repay the loan.[25]

13. If the borrower provides collateral of sufficient value (to cover both the principal and the interest charges),[26] the broker is not required to tell the lender that he is acting as an agent for the borrower. In this case,

---

21. *Rema* 168:21; the non-Jewish trustee is responsible if an unauthorized loan defaults. (This would be a case of 'willful misconduct.') Whenever a non-Jew is responsible for the loan, it is considered his loan, as we have seen in Paragraph 7.

22. Y.D. 160:18; this is part of the general exemption from Rabbinically prohibited Ribbis, which applies to all charities (see Chapter 5, Paragraphs 11-20, for additional details). This is permitted even if the orphans are over 13 years old, as long as they are not yet capable of managing their own financial affairs (*Rema* 160:18), and even if they have been left a large sum of money more than adequate to provide for their needs (*Bris Yehudah* 7:n9).

23. Y.D. 168:17. [This is similar to the case of a money manager, except that the money manager is an agent for the lender, while the loan broker is an agent for the borrower. The Rabbinic prohibition of *maris ayin* (see Paragraph 1) does not apply to this situation (see *Darkei Moshe*, end of 168 and *Bris Yehudah* 31:n14).]

24. *Bris Yehudah* 31:n12.

25. Y.D. 168:17.

26. *Chochmas Adam* 137:21.

the lender relies on the collateral for repayment, and since the collateral belongs to the borrower, it is considered a direct loan to him.[27]

14. Mortgage Brokers: The rules regarding Jewish mortgage brokers and Jewish-owned mortgage companies are much more complex. For this reason, it is especially important to use a Heter Iska when securing a loan through a mortgage company. These laws are discussed in Chapter 13, Paragraphs 24-25.

Borrowing a Credit Card

15. It is a fairly common practice for someone who is short of cash to borrow a credit card from a friend or relative, and make purchases with it. When this happens, the person using the card must pay the card owner only the amount of money he actually used for his purchases. He may not pay the finance charges which accumulate as a result of his purchase. This prohibition applies even if he pays the bank directly.[28]

In general, expenses which are incurred due to a loan may be passed on to the borrower; however, this does not apply to interest expenses. [See Chapter 4, Paragraphs 1-5.]

16. Many credit card agreements allow for a grace period (often for a 30-day period), stipulating that if payment is received during this period, no interest is charged. Someone who borrows a credit card

---

27. *Shach* 168:51, *Chochmas Adam* ibid., *S.A. Harav* §66. [Cf. *Bris Yehudah* 31:n13 that there is an opinion which maintains that even in this situation it is preferable that the lender be informed who the borrower is. This is clearly in dispute with *Shach* and the other poskim who quote him.]

An example of this type of arrangement is the case discussed in Chapter 13, Paragraph 39, where a bank issues a mortgage, using the property to secure the loan. If the bank does not require the borrower to personally guarantee the loan, the broker may serve as the borrower of record to secure a mortgage for someone else. (See Chapter 13, Note 59.)

28. This is an application of Y.D. 168:17; *Mishnas Ribbis* 17:7. The reason that this is prohibited is that the bank (or credit company) which issued the card is lending money to the cardholder. He, in turn, is lending the money to his friend, so that he can make a purchase. This must be viewed as two distinct loans. The first loan was issued by the bank to the cardholder, and he is responsible to make payments to the bank. Interest which is charged on that loan is charged to him. The person who used the card borrowed money from a fellow Jew, and is prohibited from paying more than the exact amount which was borrowed.

This prohibition applies even when the person using the card pays the bank directly, because payments which are made to the account of the cardholder are considered payments made directly to him.

should avoid the Ribbis problem by making payment within this period.[29]

Passing a Loan on to Someone Else

17. When a Jew borrows money from a non-Jewish individual or bank for interest and he later lends those funds to a fellow Jew, he may not stipulate that the new borrower is responsible for all interest payments which accrue while the money is in his possession.[30] This prohibition applies even if the loan was originally taken with the specific intent of passing it on to the second individual.[31]

18. This prohibition applies even if the second borrower draws a contract which obligates him to make payments directly to the original non-Jewish lender.[32]

---

29. If the person using the card honestly pledges to make payment during the 30-day period, and then neglects to do so, interest charges would accrue. The owner of the credit card had relied on the borrower to make payment, and he is not even aware that interest is being charged to his account. In this case, one could argue that the person who borrowed the card should be permitted to make these payments, inasmuch as he caused these costs to accrue by neglecting to honor his agreement. (Here he would be paying because he is a *gorem hezek*, someone who caused damage. One could argue that in this case payment would not only be permitted, but would be required *latzeis yidei shamayim*.)

See *Mishnas Ribbis* 17:n11 who discusses this without coming to a clear conclusion. He notes that if the card owner did make the interest payments, the person who borrowed the card could later compensate him by sending him a gift, provided that he stays within the guidelines of the laws of Ribbis Me'ucheres, which were outlined above in Chapter 4, Paragraph 24.

30. Y.D. 168:1. In this case, the original lender (the non-Jew) has not extended credit to the second individual. The person who borrowed from the bank is still its borrower of record. What has actually happened is that two loans have taken place: The bank has lent money to the first individual and he has then loaned the funds to the second individual. The first loan is between Jew and non-Jew and Ribbis may be charged. However, the second loan is made between two Jews. The second borrower may not pay interest, since he has borrowed from a Jew. When he pays interest to the non-Jew, he is benefiting his lender by paying a debt for which the lender is legally responsible. This is prohibited as Ribbis Ketzutzah (Y.D. 160:14).

31. Unfortunately, this is a common practice. Where an individual is unable to secure credit, a friend or relative who has a good credit standing will often take the loan and pass it on to him. Interest which is paid by the person who receives the money is Ribbis Ketzutzah. (A Heter Iska may be used to permit this arrangement.) See Chapter 13, Paragraphs 37-39, regarding mortgages which are taken in this manner, and for the appropriate manner of setting up a Heter Iska in this situation.

32. Y.D. 168:1.

19. If this situation already occurred, and the second individual has already made interest payments to the non-Jew, the original borrower is obligated to reimburse him for these payments.[33]

20. A non-Jew who is owed money makes arrangements for the loan to be passed on to a second Jew. If he then directed his borrower to pass the funds on to the second Jew, this is prohibited.[34] The first borrower must first retire the original debt by repaying the non-Jew (or his agent).[35]

---

33. *Rema* 168:1. Whenever Ribbis has been paid, the payer is entitled to reimbursement.

Mechilah: If the second borrower has already repaid the entire loan, plus additional interest, he may choose to forgo this reimbursement. This constitutes *mechilah*, which exempts a lender from any obligation to return Ribbis which he had already received (Y.D. 160:5; see also Chapter 20, Note 20).

If only a portion of the loan was repaid and there is still an outstanding balance on the loan, the option of *mechilah* would not apply. This is based on *Igros Moshe* (Y.D. 3, notes to Ribbis 162:23; see also *Pischei Teshuvah* 161:6), who rules that any payments which were made to the non-Jew (even if designated as interest payments) must be calculated as payment of principal. This affects the halachah in regard to *mechilah*, as follows:

Suppose a $10,000 loan was made and the second borrower has already paid $2,000, of which $1,000 is for interest and $1,000 is for principal. Halachah requires that the entire $2,000 be figured as payment of principal. Therefore, the second borrower owes a balance of only $8,000. If the second borrower were to be *mocheil* the interest which he has already paid, he would erroneously calculate the balance due at $9,000. The problem is that once he pays $8,000 of this balance, halachah considers the loan to be completely repaid and the additional $1,000 would be Ribbis. *Mechilah* would not permit this, because it can only allow a borrower to forgo reimbursement for Ribbis payments previously made; it cannot permit additional payments.

[This calculation, which automatically considers Ribbis payments as payment of outstanding principal, applies only to the account between the two Jews. The non-Jew is permitted to receive Ribbis. In calculating the money owed to him, he counts $1,000 as interest, leaving a balance of $9,000. When the second borrower pays his balance of $8,000, an additional $1,000 of debt still remains. The original borrower would be responsible to repay this debt; the second borrower may not make this additional payment.]

34. Y.D. 168:1. Money is being passed from one Jew to another; this gives the impression that the second Jew is paying Ribbis for the first borrower (*Tur* quoted by *Taz* 168:2 and *Shach* 168:4; *Pnei Yehoshua* refers to this as a form of *maris ayin*).

This applies even if the money is passed on in the presence of the non-Jew (*Bris Yehudah* 31:n24 citing *Nesivos HaMishpat* 126:3 that the concept of *maamid sheloshtan* does not apply here).

35. Even if the non-Jew does not take possession of the money, but says, "Place the money on the ground and you are relieved of your obligation to repay," this is sufficient to terminate the debt. The second borrower may then take the money off the ground to initiate his loan (*Shach* 168:7, *Chachmas Adam* 137:3, *Chavos Daas* 168:3; *Shulchan*

Only then may the funds be issued to the second borrower, as a new loan.[36]

21. Assuming a mortgage: A mortgage is a bank loan, and also may not be passed from one Jew to another Jew. Therefore, a person who purchases a property may not assume the mortgage which was originally issued to the seller, if it remains recorded in the name of the seller. A Heter Iska may be used in this situation.[37]

However, when both the property and the mortgage are recorded in the name of the buyer, this is permitted.[38]

Purchasing Debt

22. A Jew is permitted to borrow money from a non-Jew under terms which require interest payments. If the non-Jew were then to sell this debt to a Jew, the status of the loan would change. It now becomes a loan between two Jews, and interest may not be paid for the period that the debt is the property of the Jewish purchaser. This is identical to the case discussed in Chapter 13, Paragraphs 44-46, regarding the purchase of a mortgage. The exceptions outlined there apply here as well.[39]

Aruch 168:3 maintains that it is not necessary that the lender specifically state, "and you are relieved...").

In this case, cash or merchandise should be used to repay the loan; it is not clear that the loan would be terminated by the placing of a check on the ground (*Mishnas Ribbis* 17:n8).

36. Y.D. 168:2. [This is permitted even if the first borrower is then assigned to collect payment for the non-Jew (ibid. and *Taz* 3).]

See *Bris Yehudah* 31:n30 who questions whether this is true even when the non-Jew did not take physical possession of the money, but instructed that the money be placed "on the ground..." (as in the previous note) and that the second borrower take it from there.

37. Any of the three methods outlined in Chapter 13, Paragraphs 28-35 may be used. See also Notes 51-53.

38. *Chelkas Yaakov* 3:196:n3, *Keren HaTorah* (Introduction), *Bris Yehudah* 31:n18, *Mishnas Ribbis* 18:n14. If the mortgage remains recorded in the name of the seller (for example, if the bank was not notified that the property was sold), this is prohibited. This is true even if the mortgage payments are made directly to the bank, and funds do not pass directly between two Jews (as in Paragraph 18).

39. We have seen there, in Paragraph 47, that if the original loan agreement does not allow for prepayment of the debt, a Jew may purchase the debt and continue to collect interest until the date that the debt is due. This leniency is not limited to mortgage situations; it also applies to debt which is not secured by collateral (*Mishnas Ribbis* 17:n13, based on *S.A. Harav* §70).

23. A Jew may borrow money from a non-Jew and agree to pay interest. The non-Jew is then permitted to use this debt as collateral for a loan he takes from another Jew, even if the second loan calls for interest payments. Since the non-Jew is the person borrowing the money, interest may be paid.

Later, if the non-Jew were to fail to make payment, the money he owes may be collected from the collateral. However, the Jewish lender may not collect any of the interest which accrued after the debt was designated as collateral, directly from the Jewish borrower. This money may only be collected by the non-Jew and then passed on to the lender.[40]

Charitable Trusts

24. Section 170 of the Internal Revenue Code sets forth the United States federal tax regulations for charitable contributions. These allow for various methods of receiving tax benefits when making charitable contributions. Setting up a charitable trust is one method that can provide significant tax relief for people in specific situations.[41] Two of the most popular methods of establishing a charitable trust are the *Charitable Remainder Trust* and the *Charitable Lead Trust*.

The *Charitable Remainder Trust* works in the following manner. A trust is set up, with a charitable organization named as beneficiary. The donor gives cash or property to this trust. When the donor dies, these funds become the property of the charity. However, as long as he is alive, the donor receives interest stipends which are generated by the trust. He also receives an immediate income tax and gift tax deduction for the year in which the funds are placed into the trust.[42]

---

40. *Mishnas Ribbis* 17:n13 based on *Taz* 168:12. This is because of the concern that if the Jew were to collect this money it would seem to be interest which accrued to him. This is not a question of Ribbis Ketzutzah.

41. [Trusts are important options for people with large estates who have assets in a pension plan. Under current U.S. law, if a person has more than $600,000 in assets, all benefits of his pension plan would be taxed twice when he dies. First, income tax would take as much as 50%, depending on the person's tax bracket. Estate taxes may take an additional 40% of the gross inheritance. This means that a pension plan which has $200,000 may be worth only $20,000-$30,000 to its heirs. In this case, someone who places his pension plan in a trust (or wills it to charity) actually makes a large contribution at a relatively small cost.

See also *Ahavas Chessed* 3:4, where the Chofetz Chaim strongly advises that generous gifts should be left to charity as part of one's will.]

42. The actual tax savings is based on IRS tables and would vary, depending on the age of the person receiving the stipends.

It should be stressed that anyone setting up a trust should verify that the charity

According to many poskim, this situation raises Ribbis problems.[43] Nevertheless, this arrangement is permitted in either of the following cases:

a) **Where the donor's stipends do not exceed the amount which was donated:** Consider, for example, the case of someone who donated $100,000 to a charitable remainder trust, and receives an annual interest stipend of $5,000. If he receives this stipend for twenty years, he will have received $100,000. Even if we were to consider the trust as an entity which borrows the donor's money, this would be permitted, since the donor has not received more than he contributed.[44]

b) **Where the donor receives more than the amount he donated:** For example, in the previous case, if he receives a $5,000 payment in the twenty-first year of the trust, this is permitted only in limited cases.

   If the trust had been set up in a manner which guarantees that the donor will receive his annual stipend even if the trust

---

which is designated as beneficiary is a qualifying charitable organization, recognized by the IRS. This can be verified by checking the IRS publication listing recognized organizations ('Culmative List of Exempt Organizations').

43. When establishing a trust, a donor offers a gift to the charitable trust with the stipulation that he receive benefits in return. One might argue that this donation is a gift, rather than a loan, and that none of the Ribbis prohibitions apply.

In fact, this arrangement does pose a Ribbis problem, in cases where the trust pays the donor (over time) more money than he contributed to the trust. This is similar to a case cited by *Pischei Teshuvah* (160:5), involving the following arrangement:

Reuven told Shimon, "I hereby give you $100 as an outright gift. However, this is contingent on you giving me a gift of $120 in thirty days."

By stipulating that the funds which were given are gifts, Reuven hoped to avoid the prohibition of Ribbis. In the ruling cited by *Pischei Teshuvah*, this is considered a loan and is a form of Ribbis Ketzutzah, despite the fact that the principals never used the word 'loan.'

Here too, a gift which is contingent on a regular rate of return does pose a Ribbis problem, except in the cases cited in Paragraph 24.

It should be noted that *Igros Moshe* would permit all types of *Charitable Remainder Trusts*. Since *Igros Moshe* maintains that a borrower is defined as someone who has personal responsibility to pay a loan, when a loan is not guaranteed by any individual, the arrangement does not have the status of a loan, and Ribbis may be paid. This is the basis for the ruling permitting corporations to pay Ribbis (*Igros Moshe* Y.D. 2:63; see Chapter 5, Paragraph 27) and would apply to trusts as well, since the trustee does not personally guarantee the principal.

44. [Tax benefits which the donor receives are not considered Ribbis and are not included in this calculation.]

does not actually earn that amount in profits (i.e., money would be taken from the principal), this payment is considered Ribbis. However, if the donor is only entitled to receive the stipend if the trust actually earns a profit of that amount, this arrangement is permitted.[45]

c) **When a Heter Iska is used,** this trust is permitted in all cases. The donor and the trustee would be the parties to the Heter Iska. The standard Heter Iska form (Chapter 23, 'Iska A') may be used.

25. The *Charitable Lead Trust* is an arrangement which allows a donor to reduce his tax liability during a year in which he has a large amount of income. The donor creates a trust to which he transfers cash or property for a predetermined length of time. He designates a charitable organization, which receives a guaranteed annual payment, based on the expected earnings of the trust. At the end of the designated period, the cash or property of the trust reverts back to its original donor (or to a designated third party).[46]

This arrangement is the reverse of the *Charitable Remainder Trust*, in that the principal is always designated to be returned to its owner. This situation presents no Ribbis problem.[47]

---

45. Based on *Bris Yehudah* 7:17.

Annuity Trusts and Unitrusts: Two popular versions of the *Charitable Remainder Trust* are *Charitable Remainder Annuity Trusts* and *Charitable Remainder Unitrusts*. One of the basic differences between these two forms of trust is that an annuity trust must pay its scheduled stipend, even if the income is not sufficient to cover this payment. The stipend would be paid out of principal. This presents a Ribbis problem.

Unitrusts may be set up in a manner which limits payments to revenue which is earned by the trust. This avoids the Ribbis problem.

46. The donor is permitted to take a current deduction (subject to certain limitations) for the value of the income interest which is being extended to the charity.

47. In a *Charitable Lead Trust*, the principal always remains the property of the donor, in the sense that he is liable if there is any loss of principal. He has only surrendered control of the money by transferring it to the trust. This has the halachic status of a *pikadon* and none of the Ribbis prohibitions apply.

It may be that the trust will earn more than the amount designated for charity. For example, the trust may have guaranteed the charity 5% annually. The trust may actually earn 7%. These extra earnings would accrue to the trust and ultimately become the property of the donor, as his profit. Since no loan has taken place, this profit is permitted (heard from the author of *Vechai Achicha Imach*).

CHAPTER EIGHTEEN

On the Farm

- ☐ Advance payment for produce (1-2)
- ☐ Selling produce which is not sufficiently grown (3-4)
- ☐ Lumber (5)
- ☐ Wine (6-7)
- ☐ Farm products which do not grow (8)
- ☐ Using produce as payment (9)
- ☐ Accepting risk (10-11)
- ☐ Young sheep or cattle (12)
- ☐ Paying farmworkers (13)

Introduction

A farmer invests money in his field and does not see a return until his crops are grown and marketed. Until this time, farmers have a special need for funding and are often willing to offer inducements to customers so that they would pay in advance. We have seen, in Chapters 7 and 8, that this is generally prohibited.

In this chapter we will examine how the rules of Ribbis affect the farmer, and in which areas the rules relating to the sale of agricultural products differ from the rules which have been established in the previous chapters of this book. Other aspects of the laws of Ribbis, outside of those recorded here, apply to a farm situation in the same way that they apply elsewhere.

There is a major difference between products which are produced in a factory and those which are produced by agriculture. When a product is manufactured, people cause it to take shape. The product is bent, cut, stretched, twisted or assembled according to the specifications determined for the manufacture of the product. When the human has completed his work, the product is complete.

On the farm, produce is planted, and nurtured by the farmer. After a farmer has finished planting, the fruits or vegetables grow on their own because of the force of nature. We will see how this affects the laws of Ribbis.

Advance Payment

1. A farmer may sell his produce before it is fully grown. For example, if the apples on his trees are only half grown, he would be permitted to offer them for sale. The customer would make immediate payment, and would receive the apples after they are fully grown. In exchange for making advance payment, the customer would be charged for the apples at the present market rate (i.e., at the time of payment). This protects him from future increases in the market price of apples.[1]

---

1. Y.D. 173:8. Manufacturers are generally prohibited from doing this. We have seen, in Chapter 8, that prices may be guaranteed (in exchange for advance payment) only under certain conditions. One of those conditions was called *yesh lo*, where a seller has the particular item in stock and is therefore permitted to sell it at the current price, even if it will not be delivered until a future time. Produce which has begun to grow is not yet ready for delivery, and should therefore not qualify as *yesh lo*. Still, there is a major difference between manufactured goods which are incomplete and produce which is not fully grown (as has been pointed out in the introduction to this chapter). Produce can

2. This is permitted under the following conditions:

    a) The most the farmer may guarantee is the market price in effect at the time the produce is ordered.[2] He may not offer an additional discount because he is receiving advance payment.[3]

    b) The farmer must deliver the same produce which had already begun to grow at the time of purchase. He may not substitute other apples at the time of delivery.[4]

---

grow on its own, and it will become ready for delivery even if the farmer does not do anything to assist it. Thus, the produce qualifies as *yesh lo,* and the deal is permitted.

After receiving payment for the produce, the farmer is permitted to perform the minor farming tasks which may still be needed in the field (see *Chochmas Adam* 139:17).

2. There are two benefits to the buyer: First, that the current price is charged. Secondly, that the farmer can charge the price of small apples, despite the fact that the customer will later receive large apples (Y.D. ibid.).

3. *Gedulei Terumah* 4:43, quoted by *Bris Yehudah* 25:n2.

There is a general prohibition against offering discounts in exchange for advance payment (Y.D. 173:7). However, where the item is in stock, the exception of *yesh lo* applies and discounts are permitted. If partially grown produce is considered *yesh lo,* as we stated earlier, it would seem that a discount should be permitted. Still, *Gedulei Terumah* rules that this is prohibited. [He apparently holds that since this is not a true *yesh lo,* only the smaller prohibition (of guaranteeing prices) is removed and not the greater prohibition (on offering discounts).] This ruling is based on the fact that the *Shulchan Aruch* does not mention that a discount is permitted when discussing the halachah of produce.

It is not clear why the ruling of *Gedulei Terumah* is not mentioned by other poskim.

It should be noted that the *Shulchan Aruch* records the halachah of selling produce which is not fully grown just after it discusses the laws of selling items at a discount (in exchange for advance payment). This juxtaposition would seem to imply that it would even be permitted for a farmer to offer a discounted price. *Bris Yehudah* (ibid.) writes that "were it not for his (*Gedulei Terumah's*) words, it would seem to me that (offering a discount) is permitted, just that (the *Shulchan Aruch* does not mention this) because it is unusual to offer a discount."

4. *Taz* 173:13, *Shach* 173:20. "It is as if he had conferred ownership of the produce from the time (of payment) and loaned him the use of the earth until the produce grows" (*Chochmas Adam* 139:15).

[If all of the farmer's produce would become ruined in the interim, he would be prohibited from purchasing produce in order to make the delivery. In this case, it is not clear if the farmer would be permitted to refund the original payment to the customer (see *Chavos Daas* 173:18).]

Divrei Sofrim asks why, if the fruit belongs to the buyer, the farmer may allow the buyer to grow the produce in his field; this should constitute Ribbis, since the customer is receiving free use of the field in exchange for his advance payment.

This difficulty is answered in that the produce actually belongs to the farmer, even after payment. Although, with regard to the laws of Ribbis, we view the produce as if it were sold, the buyer does not actually take legal title to the item which he is ordering.

Now, no matter how we look at this transaction, the farmer is permitted to allow use

c) The produce must be fully formed and must be suitable for use in its present size. Items such as unripe grapes, which cannot be marketed until they are fully grown, may not be sold in this manner.[5]

3. Produce which is not sufficiently grown to be marketable (even if it is edible) may not be sold in this manner.[6]

A farmer who wishes to sell such produce may still do so in the following way. The customer pays for the produce, but actually purchases the trees (or vines) on which it is growing. The farmer stipulates that the trees are only being sold for the fruit which it produces in the coming year, and that once the trees are harvested, they revert back to their original owner. The customer would then make a formal *kinyan* to acquire the trees (or vines).[7]

4. During the summer season, when produce is available at specific market prices, a farmer may guarantee orders at the market price, even if delivery is scheduled for the winter when prices tend to rise. This is permitted even if the seller does not actually have produce in stock at the time that payment is made.[8]

5. Lumber: A farmer may plan to sell his vines or trees to someone who will cut them down for use as lumber. He may wish to sell them in advance (while they still have fruit on them), and stipulate that the

---

of his field. If the payment is viewed as if it were a purchase, and the produce is seen as if it already belongs to the buyer, no loan has taken place and the farmer could benefit his customer. If the payment is seen as an advance for the future transfer of the produce, the produce still belongs to the farmer and could continue growing in his field.

5. Y.D. 173:10 and *Rema* 173:8.

6. Y.D. 173:10.

7. *Kesef Mishnah* quoted by *Yad Avraham* to 173:10 and *Bris Yehudah* 25:4. Cf. *Chavos Daas* 173:14 who rules that any work to be done for the trees or vines before harvest must be the responsibility of the purchaser.

8. Y.D. 175:1. The reason for this leniency has been explained in Chapter 8, Note 18.

This is permitted only when the customer makes payment in cash. If the farmer owes money to the customer and that debt is used for payment, this is prohibited (*Shach* 163:1 based on *Beis Yosef, Darkei Moshe*, and *Bach; Gra* 163:1; cf. *Taz* 163:4 and *Chasam Sofer* C.M. 170 who rule that this is permitted).

The customer might wish to stipulate that only produce which will actually grow in the seller's field is to be used for delivery. This guarantee may not be made, even if similar produce is presently available in the marketplace (*Maharsham* 5:51, *Bris Yehudah* 24:10; this is because the exception regarding items which are available at a set price applies only in cases where the merchandise which is being paid for could have actually been bought at the time of payment).

buyer actually take the trees at a future date. The farmer may not induce the buyer to pay in advance by guaranteeing a low price.[9]

6. Wine: After juice has been squeezed from grapes, it is allowed to ferment and turn to wine. During the fermentation process, not all the grape juice turns to wine; some grape juice sours and becomes unusable.

The owner of the grape juice may wish to raise capital by selling the barrels before or during the fermentation process. If customers want to be guaranteed that their barrels of grape juice will not spoil, the seller would be permitted to accept payment in advance and agree to refund the payment if the grape juice were to spoil.[10]

However, the seller is not permitted to guarantee against the price of the wine falling prior to delivery. For example, if the price of wine is set at five dollars a bottle at the time of payment and the market price drops to four dollars a bottle by the time it is delivered, the seller may not refund the difference.[11]

---

9. Y.D. 173:11. This is similar to the case cited previously, involving produce which is not sufficiently grown. Here too, the lumber which is being sold is not considered suitable for use as lumber until its fruits are harvested (*Taz* 16).

10. Y.D. 173:13. This is permitted because good grape juice does not spoil during the fermentation process. Only grape juice which was originally defective would later spoil. Thus, the seller is actually guaranteeing the quality of the grape juice which he is selling (*Tosafos* 64b, quoted by *Taz* 173:17 and *Shach* 173:23).

Yad Avraham 173:13 rules that if the grape juice were to spoil during the fermentation process, the seller may only refund the value of the juice at the time it spoils (i.e., the current payee for good grape juice), not the entire purchase price. *Erech Shai* disagrees, maintaining that the entire purchase price may be refunded. *Bris Yehudah* (24:n83) points out that this is also the opinion of *Chavos Daas* 173:19.

11. Y.D. 173:13. This is prohibited whenever the seller guarantees that the grape juice will ferment properly, even if the buyer takes physical possession of the grape juice.

This is not consistent with the rules involving prepayment for merchandise, as outlined in Y.D. 175:7. There, we rule that when payment is advanced for a product which is available at a set market price, the seller is permitted to guarantee that the price will not fall. For example, if an item is sold for $10, with delivery in six months, the seller may stipulate that if the price will drop below $10 by the time of delivery, he will honor the lower price.

Commentators offer divergent explanations for this ruling. The most commonly accepted explanation is that of *Tosafos* (quoted by *Taz* 173:17 and 175:9). This opinion holds that prices may be guaranteed against falling in most situations, because most agreements involving payment for future delivery do not limit the seller. He may buy or sell the merchandise at any time until the delivery date so long as he replaces it with identical merchandise. In these cases, the merchandise really belongs to the seller; thus he may agree to suffer the loss if its value dropped.

When wine is sold, the situation is different. In this case, the agreement limits the seller. He may not sell this barrel of grape juice, but must hold it until the delivery time. This

7. An alternative agreement for the sale of wine is for the seller to guarantee the price, but not the spoilage of the grape juice. Whenever the buyer accepts some risk (whether for spoilage or price fluctuations), other risks may be guaranteed by the seller.[12]

8. Other products which are produced in a farm (such as milk, wool and honey) are fundamentally different from produce. When produce grows, the original fruit becomes larger. If the original fruit is removed, no new growth takes place. This is not true in the case of farm commodities like milk, honey or wool. When these products grow, the additional material is not actually a part of the original product. For this reason, the leniency which is allowed for produce (in Paragraph 1) does not apply to these items.[13]

If a farmer wishes to sell these products before they are produced, he may not offer the customer a discount for making advance payment. For example, before milking his cows, he may not offer to sell the milk at a reduced price per gallon in exchange for advance payment.[14]

9. Using produce as payment: When farmers are unable to pay in cash, they may barter by offering their produce as payment. For example, a farmer may order a load of seeds and offer payment in the form of produce which will later grow.

In this case, the amount of produce which will be delivered at the time of payment must be based on its market value at the time of delivery time. If the farmer receives a hundred dollars worth of seeds, he may later send a hundred dollars worth of produce as payment. However, the farmer may not guarantee a specific amount of merchandise as payment, since the product may turn out to be worth more at the time it is delivered.[15]

---

is viewed as a true sale and the merchandise is considered to be in the buyer's possession. The buyer must therefore suffer the loss if its price were to fall (as explained by *S.A. Harav* §34).

12. *S.A. Harav* §34, *Bris Yehudah* 24:26 and n84.

13. *Taz* 173:14, *Shach* 173:21. This is why these items do not fall under the category of *yesh lo*.

14. Y.D. 173:9. The farmer may offer milk, wool or honey at the present price, despite the fact that he is guaranteeing the price for future delivery. This is permitted because these products usually have set market prices and are readily available (*Bris Yehudah* 25:4, based on *Meiri* to B.M. 64a). Prices may be guaranteed for any product which has a set market price (Y.D. 175:1).

15. In this scenario, the farmer is in fact selling the produce and accepting the seeds as advance payment. Whenever advance payment is made, a farmer may not guarantee the price of produce which he will later deliver (Y.D. 173:10). This applies in any situation

Accepting Risk

10. A seller may not offer discounts for advance payment because he is benefiting the customer for extending funds in advance. However, when it is not clear that a discount is being offered, this is permitted. Therefore, in situations where the customer accepts a degree of risk by paying in advance, he may be offered a discounted price.[16]

For example, a customer may agree to buy all of the produce which a farmer will grow in a given field during the following year. He is willing to pay a set price in advance, and receive whatever amount of produce the field produces. The farmer may ask for a low price because he knows that the buyer is paying in advance. In this case, since there is a possibility that the field will produce less than anticipated, it is not clear that a discount is being offered. The prohibition therefore does not apply.[17]

11. Other farm products, such as milk, wool or honey, may also be sold in this manner.[18]

12. Young sheep or cattle: A farmer is permitted to sell a young animal, with the customer paying in advance and taking delivery only after the animal is fully grown. The farmer may offer a discounted price for the animal because of the advance payment. This is permitted because the customer accepts a degree of risk in making this investment. There is a possibility that the animal will become sick or die, in which case the farmer would not be obligated to return his money.[19]

Paying Farmworkers

13. All the laws regarding the timely payment of employees apply to farmworkers as well. The *Shulchan Aruch* describes the following

---

where merchandise is used as payment, since the farmer is actually selling the merchandise (which will be delivered later) for the value which is set at the time of the purchase (*Chazon Ish* 72:5, *Bris Yehudah* 22:17; see also *Chavos Daas* 162:1).

[If the farmer had this produce in stock, he would be permitted to guarantee its price (as explained in Chapter 8, Paragraph 5).]

16. The possibility that a loss may be incurred must be real. It is not sufficient if there is only a theoretical possibility of loss (Y.D. 173:10).

17. Y.D. 173:9. *Nesivos HaMishpat* 209:1 adds that this is permitted even when the seller is motivated by his need for advance funding, as long as he does not say so.

18. Y.D. ibid.

19. Y.D. 173:10. This is permitted because it is not uncommon for the animal to become sick or die. The investment therefore involves a real risk.

situation involving farm workers, in a situation where the employer does not have capital to pay their wages until the produce is sold:

A watchman was hired to guard a field of produce until the harvest is completed. When the harvest is finished, his work is done and his wages become due. If the employer is unable to pay his employee's wages on time, he may not offer to pay the worker additional monies as inducement to agree to a delay in receiving his pay.[20]

The employer may use the following option to delay payment. He may extend the worker's job to include participation in the threshing process. In this case, the employee's wages are not due until later, when the threshing is completed.[21] At that time, the employer is permitted to add to his employee's wages to compensate him for the delay in receiving payment. Since these wages are being paid at the time that they are legally due, no debt ever existed. The rules of Ribbis therefore do not apply.

---

20. Y.D. 173:12 and *Chavos Daas* 16. If the employer offers to pay his workers for waiting, it may constitute Ribbis Ketzutzah (*Bris Yehudah* 26:n15. This is based on *Beis Yosef* 176, discussing a similar situation, who raises the possibility that this is a Biblical prohibition).

21. This is because someone who is hired by the job (and not by the hour) is entitled to payment only when the job is completed.

[It should be noted that the employee's term of employment can only be extended with his consent.]

CHAPTER NINETEEN

Starting a Gemach

Introduction

In *Ahavas Chessed*,[1] the Chofetz Chaim urges that everyone set aside funds to establish a free loan fund, so that he will have funds available in case someone requests a loan. [A free loan fund is commonly referred to as a Gemach; Gemach is an acronym for **gem**il **as ch**essed, which is the Hebrew term for performing kind deeds.]

He explains, "So that it not seem strange in the eyes of the reader, that I urge every individual, whether wealthy or poor, to have an established Gemach in his home, I will explain this to you, my brothers. . . .We are assured that when we are involved in this [mitzvah] properly, our sins will be forgiven just as they were once [forgiven] through sacrifices [in the Beis HaMikdash], and even more so. As it is told in *Avos DeRav Nosson* (4:1): Rabbi Yochanan ben Zakai was leaving Yerushalayim and Rabbi Yehoshua was following him. They observed the site of the Temple, which lay in ruin. Rabbi Yehoshua said, 'Woe to us! This place, where Israel's sins were forgiven, is destroyed!'

Rabbi Yochanan ben Zakai replied, 'Do not be saddened, my son, for we have another means of attaining forgiveness, which is equal to this. This is *gemilas chessed*, as it states, 'For I desire kindness, rather than sacrifices.'

Certainly then, everyone whom G-d has granted intelligence will be sure not to procrastinate and will set up a Gemach in his home, each person according to his ability. This will serve as a source of atonement, similar to the Inner Altar [of the Beis HaMikdash] (ibid., Chapter 15)."

---

1. 2:13.

In a note to Section 2, Chapter 15, the Chofetz Chaim stresses the worthiness of establishing a Gemach in the memory of a relative who has passed away. He writes, "There are people who wish to erect a memorial in eternal memory of the souls of their parents. They build expensive marble monuments [over their parents' graves], with silver etchings or the like, with designs and many flowers. Some add nice plants. They spend a lot of money on these things and think that this brings pleasure to the soul of the deceased.

"How people blunder with these plans! When a soul leaves this world it lives in a world of truth, where it recognizes the ideals of Torah and Mitzvos, for this is the only merchandise which is accepted in those worlds. . .It would be better for a cheaper monument to be erected, with simple lettering and without designs or flowers or plants. The money which is saved should be used to purchase *sefarim* for a *Beis Hamedrash* with the name of the deceased inscribed in them, or to create a Gemach in memory of the parent's soul. This would cause their souls to benefit. With each loan, which fulfills a Biblical mitzvah, merit is added to the departed parent."

The Importance of This Mitzvah

1. The mitzvah of making free loans available to poor people takes precedence over the mitzvah of offering them charity.[2]

2. It is proper to set aside moneys for use in a free loan fund. The Chofetz Chaim recommended that people set aside one third of their *maaser* (tithe) moneys for contributions to such a fund.[3]

3. It is preferable to set up a communal Gemach rather than to offer loans as an individual.[4]

Running a Gemach: Ribbis Problems

4. The Biblical prohibition of Ribbis applies to loans which are extended by free loan funds. It is therefore prohibited for a Gemach to lend its

---

2. *Shulchan Aruch* C.M. 97:1.

See, however, *Pischei Choshen* to *Hil. Halvaah* 1:n2, who maintains that it is preferable to donate money to charity rather than to lend it out. It is difficult to reconcile this opinion with the language of the *Shulchan Aruch*. In addition, *Pischei Choshen* himself points out that *Taz* (to C.M. 97 s.v. *b'tur*) rules that a loan takes precedence.

Pischei Choshen's contention that charity takes precedence is probably based on the fact that donations to charity involve an added level of giving, in that the money will never revert to the giver. This would seem to be more significant than the extension of a loan, where the money is returned to the lender when the loan is repaid.

When donating to a Gemach, a person has both benefits: The donation is a permanent one and his money is extended as a loan. The *Chofetz Chaim* (quoted below in Note 4) points this out as an advantage of contributing to a Gemach. This would certainly take precedence.

3. *Ahavas Chessed* 2:18. Once the fund has sufficient capital to satisfy the loan needs of a community, these contributions may be suspended (ibid.). *Eliyahu Rabbah* (O.C. 156) also rules that *maaser* money may be used to establish a Gemach.

This ruling is based on the opinion of *Rambam* who classifies loan moneys as charity. *Maaser* funds may therefore be used. *Ramban* disagrees, maintaining that this is a separate mitzvah, totally independent of the mitzvah of charity. According to this view, *maaser* moneys may not be used to establish a Gemach. *Ahavas Chessed* notes that *Shulchan Aruch* accepts the opinion of *Rambam*. He nevertheless recommends that one who undertakes to tithe his money should explicitly state that he may offer some of these funds to a Gemach.

4. *Ahavas Chessed* 2:16. There are several reasons for this. First, someone who contributes to a communal Gemach has a share in extending many more loans, even if his own contribution is a small one. In addition, when donating to a Gemach, a contributor is parting with his money. This is a greater mitzvah than offering a loan, where the lender intends to get his money back. Moreover, a communal Gemach is more accessible to a poor man; when individuals establish loan funds, it is possible that a poor man will find them busy and return home without a loan.

funds on the condition that the recipient offer a donation[5] (even if the donation is to another charity[6]).

5. Someone who receives a free loan from a Gemach may subsequently choose to show his appreciation by making a donation to the Gemach. Since the donation was not a condition of the loan, it is not Ribbis Ketzutzah. This is permitted even if the donation is clearly being offered in gratitude for the loan.[7]

6. A Gemach may not charge membership fees and restrict loans only to members because this fee is in effect a charge for a loan. This is prohibited even when the fees are to be used by the fund to offer loans.[8]

---

5. Y.D. 160:18. See also *Minchas Yitzchak* 6:78 and *Bris Yehudah* 6:n29. Even if the Gemach does not demand a donation, the borrower should not offer one when requesting a loan.

If someone who is receiving a free loan from a Gemach pledges to make a donation at a later time, may he subsequently make that donation?

This depends on whether this donation is considered Ribbis Ketzutzah. *Machneh Ephraim* §18 cites a dispute among Rishonim in cases where a borrower is given a loan unconditionally, but the borrower, when receiving the loan, states that he will give the lender a gift for his kindness. While all agree that this is prohibited, there is a dispute as to whether this gift is considered Ribbis Ketzutzah. (See also *Bris Yehudah* 3:n11 and 12.)

This situation involving a Gemach presents a unique problem. In general, where a question of Biblical law is involved we follow the more stringent opinion, in order to avoid the possibility of violating a Biblical prohibition. On one hand, this means that the borrower may not make a donation to the charity, since this may be a form of Ribbis Ketzutzah. On the other hand, if this is actually Ribbis DeRabbanan, the obligation stands and failure to pay is a violation of another Biblical injunction on failing to pay one's pledge to charity.

The borrower would have to find a way out of this dilemma, perhaps by telling a friend of his problem and hoping that the friend would make the donation on his behalf. (A third party is permitted to pay a lender, in appreciation of a loan which was extended to someone else — see Chapter 4, Paragraph 11.)

6. The Biblical prohibition applies whenever the lender requires that a payment be made, even if the payment is made to others (Y.D. 160:14).

7. *Bris Yehudah* 7:n45. This is not Ribbis Ketzutzah since it was not a condition of the loan. *Bris Yehudah* recommends that if a donation is made to the Gemach, it is preferable that it be made before the loan is granted or after it is repaid. Although we rule that where charities are involved all forms of Ribbis DeRabbanan are permitted, it is preferable that the donation take the form of a more lenient type of Ribbis.

8. Charities are prohibited from charging interest for their loans, even when the interest benefits the charity itself (Y.D. 160:18). These charges are prohibited even if they are labeled as membership fee or as a mandatory donation (*Bris Yehudah* 7:n45).

7. It is the practice of some free loan funds to require that individuals lend money to the Gemach in order to become members. Members are then entitled to receive loans from the Gemach. Although some poskim permit this practice,[9] it is preferable that a Heter Iska be used at the time that members offer their loans to the Gemach.[10]

---

9. *Bris Yehudah* 11:n13, based on *Maharam Shick* Y.D. 157.

This practice should be prohibited based on the rule of *halveini v'elveh lach* ('lend me and I'll lend you'), which prohibits two individuals from entering into a deal to trade loans (i.e., where the borrower says, "If you lend me money today, I will obligate myself to lend you money when you request it, at some future time"). The status of *halveini v'elveh lach* is a subject of disagreement among earlier poskim. Most poskim rule that it is Ribbis, as discussed in Chapter 3, Paragraph 20. This being the case, why do these poskim permit such an arrangement in the case of a Gemach?

Maharam Shick (as applied by *Bris Yehudah* to our situation) ruled that this is permitted, based on the following consideration. *Halveini v'elveh lach* is prohibited where an agreement requires that a loan be given in order for a loan to be received. Someone who lent money to the Gemach fund has not actually extended a loan until someone else borrows those funds. It is possible that before his funds are ever used by others, he would borrow money from the Gemach, perhaps even more than he put in. It is also possible that his loan will continue on a constant basis, and that he will be unable to repay the loan. This individual would constantly be a borrower, and never a lender, and therefore is clearly not involved in a *halveini v'elveh lach* situation. Thus, the Gemach agreement does allow for the possibility that a loan would be offered without a condition of *halveini v'elveh lach*.

[Of course, it is unlikely that this scenario would actually take place. Still, the fact that it is even possible is sufficient, because any of the members could have used this opportunity. This means that anyone who receives a loan was not *required* to leave funds in the Gemach in order to receive the loan.]

It should be noted that since the entire prohibition of *halveini v'elveh lach* is a subject of dispute, one who relies on the lenient opinion of *Maharam Shick* cannot be faulted. Still, since a Heter Iska is available, this is the proper procedure for a Gemach to use.

10. *Bris Yehudah* ibid. A standard Heter Iska form (Iska A in Chapter 23) is used. The Gemach is designated as the managing partner, with the member as the investing partner. Where the Heter Iska reads, "It is agreed that if I return the above-mentioned principal to the investing partner, together with an additional _____ as payment for his share of the profits which are generated, then I will not be required to make any further payment nor will I be required to take an oath," it should be amended to read, "It is agreed that if the Gemach makes a loan available to the investing partner, and returns the above-mentioned principal on demand, then it will not be required to make any further payment nor will an oath be required."

The paragraph which begins, "I am obligated to make this payment...," should be deleted from the Iska.

The Gemach should keep its excess funds in a revenue-bearing account, so that the terms of the Iska (which stipulate that funds are being invested for profit) would apply. If the Gemach does not have the potential of realizing revenues from any of its funds, the Heter Iska may not be used (as explained in Chapter 22, Paragraph 31).

8. The Gemach may not require that borrowers raise money for the Gemach. Some poskim permit this when a Heter Iska is used.[11]

Charging for Expenses

9. Although loan funds may not charge interest for their loans, they are permitted to pass on their expenses in the form of a charge for each loan.[12] This may be done in one of the following ways:

    a) By calculating the actual expenses involved in each loan (e.g., legal expenses, billing costs) and charging the borrower;

    b) By calculating the total expenses for a given year and dividing this by the number of loans which are extended. If this method is used, the charge is identical for each loan, regardless of the expenses involved for that particular loan or the size of the loan;[13]

    c) Expenses may be divided among the borrowers based on the sum loaned to each individual, so that an individual who borrows more money from the fund is paying a greater share of the expenses.[14] This method is the most questionable form of billing and should not be used except on the advice and

---

11. *Minchas Yitzchak* 6:78. A standard Heter Iska form (Iska A in Chapter 23) is used. The person receiving funds is designated as the managing partner, with the Gemach as the investing partner. Where the Heter Iska reads, "It is agreed that if I return the above mentioned principal to the investing partner, together with an additional _____ as payment...," it should be amended to read, "It is agreed that if I raise donations of $ _____ for the investing partner then I will not be required to make any further payment nor will I be required to make an oath."

    It should be noted that a Heter Iska is suitable for use only when the borrower is using the funds for investment purposes or (if the loan is for personal use) if he has other investments. When the borrower has no investments, a Heter Iska should not be used (this has been explained in Chapter 22, Paragraph 31).

12. Although this is permitted, Gemach funds traditionally do not charge for their loans. *Bris Yehudah* quotes Rabbi Yosef Chaim Sonnenfeld who was opposed to the practice of passing along expenses, despite the fact that it is clearly permissible.

13. *Minchas Yitzchak* 5:109. The Gemach must be careful not to charge more than the actual expenses which it incurs. [See *Doveiv Meisharim* Responsa 10, who advised a Gemach to use a Heter Iska when billing for expenses. *Minchas Yitzchak* and *Bris Yehudah* 9:7 rule that this is not necessary. It would appear that even *Doveiv Meisharim* requires the Heter Iska only in the particular type of case he is discussing.]

14. *Maharam Shick* Y.D. 158 implies that this is permitted.

guidance of a competent Rav who is knowledgeable in the laws of Ribbis.[15]

10. **Optional expenses** of a Gemach, such as advertising costs or signs, should not be passed on to the borrowers.[16]

If a Gemach borrows money from a bank (or other non-Jewish source) and pays interest for these funds, the interest costs may not be passed on to borrowers.[17]

11. **Fund-raising expenses** are not directly related to the loans and may not be passed on to borrowers.[18]

12. Losses incurred because of defaults on loans are not considered expenses. The Gemach must therefore absorb these losses and may not pass them on to other lenders.[19]

Ribbis DeRabbanan

13. Communal free loan funds are charities. We have already seen (in Chapter 5) that Rabbinical prohibitions of Ribbis do not apply where a charity's moneys are involved. A Gemach is therefore permitted to invest funds in ways which would otherwise be prohibited by Rabbinic law.[20]

---

15. *Bris Yehudah* 9:n15 quotes *Maharam Shick* but reports that R' Isser Zalman Meltzer objected to this practice because charges are determined by the amount being borrowed. Expenses do not increase because of the larger amount being loaned to any individual (recording and billing costs are the same, no matter how large the loan is). The extra charge is therefore unwarranted, and is considered a Ribbis charge for the additional amount of the loan.

16. *Chazon Ish* questioned the permissibility of passing on non-essential expenses (quoted by *Bris Yehudah* 9:n13). Even many commonly accepted expenses, such as the printing of stationery, are not truly essential to the operation of the Gemach.

17. *Vechai Achicha Imach* §108.

18. *Mishnas Ribbis* 2:17.

19. The many poskim who permit a Gemach to charge for expenses do not include a defaulted loan in their list of expenses, because this is a loss which is incurred by the Gemach, rather than an expense.

20. *Rema* 160:18. Nevertheless, individual borrowers should not be charged Ribbis, even in forms which are Ribbis DeRabbanan, because the donors who contributed money to the Gemach did so with the understanding that free loans will be offered (*Bris Yehudah* 7:n45).

However, a Gemach's excess funds may be invested in ways which earn interest, even if these investments constitute Rabbinic Ribbis. Examples of permissible investments are presented above, in Chapter 5, Paragraphs 15 and 16.

Free loan funds which are an individual's personal property, and which may be diverted for personal use (under conditions which do not require repayment), are not considered charities. Therefore, these funds may not be invested in a manner which would violate Rabbinic law.[21]

Benefiting the Chairman of a Gemach

14. The Torah prohibits Ribbis only when the borrower pays the lender for a loan. Therefore, when seeking a loan, it is permitted to hire a third person to influence the lender to offer a loan.[22] The chairman of a Gemach may therefore accept payment to influence the officers of the Gemach to agree to extend a loan.[23] However, he may not do so if he is personally involved in extending the funds to the borrower. This is prohibited because it would create an appearance of Ribbis, since both the loan and the payment are being passed between the same people.[24]

Running a Gemach: General Rules

15. Every Gemach should set up rules to insure that its loans will be repaid. Borrowers should be required to furnish collateral or arrange cosigners for their loan. This requirement should be applied uniformly to all borrowers, regardless of their wealth.[25]

---

21. *Bris Yehudah* 7:n45.

Many communal Gemach funds receive loans from individuals, which they then lend out. These Gemachs are a combination of personal and communal moneys. May these funds be invested in a manner which constitutes Ribbis DeRabbanan?

Mishnas Ribbis 2:n15 cites R' Akiva Eiger (to *Rema* 160:18) who rules that the Talmudic concept of *bereirah* (retroactive designation; this concept allows determinations to be made retroactively) applies in cases of Ribbis DeRabbanan. In our case *bereirah* allows us to say that the portion of the loan fund which was donated by individuals is not being loaned for Ribbis; that only the portion which belongs to the community is being used for this loan. According to this opinion, a Gemach is permitted to loan its funds for Ribbis DeRabbanan, provided that the amount which is loaned in this manner does not exceed the communal portion of the fund's assets.

22. Y.D. 160:16.

23. [This is permitted only where the bylaws of the Gemach do not explicitly prohibit it. In general, it is a good idea for the Gemach to restrict such payments, since they obviously create a conflict of interest and influence the judgment of the Gemach officers. This may cause a loan to be offered in a situation where the loan would present an undue risk.]

24. *Bris Yehudah* 7:n45, based on *Mishnah LaMelech* (to *Hil. Malveh* 4:14, s.v. *v'da*).

25. *Ahavas Chessed*, note to 2:16: "It is appropriate to act this way and to write this as a regulation of the Gemach, for without this the Gemach's funds will disappear over time. . . ."

Ahavas Chessed (note to 2:21) prefers the use of collateral to the use of a guarantor, because of the chance that guarantors will not make good on their pledge.

16. An individual who extends a loan may insist that it be repaid in one lump sum. He is not obligated to extend a loan to a borrower who intends to make numerous incremental payments. This is because a person who receives numerous smaller payments tends to spend the money more easily.[26]

This concern should not apply to a Gemach, since the money which is returned may not be spent. Borrowers may therefore arrange for payments to be made in installments. This arrangement is an added generosity, since a borrower finds it easier to pay in this manner.

17. Terms of the loan: No clear guidelines are offered in halachah for the amount of money which should be loaned to each applicant, or for the period of time that loans should be granted. *Ahavas Chessed* therefore concludes that this depends on circumstances. In the case of a Gemach, one must take into consideration both the needs of the borrower and the Gemach's anticipation of the need for future loans.[27]

18. There is no limit on the number of times that loans may be offered to the same individual. The lender should not resent lending money numerous times, just as he would not resent the constant visits to his store by a regular customer. A person who offers a loan should remember that he enjoys a spiritual 'profit' from each loan that he extends.[28]

---

26. *Ahavas Chessed* 1:1:10. It is nevertheless preferable that the lender extend himself beyond what halachah demands, and accept incremental payments (ibid.).

[*Pischei Choshen* 1:n21 questions this ruling. He reasons that if someone is supposed to forgo potential interest earnings to perform the mitzvah of lending money to a fellow Jew, he should certainly be obligated to forgo the inconvenience of being paid in installments.

This difficulty can be answered as follows. Although it is true that inconveniences should not forestall someone from offering a loan, this case is different. Here, the lender is prepared to extend a loan. It is the borrower who insists on the convenience of making payment in installments. Since the inconvenience associated with the method of payment must be borne by one of them, it is fair that the borrower and not the lender should accept this inconvenience.]

If a loan was already extended, Shulchan Aruch 74:4 rules that although it is wrong for the borrower to insist on making incremental payments, the lender is not entitled to refuse these payments. *Shach* 74:17 maintains that these payments may be refused. *Nesivos HaMishpat* 74:15 and *Aruch HaShulchan* 74:6 accept the ruling of *Shach*.

27. *Ahavas Chessed*, note to 2:16. (This also appears in 1:1:4 and 6, in regard to individuals who offer loans.) A source for this can be found in *Shulchan Aruch* (C.M. 97:1) which states that loans which are extended to wealthy people who are in need of cash, should be extended *'lefee shaah'* — for a brief period of time. Thus, we see that the period of the loan should be set according to the need.

28. *Ahavas Chessed* 1:1:7.

19. A Gemach must protect its ability to collect payment every time it extends a loan. Therefore, the Gemach should establish proof of its loan by having witnesses observe the transaction, demanding collateral for the loan,[29] or by requiring that a promissory note be signed by the borrower.[30]

20. Once a person has consented to offer a loan, he may not retract the offer. This is because a pledge to perform a mitzvah is binding.[31]

Who May Be Refused by a Gemach?

21. A Gemach is established to provide free loans to members of the Orthodox Jewish communities. Loans to non-observant Jews (or

---

29. C.M. 70:1. The Talmud teaches that one who lends without witnesses violates the Biblical injunction of *Lifnei iver lo setain michshol* (lit., before a blind person do not place a stumbling block). This is a general prohibition on causing someone to violate any Biblical law. One who lends money without securing proof of his loan is tempting the borrower to deny the loan. All loans (whether given by an individual or by a Gemach) should therefore be extended in the manner described here.

[When people extend loans for insignificant amounts of money (e.g., lending someone a quarter for a phone call) this certainly applies, since it is common for people to forget to repay such loans. It is therefore important that someone who extends this type of loan without witnesses should decide that if the borrower does not pay the loan he is *mocheil* the debt.]

Numerous poskim express amazement that people ignore this halachah and routinely offer loans without witnesses, collateral or a note of debt, see *Pri Yitzchok* 1:48 and 2:49, *Erech Shai* and *Aruch HaShulchan* C.M. 70:1. [See also *Ritva* to *Megillah* 28a, who holds that the Talmud did not mean to establish this as an absolute requirement; see also *Ohr Lee* 78 and *Sdei Chemed* Vol. 9, p. 188.]

In the case of a Gemach, where communal money is at risk, one must certainly be careful to satisfy these conditions.

30. The preferable method is to use a promissory note. This is better than using witnesses since a note is always available to the lender, while witnesses might become unavailable (*S.A. Harav Hil. Halvaah* §6). This is also better than collateral, because when someone relies on collateral, a dispute might still ensue regarding the precise amount that was loaned. When a note is used, this is established clearly (*Sma* 70:4). *Shach* 70:2 permits a promissory note which is signed by the borrower, even if there are no witnesses.

31. *Ahavas Chessed* 1:1:11, based on Y.D. 213:2.

S. A. Harav (*Hil. Mechirah U'Matanah* §1) goes further, maintaining that if a person decided in his own mind to do someone else a favor, and he remains capable of doing this favor, he is expected to carry out his intention.

[If the lender subsequently finds out that the borrower is careless with other people's money and is not careful to pay his loans, the pledge may be retracted. This is because the pledge was originally made based on false pretenses. In the case of a Gemach, there is an additional factor in that the person running the Gemach does not have the authority to issue bad loans.]

to gentiles) fall outside the mandate of a Gemach and may not be extended.[32]

22. There is no obligation to lend money to someone who will not repay the loan, even if he is a poor person.[33] A Gemach has a mandate to offer loans, not donations.

23. A Gemach may blacklist those who have defaulted on previous loans, and refuse to extend loans to them ever again. This is true even if the previous loan was paid by a guarantor.[34]

Who Takes Precedence in Receiving Loans?

A. Needs Which Take Precedence

24. Helping someone earn a livelihood: The greatest kindness occurs when a loan is offered to someone who can use this money to forestall the collapse of his source of income. This loan allows the person to remain financially solvent and, with time, to reestablish his business and earn a livelihood.[35]

25. Numerous small loans: Where there are many applicants for loans, and the Gemach has the choice of offering many small loans or one large loan, the lending of numerous small amounts takes precedence.[36]

---

32. *Ahavas Chessed* 1:3 rules that the mitzvah of offering free loans applies only when loans are extended to observant Jews. He defines an observant Jew as "anyone who subscribes to the thirteen basic principles of our faith." Since a Gemach is established for the purpose of fulfilling the Biblical commandment of offering free loans, its activities are limited to situations where the loan fulfills this commandment. Naturally, if the original mandate of the Gemach explicitly called for loans to be offered to all people, this would be permitted.

Chochmas Adam 130:7 and *Pischei Teshuvah* 159:4 cite additional reasons for withholding loans from non-observant Jews. However, this objection does not apply to all non-observant Jews; it is limited to loans which are offered to a Jew who was raised in an observant home but has become so far removed from his people that he no longer considers himself part of the Jewish nation (this has been explained in Chapter 5, Paragraph 10).

33. *Chochmas Shlomo* (C.M. 97:1, based on *Rashi* to *Shevuos* 39b), *Ahavas Chessed* 1:1:8, *Pischei Choshen* 1:5. This does not hold true if the borrower is willing to offer collateral to guarantee the loan (*Ahavas Chessed* 2:8).

34. *Ahavas Chessed*, note to 2:21.

35. *Ahavas Chessed* 1:1:14, 1:6:10 and 2:21. This loan accomplishes the added mitzvah of *and you shall strengthen him* (Lev. 25:35).

36. *Ahavas Chessed* 1:1:14. This is based on the *Rambam* to *Pirkei Avos* (3:15) who writes that the performance of many good deeds is preferable to the performance of one

When the lender has the choice of offering a single loan which would help a person forestall the collapse of a business, this takes precedence over offering many small loans.[37]

26. Loans may be extended to wealthy people who are in need of cash. However, the loan should only be extended for a limited period of time.[38]

27. Poor people who are in need take precedence over wealthy people who need a loan. Where one person needs the loan for food, and another person needs the loan for clothing, the loan should be extended to the person who needs the loan for food.[39]

B. People Who Take Precedence[40]

28. Where needs are equal, precedence is established on the following basis:

1) **Talmid Chacham** — A Torah scholar (or his wife)[41] takes precedence over others.[42]

---

extraordinary mitzvah.

This is explained further in *Ahavas Chessed* 2:13, "One man had given out many small amounts as charity to each of many people. The total added up to a ruble. Another person gave a single donation of a ruble. . .the merit of the first person far exceeds his. . .the first person has, by his many acts, habituated himself to do good, and this trait has become ingrained in his soul much more than the second person, who overcame his *yetzer* [*hara*] only once. . .[this applies] in our case too, where a person separates a sum of money for the mitzvah of Gemach. . . ."

37. *Ahavas Chessed* 1:1:14.

38. C.M. 97:1; *Pischei Choshen* 1:n5 quotes poskim who set a period of under thirty days for these loans. See also the introduction to *Ahavas Chessed*, Note 9.

The parameters of the mitzvah of lending money, as it applies to wealthy people, is the subject of discussion among later poskim; see *Ahavas Chessed* 1:6:n3, *Even Haazel* to beginning of *Hil. Malveh*, *Sefer HaMitzvos LeR' Saadya Goan*, notes to *Asei* 25 (p. 165 in the popular edition).

39. *Ahavas Chessed* 1:6:1, based on Y.D. 251:7 in regard to precedence in receiving charity. This applies even if the person who is in need of clothing is a member of the community and the person who is in need of food lives outside the city (*Chasam Sofer* Y.D. 234).

40. These rules apply to a communal Gemach. When an individual offers a loan, there are two categories which precede those presented here. They are: a teacher who taught the individual most of his Torah knowledge in any single level of Torah study (*rabbo muvhak*), and a relative.

41. *Ahavas Chessed* 1:6:6.

42. *Ahavas Chessed* 1:6:n14; cf. *Pischei Teshuvah* Y.D. 251:3.

2) **Bnei Earo** — Members of that particular community take precedence over outsiders.[43]

3) **Kohen VeLevi** — A Kohen takes precedence over others, and a Levi takes precedence over a Yisrael. A Yisrael takes precedence over a *mamzer*.[44]

4) **Someone with no wealthy relatives** — A person who does not have wealthy relatives takes precedence over someone who does. This is true whenever the relatives are capable of extending a loan, even if they are not willing to do so.[45]

Checks Which are Given as Surety

29. Many Gemachs ask that the borrower give a post-dated check for the amount of the loan. If it is stipulated that this check will be used for payment, the Gemach may cash the check (at the proper date) without notifying the borrower.

However, if a check was given only as surety, the Gemach may not cash the check without first notifying the borrower that it intends to do so.[46]

Pruzbul

30. After the Shemittah year has passed, the Torah prohibits a person from collecting debts which had come due before the end of the Shemittah year. This provision effectively cancels these outstanding debts. It is common practice for lenders to write a *pruzbul* during the Shemittah year, to enable them to collect these debts.[47] A Gemach is not affected by the passing of Shemittah, and therefore does not need to execute a *pruzbul*.[48]

---

43. *Ahavas Chessed* 1:6:2; a member of the community is someone who is there for twelve months, or someone who plans to live in the community on a permanent basis.

[When a wealthy member of the community requests a loan, it is not clear if he takes precedence over a poor person from outside the community (see *Ahavas Chessed* 1:6:n10. Where the bylaws of the Gemach give precedence to city members, this is certainly binding).]

44. *Ahavas Chessed* 1:6:6. This is true only if all are equal in Torah knowledge. If not, a learned person, even a *mamzer*, takes precedence over an unlearned Kohen.

45. *Ahavas Chessed* 1:6:12.

46. *Pischei Choshen* 3:n6. He maintains that if a check is cashed without the borrower's knowledge, this may violate the Biblical prohibition of *lo savo el beiso laavot avoto* (*Deut.* 24:10). This prohibits a lender from seizing payment without due process of Beis Din.

47. The laws of Shemittah and *pruzbul*, as they pertain to individuals, are presented in Chapter 21.

48. *Yichaveh Daas* 4:64.

CHAPTER TWENTY

Returning Ribbis

- ☐ The rule (1)
- ☐ When Ribbis Ketzutzah was accepted (2-4)
- ☐ Ribbis in the form of services (5)
- ☐ Ribbis in the form of goods (6-7)
- ☐ Tovas Hanaah (8)
- ☐ Ribbis collected by a minor (9)
- ☐ Ribbis paid by a minor (10)
- ☐ Shemitah (11)
- ☐ Mechilah (12-14)
- ☐ The repentant moneylender (15-18)
- ☐ Returning Rabbinically Prohibited Ribbis (19-21)
- ☐ Exceptions (22)
- ☐ Heirs (23-25)
- ☐ Trading loans (26)
- ☐ Less stringent forms of Ribbis (Ribbis Mukdemes; Ribbis Me'ucheres; haaramas Ribbis; Ribbis B'Shas Perayon) (27)

Introduction

Although the Torah prohibits the paying of Ribbis, once a borrower makes a Ribbis payment, it becomes the property of the lender. Thus, money or objects received as Ribbis belong to the lender.[1]

A separate Biblical mitzvah requires a person who accepts Ribbis to return it to the borrower. This is derived from the verse (*Lev.* 25:36), *Do not take from him interest. . .and your brother shall live with you.* We understand this to mean that Ribbis must be returned, so that the effect of the financial drain that the Ribbis payments have had on the borrower's quality of life can be reversed. In earlier times (when Beis Din had the legal jurisdiction to enforce halachah), Jewish courts would force compliance with this commandment by flogging the lender until he agreed to return the Ribbis funds which he had received.[2]

The applications of this commandment (and exceptions to it) are the subject of this chapter.

The Rule

1. The Torah requires a person who accepts a Ribbis payment to return it to the original owner. This applies to all Ribbis Ketzutzah

---

1. *Ritva* (to *Kiddushin* 6b and B.M. 61a) explains that since Ribbis payments are given willingly, the lender takes legal possession when it is paid. *Ritva* maintains that this is why Ribbis moneys pass onto heirs on the death of the lender (see Paragraph 23 below). In a similar situation involving stolen funds, the heirs are obligated to return the funds to their rightful owner. This is not true regarding Ribbis funds, since they are the legal property of the lender. The Biblical mitzvah to return Ribbis funds is incumbent only on the individual who actually received the Ribbis; heirs are not obligated to return moneys which their father improperly received as part of a Ribbis transaction.

Ritva's explanation of Ribbis as becoming the property of the lender is fundamental to the laws of Ribbis. Other applications of this explanation appear throughout this chapter (see Notes 11 and 19). See also *Avnei Meluim* 28:22, *Chavos Daas* 161:10, *Pnei Yehoshua* to B.M. 61b (s.v. *Begemara elah* and s.v. *amar Rav*), *Shaar Hamelech* to Hil. *Ishus* 5:15, R' Akiva Eiger (notes to *Rambam*, to Hil. *Malveh* 8:15) and *Chazon Ish* (Y.D. 70:2) who accept the *Ritva's* concept. Cf. *Tosafos* (to B.M. 112a), *Machneh Ephraim* (Ribbis §2), and *Igros Moshe* (Y.D. 3, notes to Ribbis 161:25) who disagree.

One practical difference between these opinions involves an individual who received an esrog as Ribbis payment, and wishes to use it to fulfill his obligation during Succos. Since the Torah requires a person to own the esrog he uses on the first day of Succos, *Tosafos* would not permit its use, while *Ritva* would permit it (*Binyan Zion* 1:66).

2. Y.D. 161:5.

(Biblically prohibited Ribbis), whether it was given in the form of cash, goods or services. It does not apply to Rabbinically prohibited forms of Ribbis.[3] The guidelines for determining whether Ribbis is Biblically or Rabbinically prohibited have been spelled out above, in Chapter 2.

When Ribbis Ketzutzah Was Accepted

2. Cash payments: Money which was received as interest on a loan must be returned to the borrower. This is both a remedy to the transgression which already occurred[4] and a separate fulfillment of a Biblical mitzvah.[5]

3. In cases where interest payments were made before the principal was fully repaid (e.g., the borrower made monthly mortgage payments, which include interest payments, even when the principal was still partially unpaid), the borrower may compel the lender to repay the Ribbis by calculating his interest payments as a credit toward the unpaid balance. For example, $10,000 was borrowed, and the first payment of $200 was made. If that payment consisted of $100 in interest payments and an additional $100 for payment of principal, the borrower may calculate this as a $200 payment on principal, leaving only a balance of $9,800 to be repaid on the loan.[6]

4. Similarly, whenever the outstanding balance has not yet been repaid to the lender, the lender does not actually have to return the cash which he received as interest. He may keep the money and apply it as a

---

3. Y.D. 161:1 and 5. In most instances there is a moral obligation to return even Rabbinically prohibited Ribbis (*latzeis yidei shamayim*). These guidelines are detailed later in this chapter.

In situations where the status of Ribbis is an issue of dispute among the poskim, the borrower cannot be compelled to return Ribbis when there are poskim who consider the payment to be a form of Rabbinic Ribbis. (This is based on the Talmudic principle of *hamotzi meichaveiro alav haraayah*, one who seeks to collect must prove the obligation.) Nevertheless, a person should return such Ribbis since this is a question of Biblical law. If he neglects to do so, Beis Din should impress on the person that he is violating a prohibition by failing to return it (*Chochmas Adam* 142:27, based on *Shach* 177:65).

4. This is the subject of discussion in *Bava Metzia* 62a, see *Tosafos* and other Rishonim there.

5. See the introduction to this chapter.

6. See footnote which follows. This rule certainly applies when Ribbis Ketzutzah was paid. *Shulchan Aruch* (Y.D. 166:3) records a dispute as to whether this extends even to Rabbinically prohibited Ribbis (see Paragraph 21 below).

credit towards the portion of the outstanding balance which has not been repaid.[7]

The lender may keep the Ribbis payment as payment for principal, even if the borrower is not yet obligated to repay the principal (i.e., the principal is not due until a later date).[8]

5. Services: When the terms of a loan require that in addition to repaying the loan, the borrower must provide non-material services to the lender without charge (or at a discount), these services are also Ribbis Ketzutzah. The lender must therefore reimburse the borrower the fair market value of the services (at the time they were received by the lender).[9] For example, if the terms of the loan called for the borrower to paint the lender's home, the borrower must be paid a fair price for his

---

7. *Igros Moshe* (notes to Ribbis 161:23) explains that, from a halachic standpoint, it is *not possible* to make a Ribbis payment when there is principal which has not yet been repaid. Any moneys which were passed from the borrower to the lender, even if given as interest, are automatically reckoned as a payment of principal. Since these moneys are not considered interest payments, there can be no obligation to return them to the borrower. [See also Note 21, below.]

Similarly, in the situation in the previous paragraph, where the lender is not willing to repay the Ribbis which he received, the borrower may simply deduct it from the outstanding balance which he owes. [Regarding a similar situation involving Ribbis DeRabbanan, see Paragraph 21, below.]

The concept introduced by *Igros Moshe*, that Ribbis payments are automatically reckoned as payment of principal, actually appears in the *Teshuvos R' Akiva Eiger* (1:80), although he discusses this question without arriving at a clear conclusion. In his case too, the borrower had made Ribbis payments, but had not repaid the principal. However, before the principal was repaid, the lender died. His heirs argued that since they were not obligated to repay Ribbis which their father had accepted (heirs have no such obligation; see below), the borrower was obligated to repay the principal and could not make deductions for Ribbis Ketzutzah which had previously been repaid. R' Akiva Eiger questions whether this is so, since the Ribbis payment could be automatically deducted from the balance of principal. However, in concluding his letter, R' Akiva Eiger writes that time pressures did not allow him to examine this topic sufficiently so as to come to a definite halachic conclusion.

Pischei Teshuvah (161:6) quotes *Tiferes Tzvi* Y.D. 48:1 who rules that the heirs may not collect the full principal because the Ribbis payments must be deducted. This is consistent with the ruling of *Igros Moshe*.

8. The lender agreed to the loan because he felt that it would earn interest. Later, when he realizes that he is not permitted to take the interest payment, he has the right to demand the immediate return of the *entire* loan. This is because he could argue that the loan was given on an erroneous premise, and that he would never have agreed to offer a free loan (*Mishnah LaMelech*, quoted by *Chavos Daas* 161:5 and R' Akiva Eiger to Y.D. 173:1). Thus, he may certainly retain partial payment prior to the original due date.

9. *Pischei Teshuvah* 161:9.

work. Similarly, if the borrower was required to give the lender free use of his property, the lender must subsequently pay rent for the property which he used.[10]

6. Goods: When the terms of a loan call for specific goods to be given to the lender as interest, this is also Ribbis Ketzutzah and must be returned. Some poskim require that the item itself (when the lender still has it in his possession) be returned. Others maintain that it is sufficient for the lender to pay the fair market value of the item.[11] If the borrower has no interest in the item itself, he may certainly accept cash payment in its place.

7. When a loan agreement originally required interest payments in the form of cash, and the parties subsequently agreed to substitute the cash with goods (or services), all poskim agree that reimbursement may be made in cash form. In this case, the agreement to substitute goods for cash was not part of the Ribbis agreement and therefore remains valid.[12]

When the substitute item is distinctive or unusual, to the extent that people who observe it in the possession of the lender would recognize it as having been received from the borrower, the object itself must be returned to the borrower. This is because it is improper to flaunt assets which were received as a result of a Ribbis transgression. This is a Rabbinic obligation, instituted to protect the honor of the law.[13]

---

10. Y.D. 161:5, *Bris Yehudah* 8:10. [This applies only where the property which was given to the lender has a rental value (*kayma l'agra* — see *Shach* 161:9).] If the lender paid a discounted rate for the services (or for use of the property) as part of their agreement, the lender is obligated to refund the discount to the borrower (Y.D. ibid.).

11. *Mishnah LaMelech* (*Hil. Malveh* 8:16, quoted in *Pischei Teshuvah* 161:9) requires that the object itself be returned. Numerous poskim disagree with this ruling. They argue that items given as Ribbis become the legal property of the receiver. (This concept has been outlined in the introduction to this chapter.) Since the obligation to reimburse the borrower is a separate Biblical mitzvah, this can be accomplished with a cash payment (*Chavos Daas* 161:10, *Shaar HaMelech* to *Hil. Ishus* 5:15 and quoted in *Pischei Teshuvah* 161:9, *Avnei Meluim* 28:22, *Maharsham* 2:228).

Chazon Ish 70:2 explains that *Mishnah LaMelech* agrees with the underlying concept that a Ribbis payment becomes the property of the receiver. Nevertheless, he holds that the very agreement to provide the particular item is itself a benefit to the lender, which is offered in exchange for the loan. This agreement itself is also Ribbis, and the benefit of receiving the particular item must also be returned. (Cf. *Igros Moshe* notes to *Hil. Ribbis* 161:25.)

12. Y.D. 161:8.

13. Y.D. 161:9. (See also Paragraphs 17 and 23, below, where a similar ruling applies.) This prohibition would apply, for example, to a unique item of clothing (see *Bris*

8. Tovas hanaah: If the lender has a business, he may not stipulate that the borrower patronize his business in exchange for the loan. This is known as *tovas hanaah*, and is a real benefit, which may not be offered to the lender.[14]

After receiving this benefit, the lender is obligated to return its value to the borrower. He is *not* obligated to return the entire profit which was generated by the borrower's patronage. Rather, he must only return the market value of a broker's services which would generate this amount of business.[15]

9. Ribbis Ketzutzah which is collected by a minor must be returned.

However, if he has already spent the Ribbis he cannot be compelled to repay it, even if he has other funds.[16]

Later, when he grows up, some hold that he is obligated to return

---

Yehudah 8:n35). A car or truck, even if not unusual, would also fall into this category, since people are generally aware of the identity of its owner (*Toras Ribbis* 2:B.H.12).

14. Y.D. 160:23. This prohibition applies to patronizing both a business which sells goods (such as a grocery store) and a business which offers a service (such as a repair shop) (*Bris Yehudah* 11:24 and 25). Similarly, the lender may not offer a loan on the condition that he be offered a job, even if he will be paid a fair salary for his work (*S.A. Harav* §14).

In Chapter 3, Note 33, we have seen that there is a dispute regarding *tovas hanaah.* Some consider it Ribbis Ketzutzah, while others consider it a Rabbinic form of Ribbis. The opinions recorded here, which discuss the obligation to return this type of Ribbis, follow those who consider it Ribbis Ketzutzah.

15. *Maharsham* 4:95, *Bris Yehudah* 11:n46. *Maharsham* discusses the case of a teacher who had extended a loan on the condition that the borrower send his children to study under him. Later, after the children had already enrolled in his school, the parties realized that this agreement involved Ribbis. *Maharsham* suggests that the lender pay a fee to the borrower as compensation for inducing him to send the children to study under him. This fee would be based on the market value of arranging for students to attend a school (*Maharsham* sets this fee at 1-2%). *Maharsham* permits this fee to be deducted from the tuition which is owed the teacher.

Teshuvah MeAhavah (3:notes to Y.D.; quoted in *Bris Yehudah* 11:n53) discusses the case of a loan which was extended on the condition that the borrower offer a job to the lender. If the borrower later satisfied his part of the agreement and offered a job to the lender (for example, he had given the lender a utensil to repair), but the lender had not yet done the work, we would require that the job be taken from him and be given to someone else. (This follows the opinion that this constitutes Ribbis Ketzutzah.)

16. *Rashba*, quoted by *Mishneh LaMelech* (to *Hil. Milveh* 4:14, s.v. *v'eicha*h), *Rivash*, quoted by *Beis Yosef* 160 and R' Akiva Eiger 160:20. If the Ribbis is still in his possession, many poskim rule that the minor can be compelled to return it (*Rashba*, Y.D. 160:20, as explained by R' Akiva Eiger; see also *Gra* 160:49; R' Akiva Eiger also quotes a dissenting opinion which holds that a minor can never be compelled to return Ribbis).

the Ribbis (*latzeis yidei shamayim*), but all agree that he cannot be compelled to do so.[17]

10. If a minor borrowed money and paid Ribbis, the lender (even if he is an adult) cannot be compelled to return it.[18] However, he should do so on his own (*latzeis yidei shamayim*).

Shemittah

11. Every seventh year is Shemittah, the Sabbatical year, when most types of outstanding loans automatically become voided. This does *not* affect the lender's obligation to repay Ribbis. Thus, even after Shemittah (or many Shemittos) passes, the lender remains obligated to reimburse the borrower.[19]

Mechilah

12. After paying Ribbis Ketzutzah, a borrower may choose to forgo his right to reimbursement. This is called *mechilah* and exempts the lender from any obligation to return the Ribbis which he had already received.[20] However, it does not permit further interest

---

17. *Bris Yehudah* 8:n61. The case discussed there involves an agent who was appointed to manage the minor's affairs and collected Ribbis for him. The same rule should also apply to a minor who collected Ribbis on his own. Cf. *Bris Yehudah* 3:11 who presents a dispute concerning this situation, including the opinion of some poskim who consider it to be Ribbis Ketzutzah.

18. *Bris Yehudah* 3:12, because this is not considered Ribbis Ketzutzah. [This applies to Ribbis paid by a child who is at least six years old and understands business affairs. Payments made by a younger child are not legal transactions and must be returned (C.M. 235:1).]

19. *Bris Yehudah* 8:17. Shemittah cancels most outstanding debts. However, the obligation to repay Ribbis is not included, because it is a separate mitzvah obligation (as explained in the introduction to this chapter), not debt or any other type of financial obligation. The rules of debt cancellation of Shemittah therefore do not apply.

20. Y.D. 160:5. *Shulchan Aruch* does not actually state that one is permitted to be *mocheil* the reimbursement; it deals only with *mechilah* after it has taken place. One could argue that the *mechilah* itself should be prohibited as Ribbis, since it benefits the lender. Still, the language used by *Levush* implies that one is permitted to forgo reimbursement. (After quoting the language of *Shulchan Aruch*, *Levush* adds that this is "similar to a case of theft, where one may be *mocheil*.") Additionally, *Taz* (quoted below in Paragraph 14) maintains that *mechilah* may be assumed in certain conditions. If *mechilah* were prohibited, one could not make such an assumption.

Does *mechilah* exempt a person from the moral obligation to return Ribbis?

Perishah 160:8 holds that *mechilah* satisfies only the financial obligation of the lender. The Biblical prohibitions which were transgressed are not rectified unless the

payments to be made, even if they are in connection with the same loan.[21]

13. *Mechilah* is valid only in cases where the borrower chooses to forgo reimbursement by his own free choice. If he was compelled to do so, or if the loan was originally extended with the understanding that the borrower would subsequently be *mocheil* his right to retrieve his Ribbis payment, the *mechilah* is not valid and the Ribbis payment must be returned.[22]

14. Some poskim maintain that one is obligated to return Ribbis only if the borrower requests reimbursement. They see the borrower's failure to solicit reimbursement as an indication that he has exercised his right to forgo reimbursement (*mechilah*). Most poskim disagree and maintain that only an explicit *mechilah* is valid. One should follow this opinion.[23]

---

money is actually returned. According to this opinion, a moral obligation remains even after *mechilah*. See also *Avnei Nezer* (Y.D.:end of 135) who rules that it is preferable to actually repay the loan.

Gra (160:7) and *S.A. Harav* (§5) rule that after *mechilah* there is not even a moral obligation (*latzeis yidei shamayim*) to return Ribbis. This implies that *mechilah* is the equivalent of repayment in rectifying the Ribbis transgression which had taken place. *Bris Yehudah* (1:n41) cites *Minchas Chinuch* and *Shaar HaMishpat* (C.M. 9) who support this opinion.

Minchas Yitzchak 2:79 and *Mishnas Ribbis* (21:n9) suggest that when the lender is prepared to return the Ribbis, and the borrower refuses to accept repayment and states clearly, "I consider it as if I have been repaid," this would be sufficient according to all opinions.

21. There is one situation where the borrower could not be *mocheil* this money. This is in the case outlined in Paragraphs 3 and 4 above. In that case, Ribbis payments were made before the loan itself was repaid. Since these payments are automatically counted as payment of principal, the outstanding balance is reduced. In this way, the borrower automatically recovers the Ribbis which he had paid. When the borrower repays the balance, at this reduced calculation, he has recovered the moneys which he paid as interest. He would then be prohibited from making any additional payments, as these new payments would constitute Ribbis.

22. *Beis Yosef*, in *Bedek Habayis*, 160.

23.*Taz* (161:3) maintains that one is obligated to return Ribbis only if the borrower requests that he do so. This opinion is accepted by *Chavos Daas* (161:Chidushim 7), *Shaar HaMishpat* (C.M. 9:1) and *Shevus Yaakov* §135.

Sma (C.M. 9:1) disagrees and requires that the lender take the initiative and repay Ribbis Ketzutzah even when no request is made. This is also the opinion of *Birkei Yosef* (C.M. 9:1), *Ketzos HaChoshen* (ibid.), *Kenessess HaGedolah* (to Y.D. 161), *Beis Lechem Yehudah* (ibid.), *Haflaah* (to *Kesubos* 105). *Maharsham* 1:20 refers to this as the majority opinion of the poskim.

Igros Moshe (Y.D. 3, notes to Hil. Ribbis 160:6) also points out that Ribbis payments

An Exception: The Repentant Moneylender

15. Although the Torah obligates a lender to return Ribbis Ketzutzah in all cases, there is one situation where we generally do not accept reimbursement. This involves a professional moneylender, who had collected Ribbis on a routine basis as his regular source of income. When this individual seeks to repent, the obligation to repay all of the interest which he had collected would be too great a burden, and may very well dissuade him from repenting. For this reason, the Rabbis instructed that we should not accept reimbursement from someone in this situation, "to open the path of repentance to him."[24]

16. This applies even when the lender is a wealthy man, who has sufficient funds with which to make reimbursement.[25]

17. This exception applies only where the following conditions are present:

☐ The moneylender repented on his own accord, without being compelled to do so. If he offers to repay Ribbis only after being summoned to Beis Din, his reimbursement is accepted.[26]

☐ The individual's major source of income involved the collecting of Ribbis. This does not apply to someone who had another occupation, but frequently lent money as a secondary source of income.[27]

---

are generally made willingly by a borrower who wishes to honor his commitment to do so. His subsequent failure to request reimbursement is no more than an extension of that attitude, and cannot be seen as reflecting a decision to be *mocheil* his right to reimbursement.

24. Y.D. 161:7. [An identical practice is applied to a repentant thief, see C.M. 366:1.] One who does accept reimbursement is in violation of this ruling, and the Rabbis express displeasure with his conduct (*'ein ruach chachamim nochah heimenu'*). However, he is not considered a thief, since he accepted money to which he is truly entitled. He is certainly not obligated to return this money to the lender.

25. *Sma* (C.M. 366:1). This is because the enormous expenditure is a deterrent to his repentance.

26. Y.D. ibid.; *Shach* (161:12) adds, "But if he is unrepentant, we force him to return (the Ribbis)." This leaves unclear the status of an individual whose repentance was precipitated by his being called to Beis Din. *Rema* (to C.M. 366:1) implies that in this case reimbursement may be accepted (*Bris Yehudah* 8:75 rules this way, based on *Shitah Mikubetzes* to *Bava Kama* 94b).

27. Y.D. ibid.

□ The Ribbis payment was not made with an unusual or distinctive item. If such an item was given as Ribbis and it is still in the lender's possession, its return should be accepted.[28]

18. Although we do not require a repentant moneylender to return Ribbis, he has a moral obligation (*latzeis yidei shamayim*) to do so.[29] Therefore, if he presses the borrower to accept reimbursement even after the borrower refuses to accept it, the payment may be accepted.[30]

Returning Rabbinically Prohibited Ribbis

19. The obligation to return Ribbis was not extended to Rabbinically prohibited forms of Ribbis. However, there is a moral obligation (*latzeis yidei shamayim*) to return Ribbis DeRabbanan.[31]

The borrower may not compel the lender to fulfill his moral obligation to return Ribbis DeRabbanan. If the borrower seizes the money or item which he had given the lender as Ribbis, the borrower must return it to the lender.[32]

20. If the lender offers to return Ribbis DeRabbanan because he believes that halachah requires that he do so, the borrower may not accept reimbursement unless he first informs the lender that returning it is only a moral obligation.[33]

21. A borrower can retrieve Ribbis DeRabbanan, even without the lender's consent, in the following situation. When the loan itself (i.e., the principal) was not yet repaid, and Ribbis for the loan had already been paid, the borrower is entitled to deduct the Ribbis payment

---

28. Y.D. ibid. with *Shach* 11 and *Nekudas HaKesef*. [This is similar to the ruling in Paragraph 7, above. See Note 13 for examples of 'distinctive items.']

29. *Shach* 161:13. If the borrower is truly willing to forgo his right to reimbursement, this constitutes *mechilah,* and most poskim rule that there is no moral obligation to repay (see Note 20).

30. *Sma* 366:4, *Bris Yehudah* 8:26.

31. Y.D. 161:2. For example, when a free loan was issued, and the borrower adds a gift at the time that he repays the loan, this is Ribbis DeRabbanan. If additional cash was added at the time of repayment, and the lender was unaware of this until he returned home and counted the money, see Paragraph 27, below.

32. Y.D. 161:3.

33. *Pischei Teshuvah* 161:3.

from the balance which he owes on the loan. For example, if he received a $1000 loan, and gave the lender a gift worth $100 in appreciation of the loan, the borrower is only obligated to repay $900 for the original loan.[34]

This applies only to an outstanding balance on the same loan for which Ribbis was paid. A borrower may not reclaim Ribbis DeRabbanan by withholding money owed to the same lender for other debts.[35]

Exceptions

22. One is obligated to return Rabbinically prohibited Ribbis in the following situations:

☐ The Ribbis was not paid willingly; for example, if the lender took Ribbis without the borrower's knowledge or if he compelled the borrower to make a Ribbis payment by threatening him. This is considered larceny, not a Ribbis payment, and reimbursement is an obligation.[36]

☐ A secular court compelled the borrower to pay Ribbis. This also applies where a Beis Din compelled payment because of an error in knowledge of the law.[37]

☐ The borrower was unaware that the payment is prohibited because of the laws of Ribbis.[38]

---

34. *Rema* 166:3. This is actually a subject of dispute among Rishonim, and *Shulchan Aruch* quotes both opinions. *Noda BeYehudah* (2:76) explains that *Rema's* ruling is based on the fact that the borrower is in possession of the money and cannot be compelled to make full payment where his obligation to do so is doubtful (*'hamotzi meichaveiro alav haraayah*). [A similar situation involving Ribbis Ketzutzah was discussed above, in Paragraph 3.]

35. *Mishnas Ribbis* 21:13, from B.M. 67.

36. Y.D. 161:4. This does not apply when the borrower willingly handed the Ribbis to the lender, even if he did so because the lender pressured him (*Igros Moshe*, notes to *Hil. Ribbis* 161:22).

37. Y.D. ibid.. This does not apply where the Beis Din made an error in judgment (*Chavos Daas* 161:3). If the Beis Din required payment of Ribbis DeRabbanan because evidence that this was a Ribbis payment was not available to them, and that evidence was later presented, some poskim require the lender to return the Ribbis (*Shach* 161:6; cf. R' Akiva Eiger who quotes a dissenting opinion).

38. *Bris Yehudah* (8:28), based on *Imrei Binah* (Responsa 2:15) and *Tiferes LeMoshe* (to Y.D. 161).

Heirs

23. If an individual collected Ribbis and then died, his heirs have no obligation to return the Ribbis, even if he had taken Ribbis Ketzutzah.[39]

The only case where heirs are obligated to this rule is when *all* the following factors are present:[40]

    a) When Ribbis Ketzutzah was collected;[41]

    b) when the lender regretted collecting Ribbis and indicated a desire to return the Ribbis before he died;

    c) when an unusual or distinctive item was given as Ribbis, and the item was still in the lender's possession when he died.[42]

24. If someone lent money for Ribbis and died before actually collecting it, his heirs may not accept the Ribbis payment. This is even true where the Ribbis had already accrued to the person's account before he died.[43] This applies to both Ribbis Ketzutzah and Ribbis DeRabbanan.[44]

25. If the borrower died after paying Ribbis, it is not clear that the mitzvah to return Ribbis still applies. Therefore, his heirs cannot compel the lender to return the Ribbis which was collected.[45]

---

39. Y.D. 161:6. The mitzvah to repay Ribbis is incumbent on the lender himself, and does not apply to anyone else. This has been explained above, Note 1. The heirs do not even have a moral obligation (*latzeis yidei shamayim*) to return Ribbis (*Bris Yehudah* 8:n41). If the heirs choose to return the Ribbis, they may certainly do so.

    If Beis Din had ordered the lender to return the Ribbis, but he died before complying with their ruling, *Shaar Deah* maintains that the heirs are obligated to return the Ribbis. Cf. *Imrei Binah* who disagrees.

40. Y.D. 161:6. In this case, the obligation to return Ribbis is as an expression of respect for the deceased father, and not because of the mitzvah to repay Ribbis (*Shach* 10). *Machneh Ephraim* §8 rules that this obligation applies to all heirs, and is not restricted to cases where the heirs are the deceased's children.

41. Where Ribbis DeRabbanan was involved, the obligation *latzeis yidei shamayim* extends to the heirs (*Shitah Mikubetzes* 61b, *Mishnah LaMelech* to *Hil. Malveh* 4:4, *Divrei Sofrim* 161:40).

42. This is identical to the exception regarding unusual items which was mentioned above in Paragraphs 7 and 17. (See Note 13.)

43. *Bris Yehudah* 8:17. If heirs did collect this type of Ribbis, *Bris Yehudah* is not sure if reimbursement is required.

44. R' Akiva Eiger to Y.D. 160:18.

45. *Pischei Teshuvah* 161:6, quoting *Dagul MeiRivavah*.

Trading Loans

26. According to many poskim, individuals may not trade loans. This means that Reuven may not lend money to Shimon, with the provision that Shimon will lend him funds at a later time, should he request a loan. This is prohibited even if both loans are for equal amounts.[46]

If loans were traded, the second loan (which Shimon gave Reuven) is seen as a Ribbis payment for Reuven's loan.[47] One who wishes to satisfy all opinions should 'repay' the favor which was given to him in the form of the second loan, by promising his lender (in this example, Shimon) a loan of equal amount, when he needs it.[48]

Less Stringent Forms of Ribbis

27. There are forms of Ribbis DeRabbanan which are on a more lenient   level, where there is not even a moral obligation to return the Ribbis. These include:

a) **Ribbis Mukdemes:** Gifts sent to a friend, in anticipation of a loan request, before a request for a loan was actually made. These gifts do not have to be returned.[49]

b) **Ribbis Me'ucheres:** Gifts sent to a lender after the loan has already been repaid.[50]

c) **Haaramas Ribbis:** This is a terminology used to describe various forms of Ribi. Where this phrase is used, it indicates a lenient level of Ribbis, regarding which there is no obligation to

---

46. This type of Ribbis is known as 'Halveini V'elveh Lach.' Y.D. 160:9 presents two opinions regarding this transaction. This was discussed above, Chapter 3, Paragraph 20.

47. According to some poskim, this constitutes Ribbis Ketzutzah (*S.A. Harav* §6).

48. See *Igros Moshe* (notes to *Hil. Ribbis*, 160:9, s.v. *uli'aniyas dati*); See also R' Akiva Eiger to Y.D. 160:9, who discusses whether the cash value of the loan should be given as a form of repayment. [Although it is recommended that one repay the lender in the manner described above, we cannot rule that this is obligatory. This is due to the many questions regarding *Halveini V'elveh Lach:* 1) whether it is prohibited at all; 2) whether it is a form of Ribbis Ketzutzah according to those who do prohibit this; 3) whether there is an obligation to return the Ribbis in this type of situation, and in what manner this should be done.]

49. Y.D. 161:2. The laws of *Ribbis Mukdemes* have been discussed in Chapter 2.

50. Ibid.

reimburse the borrower.[51] A penalty payment is an example of *haaramas Ribbis.*[52]

d) ***Ribbis BeShaas Perayon***: When the borrower repays his loan and intentionally adds money to the repayment, many poskim hold that there is no obligation to return the extra moneys to the borrower.[53]

---

51. See Y.D. 163:3, where there is an opinion that agreements to pay *haaramas Ribbis* are actually enforceable in Beis Din. Although this is a matter of dispute, it would seem clear that there is no obligation to return *haaramas Ribbis* once it has been paid (*Bris Yehudah* 8:1). This applies only where the designation of Ribbis as *haaramas Ribbis* appears in the Gemara or in the earlier poskim (*Bris Yehudah* 8:n3, quoting *Sma*).

52. See Y.D. 177:14. This applies to one-time penalties which are imposed when a loan is not repaid on time. This does not apply to penalties which continue to accrue every week or month. These would be a regular form of Ribbis DeRabbanan, where there is a moral obligation to offer repayment. (The laws of penalty payments are outlined in Chapter 9.)

53. *Chavos Daas* 160:2, in explanation of *Shulchan Aruch* (C.M. 232:2), maintains that this is a form of *Ribbis Me'ucheres*. Although there are other explanations of the *Shulchan Aruch* (see *Taz* 160:2 and *Shach* 160:4), numerous poskim accept the ruling of *Chavos Daas* (*Shaar Deah* 160:1, *Tiferes LeMoshe* to *Shach* 160:4, *Imrei Baruch* to *Chavos Daas*; see also *Pilpulei Charifta* to *Rosh* 67:7).

CHAPTER TWENTY-ONE

Shemittah*

A. The prohibition on collecting debt (1-15);
- When debt may not be collected (1-2)
- Loans (3)
- Borrowing household items (4)
- Guarantors (5)
- Collateral (6)
- Iska partnerships (7)
- Heter Iska (8)
- Bills for goods and services (9-10)
- Doctor bills (11)
- Debt which is not affected by Shemittah (12)
- Minors (13)
- Stipulating that a loan not be affected by Shemittah (14-15)

B. Pruzbul (16-30):
- Hillel's Enactment (16-17)
- The Beis Din (18-20)
- Someone who is unable to appear before Beis Din (21)
- Transferring real estate to the debtor (22)
- Language of the pruzbul contracts: three versions (23)
- Oral pruzbul (24)
- Dating the pruzbul (25)
- When is the pruzbul written? (26-29)
- After the pruzbul is written (30-32)

Appendix: Pruzbul forms

---

* The laws of Shemittah have no direct connection to the laws of Ribbis. They are included here because they relate specifically to the laws of loans.

Introduction

The Torah teaches that beginning from the time the Jews first settled Eretz Yisrael,[1] every seventh year, is a Sabbatical year, or Shemittah. The primary aspect of Shemittah is the injunction against tilling the land of Eretz Yisrael and purchasing produce which was grown in violation of this ban.

There is a second aspect of the Shemittah year which applies in all countries. This is a prohibition against collecting debts which come due before the end of the Shemittah year. This provision effectively cancels such outstanding debts.[2]

There is dispute among the poskim regarding the Shemittah prohibition on working the land. Some hold that the Biblical prohibitions remain in effect even today, while others hold that the modern-day prohibitions are Rabbinic. There is no such dispute in regard to the Biblical prohibition on collecting debt. All poskim agree that this applies only when most of the Jewish people reside in the land of Eretz Yisrael.[3] Since the time of the destruction of the first Beis HaMikdash, a majority

---

1. The Jewish people first entered Eretz Yisrael in the year 2488. They settled the land fourteen years later, in 2502, and the first Shemittah cycle began at that time. Many centuries later, after the Jews were exiled from Eretz Yisrael, there was a great deal of confusion regarding the precise determination of the Shemittah year (see *Darkei Moshe* C.M. 67:3, *Teshuvos Maharalbach* 143 and *Perishah* 67). In the sixteenth century, an assemblage of Torah authorities in Eretz Yisrael was convened to determine the Shemittah year. Our calculation today is based on their ruling (*Birkei Yosef* to Y.D. 330:137, quoting *Avkas Rechel*).

2. R' Moshe Feinstein zt''l (*Dibros Moshe* to Gittin haarah 52) presents a detailed explanation of this law. He explains that Shemittah does not directly cancel debt. The debt actually exists, but the Torah obligates a creditor to cancel it. [R' Yaakov Kaminetsky zt''l, in *Emes LeYaakov* to Gittin 36, offers a similar explanation.] For ramifications of this interpretation, see below Notes 5 and 29.

3. C.M. 67:1.

The Talmud (*Gittin* 36a) teaches that the prohibition of collecting debt is applicable only when the laws of Yovel (the Jubilee Year) are in effect. Elsewhere, the Talmud (*Erichin* 32b) demonstrates that Yovel is in force only when the majority of Jews live in Eretz Yisrael. Today, since most Jews live outside of Eretz Yisrael, the laws of Yovel are not in effect. For this reason, the Biblical prohibition on collecting debts after Shemittah is also suspended. [Although the Rabbis extended the prohibition of collecting debts, they did not extend the laws of Yovel; see *Tosafos* to Gittin ibid. and *Sma* C.M. 67:2, who explain why Yovel was not extended.]

Today, nearly a third of world Jewry resides in Eretz Yisrael, and it is conceivable that a majority of the Jews in the world will some day live in Eretz Yisrael. In the event that

of Jews have lived in the Diaspora. During this entire period, the prohibition is only Rabbinic.

In this chapter, we will examine the laws of this prohibition, as well as the popular mechanism, known as *pruzbul*, for allowing debts to survive the Shemittah year.

A. The Prohibition on Collecting Debt

When Debt May Not Be Collected

1. Once the Shemittah year has passed, one may not collect any outstanding debts. This prohibition does *not* apply during the Shemittah year, when a person is permitted to collect debt. It applies only after the last moment of Shemittah has passed and Rosh Hashanah of the following year begins.[4]

---

this happens, would the laws of *Yovel* (and the prohibition of collecting debts after Shemittah) once again become Biblical in nature?

[This question impacts other laws as well. For example, the Biblical mitzvah of separating *challah* from dough is also associated with the settlement of Eretz Yisrael by a majority of the world's Jews.]

Chazon Ish (Y.D. 64:2) rules that even if a majority of Jews were to reside in Eretz Yisrael, the Biblical prohibition would not be in effect. This is based on the Talmud (*Erichin* 32b) which teaches that *Yovel* takes effect only when the majority of Jews return to their tribal plots in Eretz Yisrael. *Chazon Ish* cites Rishonim who rule that the tribal division of Eretz Yisrael was abolished by the conquest of Eretz Yisrael at the time of the destruction. It would therefore be impossible for *Yovel* to take effect before the coming of Mashiach.

4. C.M. 67:30. The Biblical prohibition reads, *At the end of seven years, observe Shemittah. And this is the rule of Shemittah, every creditor who is owed by his friend shall restrain his hand, he shall not demand it of his friend* (Deut. 15:1-2). The words *At the end of seven years* imply that the prohibition begins after the seventh year had already ended. *Rashba* (Responsa 1:9) explains that it is the end of the seven-year Shemittah cycle, and not the Shemittah year per se, which affects the debt. This is why it is at the end of the cycle, which is at the end of Shemittah, that debt may not be collected.

[There is an opinion which holds that the prohibition of collecting debt begins at the onset of the Shemittah year. This is the opinion of *Rosh* (*Gittin* 4:18) and is based on *Tosefta* 8:11. *Shulchan Aruch* follows the ruling of virtually all Rishonim who reject this opinion. See also *Beis Yosef*, who points out that *Rosh* had an erroneous version of the *Tosefta* (see *Rash* to *Sheviis* 10:1). (See also Note 50, below.)]

When payment is made before Rosh Hashanah, Shemittah does not cancel the loan. However, if payment is made by check, and the check had not cleared before Rosh

2. If a debtor offers payment after Shemittah has passed, the creditor is obligated to inform him that he is canceling the debt because of the intervening Shemittah. If the debtor insists on paying, the lender may accept it.[5] It is recommended that a person pay his debts even if Shemittah has passed.[6]

To Which Debt Does This Apply?

3. Loans: This applies to all debt which results from a loan, whether a promissory note was written or not, and whether it was extended by an individual or by a corporation.[7]

If a loan had not yet come due when Shemittah ended, it is not affected by Shemittah. Therefore, if someone extended a ten-year loan, he could collect the debt at the end of the ten years, despite the fact that Shemittah had passed while the loan was outstanding.[8]

Hashanah, the loan is not considered paid and may therefore not be collected. This is true even if there are sufficient funds in the borrower's account to cover the check. The reason is that under American banking regulations a check does not represent a transfer of funds (as explained in Chapter 12, Paragraph 32, regarding the laws of Ribbis). It is simply an order of payment which instructs the bank to release funds to a particular individual. Until those funds are actually released, the debt remains unpaid. Consequently, when Rosh Hashanah subsequently passes, the loan may no longer be collected.

5. C.M. 67:36; the debtor should refer to the payment as a gift rather than as a settlement of debt (ibid.). The creditor may pressure the debtor to offer this payment (as long as he does not mislead him into thinking that he is obligated to do so) (*Shach* 67:11).

Dibros Moshe (cited above, Note 2) quotes *Tosafos Rid* who explains that the Biblical mitzvah of restraining one's hand from collecting debt is accomplished when a creditor informs his debtor that he is not obligated to pay the debt. If the debtor wants to pay anyway, the creditor may accept it, since he has already fulfilled his mitzvah by refusing payment.

6. *Chochmas Adam* (in *Shaarei Tzedek* 21:11), from *Sheviis* 10:9. This is also apparent from the Talmud (*Gittin* 37b; the incident involving Rabbah and Abba bar Minyomei). It is not clear why the *Shulchan Aruch* does not record this. (See *Dibros Moshe* ibid., for an explanation of this halachah.)

7. If a promissory note had been given to the lender, he must return it after Shemittah (C.M. 67:37).

Yichaveh Daas 4:64 requires that a bank write a *pruzbul* to collect on its loans. He rules that a single *pruzbul* is sufficient, despite the fact that the bank offers loans on behalf of its many shareholders.

8. C.M. 67:10. This is based on the aforementioned verse, *he shall not demand it of his friend* (Deut. 15:1-2), which implies that the creditor could otherwise have demanded payment. In the case of a loan which is not yet due, the creditor could not demand payment, even if it were not Shemittah (*Makkos* 3a-b).

This case is actually a subject of contention in the Talmud, which presents two contrary rulings without establishing a conclusion. The lenient ruling of *Shulchan Aruch* is

Even if the loan had come due (i.e., before Shemittah ended), if the lender and borrower agree to extend the due date past Rosh Hashanah, this would suffice to allow the debt to be collected after Shemittah has passed.[9]

If a loan has no due date, but is payable on (for example) seven days' notice, Shemittah does not affect the loan as long as notice is not given.[10]

4. Borrowing household items: People routinely borrow household items (such as milk or eggs) from neighbors. The laws of Shemittah apply here as well.[11] Therefore, if the borrower repays the item after Shemittah passes, the neighbor is obligated to inform him that he has canceled the debt because of the intervening Shemittah. If the borrower nevertheless insists on paying, the neighbor may accept it.

5. Guarantors: When a guarantor pays a borrower's debt, he becomes the creditor, and the borrower must pay him. The rules of Shemittah apply to this debt.[12]

---

based on the opinion of *Rosh* who maintains that this is a case of doubt, and since the issue is one of Rabbinic law, we rule leniently (*safek derabbanan lekula*) and the prohibition does not apply.

9. R' Moshe Shternbuch, in *Teshuvos Vehanhagos* 2:707.

10. [I have not found this case discussed explicitly in the poskim. However, this ruling can be deduced from the words of R' *Tam* (quoted by *Rosh* to *Makkos* 3b, in his discussion of a loan which had not yet come due by Shemittah). He discusses the case of a Yisrael who had loaned money to a Kohen with the stipulation that when the Yisrael has *terumah* which he is obligated to give the Kohen, he would keep the *terumah*, counting the money as payment. The Talmud (*Gittin* 30a) teaches that Shemittah does not affect this loan. R' *Tam* explains that this is a case of a loan which has not yet come due, and that this is why the debt is not affected by Shemittah. We see from this ruling that a loan which comes due upon fulfillment of a specific condition is not considered to have come due until that condition was met. (Although Rishonim question R' *Tam's* explanation, they do not challenge the basic consideration of this debt as debt which is not due.) It therefore follows that when debt comes due only after prior notification of a desire to collect, that Shemittah does not affect the debt until notification has been made and the debt has actually come due.]

11. *Chaim Shaal* 2:38:13, *Ben Ish Chai Ki Savo* 1:26. [This is similar to the laws of Ribbis, where we have also seen that these laws apply to the borrowing of household items.]

12. C.M. 67:5. A guarantor who pays a non-Jewish lender is entitled to receive the promissory note which was written to the lender, so that he can use it to demand payment from the borrower. He may then use the note to collect, even after Shemittah has passed. This is because the note represents debt which is owed to a non-Jew and this type of debt is not affected by Shemittah (*Rema* 67:17).

6. Collateral: When a creditor receives collateral for a loan, Shemittah does not affect the loan.[13]

7. Iska partnerships: In the next chapter we will be introduced to the concept of an Iska partnership. This partnership exists when an investor puts up capital and his partner uses the capital to establish and run a business. We will see that when the two partners agree to divide the profits equally, half of the capital is seen as a loan to the managing partner. This creates debt between the investing partner and the managing partner; the laws of Shemittah apply to this portion of the Iska partnership.[14]

8. Heter Iska: There are two basic types of Heter Iska forms. The more popular form is known as the *palga milveh u'palga pikadon* (half loan-half investment) form. [This can be recognized by the words 'profits and losses will be shared equally,' which appear exclusively in a *palga milveh u'palga pikadon* form.] When this form is used, the money which is invested is considered half loan and half investment. Shemittah affects the half loan portion, and it may not be collected after Shemittah has passed.[15]

Bills for Goods or Services

9. Businesses which offer credit for purchases (for example, grocery stores or supermarkets which allow customers to charge their purchases) are not affected by the passing of Shemittah, because when the customer pays, he is paying for a purchase rather than a debt. The laws of Shemittah therefore do not apply.[16]

---

13. C.M. 67:2 and 12. *Shulchan Aruch* records a dispute if this is limited to the value of the collateral, or if the existence of collateral changes the status of the entire debt.

14. C.M. 67:3. *Tumim* 67:6 cites the view of *Radvaz* (4:214) who disputes this ruling. The view of *Shulchan Aruch* is nevertheless accepted as halachah (*S.A. Harav Hil. Halvaah* §37, *Chasam Sofer* C.M. end of 50, *Kitzur Shulchan Aruch* 180:2; see also *Ein Yitzchak* O.C. 21 who points out that *Radvaz* himself, in another letter (3:564), accepts the ruling of the *Shulchan Aruch*).

15. A Heter Iska creates an Iska partnership and it therefore has the same status as an Iska (*Tumim* 67:6; Cf., *Ohr Zarua* quoted by *Maharsham* 1:52 s.v. *shuv chazar*).

16. C.M. 67:14.

This explanation is based on *Bach* 67, who cites *Tosafos, Rosh* and *Ran* who explain the exception of purchase credits in the manner presented here. *Tumim* 67:15 and *Shaar Mishpat* 67:6 cite additional Rishonim who concur with this explanation. [This is similar to the laws of Ribbis where we have also considered purchase payments as distinct from debt payments (Chapter 2, Paragraph 18).]

Another explanation: *Sma* 67:26 and *S.A. Harav Hil. Halvaah* §39 support a different explanation of this halachah. According to this view, Shemittah does not affect

This exception applies only if Shemittah passes soon after credit was extended. If the credit was extended earlier, and the merchant formally establishes the payment as debt before Shemittah passes, it has the same status as a loan.

An obligation is formally established as debt when the customer is billed. If Shemittah passes after this, the merchant may no longer collect his debt. According to some opinions, when the merchant totals the money he is owed by an individual customer, even if he does not actually send out a bill, this also formally establishes the debt.[17]

These rules also apply to wages which are owed.[18]

10. When an individual sells merchandise on credit, many poskim hold that Shemittah does affect the debt. According to this opinion, only purchase credits which are extended by businesses are not affected by Shemittah. This is because a business generally allows time for payment, and payment is not due until billing. However, a private seller generally expects payment right away; his credit is therefore considered debt, and is affected by Shemittah.[19]

---

purchase credits because payment for purchases are not due until they are billed. Usually, businesses ask for payment only after a period of time has passed; purchase payments therefore fall under the category of loans which have not yet come due. We have already seen that loans which have not come due are not affected by Shemittah (Paragraph 3). See also *Kesav Sofer* C.M. 8, s.v. *u'lfi aniyus daati*, who discusses both explanations.

The former explanation is accepted by *Bach*, *Tumim* 67:15 and *Shaar Mishpat* 67:6, and appears to be the opinion of at least nine Rishonim.

[*Rema* also seems to concur with this explanation. This is apparent from the opinion cited by *Rema* (and quoted above) that after a merchant totals the money he is owed by an individual customer, even if he does not actually send a bill, he formally establishes the debt. Subsequently, the debt is affected by Shemittah. This could only be based on the first explanation, since the customer's subsequent payment would be called a settling of debts; according to *Sma*, the totaling of debt should not affect Shemittah, since this does not directly affect the due date of the loan.

Kesav Sofer (C.M. 8) also points out that there is an opinion in the Talmud which maintains that Shemittah does affect loans which have not yet come due. This would indicate that the Mishnah's exception regarding purchase credits is not based on the law of loans which are not yet due. (*Kesav Sofer* nevertheless bases the second explanation on a source in *Yerushalmi*.)]

17. C.M. 67:14 and *Rema*. This concept is known as *zakfan alav bemilveh*, formally establishing a debt.

18. C.M. 67:15. [This applies to rental payments as well.]

19. *Beis Yosef* 67, *Sma* 67:26, *S.A. Harav Hil. Halvaah* §39, *Kitzur Shulchan Aruch* 180:10.

[*Sma* explains this ruling in a manner which is consistent with his explanation, presented above in Note 16, of the exception regarding businesses. We have seen that

11. Doctor Bills: If a doctor is owed money for services, this debt is not affected by Shemittah, unless the patient has been billed. Therefore, a doctor who treats patients after he has executed a *pruzbul*, but before Shemittah has ended, should not bill for his services until after Rosh Hashanah.[20] Bills should not even be prepared for mailing until Shemittah has ended.[21]

Debt Which Is Not Affected by Shemittah

12. Shemittah does not affect the following obligations:

☐ **Pikadon:** Money which was given to someone for safekeeping must be returned even after Shemittah has passed:[22]

☐ **Business Partners:** When partners run a business, it is common for one partner to have some of the business money or merchandise in his possession. Shemittah does not affect his obligation to return this to the business.[23]

---

numerous poskim disagree with this explanation. Still, since it is possible that they would agree with this ruling for other reasons, one should act stringently. Cf. *Tumim* 67:15 who rules leniently, based on his disagreement with *Sma's* explanation.]

20. This is sufficient to prevent Shemittah from affecting the debt, according to both explanations of the law of purchase debt.

According to the first explanation, payment for goods or services are not considered debt payment until billing. Shemittah therefore does not affect doctor fees prior to billing.

Even according to the second explanation (of *Sma*), where it is accepted that the doctor's fees are not due until the patient is billed, Shemittah would not affect the fees. When a doctor does not demand payment at the time of his visit, it is generally accepted that payment is not due until it is billed (or until the subsequent visit).

[**Billing insurance companies:** If a doctor accepts a patient on assignment and agrees to accept whatever the insurer pays, the fees are owed to him by the insurance company (and not by the patient). Since these are not Jewish companies, they may be billed before Shemittah ends. However, if the patient is personally responsible for payment, the doctor should not bill the insurance company before Rosh Hashanah since this would formally establish the fee as a debt. If he did bill the insurer and the insurer did not make full payment, he could not collect the balance from the patient after Shemittah passes.]

21. This is based on the second opinion in *Rema*, quoted in Paragraph 9, which holds that when the merchant totals the money which he is owed by an individual customer, even if he does not actually send out a bill, this is enough to formally establish the debt.

22. If a loan was given, but the promissory note refers to the debt as a *pikadon*, Shemittah would not affect the loan. This is because the contract is seen as an explicit stipulation that the loan would not be affected by Shemittah. As we will see in Paragraph 14, an explicit stipulation works to prevent the Shemittah prohibition (*Rema* 67:9).

23. C.M. 67:4. This is considered a *pikadon* (*Sma* 67:12).

- **Charities:** Money which is owed to charity is not affected by Shemitah.[24] This also applies to the loans which are issued by a Gemach (free loan fund).[25]

- **A thief's** obligation to repay his victims is not affected by Shemittah.[26]

- **Money awarded in Beis Din:** If a dispute was settled in Beis Din, and the Beis Din issued a written declaration obligating payment, Shemittah does not affect the obligation to pay. This is true even if the obligation is based on a loan, which was denied by the borrower. When Beis Din finds the borrower culpable, his obligation is not absolved by Shemittah.[27]

- **Ribbis:** Someone who collects Ribbis Ketzutzah is obligated to return the Ribbis to the borrower (these laws were explained in the previous chapter). Shemittah does not affect the status of one's obligation to repay Ribbis. Thus, even after Shemittah (or many Shemittos) passes, the lender remains obligated to reimburse the borrower.[28]

---

24. C.M. 67:28. Pledges which were made to benefit a needy individual are not affected by Shemittah, even if the pledge was already established as a debt (e.g., it was billed; see Paragraph 9). This is because pledges to charity have the legal status of an oath. Shemittah affects only monetary obligations and not obligations which are established as an oath (*Aruch HaShulchan* 67:8).

Gifts: For the same reason, if someone swears that he will give a gift, even to a wealthy person, this obligation is not affected by Shemittah (ibid.).

An oath that a loan will be paid: If the borrower swore that he would pay the loan (without explicitly mentioning Shemittah), and Shemittah passes, many poskim rule that he is not obligated to pay. This is because we understand the oath to mean that as long as the debt is outstanding, the borrower is committed to pay. If the loan is canceled for other reasons (e.g., if the creditor would *mocheil* the debt), the borrower certainly does not mean that he would obligate himself to pay. This applies when Shemittah passes; the oath does not cause the debt to continue (*Rashba* 1:775, *Maharik* 81, *Maharit* 2:69; see also *Noda BeYehudah* C.M. 1:31 s.v. *v'ode*).

25. *Yichaveh Daas* 4:64.

26. *Gra* 67:13, quoting *Sifri*.

27. C.M. 67:8. If the borrower confessed to the debt, Beis Din may choose not to issue a written statement, and the debt would be affected by Shemittah (C.M. 67:7 and *Sma* 17).

28. *Bris Yehudah* 8:17. Shemittah cancels most outstanding debts. However, the obligation to return Ribbis is not a debt, because this is not considered a financial obligation. Rather, it is a separate mitzvah obligation (as explained in the Introduction to Chapter 20), to which the rules of debt cancellation on Shemittah do not apply.

13. Minors: Loans made by minors are not affected by the passing of Shemittah.[29]

Stipulating that a Loan Not Be Affected by Shemittah

14. When extending a loan, if the lender stipulates that the loan is being offered on the condition that the borrower does not exercise his option of not paying after Shemittah, the borrower would be obligated to honor this stipulation and pay the loan even after Shemittah.[30]

15. If the creditor contends that this stipulation was made at the time of the loan, he is believed even if the debtor denies it.[31]

---

29. C.M. 67:28 as explained by *Tumim* 67:25. *Tumim* maintains that this applies even if the minor reached the age of thirteen before collecting the debt. [Cf. *Minchas Chinuch* 477:1 who maintains that debt is canceled by Shemittah regardless of its owner's obligation to observe the mitzvah. This view differs with the explanation offered by R' Moshe Feinstein, presented above in Note 2. According to the view of R' Moshe Feinstein, Shemittah never serves to cancel debt. Rather, the creditor has a mitzvah to cancel the debt. When the creditor is a minor, he has no such obligation and the debt stands.]

A **non-observant Jew:** If someone owes money to a non-observant Jew and Shemittah passes, he remains obligated to pay. This is based on the above explanation of R' Moshe Feinstein. As quoted earlier, in Note 5, R' Feinstein maintains that Shemittah does not cancel a debt. It merely obligates the creditor to inform the debtor that he is not obligated to pay. It would follow that when the creditor does not offer to cancel the debt, the debt remains in effect. Thus, although the creditor has violated the Biblical prohibition, the debtor's obligation to pay remains intact.

[A person must try to avoid this situation, since he is causing the non-observant creditor to violate a Biblical prohibition. This may cause the borrower himself to be in violation of the Biblical prohibition of *Lifnei iver lo setain michshol*, which is a general prohibition on causing someone to violate *any* Biblical law. It is certainly preferable that someone who takes a loan from a non-observant Jew should stipulate that he will not enforce the laws of Shemittah, in regard to the loan (as in Paragraph 14).]

30. C.M. 67:9. The Hebrew phrase for this stipulation is עַל מְנָת שֶׁלֹּא תַשְׁמִיטֵנִי בַּשְׁבִיעִית״. (See *Kehilos Yaakov* to *Makkos* §3, for an explanation of how this works.)

This applies only when the stipulation uses the phrase presented here (whether in Hebrew or English), which states that the borrower will not exercise his rights after Shemittah. If the stipulation states that the loan is given on the condition that Shemittah does not affect the loan [עַל מְנָת שֶׁלֹּא תַשְׁמִיטֵנִי שְׁבִיעִית], this stipulation is not valid because it contradicts the Torah rule that Shemittah affects the loan. Such a condition (*masneh al mah shekasuv baTorah*) is not valid (ibid.).

31. C.M. 67:34.

The Pruzbul

16. The laws of Shemittah apply to a loan when the debt is in the possession of an individual lender. When a loan has been entrusted to Beis Din, these laws do not apply.[32]

17. The Tanna, Hillel, observed that people were reluctant to offer loans, for fear that they would lose their money because of Shemittah.[33] He recommended that people execute a contract to formally transfer their loans to Beis Din for collection, so that Shemittah would not cancel these loans. The contract which Hillel devised to expedite this process is known as a *pruzbul*. (This is an Aramaic phrase, meaning 'relief for the wealthy.') This contract is used by lenders who want to collect their debt after Shemittah. *Pruzbul* forms appear at the end of this chapter.

The Beis Din

18. **Must a Beis Din be present** when the *pruzbul* is signed?

This is a dispute between Rishonim. Some permit loans to be transferred to Beis Din, in the presence of witnesses, even if the Beis Din is unaware that this is happening. Although this opinion is accepted as halachah, the prevalent Ashkenazic custom is to convene a Beis Din and have them sign the *pruzbul*.[34]

---

32. *Sifri* (quoted by *Tosafos* to *Gittin* 36a) deduces this from the verse, *And this is the rule of Shemittah, every creditor who is owed by his friend shall restrain his hand, he shall not demand it of his friend* (Deut. 15:1-2). *Rambam* (to *Sheviis* 10:2) explains that when Beis Din is involved, collection is no longer an issue between the creditor and his friend, and the laws outlined in this verse do not apply.

33. This violates the Biblical injunction which appears in *Deut.* 15:9: *Beware, lest your heart have an improper thought, saying, the seventh year, the year of Shemittah is at hand, and your eyes will look at your poor brother in a bad way, and you will not give him. . .*

34. *Yerushalmi Sheviis* 10:3 states that a *pruzbul* is valid "even if they are in Rome." *Pnei Moshe* understands this to mean that even if the Beis Din is in Rome, creditors in Eretz Yisrael could give their debt to the Beis Din. This opinion maintains that the Beis Din need not be present when the *pruzbul* is signed. This is also the opinion of *Mordechai* to *Gittin* §379.

 Ramban (to *Gittin* 36b, see also *Ramban* to *Chullin* 4b), *Ran* (to *Gittin* 36b) and *Rashba* (Responsa 2:313) understand the words of *Yerushalmi* differently. "Even if they are in Rome" refers to the promissory notes; even if they are in Rome, a person in Eretz Yisrael may give them to Beis Din by using a *pruzbul*. According to this opinion, we have no basis for permitting a *pruzbul* to be signed by witnesses without the presence of a Beis Din.

 C.M. 67:21 brings both opinions, apparently favoring the former opinion, which

19. Some Rishonim require that the *pruzbul* be executed in the presence of a Beis Din which consists of people who are familiar with the laws of Shemittah and who serve as an official Beis Din of the community. Others maintain that a simple Beis Din of three people is sufficient. The Ashkenazic custom is to follow this opinion.[35]

20. Most poskim permit relatives of the borrower or lender to serve on the Beis Din which executes the *pruzbul.*[36]

21. **Someone who is unable to appear before Beis Din** may write a letter to Beis Din, transferring his loans to them. Beis Din would then write a *pruzbul,* which would be effective based on the day that the letter was written.[37] Another option would be for him to appoint an agent to execute the *pruzbul* for him.[38]

---

permits the *pruzbul* to be signed by witnesses outside of Beis Din. This is the ruling of *Aruch HaShulchan* 67:10. *Chasam Sofer* C.M. 50 writes that his teacher Rabbi Nosson Adler used this method: "He submitted his [loans to a Beis Din] through me and one other with me, at the end of the year 5544."

Since a Beis Din requires three people, Rabbi Adler clearly relied on the opinion that two witnesses are sufficient. This is also the ruling of *Yichaveh Daas* 4:63.

A *pruzbul* form which is drawn for use in this case appears in *Chochmas Adam* (in *Shaarei Tzedek* 21:6; see also in *Yichaveh Daas* 4:63, *Moadim Uzmanim* 6:18 and *Tzitz Eliezer* 12:85).

35. *Shulchan Aruch* accepts the first opinion, while *Rema* accepts the lenient opinion. The Ashkenazic custom is to approach three people and ask them to serve as a Beis Din specifically for the purpose of executing the *pruzbul* (*Kitzur Shulchan Aruch* 180:15 writes that they should be *Bnei Torah*, i.e., people who study Torah regularly; *S.A. Harav* §35 requires only *anashim kisheirim*, observant Jews).

This opinion is difficult to justify, in that the Talmud appears to require a Beis Din of *talmidei chachamim*. See *Chasam Sofer* C.M. 113 who offers a basis for the Ashkenazic custom.

36. *Minchas Yitzchak* 10:140, *Yichaveh Daas* 4:64, *Tzitz Eliezer* 6:39.

Minchas Yitzchak explains that the simple transferring of loans to Beis Din involves no decision on the part of Beis Din and that relatives are therefore not disqualified. (This is similar to a Beis Din which is convened for annulling vows, where relatives may serve.) If there would be a dispute between borrower and lender, they would approach another Beis Din. Cf. *Tumim* 67:23 who questions whether relatives may serve on this Beis Din, and does not come to a conclusion.

37. *Chasam Sofer* C.M. 113, quoted in *Pischei Teshuvah* 67:3. [In *Chasam Sofer's* case, the Beis Din recognized the signature of the sender. It is not clear if this is a requirement. It would certainly suffice if the Beis Din was presented with witnesses who recognize the signature.] An appropriate letter and *pruzbul* form, for use in this case, appears at the end of this chapter.

38. *Birkei Yosef* 434:5, *Yichaveh Daas* 4:64, *Tzitz Eliezer* 6:39. See *Yichaveh Daas* who explains why this works. It is not clear if all poskim would agree. The first method is

Transferring Real Estate to the Debtor

22. A *pruzbul* works only when the borrower owns real estate. Even a small amount of real estate is sufficient to satisfy this condition.[39] If the borrower does not own real estate, the lender may transfer a portion of his real estate to him. Since lenders are often unsure if their debtors have real estate, it is customary for a person who is executing a *pruzbul* to convey real estate to any debtor who does not own any land, by making a *kinyan* (usually through the members of the Beis Din).[40]

Language of the Pruzbul Contracts

23. There are three versions of *pruzbul* contracts:

a) **The short version:** This appears at the end of this chapter as *Pruzbul C*. This version incorporates the simple language of the *Mishnah* and *Shulchan Aruch*, and is valid according to all opinions.[41]

b) **A longer version:** Many Jewish communities added to the text of the *pruzbul*.[42] They included a statement that land had been transferred to the borrowers by the lender. They also included a short explanation of the mechanics of the *pruzbul*. This *pruzbul* appears below as *Pruzbul A*. This version may not be used by a person who does not own land, since he cannot

---

therefore preferable (i.e., the person would give a written note to the agent who brings it before Beis Din).

39. C.M. 67:22. *Shach* 41 offers the reason for this requirement.

This condition is satisfied even if the debtor only has use of someone else's property, whether he rents or was offered its use for free (C.M. 67:23). *Rashba* (1:934-5) rules that even if a person purchased a seat in the synagogue this is sufficient.

It is therefore rare that a debtor does not have real estate. Only someone who lives as a house guest with other people (e.g., immigrants who do not yet have a place of their own) or people who live in property which belongs to others would fall under this category (*Chasam Sofer* C.M. 50, quoted in *Pischei Teshuvah* 67:4).

40. If the lender owns no real estate, he would request that a third person transfer a piece of their real estate to the debtors. Most people would be willing to do this, since this involves only the transfer of only the smallest amount of real estate (worth a *perutah*, or one cent, to each debtor).

41. See for example, *Igros Moshe* C.M. 1:19, who writes that he used this type of *pruzbul*.

42. *Chikrei Lev*, cited in *Yabia Omer* C.M. 3:6. *Chochmas Adam* (in *Shaarei Tzedek* 21:5 and 8) also uses a longer version, containing a brief explanation of the *pruzbul* [and adding the words בֵּין בִּשְׁטָר בֵּין בַּעַל פֶּה. He also indicates (in 21:7) that when real estate is transferred to the borrower, this would be stated in the *pruzbul*.

transfer title to the borrower. However, he may use a version which contains the added explanation, without mentioning the transfer. This appears below as *Pruzbul B.*

c) ***Baal HaTerumos* version:** *Beis Yosef* cites a version of *pruzbul* which was used by earlier Rishonim. This *pruzbul* requires that a lender use a *kinyan* to transfer his loans to the Beis Din. *Minchas Yitzchak* [43] preferred this version and introduced it to his community in Yerushalayim. *Igros Moshe,* [44] however, is opposed to this version. This *pruzbul* has not gained widespread acceptance outside Yerushalayim.

24. Oral *pruzbul*: *Talmidei chachamim* may rely on an oral statement to transfer their loans to Beis Din (provided that this statement is made in the presence of the Beis Din). [45] Many poskim permit anyone to use this leniency. [46]

Although it is preferable that a written *pruzbul* be used, someone who is unable to do so (e.g., he forgot to write a *pruzbul* until the last moment before Rosh Hashanah) may rely on this opinion. [47]

25. Dating the *pruzbul*: A *pruzbul* must be dated accurately. If the *pruzbul* is not written on the day that the loans are transferred to Beis Din, the Beis Din must still enter the date of the transfer on the *pruzbul.* [48]

A predated *pruzbul* is valid; however, a postdated *pruzbul* is not valid. [49]

---

43. *Minchas Yitzchak* 6:160; it should be noted that the *pruzbul* form which appears in this Responsa contains numerous errors. A corrected version appears in *Minchas Yitzchak* Volume 10. (In the corrected version the creditor must transfer his loans by means of *kinyan agav karka.*)

44. *Igros Moshe* C.M. 1:19 and 21. See also *Chochmas Adam* (in *Shaarei Tzedek* 21:7) who indicates that it is not the custom to use this version.

45. *Chasam Sofer* C.M. 113.

46. *Shulchan Aruch* 67:20 limits this to *talmidei chachamim. Rema* extends this to everyone, even to someone who is in a different city than the Beis Din.

47. *S.A. Harav Hil. Halvaah* §35, *Kitzur Shulchan Aruch* 180:15, *Tzitz Eliezer* 5:11.

48. *Chasam Sofer* C.M. 113.

49. C.M. 67:32. Loans which are issued after the creditor transferred his loans to Beis Din are not protected by the *pruzbul,* and may therefore not be collected after Shemittah ends. A dishonest person could use a postdated *pruzbul* to collect these loans, since people would assume that they were included in the *pruzbul's* transfer to Beis Din. The *pruzbul* is therefore not valid. (This concern does not exist with a predated *pruzbul.*)

A postdated *pruzbul* is not even valid for loans which existed at the time that the

When Is the Pruzbul Written?

26. A *pruzbul* may be written any time before the end of the Shemittah year. However, the *pruzbul* is only valid for loans which predate it. For example, if someone writes a *pruzbul* six months before Shemittah ends, he may not collect payment of loans which were extended during those six months, unless he later wrote a second *pruzbul*. For this reason, it is customary to write a *pruzbul* during the last month (i.e., during Elul), before the Shemittah year ends.[50]

27. The latest time that a *pruzbul* may be written is the last moment of Erev Rosh Hashanah, at the end of the Shemittah year.

However, when money has been lent to borrowers living in another city where the sun sets earlier, a lender must be careful to write his pruzbul before Rosh Hashanah begins in that city.[51]

---

pruzbul was actually executed (R' Akiva Eiger to C.M., quoting *Ran* and *Tosafos Yom Tov*).

Tumim 67:27 questions this ruling. He points out that an oral *pruzbul* is sufficient. If so, even if we invalidate the *postdated pruzbul* contract, the *pruzbul* should still be valid on the basis of the creditor's oral statement to Beis Din.

Tosafos Yom Tov (*Sheviis* 10:5) explains that a postdated *pruzbul* is invalidated as a penalty for drawing a contract which could be used to cause people undue loss. This would answer *Tumim's* objection and explain why someone who writes such a contract is penalized so that he may not even rely on his oral statement to Beis Din.

50. *Dvar Avraham* 1:32, *Yichaveh Daas* 4:62.

The Talmudic principle of *stam halvaah shloshim yom* teaches that when a loan is issued and no payment date is set, the loan is due thirty days later. Since the month of Elul begins twenty-nine days before Rosh Hashanah, any loan which is issued during Elul of the Shemittah year is not due until after Rosh Hashanah has passed. As we have already seen, Shemittah does not affect loans which come due after Rosh Hashanah; therefore there is no need to write a *pruzbul* for loans issued during the month of Elul (*Rishash* to *Makkos* 3b). This is the source for the practice of writing a *pruzbul* during Elul.

This ruling is the subject of considerable controversy; see *Bach* 67, *Tumim* 67:16, *Shaar Mishpat* 73:2, *Kesav Sofer* C.M. 8 s.v. *v'ayin* and *Minchas Chinuch* 477.

Dvar Avraham (ibid.) maintains that this dispute is academic. He cites *Magen Avraham* 307:14 who notes that it is the practice in most communities today to repay loans within thirty days, and that this practice supersedes the principle of *stam halvaah shloshim yom*. One who writes a *pruzbul* and then issues a loan should therefore clearly set a payment date. If he desires that Shemittah not affect the borrower's obligation to pay, the due date should be set for after Rosh Hashanah.

For this reason, many people wait until a few days before Rosh Hashanah to execute a *pruzbul*, so that all their loans would be covered by the *pruzbul*.

51. *Minchas Shlomo* 47:2 discusses the case of an American who loaned money to a resident of Israel. He suggests that the Shemittah laws may affect the loan at the time

28. Some communities have the custom of writing a *pruzbul* before Shemittah begins. People who follow this custom must be careful to write a second *pruzbul* before the end of the Shemittah year, if they intend to collect payment on loans which are extended during Shemittah.[52]

29. At night: Most poskim allow a *pruzbul* to be written at night.[53]

After the Pruzbul Is Written

30. A *pruzbul* is not valid for loans which are extended after it is signed. If the lender wishes to collect on those loans he should stipulate that the loan is being offered on the condition that the borrower does not exercise his option of not paying after Shemittah [עַל מְנָת שֶׁלֹּא תַשְׁמִיטֵנִי בַּשְׁבִיעִית]. The borrower would be obligated to honor this stipulation and pay the loan.[54]

---

that Rosh Hashanah begins in Israel, which is approximately seven hours earlier than in the eastern United States.

52. This custom is based on the opinion of *Rosh* (quoted above, Note 4), who holds that the laws of Shemittah apply at the beginning of the year. *Shulchan Aruch* clearly rejects this opinion. The is also the opinion of virtually all poskim (*Radvaz* 5:2238, *Panim Me'iros* 2:174, *Yehudah Yaleh* 3:179, *Kitzur Shulchan Aruch* 180:13, *Rav Pialim* in *yisod yishurin* 1:11, *Yichaveh Daas* 4:62. This was also the practice of Rabbi Nosson Adler, quoted by his disciple *Chasam Sofer* in C.M. 50).

Still, there are poskim who recommend writing a *pruzbul* twice, once before Shemittah begins and again before Shemittah ends (*S.A. Harav Hil. Halvaah* §36, *Tumim* 67:26). The opinion of *Chasam Sofer* is unclear. Although he writes, in C.M. 50, that a *pruzbul* should be written only at the end of Shemittah, elsewhere (in O.C. 15) he derides those who do not take the precaution of writing a *pruzbul* before Shemittah begins (see *Tzitz Eliezer* 9:29, *Likutei Haaros* to *Chasam Sofer* O.C. 15 and *She'arim HaMitzuyanim BeHalachah* 180:25).

53. *Yabia Omer* C.M. 3:6, *Yichaveh Daas* 4:64, *Tzitz Eliezer* 6:39. Executing a *pruzbul* involves a transfer of loans and is not a formal act of Beis Din, which could only take place during the day.

54. See Paragraph 14 (and Note 30) where this was explained.

It should be noted that *Chasam Sofer* (C.M. 113) maintains that one is not permitted to attach this stipulation to the loan. *Chasam Sofer* argues that *Shulchan Aruch* rules only that this stipulation is valid, not that one is permitted to attach it to a loan. According to this view, someone who does so violates the prohibition of *Beware, lest your heart have an improper thought, saying, the seventh year, the year of Shemittah is at hand, and your eyes will look at your poor brother in a bad way, and you will not give him* (Deut. 15:9). As proof of his position, *Chasam Sofer* questions why it was necessary for Hillel to introduce a *pruzbul* when the Shemittah injunction could easily be avoided by expressing this stipulation. He therefore concludes that this stipulation is not a proper option.

Pischei Teshuvah (67:2) expresses surprise that *Chasam Sofer* fails to note that *Ritva* already questioned the need of a *pruzbul* when this stipulation would suffice. His answer,

31. It is the custom of certain communities for individuals to extend small loans after executing a *pruzbul*. These loans are not included in the *pruzbul* and are therefore affected by Shemittah. This is done to give people the opportunity of performing the mitzvah of canceling loans after Shemittah.[55]

32. The lender is given the *pruzbul* contract. It is the custom to save the *pruzbul*, at least until Rosh Hashanah passes. However, even if the *pruzbul* is lost before Rosh Hashanah, the lender is permitted to collect his debt.[56]

---

quoted by *Beis Yosef* (in *Bedek Habayis* to C.M. 67), is that a lender does not always desire to use this stipulation. For example, if he issues a thirty-day loan, a year before Shemittah, he wants to receive payment long before Shemittah ends. If he were to attach this stipulation to the loan, the lender would be intimating to the borrower that he anticipates that the loan would remain outstanding for a year. A lender would not want to convey this impression.

It is clear from the words of *Ritva* that a person may attach this stipulation to a loan. The fact that *Beis Yosef* quotes this without dissent indicates that he agrees with this ruling. *Pischei Teshuvah* also quotes *Tevuas Shor* who offered another answer to the question of why a *pruzbul* is needed. This indicates that he too holds that this stipulation may be used.

Another option: One who wishes to satisfy the opinion of *Chasam Sofer* and still collect payment may stipulate that the loans become due on the day after Rosh Hashanah. We have already seen (in Paragraph 3) that when payment is due after the Shemittah year, the debt is not affected by Shemittah.

55. *Ben Ish Chai* to *Ki Savo* 1:26.
56. *Mahari Asad* (also known as *Yehudah Yaleh*) 2:179.

Appendix to Chapter Twenty-One:
Pruzbul Forms

Pruzbul A:
For Use by One Who Owns Real Estate

פרוזבול למי שיש לו קרקע

במותב תלתא כחדא הוינא כד אתא _____ המלוה ואמר לפנינו:

_____ מוסרני לכם

הדיינים שבעיר _____ , שכל חוב שיש לי בין בשטר בין בעל פה

שאגבנו כל זמן שארצה. וגם אני מודה שהקניתי קרקע מארעא דאית לי לכל

לוה שאין לו קרקע. ואם לא תגבוהו אתם, כיון שמסרתי לכם פרוזבול זה, הרי

אני גובה כל חוב שיש לי עד היום אצל כל אדם כל זמן שארצה.

ואנחנו ב"ד שמענו דבריו ויפינו כחו דלא תשמט ליה ויגבה כל חובותיו על ידי

פרוזבול זה כתקנת הלל וחז"ל.

ועל זה באנו על החתימה יום _____ לחודש אלול שנת תש _____ .

_____ נאום

_____ נאום

_____ נאום

Directions for using the pruzbul:

- ☐ Fill in the spaces on the *pruzbul*.
- ☐ Make a *kinyan*, giving a portion of your real estate to each debtor.
- ☐ Read lines two through six of the *pruzbul* to the *dayanim*.
- ☐ Have the *dayanim* sign the *pruzbul*.

IMPORTANT: This *pruzbul* is not valid for loans which are extended after it is signed. If additional loans are offered, be careful to say, "עַל מְנָת שֶׁלֹּא תַשְׁמִיטֵנִי בִּשְׁבִיעִית".

Pruzbul B:
For Use by One Who Does Not Own Real Estate

פרוזבול למי שאין לו קרקע

במותב תלתא כחדא הוינא כד אתא _____ _____ המלוה ואמר לפנינו:
מוסרני לכם _____
הדיינים שבעיר _____, שכל חוב שיש לי בין בשטר בעל פה
שאגבנו כל זמן שארצה. ואם לא תגבוהו אתם, כיון שמסרתי לכם פרוזבול זו,
הרי אני גובה כל חוב שיש לי עד היום אצל כל אדם כל זמן שארצה.
ואנחנו ב״ד שמענו דבריו ויפינו כחו דלא תשמט ליה ויגבה כל חובותיו על ידי
פרוזבול זו כתקנת הלל וחז״ל.

ועל זה באנו החתימה יום _____ לחודש אלול שנת תש _____ .

נאום _____

נאום _____

נאום _____

Directions for using the pruzbul:

☐ Fill in the spaces on the *pruzbul*.

☐ Have someone make a *kinyan*, giving a portion of his real estate to each of your debtors.

☐ Read lines two through five of the *pruzbul* to the *dayanim*.

☐ Have the *dayanim* sign the *pruzbul*.

IMPORTANT: This *pruzbul* is not valid for loans which are extended after it is signed. If additional loans are offered, be careful to say, "עַל מְנָת שֶׁלֹּא תַּשְׁמִיטֵנִי בַּשְּׁבִיעִית".

Pruzbul C:
Short Pruzbul Form

פרוזבול

במותב תלתא כחדא הוינא כד אתא _____ המלוה ואמר לפנינו:

מוסרני לכם _____

הדיינים שבעיר _____ שכל חובות שיש לי שאגבה אותם כל זמן

שארצה.

ועל זה באנו על החתימה יום _____ לחודש אלול שנת תש_____

נאום _____

נאום _____

נאום _____

Directions for using the pruzbul:

☐ Fill in the spaces on the *pruzbul*.

☐ Make a *kinyan*, giving a portion of your real estate to each debtor. If you do not have real estate, ask the *dayanim* to do this for you.

☐ Read the second and third lines of the *pruzbul* to the *dayanim*.

☐ Have the *dayanim* sign the *pruzbul*.

IMPORTANT: This *pruzbul* is not valid for loans which are extended after it is signed. If additional loans are offered, be careful to say, "עַל מְנָת שֶׁלֹּא תַשְׁמִיטֵנִי בַּשְׁבִיעִית."

Pruzbul D:
When One Is Unable to Appear Before Beis Din

Form of Letter to Be Sent to Beis Din

מוסרני לכם _____ הדיינים

שבעיר _____ שכל חובות שיש לי בין בשטר בין בעל פה,

שאגבנו כל זמן שארצה.

יום _____ לחודש _____ שנת תש _____.

חתימה: _____

Directions for using this letter:

Fill in the spaces, and mail to a member of the Beis Din, together with proof of signature (e.g., names of people accessible to the Beis Din, who recognize the signature). Leave sufficient time for this to arrive before Rosh Hashanah.

Pruzbul Form to Be Used by Beis Din

פרוזבול למי שאין יכול לבוא לפני ב״ד

במותב תלתא כחדא הוינא ואתא קדמנא מכתב הנודע לנו שהוא בחתימת יד

החתום מטה, וזה היה נוסח הכתב ההוא:

מוסרני לכם _____

הדיינים שבעיר _____ שכל חובות שיש לי בין בשטר בין בעל פה,

שאגבנו כל זמן שארצה, חתימה: _____ .

ומדאתברר לן שכן הוא, אשרנוהו וקיימנוהו כדחזי ויהיה לפרוזבול זה כל תוקף

ועוז עד יום חתימת כתב הנ״ל, יום _____ לחודש _____ שנת תש____ .

ועל זה באנו על החתימה יום _____ לחודש _____ שנת תש____ .

נאום _____

נאום _____

נאום _____

Directions for using this pruzbul:

- ☐ Fill in the spaces on the *pruzbul*, writing the sender's name at the end of line 5, the date of the signing of the *pruzbul* on line 7 and the date of his letter on line 8.

- ☐ Have someone make a *kinyan*, giving a portion of his real estate to each of the sender's debtors.

- ☐ The *dayanim* sign the *pruzbul*, and mail it to the sender.

IMPORTANT: This *pruzbul* is not valid for loans which are extended after the letter was signed. If additional loans are offered, be careful to say, "עַל מְנָת שֶׁלֹּא תַשְׁמִיטֵנִי בַּשְׁבִיעִית."

CHAPTER TWENTY-TWO

Understanding A Heter Iska

Introduction

The Heter Iska form is known to most people as a contract which allows a person to avoid the restrictions posed by the Ribbis prohibitions. Although a Heter Iska does usually accomplish this, it must be understood that a Heter Iska does not permit Ribbis charges. *Igros Moshe* admonishes us to understand that a Heter Iska "is not a magic incantation or lucky charm which works (to dispel the prohibition of Ribbis)."

A Heter Iska operates in a specific manner: to structure the 'loan' as an investment for which profits may be paid. Many poskim[1] require that both sides understand the concept of a Heter Iska before they can enter into such an agreement. In this chapter, we will explain the mechanics of a Heter Iska. Heter Iska forms and specific instructions will be presented in the chapter which follows.

The concept of Heter Iska appears nowhere in the Talmud. The Talmud does discuss the laws of an Iska, which is a partnership agreement. The rules which pertain to an Iska agreement were later modified and adapted to form the Heter Iska agreement with which we are now familiar. A proper understanding of a Heter Iska must therefore begin with the study of the laws of a partnership agreement, known as an Iska. This is presented in the first section of this chapter.

A. Iska: A Partnership Agreement

The Concept

1. The concept of an Iska appears in *Bava Metzia* 104b, where the Talmud discusses a business partnership between two individuals. The first individual invests the funds which are needed for the project, but does not actually participate in running the business. We will refer to him as the investing partner. The second individual does not invest any funds in the business; rather, he receives the funds and uses them to purchase merchandise with which he runs the business. We will refer to

---

1. *Kuntres HaSma* 4, *Shelah Chullin* 84, *Chochmas Adam* 143:3, *Tzemach Tzedek* Y.D. 88, *Chasam Sofer* C.M. 48, *Igros Moshe* Y.D. 2:62, *Bris Yehudah* 35:4. If a Heter Iska was already used but the people involved did not understand what the Heter Iska accomplishes, see Chapter 23, Note 3.

him as the managing partner. The agreement calls for all profits and losses to be divided equally between these two partners.[2]

The Talmud calls this arrangement *'palga milveh u'palga pikadon,'*[3] half loan-half investment.

The concept of 'half loan-half investment' is based on the principle that each partner in a business is entitled to profits which are generated by his money. The Iska agreement entitles the managing partner to receive 50% of the profits, despite the fact that he did not actually invest money into the business. This means that the agreement treats 50% of the invested funds as if they were the managing partner's. This is because half of the money which was given by the investing partner is considered a loan to the managing partner, which he then uses to realize profits.

The agreement also calls for the investing partner to receive 50% of the profits which are generated. This means that 50% of the business funds

---

2. The case discussed in the Talmud involves an agreement which calls for a 50%-50% division of profits. This is the case described here. If the parties wish, they may arrange for profits to be divided in any manner they choose.

For example, the agreement may call for the investing partner to receive ³⁄₄ of the profits. In this case, the arrangement would be viewed as 25% loan-75% investment, and losses would also be divided, based on this same 25%-75% arrangement (*Rambam Hil. Shiluchin* 6:5; *Chochmas Adam* 142:23). In this case, it would be prohibited to divide the losses evenly, because doing so would unduly benefit the investing partner. Since he lent money to the managing partner (i.e., the 25% which is loan), this would constitute Ribbis (*Chochmas Adam* ibid.).

Alternatively, the agreement may call for the managing partner to receive ³⁄₄ of the profits. In this case, the arrangement would be viewed as 75% loan-25% investment, and losses would also be divided, based on this arrangement. Here, though, they may agree to divide losses evenly. This is permitted because it benefits the managing partner, not the investing partner; therefore there is no problem of Ribbis.

In addition, in the case described in the Talmud, the managing partner does not invest his own funds in the business. However, two people can arrange an Iska contract even if the managing partner does invest his own funds. In this case, his share in the business would grow, based on the amount of money he invests. The investing partner's liability would still be based on his share in the profits (*Rema* 177:3, *Shach* 177:13, as explained by *Chavos Daas* 177:4).

3. *Palga milveh* refers to the 50% of the money which is a loan to the managing partner. The managing partner must return this money, even if it is lost in the investment. However, profits earned by this money are his, and may not be paid to the investing partner, since this would constitute Ribbis.

Palga pikadon refers to the 50% of the money which is invested with the managing partner. All profits and losses involving this money belong to the investing partner. (The managing partner runs the investment; the investing partner does not have to be aware of the details of his investment. This works in the same way as any other investment, such as an investment that a stockbroker makes on behalf of his clients.)

are considered his. Although he has actually advanced all of the business funds, the agreement treats only half of the money as the investing partner's. This is the 'half investment' portion of the business.[4]

2. **Guaranteed profits:** The managing partner may not guarantee that the investor will receive a profit.[5]

Rules Regarding Liability

3. **Losses which are shared equally:** There is a possibility that this business deal will not earn any profits. It may even be that some of the principal will be lost. Since this arrangement is half loan-half investment, both parties would share all losses equally. This applies to all normal business losses, whether they are a result of ordinary business problems (e.g., the business is unable to sell all of its merchandise) or general market conditions (e.g., the value of real estate goes down). In these cases, the investing partner and managing partner would share all losses equally.

4. **Losses which are the responsibility of the managing partner:** The managing partner controls the business funds. He is considered a *shomer*, or guardian, of the investing partner's moneys.[6] The Torah

---

4. To state this more clearly: Reuven invests $100 in a business deal, with Shimon acting as managing partner. They are to share all profits equally. Reuven is actually telling Shimon, "I am giving you $50 as an investment. All profits which are earned by these $50 belong to me. In addition, I am giving you $50 as a loan, which you are to invest in the business. All profits earned by these $50 are yours."

Later, if the business deal earns a profit of $60, we credit each partner's $50 with a $30 profit. The investing partner would receive $80 for his share of the business. Of the remaining $80, the managing partner would keep $30, and return the $50 which he had borrowed from the investing partner.

5. Y.D. 177:6.

Some poskim permit the following arrangement. The managing partner sets the anticipated profits at a specific sum; for example, $100. If the investing partner's share of the business profits exceeds this sum, he would still receive only $100. If the business were to earn $100 or less, the entire profit would belong to the investing partner. If there were no profits, he receives nothing. This arrangement is permitted because it does not obligate the managing partner to use his own money to pay the investing partner (*S.A. Harav* §41 quotes two opinions which disagree regarding this arrangement but writes, "The prevalent custom in these communities is to rule leniently, to make a Shtar Iska based on this, provided that liability for *oness* and losses is on both parties equally...").

6. There are two classes of *shomer*. A *shomer chinam* (unpaid guardian) receives no compensation for his work. His liability is limited. A *shomer sachar* (paid guardian) does receive compensation. His liability is greater.

Where an Iska is concerned, the managing partner is considered a *shomer sachar* (Y.D. 177:5 and *Taz* 177:9). The rules outlined above reflect the managing partner's status as a *shomer sachar*.

delineates specific rules of liability for situations involving guardianship, as follows.

A guardian is responsible for all forms of avoidable loss (*geneivah v'aveidah*), even in situations where negligence is not involved. If the business suffered a loss of this type, the managing partner would be obligated to repay the entire loss to the investing partner. However, if the loss is unavoidable and unpredictable, he is not responsible (this is known as *oness*). In this case, the investing partner would absorb half the loss.

5. These rules apply when the two parties made no other agreement.

However, the Torah permits individuals to draw up their own agreement, even if it deviates from the Biblical guidelines for liability. For example, a guardian who watches someone else's property has only limited liability, according to the Biblical guidelines. Still, if he agrees, he may accept full liability. This is a Talmudic principle known as *masneh shomer chinam lehiyos keshoel*, lit., a guardian may contract (to be liable) as (if he were) a borrower.

This principle does not apply to situations involving loans, if the agreement would violate the laws of Ribbis. In the case of a Heter Iska, this means that the parties may agree to hold the managing partner to a lesser degree of responsibility (since this does not violate the laws of Ribbis). However, the managing partner may not accept total responsibility, including responsibility for the portion of the money which belongs to the investing partner (since this would violate the laws of Ribbis).[7]

6. If an agreement was already made: If the managing partner accepts liability for the entire investment, while stipulating that he receive only half the profits, this contract may not be honored.[8] One of the two

---

7. *Rema* 177:2.

An investing partner receives profits because of the 'half investment' portion of the funds which he has advanced. This portion of the funds belongs to him (in the same way that funds which are invested through a stockbroker remain the property of the investor). An investment carries with it, by definition, a possibility of loss. If the managing partner would guarantee these funds against loss, this would no longer be a 'half investment.' Instead, this would be a loan to the managing partner. In this case, the investing partner would not be entitled to a share of the profits, since the laws of Ribbis prohibit the paying of 'profits' for loans.

We have therefore established an important concept: An investing partner is eligible to realize a profit on his investment only in situations where he risks a loss on that investment. As we shall see, this principle is crucial to the understanding of a Heter Iska.

8. *Rema* 177:25 states, as a rule, that an Iska agreement is not viable unless it conforms to the rules outlined here.

clauses (either the clause regarding profits or the clause regarding losses) must be struck from the agreement. Poskim disagree on how this is accomplished.[9]

Insurance

7. The parties to an Iska may protect themselves against loss by purchasing insurance. When purchasing a policy, both partners would share the cost of the insurance.[10] However, the managing partner

---

9. *Chacham Tzvi* 127 rules that the part of the agreement dealing with profits is left intact, and profits are shared equally. The part of the agreement dealing with liability is changed, leaving the investing partner liable for half of any loss.

Shaar Deah 177:1 quotes *Chacham Tzvi*, but disagrees. According to his opinion, the part of the agreement dealing with liability is left intact, so that the managing partner remains liable for the entire investment, as in the original agreement. The part dealing with profit sharing is changed, so that all the profits belong to the managing partner.

Shaar Deah's ruling is based on Y.D. 173:4, where someone sold a promissory note at a discount and guaranteed its payment. This agreement is not permissible. (When a note is sold at discount, the buyer must accept liability; see Chapter 12, Paragraph 2.) There, *Shulchan Aruch* rules that the part of the agreement pertaining to liability is honored, and the seller remains liable if the note could not be collected. The part of the agreement pertaining to profit is adjusted, so that all profits which are realized when the note is collected must be given to the seller. *Shaar Deah* applies this ruling here, and adjusts the portion of the agreement which deals with profits, while leaving the liability agreement intact.

This opinion is also consistent with the general rule for Ribbis agreements, which requires that any part of an agreement which calls for Ribbis payments may not be honored. Here too, we void the clause which calls for payment to the lender, according to *Shaar Deah*.

Since this is a matter of dispute, the principle of *hamotzi meichaveiro alav haraayah* applies. This principle teaches that in cases of doubt a person cannot be compelled to make payment. Therefore, if there is a loss, the managing partner could not be compelled to honor his agreement regarding liability (*Erech Shai* 177:1, quoted in *Bris Yehudah* 37:n14).

[The fact that the managing partner could not be compelled to pay, even if only because of doubt in establishing halachah, yields an interesting result. Once the managing partner cannot be compelled to honor his agreement regarding liability, this part of the agreement is effectively nullified. Once this is nullified, there should be no question that profits may be shared, since the managing partner does not have full liability. Thus, even though *Shaar Deah* disagrees in theory with this ruling, he should concede that once we nullify the managing partner's liability, the profit payments do not constitute Ribbis. This point requires further study.]

[In the case under discussion, the managing partner received payment for his efforts in connection with the investment, as is required (see Paragraph 8).]

10. *Bris Yehudah* 37:5 and Note 13 there. The managing partner may only pay the share of the insurance costs which is equal to his share of the profits and losses. (For example, when he is liable for 50% of the losses, he may pay only 50% of the insurance costs.) However, only the managing partner is limited to paying his share of the insurance; if the investing partner wishes to pay the entire cost of the insurance, he may do so (ibid). [This

may not act as the insurer, even if the investing partner pays him to do so.[11]

Compensation for Time and Effort

8. As we have seen, an Iska agreement creates a 50%-50% of partnership in which all profits and losses are shared equally. Still, the managing partner does all the work required for the investment. This work presents a Ribbis problem; since the managing partner has borrowed money from the investing partner (the 'half loan' part of the investment), he may not work for him without compensation. The investing partner must therefore compensate the managing partner for the time and effort which he expended on behalf of the investing partner's portion of the investment.[12]

9. Setting the amount of compensation: Arrangements for this compensation should be made at the time the investment begins. If this is done, it is sufficient for a token payment to be made.[13] [Many Iska agreements call for a token payment of one dollar.[14] This

---

is because the managing partner is a borrower. He is prohibited from protecting the investing partner from liability which affects his share of the business. The investing partner is a lender and he is not prohibited from benefiting the borrower.]

11. This is the subject of dispute between *Derishah* 167:1 and *Taz* 167:1 and 172:8. *Derishah* allows the managing partner to insure the principal, provided that he is paid for doing so. According to this view, the insurance deal is not part of the Iska. Rather, it is a separate business arrangement.

Taz disagrees. We have already seen that whenever the managing partner accepts liability, all profits which the investing partner receives are considered Ribbis. It should make no difference that the managing partner receives compensation for accepting liability. "This is similar to giving someone a gift (to influence him) to borrow from you for interest (which is certainly prohibited). This case is identical."

All later poskim follow the opinion of *Taz* who prohibits the managing partner from personally insuring the investment.

12. Y.D. 177:2. This payment is required to avoid Ribbis. For this reason, the managing partner may not elect to forgo payment (*mechilah*), even if he genuinely wishes to do so.

13. Y.D. 177:3. All Heter Iska agreements contain a provision for this payment. Where arrangements were not made, see Y.D. 177:2-4.

14. Many poskim hold that any token payment is acceptable (*Perishah* 177:6, *Beis Meir* 177:4, *Ginas Veradim* 6:4; *Darkei Teshuvah* requires only that the payment be worth a *perutah*). Others require a minimum payment of one *dinar* (this is the language used by *Shulchan Aruch*; *Birkei Yosef* and *Ben Ish Chai* to *V'eschanan* apparently understand this literally).

[A *dinar* is equivalent to 4.8 grams of silver. When the price of silver is $7 an ounce, the value of 4.8 gram would be $1.08. The price of silver is generally well below this level. The one-dollar payment therefore satisfies both opinions (*Mishnas Ribbis* 22:n5). In general, payment is usually made at the time that the partners enter into the agreement.]

10. An alternative manner of compensating the managing partner is for the Iska agreement to assign him an increased percentage of profits. For example, the agreement might assign 55% of the profits to the managing partner, with this additional 5% in consideration of his efforts on behalf of the business (losses are still divided 50%-50%).[15]

Compensation for Merchandise

11. The managing partner must be compensated for any personal property which he contributes to the partnership. This includes mailing or phone costs, merchandise which is sold by the business and materials which are used to conduct business. He must be paid their fair market value. If the managing partner purchased an item for himself, when it was inexpensive, and decided afterwards to sell it to the business, he must charge the business its full market value.[16]

---

the payment should be set at approximately one sixth the cost of an ounce of silver, to satisfy this opinion. See Note 41.]

15. *Rambam* to *Hil. Shiluchin* 6:4; *Taz* 177:5, *Shach* 177:9. *Bris Yehudah* 36:3 accepts this as the opinion of most poskim. [In 40:n12, *Bris Yehudah* wonders, "I do not know why those who draft Heter Iska contracts have refrained from using this method..."]

The usual method of compensation for time and effort would require a separate payment for each transaction. When a bank or business uses a Heter Iska Klali for all its transactions, it is cumbersome to require a separate payment each time the Heter Iska applies. For this reason, *Rambam's* method of computing compensation is sometimes incorporated into a Heter Iska Klali (*Mishnas Ribbis* 22:20). This method is used in the Heter Iska Klali found in Appendix II to Chapter 6, Clause IV and in Appendix II to Chapter 12, Clause IV.

Under normal conditions, an Iska calls for both profits and losses (or expenses) to be divided evenly. In that case, there is no difference if expenses are charged before profits are divided, or if the expenses are shared afterwards. Since everything is divided 50%-50%, there is no net difference in how this is done. However, when the arrangement described here is used, expenses are divided 50%-50%, but profits are divided 55%-45%. In this case, extra care must be taken to deduct all expenses before the profit is divided. Here, there is a difference if expenses are deducted before disbursement or afterwards. An illustration of this difference appears below, in Note 19.

16. Y.D. 177:22.

[However, if the managing partner purchases goods specifically for the business, any discount which he receives would belong to the business. If the business does not need a large quantity of this item, but the managing partner purchases a large quantity (for example, by finding others to purchase the extra amount from him) and receives a bulk-rate discount, *Bris Yehudah* 38:n56 questions whether this discount may be passed

Compensation for Expenses

12. The managing partner must bill all legitimate business expenses to the business. For example, if there are costs involved in transporting merchandise, he may not pay these freight costs on his own. Even if he receives full compensation for his time and effort, he must be compensated for all out of the pocket costs separately.[17]

Rules Regarding Profits

13. In an Iska arrangement, the investing partner lends funds to the managing partner (i.e., the 'half loan' portion of the investment). Thus, a lender/borrower relationship between the business partners is created. For this reason, the investing partner may not receive more than the amount of profit stipulated by the agreement. Many poskim also prohibit the managing partner from benefiting the investing partner in ways which are not directly connected to the investment. This includes all the prohibited benefits which have been outlined in earlier chapters.[18]

---

on to the business. However, if this type of arrangement is a common business practice, it appears that *Bris Yehudah* would concede that the discount may be passed on to the business.]

17. Y.D. 177:21 and *Shach* 45, requiring that the partner be compensated for transporting the goods. This refers to a community where it is the standard practice to hire people to transport merchandise. In this case, the managing partner is entitled to compensation even if he transports the merchandise himself. If the managing partner did absorb these costs by transporting the merchandise himself or by paying these costs out of his own pocket, he would be benefiting his partner (by absolving him of his share in the expense). This is prohibited, since the investing partner loaned money to the managing partner.

18. *S.A. Harav* §39, *Maharsham* 4:95, *Tuv Tam Vodaas* 3:35 regarding cases where a Heter Iska is used. See *Bris Yehudah* 10:n7 where this is discussed at length.

Chavos Daas (166:1) suggests that not all prohibitions apply to the Iska situation. He refers specifically to the *befarhesya* prohibition outlined above in Chapter 1, Paragraph 2 (where the lender is prohibited from receiving benefits which are technically permitted, because they are extended in a publicly noticeable way). As *Chavos Daas* points out, that case does not involve an actual Ribbis prohibition. Rather, the prohibition is based on the fear that it would appear as Ribbis; people who observe the situation may think that the benefits are being extended in appreciation for the loan. *Chavos Daas* suggests that this consideration may not apply in the case of an Iska, since it does not involve a routine loan. Since this is a case which only involves an investment, there is no fear of people thinking that the managing partner is indebted to the investing partner or that the benefits are being offered in appreciation of a loan. [*Chavos Daas* does not offer a definitive ruling.]

14. Business taxes are deducted from the profit before it is divided.[19] Income taxes are *not* taken into account when the profits are divided.[20]

15. Charitable donations: When the business donates money to charity, both partners must have an equal say in these disbursements. Where it is the custom of both partners to tithe their profits, each partner must be allowed to decide where to donate the tithe of his share in the profits.[21]

Similarly, one partner may not offer merchandise which belongs to the partnership as a gift to a friend. If either partner does this without the other partner's consent, he must pay the other partner for his share in the value of the gift. If he is unable to pay, the receiver is obligated to return the gift to the business.[22]

Diverting Iska Funds for Personal Use

16. The managing partner may not divert Iska funds for personal use. This applies even to the 'half loan' portion of the Iska and even if

---

19. *Rema* 177:34.

[In some cases, this would make a difference in the amount of profit received by each partner. For example, in the case mentioned above, Paragraph 10, the managing partner receives 55% of the profit, but losses are divided equally. Consider the case of a business which realizes a $1500 profit, but has a tax bill of $500. If the profit is divided before taxes are paid, the managing partner would receive $825 while the investing partner would receive $675. If each then pays his $250 share of the taxes, the net result is that profits were divided $575-$425. However, if the taxes were paid first and the remaining $1000 was then divided, the managing partner would receive $550, while the investing partner would receive $450.]

20. *Bris Yehudah* 38:n57. This means that if one of the partners is in a higher income tax bracket, he will actually receive a smaller net benefit from the partnership. [This is because income tax is a personal expense and not a business expense. Personal expenses are not reckoned in computing the business profit which is to be shared.]

21. *Rema* 177:22.

22. *Y.D.* 177:32. Giving a gift without the partner's consent is prohibited as theft.

[This prohibition appears to be independent of the laws of Ribbis. It is therefore not clear why *Shulchan Aruch* cites this law in Hilchos Ribbis. Perhaps the *Shulchan Aruch* is making the statement that this is not a true business expense. It would then follow that if the managing partner allows the investor to offer a gift from business funds (or merchandise), this would constitute Ribbis, because he is benefiting the investing partner. In addition, if the partners agreed that each of them could give a specific amount of the merchandise as gifts, this would not be considered a business expense, but a dividing of profits. In the case described above, where the agreement called for an even division of expenses, but gave the managing partner 55% of the profits, the right to give gifts would also have to be divided on a 55%-45% basis.]

all of the profits which accrue to the investment portion are paid to the investing partner.[23]

Attaching Conditions to the Iska[24]

1. Attaching Conditions Which Relate to Principal

17. The investing partner may attach any condition to his investment.

For example, he may stipulate that his money be invested only in a specific investment, or in a specific type of investment. The agreement may hold the managing partner liable if he were to deviate from these instructions. If it were to happen that he did deviate from the instructions, the investing partner would still be eligible to receive profits, if there are any. However, he would not lose any money if the investment sustained a loss of principal.[25]

18. The managing partner may deliberately violate the conditions of the investment, provided that he is doing so with the intention of

---

23. Y.D. 177:30. It is generally assumed that an investing partner prefers that the managing partner's funds remain in the investment, because this assures him that the managing partner will manage the investment with the proper care and effort (*Rashi* to B.M. 104b, quoted by *Taz* 177:37).

If it is the normal practice of partners to allow one partner to divert a [small] amount of money for his personal use, this is permitted (*Rema* 177:5).

24. It is important to fully understand the conditions which are outlined here. These two types of conditions (one relating to principal and the other to profit) form integral parts of the Heter Iska contract.

25. Y.D. 177:5. These types of conditions are permitted, since they are normal business conditions. As we shall see, these conditions are sometimes added with the deliberate intention of having the managing partner violate them, thereby allowing him to accept full responsibility for the funds. However, these must be normal business conditions. The following conditions may not be attached to an Iska.

- **Impossible conditions:** Conditions which the managing partner could not possibly keep may not be part of the agreement. For example, the agreement may not require the managing partner to be in two places simultaneously (i.e., when the funds are invested in two businesses, the managing partner could not be required to personally supervise both investments on a continuous basis) (*Chochmas Adam* 142:6, *Ginas Veradim* 6:9, *Bris Yehudah* 37:n18).

- **Unreasonable conditions:** Conditions to which businessmen would never agree, in the normal conduct of business, may not be added to an Iska (*Ginas Veradim* ibid.).

- **Unrelated conditions:** Conditions which have no relation to the investment may not be added to the agreement. For example, the agreement may not stipulate that if the managing partner eats grapes he would become responsible for the entire investment (*Chazon Ish* 66:1).

improving the value of the investment. For example, if the agreement required that the funds be placed in a specific investment, the managing partner may choose a different investment. In this case, the investing partner could only gain, since the agreement holds the managing partner completely liable for any loss of principal, but requires that he share any profits with the investor.[26]

19. When the managing partner violates the conditions of the investment, he becomes liable for the loss of all principal. However, he is not liable for the loss of revenue which he caused by withholding the funds from the planned investment.[27]

20. Another condition which may be included in the original Iska agreement states that if the managing partner claims that the investment sustained a loss of principal, he must prove it by presenting two witnesses to support his claim.[28] If he is unable to provide

---

26. *Rema* 177:5 and *Taz* 10. The managing partner may not violate the conditions of the agreement if his intention is to use the funds for his personal benefit (for example, if funds were diverted to help a family business). This would constitute theft, and the conditions of the Heter Iska would then be violated. Our discussion here involves cases where the managing partner's intent was to benefit the investing partner (*Rema*).

When the managing partner violates the conditions of the investment, he is liable only for the losses which are a result of this deviation. Losses which would have occurred even if he had not violated the agreement must be shared equally (*S.A. Harav* §44, *Chazon Ish* 76:1).

There is a dispute regarding a situation where the original agreement states explicitly that if the managing partner deviates from the terms of the investment, he becomes liable for any loss, even those which are not related to the deviation. *S.A. Harav* maintains that if this was part of the original agreement, it is a binding condition. *Chazon Ish* maintains that this may not be honored. [See *Bris Yehudah* 37:n19, who quotes both opinions but does not issue a ruling regarding the dispute. Since there are opinions (also quoted there) who disagree with *Rema* and disapprove of this entire arrangement, it would seem that it is sufficient to rely on *Rema's* ruling in regard to losses which are tied to the change of investment. It is certainly preferable that this leniency not be stretched to include other losses.]

27. *Bris Yehudah* 37:n20, based on *Kuntres HaSma* 4.

28. *Taz* 167:1, quoting *Terumas HaDeshen*. *Terumas HaDeshen* actually goes a step further, and allows the contract to name two specific individuals who must testify to verify any loss of principal, and precludes anyone else from testifying to a loss. This condition would make it extremely difficult for the managing partner to prove that his investment lost money.

Even when the Iska agreement does not designate specific witnesses, the Iska may exclude friends or relatives of the managing partner from eligibility as witnesses (*Chochmas Adam* 142:6).

Kuntres HaSma 8 and *Taz* point out that even *Terumas HaDeshen* permits this only

witnesses, he would be required to repay the principal to the investing partner.[29]

21. Bankruptcy: If the agreement requires the managing partner to produce witnesses to testify to the loss, and he is unable to do so, he would remain liable even if he claimed bankruptcy, and even if the courts accepted this claim.[30]

22. *Igros Moshe* expresses concern that in today's society, where many people are not scrupulous in their financial dealings, the managing partner may be able to find witnesses to testify falsely, particularly if they trust the managing partner's claim that a loss took

---

when there is a possibility that the two individuals who are named will be aware of a loss. The contract may not name two individuals who live in a distant town and require that they testify to a loss. Furthermore, the two individuals who are named should have some knowledge (*yediyah ketzas*) of the investment, so that it would be possible that they would be aware of a subsequent loss. Thus, the contract may set difficult conditions on the managing partner, but it may not set impossible conditions.

Some poskim object to this condition, even when the contract allows any witness to testify to a loss. They argue that this condition is indeed an impossible condition. Even if witnesses were aware of a specific loss, it is impossible for them to know with certainty that no profits were generated with these moneys during the entire time that they were under the control of the managing partner. Accordingly, *Erech Shai* (to 167) recommends that the agreement require the managing partner to swear to verify a loss, and that there be no requirement that he bring witnesses.

Still, virtually all poskim allow this condition to be included in an Iska. It should also be noted that the prohibition on accepting liability in Iska agreements is never Ribbis Ketzutzah, since the agreement does not guarantee that the investing partner will receive money if the business does not generate a profit (*Shach* 177:2). Since this involves only Ribbis DeRabbanan, one may rely on the lenient opinion.

29. The investing partner may insist that the managing partner produce witnesses (even though he knows that witnesses are not available and that this will obligate the managing partner to absorb the entire loss) even if he really believes that the managing partner is telling the truth and that there was a loss. Still, the contract requires the managing partner to repay the principal whenever he is unable to produce witnesses, and the investing partner may insist that this condition be honored (*S.A. Harav* §45, *Maharshag* 1:3).

However, if the investing partner has personal knowledge regarding the loss, he may not demand that witnesses be produced to attest to this (*Igros Moshe* Y.D. 2:62; *Bris Yehudah* 38:n6 cites additional sources for this ruling). For this reason, it is in the interest of the investing partner that he not know the details of the particular investment. In this way, he could not know if a loss was sustained (*Igros Moshe* ibid.).

30. *Mishnas Ribbis* 22:n15. The contract specifically obligates the managing partner to produce witnesses. The investing partner is not obligated to accept the findings of a court, even if the court investigated the investment.

place.[31] For this reason, it is a good idea for the Iska contract to specifically state that only qualified witnesses who are acceptable to an Orthodox Beis Din may be trusted to bear testimony.[32]

2. Attaching Conditions Which Relate to Profits

23. Since an investing partner anticipates earning profits from his investment, the Iska agreement may make provisions for a specific amount of anticipated profits. It may stipulate that if the managing partner claims that these profits were not realized, he would be required to attest to this claim under oath. The contract may even require that he make a solemn oath in the presence of a Beis Din, while holding a Torah scroll.[33] Since Orthodox Jews traditionally avoid making this type of oath, even though they are swearing truthfully, the investing partner would be reasonably confident that he will receive his anticipated profit.[34]

---

31. *Igros Moshe* Y.D. 2:62 and 3:39. *Igros Moshe* also points out that the managing partner may bring non-Orthodox Jews as witnesses, and cite their eligibility to testify in secular court as grounds for qualifying their testimony in Beis Din. He therefore recommends that the Iska require the managing partner to swear that a loss took place, just as he is required to swear if the investment did not realize its anticipated profit (in Paragraph 23). *Igros Moshe* assumes that the managing partner would be more reluctant to swear than to bring false witnesses.

This option has not been adopted by most Batei Dinim, who draw Iska agreements in the way it has been drawn for generations, requiring the testimony of witnesses. Still, it is a good idea to forewarn this problem in the manner outlined above.

32. This language has been incorporated into the Heter Iska agreements which appear in the following chapter.

33. *Taz* 167:1 and *Shach* 167:1, quoting *Levush*. Earlier poskim had allowed the contract to require that two witnesses verify that the anticipated profit was not realized. This was patterned after the Iska of *Terumas HaDeshen* (quoted above), which requires the testimony of two witnesses to verify loss of principal.

Levush objected to this. He argued that it is appropriate to require testimony of witnesses only where loss of principal is involved. There, the investing partner knows for certain that a specific sum was invested, and he may demand the most stringent safeguards to protect it. This is not true in regard to profits. The Iska contract set profits, based on the anticipation that the profits will be realized. It is not appropriate to require the testimony of witnesses to verify that this anticipated profit did not materialize. Because of these objections, *Kuntres HaSma* 9 changed this clause to allow for an oath to verify profits. This was accepted by *Levush* (as indicated in *Kuntres HaSma*) and virtually all later poskim.

34. This is the condition which is generally used in a Heter Iska. If the investing partner is afraid that the managing partner may actually take this oath, he may add conditions to the contract which serve to dissuade him from doing so. For example, some poskim allow a condition which requires that the oath be made at the time of the Torah reading in the synagogue, in the presence of the entire congregation (*Binas Adam* 9, *Igros Moshe*

B. The Heter Iska Contract

Creating an Iska

24. The first part of this chapter detailed the case outlined in the Talmud, where two parties were involved in a business deal which had been drawn as a half loan-half investment. In that case, the investing partner was entitled to receive profits from the investment portion of the moneys which he had advanced.

A Heter Iska works on the same principle of this Iska agreement. Suppose Reuven approaches Shimon for a loan, which he needs for business purposes.[35] Shimon would like to charge interest for the loan, but he knows that this is prohibited. He therefore refuses to offer the loan. Instead, he proposes that Reuven allow him to invest in Reuven's business, under the Iska guidelines outlined above, by offering half the funds as a loan and the other half as an investment. By becoming an investing partner, Shimon is entitled to share the profits which result from his investment.

This is essentially what occurs when a Heter Iska is used: A half loan-half investment (*palga milveh u'palga pikadon*) Iska is created. To protect the investing partner, certain conditions are included in the Heter Iska, as explained below.

25. Protecting the principal: When taking a loan, a borrower guarantees that the loan will be repaid. When a Heter Iska is used, the investor may not be guaranteed that he will be repaid. If the investing partner were to lose money, half of the principal (the *palga pikadon* half) would be lost. Most investing partners would be reluctant to use a Heter Iska if it involved this risk.

Y.D. 2:62). *Kuntres HaSma* 3 prohibits this, apparently because he considers this to be a condition which the managing partner would not possibly fulfill. Impossible conditions may not be attached to the contract. (*Binas Adam* and *Igros Moshe* maintain that since it is possible for the condition to be fulfilled, this is sufficient.)

If the managing partner is not an Orthodox Jew: It is the common practice to permit use of a Heter Iska (which includes this requirement for an oath) even when the managing partner is not an observant Jew (*Igros Moshe* 3:39). However, Beis Din generally does not allow a non-observant person to swear. For him, this would therefore be an impossible condition. See *Tam Ribbis* (*kuntres achron* 32) and *Mishnas Ribbis* 22:n11 who question why this agreement is valid.

35. See below, Paragraphs 30-34, for a discussion regarding a loan which is not intended for business purposes.

The standard Heter Iska form protects the investing partner by incorporating the condition outlined by *Terumas HaDeshen* (Paragraph 20, above) into the contract. This condition requires that any loss to principal be verified by two trustworthy witnesses. Although it is possible that such witnesses will be produced, it is highly unlikely. When witnesses are not produced, the investing partner is entitled to assume that a loss has not occurred, and his principal is returned to him. This greatly reduces the investing partner's risk to the point where most people would be comfortable making this investment.[36]

26. Protecting the profits: When investing money, a person is not sure that he will earn a profit. Before making this investment, the investing partner may request that a profit be guaranteed. While it is impossible to actually guarantee a profit, a Heter Iska provides for the likelihood that the profit will be realized.

The standard Heter Iska form protects the investing partner by incorporating the condition outlined by *Kuntres HaSma* (Paragraph 23, above) into the contract. The contract stipulates that the parties anticipate a specific amount of profit. It also stipulates that the investing partner has the right to assume that these profits were realized. If the person receiving the money (the managing partner) contends that the profits were not realized, the contract requires that he verify the loss under solemn oath in the presence of a Beis Din. Since Orthodox Jews traditionally refrain from uttering this type of oath, the investing partner is relatively certain that he will receive his profits (even if the managing partner will have to pay from his own funds).[37]

---

36. There is still one scenario under which the investing partner could lose his principal. If he has firsthand knowledge of the particulars of the investment and that a loss was sustained (for example, if he saw that the investment property was destroyed by fire), he could not require that witnesses be produced to prove this. For this reason, it is preferable that the investing partner not be familiar with the particulars of the investment [or that the Heter Iska be drawn up to explicitly include him in other investments which belong to the managing partner] (*Igros Moshe* Y.D. 2:62, *Bris Yehudah* 38:n6).

[Even if the investing partner saw the investment property destroyed by fire, he could argue that it may have been insured. In this case, there would not be a loss to principal. The managing partner would have to prove, by calling witnesses, that there was no insurance. This is a difficult thing to do.]

37. If the investing partner is afraid that the managing partner will swear, he may toughen this provision by requiring that he swear in the synagogue at the time of the Torah reading, when the entire congregation is present (*Binas Adam* 9, *Igros Moshe* 2:62; see Note 34, above).

27. This clause may be used only because it leaves the managing partner the option of making an oath. The standard Heter Iska form reads, "It is agreed that if the managing partner shall return the principal plus an additional $ _____ [the anticipated profit] for his share in the profits, the managing partner shall be relieved of the above-mentioned oath."[38]

Both parties understand that this option will be used, and that the managing partner does not intend to swear. This is nevertheless permitted, because the managing partner has the option of swearing and is therefore *not obligated* to make this payment.[39]

An Erroneous Heter Iska Form

28. An English-language Heter Iska form has been circulated with this clause: "It is agreed that in lieu of the aforementioned oath, the managing partner will return the principal to the investing partner, with an additional $_____ [the anticipated profit] for his share in the profits."

This language implies that the managing partner is *obligated* to pay, in lieu of making an oath. This is not a proper Heter Iska, and may actually entail a Biblical Ribbis prohibition.[40]

---

38. **A dispute:** The standard Heter Iska form calls for a one-time payment. May this form call for monthly or weekly profit payments?

Taz 177:21 prohibits this, although his reason is not clear. *S.A. Harav* §48 concurs with *Taz's* ruling and explains that this is prohibited "because when a set weekly or monthly amount is mentioned, it is obvious that this is interest and that the Heter (Iska) is only a subterfuge...".

Nekudas HaKesef (to *Taz*) disagrees, and maintains that it is permitted "and this is the custom." *Beis Meir* and *Shoel U'Meishiv* 3:2:147 concur with this ruling. Although *Tzemach Tzedek* generally follows the rulings of his grandfather, the author of *S.A. Harav*, in this case he concedes (in Y.D. 102) that the custom is to follow the ruling of *Nekudas HaKesef*. This is also the custom of contemporary poskim.

39. *Teshuvos HaRema* 80, *Teshuvos Maharam* 135, *Kuntres HaSma* 2. This has been accepted by virtually all the later poskim (see, for example, *Chochmas Adam* 142:7).

40. *Chochmas Adam* 142:12, *Bris Yehudah* 35:n54. This distinction is also explained clearly in *Teshuvos HaRema* 80. See also *Mishnas Ribbis* 22:n12, who alludes to this erroneous Iska form.

This form can be amended, as follows: "It is agreed that in lieu of the aforementioned oath, the managing partner has the option of returning the principal to the investing partner, with an additional $ _____ [the anticipated profit] for his share in the profits."

Bris Yehudah (40:n1) writes, "We see from the words of later Rabbis that many Heter Iska contracts were written without the advice of experts, and these (Rabbis) raised a cry regarding many which were not written in accordance with halachah. One should only rely on an Iska contract if he knows from whom (the wording of the Iska originated) and on which form it was based."

A One-dollar Payment

29. Most Heter Iska forms require the investing partner to pay one-dollar to the managing partner.[41] This dollar is not part of the investment and it is not returned to the investing partner, even if the investment realizes a profit. The reason for this payment has been outlined above, in Paragraphs 8 and 9. When using a Heter Iska form, the parties must remember to actually make this payment.[42]

---

41. A Heter Iska form in *Igros Moshe* Y.D. 3:41 calls for a fifty-cent payment. See Note 14, above, that the payment should preferably be the equivalent of (approx.) one sixth the cost of an ounce of silver. Thus, when the price of silver is under $3 an ounce, a fifty-cent payment would suffice according to all opinions. In fact, the price often fluctuates higher. This is why most Heter Iska contracts call for a one-dollar payment. [If the price of silver were to rise above $6.30 an ounce, this should be increased.]

42. This dollar payment is made to compensate the managing partner for the time and effort which he exerts for the benefit of the joint investment. This payment is required; the managing partner is not permitted to forgo this payment, even if he genuinely wishes to do so (the reason for this has been explained above).

Some Iska forms state that the managing partner has received a one-dollar payment, but do not actually instruct that this payment be made. Even if the managing partner signs this contract, thereby attesting to having received this payment, this is not sufficient. The managing partner must actually receive the dollar (*Bris Yehudah* 40:n3; Cf., *Chelkas Yaakov* 3:208).

This token payment is sufficient only when it is part of the original Iska agreement. If the original agreement did not include compensation, the *Shulchan Aruch* requires that proper payment be made (see *Shach* regarding the method of calculating this payment). Therefore, at this point, a one-dollar payment is no longer sufficient.

[*Shach* 177:14 adds that in communities where there is an accepted method of compensation, it is automatically assumed that the parties meant to use that method, even if this was not included in the Heter Iska. The author of *Mishnas Ribbis* argues that in our communities, it has become the accepted practice for a Heter Iska to require a one-dollar payment. Thus, today this payment should be sufficient even if not included in the Heter Iska.]

A second method of compensation: Not all Heter Iska contracts call for a cash payment. An alternative form of compensation has been described in Paragraph 10. That arrangement grants the managing partner a greater share in the profits, as compensation for his time and effort. This arrangement is usually used in a Heter Iska Klali, where a single Heter Iska covers many transactions. In that case, it would be cumbersome to arrange for a one-dollar payment every time an investment is made. This method is therefore favored. Most standard Heter Iska forms other than Heter Iska Klali forms use the one-dollar payment method.

An improper method of compensation: A third form of compensation would designate that any profits which are in excess of the anticipated profit would be payable to the managing partner as compensation for his time and effort. This is not a satisfactory option (*Kuntres HaSma* 2).

A Guarantor

30. When two Jews enter into a Heter Iska agreement, a third Jew may guarantee both the principal and the profit payments, subject to the terms of the Heter Iska.[43]

When he is guaranteeing the profits, many poskim require that the guarantor obligate himself by making a *kinyan*.[44]

Loans for Personal Use

1. When the borrower owns no investments

31. We have seen that when a Heter Iska is used, money is advanced as an investment. When someone borrows money for non-business purposes, such as to pay off household debt, there is no investment which generates profit. In this case, a Heter Iska should not be used (except as outlined in Paragraph 33). According to many poskim, if a loan was extended using a Heter Iska, it is not valid and the borrower would be prohibited from making payments.[45]

---

43. *Shoel U'Meishiv* 2:4:114, *Bris Yehudah* 38:7. The *areiv* would be required to pay only under conditions where the managing partner would have this obligation. Thus, if the managing partner is absolved from paying because he satisfied the terms of the Heter Iska (by bringing witnesses to attest to a loss, or by swearing that there was no profit), the *areiv* would not pay.

There is significant discussion regarding the technicalities of a guarantor to a Heter Iska. Under the terms of a Heter Iska, no payment is required when the managing partner swears that there were no profits. If the managing partner does make this oath, so that he is not obligated to pay, is the guarantor also absolved from his obligation to pay? Or does the guarantor's obligation remain intact unless he himself swears that there was no profit? See *Maharsham* 1:20, *Imrei Yosher* 1:189 *Bris Yehudah* 38:14, *Mishnas Ribbis* 22:39 and *Toras Ribbis* 16:18-23.

[As a matter of halachah, it would be preferable that the guarantee be attached to the Heter Iska document (or that the guarantor write 'done according to the Heter Iska' before his signature — *Divrei Sofrim* 177:E.D. 275), and that the guarantor state explicitly that he is appointing the managing partner to be in charge of the funds and that his oath would be believed in regard to profits.]

44. *Shach* to C.M. 129:12. Although *Ketzos HaChoshen* 129:2 disagrees, see *Nesivos HaMishpat* who defends the need for a *kinyan*.

45. *S.A. Harav* §42, *Ginas Veradim* 6:4, *Kitzur Shulchan Aruch* 66:10.

If the Iska money was already given for personal use, how can the parties correct this?

S.A. Harav explains that the person who received the money (the managing partner) should repay these funds to the Iska, by giving the moneys to a third party who takes possession for the investing partner. This money is then returned to the managing

32. In a *palga milveh u'palga pikadon* type of Heter Iska (the type described throughout this chapter), half the funds are advanced as a loan to the managing partner, with profits accruing to him. If these funds (up to 50% of the total) are used for personal purposes, with the remaining moneys invested, this does not affect the validity of the Heter Iska.[46]

2. When the borrower has other investments

33. A person who owns numerous income-producing assets may nevertheless find himself short of cash. He may be forced to sell some of his assets in order to raise cash, so that he can satisfy his creditors. If someone advanced money to him, he would be able to pay his creditors and still retain the income-producing assets which he owns.

According to many poskim, it would be permissible for this individual to use a Heter Iska to receive money for personal use. He would use this money to pay off his personal debts. The terms of the Heter Iska would then be applied to the profits which are produced by his assets.[47]

---

partner and invested, with profits shared in accordance with the Iska agreement. [Profits could not be paid for the period that the money was not invested.]

This applies when Iska funds were given for personal use. If the funds were given for investment, and the managing partner diverted them to personal use without authorization, *S.A. Harav* requires that the funds be returned directly to the investing partner (and not to a third party).

46. *Bris Yehudah* 38:9. In recording the prohibition on using Iska funds, *S.A. Harav* clearly states that this prohibition applies when the managing partner "spent more than half of the moneys...".

The managing partner would only be permitted to use these funds for non-investment purposes if he has the permission of the investing partner, as explained above, Paragraph 16.

47. *Shoel U'Meishiv* 3:1:137, *Maharsham* 2:216, *Imrei Yosher* 108, *Igros Moshe* Y.D. 2:62.

The leniencies of Shoel U'Meishiv: *Shoel U'Meishiv* goes even further. He maintains that even if the person who receives the money does not own any income-producing assets, a Heter Iska may be used. This applies whenever the money which is received is used to save other expenses. For example, if money had not been advanced, the person would be forced to sell his home to satisfy his creditors, and he would then have to begin paying rent. The money which he received allowed him to save this expense. This is sufficient grounds to allow for the use of a Heter Iska, and the sharing of 'profits' (- the 'profits' are the saved expenses). See also *Maharsham* 2:252 who concurs with this ruling.

Elsewhere, *Shoel U'Meishiv* (1:3:160) adds that whenever funds are advanced to someone who owes money, this saves him the time which he would have had to spend trying to collect this money. If the person is now able to use this time earning money, this time has a financial value. *Shoel U'Meishiv* rules that this is sufficient grounds for

3. Loans for the purchase of a home

34. Real estate which has a rental income: A Heter Iska may be used for the purchase of real estate which is a true investment. This includes the purchase of development properties and income producing properties.[48]

35. Real estate which has no income: When the money is used for the purchase of a one-family home, this practice is questionable. In areas where real estate prices fluctuate greatly, a Heter Iska may be used.[49] However, use of the standard Heter Iska presents various problems. The Iska may only allow the sharing of profits which the property actually shows. In addition, if the investing partner is aware that the value of the property did not increase during the period of the Iska, he may not collect the profits which were anticipated by the Iska.[50]

---

allowing the use of a Heter Iska. According to this ruling, even people who do not have income-producing assets would be permitted to use a Heter Iska in these cases.

Most of the later poskim dispute these leniencies. They maintain that indirect savings are not profits which can be shared by use of a Heter Iska (*Erech Shai* 177:7, *Teshuras Shai* 1:88, *Imrei Yosher* 108, *Maharshag* Y.D. 4, *Tuv Tam Vodaas* 3:2:40, *Igra Ramah* 19, quoted by *Maharsham* 2:252).

Bris Yehudah 38:n18 concludes his discussion of this topic with the words 'tzarich eiyun lemaaseh' (i.e., that it is difficult to give a ruling on this dispute).

48. *Maharsham* 2:216.

49. *S.A. Harav* §42, who maintains that a Heter Iska may not be used to finance the purchase of a home, because this is not a revenue-producing investment. A Heter Iska may be used only where there is a potential for profits to be realized by the investment.

Tam Ribbis (*kuntres acharon* §23) points out that in the time and place that the ruling of *S.A. Harav* was written (Eastern Europe, *circa* 1750) real estate prices did not fluctuate greatly. In situations where the market is such that the value of real estate may significantly increase in price, the purchase of real estate is actually an investment. Therefore, when there is potential for the profit margin stipulated in the Heter Iska to actually be realized, the objections of *S.A. Harav* would not apply. This is also the opinion of *Bris Yehudah* 38:n18 (s.v. *u'mekol makom*), based on *Teshuras Shai* 1:23.

50. *Mishnas Ribbis* 22:n22. [This is based on *Igros Moshe* 2:62, quoted above Note 29, who rules that the Heter Iska requires the managing partner to prove the amount of loss (and to swear that there were no profits), only if the investing partner does not have independent knowledge of this.]

Tam Ribbis (ibid.) reports that *Chazon Ish* also ruled that if a Heter Iska is used, and the investing partner is certain that the value of the real estate did not increase, he may not collect the profit to which he would be entitled under the terms of the Heter Iska.

When the standard *palga milveh u'palga pikadon* form is used, the investor is only entitled to half of the profits. Thus, a 15% return could be anticipated on the Iska, only if there was a possibility that the property value increased by 30%. For this reason, R'

36. *Igros Moshe* designed a special form for use when money is advanced for the purchase of a home.[51] This contract does not use a Heter Iska formula. Instead, *Igros Moshe* recommends that a sale-lease agreement be used. This works in the following manner.

In his example, a home is purchased for $20,000, with half paid at closing and the other half to be paid over time. The seller wishes to receive interest for the $10,000 credit; however, he is not permitted to receive interest. R' Feinstein suggests that the seller retain ownership of 50% of his home. He would sell only half his home for the $10,000 cash which he receives. Over time, the buyer makes monthly payments to him, until these payments total $10,000. With each payment, the buyer acquires additional ownership in the property, until he has paid the full $10,000 and becomes its sole owner.

In the interim, the buyer is living in a home which is only partially his. The seller is allowing the buyer to live in a home in which he has partial ownership, and he is entitled to a rental fee from him. Thus, each month, the buyer makes a payment to the seller which contains two parts: a payment of principal towards ownership of the house, and a rental payment for its use. This fee can be set at an amount equal to the interest rate which the seller desires. For example, if there is a prevailing interest rate of 8% (or $850 per $10,000 loaned), the seller may charge $850 per year as rental for his portion of the home (see note below for additional points regarding these payments). In this manner, the seller receives his desired revenue without actually making a loan.[52]

Shlomo Zalman Auerbach zt"l (quoted in *Tam Ribbis* 26) advised that a *kulo pikadon* form be used. For details regarding use of this form, see Chapter 23.

An option: If the managing partner has other investments, a standard Heter Iska form would be used, to give the investing partner a share in those investments. This would operate in the same manner as any Heter Iska, where the investing partner does not have to be aware of the particular nature of the investments. He would then be entitled to a share in the profits, based on the provisions of the Heter Iska.

51. *Igros Moshe* (2:62). The advantages and disadvantages of this method have been discussed in Chapter 13, Paragraphs 31 and 32. A contract suitable for use when buying a home appears in the next chapter.

52. A practical method of expediting this procedure would be to secure a schedule of payments (the type used by all banks in scheduling mortgage payments) for, in our example, a $10,000 loan. This schedule of payments contains two columns, one which calculates the monthly interest payment and the other which calculates the monthly payment of principal. Although the total payment for eachmonth is identical, the portion which is paid towards principal and the part paid for

C. Common Questions Regarding a Heter Iska

How Much Profit May a Heter Iska Pay?

37. A Heter Iska does not permit interest payments. The payments which are stipulated in the Heter Iska reflect the anticipated profits from the investment. The amount of profit which the Iska anticipates may be an optimistic projection, but it must be realistic. The Iska may not set payments at a rate which is greater than the profits which the investment can potentially realize.[53]

The standard Heter Iska form, which has been discussed throughout this chapter, is the *palga milveh u'palga pikadon* form. This form calls for profits to be divided fifty-fifty (as explained above, Paragraph 1). For example, the investing partner may advance $1000 and wish to receive a profit of 10% of this amount, which is $100. Since the Heter

---

interest change gradually. Each month, the principal portion increases while the interest portion decreases (since the amount of outstanding principal decreases every month, the amount of interest also decreases). This is true of all routine payment schedules.

This schedule should be incorporated into the sale-lease agreement, but the interest fees should be relabeled as rental charges. Thus, every month the buyer pays a set sum, identical to the sum he would have paid if he had actually taken a loan. The portion labeled 'principal' is used to acquire additional ownership in the home, until the entire $10,000 is paid and he acquires complete ownership. The portion labeled 'rental charges' is due to the seller because the buyer is using his portion of the home. As each month passes, the buyer owns a greater and greater percentage of the home. He is therefore renting a smaller and smaller portion from the seller. It is therefore appropriate that the amount of money paid as rental charges decreases each month, as shown in the schedule of payments.

A contract based on this concept, but with some variations, appears in Rabbi Bleich's *Contemporary Halachah*, Appendix to Volume 2.

53. *Igros Moshe* Y.D. 2:62 and 63, 3:40, *Tam Ribbis* 177:12.

Fortunately, in modern times there are many investments which have the potential of producing extraordinary rates of return. If the investing partner specifically stipulates that the managing partner is free to invest in any investment he chooses (most Heter Iska forms contain this language), the Heter Iska may contain a high anticipated return. However, in cases where the investment is clearly being advanced for use in a specific business, the contract must be drawn carefully to reflect the potential profit of the investment.

Iska calls for profits to be divided, this would only be permissible if the anticipated profit is $200, or 20%.[54]

38. The managing partner may not begin making payments until he has had an opportunity to use the investment to earn a profit.[55]

It is therefore questionable whether a Jewish bank is permitted to offer free gifts to depositors, if the gifts are actually delivered at the time that the deposit is made.[56]

If There Is No Profit, Will the Investing Partner Be Paid?

39. There is a possibility that this business deal will not earn a profit or that some of the principal will be lost. If this happens, the managing partner is still permitted to pay the investing partner the amount of profit which is stipulated in the Iska contract. This is because the Iska agreement requires the managing partner to swear that there was no profit in order to be absolved from his obligation to pay. He may

---

54. *Chasam Sofer* C.M. 63, *Igros Moshe* ibid. This Heter Iska may contain language which refers to a 10% rate of return, because it is understood that this refers to the investing partner's share of the profits (*Chasam Sofer* ibid.).

An option — the *kulo pikadon* Iska form: If the investing partner is not willing to advance funds unless he receives (for example) a 10% profit, the anticipated profit of the business must be 20%. If the partners realize that it is not realistic that they will realize this rate of profit, the Heter Iska form which has been described in this chapter could not be used. However, there is an alternative form of Heter Iska, known as the *kulo pikadon* form, which may be used. This form is described in Chapter 23, Paragraphs 8-11. When it is used, the investing partner may receive a profit which is equal to the total profit of the investment. Thus, if it is anticipated that the investment will realize a 10% profit, he may receive the entire 10%.

55. *Maharsham* 2:notes to index 216, *Bris Yehudah* 38:6. The managing partner may pay the investing partner, if he stipulates that the payment is being made on the investing partner's account and that this amount will be deducted from whatever moneys he will be owed at the time that payments are due (*Imrei Yosher* 1:189, *Bris Yehudah* ibid.).

56. This refers to Jewish banks which use a Heter Iska for transactions involving Jewish depositors. *Bris Yehudah* 38:n10 questions whether a Heter Iska serves to permit these gifts. We have seen (Chapter 5, Paragraph 27) that *Igros Moshe* permits corporations (such as banks) to make Ribbis payments. We have also seen that this is a matter of dispute. Since this is a question of Ribbis Ketzutzah, one should act stringently.

[If the depositor chooses the gift but does not actually take possession until a day (or more) has passed, this would be permitted. Thus, a depositor would have the option of arranging with the bank to pick up his gift the following day.]

elect to pay the anticipated profit (from his personal funds), rather than to swear.[57]

However, if the investing partner has firsthand knowledge that there was no profit, he may not demand that the managing partner make an oath to attest to this. In this case, profit may not be paid.[58]

Are There Reasons to Avoid Using a Heter Iska?

40. One who offers a free loan performs numerous Biblical mitzvos.

This is especially true when the borrower is a needy person. One who uses a Heter Iska is trading these mitzvos for the profit which the Iska pays. The *Chofetz Chaim* strongly advises that a lender choose the spiritual gain, by offering a free loan, rather than the monetary gain which results from use of a Heter Iska. He adds that the original intent of the poskim who encouraged the use of a Heter Iska was for loans which involved extraordinarily large sums of money, where offering a free loan was not an option. However, when one can afford to offer a free loan, this is certainly preferred.[59]

This consideration should serve to encourage people to offer free loans; it is not meant to discourage use of a Heter Iska in cases where a free loan would not be offered anyway.

41. When money is advanced for use in a business venture or investment, one need not hesitate to use a Heter Iska. In these cases, the Heter Iska represents a true investment agreement.

Even in situations where money is being advanced for the personal use of the 'managing partner,' most poskim permit the use of a Heter Iska. Still, there were poskim who were opposed to use of a Heter Iska

---

57. *Chochmas Adam* 142:10, *Kitzur Shulchan Aruch* 66:3, *Bris Yehudah* 38:5.

58. *Igros Moshe* Y.D. 2:62 and 63, *Bris Yehudah* quoting *Panim Me'iros* 2:36, *Tuv Taam Vodaas* 3:2:40 and *Divrei Chaim hashmatos* to 2:16.

59. *Ahavas Chessed* 2:15. "My brothers and friends, this is not God's chosen way ... even when the Heter Iska is used properly, this causes the attribute of compassion to be diminished in the world. The Holy Books have taught that one of the reasons for the Torah's prohibition on Ribbis was to strengthen the attribute of compassion in the world...and this is one of the causes of poverty among Jews. In times when most loans among Jews were offered for compassionate reasons, God dealt with us with the attribute of compassion ..."

The son of the *Chofetz Chaim* writes (in *Kol Kisvei Chofetz Chaim, meluim* to Vol. 3, P. 75) that although his father sometimes borrowed money through the use of a Heter Iska, when lending money he never used a Heter Iska.

in this type of situation. They view the Iska contract as a subterfuge which is used to evade the Ribbis restrictions.[60]

Is a Written Iska Contract Necessary?

42. When two parties agree to the terms of a Heter Iska and money changes hands on the basis of this understanding, it is not necessary to have a written contract.[61] Still, it is preferable to have a written Heter Iska contract.[62]

43. If the person who receives the money (the managing partner) signs a note of debt to the investing partner, he must also have a written Heter Iska.[63] If the note itself states that the debt is being established

---

60. *Bris Yehudah* (40:n1) cites three earlier authorities who questioned the validity of a Heter Iska because they considered it to be a *haaramah*, a subterfuge (*Sefer Zichronos*, *Ginas Veradim* and *Shulchan Gevoah*). This is more than offset by the preponderance of poskim who encouraged the use of a Heter Iska and actually wrote and published Heter Iska forms.

Bris Yehudah (ibid.) writes, "I have not found, among the later poskim, one who questions this. On the contrary, whenever the poskim saw questions of prohibition, they advised the use of an Iska. Nevertheless, one who fears and trembles before the word of God and refrains from lending (through the use of a Heter Iska), except where it is a true investment, is not considered to be acting in excess stringency. . .if he cannot lend in the manner of a true investment, he should offer a free loan, and should not refrain from lending because of this (stringency)."

61. *Tzemach Tzedek* Y.D. 88, *Kitzur Shulchan Aruch* 66:7, *Divrei Chaim* 2:16 (in *hashmatos*), *Tuv Tam Vodaas* 3:2:43, *Bris Yehudah* 35:4. *Chasam Sofer* C.M. 48 writes that when lending the moneys of orphans, which had been entrusted to him, he would write a regular note of debt and add to it the words, 'Done by the Heter of Maharam, as discussed between us, for the amount of _____ .' Both parties would then sign this notation. (It should be noted that the Heter Iska of Maharam is *not* the type of Heter Iska which is in common use today. Today, someone who explains that he is using a Heter Iska, as described here, should write simply 'Done by Heter Iska. . .'. If he already used the inaccurate language 'of Maharam,' *Bris Yehudah* 40:n10 rules that this is valid.)

Once the money already changed hands (for example, it was originally given as a loan) and the parties afterwards made an oral agreement to change this to an investment under the terms of a Heter Iska, this new agreement is not binding. All subsequent losses or profits are the responsibility of the managing partner (*Shach* 177:41).

62. *Kitzur Shulchan Aruch* 66:7, *Bris Yehudah* 40:9. All the poskim who dealt with the issue of Heter Iska actually wrote Iska contracts. One objection to use of a Heter Iska is that it is a subterfuge which is used to circumvent the laws of Ribbis. In light of this objection, it is clear that we should try our best to establish the Heter Iska as a genuine agreement. Using a written Iska contract allows for a greater understanding of the agreement and lends it a sense of authenticity.

63. Y.D. 177:24. Although it is not necessary to have a written record of the Iska, if there is a document which refers to the transaction, a record of the Iska must also be made. If

according to the rules of a Heter Iska, this is sufficient.[64]

44. Witnesses are optional in any Heter Iska agreement. Here, as in virtually all financial agreements, witnesses are not required for the agreement to be valid. The parties may prefer to have witnesses who could later verify the transaction. For this reason, many Heter Iska contracts leave space for the signature of witnesses. If these documents are used without having witnesses sign, this does not affect the validity of the contract. Even when a *kinyan* is required, witnesses need not observe the *kinyan*.[65]

Is a Kinyan Necessary?

45. Whenever a Heter Iska agreement is concluded before the money changes hands, no *kinyan* is necessary.[66] Still, many Heter Iska forms contain language directing that a *kinyan* be made.

---

the only record of the transaction was one which did not refer to the Iska, and the investing partner dies, his heirs would find the contract and use it to collect. They would be unaware that if the investment lost money (and the managing partner could bring witnesses to prove it), they are not entitled to recover their money (as explained by *Be'er HaGolah*).

If this rule was violated and a note of debt was written without reference to a Heter Iska, this does not affect the status of the investment (*Chochmas Adam* 142:13).

64. *Beis Yosef* 177, *Chasam Sofer* C.M. 48. *Beis Meir* to 177:24 and *Shaar Deah* 177:12 permit this even if the reference to the Heter Iska appears as a notation at the bottom of the note of debt.

Shach suggests two other options:

- **Witnesses:** Many poskim hold that it is not necessary to have a written record of the Iska if there are witnesses who are aware that the note is subject to the provisions of the Heter Iska (*Bach, Shach* 177:49 and *Kitzur Shulchan Aruch* 66:9). Others disagree and maintain that witnesses are not sufficient (*Taz* 177:33 and *Chochmas Adam* 142:13). Although it is preferable that a Heter Iska be written, in case of need one may rely on the lenient opinion (*Chochmas Adam* ibid.; *Divrei Chaim* in *hashmatos* to 2:16 and *Maharil Diskin* 21 report that the custom is to rely on the lenient opinion of *Shach*).
- If the note of debt is entrusted to a third party, who is aware that it is subject to the provisions of a Heter Iska, no written Heter Iska is needed (*Shach* 177:47, *Chochmas Adam* ibid.).

65. *Kuntres HaSma kitzarah* 6, who writes: 'Witnesses were created only for (protection against) deceit.'

66. *Tzemach Tzedek* Y.D. 88, *Bris Yehudah* 35:4.

There are cases where a *kinyan* is required, because money does not change hands. A common example:

A supplier sold merchandise on credit, and delivered the goods to the customer. The supplier may later wish to enter into an Iska agreement with his customer. To do this, he

Changing a Loan to an Iska

46. If money changed hands as a loan, and the parties later decided to use a Heter Iska to change this to an investment, the loan must first be paid. The funds are then invested under the terms of a Heter Iska. If it is difficult to actually return the borrowed cash, this can be accomplished by a *kinyan*, as described in the note below.[67]

47. An investing partner may wish to enter into an Iska agreement involving merchandise. For example, a businessman has merchandise which he plans to sell at a profit. An investing partner may advance funds to the businessman; instead of making this a loan, the investing partner would purchase some of the merchandise, using a Heter Iska to acquire partnership. Later, when the merchandise is sold, they would divide the profits in accordance with the guidelines of the Iska agreement. In this case, no *kinyan* is needed.[68]

Can a Heter Iska Agreement Be Terminated Prematurely?

48. A Heter Iska agreement usually stipulates a period of time for which it remains in effect. The investing partner may not terminate

---

would use the merchandise which he delivered as capital for the Iska. Since the contract is being put into effect after the merchandise was already delivered, a *kinyan sudar* is required to make the contract binding (*Bris Yehudah* 35:n11; Cf., *Ginas Veradim* quoted there). Heter Iska forms for this type of arrangement appear at the end of Chapter 6. These forms require a *kinyan sudar*, with the supplier handing a handkerchief or other utensil or item of clothing to the customer. In exchange, the customer gives the supplier a share in his business profits under the terms of the Heter Iska.

67. *Chavos Daas* 167:3, *Dagul MeiRivavah* to *Shach* 177:41.
[If the borrower owns real estate, he can accomplish this *kinyan* as follows. He would repay the loan by giving the lender possession of his real estate, in the value of the amount he owes. He makes the transfer with a *kinyan sudar*. The lender now becomes an investing partner, by returning this portion of the real estate to the borrower (by making a new *kinyan sudar*) under the terms of a Heter Iska. This *kinyan* does not have to be done with the lender himself. A third person may act as his agent for these transactions (*Chavos Daas*).]
If a Heter Iska contract is written and passed between the parties, *Dagul MeiRivavah* does not require a *kinyan*. It is not clear why this would not be required.
68. *S.A. Harav* §43, *Maharsham* 2:notes on index page, to 216.

the agreement prematurely.[69] However, the managing partner may terminate the agreement at any time,[70] provided he returns the principal and profits to the investing partner.[71]

---

69. Y.D. 177:36. Similarly, if the investing partner dies, his heirs could not terminate the agreement (*Bris Yehudah* 38:19).

If the original Heter Iska contains a clause which allows the investing partner to terminate the agreement, this would be permitted. [It is highly questionable if this clause could be added later. Since the investing partner has loaned money to the managing partner (i.e., the *palga milveh* portion of the investment), the managing partner may not extend an unusual courtesy to him. Allowing this clause to be added would constitute an unusual courtesy, which is Ribbis. (This concern does not apply when a *kulo pikadon* form is used — see Chapter 23, Paragraphs 8-11.)]

70. Y.D. 177:36 and C.M. 176:23. This is based on the Biblical law which permits an employee to terminate his employment prematurely. The managing partner has the status of an employee who is managing the investing partner's funds and he is therefore entitled to quit prematurely.

Sma to C.M. 72:7 and *Shach* to C.M. 74:12, referring to a specific type of Heter Iska agreement, rule that the managing partner may not terminate the agreement. However, it is not clear what type of Heter Iska they were referring to and what the basis of this objection is. Numerous explanations are offered:

- *Shevus Yaakov* 2:184 (quoted by *Pischei Teshuvah* to C.M. 176:27) maintains that this applies to all standard Heter Iska agreements. Since these agreements do not actually obligate the managing partner to be involved in an investment, there is no employment; therefore the managing partner may not quit. When an investment does require personal involvement in a business, it is considered employment and the managing partner may quit at any time.

- *Shaar Deah* 177:15 (also quoted by *Pischei Teshuvah* to C.M. 176:27) explains the *Sma* and *Shach* differently. The rule is that an employee is entitled to quit prematurely only if he decides that he no longer wishes to be employed in that particular line of work. An employee may not quit to switch to a different employer who will pay him more for the same work. In this case, the worker is obligated to honor his contract (*Rema* to C.M. 333:4). This applies to an Iska as well; a managing partner would not be permitted to terminate an Iska agreement when he is motivated by his ability to enter into an Iska elsewhere, under better terms. *Sma* and *Shach* are referring only to this type of termination.

Most poskim reject the ruling of *Shevus Yaakov* and follow the simple meaning of Y.D. 177:36 which allows a managing partner to terminate an Iska (*Tumim* 74:6, *Nesivos HaMishpat* 74:4, *Beis Ephraim* C.M. 17).

71. *Bris Yehudah* 38:15.

How much profit must be paid?

A Heter Iska agreement allows the managing partner to make an oath regarding the profits which had accrued. If he decided to exercise this right, the managing partner would swear and pay the amount of profit which had accrued up until that time. In fact, the managing partner generally does not swear. The Heter Iska allows him to pay a set sum instead of swearing. If the Iska set this sum at a percentage (of the principal) per day

What Happens if the Payment
Is Not Made on Time?

49. A Heter Iska usually stipulates a date for payment. If payment is not made on that date, the managing partner would continue holding the investing partner's money. Many poskim hold that the terms of the Heter Iska would continue, so that the investing partner would continue receiving profits until the debt is paid.[72] Since this is a matter of dispute,[73] it is preferable that the Heter Iska state explicitly that if payment is not made on time, the terms of the Heter Iska continue (most standard forms contain this provision).

50. Regarding the procedure for selling an Iska, see Chapter 12, Paragraph 21.

51. Regarding the question of whether a minor may be involved in a Heter Iska, see Chapter 5, Paragraph 39.

---

or week, the managing partner would pay the amount which accrued at the time of payment. However, a Heter Iska is often drawn to pay a specific sum of money in place of an oath. In this case, the managing partner would be required to pay this entire amount when terminating the contract, despite the fact that he actually had the investment funds for a shorter period of time than anticipated. If the Heter Iska set a specific amount per month or per year, he would be obligated to pay for the entire month or year (*Nesivos HaMishpat* 74:4, *Beis Ephraim* C.M. 17).

72. *Taz* 177:14 and 31, *Kuntres HaSma* 10, *S.A. Harav* §41.

If the Iska suffered a loss after the payment date which was verified by witnesses (in accordance with the requirements of the Heter Iska), some poskim hold that the investing partner could not be compelled to share in the loss. This is because the managing partner was obligated to return the investment moneys on the stipulated date, and he continued the Iska without authorization. The investing partner is therefore permitted to benefit if a profit is realized, but is not obligated to share in the losses (*Kuntres HaSma* 10, *Maharam Alshich* 117). See *Bris Yehudah* 38:n62 who quotes a dispute regarding this. In order to avoid this problem, it is important that the investing partner decide if he wishes the Iska to continue. He should then inform the managing partner of his wishes.

73. *Pischei Teshuvah* 177:2, quoting *Levushei Serod*, maintains that while the managing partner is *permitted* to continue under the terms of the Heter Iska, he is not *obligated* to continue sharing the profits of the investment. *Bris Yehudah* 38:n61 points out that this also appears to be the opinion of *Chavos Daas*.

CHAPTER TWENTY-THREE

Using a Heter Iska

Index of Heter Iska Forms:

Introduction

This chapter contains directions for use of a Heter Iska. In addition, two alternative Iska forms, the *kulo pikadon* form and the Heter Iska Klali, are described at length.

It is worth noting the warning of the *Yaaros Divash* (P. 124), 'Our sages have designed the formula of Heter Iska, but one must be careful to use it properly, for (the Heter Iska) has many laws, and there is not enough time or parchment to teach them publicly. One who chooses life and wishes to stand up at *techiyas hameisim* should seek the advice of a learned person when involved in this type of loan.'

General Rules for Use of a Heter Iska

1. The terms 'loan,' 'interest' or 'borrowing' should not be used when money is advanced through use of a Heter Iska. The Iska contract changes the loan to an investment. It should therefore be referred to as an Iska or investment, with payments referred to as profits.[1]

2. Both parties must be aware that a Heter Iska is being used.[2] Both

---

1. *Bris Yehudah* 40:8. If these terms were used, even in writing, this does not invalidate the Heter Iska (*Maharsham* 2:252, *Bris Yehudah* 40:n15).

2. While it should be obvious that a financial agreement must be accepted by both parties, the poskim discuss the possibility of one party incorporating a Heter Iska without the knowledge of the other.

A Heter Iska Klali which is entered into, unilaterally, by the managing partner, is not valid according to most poskim. cf. *Maharam Shick* Y.D. 164 who held that a unilateral Heter Iska is valid; virtually all poskim dispute this. See, for example, *Maharshag* Y.D. 5 and 52 (who was a disciple of *Maharam Shick* but disputed this ruling).

A Heter Iska Klali which is entered into, unilaterally, by the investing partner: *Maharsham* (1:20 s.v. *vesham*) permits the investor to attach a Heter Iska agreement without the knowledge of the managing partner. He bases this on the Talmudic rule of *zochin le'adam shelo befanav*. This principle allows someone to act on another person's behalf, even without his knowledge, if his action benefits that person. Since the person entering into the Heter Iska intends to benefit the managing partner, this is permitted. *Maharsham* explains that although the managing partner is not aware of it, if he were to swear that there were no profits, the investing partner would not take money from him. This Heter Iska therefore represents a gain for him.

This ruling is a controversial one.

Bris Yehudah 6:n53 cites others who dispute this ruling. They argue that it is not at all clear that the managing partner is benefiting from this Heter Iska. If the Heter Iska were not valid, he would not be obligated to pay any profits to the investing partner (since this would constitute Ribbis). Thus, use of the Heter Iska causes him a loss. *Maharsham* would undoubtedly argue that if the Heter Iska were not valid, the loan would not have been extended in the first place. The managing partner therefore gained

should also understand the concept of Heter Iska and its basic provisions.[3]

3. A Heter Iska is signed by the person receiving the money (the managing partner). The investing partner holds the contract so that he will later be able to prove that he invested money with the managing partner.[4] The investing partner does not sign the Heter Iska (except in the case where a note of debt, such as a mortgage, was also signed — see the paragraph which follows).

4. If, for legal reasons, the parties wish to use documents which refer to the investment as a loan, they may do so.[5] However, if they do, they must write a Heter Iska as well.[6]

---

in receiving the loan because of the Heter Iska. Still, once the loan was extended, the conditions of Heter Iska do not benefit the managing partner (*Bris Yehudah* ibid.).

See also below, in our discussion of Heter Iska Klali, where the issue of a one-sided Heter Iska is discussed.

3. *Kuntres HaSma* 4, *Shelah Chullin* 84, *Chochmas Adam* 143:3, *Tzemach Tzedek* Y.D. 88, *Chasam Sofer* C.M. 48, *Igros Moshe* Y.D. 2:62, *Bris Yehudah* 35:4. *Chofetz Chaim* (*Ahavas Chessed* 2:15) advises that people who use a Heter Iska should study the laws of Heter Iska in *Chochmas Adam*.

If a Heter Iska was already used: If money was advanced through use of a Heter Iska, but the people involved did not understand how the Iska contract works, *Shelah* (ibid.) holds that it is invalid. *Bris Yehudah* 40:n14 writes that most poskim rule that the Heter Iska is valid, since the parties obligated themselves to the provisions of the Heter Iska. However, if the parties involved think that the Heter Iska does not affect the investment, and that it is only a means of permitting the loan, *Bris Yehudah* concedes that this is not valid.

Igros Moshe 3:41, in drawing a Heter Iska Klali for use by a bank, explicitly writes that it applies to people 'who do not know at all, what an Iska is.' This would appear to contradict the ruling of *Bris Yehudah*, who does not allow use of a Heter Iska in such cases.

[These two rulings can be reconciled. *Igros Moshe's* ruling is valid in his case, involving a bank. People who do business with a bank usually know that their deposits and/or loans are subject to the bylaws of the bank. When doing business with the bank they are agreeing to accept its bylaws, despite the fact that few depositors ever read these rules. In that case, therefore, it is as if they agreed to the Iska, which is incorporated into the bank's bylaws, even without knowledge of its provisions. This does not necessarily apply to individuals who enter into an Iska agreement, but think that it has no effect on the terms of the investment.]

4. This is not required by halachah. We have already seen (in Chapter 22, Paragraph 41) that a written contract is not technically required.

5. The purpose of signing such a legal document is to expedite legal redress in the event that the terms of the Heter Iska are violated.

6. Y.D. 177:24. These loan documents may contain references to interest payments. It is preferable that the Heter Iska be written before the loan documents are signed (*Chasan Sofer*, quoted in *Mishnas Ribbis* 22:n33).

In this case, many poskim hold that it would not be permissible to leave the Heter Iska in the hands of the investing partner. This is because of the fear that if there is a loss (and witnesses attested to the loss, so that the investing partner would lose money under the terms of the Iska) the investing partner could hide the Heter Iska and demand payment based on the note of debt. For this reason, a duplicate Heter Iska must be signed by the investing partner and given to the managing partner. Alternatively, the Heter Iska may be entrusted to a third party.[7]

5. When a note of debt has been written, it is important that the following clause be inserted into the Heter Iska:

'In the event of any conflict between the terms of this Iska agreement and the terms of any other agreement signed by the two parties relating to the above-mentioned funds, the terms of this agreement shall prevail.'[8]

---

7. *Chochmas Adam* 142:13, *Kitzur Shulchan Aruch* 66:9. *Maharsham* 5:83 also recommends that the managing partner have a copy of the Heter Iska (cf. *Maharsham* 3:262 that this is not absolutely required). This applies even if the investing partner is an honest person and the managing partner does not really suspect that he would hide the Heter Iska (*Chochmas Adam* and *Kitzur Shulchan Aruch*, ibid.).

Darkei Teshuvah 177:72 quotes many poskim who dispute this and allow the Heter Iska to be held solely by the investing partner. See also *Minchas Yitzchok* 4:16.

[Where the investing partner is a non-observant Jew or an unscrupulous individual and there is a valid reason to suspect that he might deny the existence of the Heter Iska, these precautions are certainly necessary (*Mishnas Ribbis* 22:n33).]

If the note itself states that the debt was established according to the rules of a Heter Iska, this is sufficient (*Beis Yosef* 177). Others add that this is permitted even if the reference to the Heter Iska appears as a notation at the bottom of the note of debt (*Beis Meir* to 177:24, *Chasam Sofer* C.M. 48 and *Shaar Deah* 177:12).

Many poskim hold that it would be sufficient to have witnesses who are aware that the money was given in accordance with a Heter Iska. Others dispute this (this has been detailed in the previous chapter, Note 64).

8. *Kol Kisvei Rav Henkin* 2:50:3, *Igros Moshe* Y.D. 2:62 and 3:38.

See also *Chasam Sofer* C.M. 48 who writes that it was his regular practice to lend the funds of orphans, using a Heter Iska. Because he wished that the contract remain enforceable by secular law, he would not actually write a Heter Iska. Instead, the terms of Heter Iska would be explained orally to the person receiving the moneys. The letter of debt would contain a notation which read, 'Done by the Heter of Maharam, as discussed between us, for the amount of _____ .' Both parties would then sign this notation.

(It should be noted that the Heter Iska of Maharam is *not* the type of Heter Iska which is in common use today. Today, someone who explains that he is using a Heter Iska as described here, should write simply, 'Done by Heter Iska. . .')

Directions for Filling Out a Heter Iska Form

6. The following information must be inserted into a standard Heter Iska form:[9]

- ☐ **Names:** The name of the person extending the funds is inserted into the space which refers to the investing partner. Some Heter Iska forms also contain a space for the name of the person receiving the funds. This is the space which refers to the managing partner. Many Heter Iska forms do not actually leave space for the name of the managing partner, except at the end, where he signs the Heter Iska.[10]

- ☐ **Principal:** The Heter Iska allows space for the principal which is invested ('. . .have received the sum of $ _____'). This should contain the entire principal amount (both the 'half loan' and the 'half investment'). If merchandise was given for investment, the words 'the sum of' should be removed and the following should be inserted: 'merchandise valued at $_____ .'

- ☐ **Payment:** The Heter Iska contains a space for a description of the payment which the managing partner will make at the time that the Iska terminates.[11] The description may be a sum of money or it may describe the method of calculating the payments. For example, it may be filled in to read: 'an amount equal to 10% of the outstanding balance.'[12]

- ☐ **Date of payment:** The date on which payment is due is inserted. If the agreement does not call for the payment to be made in a single lump sum, this may read: 'as stated in the promissory note' or 'on demand.' It is important that this be

---

9. This information (with the exception of the signatures) may be inserted in advance; the presence of the parties is not required.

10. In this case, it would be prudent to include a full identification of the managing partner, so that it would be easier for the investing partner to use the Heter Iska to prove the managing partner's identity.

11. This is the space which is followed by the words, 'as payment for his share of the profits.'

12. This amount may be tied to the Consumer Price Index (*Bris Yehudah* 40:19) or to the prime rate (*Mishnas Ribbis* 22:n47).

All benefits which are paid to the investing partner must be included. Thus, if there are 'points' payments, these must be included here. Even non-cash benefits may be added.

followed by the following sentence: 'If payment is not made by the due date, the terms of this Heter Iska shall continue.'[13]

☐ **Name of arbitrator:** An optional clause, which appears in some Heter Iska forms, allows the parties to agree to a third party whose decision would be binding if any disputes were to arise. It is not halachically necessary to insert a name, even if the form which is being used contains space for it. If this is not filled in, the space should be crossed out (or the words 'a mutually acceptable person' may be inserted).

☐ **Signature:** The managing partner signs the Heter Iska and gives it to the investing partner in exchange for the moneys which are advanced. The investing partner's signature is not required (except as outlined above, Paragraph 4).

☐ **Date:** The date on which the Heter Iska is signed is filled in. This should be the same date on which the funds are advanced. The Heter Iska may not be predated. A postdated Heter Iska is valid.

☐ **Witnesses:** This is an optional part of a Heter Iska. This does not have to be used, even if the form which is being used contains space for it.

7. Payment: The investing partner should give one dollar to the managing partner, as required by the Heter Iska.[14]

The Kulo Pikadon Form[15]

8. There are two basic Heter Iska forms. The form which has been described up to this point is known as the *palga milveh u'palga pikadon* (half loan-half investment) form. This can be recognized by the words 'profits and losses will be shared equally.' Any form which contains this clause is a *palga milveh u'palga pikadon* form, and all the rules which have been outlined until this point apply. This is the traditional Heter Iska form, which has been in use for generations.

---

13. This is explained in Chapter 22, Paragraph 49.

14. The reason for this payment is explained in Chapter 22, Paragraphs 8 and 29.

15. This is the subject of much discussion among contemporary poskim. What follows is a brief synopsis of the basic points which relate to a *kulo pikadon* form. For further discussion, see *Vechai Achicha Imach* 108-109, *Tam Ribbis* in *kuntres acharon* 27 and 28, R' Moshe Shternbuch Shlita in *Daas VeHalachah* and in the introduction to *Kitzur Dinei Ribbis*, and *Toras Ribbis* 16:48.

A second type of Heter Iska is known as the *kulo pikadon* form. This form is virtually identical except that all of the funds (rather than just half) which are advanced are investment moneys.[16] This contract calls for all profits and losses to be assigned to the investing partner (and not 'shared equally'). All other clauses in the form are identical to a *palga milveh u'palga pikadon* form. Assuming that the managing partner does not exercise his right to swear or bring witnesses, the payments are identical no matter which form is used.

9. The advantages of the *kulo pikadon* form: Every Heter Iska form calls for the managing partner to make a payment if he chooses not to take an oath. This payment represents the investing partner's anticipated profit. In a *palga milveh u'palga pikadon* form, the profits are shared equally. Thus, if the Iska calls for the investing partner to receive 15% of the invested moneys, this means that the anticipated profits are 30% (so that the investing partner's share is 15%). When interest rates are high, the investing partner would want a high return for his investment. Since this rate would have to be doubled when using a *palga milveh u'palga pikadon* form, this would result in an unrealistic anticipated profit rate. If a *kulo pikadon* form is used, this concern is alleviated, since the investing partner's return is equal to the total anticipated profit.[17]

A *palga milveh u'palga pikadon* form creates both a loan and an investment. Since the managing partner is also a borrower, he is prohibited from benefiting the lender/investor. Because they have a borrower / lender relationship, any benefit which is extended to the investing partner would constitute Ribbis.[18] This means that the

---

16. To properly understand this difference, it is necessary to understand how a *palga milveh u'palga pikadon* form works. This has been explained in Chapter 22, Paragraph 1.

17. It is for this reason that the *kulo pikadon* form became increasingly popular in Eretz Yisrael during their periods of hyper-inflation. In addition, when moneys are forwarded for modest investments, such as the purchase of a home, the anticipated profit is modest in any event, and it is totally unrealistic to anticipate that the profit would be twice the investor's rate of return. For this reason, R' Shlomo Zalman Auerbach zt"l (quoted in *Tam Ribbis* 26) encouraged the use of a *kulo pikadon* form when moneys are advanced for the purchase of a home.

18. *S.A. Harav* §39, *Tuv Taam Vodaas* 3:35, *Maharsham* 4:95. This also appears to be the opinion of *Gra* in his notes to *Yerushalmi* (*Dmai* 6:4).

[We have seen, in Chapter 3, Paragraphs 25-29, that no-cost benefits, known as *tovas hanaah* (such as the giving of *terumos* and *maasros* to the lender), are also included in the Ribbis prohibition. *Gra* (ibid.) holds that in situations involving a Heter Iska, *terumos* and *maasros* may be given to the investing partner. *Divrei Sofrim*, in *Emek*

managing partner may not benefit the Iska partnership since this would create profit for the investor.[19]

We have seen that the parties to a Heter Iska must understand how the Iska works. Where the people involved have no understanding of the Iska, it is simpler to explain a *kulo pikadon* form, since this is a straight investment.[20]

10. The disadvantages of this form: As we have noted in the previous chapter, there were poskim who objected to a Heter Iska on the grounds that it is a subterfuge (*haaramah*) which is designed to permit interest payments. Most poskim reject this argument, because a Heter Iska creates a business arrangement. A conventional Heter Iska creates a partnership, with the managing partner entitled to half the profits. This is a true business arrangement and is therefore not seen as subterfuge. When a *kulo pikadon* form is used, all profits belong to the investing partner. Why, then, is the managing partner involved? This gives a greater appearance of subterfuge.[21]

An additional problem: Whenever a Heter Iska is used, there is a possibility that the investing partner will lose the money he invested. When a *palga milveh u'palga pikadon* form is used, the maximum loss which he may suffer is half his investment. This is because this contract assesses losses equally, with the managing partner responsible for half the money. When a *kulo pikadon* form is used, the investing partner may, conceivably, lose all of his money. Although it is unlikely that this will happen, the investing partner would naturally prefer the *palga milveh u'palga pikadon* form.

Davar 177:265, cites this *Gra* as a source for permitting all types of *tovas hanaah* benefits in situations involving a Heter Iska. This quote seems to be inaccurate. *Gra* is referring specifically to the *tovas hanaah* benefits associated with *terumos* and *maasros*, where there is a separate prohibition on taking money for *tovas hanaah* benefits. *Gra* implies that all other cases of *tovas hanaah* are prohibited.]

19. See Chapter 22, Paragraphs 11 and 12, for common situations where this is problematic.

20. *Chelkas Yaakov* 3:189:9.

21. *Minchas Yitzchak* 4:18:2, *Bris Yehudah* 40:n2. This is supported by the fact that the different Heter Iska forms, which were written by poskim of the previous generations, all used the *palga milveh u'palga pikadon* method.

A defense of the *kulo pikadon* form: It is rare that a businessman uses only borrowed funds to start a business. Often, he has his own funds, but needs additional moneys to get started. Thus, a businessman who has $100,000 may need another $50,000. It would be normal for the businessman to take these moneys from the investor and allow him to collect all of the profits. This is a normal business arrangement (and not a subterfuge) since this businessman *does* gain, despite giving all profits to the investing partner.

11. As a matter of halachah, the *palga milveh u'palga pikadon* form is preferred. In cases where there are specific problems with the use of a *palga milveh u'palga pikadon* form, most poskim permit the use of the *kulo pikadon* form in its place.[22]

Heter Iska Klali

12. The traditional Heter Iska form is used on an individual basis. Each time money is advanced, the parties come together and sign an Iska agreement.

This is not a practical arrangement for businesses which are constantly dealing with loans or credit arrangements. It would be too cumbersome and time consuming for these businesses to arrange a Heter Iska for each transaction. For this reason, many businesses use a Heter Iska Klali. This is a document which specifically states that all the company's transactions with Jewish customers are subject to the Heter Iska agreement, as described in the Heter Iska Klali.[23]

---

22. This is the approach used by *Minchas Yitzchak* 7:66. Although *Bris Yehudah* is opposed to the use of this form, *Divrei Sofrim* (p.341) reports that the author of *Bris Yehudah* does allow use of a *kulo pikadon* form in specific situations.

23. An interesting form of Heter Iska Klali was drawn up by R' Ezriel Meir Eiger, the Rav of Lublin, in 1924. In response to the growing problem of Ribbis transactions at that time, R' Eiger proposed that every businessman write a Heter Iska Klali which states that all business transactions into which he enters are being done under the rules of a Heter Iska. A businessman would write this Iska once, when going into business, and it would remain in effect for his entire business career. This Heter Iska Klali would cover all business transactions, even if the Heter Iska was not mentioned at the time and even if the businessman had forgotten about the Heter Iska Klali.

This proposal was originally published in *Kovetz Derushim*, a publication of the Agudas Rabbanim of Poland. In subsequent issues, numerous Rabbanim commented on the proposal, both pro and con. Many Rabbanim objected to the concept of entering into an Iska once for a lifetime. They proposed that the Iska be renewed annually. However, most Rabbanim supported the proposal of using a Heter Iska Klali, although it is clear that they did so only because of the great need of the time (see *Bris Yehudah* 40:n19).

Many Rabbanim, including R' Isser Zalman Meltzer and R' Aaron Kotler, opposed this plan. They argued that a Heter Iska Klali is not valid for loans which clearly call for interest payments, unless the Heter Iska is specifically drawn for that transaction (*Mishnas R' Aaron* Y.D. 20). R' Isser Zalman Meltzer proposed that businessmen be encouraged to make oral stipulations each time they make a deal, stating that the deal is subject to the rules of Heter Iska. He stressed that in cases where oral statements could not be made because the second party to the deal would not agree to it, the Heter Iska Klali would also not be valid because of the objections of the second party. *Maharshag* (Y.D. 5) also forbade use of a Heter Iska Klali where only one side was

According to most poskim, the customer must be notified that his dealings are subject to a Heter Iska Klali. For example, bills may state (even in fine print, so long as it is clearly legible), 'Subject to our Heter Iska Klali.' If customers are not notified that a Heter Iska Klali exists, most poskim prohibit its use.[24]

13. Banks and other corporations which are chartered by government agencies have a unique status. They may use a Heter Iska Klali even if customers are not specifically notified of this, for the following reason.

Poskim require that customers be notified of the existence of a Heter Iska Klali, because the Iska contract is not binding when the customer does not agree to it. Banks tend to have long and complicated bylaws. Most depositors do not bother studying these bylaws, but agree to be bound by these regulations. This agreement is considered routine and is binding. Since all of the institution's dealings are subject to its bylaws,

---

aware that it existed (a letter to R' Ezriel Meir Eiger, on this topic, also appears in *Har Tzvi* Y.D. 141).

Bris Yehudah (40:n20) points out that it is clear, from the voluminous discussion regarding R' Ezriel Meir Eiger's proposal, that a Heter Iska Klali would be acceptable if both parties to the transactions agreed to it, even if they did not discuss the Heter Iska each time they concluded a transaction. This is a basis for use of a Heter Iska Klali, as outlined in the following note.

24. Some poskim require that the Heter Iska Klali be mentioned each time a deal is completed; others hold that it is sufficient that the parties are aware that the Heter Iska Klali exists.

One of the earliest forms of Heter Iska Klali appears in *Maharsham* 1:20 (s.v. *u'beguf*). This Heter Iska Klali was written for use by a Jewish-owned bank, for loans to people of that town. *Maharsham* notified the townspeople that the Heter Iska exists, by having announcements made in all of the town's synagogues and study halls. He also relied on the fact that the Heter Iska was drawn in Beis Din and that word of such events tends to be spread around town. (This is an assumption which is also found elsewhere in halachah.) *Maharsham* states explicitly that he did not require that the Heter Iska be entered into the bank's constitution, nor that it be displayed in the bank.

Imrei Yosher 1:189 concurred with this arrangement.

Bris Yehudah 40:n21 cites poskim who require that the Heter Iska Klali be incorporated into the bank's bylaws. He points out that under the modern-day banking procedures, where government regulators keep tight control over bank transactions, agreements which are not legally part of the bank's regulations are meaningless. He argues that in today's situation, even *Maharsham* would probably require this.

Bris Yehudah adds that it is not sufficient for a local branch manager to sign a Heter Iska Klali on behalf of a bank. Local managers often do have the authority to enter into individual agreements, at their own discretion, and their authority would suffice for an individual Heter Iska. However, a Heter Iska Klali is a broad document. The signature of a local manager on this type of document may not be upheld. It is therefore necessary for the bank's board of directors to approve a Heter Iska Klali.

the Iska Klali is automatically attached to every loan. (This is the practice of most Israeli banks.)[25]

It is preferable that the banks display their Heter Iska Klali, so that depositors would be aware that it exists.[26]

14. If a Jewish-owned bank does not use a Heter Iska Klali for all its deposits, but it is willing to enter into a Heter Iska agreement with individuals who request it, an individual may borrow money from the bank, using a regular Heter Iska. However, he may not use a Heter Iska to deposit money with the bank. This is because the bank collects Ribbis on the loans it makes to other Jews (who do not request a Heter Iska). The depositor is prohibited from collecting the profits of the bank, since these profits are the result of Ribbis collections.[27]

---

25. *Bris Yehudah* 40:n21. The Heter Iska Klali is valid only if it is approved by the bank's board of directors and incorporated into its bylaws.

Igros Moshe (Y.D. 3:41) permits the use of a Heter Iska Klali for a bank, and explicitly applies it even to customers who do not know what a Heter Iska is.

Depositing money in a Jewish bank: It should also be noted that according to the opinion of *Igros Moshe*, all corporations are permitted to pay Ribbis for loans they receive. Others dispute this ruling. Still, someone who wishes to practice a personal stringency and refrain from relying on a Heter Iska Klali may still choose to deposit money with these banks, since he has the added weight of *Igros Moshe* who permits this, even without a Heter Iska. [Regarding someone who prefers not to rely on this, see the paragraph which follows.]

Borrowing money from a Jewish bank: *Igros Moshe's* leniency would not apply to someone who takes a personal loan from a Jewish bank, since he does not permit an individual to pay Ribbis to a Jewish corporation. Someone who wishes to act stringently may ask the bank to attach a separate Heter Iska to his agreement, or to write 'done according to the rules of the Heter Iska' on his loan agreement (*Bris Yehudah* ibid.).

26. *Bris Yehudah* ibid.

Free gifts to depositors: *Bris Yehudah* adds that even when a bank uses a Heter Iska, this does not permit the bank to offer free gifts to depositors, if the gifts are actually delivered at the time the deposit is made. This is because a Heter Iska works only for payments which are made *after* the investment has had the opportunity to earn a profit (*Bris Yehudah* 38:n10, based on *Maharsham* 2:notes to index 216). [If the gift is chosen at the time of deposit, but it is not delivered until later, this would be permitted.]

27. *Bris Yehudah* ibid. The depositor could not argue that his profits are the result of interest paid by gentiles, since all of the bank's profits are combined. (The Talmudic principle of *bereirah*, retroactive designation, could not be used to establish that the gentile's interest is being paid to the Jewish depositor, since this transaction is a case of Biblical Ribbis and the leniency of *bereirah* does not apply to cases of Biblical law — *Bris Yehudah*.)

Indeed, it would seem that a depositor is better off *if he does not use a Heter Iska!* Banks are incorporated, and there is no personal liability for the loans which they take. According to the opinion of *Igros Moshe*, all corporations are permitted to pay

15. For this reason, it would also be prohibited to buy shares in a publicly traded bank which has a majority of Jewish owners and does not use a Heter Iska Klali.[28]

16. Compensation: A routine Heter Iska calls for a one-dollar payment as compensation for the time and effort of the managing partner. When a Heter Iska Klali is drawn, this provision may also be used. However, since this would require a separate payment for each transaction, a Heter Iska Klali usually uses an alternative method of compensating the managing partner. The most common method is that of *Rambam*, which has been described in Chapter 22, Paragraph 10.

INDEX OF HETER ISKA FORMS
Standard Forms

Iska A: Where Money Is Advanced for Business Use
Iska B: Where Money Is Advanced for Personal Use
Iska C: Standard Iska Calling for Monthly Payments

Kulo Pikadon Iska Forms

Iska D: Where Money Is Advanced for Business Use
Iska E: Where Money Is Advanced For Personal Use

The Following Forms Appear in
Other Chapters of This Book

Chapter 6: Heter Iska for Credit Purchases
            Heter Iska Klali for Credit Billing
Chapter 7: Heter Iska for Prepayment Discounts
Chapter 8: Heter Iska Form for Commodity Trading
Chapter 12: Heter Iska Form for the Sale of Debt
             Heter Iska Form for Selling Notes at Discount
Chapter 13: Sale-lease Agreement (for Private Mortgages)
Chapter 16: Contract for Use in Establishing Partnerships
             Between Jews and Non-Jews

---

interest. Someone who does not use a Heter Iska would be collecting interest from the bank, and would not be sharing the bank's profit. He has a halachic opinion to rely on when taking interest. If a depositor does use a Heter Iska, the profits which he collects would not be permitted, even according to this opinion.

28. *Bris Yehudah* ibid. Here too, the shareholder is profiting from Ribbis payments.

Iska A: Where Money Is Advanced for Business Use

Iska Contract[1]

I, the undersigned, have received the sum of $ _____ from _____ (hereafter referred to as the "Investing Partner"), to be used for business purposes. I obligate myself to utilize these funds in a manner which I believe will generate profits. Any profits realized or losses sustained shall be shared equally between the investing partner and myself.

Any claim of loss must be verified through the testimony of two qualified witnesses in, and under conditions acceptable to, an Orthodox Jewish court of law. Any claim regarding the amount of profit generated by these funds shall be verified under solemn oath, before and under conditions acceptable to, an Orthodox Jewish court of law.

It is agreed that if I return the above-mentioned principal to the investing partner, together with an additional _____ as payment for his share of the profits which are generated, then I will not be required to make any further payment nor will I be required to make an oath.

I am obligated to make this payment on or before _____ . If payment is not made by this time, the terms of this Iska shall continue.

I have received one dollar from the investing partner as payment for my services during the term of our partnership.[2]

In the event of any conflict between the terms of this Iska agreement and the terms of any other agreement signed by the two parties in regard to these funds, the terms of this agreement shall prevail.

This agreement shall follow the guidelines of Heter Iska as explained in *Sefer Bris Yehudah*. It is agreed that any dispute which may arise in connection with this agreement shall be submitted before _____ .[3] Judgment rendered by the aforesaid authority may be entered in any court having jurisdiction thereof.

Dated _____

Signature of the Recipient _____

Signature of the Investor _____

Witnesses[3]

In witness whereof the above-mentioned parties have entered into this Heter Iska agreement on this _____ day of _____ .

Signature of Witness _____

Signature of Witness _____

---

1. Hebrew versions of a Heter Iska suitable for use in this situation appear in *Tam Ribbis* p. 307 and *Mishnas Ribbis* p. 256.
2. The investing partner pays one dollar to the managing partner, in addition to the funds which are invested. The reason that this payment is necessary is explained above, Chapter 22, Paragraph 29.
3. This part of the contract is optional.

Iska B:
Where Money Is Advanced for Personal Use

Heter Iska B (which appears on the following page) is suitable for use when someone needs money for personal use and wishes to enter into an Iska agreement with an investor who is providing these funds. The person investing these funds acquires a portion of the investments which are owned by the receiver. This Heter Iska is drawn so that it can be used even in cases where the person receiving the money owns no investments at all. However, this case, the Heter Iska should not be used, except under the advice and guidance of a Rabbi who is an expert in these laws.

PLEASE NOTE: If the parties wish to have witnesses attest to the Heter Iska, the final portion of Iska A may be added at the end of the contract.

Iska C:
Standard Iska Calling for Monthly Payments

This Iska form is identical to the form which appears above (Iska A), except that it is drawn in a manner which requires monthly payments. This form, which appears on page 422, should only be used when the monthly payments do not include principal payments. Payment of principal is due at the date designated in the Heter Iska.

If the monthly payments do include payment of principal, a separate schedule of payments should be drawn up. The Iska A or B form should be used with the following insertion. In the space which reads '. . .make these payments on or before _____ ,' the following words should be added: 'the dates specified on the schedule of payments.'

PLEASE NOTE: If the parties wish to have witnesses attest to the Heter Iska, the final portion of Iska A may be added at the end of the contract.

Iska B: Where Money Is Advanced for Personal Use

Iska Contract

I, the undersigned, have received the sum of \$_____ from _____ (hereafter referred to as the "Investing Partner"), for investment in an Iska partnership, subject to the following terms:

In exchange for the aforementioned sum, the investing partner shall acquire a share (in the value of the funds received) in any investment, real estate or business which I own. In the event that no such investments exist, the investing partner will acquire partnership (in the value of funds received) in any future investment which I shall make. The investing partner hereby appoints me as an agent to execute this investment (or investments), as I deem appropriate, on his behalf. This investment (or investments) shall be owned jointly by the investing partner and myself. Any profits realized or losses sustained shall be shared equally between the investing partner and myself.

Any claim of loss must be verified through the testimony of two qualified witnesses in, and under conditions acceptable to, an Orthodox Jewish court of law. Any claim regarding the amount of profit generated by this investment (or investments) shall be verified under solemn oath, before and under conditions acceptable to, an Orthodox Jewish court of law.

It is agreed that if I return the above-mentioned principal to the investing partner, together with an additional _____ as payment for his share of the profits which are generated, then I will not be required to make any further payment nor will I be required to make an oath. I am obligated to make this payment on or before _____ . If payment is not made by this time, the terms of this Iska shall continue.

I have received one dollar from the investing partner as payment for my services during the term of our partnership.[1]

In the event of any conflict between the terms of this Iska agreement and the terms of any other agreement signed by the two parties in regard to these funds, the terms of this agreement shall prevail.

This agreement shall follow the guidelines of Heter Iska as explained in *Sefer Bris Yehudah*. It is agreed that any dispute which may arise in connection with this agreement shall be submitted before _____ .[2] Judgment rendered by the aforesaid authority may be entered in any court having jurisdiction thereof.

Dated _____

Signature of the Recipient _____

Signature of the Investor _____

---

1. The investing partner should pay one dollar to the the managing partner. The reason that this payment is necessary is explained above, Chapter 22, Paragraph 29.
2. This part of the contract is optional.

Iska C: Standard Iska Calling for Monthly Payments

Iska Contract

I, the undersigned, have received the sum of $ _____ from _____ (hereafter referred to as the "Investing Partner"), to be used for business purposes. I obligate myself to utilize these funds in a manner which I believe will generate profits. Any profits realized or losses sustained shall be shared equally between the investing partner and myself.

Any claim of loss must be verified through the testimony of two qualified witnesses in, and under conditions acceptable to, an Orthodox Jewish court of law. Any claim regarding the amount of profit generated by these funds shall be verified under solemn oath, before and under conditions acceptable to, an Orthodox Jewish court of law.

The amounts due hereunder, if any, to the investor shall be payable monthly, on the first of every secular month. If these profits are being paid in a timely manner, the return of the sum invested herewith shall not be required until _____ .[1] If there are no profits during any given month, the investor shall be notified of this immediately.

It is specifically agreed that if I pay, to the investing partner, the monthly sum of _____ as payment for his share of the profits which are generated, then I will not be required to make an oath, nor will I be required to notify the investing partner regarding the profits which were realized. Additional profits, if any, shall be my sole property.

The investing partner shall be entitled to the presumption of credibility in any claim regarding compliance of the terms herein. This provision shall survive the termination of this Iska. In the event that the monthly payment or notice which is required herein is not given, the presumption shall be that the moneys invested have continued to generate a profit equal to or greater than the amount required by the monthly payment.

I have received one dollar from the investing partner as payment for my services during the term of our partnership.[2]

In the event of any conflict between the terms of this Iska agreement and the terms of any other agreement signed by the two parties in regard to these funds, the terms of this agreement shall prevail.

This agreement shall follow the guidelines of Heter Iska as explained in *Sefer Bris Yehudah*. It is agreed that any dispute which may arise in connection with this agreement shall be submitted before _____ .[3] Judgment rendered by the aforesaid authority may be entered in any court having jurisdiction thereof.

Dated _____

Signature of the Recipient _____

Signature of the Investor _____

---

1. Enter the date on which payment of principal is due, or the words "on demand."

2. The investing partner pays one dollar to the managing partner, in addition to the funds which are invested. The reason that this payment is necessary is explained in Chapter 22, Paragraph 29.

3. This part of the contract is optional.

Iska D: Kulo Pikadon Form
Where Money Is Advanced for Business Use

We have seen that there are cases where a *kulo pikadon* form is desirable.[1] This form appears below and is suitable for use in the same cases as Heter Iska A ('business use').

PLEASE NOTE: If the parties wish to have witnesses attest to the Heter Iska, the final portion of Iska A may be added at the end of the contract.

Iska Contract

I, the undersigned, have received the sum of $ _____ from _____ (hereafter referred to as the "Investing Partner"), to be used for business purposes. I obligate myself to utilize these funds in a manner which I believe will generate profits.

Any profits realized or losses sustained as a result of this investment shall be allocated to the investing partner. However, five percent (5%) of the profits shall be retained by the undersigned for his services during the term of this Iska.

Any claim of loss must be verified through the testimony of two qualified witnesses in, and under conditions acceptable to, an Orthodox Jewish court of law. Any claim regarding the amount of profit generated by these funds shall be verified under solemn oath, before and under conditions acceptable to, an Orthodox Jewish court of law.

It is agreed that if I return the above-mentioned principal to the investing partner, together with an additional _____ as payment for the profits which are generated, then I will not be required to make any further payment nor will I be required to make an oath. The balance of the profits, if any, shall be my sole property. I am obligated to make this payment on or before _____ . If payment is not made by this time, the terms of this Iska shall continue.

In the event of any conflict between the terms of this Iska agreement and the terms of any other agreement signed by the two parties in regard to these funds, the terms of this agreement shall prevail.

This agreement shall follow the guidelines of Heter Iska as explained in *Sefer Bris Yehudah*. It is agreed that any dispute which may arise in connection with this agreement shall be submitted before _____ .[2] Judgment rendered by the aforesaid authority may be entered in any court having jurisdiction thereof.

Dated _____

Signature of the Recipient _____

Signature of the Investor _____

---

1. This was explained above, Paragraphs 8-11.
2. This part of the contract is optional.

Iska E: Kulo Pikadon Form
Where Money Is Advanced for Personal Use

We have seen that there are cases where a *kulo pikadon* form is desirable.[1] This form appears below and is suitable for use in the same cases as Heter Iska B ('personal use').

PLEASE NOTE: If the parties wish to have witnesses attest to the Heter Iska, the final portion of Iska A may be added at the end of the cotnract.

Iska Contract

I, the undersigned, have received the sum of $ _____ from _____ (hereafter referred to as the "Investing Partner"), for investment in an Iska partnership, subject to the following terms:

In exchange for the aforementioned sum, the investing partner shall acquire a share (in the value of the funds received) in any investment, real estate or business which I own. In the event that no such investments exist, the investing partner will acquire partnership (in the value of funds received) in any future investment which I shall make. The investing partner hereby appoints me as an agent to execute these investment(s), as I deem appropriate, on his behalf. These investment(s) shall be owned by the investing partner.

Any profits realized or losses sustained shall be allocated to the investing partner. However, five percent (5%) of the profits shall be retained by the undersigned for his services during the term of this Iska.

Any claim of loss must be verified through the testimony of two qualified witnesses in, and under conditions acceptable to, an Orthodox Jewish court of law. Any claim regarding the amount of profit generated by this investment (or investments) shall be verified under solemn oath, before and under conditions acceptable to, an Orthodox Jewish court of law.

It is agreed that if I return the above-mentioned principal to the investing partner, together with an additional _____ as payment for his share of the profits which are generated, then I will not be required to make any further payment nor will I be required to make an oath. I am obligated to make this payment on or before _____ . If payment is not made by this time, the terms of this Iska shall continue.

In the event of any conflict between the terms of this Iska agreement and the terms of any other agreement signed by the two parties in regard to these funds, the terms of this agreement shall prevail.

This agreement shall follow the guidelines of Heter Iska as explained in *Sefer Bris Yehudah*. It is agreed that any dispute which may arise in connection with this agreement shall be submitted before _____ .[2] Judgment rendered by the aforesaid authority may be entered in any court having jurisdiction thereof.

Dated _____

Signature of the Recipient _____

Signature of the Investor _____

---

1. This was explained above, Paragraphs 8-11.
2. This part of the contract is optional.

❧ Source Index
❧ Topic Index

Source Index

for Yoreh Deah 159-177

Column on left (in bold) refers to Chapter:Paragraph in Shulchan Aruch Yoreh Deah.
Column on right indicates Chapter:Paragraph or Chapter:Note in this book.

Topic Index

can it be sold? 12:n42;

cashing at discount 12:26-29;

cashing to repay loan, without owner's consent 19:29;

charging borrower cost of returned checks 4:1;

difference between U.S. law and Israeli law 12:n51;

different than a promissory note 12:n42;

drawn on foreign bank 8:29;

drawn on foreign currency 12:33;

fees for cashing 12:34;

for *kinyan kesef* 11:n32;

given before end of Shemittah, but cashed after 21:n4;

kinyan for sale of 12:29;

liability of seller 12:28;

surcharge for payment by 6:9;

understanding mechanics of 12:n41;

child;

parent charging Ribbis with intent to return 5:33;

parents paying Ribbis to 5:34

see 'minors'

closing; see 'real estate'

collateral;

bonds as 12:n60;

non-Jew using interest loan as 17:23;

paying third party to provide 4:27;

prevents Shemittah laws 21:6;

promissory notes as 12:17;

real estate 9:17;

requiring that the borrower sell to lender 3:29;

surrendering as payment 9:16-17;

to be used for mitzvah 5:n36;

transferring when debt is sold 12:6;

worth more than loan 9:16-17;

commodity trading 8:21-22

common courtesies 3:16;

compensating; see 'reimbursing'

Consumer Price Index;

Heter Iska tied to 23:n12;

interest tied to 2:3;

contract

contains Ribbis, what to do? 13:49;

for partnership between Jews and non-Jews 16:*Appendix*;

sale-lease contract form 13:*Appendix I*;

to establish proper ownership of property 13:*Appendix II*;

which calls for Ribbis must be destroyed 2:26;

contractor;

reduced rate for advance payment 10:24;

convert; see Ger

corporations;

status of 5:27;

synagogues which are incorporated 5:n20;

cosigner;

may be paid 4:28;

see also 'guarantor'

court fees,

charged to borrower 4:1;

court-obligated Ribbis payment 20:22;

credit;

asking higher price because of 6:13-14;

charging for 6:5;

extended on condition of prepaying old loans 6:23-24;

extending terms of credit is considered new loan 6:25;

permitted forms of charges 6:11;

storekeeper totaling debt 6:n47;

see also 'merchandise sold on credit'

credit cards;

borrowing a credit card and paying interest fees for owner 4:5, 17:15-16;

higher price for credit card purchases 6:5;

passing on processing costs 6:n15;

credit for purchases;

canceled by Shemittah? 21:9;

charging interest 6:1;

extending due date 2:8;

offering discount for immediate payment *after* sale completed 3:n45;

penalty for late payment 9:7;

restructuring payment schedule 3:34;

Ribbis Ketzutzah? 2:8;

credit for services;

Ribbis Ketzutzah? 2:n13;

currency;

    defining legal 14:n3;

    definition of 14:n3;

    devalued during loan 2:n6;

    losses value 14:n3;

    maaser kesafim when losses value 14:n3;

    status of our coins and bills 14:n3;

D

damages;

    penalty for late payment 9:n35;

debt balance not known 4:25;

debt;

    sale of; see 'promissory notes'

    sold at discount 12:1-5;

delivery;

    charging for delivering loan 4:3;

    payment due at time of 10:5;

    penalty if delivered late 9:7;

deposits;

    at time purchase order is placed 7:3;

    for soda bottles, shopping carts 4:31;

    given to guarantee wages 10:20;

    required to guarantee price 8:2-3;

    see 'security deposits'

devaluation of currency 2:n6;

differences between Ribbis Ketzutzah and Rabbinic Ribbis 2:n1; 4:n38;

dina demalchusa dina;

    establishing legal currency 14:n3;

dinar;

    value of 22:n14

discount benefits offered to lender 3:7;

discount for cash payment 6:5-10;

discount for prepayment;

    animals, cattle 18:12;

    cantors 10:28;

    contractors 10:24;

    doctors 10:n28;

    employees 10:17-19;

    for early registration 7:22;

    for labor with no set value 10:28;

    for larger down payment 13:3;

    for magazine subscriptions 8:24;

    for multiple rides 7:23;

    for prepaying credit bill ('²/₁₀ net 30') 6:n41;

    for prepayment of loan 12:41;

    for prepayment of real estate 13:1;

    for produce 18:2;

    if prohibited discount was already given 7:20-21;

    of rental fees 11:14-16;

    permitted for prepayment on purchase 7:6-18;

    prohibited for prepayment on purchase 7:1-2;

    professional entertainers 10:28;

    use of *mikveh* 4:n46;

    using a Heter Iska 7:19;

    when offered by corporation 7:5;

discounting a debt 3:35;

    bank checks and money orders 12:25;

    guarantor for debt 15:24;

    personal checks 12:30-31;

    selling notes 12:24;

    third-party checks 12:27 and 32;

doctor's fees;

    affected by Shemittah 21:12;

    charging reduced rate for prepayment 10:n28;

dollar;

    considered a currency in Israel? 1:n29;

down payment;

    discount if larger 13:3;

    see also 'deposits'

dowry; see 'wedding'

due date;

    extension on credit debt 6:25;

E

early payments to compensate for late payments 3:24;

eggs;

    bloodspots in borrowed egg 1:n10;

    borrowing 1:5;

employee billing Ribbis for employer 2:n25;

employer; see 'wages'

escape clause;

    adding later 13:20;

    as a non-binding pledge 13:23;

    drawn to avoid Ribbis problems 13:22;

    on sale of real estate 13:17-18;

escrow funds;
    lawyers using 1:23, 13:n10;
    paying for use of 13:5;
    reimbursing interest of 1:23, 13:5;
esrog;
    discount for prepayment 7:15
    given as Ribbis 20:n1;
establishing value of currency 1:20;
exchange policy 1:18
expenses;
    cashing checks 12:34;
    see also 'charging for expenses'
    see also 'reimbursing lender'
extension on date loan is due 2:2;

F

"fair" Ribbis 1:23
family members;
    charging Ribbis 5:33;
farm issues Chapter 18;
favors offered to the lender 1:1-4;
    publicly 1:2;
foreign currencies;
    bank sets value 14:n26;
    borrowed, may pay same amount? 14:14;
    borrowed in one country, paid in another 8:n38;
    loans of 1:20, 8:20;
    payment using 8:27;
    trading 8:19-20;
foreign currency checks;
    establishing value of 12:n52;
    may be sold? 12:33;
    processing fees 12:n54;
forgoing payment; see 'mechilah'
free loan fund;
    advantage of communal fund 19:3;
    benefiting officers of 19:14;
    blacklist those who default 19:23;
    for paid members only 19:6;
    how much to lend each? 19:17;
    importance of 19:Introduction;
    in memory of 19:n1;
    loans to non-observant Jews 19:21;
    may collect Ribbis DeRabbanan? 19:13;
    multiple loans to same person 19:18;

passing on expenses 19:9-12;
pledge to donate at time of loan 19:n5;
precedence in offering loans 19:24-28;
precedence over charity 19:1;
refusing because cannot repay 19:22;
require proof of loan 19:19;
requiring donation 19:4;
requiring loan to Gemach 19:7;
Shemittah 19:30;
to wealthy people? 19:26;
using Heter Iska 19:7-8;
voluntary donation 19:5;
free loans;
    changed to interest loan 1:2;
    obligation to extend if losing interest from bank 5:n7, n8;
    to non-observant Jews 5:n19;
    see also 'free loan fund'
friends involved in a loan;
    continuing to do favors 1:1;
    gift at time loan is paid 2:n26;
    inviting for a meal 1:11;
    purchasing an aliyah 1:2;
    relationship after loan 1:1-4;
    using borrower's utensils 1:4;
fruits;
    borrowing during season to return off season 14:n7;

G

gas stations;
    charge extra for credit card purchase 6:5;
Gemach see 'free loan fund'
Ger 5:6-8;
    rules for loans extended as non-Jew 5:7;
    rules for loans taken as non-Jew 5:8;
    status during Geirus process 5:n10;
gift to lender;
    after loan is repaid 2:22-24;
    at time of payment, when permitted 4:22;
    at time of payment 2:n26;
    before loan is offered 2:19-21;
    between friends 1:1-3;
    many years later 2:25;
    offered during period of loan 2:16-17;

to merchant who offered credit 4:22-23;
    unrelated to loan 1:n8;
    when lender is charity 4:20;
    when lender is child 5:34;
gift;
    was delivered late 9:18;
gift;
    which causes loss to receiver 14:n20;
Ginnie Mae;
    investing in 13:48;
    who owns mortgages? 13:n71;
Government National Mortgage Association;
    see 'Ginnie Mae'
greeting the lender 3:10-11;
    after loan is paid 3:18;
    returning greetings 3:11;
    the obligation to respond to greetings 3:n17;
guaranteeing a price;
    for prepayment 8:1;
    if improper agreement was already made 8:30;
    if price falls 8:13;
    lumber 18:5;
    milk, wool, honey 18:8;
    produce 18:1-3;
    requiring a deposit 8:2-3;
    wine 18:6-7;
guarantor;
    agreement already signed 15:11;
    corporation serves as 15:n35;
    delay in reimbursement to 15:9;
    different categories 15:*Introduction*;
    for bank loan 15:15-17;
    for mortgage 15:19-20;
    for loan between Jews 15:1-8;
    for loan involving Ribbis DeRabbanan 15:3;
    for loan sold at discount 15:4;
    for mortgage 13:40;
    for partnership loan 15:17;
    for sale of promissory note 12:6, 15:28;
    Heter Iska to permit 15:20;
    if lender pursues collateral 15:19;
    if non-Jewish borrower put up collateral 15:27;

loan between non-Jews 15:29;
loan from Jew to non-Jew 15:21-28;
loan from non-Jew to Jew 15:9-20;
may be paid 15:6-7;
on business loan 16:n4;
on Heter Iska 15:5, 22:30;
paid loan, then Shemittah passed 21:5;
prohibition if *areiv* does not pay? 15:n23;
reimbursing for Ribbis paid to non-Jew 15:11, 13;
takes promissory note 21:n12;

H

haaramah;
    disguising loan as gift 2:n8;
    Heter Iska 22:n60;
haaramas Ribbis;
    different than other forms of Ribbis 9:n1, 9:2-3;
    may be collected if already set 9:n4;
    obligation to return 20:27;
    when surrendering collateral 9:16;
heirs;
    of borrower, returning to 20:25;
    of lender returning Ribbis 20:22-24;
    terminating Heter Iska agreement 22:n69;
Heter Iska;
    adding 'by Heter Iska' to a bill 6:n43;
    adding to loan after loan was issued 13:50-51
    after Ribbis was paid, on mortgage 13:52;
    canceled by Shemittah? 21:8;
    changing loan to 22:46-47;
    conditions which may be added to 22:17;
    conflict between legal documents and 13:29;
    debt changed to 22:n66;
    difference between *kulo pikadon and palga pikadon* 23:8-11;
    directions for filling out 23:6-7;
    disadvantage of 13:31;
    for '²/₁₀ net 30' 6:n41;
    for advance on sale of real estate 13:4;

for selling notes at discount
12:Appendix II;
Kulo pikadon form for business use
23:Iska D;
Kulo pikadon form for personal use
23:Iska E;
requiring monthly payments 3:Iska
C;
sale-lease form for private mortgages 13:Appendix I;
see also 'Heter Iska Klali forms'
Heter Iska Klali;
explanation of 23:12;
incorporated in company's bylaws?
23:n24;
mentioned each time? 23:n24;
notifying investor 23:12;
one for entire business career 23:n23;
oral 23:n23;
without knowledge of investor 23:n2;
without knowledge of managing partner 23:n2;
see also 'Heter Iska Klali forms'
Heter Iska Klali forms;
for '²/₁₀ net 30' 6:Appendix;
for business which sells on credit
6:Appendix;
for selling notes at discount
12:Appendix II;
of R' Ezriel Meir Eiger 23:n23;
honoring commitment;
mental decision 12:n19;
oral commitment 12:n19;
Ribbis commitment 13:49;
advice for dealing with problem
4:n17;
hotels;
discounts for early registration 7:22;
house; see 'real estate'
household situations 1:5-8;
borrowing food 1:5;
see also 'neighbors'

I

IOU; see 'promissory notes'
incremental payments 19:16;
inflation;
protection against 6:19;

reimbursement for loss of money's
value 2:3;
see also 'Consumer Price Index'
influencing lender to offer loan;
gift by others 3:11
gift from borrower 2:19-21;
insurance;
for item being rented 11:5;
for Heter Iska agreement 22:7;
insurance companies;
service charges 6:n37;
interest-free loan; see 'free loan'
interest payments calculated as principal
17:n33;
interest which is paid only if borrower
profits 2:12-13;
one-time payment 2:4;
investing in company which loans for
interest 17:8;
investment;
money is later changed to loan 2:n4;
Iska partnerships 22:1-23;
affected by Shemittah? 21:7;
bankruptcy 22:21;
compensating managing partner 22:8-
12;
conditions of 22:17-23;
diverting funds for personal use 22:16;
donations by 22:15;
if made improperly 22:6;
insurance 22:7;
rules regarding liability 3-6;
rules regarding profits 22:13—15;
tax payments 22:14;
understanding the concept 22:1;
Israel;
government loans 5:30;
is dollar considered currency? 1:n29;
Israeli bonds 5:30;

J

jewelry;
paying for use of 11:4;
Jews, non-observant;
and Shemittah 21:n29;
as witnesses for Iska 22:n31;
definition of 19:n32;
do Ribbis prohibitions apply? 5:9-10;

Gemach loan to 19:20;
interest loan inherited by observant
   son 5:n18;
repentant Jew who took Ribbis 20:12-
   15;
using a Heter Iska 22:n34;
witnesses for a Heter Iska 22:n31;
Job,
   offering the lender in exchange for
      loan 3:25;
joint loan;
   guaranteeing entire 15:16;
   mortgage 13:42;

K

"Keep the change";
   when paying for a purchase 1:22;
   when repaying loan 1:21;
kinyan;
   checks as kesef? 11:n32;
   for sale of bank account funds 12:n37;
   for sale of checks 12:29;
   for sale of Heter Iska 12:21;
   for sale of mortgage 13:44;
   maamad shiloshton 12:14;
   oral agreements 12:n19;
   'pay to bearer' notes 12:n38;
   postscript to old note as shtar 12:14;
   real estate always requires shtar?
      13:n76;
   shtar, by signing note 12:24;
   situmta for sale of contract 12:14,
      12:19;
   standard contract as kinyan situmta
      9:24;
   sudar, how it is done 10:25;
   to change loan to Iska 22:46-47;
   to finalize rental agreement 11:n32;
   to obligate contractor 10:25, 27;
   to sell debt 12:13;
   transfer of debt 12:14;
   transfer of non-Jew's debt 12:19;
   transfer of real estate 13:51;
   with Heter Iska 22:45;

L

late payment;
   charge for 6:2-3;

compensating by paying other obligations early 3:24;
compensating lender for damage
   caused 4:7;
compensating lender for lost earnings
   4:6;
due to oness 9:13;
for purchase, penalty permitted 9:7-8;
payment for damages 9:n35;
penalty 9:1-5;
surcharge by contractor or repairman
   10:29;
to orphans or tzedakah 9:n3;
voluntary compensation for 9:14, 9:n2;
wages Chapter 10;
see also 'penalties'
lawyers;
   collecting Ribbis payments 2:n25;
   preparing documents for Ribbis deal
      2:15;
   using escrow accounts 1:23, 13:n10;
lease agreements;
   penalty for late payment 6:4, 9:6,9;
   see also 'real estate'
legal expenses of lender,
   cost passed on to borrower 4:1;
lender;
   who is a friend 1:1;
   who is a tenant 1:2-3;
liability;
   of renter for rented utensil 11:2;
   for sold check 12:28;
lien,
   cost passed on to borrower 4:1;
Lifnei iver;
   guaranteeing Ribbis loan 15:n6, n8;
   guidelines 2:n25;
   loan without witnesses 19:n29;
   witnesses to a Ribbis loan 2:n23;
loan;
   changing to Heter Iska 22:46-47;
   disguised as gift 2:n8;
   honoring pledge to loan 19:20;
   lender may require lump payment
      19:16;
   may be offered in gratitude for favor
      or gift 2:21;
   of goods 2:6;

of services 2:7;
offered without witnesses 19:n29;
passed to a friend who paid interest,
what now? 17:19;
taken from non-Jew
for use of third person 17:17,
if situation already occurred 17:19;
taken to pass to friend, who pays
interest? 17:17-20;
trading loans 3:20-23;
unsure how much borrowed 1:6;
who takes precedence? 19:24-28;
see also 'Heter Iska'
loan broker;
arranging loan from non-Jew 13:n35
see also 'mortgage broker'
loans for investment;
Ribbis also prohibited 1:23;
sharing profits 2:12;
lost earnings because loan was not repaid
1:23;
lumber;
sold in advance 18:5;

M

maamad shiloshton 12:14
maaser kesafim;
deducting loss due to inflation 14:n3;
one third to Gemach 19:2;
to free loan or to charity? 19:1;
when interest costs may be deducted
4:n7;
when lost interest may be deducted
1:n36;
magazine subscriptions;
at discount 8:24;
rate is guaranteed 8:24;
recommended method 8:n43
maris ayin;
helping Jew receive loan from non-
Jew 5:n6;
helping non-Jew arrange interest 17:1-
2;
non-Jewish lender directs that loan be
passed on 17:20;
meals;
exchanging invitations 1:11;
inviting the lender 1:n1;

mechilah;
does moral obligation remain after?
20:n20;
minors 9:n4;
of obligation to return Ribbis 20:12-
14;
to benefit lender 20:n20;
where principal is still owed 17:n33;
mechirah al minas lihachzir; 1:n24;
merchandise sold on credit;
'²/₁₀ net 30' 6:20;
charges for billing 6:18;
charging extra 6:5-10;
late penalty permitted 9:7-8;
protecting against inflation 6:19;
merchandise;
as penalty for late payment 9:5;
borrowed to sell 14:1-3;
calculating value of 4:21;
offered as loan in place of cash 3:9;
payment in foreign currency 8:28-
29;
returned to seller 1:15-16;
setting value of 14:n3;
trading 8:26;
used to repay loan 4:21;
value higher at place of payment
14:21;
mesayei'a ovrei aveirah, guidelines 2:n25,
15:n8;
involving Rabbinic prohibitions
2:n25, 15:n10;
to deliberate violator 2:n25, 15:n10;
mikveh;
discount for monthly fee 7:24;
minimal amount;
adding to payment 1:n10;
after loan has been repaid 2:23;
before loan is offered 2:20;
change owed to borrower 1:21;
definition of 'minimal' 2:n38;
gift at time of payment 2:n26;
gift to merchant who extends credit
4:22-23;
price fluctuations in borrowed item
1:7;
minors;
benefiting the lender's children 4:29;

exempt from Ribbis DeRabbanan 5:14;
investing orphan's money 5:15;
penalty for late payments 9:n3;
until what age? 5:19;
wealthy grandparents 5:n27;
see also 'charity funds'

P

parents;
paying a lender to offer a loan 4:11
partners,
Jewish;
can active partner obligate silent? 16:n7;
if only one active 16:5;
lending personal moneys 16:11;
leniency 16:n3;
taking business loan 16:3,
taking personal loan 16:1-2;
partnership;
between two Jews;
considered Jewish? 5:26;
dividing profits 16:13-14;
if Heter Iska signed by only one partner 16:8;
in bank 17:8;
in company which violates Ribbis 17:8;
loan to purchase merchandise 16:12;
one partner giving gift from 22:15;
taking a loan 5:29;
taking a mortgage 13:41;
using Heter Iska 16:7-10;
partnership
between Jews and non-Jews;
collecting Ribbis from Jews 16:19-20;
contract to permit Ribbis 16:21;
paying Ribbis to Jews 17-18;
status of large companies 5:26;
taking loans if more than one Jew 16:15;
taking loans if one Jew 16:16;
where non-Jew runs business 16:n26;
passing on a loan 17:17-20;
patronizing the lender's business 3:25;
getting others to patronize lender 3:26;

requiring the borrower to patronize someone else's business 3:27;
payment;
cash was not used 11:9;
designated at specific location 4:30;
discounting a debt 3:35;
due at other location, if affects value 14:21;
made directly to lender's bank account 4:30;
obligation to pay on time 4:6;
restructuring payment schedules 3:32-34;
using merchandise 14:22-23;
see also late payment.
payment delayed;
reimbursing loss 14:18;
payment for damaging someone's property;
assessing value 4:n56;
Ribbis does not apply 4:n56;
payment for stolen goods;
how to assess value 4:33;
Ribbis does not apply 4:33;
payment to money manager who arranges interest for non-Jew 17:5;
penalties for late payment;
and tzedakah money 5:16, 9:n3;
binding if agreed to 9:2;
credit for merchandise 9:7-8;
difference between one-time penalty and monthly payments 9:1 20:n52;
enforced by Beis Din 9:2;
for promised gift 9:18;
obligation to return 20:27;
of rental fees 11:20;
of wages 10:15-16;
penalty clauses Chapter 9;
reason for prohibition 9:n1;
voluntary payment 9:n2;
when permitted 9:5-8;
penalty for delaying execution of will 9:19;
pidyon haben;
borrowing coins from Kohen 3:n2;
Kohen gives coins as gift 3:n2;
using lender as Kohen where this is a condition of loan 3:n40;
using lender as Kohen where this is not a condition of loan 3:1;

utensils;
  borrowing 1:9;
  using the lender's 1:4;

V

vacation days;
  carrying over from year to year 10:31;
voluntary refund;
  sold promissory note, case where prohibited 12:n16;
sold promissory note which wasn't collected 12:9;

W

wages;
  borrow to pay? 10:6;
  compensate because paid late 10:12;
  exceptions to obligation to pay on time 10:6-11;
  higher because payment is late 10:14;
  if not requested by employee 10:9;
  lost due to time spent on loan 4:n3;
  lower because paid in advance 10:17-28;
  obligation to pay on time 10:1-5;
  partial payment 10:1, n2;
wedding
  binding dowry obligation 9:n35;
  dowry paid late 9:18;
  gift to lender's child 4:29;
  Tanaim at wedding 9:n35;
wife;
  receiving benefits due to husband's loan 4:n29;

wills;
  contains gift to non-heir 9:n37;
  donation to charity 17:n41;
  penalty for delaying execution 9:19;
wine;
  sold while still grape juice 18:6;
witness to Ribbis transaction 2:15;
witness as part of Heter Iska 22:20, 22:n33
"work for me and I'll work for you" 2:7

Y

yesh lo;
  cash to purchase considered yesh lo? 14:n11;
  creating 14:9;
  produce which began growing 18:n1;
  to allow borrowing merchandise (seah beseah) 14:6-10;
  to allow prepayment for discounts 7:7-12;
  to allow price guarantees 8:4-8;
Yeshivah;
  discounts for early registration 7:22;
  exempt from Ribbis DeRabbanan 5:13;
  paying Ribbis for a loan 5:n20;
  see also 'charity funds'

Z

zochim l'adam shelo befanav;
  where gift causes detriment 14:n20;
zakfan alav bemilveh;
  definition 21:9;
    see also 'changing debt to a loan'
  regarding Shemittah 21:n17